# Grammar, Meaning, and Concepts

*Grammar, Meaning, and Concepts: A Discourse-Based Approach to English Grammar* is a book for language teachers and learners that focuses on the meanings of grammatical constructions within discourse, rather than on language as structure governed by rigid rules. This text emphasizes the ways in which users of language construct meaning, express viewpoints, and depict imageries using the conceptual, meaning-filled categories that underlie all of grammar. Written by a team of authors with years of experience teaching grammar to future teachers of English, this book puts grammar in the context of real language and illustrates grammar in use through an abundance of authentic data examples. Each chapter also provides a variety of activities that focus on grammar, genre, discourse, and meaning, which can be used as they are or can be adapted for classroom practice. The activities are also designed to raise awareness about discourse, grammar, and meaning in all facets of everyday life, and can be used as springboards for upper high school, undergraduate, and graduate level research projects and inquiry-based grammatical analysis. *Grammar, Meaning, and Concepts* is an ideal textbook for those in the areas of teacher education, discourse analysis, applied linguistics, second language teaching, ESL, EFL, and communications who are looking to teach and learn grammar from a dynamic perspective.

**Susan Strauss** is Associate Professor of Applied Linguistics and Asian Studies at Pennsylvania State University, USA. Her research interests center on the interface of discourse, cognition, interaction, and culture, often from a cross-linguistic/cross-cultural perspective. She is co-author of *Discourse Analysis: Putting Our Worlds Into Words* (Routledge, 2014).

**Parastou Feiz** is Associate Professor of Applied Linguistics in the Department of English at California State University, San Bernardino, USA. Her research focuses on comparative analyses of grammatical structures across languages, particularly Persian and English. She is co-author of *Discourse Analysis: Putting Our Worlds Into Words* (Routledge, 2014).

**Xuehua Xiang** is Associate Professor of Applied Linguistics in the Department of Linguistics at the University of Illinois at Chicago, USA. Her research focuses on using empirical lenses, such as discourse analysis, corpus tools, and cognitive-functional perspectives to study the interaction of language, culture, and communication.

# Grammar, Meaning, and Concepts

A Discourse-Based Approach to English Grammar

Susan Strauss, Parastou Feiz, and Xuehua Xiang

NEW YORK AND LONDON

First published 2018
by Routledge
711 Third Avenue, New York, NY 10017

and by Routledge
2 Park Square, Milton Park, Abingdon, Oxon, OX14 4RN

*Routledge is an imprint of the Taylor & Francis Group, an informa business*

© 2018 Taylor & Francis

The right of Susan Strauss, Parastou Feiz and Xuehua Xiang to be identified as authors of this work has been asserted by them in accordance with sections 77 and 78 of the Copyright, Designs and Patents Act 1988.

All rights reserved. No part of this book may be reprinted or reproduced or utilised in any form or by any electronic, mechanical, or other means, now known or hereafter invented, including photocopying and recording, or in any information storage or retrieval system, without permission in writing from the publishers.

Every effort has been made to contact copyright-holders. Please advise the publisher of any errors or omissions, and these will be corrected in subsequent editions.

*Trademark notice*: Product or corporate names may be trademarks or registered trademarks, and are used only for identification and explanation without intent to infringe.

*Library of Congress Cataloging-in-Publication Data*
Names: Strauss, Susan G., author. | Feiz, Parastou, author. | Xiang, Xuehua, 1976– author.
Title: Grammar, meaning, and concepts : a discourse-based approach to English grammar / Susan Strauss, Parastou Feiz and Xuehua Xiang.
Description: New York, NY : Routledge, [2018] | Includes bibliographical references and index.
Identifiers: LCCN 2017052956 | ISBN 9781138785267 (hardback) | ISBN 9781138785274 (pbk.) | ISBN 9781317665045 (epub) | ISBN 9781317665038 (mobipocket/kindle)
Subjects: LCSH: English language—Discourse analysis. | English language—Grammar. | Semantics.
Classification: LCC PE1422 .S77 2018 | DDC 425—dc23
LC record available at https://lccn.loc.gov/2017052956

ISBN: 978-1-138-78526-7 (hbk)
ISBN: 978-1-138-78527-4 (pbk)
ISBN: 978-1-315-76797-0 (ebk)

Typeset in Galliard
by Apex CoVantage, LLC

This book is dedicated to the memory of Noriko Akatsuka (1937–2016). Noriko's influence abounds in how we and our students view language, grammar, and discourse.

# Contents

*List of Illustrations* — ix
*Acknowledgments* — xiii

1 Meaning Beyond Syntax: Discourse and Conceptualization — 1

2 The Nuts and Bolts of Grammar — 6

3 The Basic Grammar for Mentioning People, Ideas, Values, Objects, Concepts, and Things: Nouns and Their Meanings in Discourse — 48

4 Referring to, Identifying, Specifying, Underspecifying, Possessing, and Quantifying Things, People, and Ideas in Discourse: Determiners — 78

5 Alternate Ways to Identify, Specify, Underspecify, Focus On, and Quantify Things, People, and Ideas in Discourse: Pronouns — 118

6 The Grammar of Events, States, Identities, Actions, Power, Control, and Spontaneity in Discourse: Verbs — 143

7 The Grammar of Time, Fact, Habit, Changeability, Permanence, Sequence, and Relevance in Discourse: Tense and Aspect — 177

8 The Grammar of Directives, Permissions, Obligations, Opinions, and Mitigations: Imperatives and Modals — 219

9 The Grammar of Agency, Control, Responsibility, Passivity, Non-Agency, and Non-Accountability: Voice — 264

10 The Grammar of Juxtaposing, Contrasting, Denying, Excluding, Contradicting, and Reversing: Negation — 289

11 The Grammar of Inquiry and Apparent Inquiry in Discourse: Yes-No Questions, *Wh-* Questions, Alternative or Choice Questions, and Tag Questions — 324

12 The Grammar of Situating Entities in Space, Time, and
   Abstractness, Hanging On, Burning Up, and Cooling Down:
   Prepositions and Phrasal Verbs                                   352

13 The Exquisite Grammar of Descriptions—Being Bellicose or
   Bubbly, Feckless, or Fearless: Adjectives                         403

14 The Grammar of Connecting, Adding, Conjoining, Contrasting,
   Indicating Alternatives, and Expressing Stance: Conjunctions     437

15 The Grammar of Exquisitely Evoking Events, How Things
   Happen, When Things Happen, If Things Happen, and How We
   Portray Such Views in Discourse: Adverbs                         453

   *Index*                                                           471

# Illustrations

## Figures

| | | |
|---|---|---|
| 1.1 | "How I spent my summer vacation" | 1 |
| 1.2 | "Just bark. The app automatically translates it to English!" | 4 |
| 2.1 | "The first human was cloned in 2002. When he found out, he was beside himself." | 6 |
| 2.2 | "More walking, less flying." | 32 |
| 3.1 | "I'm taking an innovative approach to teaching this semester. I'm using books!" | 48 |
| 3.2 | Conceptual meaning—Type 1 | 54 |
| 3.3 | Conceptual meaning—Type 2 | 56 |
| 3.4 | A *strawberry*/one *strawberry*/red, ripe *strawberries* (Type 1) | 62 |
| 3.5 | *Strawberry* jam (Type 2) | 62 |
| 3.6 | *Coffee* (Type 2). General term, concept, ingredient, flavor. | 63 |
| 3.7 | *Coffees* (Type 1). Coffee in cups, various styles of serving. | 63 |
| 3.8 | Foregrounds the UNIT as a whole (Type 3a). Takes SINGULAR verb form. | 65 |
| 3.9 | Foregrounds the MEMBERS (Type 3b). Takes PLURAL verb form. | 65 |
| 3.10 | "A good retirement fund should include bones, rawhide, beefy treats, a few toys and an assortment of kitchen trash." | 71 |
| 4.1 | "Don't slice the pizza. My diet says I'm only allowed to eat one piece!" | 78 |
| 4.2 | "This light warns you that your battery may be critically low. And *this* light warns you that your conversation may be critically dull." | 94 |
| 4.3 | "Nurses work 12 hours a day: 4 hours caring for patients and 8 hours washing our hands." | 112 |
| 5.1 | "IPOD/YOUPOD/WEPOD/THEYPOD" | 118 |
| 5.2 | ". . . and *that's* why you need to raise my allowance!" | 137 |
| 6.1 | "I love you and enjoy our time together, but I'm still young and I've decided to start seeing other bears." | 143 |
| 6.2 | "What cellphone service are you using? It sounds like you're talking under water!" | 166 |
| 6.3 | Icon meaning "Walk Your Bike" | 169 |
| 6.4 | Sign, "Shuffle Your Feet for Stingrays." | 170 |
| 7.1 | "When you're trying to fall asleep, does it ever feel like your thumbs are still texting?" | 177 |
| 8.1 | "Employees must wash hands" | 219 |
| 8.2 | "Don't spend more than you earn" | 226 |
| 8.3 | Gradience in meanings for deontic modals | 233 |
| 8.4 | Gradience in meanings for epistemic modals | 235 |

x  *Illustrations*

| 8.5 | Sign by New Jersey Department of Health | 238 |
| --- | --- | --- |
| 8.6 | Sign by Kansas Department of Health and Environment | 238 |
| 8.7 | "Did you hear? They *might make* us wear uniforms to school next year!" | 239 |
| 9.1 | "Conspiracy theorists say Humpty Dumpty was pushed." | 264 |
| 9.2 | "The world's greatest hoax was exposed today when it was revealed that algebra will *never* be useful to you later in life." | 271 |
| 9.3 | Sign in front of a café in State College, Pennsylvania: "Bikes *Park* Free" | 280 |
| 9.4 | Road sign in the northeast US: Bridge *Ices* Before Road | 280 |
| 10.1 | "Your brain *is* like a sponge that absorbs knowledge, but that's not exactly how it's done." | 289 |
| 10.2 | "I'm reading an updated version of *Romeo and Juliet*. This time their relationship comes to a tragic end when she unfriends him on Facebook." | 305 |
| 10.3a | Odorless garlic supplement label | 310 |
| 10.3b | Odor-free garlic supplement label | 310 |
| 10.4 | "My doctor told me to increase my exercise program, so I switched from not exercising three times a week to not exercising six times a week." | 314 |
| 10.5 | "Young Lungs at Play" sign | 320 |
| 10.6 | "One Way" sign | 321 |
| 10.7 | "Warning: Pesticide" sign | 321 |
| 11.1 | "For my Current Events class, I'm supposed to read a newspaper every day. What's a newspaper?" | 324 |
| 11.2 | "Want to settle your case FAST? Call the law firm of Rock, Paper & Scissors!" | 342 |
| 11.3 | "Why didn't you tell me your relatives were coming for the holidays?!" | 344 |
| 12.1 | "They're adding fluoride to the drinking water in Washington to help fight truth decay." | 352 |
| 12.2 | *from*: movement—part of a whole—leaving a source | 355 |
| 12.3 | *of*: part of a whole | 356 |
| 12.4 | *in*: enclosure | 356 |
| 12.5 | *to*: movement in the direction of a goal, end point, or target | 357 |
| 12.6 | *into*: entering an enclosure from a source location | 359 |
| 12.7 | *inside*: enclosure with defined boundaries | 359 |
| 12.8 | *out*: beyond an enclosure | 360 |
| 12.9 | *outside*: beyond an enclosure with defined boundaries | 360 |
| 12.10 | *for*: connection to a purpose, intention, recipient, destination, stand-in, or continuous duration | 360 |
| 12.11 | *on*: contact with a surface | 362 |
| 12.12 | *off*: disconnect from surface | 364 |
| 12.12a | Electrical circuit metaphor—*on* | 364 |
| 12.12b | Electrical circuit metaphor—*off* | 364 |
| 12.13 | *onto*: movement resulting in contact with a surface from a source location | 365 |
| 12.14 | *at*: a point that is located in space | 365 |
| 12.15 | *by*: connection of a place to a place, an action to a time, a result to a process, an action to an agent, a unit to an equal unit, an action to a supported position | 371 |
| 12.16 | *around*: motion that follows the perimeter of something | 372 |
| 12.17 | *about*: non-specific motion in any direction but that which designates a perimeter | 373 |
| 12.18 | *as*: in the capacity of, equaling in total identity to | 373 |
| 12.19 | *like*: similarity | 374 |

| | | |
|---|---|---|
| 12.20 | *through:* movement traversing an entire trajectory within an enclosure or partial enclosure | 374 |
| 12.21 | *after:* sequentially next, following | 375 |
| 12.22 | *before:* sequentially preceding, prior | 375 |
| 12.23 | *before:* in physical space only, with a limited inventory of verbs, such as *stand before, appear before, kneel before, come before, go before* | 376 |
| 12.24 | *over:* arched trajectory and any point on that trajectory | 376 |
| 12.25 | *under:* at a lower vertical point | 377 |
| 12.26 | *with:* link | 378 |
| 12.27 | *without:* linkless | 379 |
| 12.28 | *on:* contact with a surface | 387 |
| 12.29 | *on* as a phrasal verb particle: continuative aspect, continuous metaphorical contact | 388 |
| 12.30 | *off:* disconnect from surface | 389 |
| 12.31 | *off* as a phrasal verb particle: completive aspect—complete metaphorical disconnect | 389 |
| 12.32 | *out:* beyond an enclosure; *out* as a phrasal verb particle: completive aspect, completely beyond metaphorical enclosure | 390 |
| 12.33 | *up:* toward a higher vertical position (as a preposition or adverb); *up* as a phrasal verb particle: completely, to the extreme metaphorical upper limit | 391 |
| 12.34 | *down:* toward a lower vertical position (as a preposition or adverb); *down* as a phrasal verb particle: completive aspect, to the extreme metaphorical lower limit as a gradual process | 391 |
| 12.35 | *through* as a preposition: movement traversing an entire trajectory within an enclosure or partial enclosure; *through* as a phrasal verb particle: movement traversing a metaphorical trajectory within an enclosure or partial enclosure | 393 |
| 12.36 | *by:* as a preposition: connection to a place, an action, an idea; *by* as a phrasal verb particle: metaphorical connection to a place, an action, an idea, a duration | 393 |
| 12.37 | *after* as a preposition: sequentially next, following; *after* as a phrasal verb particle: metaphorical sequence of next or following | 394 |
| 12.38 | "I'm supposed to eat kale for smother skin, turkey for stronger nails, fish for thinner thighs, oats for cardiovascular benefits...." | 396 |
| 12.39 | Line drawings for preposition activity #5 | 399 |
| 12.40 | Line drawings for preposition activity #5 | 399 |
| 12.41 | Line drawings for preposition activity #5 | 399 |
| 12.42 | Line drawings for preposition activity #5 | 399 |
| 13.1 | "I should go on a diet, but I'm afraid my brain will get thinner and I'll become narrow-minded!" | 403 |
| 13.2 | "The good news is, you'll be spending Thanksgiving with a large group of happy people." | 424 |
| 14.1 | "I clawed my way to the top of the corporate ladder, but I couldn't get back down and they had to call the Fire Department." | 437 |
| 14.2 | "Our ads promise you the biggest tax refund possible, so we're instructing your employer to withhold 300% of your paycheck this year." | 444 |
| 14.3 | "The college of my choice is very expensive, but when you graduate , they give you a home in the suburbs, a minivan, a lovely wife, two beautiful children and a golden retriever." | 445 |
| 15.1 | "For richer or poorer, in sickness and health, until one little thing goes wrong and you give up on each other?" | 453 |

xii  *Illustrations*

15.2  "When your price is very high, people assume that your product must be very good!" 463
15.3  "If a bus built in 1987 leaves Pittsburgh at 9:14 and Robert sets his crockpot to start cooking a 6-pound roast at 2:09, how long will it take your parents to stop helping with your homework?" 465

## Tables

3.1  More proper nouns, according to category 51
3.2  Prototypical "count" nouns: Singular and plural forms 53
3.3  Prototypical "non-count" or "mass" nouns: No plural forms possible 56
3.4  Traditional "non-count"/"mass" nouns denoting substances, materials, liquids, solids, gases, and abstract concepts 59
4.1  Determiner types and examples 79
5.1  The referential concept of *person*—encapsulated 119
12.1  Core meanings of select prepositions 354

# Acknowledgments

This book has been made possible thanks to our outstanding relationship with Routledge/Taylor and Francis, and especially current and former editors, including Kathrene Binag, Elysse Preposi, Judith Newlin, Rebecca Novack, and Leah Babb-Rosenfeld. We also appreciate the supportive relationship with ApexCoVantage throughout the copy editing and typesetting processes.

We thank Glasbergen Cartoon Service for their permission to reproduce all the cartoons in this volume, all of which are Copyright © Randy Glasbergen. We also thank A. J. Schuler, Psy.D., for his permission to reproduce text extracts from his website on intercultural communication, https://wenku.baidu.com/view/3e9371906bec0975f465e2d2.html, in Chapter 5.

Susan extends her deepest gratitude, love, and appreciation to her six children, Tenaye, Mihret, Addie, Biniyam, Bereket, and Terefech, for their patience, understanding, and love during the nearly three years that this book was being written, and always. She is indebted to Jungwan Yoon and Bonnie Alco for reading multiple early drafts of many chapters and for their insightful feedback. And she thanks her former students who took the Discourse-Functional Grammar class with her at Penn State over the past two decades. Their never-ending enthusiasm and excitement of discovering meaning in grammar and discourse are both the impetus and inspiration for writing this book, making it possible to share these approaches with other prospective teachers and students of language.

Parastou thanks her family for their immense love and constant support throughout the process of writing this book, and always. She extends her warm thanks to Sunny Hyon for her words of encouragement and wisdom. Parastou is especially grateful to Brian for being by her side through the best and hardest parts of this process, and always.

Xuehua thanks her family for being such good friends and sources of kindness and support.

# 1 Meaning Beyond Syntax
## Discourse and Conceptualization

*Figure 1.1* "How I spent my summer vacation"
© Randy Glasbergen. Reproduced with permission of Glasbergen Cartoon Service.

This is a book on grammar and its relation to discourse and meaning. One of the main underlying philosophies of the book is that grammatical structures are meaningful in and of themselves and that, similar to our word choices, our grammatical choices have the power to create and communicate meaning. Even the smallest bits of grammar, like determiners *a*, *the*, *each*, and *every*, are conceptually meaningful in systematic and potentially powerful ways.

We present an approach to grammar and discourse that reveals meaning from a conceptual perspective, focusing on the ways in which users of language express viewpoints, stances, and information and depict imageries using the conceptual categories that underlie all of grammar within discourse. We introduce and work with particular grammatical categories as frameworks of meaning, often appealing to *scalar conceptual notions* of *degree*, for example, degree of individuation and specificity when referring to places, people, things, and concepts; degree of focus in picking out entities in discourse; degree of change potential in discussing events or states; degree of control over actions and outcomes; degree of intensity in descriptions; degree of personal involvement; and so forth. As you will see, much of grammar involves scalarity and gradience rather than rigidly compartmentalized categories like parts of speech and tense and aspect marking, as presented in most traditional approaches to language, both prescriptive and descriptive ones.

This book also differs from the prescriptive and descriptive accounts of English grammar in that we view grammar and conceptual meaning as integrally and inextricably linked to discourse and genre. It is within these broader contexts of discourse and genre that grammatical forms come alive and become relevant, vibrant, and meaningful, in concert with other interrelated grammatical categories and/or parts of speech. Grammar involves the choice of certain forms over other possible competing forms, each evoking a difference in the speaker's or writer's perspective or perception of an event, a difference in the degree of responsibility assigned to an entity active in the discourse, or a difference in stance vis-à-vis the topic or issue at hand. Grammatical choice influences how we shape, create, organize, and understand discourse within the multiplicity of discourse genres.

The book addresses individual parts of speech, like nouns and determiners, and individual grammatical categories, like negation, transitivity, and voice, as interrelated with other parts of speech and other grammatical categories and as integral components of discourse and genre. In this way, the book is designed dually to introduce the various elements of grammar as parts of coherent wholes as well as to present grammar as an all-encompassing construct of language and discourse that is present in all facets of our everyday lives. That is, unlike the traditional accounts and reference materials on grammar that isolate parts of speech and grammatical categories as independent and isolated linguistic components, the explanations and review sections in this book cycle back and re-introduce other relevant and related bits of grammar that contribute integrally to the meaning and imageries expressed in the data samples—pointing out and asking our readers to also notice, for example, how, within the discussion of adverbials, other grammatical categories like conjunctions, adjectives (including relative clauses), nouns, determiners, and verbs (and verb types) work together to depict the beautifully crafted scene in the opening paragraphs of a novel.

The traditional rules of grammar can be confusing. They seem and sometimes truly are superficially arbitrary. And they often occur as long lists of proper usages associated with one type of grammatical construction or another, followed, as we all know, by other lists that are full of exceptions. In fact, when we think of the term *grammar rule*, what may come to mind just as easily and just as spontaneously is the word *exception*, or more accurately, the plural form of the word, *exceptions*, because there are usually so many of them for each traditional grammar rule. Sometimes, there are even more exceptions to the rules than there are "proper usages."

By tweaking the generalizations of the so-called grammar rules and incorporating meaning based on conceptual representations of grammatical categories and parts of speech, we re-evaluate the regularities in grammar patterns. In this way, many of the traditional exceptions are incorporated into the new generalizations. This approach to grammar is based on more flexible rules, more dynamic ones that are linked to conceptual meaning. As such, the rules become simpler, and the exceptions to those rules fewer and easier to explain.

In this book, grammar is not simply discussed from the perspectives of right vs. wrong, grammatical vs. ungrammatical, proper vs. sloppy, "good grammar" vs. "poor grammar," and especially not from the point of view of "That's just the way it is, because the rules say so." Instead, rules of grammar are presented as the system of language through which speakers and writers organize thoughts, experiences, ideas, perceptions, and stances.

The book's content and approach evolved from our nearly two decades of teaching grammar to students who enter our classes with the expectation that the term *grammar* is equivalent to "diagramming sentences," "rules of word order and syntax," and even "standards by which to judge how people use language." Students enter our courses expecting more of the same: rules and exceptions, or what constitutes "proper" vs. "improper" structures or "right" vs. "wrong" choices. And more than that, students leave our courses and workshops with a keen sensitivity to the *nuances of meaning* created through choices of grammatical forms and structures and, generally, a keen sensitivity to how language is used—everywhere.

For speakers and writers, teachers, learners, and users of language, this enhanced awareness of language and discourse not only improves our skills in oral and written communication but also helps us see beyond the words, beyond the literal, and beyond the surface, while attending to choice-making and concepts, meaning and stance, within the wide range of genres and registers that permeate all of our discourse throughout all of our lives.

A simple illustration is the opening cartoon, Figure 1.1. One classic back-to-school genre of discourse is the oral report or essay in which students share what they did during their summer break. Often these essay types are reduced to cliché titles like "How I Spent My Summer Vacation." In the cartoon, instead of describing his summer activities, the student itemizes his full list of expenses—playing on the literal meaning of the verb *spend* as it pertains to money and the figurative meaning as it pertains to time.

Our approach to grammar is designed to guide learners and teachers of English to become more keenly aware of meaning and its connection to grammar—from the more obvious types of distinctions like singular vs. plural or present tense vs. past tense to the more subtle ones like *Has the plane from Newark arrived?* vs. *Did the plane from Newark arrive?* and further variations in which grammatically optional adverbials appear, for example, *Has the plane from Newark arrived yet?* vs. *Has the plane from Newark arrived already?* Contrasts like these are most clearly disambiguated by examining the actual discourse and genre in which they were produced and by considering the various possible *stances* (or attitudes) of the speaker or writer. That is, distinctions in sentence-based examples like these cannot really be accounted for without considering the surrounding discourse. We also address, as grammar, seemingly subtle distinctions in word meanings like *tall* vs. *high* or *big* vs. *large*, and gradable adjectives like *cold* and *cool* or *happy* and *glad* vs. absolute adjectives denoting upper limits, like *freezing* or *delighted*. Most of our illustrative examples draw on actual spates of discourse from a multiplicity of sources such as public signage, emails, policy documents, classroom lectures, essays, news reports, poetry, encyclopedia entries, novels, and so forth.

With regard to meaning, we also point out in multiple sections throughout the book that literal, strictly denotative meanings of words are actually quite uncommon, since genre, context, and surrounding discourse all affect and color the meanings of words. The following quote from Lemony Snicket will illustrate:

> It is very useful, when one is young, to learn the difference between "literally" and "figuratively." If something happens literally, it actually happens; if something happens figuratively, it feels like it is happening.
>
> If you are literally jumping for joy, for instance, it means you are leaping in the air because you are very happy. If you are figuratively jumping for joy, it means you are so happy that you could jump for joy, but are saving your energy for other matters.
>
> (Snicket, 1999, p. 68)

For someone to "jump for joy," literally, as the passage describes, he or she is springing upward into the air out of happiness, feet off the ground. How often have you actually (and literally) witnessed something like this? In what sorts of contexts might people literally jump for joy? Possibly, in scenarios like these:

> Employees receiving a huge raise, prospectors finding gold, students on the last day of school just before summer vacation . . .

## 4  Meaning Beyond Syntax

Figuratively, though, "jumping for joy" expresses a high degree of happiness in which a person *feels like* leaping into the air but doesn't actually do it in a realistic context. Literal interpretations of language make for interesting imaginary scenarios but often not realistic ones.

If you think about the disparity in pay between male and female professional athletes, you might be *opening up a huge can of worms*, but not literally, of course. It just means you'd be opening up a controversial or problematic issue, one that could be immensely difficult to resolve.

The meanings of phrasal verbs change significantly with literal and figurative interpretations: You can *pull* your socks, boots, or gloves *off*, or someone's wig can *fall off*. Both expressions yield a possible literal interpretation of an event. But if *you laugh your head off* or *cheer your lungs out*, there could be real trouble.

Also, meanings of words depend on context, the speaker(s), the addresse(s), and the genre(s). And, as you will see, there is no such thing as a true synonym in the sense of a word that has an exact one-to-one corresponding meaning with another word. While *tall* and *high* carry similar types of meanings with respect to verticality, they are near-synonyms at best, each evoking a distinct conceptual profile.

Therefore, an app that simply translates one language into another as a person speaks or as a dog barks is also impossible and potentially quite comical, as represented in the cartoon in Figure 1.2. The parody can be extended to some comical "translations" that result from such translation apps as TripLingo, Google Translate, and Waygo.

Every chapter of this book opens with a cartoon whose caption illustrates one of the main points that will be discussed in depth. The cartoon encapsulates the gist of the chapter (as this one does) or contains exemplars of the target function, part of speech, or grammatical category.

All chapters provide detailed discussions of the grammatical feature, category, or part of speech, together with robust examples from actual discourse data that elucidate and solidify the meanings and functions of those grammatical features.

All chapters contain sections called "Mini Review and Practice" and "Putting It All Together" that review the concepts and apply their meanings beyond the initial introductions and discussions. And Chapters 3 through 15 contain practice exercises that contain "Common Errors,

*Figure 1.2* "Just bark. The app automatically translates it to English!"

© Randy Glasbergen. Reproduced with permission of Glasbergen Cartoon Service.

Bumps, and Confusions" surrounding the target grammatical features (as well as those from earlier chapters), which are designed to help identify grammatical bumps and to then articulate ways that speakers and writers might revise or edit for more natural-sounding discourse. The chapters conclude with activities constructed to extend discourse- and genre-based practice and to deepen understandings of the concepts through pointed questions and suggestions for further development.

In all, this book intends to reconceive "grammar," not as a strict and unbendable set of prescriptive rules, but as a system of conceptual representation through which users of language evoke differences in perspective, opinion, and stance. Grammar traditionally gets camouflaged by "rules of structure" that not only determine "correctness" or "incorrectness" of utterances but also eclipse meaning—meaning that relates to conceptualizations of entities and events, of time and space. There is no such thing as equivalent synonyms in any language. A speaker's or writer's choice of an individual word or string of words evokes varying conceptual representations of people, objects, actions, states, habits, facts, and opinions.

# Reference

Snicket, L. (1999). *The bad beginning*. New York: HarperCollins Publishers.

# 2 The Nuts and Bolts of Grammar

*Figure 2.1* "The first human was cloned in 2002. When he found out, he was beside himself."
© Randy Glasbergen. Reproduced with permission of Glasbergen Cartoon Service.

This chapter provides a general overview of the terms that are often used in grammatical descriptions and analyses. We provide definitions of those terms as well as examples. Much of the terminology that you encounter here will be re-introduced and discussed in depth in later chapters.

## 2.1 Words

In the following quote by Gary Provost, we find some excellent advice for good writing, all of which centers on the concept of the *word*. Writing manuals and guides, like Provost (1985), often argue for the importance of varying the length of sentences. Sentence length is often determined on the basis of the number of words.

> This sentence has five words. Here are five more words. Five-word sentences are fine. But several together become monotonous. Listen to what is happening. The writing is getting boring. The sound of it drones. It's like a stuck record. The ear demands some variety.

Now listen. I vary the sentence length, and I create music. Music. The writing sings. It has a pleasant rhythm, a lilt, a harmony. I use short sentences. And I use sentences of medium length. And sometimes, when I am certain the reader is rested, I will engage him with a sentence of considerable length, a sentence that burns with energy and builds with all the impetus of a crescendo, the roll of the drums, the crash of the cymbals—sounds that say listen to this, it is important.

(Provost, 1985, p. 60)

What exactly is a word? How do you count the number of words in an English sentence? Words make up the basis of all communication. How do we define the concept of *a word*?

### What is the definition of a *word*?

A word is the smallest meaningful unit of language that stands alone and that labels or modifies a concept, an idea, an action, or a state. A word can also fulfill a grammatical function. In English, we can typically detect the beginning and end of a written word because it has blank space on each side. Boundaries in spoken words are more difficult to discern.

The relationship between the meaning of a word and the sound or shape of a word in English is typically arbitrary. That is, we understand what the word means, both literally and figuratively, through convention. Think about the words *red, shovel, vacant, run, the, tooth, forever, both,* and *spacious.* Nothing in the sound or spelling of the words will give you a hint of what the words mean. The word *red* on its own does not resemble the primary color that we find next to orange at the end of the visible spectrum.

Further, the meanings of all words are multi-layered: Every word that you find in the dictionary has a literal or objective definition. In addition, and more importantly, most, if not all, words carry a great deal of other types of meaning that extend well beyond their dictionary definitions. The literal and objective meanings that we find in a dictionary are referred to as the **denotational meanings**. The other layers of subjective meaning that are implied through the use of a particular word are referred to as the **connotational meanings**.

### Connotations

The underlined words in each pair of the following sentences have similar surface-level denotational meanings. However, the judgments or feelings associated with each word express different connotational meanings. In the following example pairs, one meaning is generally more neutral or positive, and the other has a more negative connotation.

A1: Pat has a *childish* outlook.
   connotation: immature, inexperienced (more negative)
A2: Pat has a *childlike* outlook.
   connotation: innocent, pure (more positive, neutral)

B1: Owen looked a little *sheepish*.
   connotation: not courageous, lacking strength or confidence (more negative)
B2: Owen looked a little *shy*.
   connotation: reserved, quiet, bashful (more neutral)

C1: The committee made a *weird* suggestion.
   connotation: strange, out of the ordinary, abnormal (more negative)
C2: The committee made an *unusual* suggestion.
   connotation: different, uncommon (more neutral, less negative, possibly positive)

D1: Both Alexandrine and Jannik are equally *stubborn*.
   connotation: difficult, inflexible (more negative)
D2: Both Alexandrine and Jannik are equally *persistent*.
   connotation: determined, driven (more neutral, more positive)

## Mini Review and Practice

1   Many words have similar denotational meanings, but they vary greatly in their connotations.

Think about the three-way word sets that follow (categorized according to adjectives, nouns, and verbs). Which appear to be more neutral and objective sounding? Which appear to evoke more subjective and evaluative meanings? Think about the various layers of meaning that each word can evoke. For example, the word *brother* can mean "male sibling" in its denotation, but it can also evoke multiple layers of meaning connotationally—like *emotional solidarity, shared religious affiliation, shared ethnic affiliation, male bonding*, and so forth.

As you work through these word sets, first think about the denotational meaning that all three words have in common. Which of the three feels like it is the most neutral or objective? Which two are more prone to multiple types of connotations? How does the notion of *context* affect word meaning?

How do these connotations seem to alter the meanings of the words? Do they express more **positive connotations** or more **negative connotations**? Do they express other types of evaluation or judgment like *emotion, empathy, warmth, criticism, admiration, comfort/discomfort, ostentatiousness, humility, expertise, in-group membership,* and so forth? Again, consider how context affects how words can be intended and/or interpreted.

### Adjectives:

short, pint-sized, petite
weak, frail, feeble
happy, ecstatic, overjoyed
easy, simple, uncomplicated
mean, cruel, brutal

clever, crafty, cunning
thin, skinny, emaciated
red, scarlet, bloodshot (e.g., eyes)

**Nouns:**

house, residence, home
immigrant, foreigner, alien
gold, jewelry, bling
sibling, brother, friend

**Verbs:**

read, skim, peruse
speak, blabber, chat
study, cram, memorize
eat, devour, consume
drink, sip, gulp
plan, calculate, plot

2   Colors and their meanings

Think about the following colors and how they are used in English discourse:

red, white, blue, green, yellow, orange, violet, purple, pink

First, think about how color terms are used denotationally—that is, in what types of contexts and in describing what types of visible objects are these color terms used (e.g., red rose, blue sky, white cloud)?

Now, find other expressions in English that use these and other color terms in connotative or figurative ways. For example, what other meanings does *red* evoke? (anger, political affiliations, embarrassment) How about *green*? (envy, immaturity, unripe fruit, lack of expertise)

You might also want to conduct an internet search for expressions that use these color terms to evoke various feelings, opinions, and perceptions beyond their denotational meanings.

Try to find examples of how color terms are used both denotationally and figuratively in other languages that you know.

### 2.1.1 Words That Sound Like Their Meanings: Onomatopoeia

As we have seen, the relationship between word meaning and the sounds or shapes of words is typically an arbitrary one. An exception to this is the category of *onomatopoeia*. One defining criterion of this category is that the sound of the word resembles the meaning of the word. Typical sub-categories of onomatopoetic expressions include the following sounds:

**animal sounds:**

bird: *tweet*                duck: *quack*
chicken: *cluck*             rooster: *cock-a-doodle-doo*
cow: *moo*                   pig: *oink*
cat: *meow, purr*            dog: *arf, woof, bowwow*

**anatomical sounds:**

*snort, sniff, achoo, tsk, burp, lub-dub*

**machine sounds:**

car engine: *vroom*          train: *choo choo, chooga chooga chooga*
fan: *whir*                  clock: *ticktock*
bell: *jingle, clang, dingdong*   jackhammer: *rat-a-tat-tat, grrakkka kkkaak*

**impact sounds:**

*thud, wham, pow, smack, clink, crash, crack, crunch, crackle, clip-clop, pitter-patter, snap, splat, boom, kaboom, splash, splish-splash*

**nature sounds:**

rain: *pitter-patter*        wind: *whoosh*
fire: *crackle*              thunder: *boom, crack*

What other types of onomatopoetic sounds can you think of in English? In what sorts of contexts or genres of discourse do you expect to see these types of words in English, for example, in children's books, fictional writing and storytelling, *manga*, *anime*, comics, or theatrical scripts?

How do these types of words pattern in other languages that you may know, like Spanish, French, Japanese, Mandarin, Korean, Persian, Vietnamese, Arabic, and so forth? Do you find mimetic or onomatopoetic expressions to be more or less frequent in those languages in comparison to English? What are some notable examples of mimetic expressions in languages other than English?

## 2.2 Basic Parts of Speech

The basic parts of speech for English are as follows:

**Nouns**        words that label things, people, places, ideas, and concepts
                 Common nouns:   *book, chapter, history, time, table, democracy*
                 Proper nouns:   *Boston, Audi, Louvre, David, Dr. Ross*

**Determiners** words that precede nouns that indicate number/quantity, specificity, focus, possession/affiliation, identifiability, and gender
                 *this, that, these, those, each, every, my, his, her, our, two, such, one fourth of*

| | |
|---|---|
| **Pronouns** | words that replace a noun or a noun-like referent |
| | Subject: *I, you, he, she, it, we, they* |
| | Object: *me, you, him, her, it, us, them* |
| | Reflexive: *myself, yourself(ves), himself, herself, itself, ourselves, themselves* |
| | Reciprocal: *each other, one another* |
| **Verbs** | words that express events, states, identities, and actions |
| | *run, walk, read, eat, play, jump, be, become, receive, have, give, donate* |
| **Prepositions** | words that situate entities in space, time, and abstraction |
| | *from, of, at, to, for, on, off, with, without, in, inside, out, outside, over, under* |
| **Adjectives** | words that describe nouns and pronouns |
| | *blue, gray, pretty, delicious, stylish, brave, fearless, fearful, provocative, little* |
| **Conjunctions** | words that join two or more units (words, phrases, or clauses) together |
| | *and, or, but, nor, yet, so, for, either, both, nevertheless, besides* |
| **Adverbs** | words that describe and modify verbs, adjectives, and other adverbs |
| | *luckily, maybe, tomorrow, correctly, now, here, soon, very, really* |

Words that are categorized into one part of speech might also be used as other parts of speech. For example, the word *book* is commonly used as a noun. But *book* can also be used as a verb meaning "to establish on record," "to reserve," or "to enter into the record books."

*book* = verb
  We <u>booked</u> a room at the Hyatt Hotel.
  The police caught the thief and <u>booked</u> him the same day.

Similarly, the word *plot* can be used as a noun with multiple meanings:

*plot* = noun  "the main events of a story, film, or play"
  "an expanse of land"
  "a plan made in secret"

*Plot* can also be used as a verb meaning "to plan something [usually bad or unpleasant] in secret."

From Miami, these fierce opponents of Fidel Castro <u>plotted</u> to overthrow the Cuban dictator and channeled funds to dissidents.

(Levy, 2015)

Here, the verb *plot* has a negative connotation (particularly for the target of the plot).

Now, have a look at the following crossword puzzle clue that appeared in the *Los Angeles Times* on January 6, 2017:

4-letter word that means "plot to plow" ___ ___ ___ ___.

Is *plot* used here as a noun or a verb?
[It's used as a noun.] How do you know?
(It is actually possible to interpret the clue with *plot* used as a verb, which makes crossword puzzles a little tricky to solve.)

[*Answer:* ACRE]

## 2.3 Forming Words

### 2.3.1 Adding Morphemes to Words: Affixation

The most common way to expand our inventory of words or to change meanings of existing words is by adding morphemes in the form of prefixes and suffixes. This process of adding prefixes and suffixes (affixes) to words is known as **affixation**.

A **morpheme** is the smallest unit of language that conveys meaning. A morpheme can be **free**—that is, it can **stand alone** and convey a **comprehensive meaning**, like *paper, key, write, walk,* and *pretty*. This means that an entire word can be a morpheme.

Or, a morpheme can be **bound**—that is, **it must attach or be affixed to another part of the word** in order for its meaning to be expressed, like *-s* (plural marker), *-ed* (past tense marker), *un-* (negative prefix), *mega-* (prefix of size), *-ness* (suffix that changes an adjective into a noun), and *-ly* (suffix that changes an adjective into an adverb). The **meanings of bound morphemes** are **partial** in that they express limited bits of meaning that cannot stand on their own like free morphemes can.

#### 2.3.1.1 Inflectional Morphemes

Inflectional morphemes constitute a finite set of morphemes that influence word meaning. **Inflectional morphemes provide grammatical meaning** to words, meanings like plural, possessive, tense and aspect, and comparative and superlative. There are only eight inflectional morphemes for English. They are all **suffixes**—that is, they are added to the ends of the words in question.

ADDED TO NOUNS: TWO FORMS

    1  -s plural marker

        *books*
        [FREE] + bound

        *cartoons*
        [FREE] + bound

    2  -'s possessive marker

        *Jack's* pencil
        [FREE] + bound

        the *jar's* contents
        [FREE] + bound

Here are some examples of nouns that are **inflected** for **both plural and possessive**:

    Some teens have trouble understanding their *parents'* rules.
      [FREE = parents] + bound [pl.] + bound [poss.] = parents'

    The *bands'* lead singers tested the microphones before the show.
      [FREE] + bound [pl.] + bound [poss.] = bands'

ADDED TO VERBS: <u>FOUR</u> FORMS

    1 -s <u>third-person singular present tense</u>

        Malcolm Gladwell *writes* essays.
                [<u>FREE</u>] + **bound**

        Sonia *bakes* blueberry scones.
                [<u>FREE</u>] + **bound**

In English, for the present tense, <u>**only the third-person singular form changes by adding -s**</u> (except for the verbs *be* and *have*, which are irregular—see Chapter 7).

The other forms are identical, with no change to the verb form.

| | | | |
|---|---|---|---|
| I | play | we | play |
| you (s.) | play | you (pl.) | play |
| he/she/it | play**s** | they | play |

    2 -ed <u>past tense</u>

Note: For regular verbs, -ed is the morpheme for the past tense.

        Pete Conrad *walked* on the moon.         [regular past tense]
            [<u>FREE</u>=walk] + **bound**

        Marie Curie *discovered* radium.          [regular past tense]
            [<u>FREE</u>=discover] + **bound**

Irregular past tense verbs do not follow this pattern but are still understood as evoking **the basic meaning** of that verb **plus past tense**:

| | | | |
|---|---|---|---|
| sing | → | *sang* | [<u>FREE</u>=sing] + **past tense meaning** |
| bring | → | *brought* | [<u>FREE</u>=bring] + **past tense meaning** |
| take | → | *took* | [<u>FREE</u>=take] + **past tense meaning** |

        Chuck Yeager *broke* the sound barrier in 1947.    [irregular past tense]
                [<u>FREE</u>=break] + **past tense meaning**

        Orville and Wilbur Wright *flew* the first airplane.    [irregular past tense]
                    [<u>FREE</u>=fly] + **past tense meaning**

    3 -en <u>past participle</u>

Note: For some verbs, *-en* is the morpheme for the past participle, regardless of whether the verb takes the past-participle form *-en* or the more common past-participle form *-ed*. The *-en* morphological designation is used to denote the past participle to distinguish that morpheme from the *-ed* past tense morpheme.

    <u>Used in perfect aspect:</u> *have/has/had/will have* + V-**en**

        Gabon *has taken* the lead over Morocco in the soccer playoffs.
                [<u>FREE</u>] + **past participle**

14   *The Nuts and Bolts of Grammar*

"The Great Oz *has spoken*," bellowed the Wizard of Oz.
[FREE] + **past participle**

Malala and her family *have donated* millions to charities.
[FREE] + **past participle**

Used in passive voice: *be/is/are/was/were* + V-**en**

Eva Perón's tiara *was stolen* and *was* later *recovered* by police in Milan.
[FREE] + **past participle** [FREE] + **past participle**

The national anthem *was sung* by Beyoncé at Obama's 2013 inauguration.
[FREE] + **past participle** [irregular: *sing* → *sung*]

  4  -ing present participle

Used in progressive aspect: *be/is/are/was/were* + V-ing (see Chapter 7)

Do you know what language he *is speaking*?
[FREE] + **present participle**

Christiane Amanpour *is reporting* the news live from Cairo.
[FREE] + **present participle**

ADDED TO ADJECTIVES AND ADVERBS: TWO FORMS

  1  -er comparative

Used when comparing and contrasting a quality or state to another quality or state. The comparative is used when **two entities** (or qualities or states) are being compared or contrasted. Note minor variations in spelling when adding morphemes, for example, *y* → *i*, the doubling of some final consonants, and the addition of only *-r* (instead of *-er*) when words end with the letter e.

| happy → *happier* | strange → *stranger* |
|---|---|
| [FREE] [FREE] + **comparative** | [FREE] [FREE] + **comparative** |
| red → *redder* | green → *greener* |
| [FREE] [FREE] + **comparative** | [FREE] [FREE] + **comparative** |
| hot → *hotter* | mild → *milder* |
| [FREE] [FREE] + **comparative** | [FREE] [FREE] + **comparative** |

Chicago is even *colder* than Mars today.
[FREE] + **comparative**

Some posts on Facebook now appear in *larger* and *bolder* font.
[FREE] + **comparative**   [FREE] + **comparative**

  2  -est superlative

Used when describing **the extreme upper limit or extreme lower limit** of a quality or state. The superlative is not used when there are only two entities being compared or contrasted.

For only two entities, use comparative forms. Again, note variations in spelling, as with the comparative: *y → i*, the doubling of some final consonants, and the addition of only *-st* (instead of *-est*) when words end with the letter *e*.

| clean → | <u>clean</u>*est* | dirty → | <u>dirt</u>*iest* |
|---|---|---|---|
| [FREE] | [FREE] + **superlative** | [FREE] | [FREE] + **superlative** |
| funny → | <u>funn</u>*iest* | sad → | <u>sad</u>*dest* |
| [FREE] | [FREE] + **superlative** | [FREE] | [FREE] + **superlative** |
| large → | <u>larg</u>*est* | dry → | <u>dri</u>*est* |
| [FREE] | [FREE] + **superlative** | [FREE] | [FREE] + **superlative** |

February 2016 was Earth's <u>warm</u>*est* month on record.
[FREE] + **superlative**

Here is a list of 15 universities with the <u>high</u>*est* tuition in the US.
[FREE] + **superlative**

### 2.3.1.2 Derivational Morphemes

Derivational morphemes are far more varied and more numerous than inflectional morphemes. Derivational morphemes alter the meanings of words through both prefixes (attached before the root word) and suffixes (attached after the root word).

Sometimes derivational morphemes change parts of speech, for example, from nouns to adjectives, from adjectives to adverbs, from adjectives to nouns, and so forth. Derivational morphemes also can change the meanings of words from affirmative to negative, and they can add other types of meanings like *approximation* (*-ish*), *the process of* (*-ize, -[i]fy*), *evaluative commentary of quantity* (*under-, over-*), and so forth.

| success → | <u>success</u>*ful* → | un<u>success</u>*fully* |
|---|---|---|
| [FREE] | [FREE] + **bound** | **bound** + [FREE] + **bound** + **bound** |
| NOUN | ADJECTIVE | ADVERB: NEGATIVE + noun + ADJ + ADVERB |
| achieve → | <u>achieve</u>*ment* → | over<u>achieve</u>*ment* |
| [FREE] | [FREE] + **bound** | **bound** + [FREE] + **bound** |
| VERB | NOUN | NOUN: evaluative commentary |
| teach → | <u>teach</u>*er* | |
| [FREE] | [FREE] + **bound** | |
| VERB | NOUN | |
| hospital → | <u>hospital</u>*ize* | |
| [FREE] | [FREE] + **bound** | |
| NOUN | VERB | |
| brown → | <u>brown</u>*ish* | |
| [FREE] | [FREE] + **bound** | |
| ADJECTIVE | ADJECTIVE (+ approximation) | |

## COMMON DERIVATIONAL PREFIXES IN ENGLISH

(Note that these prefixes do not typically change the part of speech of the original word.)

- re-      'to do again,' 'back, backward'
  *re-write, redesign, retell, reread, replay, reiterate, retake, retreat*

- mis-     'to do in error'
  *misspeak, misquote, misremember, mislay, mistake, misrepresent*

- bi-      'two'
  *bicycle, binary, bilateral, bipartisan, bimonthly, biped, biracial*

- mono-    'one'
  *monorail, monocle, monopoly, monogamy, monotone, monochrome, monarchy*

- over-    'to do too much of something, to do to excess'
  *overestimate, overdo, overrate, overanalyze, overcook, overachiever*

- under-   'to do or represent something as less than, inferior, or insufficient'
  *underestimate, understate, undersell, underplay, underrate, undercook*

- pre-     'in advance of something'
  *preapprove, prepay, preaddress, preview, pre-assign, preposition*

- post-    'after something'
  *postpone, post-graduation, postpartum, postindustrial, postmodern, postposition*

- anti-    'against'
  *anticancer, antibullying, anticorrosion, antithesis, antisocial, antifreeze*

- negative prefixes (see Chapter 10)

  - non-
    *nonpartisan, nonissue, nonprofessional, nondescript, noncritical*
  - un-
    *unprofessional, undo, untie, uncritical, unimaginative, unpatriotic, unsay*
  - im-, in-, il-, ir-
    *impossible, imbalance, insane, inept, innocuous, illegal, illegitimate, irregular*
  - a-, an-
    *amoral, atheoretical, asynchronous, asexual, anarchy, anonymous*
  - dis-
    *dislocate, displeasure, dissuade, disbar, disband, disagree, disown, disappear*

## COMMON DERIVATIONAL SUFFIXES IN ENGLISH

(Note that these suffixes DO typically change the part of speech of the original word.)

- -ly  'in the manner of' (adjective to adverb)
  *quickly, daintily, rapidly, readily, joyfully, mercifully, comfortably, softly*

- -er  'the person or thing that does the action of the verb' (verb to noun)
  *print* = V   *printer* = person or thing that prints something.
  *admire* = V   *admirer* = person that/who admires someone or something.
  *player, writer, gardener, teacher, explorer, designer, performer, typewriter*

  - -or (variation) *instructor, actor, investor, creator, assessor, curator, conductor*

- -ment     'means or result of an action' (verb to noun)
  *commitment, employment, treatment, equipment*

- -tion, -ion     'condition, action, state of being' (verb to noun)
  *election, prosecution, solution, recreation, temptation*

- -ful     'having the quality of' (verb/noun to adjective)
  *joyful, playful, mindful, spoonful, watchful, fruitful, harmful, tearful*

- -ness     'an abstract concept, for example, a state, action, or quality' (adjective to abstract noun)
  *kindness, goodness, hardness, softness, laboriousness, fruitfulness, mindfulness*

- -able     'possible to do, fit for' (verb to adjective)
  *washable, translatable, laughable, teachable, playable, pleasurable*

- -al     'having the quality of' (noun/adjective to adjective)
  *electrical, fictional, promotional, historical, biblical, political*

- -ism     'the ideology of' (adjective/noun to noun)
  *activism, feminism, realism, fascism, communism, racism, sexism*

- -ist     'an expert, a professional, an ideologue' (adjective/noun to noun)
  *activist, feminist, pianist, extortionist, publicist, journalist, novelist*

- -ize     'indicating the process of change into something' (adjective/noun to verb)
  *crystallize, Americanize, dramatize, theorize, sterilize, harmonize*

- -less     'not having/without' (noun to adjective)
  *merciless, penniless, smokeless, sleeveless, careless*

## 2.3.2 Conversion

As we observed in Section 2.2 ("Basic Parts of Speech"), sometimes the notion of "part of speech" in English can be tricky, in that a word that is typically associated with **one part of speech is used as another part of speech** in discourse. This process is known as **conversion.** We illustrate the process here.

The words in the left-hand column are typically recognizable as nouns, but here we can see that they are also used as verbs:

| Noun → | Verb | Example |
| --- | --- | --- |
| water | to add, give water to | to **water** plants |
| butter | to put butter on | to **butter** toast |
| hammer | to use a hammer on, to pound | to **hammer** the nail down<br>The hail **hammered** the roof. |
| blanket | to cover heavily | The volcano **blanketed** the town in ash. |
| coat | to cover thinly | to **coat** an almond with chocolate |
| messenger | to send s.t. via messenger | to **messenger** a contract or document |
| paddle | to propel using a paddle | to **paddle** across a lake |
| bottle | to place liquid into a bottle | to **bottle** the cider |
| friend | to add s.o. to social media | to **friend** someone |
| mother | to nurture like a mother | to **mother** an injured bird |
| Google | to look up on Google | to **Google** your own name |
| plot | to lay plans for (negative) | Evans **plotted** to escape from prison. |

Conversely, in the following examples, the words in the left-hand column are typically recognizable as verbs, but here we can see that they are also used as nouns:

| Verb | → | Noun |
|---|---|---|
| laugh | | We had **a** good **laugh**. |
| steal | | If you really thought it was **a steal**, you would have bought it. |
| slumber | | She fell into **a** deep **slumber** and didn't wake up until the next afternoon. |
| abuse | | After years of **abuse**, he finally quit his job. |
| talk | | Sorry I couldn't attend **your talk** yesterday. |

### 2.3.3 Compounding

Words can also be formed by fusing two or more full words together. This process is known as **compounding**.

**noun + noun compounds**

homework, eyeglasses, eyebrow, eyelash, eyesight, toenail, fingernail, skateboard, toothbrush, pacemaker, dishwasher, bathroom, ballroom, trashcan, basketball

**other compounds: noun + verb, preposition/adverb + verb, adjective + noun, and so on**

*verbs*: handwrite, overestimate, understate, upload, backfire, foretell, crosscut
*adjectives/participles*: underground, upscale, handwritten, overstated, newfound
*nouns*: drywall, blackboard, backyard, output, comeback, wetsuit, handshake
*adverbs, adjectives, pronouns*: everyday, everyone, anybody, altogether, alright

### 2.3.4 Portmanteau or Blending: Fusing Parts of Words Together

Another way that new words are created is by **fusing parts of words together**. This process is called "portmanteau" or "blending," because it involves two parts coming together as one, resembling the old-fashioned suitcase, the *portmanteau*. Some portmanteau words have become everyday words, for example, *smog*, *brunch*, *bionic*, and *carjack*. Other blended neologisms evoke a particular position or perspective, sometimes taking on connotations of judgment and/or negative or positive evaluation:

| *smog* | smoke + fog |
| *brunch* | breakfast + lunch |
| *bionic* | biology + electronic |
| *carjack* | car + hijack |
| *Groupon* | group + coupon |
| *voluntourism* | volunteer + tourism |
| *Spanglish, Konglish* | Spanish + English, Korean + English |
| *ginormous* | gigantic + enormous |
| *hazmat* | hazardous + materials |

### 2.3.5 Other Ways of Forming Words: Shortening or Clipping and Acronyms

Some words in English appear as shortened or clipped versions of the longer words:

lab = laboratory
Lab = Labrador retriever (breed of dog)
fridge = refrigerator
flu = influenza
dorm = dormitory

Some words in English are acronyms, that is, formed by the first letter(s) of each word in a multi-word name:

laser = light amplification by stimulated emission of radiation
radar = radio detection and ranging
sonar = sound navigation and ranging
scuba = self-contained underwater breathing apparatus
zip code = zone improvement plan
Smart car = Swatch Mercedes Art

---

## Mini Review and Practice

1   Practice with **inflectional morphemes, parts of speech, compound words,** and **conversion**.

Read the following passage from *Mr. Terupt Falls Again* (Buyea, 2013, p. 234).

First, read the text for content and meaning. Then, reread to locate the previously listed target forms. Remember that the **inflectional morphemes** are strictly grammatical, indicating meanings as follows:

- -s    plural noun
- -'s   possessive
- -s    third-person singular present tense
- -ed   past tense (The regular past tense form has overt -ed. The irregular forms do not display -ed in the spelling.)
- -en   past participle, even though the form might be spelled -*ed*
- -ing  present participle
- -er   comparative
- -est  superlative

Next,

- identify the various parts of speech,
- find the compound words, and

20   *The Nuts and Bolts of Grammar*

- locate instances of conversion (in this case, nouns → verbs).

    We led our visitors to the main entrance and held the glass doors open as they filed out and boarded the yellow bus. Mr. T. went outside with Mrs. Stern. They were busy talking. I eyed Derek as he walked past me. He thought he was big and mighty for flirting with Lexie. Anger bubbled inside me.

    At some point that afternoon the sky started dropping those big, heavy very wet snowflakes. The kind you hate to shovel because the snow sticks together and weighs so much.

    (Buyea, 2013, p. 234)

**Answers:**

- inflectional morphemes:
  plural nouns: **-s**                                    *visitors, doors, snowflakes*
  past tense: **-ed** and **irregular past forms**        *led, held, filed, boarded, went, were, eyed, walked, thought, was, bubbled, started*

  present participle: **-ing**                            *talking, flirting, dropping*
  third-person singular present tense **-s**              *sticks, weighs*

- determiners:                                            *our, the, that, those*
- common nouns:                                           *visitors, entrance, doors, bus, anger, afternoon, sky, snowflakes, kind, snow*
- proper nouns:                                           *Mr. T, Mrs. Stern, Derek, Lexie*
- pronouns:
  subject pronouns:                                       *we, they, I, he, you*
  object pronouns:                                        *me*
- adjectives:                                             *main, glass, yellow, busy, big, mighty, heavy, wet*
- verbs:                                                  *led, held, filed, boarded, went, were, eyed, walked, thought, bubbled, started, dropping, hate, shovel, sticks, weighs*
- compound words:                                         *outside, inside, afternoon, snowflakes*
- conversion (nouns to verbs):                            *eyed, bubbled*

2   Practice with both inflectional and derivational morphemes.

Now, have a look at the following passage from Dwight Bolinger's (1980) classic book *Language: The Loaded Weapon—The Use and Abuse of Language Today*. Unlike the previous passage, which contained only inflectional morphemes, this passage contains a nice variety of both inflectional and derivational morphemes.

Read the passage first for content. What is Bolinger's main point here? How does he establish this point? How does it relate to what we have been discussing so far about words and word meaning?

How many morphemes does the expression *all gone* have? How many different ways could you answer this? What difference does this make in relation to Bolinger's idea?

Now, for practice, identify the inflectional morphemes. Then, identify the derivational morphemes. For the derivational morphemes, you might want to separate your categories according to prefixes and suffixes. You will definitely locate some derivational morphemes that we have not introduced here. When you do so, try to find other words that also contain those morphemes. Finally, locate the verb that is derived from a noun.

Sounds, words, and grammar are the three great layers—more like the layers of atmosphere than layers of cake, for it is impossible to cut cleanly between them. One of the earliest two-word expressions that most English-speaking children learn is *all gone*. But it is hardly two words for the child. Rather it is a two-syllable unit with a unitary meaning, something like 'disappeared'—it is learned early because of the fascination of things vanishing from sight and then reappearing. A child is not equipped either semantically or phonetically to split up the utterances that come flooding from adults.

(Bolinger, 1980, p. 25)

**Answers:**

- Inflectional morphemes:

  | | |
  |---|---|
  | -s (plural nouns): | *sounds, words, layers, expressions, children* (irregular), *things, utterances, adults* |
  | -s (third-person singular present): | *is* (irregular) |
  | -ed (past tense): | *disappeared* |
  | -en (past participle): | *loaded, gone, learned, equipped* |
  | -ing (present participle): | *meaning, vanishing, reappearing, flooding* |

- Derivational morphemes (and mixed with inflectional):

  **Prefixes**
  | | |
  |---|---|
  | ab- | *ab**use* |
  | im- | *im**possible* |
  | dis- | *dis**appear* |
  | re- | *re**appear* |

  **Suffixes**
  | | |
  |---|---|
  | -ly | *clean**ly* |
  | -sion | *expres**sion* |
  | -ary | *unit**ary* |
  | -tion | *fascina**tion* |
  | -ic + -al + -ly | *seman**tically**, phone**tically* |
  | -ance | *utter**ance* |

- Verb derived from a noun: *flood* → *utterances that come* <u>*flooding*</u> *from adults*

- Number of morphemes in *all gone*, analyzed from a traditional perspective: **three**

  *all* = FREE morpheme
  *gone* → *go* [<u>FREE</u>] + **past participle** [irregular]

3   Derivational morphemes and their meanings

The quote from Khavita Bupta Ghosh (2015) about teachers and learners contains four nouns that end in *-er*. Two instances of those *-er* endings are actually derivational morphemes that turn a verb into a noun that means "the person or thing that does the verb."

And two are not. The nouns in question have been highlighted. Which of the two contain the *-er* morpheme that turns the verb into a noun?

> A **shower** of rain rejuvenates nature; similarly a Good **Teacher** rejuvenates **learners** with the beauty of knowledge. A **shower** of rain in the desert rejuvenates the most barren wasteland and helps hibernating **flowers** to bloom with an explosion of colour and eagerness.
>
> (Ghosh, 2015)

In order to answer these questions, it is important to think about the meanings of the words.

First, is there a discernible verb (V) within the noun?
If so, does the addition of *-er* mean "a person or thing that does the action of the V"?

Can any of the following words mean more than one thing, depending upon how you analyze the morphemes?

For example, the word *better* can be used as a comparative adjective for *good* (good → better), in which case it has only one morpheme. Or, it can mean "a person who bets," in which case it would be analyzed like this:

bet         →      bett**er**
[FREE]             [FREE] + **bound**
VERB               NOUN "a person who bets"

Analyze the following words in a similar manner. How many different meanings can each word have, depending upon how you analyze the morphemes? You may want to consult a dictionary or other source(s) to find the possible range of uses of some of these words in English.

batter
ground
carpenter
taper
childspace (the ambiguous name of a day care center)
resort
sewer
chipper

4    Forming new words through portmanteau or blending

The process of fusing parts of words together creates many new meanings. In recent years, we have seen the emergence of the following expressions:

athleisure
edutainment
friendversary
infomercial
videotorial
cyborg
frenemy

> For the previously listed words, find the two noun sources that make up each fused word.
>
> What does the new word mean, and how is it used in society today?
> For example, do you see the word used in everyday language?
> Do you see it used in public media stories? In advertising? In social media?
>
> Look up the origin of the term *vlog*. Are there only two noun sources here?
> Under what circumstances was this particular term coined?
>
> Can you think of any other words that you have seen recently that have been formed through the process of portmanteau or blending? What are the origins of those words?

## 2.4 Putting Words Together: Phrases, Clauses, and Sentences

### 2.4.1 Phrases

A phrase is a grammatical unit composed of one word or more than one word functioning as a coherent grammatical whole. Within grammar and discourse, the most common types of phrases are **noun phrases, verb phrases, adjective phrases, adverb phrases,** and **prepositional phrases**.

#### 2.4.1.1 Noun Phrases

A noun phase consists of a single word that acts as the head noun or the cluster of words that enhances the meaning of a head noun. In the following examples, we will underline the head nouns. The common abbreviation for noun phrase is NP.

- Often, noun phrases are formed with a **determiner + noun** combination.

Determiners (see Chapter 4) include such words as *some, the, a, this, every, his,* and *our*.

Nouns (see Chapter 3) include such words as common nouns (*city, photograph, water, building,* and *horse*) and proper nouns (*Spain, John, Harvard, Kraft, Saturn,* and *Wendy's*).

In the following examples, the **head noun** is underlined and the entire **NP** is in bold type.

    **Some cities** in **the United States** are overcrowded.
       NP           NP

    **Our house** is located near **a synagogue**.
      NP              NP

- **Pronouns** (see Chapter 5) like *I, she, me, her, him, them,* and *they* can also be considered as NPs.

    Do **you** know Mr. Finley?    **He**  is    **our neighbor**.
       NP [pro]                NP [pro]      NP

24   *The Nuts and Bolts of Grammar*

- **An NP** can include **multiple modifiers**, like **determiners** and **adjectives**.

    Their <u>families</u> had **a joyful, exciting, and long-awaited** <u>reunion</u>.
        NP                                      NP

*2.4.1.2 Verb Phrases*

A verb phrase consists of a single verb or cluster of words that enhances or complements the meaning of a <u>main verb</u>. Note that the verb phrase does not include the subject. In the following examples, we <u>underline the main verb</u>. The common abbreviation for verb phrase is VP.

- VPs might include **only the main verb**, when the verb is **intransitive**:

    | Bats <u>sleep</u> during the day. | [*sleep*: intransitive verb] |
    |---|---|
    |     VP | |
    | The smoke <u>**dissipated**</u>. | [*dissipate*: intransitive verb] |
    |       VP | |

- VPs also include **direct and indirect objects** when the verb is **transitive** or **ditransitive** (see Chapter 6).

    | Meghan <u>**writes**</u> **poetry**. | [*write*: transitive verb] |
    |---|---|
    |       VP | [*poetry*: direct object] |
    | Felipe <u>**sent**</u> **the attachment to Keiko**. | [*send*: ditransitive verb] |
    |        VP | [*the attachment*: direct object] |
    | | [*to Keiko*: indirect object] |

- VPs include **modals and other auxiliaries** that precede the main verb (see Chapter 8).

    | All drivers **must** <u>**stop**</u> at a red light. | [*must*: modal] |
    |---|---|
    |       VP | [*stop*: intransitive verb] |
    | The fugitive **was** <u>**spotted**</u> in Paris. | [*was*: passive auxiliary] |
    |       VP | [*spot*: transitive verb] |
    | Their ship **should have** <u>**arrived**</u> by now. | [*should*: modal] |
    |       VP | [*have*: perfect auxiliary] |
    | | [*arrive*: intransitive verb] |

*2.4.1.3 Adjective Phrases*

An adjective phrase consists of a single adjective and (optionally) other words that modify or further describe the <u>head adjective</u>. In the following examples, the adjective phrases are in bold and the head adjective is underlined.

- **Adjective phrases** (AdjPs) can be single adjectives like *small, important, political, complex,* and *incredible*.

    His remarks were <u>**misleading**</u>.
                       AdjP

    Everything on Twitter is <u>**public**</u>.
                        AdjP

- **AdjPs** can consist of an adjective and other words or phrases that further modify the adjective:

    | We feel **very** <u>**lucky**</u>. | [*very*: adverb, modifies the adjective] |
    |---|---|
    |     AdjP | [*lucky*: adjective] |

He is **allergic** to cats.     [*allergic*: adjective]
   **AdjP**     [*to cats*: prepositional phrase]

### 2.4.1.4 Adverb Phrases

An adverb phrase is a single word or combination of words that describes the actions or states evoked by the VP, in terms of **how** the event or state unfolds, **when,** and **where**.

- **Adverb phrases** (AdvPs) can be single-word expressions like *carefully, carelessly, magnificently, quickly, fast, late, early,* and *today*.

   Bella Davidovich played Chopin's ballades **magnificently**.
                                                 **AdvP**

AdvPs can also consist of multiple words like *so soon, right there, unbelievably fast, later than expected,* and *quite frankly*.

   The apology came **too late**.     [*too*: adverb]
                 **AdvP**     [*late*: adverb]

   **Oddly enough**, they rejected our offer.     [*oddly*: adverb]
     **AdvP**     [*enough*: adverb]

### 2.4.1.5 Prepositional Phrases

A prepositional phrase consists of a preposition (e.g., *at, to, on, in, with, without, of*) and, most commonly, a noun phrase. These expressions typically function as adverbs or adjectives.

- **Prepositional phrases** (PPs) can consist of a single preposition and an NP, like *in the house, on the bus, in pencil, with pleasure, along the driveway, in a hurry, with no regret, to the left, at midnight, all by myself,* and *without a jacket*.

   Bojing swam **in the freezing lake** **in the middle of winter**.
               **PP** [adverb]     **PP** [adverb]
          [explains *where* Bojing swam]     [explains *when* he swam there]

   FedEx left the package **at the door**.
                     **PP** [adverb]
              [explains *where* FedEx left the package]

   This type of climate change is **without precedent**.
                          **PP** [adjective]
                   [modifies *This type of climate change*]

   Many schoolchildren in the city **of Toronto** speak fluent French.
                                   **PP** [adjective]
                               [modifies *city*]

PPs can also consist of multiple prepositions like *from inside, down from, up over,* and *back around*.

   The cat's meow came **from inside the bathroom**.
                         **PP** [adverb]
                    [modifies *from where* the cat's meow came]

   The hikers went **up over the snowy mountain** and disappeared.
                      **PP** [adverb]
               [modifies *where* the hikers went]

### 2.4.2 Clauses

Noun phrases and verb phrases combine to create clauses. A clause contains both a subject and a predicate (or verbal element).

| Corn | grows well in Iowa. | | |
|---|---|---|---|
| Subject | PRED | | |
| **NP** | **VP** | **AdvP** | **PP** [adverb] |

There are two basic types of clauses in English: **independent clauses** and **dependent or subordinate clauses**.

**Independent clauses** are called "independent" because they can **stand alone grammatically**. An independent clause can be considered a "complete sentence."

| Corn | grows well in Iowa. | [independent] |
|---|---|---|
| Subject | PRED | |
| The ice storm | will immobilize the Midwest. | [independent] |
| Subject | PRED | |

**Dependent clauses** also contain a subject and a predicate, but the idea or content expressed in a dependent clause is not complete. That is, a dependent clause contains an indicator that more information is necessary to complete the idea.

Here are a few examples of such grammatical indicators of "dependence," also known as subordinators, abbreviated here as **SUBDR**.

*when, while, as soon as, provided that, if, as if, even if, until, in order to, given that, in the event (that), although, even though, every time (that), because*

| Corn grows well in Iowa | // | **because** its soil is so fertile. |
|---|---|---|
| | | **SUBDR** |
| independent | | dependent (reason) |

| **When** it hits, | // | the ice storm will immobilize the Midwest. |
|---|---|---|
| **SUBDR** | | |
| dependent (temporal circumstance) | | independent |

There is no rule for deciding which type of clause—that is, the dependent or the independent clause—comes first in discourse. The meaning will change slightly, depending on which element of the communication writers and speakers choose to foreground.

Compare the following two sentences, and think about how the meaning shifts, even slightly, by virtue of reversing the order of the independent and dependent clauses:

**Dependent clause first:**

| **If** you follow through on your golf swing, | // | you will have more control of the ball. |
|---|---|---|
| **SUBDR** | | |
| dependent (suggestion/condition) | | independent (consequence of the condition) |

**Independent clause first:**

You will have more control of the ball,   //   **if** you follow through on your (golf) swing.
                                               **SUBDR**
independent (statement, prediction)            dependent (suggestion/condition)

In the previous examples, the dependent clauses provide information about the **reason** for a particular outcome (fertile soil in Iowa: SBDR = *because*), the **temporal circumstance** of an event (the ice storm hitting the Midwest: SBDR = *when*), or the **conditional suggestion** for an action (follow through on a golf swing: SBDR = *if*). These types of dependent clauses function as **adverbial clauses**—that is, clauses that act as adverbs within sentences. **Other types of dependent clauses** include **nominal clauses** and **relative clauses**.

**Nominal clauses** are dependent clauses that function in the same way that nouns or noun phrases do—for example, as the subject or object of the sentence. A nominal clause can begin with subordinators such as *that, what, how, who,* verb + *-ing* (gerund). Here are some examples:

Amazon announces **that** it will create 100,000 US jobs.
       **SBDR** [nominal clause (object)]

**How** you feel about him is irrelevant at this point.
**SBDR** [nominal clause (subject)]

**Playing** Minecraft helps children develop visuospatial reasoning.
**SBDR** [nominal clause (subject)]

**Relative clauses** are also dependent clauses. Their function is to enhance the meaning of the head noun. In this sense, they function as adjectives (see Chapter 13). Relative clauses are formed with relative pronouns *that, which, who, whose, whom, where,* and *when*. Relative clauses differ from other dependent clauses in that **their meanings combine information from two independent clauses**:

**Two separate independent clauses:**

Marcos  wrote an introductory paragraph.       It      is outstanding.
subject  PRED                                  subject  PRED
independent clause 1                           independent clause 2

Now, combine these two together into a relative clause using the relative pronoun *that*:

The introductory paragraph *that* Marcos wrote      is outstanding.
            relative clause [dependent]
       subject                                       PRED

**Two separate independent clauses:**

The boy  came late to class.      He      failed the test.
subject  PRED                     subject  PRED
independent clause 1              independent clause 2

28  *The Nuts and Bolts of Grammar*

Now, combine these two together into a relative clause using the relative pronoun *who* or *that*:

| The boy *who/that* came late to class | failed the test. |
|---|---|
| **relative clause [dependent]** | |
| subject | PRED |

## 2.4.3 Sentences

### 2.4.3.1 Three Sentence Types: Simple, Compound, Complex

Traditionally, sentences are defined as grammatical units that convey a complete thought or idea through, at minimum, a subject and a predicate. An independent clause is also a sentence.

| Horses | eat hay. |
|---|---|
| subject | PRED |

Sentences that are composed of only one independent clause are **simple sentences**.

| Horses | should eat hay a few times every day. | = **simple** |
|---|---|---|
| subject | PRED | |

| Kangaroos | cannot walk backward. | = **simple** |
|---|---|---|
| subject | PRED | |

Sentences that are composed of more than one independent clause and connected with a coordinating conjunction (e.g., *and*, *but*, *so*, *or*, *nor*; see Chapter 14) are **compound sentences**.

Universal Studios in Hollywood, California, opened in 1915, **and** Universal Studios in Orlando, Florida, opened in 1990.
  **compound sentence**: two independent clauses conjoined by *and*

Beef liver and other organ meats contain vitamin A, **but** some people don't like those kinds of foods.
  **compound sentence**: two independent clauses conjoined by *but*

Sentences composed of **at least one independent clause** and **one dependent clause** (including a relative clause) are **complex sentences.**

**Whenever** I pick up my dog's leash, // she wakes up from her nap.
**SBDR**
dependent clause = adverbial clause      independent clause
  **complex sentence**: one dependent clause, one independent clause

You can use Netflix anytime // **as long as** you are a subscriber.
                           **SBDR**
independent clause       dependent clause = adverbial clause
  **complex sentence**: one independent clause, one dependent clause

Did you recognize the boy **who** saved the kitten?
independent clause       dependent clause = relative clause
  **complex sentence**: one independent clauses, one relative clause

### 2.4.3.2 Elliptical Constructions in Grammar

Ellipsis in grammar refers to the leaving out of words from phrases, clauses, and sentences.

Most grammatical categories can be affected by ellipsis, as in the following examples:

**Subject pronouns**

(It's) Time for dinner!
(It's) Time for bed!
(It's) "Time to Say Goodbye" (*con te partirò*, song by Sartori & Quarantotto, 1995)
He took one look at his handiwork and (he) grinned from ear to ear.

**Object pronouns**

Call (us/me/her) when you get in.

**Auxiliary verbs**

(Are) You busy?
(Do) You have a minute?

**Subject pronouns and auxiliary verbs**

(Do you) Want to go see a movie with me?
(Do you) Wanna grab a bite?

**Relative pronouns**

"The Bathers" is one of the last pieces (that) Cézanne painted.
You should not believe every news story (that) you read on the internet.

**Prepositions**

We are bringing home a special dessert for you, (for) Stu, and (for) Murphy.
Starting (on) Friday, the president will embark on a five-day visit to South Asia.
Jaha was the spelling bee champion (for) 3 years in a row.

**Determiners**

"Every man, (every) woman, and (every) child is a partner in the most tremendous undertaking of our American history."

(Roosevelt, 1941)

**Nouns and noun phrases**

Take two (e.g., aspirin tablets) before bedtime.
The following is a list of top movie titles. Each (title, listing, entry) contains the film's name and the director's name.
This statement is true, whether it is said in the past (tense), present (tense), or future tense.

30  *The Nuts and Bolts of Grammar*

The doctor is not in (the office) today. = The doctor is not here.
We're off (work) on Monday.

**Other phrases and clauses**

It is up to all administrators, (it is up to all) teachers, and (it is up to all) parents to ensure a safe learning environment for our children.
We have fulfilled our task. They have (fulfilled their task), too.
State High won six gold medals; Bellefonte, only (won) three (gold medals).
It would be really difficult to do that. Yes, it would (be difficult).
Please (go ahead, take one, after you, etc.).
I can help, but I'm not sure how (to help, I can help).
Do what you think is best (to solve the problem, to respond to the issue, etc.).

Ellipsis in grammar is not only common, it is also necessary in discourse. Certain uses of elliptical expressions can create solidarity or distance between discourse participants, depending on such elements as context, types of ellipsis used, and aspects of the speaker-hearer or reader-writer relationship. The use of ellipsis differs according to genre and register. Ellipsis can exhibit grammatical patterns that signal lower discursive registers and grammatical patterns that signal higher discursive registers and/or more formal or technical communicative contexts. Even though ellipsis involves leaving words out, it functions to create both clarity and conciseness.

By leaving out words, phrases, and clauses (or parts of clauses), speakers and writers first and foremost avoid repetition and overstating the obvious. The use of ellipsis creates space for listeners and readers to effectively fill in the missing parts through inference. Ellipsis enhances rhythm and imagery in writing and speaking and provides for both elegance and economy in communication, as illustrated in the previous example sentences.

The following extract from Laird's (2006) novel about war and peace from the eyes of a young Palestinian boy exemplifies multiple types of ellipsis. Ellipsis is used so commonly in discourse it often goes unnoticed. Have a look:

> A woman came around the side of the house from the back. She was wearing the long traditional Palestinian dress and a white headscarf. She was leaning over to one side, bowed down under the weight of the sack she was carrying.
>
> She caught sight of Karim standing and staring at her from over the wall at the end of the vegetable plot, and shaded her eyes to see better.
>
> "You want something?" she shouted across at him. Her voice was loud and cracked, with the accent of the coast. "What are you staring at? Never seen a sack of flour before?"
>
> Taken by surprise, not knowing what to say, Karim turned and bounded away, hot with embarrassment.
>
> (Laird, 2006, p. 71)

TYPES OF ELLIPSIS ISOLATED FOR THIS ILLUSTRATION

Grammatical categories that have undergone ellipsis include conjunctions, clauses and parts of clauses, relative pronouns, auxiliaries, subject pronouns, and copular verbs.

> She was leaning over to one side, [and she was] bowed down under the weight of the sack she was carrying.
>
> She caught sight of Karim [who was] standing and staring at her from over the wall [that was] at the end of the vegetable plot.

. . . and [she] shaded her eyes to see better.

"[Do] you want something?" she shouted across [the vegetable plot] at him.

Her voice was loud and [it] cracked, with the accent of the coast [where she was from].

"[Have you] never seen a sack of flour before?"

Taken by surprise, [and] not knowing what to say, Karim turned and [he] bounded away, [feeling/he felt] hot with embarrassment.

Compare the actual piece with the version above that contains the ellipted elements of language. Which seems to flow better in your opinion? Why?

### 2.4.3.3 *Functions of Sentences (Mood)*

The sentence, as an essential communicative and grammatical construct, fulfills many types of functions. These functions are as follows:

**Declarative:** Sentences that make a statement.

> *Spotlight* won the Academy Award for Best Picture in 2016.
> The black rhino is a critically endangered species.

**Interrogative:** Sentences that ask a question or seek confirmation.

> What did you pack for lunch today?
> Wasn't Xiaoye in class this morning?

**Imperative:** Sentences that tell someone to do something. Note that there is no overt subject in the unmarked (i.e., common form of) imperative sentences. The unexpressed subject of imperative sentences is typically *you*.

> Use the intercom system to call me when you arrive.
> Read Chapters 1 and 2 by next Monday.

**Exclamatory:** Sentences that express emotion (e.g., anger, excitement, surprise).

> What an awesome job you did on your history essay!
> Look at that ice cream cone! It must have four scoops on it!

## 2.5 Gerunds

Section 2.3.2 explains one type of conversion whereby nouns are used as verbs. With **gerunds** and the gerunding process, **verbs are transformed into nouns** by adding the present participle inflectional morpheme -*ing*.

Because gerunds both derive from verbs and are formed with the present participle ending, they often resemble verbs, sometimes making them difficult to recognize as nouns.

The cartoon in Figure 2.2, which shows Superman at his doctor's office, is a nice illustration of gerunds. The doctor's advice here is "More walking, less flying," presumably because "walking" provides more of an aerobic workout and is better overall exercise for everyday health.

Another example of the gerund is illustrated by the warning often seen in movie theaters just prior to the start of the show:

**NO TALKING, NO TEXTING, NO CELL PHONES**

The nouns here are highlighted in bold: *talking* and *texting* are gerunds. They are nouns, just like the word *cell phones* is a noun.

32  *The Nuts and Bolts of Grammar*

*Figure 2.2* "More walking, less flying."
© Randy Glasbergen. Reproduced with permission of Glasbergen Cartoon Service.

**Examples of gerunds:**

**Studying** is my least favorite way to spend a Saturday afternoon.
My hobbies are **painting**, **skateboarding**, and **swimming**.
Our family loves **camping**.
**Running** a 10K will help you train for your marathon.
**Being accepted** into Harvard is my lifelong hope.
The best way to learn Japanese is by **practicing** kanji and vocabulary every day.

## 2.6 Infinitives

Like gerunds, infinitives—that is, the base form of the verb often preceded by *to*—can function as nouns:

Our family loves <u>**to take** long hikes in the nearby hills</u>.
My next-door neighbor hates <u>**to mow** the lawn</u>.
I just wanted <u>**to get up** and (to) **leave**</u>.
<u>**To be accepted** into Harvard</u> is my lifelong dream.

Infinitives can also function as **adjective**s, modifying a noun or NP in a sentence:

This is <u>a perfect essay topic</u> **to use** in your composition class.
              NP     Adj

<u>His desire</u> **to travel** to Europe this summer is growing stronger by the day.
    NP Adj

And infinitives can function as **adverbials**, modifying a verb or VP in a sentence. In these examples, the infinitive and the words that follow it to complement its meaning constitute an adverbial clause (see Chapter 15).

ByongJoon <u>has left for Seoul</u> // **to take** a teaching job in an English language academy.
               VP               Infinitive (adverbial clause = purpose)

Mr. Benveniste <u>visited the factory</u> // **to inspect** it for safety concerns.
             VP             Infinitive (adverbial clause = purpose)

## 2.7 Discourse and Grammar

As you will see throughout the remainder of this book, grammar and discourse are inseparable. One cannot exist without the other. The following categories constitute the most basic components of the discourse-grammar connection.

### 2.7.1 Genre

At the heart of all discourse and grammar is the concept of **genre**. All discourse has a purpose. All discourse requires content. And all discourse is designed to be received by a particular audience or addressee (even if the discourse is self-talk or self-reflection). Thus, all discourse is also situated in a context. The **genre** is the frame of discourse within which content, purpose, and audience design combine to convey information and messages. "Genres exhibit culturally recognizable discursive and grammatical patterns to convey essential content to some form of audience or hearer, within a particular context, and with a view to accomplish a particular communicative purpose" (Strauss & Feiz, 2014, p. 52). **Genres** are recognizable frames of discourse based on format, grammar, word choice, and register (e.g., style, technical language, formal/informal). That is, the concept of **genre** helps us better understand the discourse: its content, its purpose, its explicit meaning, and much of its implicit meaning. Discursive and grammatical elements within the frames of **genre** help us broadly distinguish, for example, recipes from science experiments, sermons from lectures, or stock predictions from weather reports (Strauss & Feiz, 2014).

Let's consider the broad literary genre of the poem. Some poems are recognizable as poems by virtue of their structures, imageries, rhymes, and rhythms. The first example is the opening stanza from "The Raven" by Edgar Allan Poe. Note these elements of structure, rhyme, rhythm, and imagery.

**Poem:** *The Raven* **(excerpt)**

> Once upon a midnight dreary, while I pondered weak and weary,
> Over many a quaint and curious volume of forgotten lore,
> While I nodded, nearly napping, suddenly there came a tapping,
> As of someone gently rapping, rapping at my chamber door.
> "Tis some visitor," I muttered, "tapping at my chamber door—
> Only this and nothing more."
>
>                                          (Poe, 1845)

Some poetry contains no rhymes but evokes poetic imageries and is visually representative of the genre of poetry (e.g., short lines, brief clauses and phrases, subject-verb inversion, ellipsis, marked instances of negation, repetition):

**Poem:** *Out of My Deeper Heart*

> Out of my deeper heart a bird rose and flew skyward.
> Higher and higher did it rise, yet larger and larger did it grow.
> At first it was but like a swallow,
> then a lark,
> then an eagle,
> then as vast as a spring cloud,
> and then it filled the starry heavens.
> Out of my heart a bird flew skyward.
> And it waxed larger as it flew.
> Yet it left not my heart.
>
> (Gibran, 1920)

The poetic **genre** of the limerick exhibits a distinctively rigid scheme of rhythm and rhyme as a means of expressing humor and wit, as in the following untitled limerick:

**Limerick:**

> There was an Old Man from Nantucket
> Who kept all his cash in a bucket.
> His daughter, named Nan,
> Ran away with a man,
> And as for the bucket, Nantucket ("Nan took it").
>
> (Voorhees, 1902)

The following list contains other genres that you will recognize on the basis of their format/structure, content, purpose, grammar, word choice, and register:

| *Genre type* | *Where these might be found* |
| --- | --- |
| Weather forecast | online weather websites, TV, radio, newspaper |
| News report | TV, radio, newspaper, online news, news sections: sports, politics, world news, local news |
| News headlines | front-page news, subheadings, clickbait on news websites |
| Movie review | newspapers, magazines, Rotten Tomatoes website |
| Restaurant review | magazines, travelogues, TripAdvisor, Yelp |
| Obituary | newspaper, Legacy.com, professional websites |
| Restaurant menu | fine dining, drive-through, coffee shop |
| Lecture | university course, public lecture, TED Talk |
| Sermon | church, synagogue, nondenominational congregation |
| Business letter | utility company, insurance, banking, auto loans |
| Fairy tale | children's books, oral tradition |

*(continued)*

| Genre type | Where these might be found |
|---|---|
| Recipe | cookbook, culinary magazine, TV cooking show, online food sites |
| Film | sci-fi, romantic comedy, drama, action/adventure |
| Music | pop, hard rock, soft rock, hip-hop, ballads, country |

Additional genres in everyday discourse include commercials (TV, radio, internet), print advertisements, magazine covers, advice columns, game rules, instruction manuals, letters to the editor and opinion pieces (in newspapers and online news), jokes (e.g., riddles, knock-knock jokes), product labels (e.g., food, cleaning products, medicines), and so forth.

The following excerpts are from three different genres: a weather forecast, a movie review, and a fairy tale. Try to identify the most obvious grammatical features—for example, sentence structure, time reference (past, present, future), word choice, contractions, imperatives, ways of describing, and formulaic expressions that stand out as being important elements of that genre.

**1 Weather forecast: Chicago, Illinois**

**"7-day forecast for January 12, 2016"**

> Let's talk about this weekend's weather. There are a couple of times when it could get icy again. There's a slight chance of some sleet or snow on Saturday morning and a greater chance of weather changing for the worse on Sunday night. That's when it could get icy again, so watch out for the freezing rain. There'll be many hours of dry weather for both days.
>
> (Baskerville, 2016)

**2 Movie review: *Blade Runner 2049***

> This is a sequel to the original 1982 film *Blade Runner* by Ridley Scott. The sequel was directed by Denis Villeneuve.
>
> Sure as it is to delight "Blade Runner" fans, this stunningly elegant follow-up doesn't depend on having seen the original. . . . As it happens, in both tone and style, the new film owes more to slow-cinema maestro Andrei Tarkovsky than it does to Scott's revolutionary cyberpunk sensibility. . . . Villeneuve deliver[s] a visually breathtaking, long-fuse action movie whose unconventional thrills could be described as many things—from tantalizing to tedious—but never "artificially intelligent."
>
> (Debruge, 2017)

**3 Fairy tale: "The Star-Child"**

> Once upon a time two poor Woodcutters were making their way home through a great pine-forest. It was winter, and a night of bitter cold. The snow lay thick upon the ground, and upon the branches of the trees: the frost kept snapping the little twigs on either side of them, as they passed: and when they came to the Mountain Torrent she was hanging motionless in air, for the Ice-King had kissed her.
>
> (Wilde, 1909)

What other types of genres in your daily life can you identify? Think about the types of language and grammar (in addition to format and structure) that are associated with each genre.

### 2.7.2 Stance and Perspective

**Stance** is generally defined as "the speaker's or writer's feeling, attitude, perspective, or position as enacted in discourse" (Strauss & Feiz, 2014, p. 4). Stance becomes visible in discourse when speakers and writers use words that reflect their opinions, judgments, and evaluations, without necessarily having to explicitly say things like "In my opinion, this is good/bad."

**Examples:**

Evaluative description of a film:
This short film on cyberbullying is **sad**.

Intensified evaluative description:
This short film on cyberbullying is **so sad/so very sad/heartrending**.

Evaluative description of a film and its effects on you as a viewer:
This short film on cyberbullying **will make you cry**.

Intensified evaluative description and its effects on you as a viewer:
This short film on cyberbullying **will make you cry your eyes out**.

Mitigated evaluative description and its effects on you as viewer:
**You will probably cry** when you watch this short film on cyberbullying.

Thoughtful suggestion to viewer regarding possible effects of the film on viewers:
**Have tissues near you** when you watch this short film on cyberbullying.

Other indicators of stance include adverbs, quantifiers, adjectives, rhetorical exclamations, exclamations, choices of specific nouns and verbs, similes, metaphors, and analogies.

**Examples:**

**More neutral stance:**

Facebook has 1.74 billion active users (as of March 2017).

**Stronger stances:**
Facebook has **as many as** 1.74 billion active users.
         [adverb]

**Can you believe it?** Facebook has **close to 2 billion** active users.
[rhetorical question]           [adverb] [quantifier]

**This is incredible!** Facebook has **almost 2 billion** active users.
[exclamation]                 [adverb] [quantifier]

**Understatement:**
Facebook has **a good number** of active users.
         [quantifier] = understatement because the actual number is very high

Let's return for a moment to the *Blade Runner 2049* film review example from the previous section. This excerpt is an example of positive, complimentary, and praising stance using a robust array of descriptors and two key juxtapositions:

**Descriptors:**

this stunningly elegant follow-up
visually breathtaking

long-fuse action movie
unconventional thrills
from tantalizing to tedious

**Juxtapositions:**

| original | : | follow-up (sequel) |
| Scott's revolutionary cyberpunk sensibility | : | slow-cinema maestro Andrei Tarkovsky |

The stance is two-pronged, swaying in one direction for the original version and in a different direction for the sequel. The author uses vivid descriptors in addition to a key juxtaposition that contrasts filmmaking techniques and filmmakers from similar decades (Ridley Scott, *Blade Runner* [1982] and Andrei Tarkovsky, *The Mirror* [1975] and *Stalker* [1979]).

### 2.7.3 Register

**Register** is an essential component of genre. **Register** refers to the ways in which speakers and writers use words and grammatical constructions in discourse. **Register** is typically associated with formality, informality, and style, as well as the use of technical or area-specific language. Often, **speakers' and writers' identities as experts, novices, learners, specialists, non-specialists, academics, conversationalists** and so forth are expressed through their choices of words and grammar.

**Informal register** includes:

**Contractions:**

| that is | → | that's |
| we will | → | we'll |
| does not | → | doesn't |
| can not | → | can't |
| he has, he is | → | he's |

**Informal variations of multiple words run together:**

| have to | → | hafta |
| going to | → | gonna |
| want to | → | wanna |
| let me | → | lemme |
| give me | → | gimme |
| look at | → | lookit |
| because | → | cuz |
| yes | → | yeah, uh-<u>huh</u> |
| no | → | nope, nah, uh-uh |

**Colloquialisms and slang (also informal):**

*yikes, no way, bucks* (dollars), *freaking* (very [euphemism for a vulgar expression]), *mess up* (ruin, make a mistake), *nuts* (crazy, insane), *be on one's back* (nag, pester), *low key* (keep something quiet, small scale), *high key* (should be said out loud and shared publicly), *totes* (totally!)

**Sentence structure and punctuation:**

> One- or two-word sentences, verbless "sentences":
> *That's me. Period. End of story.*

> Starting sentences with *And* or *But*:
> *Beau gave Mariana an engagement ring. <u>And</u> there's more. She said yes!*
> *Parents want healthier lunches in school cafeterias. <u>But</u> it's not that simple.*

**Formal register** includes:

- Absence of/limited contractions, no/limited informal variations, no/limited colloquialisms and slang

- Technical or discipline-specific words

  > **coffee consumption** vs. *drinking coffee*
  > **precipitation** vs. *rain, hail,* or *snow*
  > **digit** vs. *finger, thumb,* or *toe*

- Passive voice (see Chapter 9)

  > **Tornado activity has been detected** in parts of Florida, Georgia, and Alabama.
  > vs.
  > *We're seeing* tornado activity in parts of Florida, Georgia, and Alabama.

## 2.7.4 Collocation

**Collocations** are combinations of words that typically "go together naturally" in a language. These natural associations of words occur through convention and language use.

Here are a few common collocations:

| | |
|---|---|
| speed: | <u>fast</u> food, a <u>quick</u> bite, <u>rapid</u> heartbeat |
| things on a list: | agenda <u>item</u>, menu <u>item</u> |
| vertical measurement:<br>(<u>high</u>, not tall) | <u>high</u> taxes, <u>high</u> mountain,<br><u>high</u> expectations, <u>high</u> blood pressure |
| vertical measurement:<br>(<u>tall</u>, not high) | <u>tall</u> trees, <u>tall</u> building, <u>tall</u> person,<br><u>tall</u> grass, <u>tall</u> order, <u>tall</u> tale |
| diminutive size: | <u>small</u> town, <u>small</u> child, <u>small</u> talk, a <u>small</u> favor |
| diminutive size: | <u>little</u> boy, <u>little</u> girl, <u>little</u> finger, a <u>little</u> while |
| uncovered: | <u>bare</u> hands, <u>bare</u> feet, <u>bare</u> soil, <u>bare</u> minimum<br><u>naked</u> eye, <u>naked</u> truth, <u>naked</u> body |
| counters for plants: | <u>head</u> of lettuce, <u>head</u> of cabbage<br><u>sprig</u> of parsley, <u>sprig</u> of holly, <u>sprig</u> of mistletoe |

## 2.7.5 Pragmatics

The area of **pragmatics** concerns the ways in which **context** affects the appropriateness of the discourse. Context includes the participants and the relationships between/among them, the medium of communication (e.g., oral, written, texting, email), and the communicative environment (e.g., telephone, Skype, FaceTime; in a nightclub, doctor's office, court of law, gourmet restaurant, classroom, religious ceremony). Pragmatics is tightly linked to both genre and register. That is, if the interaction is intended to be formal, informal, academic, technical, colloquial, religious, respectful, deferential, or friendly, then there would be a certain set of expectations surrounding how language and grammar are and "should be" used.

Pragmatics also encompasses such issues as politeness, conversation topics, and speech and writing style. Pragmatics is related to grammar in the sense that even if an instance of language is *grammatically correct*, it might be *pragmatically odd* or problematic. The domain of pragmatics concerns the overall notion of contextual appropriateness in terms of social conventions, communicative style, directness/indirectness, politeness/rudeness, informal/formal registers, and so forth.

Pragmatic awareness is especially important in what is known as speech acts. The relationship between the participants as *equals* (e.g., peers, friends, family members) or *non-equals* (strangers, persons of higher status like professors, doctors, attorneys, judges, the clergy) can affect the pragmatic appropriateness of language and grammatical choice:

| *Speech act type:* | *Inappropriate in US contexts among non-equals* | *Appropriate in US contexts among non-equals* |
|---|---|---|
| Making requests | *Read this for me.* | *Can you read this for me, please?* |
| Getting attention | *Hey! Pssst! Ahem!* | *Excuse me.* |
| Giving advice | *Do a better job.* | *You should try to improve your work.* |
| Giving compliments | *You rock.* | *You did an excellent job.* |

Pragmatic awareness is an important component in all interpersonal communication. Pragmatic awareness is also important in academic communication and institutional writing, since informal registers and conversational-sounding colloquialisms can often be considered as pragmatically inappropriate. Note how grammar, word choice, and register work together in various ways to convey similar message content in the same genre of discourse.

> **Inappropriate register for email correspondence:** [inappropriate because too informal]
> Hey Prof Axelrod!
> I wasn't in class yesterday because I was sick. Can you give me the homework assignment because I wanna do it tonight and give it to you tomorrow?

> **Appropriate register:** [formal register]
> Dear Professor Axelrod,
> I apologize for not being in class yesterday. I wasn't feeling well. I am writing to ask if you could possibly send me the homework assignment, if it's not too much trouble. I'd like to work on it this evening and submit it to you tomorrow.

### 2.7.6 Markedness: Marked and Unmarked

We introduce the concept of markedness here as the degree to which language and grammar stand out as "noticeable," "uncommon," or "marked." What is **marked** is **visible** and **noticeable**. What is **unmarked** is **common** and typically does not draw any particular added attention.

Markedness comes into play in discourse when word choice or grammatical structure varies from what is common and/or expected.

The following examples illustrate the use of non-standard grammatical structures, collocations, or word choice to express stance, emphasis:

| It will never happen. | → | It *ain't gonna* happen. |
|---|---|---|
| unmarked | | marked (grammatical variant, emphatic stance) |

Good morning.
(initial greeting, not on TV)
    unmarked

→ Good morning *to you*.
    marked (*to you* is unnecessary, superfluous)
    unmarked as a TV greeting by host to audience

You <u>shouldn't</u> overwater your plants.
    unmarked

→ You *ought not* overwater your plants.
    marked (stilted, *ought not* is not often used in American English conversation and informal contexts)

<u>Have</u> a seat right there.
    unmarked

→ *You* have a seat right there.
    marked (imperative with overt *you*; the speaker is either singling out one individual from among a pair or group or expressing an aspect of emphatic stance, e.g., exasperation, impatience, excitement, or hurriedness)

### 2.7.7 *Basics of Punctuation and Sentence Structure*

| | |
|---|---|
| period, full stop (.) | Use a period (full stop) at the end of a sentence.<br>*The sentence can be a long one or a short one. This one's short.* |
| comma (,) | Use commas to separate items in a list if there are more than two items:<br>*The only students who were not in class yesterday were Samuel, Moshe, and Fabio.* |
| | Use a comma between two adjectives that don't belong together or that you don't want to connect with *and* or *but*:<br>*We had an exhilarating, fun-filled weekend.* |
| | Use a comma between two independent clauses connected by a coordinating conjunction (like *and*, *or*, or *but*):<br>*They didn't study, but they all did well on the exam.* |
| | Use a comma after an adverbial clause that starts a sentence:<br>*When you drive in Pennsylvania, you need to watch for deer.* |
| | Use a comma after an adverbial or phrase that opens the sentence:<br>*Luckily, we made it home before the storm.*<br>*As a matter of fact, it didn't hit until 10:00 p.m.* |
| | Use a comma to indicate a non-restrictive relative clause (see Chapter 13).<br>*We followed the map, which had just been updated a year ago.* |
| | Use commas to separate information in appositives (see Chapter 13).<br>*Usain Bolt, the Jamaican track-and-field star, is an 11-time world champion.*<br>[Usain Bolt = the Jamaican track-and-field star] |
| | Use a comma to separate direct quotations from the rest of the sentence:<br>*"The train is approaching," the announcer said.*<br>*The announcer said, "The train is approaching."* |
| | Use a comma to separate the day from the year in dates:<br>*Toni Morrison was born on February 18, 1931.* |
| | Use a comma to separate a city name from the state:<br>*Butte, Montana, used to be called the "richest hill on Earth."* |

| | |
|---|---|
| semicolon (;) | Use a semicolon to link two independent clauses or two sentences that are related. A semicolon is weaker than a period (or full stop) in separating two sentences and is not used frequently in written discourse:<br>*Dictionaries provide definitions of words; thesauruses provide synonyms and antonyms.*<br>*Dictionaries provide definitions of words. Thesauruses provide synonyms and antonyms.*<br><br>Use a semicolon to clearly separate larger category items from smaller category items that are connected by commas:<br>*We wanted to travel to St. Louis, Missouri; Louisville, Kentucky; and Nashville, Tennessee.*<br>*Freshmen take biology, US history, and English; sophomores take chemistry, world history, and Shakespeare; and juniors take environmental education, geography, and business.* |
| colon (:) | Use a colon to introduce something important after a full sentence. A colon typically signals to a reader, "Pay attention to what's coming next: It's important."<br>*This is all the message said: "Help me!"*<br>*We have two options: Fly to Portland or drive there.*<br>*James got exactly what he wanted: a full scholarship.* |

\*\*\*\*\*\*\*\*

## PRACTICE WITH DATA ANALYSIS: PUTTING IT ALL TOGETHER

1 The following exercises are designed to help you review inflectional morphemes (eight total that are based on grammar) and derivational morphemes (there are lots, and these change the meanings of the words). There are morphemes missing from each sentence. We have underlined the word(s) with missing morphemes. The answers are provided after the full list of sentences.

  a  Have you met <u>Kenji</u> daughter?
  b  Thanks for this <u>help</u> information.
  c  Matt is much <u>tall</u> than his brother.
  d  She <u>look</u> upset last night after <u>Joan</u> husband <u>spill</u> ink on her new carpet.
  e  The teacher <u>speak</u> <u>slow</u> and <u>soft</u> and one student <u>say</u> she's <u>have</u> trouble <u>hear</u> him.
  f  After ten <u>minute</u> of <u>argue</u> with Verizon, Ben <u>angry</u> <u>slam</u> down the phone.

**Answers:**

  a  Kenji → Kenji's (inflectional)
  b  help → helpful (derivational)
  c  tall → taller (inflectional)
  d  look → looked (inflectional); Joan → Joan's (inflectional); spill → spilled (inflectional)
  e  speak → speaks (inflectional); slow → slowly (derivational); soft → softly (derivational); say → says (inflectional); have → having (inflectional); hear → hearing (inflectional)
  f  minute → minutes (inflectional); argue → arguing (inflectional); angry → angrily (derivational); slam → slammed (inflectional)

2 The humor in the opening cartoon for this chapter, Figure 2.1, is based on a literal interpretation of language. What is the source of humor here? What does it mean to be "beside oneself," literally? What does the expression mean more figuratively, as it is used in this cartoon?

42  *The Nuts and Bolts of Grammar*

3   Gary Provost's (1985) quote in Section 2.1 beautifully illustrates not only the concepts of words and counting words in a sentence but it also illustrates independent clauses, dependent clauses, and sentence types. Most importantly, it succinctly captures the very essence of the sounds and rhythms of words and sentences in discourse.

First, reread the full excerpt. Think about what it means and what it is designed to express. Then, label each sentence according to sentence type (i.e., simple, compound, complex). As you work through this task, note also that variations on the so-called simple sentence include just one or two words, even though there might not be a discernible subject and predicate. Also, imperatives like *listen* assume that the subject is *you*.

Of the three types of sentences, which is the most frequent in the excerpt? Which is the least frequent? What effect does this variation of sentence length have on the overall sound of the discourse? How does it affect you as a reader? Does this also inspire you to vary your sentence length in your own writings?

Also, try to uncover all the instances of ellipsis in the passage. What words were left out? How does adding those words back change the rhythm and overall style of the piece?

4   News headlines and sentence types: Work through the following sets of headlines from various English language news outlets. Identify the types of sentences (i.e., simple, compound, complex) and functions of sentences or mood (i.e., declarative, interrogative, imperative, exclamatory). Is each headline actually a complete sentence? If not, why?

What effect might the headline style or structure have on readers in terms of generating interest in reading the full article? Based on the choice of words (nouns, verbs, adjectives, adverbs), can you sense the author's or the publication's stance on the issues at hand? That is, do you sense that the article might be sympathetic to the issues, against them, or neutral? Why?

*Centre Daily Times*, January 14, 2017

- Just feet from U.S. border, Cubans ponder end of dream
- Trump's plan prompts showdown on ethics

*BBC.com*, January 27, 2017

- Semi-Final: Nadal serving to win five-set thriller
- Girls lose faith in their own talents by the age of six

*Chicago Tribune*, January 25, 2017

- Immigrants, advocates vow to fight Trump orders on wall, sanctuary cities
- Political sniping won't end Chicago violence

*Los Angeles Times*, January 27, 2017

- What is a "violent crime"? For California's new parole law, the definition is murky—and it matters
- "A Dog's Purpose" [movie title] was supposed to be a hit, until animal-abuse controversy threw the studio's plan out the window.

5   The following excerpt from Toni Morrison's *The Bluest Eye* includes the following unpunctuated discourse, exactly as it appears in the novel.

*The Bluest Eye*

> Hereisthehouseitisgreenandwhiteithasareddooritisveryprettyhereisthefamily-
> motherfatherdickandjaneliveintheegreenandwhithousetheyareveryhappy
>
> (Morrison, 1999, p. 4)

Think about how the passage would both look and sound if it were punctuated according to traditional conventions. For example, where would a period, or full stop, belong? What about capitalization of the first word of every new sentence? Are there any proper nouns? Where might commas belong?

What is the most common sentence type in the passage? What genre of discourse does this sound like (e.g., a neighborhood tour, an early literacy children's book, a newspaper story)? What features of grammar and word choice help you arrive at this conclusion? Try to find some early literacy children's books. Compare and contrast the sentence structure and content of these books with what you find in the excerpt.

What follows is the passage rewritten with conventional punctuation:

> Here is the house. It is green and white. It has a red door. It is very pretty. Here is the family. Mother, Father, Dick, and Jane live in the green and white house. They are very happy.

6   Portmanteau words (i.e., fusions or blends of two or more original words) are entering our dictionaries at a rapid speed. Here are a few more examples. Try to figure out the original words that these expressions were composed of. What types of meanings (denotational and connotational) do the new words take on? Also, search the internet to see how these words have been used recently in discourse.

| Portmanteau word: | composed of: | meaning: |
|---|---|---|
| phub, phubbing | ____ + ____ | _____ |
| saleabrate, saleabration | ____ + ____ | _____ |
| screenage, screenager | ____ + ____ | _____ |
| mansplain | ____ + ____ | _____ |
| Pictionary | ____ + ____ | _____ |
| Frankenstorm | ____ + ____ | _____ |
| bromance | ____ + ____ | _____ |
| hangry | ____ + ____ | _____ |

7   Conversion is the process of linguistic change where one part of speech is used as a different part of speech in discourse. Here are a few examples of noun-to-verb conversion from actual discourse:

   a   PayPal and Visa have <u>inked</u> a broad partnership agreement under which PayPal will steer more users to link their accounts with Visa products.

   (Hook & McLannahan, 2016)

   [noun → verb: *ink*] What does *ink* mean here?

   b   Is your kid a mini Picasso? <u>Pencil in</u> a visit to an outdoor sculpture garden and pack sketchpads and crayons for an informal game of Pictionary.

   (Davies, 2008–)

   [noun → verb: *pencil* in]
   What does *pencil* mean here? How is it different from the verb *ink*?

c   A man went into a bank to <u>cash</u> a check. In <u>handing</u> over the money, the cashier, by mistake, gave him dollars for cents and cents for dollars. He <u>pocketed</u> the money without examining it.

("Switching dollars and cents," 1997)

[nouns → verbs: *cash, hand, pocket*]
What do *cash, hand,* and *pocket* mean?

What does the verb *inked* mean in a? In what ways is *inked* similar to and different from the verb *pencil in* in b? Hint: Think about the permanence of writing something in ink vs. writing something in pencil. What difference does this make in the meanings of the verbs derived from these nouns? What might the verb *pen* mean? In which contexts have you seen or read the word *pen* used as a verb?

In c, we find conversion involving three verbs: *cash, hand,* and *pocket. Cash* and *hand* are common everyday verbs that don't carry much added connotational meaning. What about the verb *pocket*? Yes, it does mean "to put something in one's pocket." But think about its connotation and the type of judgment associated with this verb. In whose favor was the mistake? The bank's or the man's? Does this verb *to pocket* typically have a positive connotation or a negative one? Why?

8   Some words look and/or sound the same but have very different meanings. Here are a few examples. Think about how the verbs in the a version differ in meaning from those in the b version:

a   Kellogg's has <u>recalled</u> some its snacks because peanut residue was found in the flour.
b   Margaret Atwood <u>recalls</u> her early life in Ottawa, Canada.

a   It's just too hot outside today. Let's go to the <u>pool</u>.
b   We've exhausted every candidate on our list. We should review the original <u>pool</u>.

What is the source of humor in the following riddle?

Q:  How do you make a snail <u>fast</u>?
A:  Take away its food.

Here are a few more examples with words that sound the same but have different meanings and different grammatical functions. Indicate the respective part of speech that each underlined word represents, and describe how the homophonous (i.e., words that sound the same) words or word groups differ from each other. In the case of contractions, write out the full forms for each first and then analyze.

<u>Your</u> friends may not think <u>you're</u> friends.

<u>It's</u> not my fault.
Each profession has <u>its</u> own vocabulary.
<u>It's</u> been a pleasure working with you.
    [Hint: The two instances of *it's* are not the same.]

I didn't see him <u>there</u>.
<u>Their</u> dog barks all day.
<u>They're</u> filing a lawsuit against the company.

I ran into him <u>some time</u> ago.
Maybe <u>sometime</u> you and I can have dinner together.
<u>Sometimes</u> I just want to quit my job and start painting again.

One <u>senator's</u> comments were taken completely out of context.
Do you know who the Ottawa <u>Senators'</u> captain is?

Try to find more examples like these and design your own sentence pairs or triplets to illustrate.

9   Practice with register.

> **formal register:** for example, technical lexicon, no contractions, longer sentences, passive voice, use of third person
>
> **informal register:** for example, contractions, imperatives, conversational style, direct address to second person "you" as listener or reader, onomatopoeia, less technical or nontechnical lexicon, starting sentences with *and* and *but*

See the two sets of discourse excerpts that follow. One involves weather reports, and the second involves a discussion relating coffee drinking to human longevity.

a   **Weather report excerpts**
   The content in excerpt a1 is from the same weather forecast that appeared earlier in Section 2.7.1.

   1   "7-day forecast for January 12, 2016"
       Local weather: Chicago, Illinois (*Chicago Tribune* online)

       > What about tomorrow? Let's move on. We'll talk about how the dry weather will stay with us, again, tomorrow, but it will be cold, so dress for the kind of weather we got today again tomorrow because the conditions aren't gonna change that much in terms of the feel of the weather. It is 24 degrees at O'Hare and later on tonight it'll get colder. It'll be down into the teens and it'll be single digit wind chills quite likely before the sun rises tomorrow morning, from one end of the area to the other. Temperatures are in the 20s.
       >
       > (Baskerville, 2016)

   2   "Weekend forecast—Eastern U.S. National Weather" (January 28, 2017)

       > Lake effect snows are going to continue today and probably tomorrow across parts of the upper Midwest, places like Michigan, Western New York State, Pennsylvania. Even farther east than there are going get some snow, with a broad counterclockwise flow over the region, some cold air aloft and the right wind direction will get some locations, probably another six inches or so, especially in parts of Western New York State not far from Buffalo and certainly the Tug Hill Plateau, just to the east of Watertown New York.
       >
       > ("Weekend forecast," 2017)

Have a look at each excerpt. Both are designed to forecast the weather conditions for viewers. What specific elements do these two excerpts share? In what way do they differ? Do you sense any difference in terms of who is being addressed in each forecast? Do you think that the "local" element for the a1 version, as opposed to the broader regional element of the a2 version, has anything to do with the register or style of the weather forecast? Why, or why not?

Identify the features of formal register and informal register in each excerpt. Which of the two is more formal? Why do you think this is the case?

b   **The relationship between coffee drinking and how long we live**

   1   NPR (National Public Radio) story about coffee and longevity

       **"Drink to your health: Study links daily coffee habit to longevity"**
       If you have a daily+18 coffee habit, here's something to buzz about: A new study finds those cups of joe may help boost longevity. . . .

The findings, published in the journal *Circulation*, build on a body of evidence linking a coffee habit to potential health benefits. . . .

As we've reported, previous research has pointed to a decreased risk of stroke. And, there's some evidence that a coffee habit cuts the risk of Type 2 diabetes, too.

(Aubrey, 2015)

2   Association of coffee consumption with total and cause-specific mortality in three large prospective cohorts

**Article published in *Circulation*, a journal addressing cardiovascular issues:**

Consumption of total, caffeinated, and decaffeinated coffee were (*sic*) non-linearly associated with mortality. Compared to non-drinkers, coffee consumption (of) one to five cups/d(ay) was associated with lower risk of mortality, while coffee consumption of more than five cups/d(ay) was not associated with risk of mortality.

(Ding et al., 2015)

Excerpt b1 is from NPR, a general-interest media outlet (radio, TV, and internet) that shares stories on various topics with a broad community of listeners, readers, and viewers. The study referred to here is the original article published in the technical journal *Circulation*. Excerpt b2 is a sample of that original article excerpted from the abstract.

Just as you did for the first data set, compare and contrast the discourse, grammar, and register in these two excerpts.

List the elements of formal and informal register from each excerpt.

What do the discourse, grammar, and register reveal to you about the relationship between audience or readers and the writing itself?

## Academic Reference

Strauss, S., & Feiz, P. (2014). *Discourse analysis: Putting our worlds into words*. New York and London: Routledge.

## Data References

Aubrey, A. (2015, December 16). Drink to your health: Study links daily coffee habit to longevity. NPR.org. Retrieved January 3, 2017, from www.npr.org/sections/thesalt/2015/11/16/456191657/drink-to-your-health-study-links-daily-coffee-habit-to-longevity

Baskerville, S. (2016, January 12). 7-Day forecast for January 12, 2016. *Chicago Tribune*. Retrieved January 10, 2017, from www.chicagotribune.com/news/weather/92324369-132.html

Bolinger, D. (1980). *Language-the loaded weapon: The use and abuse of language today*. New York: Routledge.

Buyea, R. (2013). *Mr. Terupt falls again*. New York: Random House.

Davies, M. (2008–). *The corpus of contemporary American English (COCA): 560 million words, 1990–present*. Retrieved from http://corpus.byu.edu/coca/

Debruge, P. (2017, September 29). Film review: "Blade runner: 2049." *Variety*. Retrieved December 1, 2017, from http://variety.com/2017/film/reviews/blade-runner-2049-review-1202576220/.

Ding, M., Satija, A., Bhupathiraju, S., Hu, Y. Sun, Q., Han, J., Lopez-Garcia, E., Willett, W., van Dam, R., & Hu, F. (2015). Association of coffee consumption with total and cause-specific mortality in three large prospective cohorts. *Circulation, 137*(5).

Ghosh, K. B. (2015). Kavita Bhupta Ghosh quotes. Good reads. Retrieved January 15, 2017, from www.goodreads.com/author/quotes/14590493.Kavita_Bhupta_Ghosh

Gibran, K. (1920). *The forerunner, his parables and poems.* New York: Alfred A. Knopf.

Hook, L., & McLannahan, B. (2016, July 21). PayPal and Visa ink partnership agreement. *Financial Times.* Retrieved January 15, 2017, from www.ft.com/content/eed46802-4f81-11e6-8172-e39ecd3b86fc

Laird, E. (2006). *A little piece of ground.* Chicago, IL: Haymarket Books.

Levy, P. (2015, August 12). Miami nice: Are Florida's power brokers mellowing on Cuba? *Mother Jones.* Retrieved February 2, 2017, from www.motherjones.com/politics/2015/08/miami-nice-politicians-mellow-cuba

Morrison, T. (1999). *The bluest eye.* New York: Random House.

Poe, E. A. (1845, February). *American Review, 1,* 143–145.

Provost, G. (1985). *100 ways to improve your writing.* London: Penguin.

Roosevelt, F. D. (1941). Fireside chat, December 9.

Sartori, F., & Quarantotto, L. (1995). Time to say goodbye. *Con te Partirò.*

Switching dollars and cents. (1997). The math forum: People learning math together. Retrieved January 22, 2017, from http://mathforum.org/library/drmath/view/57958.html

Voorhees, D. (1902). *The Princeton Tiger.*

Weekend forecast—Eastern U.S. national weather. (2017, January 28). Weather.com. Retrieved January 28, 2017, from https://weather.com/storms/winter/news/lake-effect-snow-great-lakes-interior-northeast-late-january-2017

Wilde, O. (1909). The star child. In O. Wilde, *A house of pomegranates: Vol. 4.* Leipzig: B Tauchnitz.

# 3 The Basic Grammar for Mentioning People, Ideas, Values, Objects, Concepts, and Things

Nouns and Their Meanings in Discourse

*Figure 3.1* "I'm taking an innovative approach to teaching this semester. I'm using books!"
© Randy Glasbergen. Reproduced with permission of Glasbergen Cartoon Service.

In this chapter, we introduce the critically important categories of nouns.

> It is often reported that children's first words are primarily nouns (Gentner, 1978; Macnamara, 1972; Nelson, 1973). This has been interpreted as evidence that the concepts referred to by nouns are particularly accessible to infants: They are different from, and conceptually more basic than, the concepts referred to by verbs or prepositions. This is a position with a long history. As far back as Aristotle, we find arguments that the kinds of things denoted by nouns are different from, and more fundamental ontologically than, the kinds of things denoted by verbs.
>
> (Gentner, 1982, p. 301)

Nouns provide labels for all things and names for all people and places. Nouns are the very essence of communication and interaction. They enable us to answer the most basic of questions: "What?" and "Who?" They give names to every object and every person around us, including us. Nouns identify and classify living things: plants, animals, species, organisms. They name solid and inorganic things: rocks, minerals, water, oxygen. And they label ideologies—for example, liberalism, conservatism, feminism, and socialism—and social values, such as freedom, justice, education, diversity, and community. Nouns enable us to categorize and differentiate between one thing or one person and another thing and another person. From the visible, solid, and tangible to the diaphanous and invisible, from the real to the imaginary, nouns enable us to make sense of the world, to understand it, to organize it, and to question it. And as our worlds change and grow and transform, so does our repertoire of available nouns. As new technology develops, as new actors enter the stage, as new nations come into being, entire inventories of new nouns enter our lexicons. As these new words emerge, they bring with them new sets of conceptual imageries and symbols and meanings.

All English nouns carry meanings that are deeply rooted in conceptual imagery, involving such elemental categories as follows:

- tangibility (*apple, orange, banana* = fruit)
- abstractness (*apple, orange, banana* = flavor; *freedom, education, perfection* = concept, ideal, value)
- individuation (*slice, segment, piece*)
- integral wholeness (*oxygen, air, merchandise, stuff, attention*)
- groups of people <u>as a unit</u> (*team, committee, government, faculty*)
- groups of people <u>as individual members</u> (*team* [e.g., players], *committee* [e.g., members], *government* [e.g., officials], *faculty* [e.g., instructors])

## 3.1 Nouns: How We Name and Conceptualize Things, People, Ideas, Values, Objects, and Concepts

Look around—what do you see? Make a mental list of the objects that are visible to you. Whether you are in a classroom, a dorm room, a public garden, a playground, a movie theater, or a café, your list will be filled with NOUNS.

Write down the names for 20 things you can see around you.

Now, shift your imagination and start thinking of things that you know are there but you can't see:

air
humidity
trust
boredom
creativity

If you can label the thing or idea with a word, that word will likely be a noun.

Now, try taking a general name for something, and then find **alternate names** for it:

SHOE: footwear, boot, sandal, sneaker, slipper, loafer, pump, high heel

And now, think of that noun in terms of its **parts**:

SHOE: heel, toe, sole, insole, vamp, tongue, eyelet, laces, aglet, chape, pin

When we label things and ideas and people in English, we choose nouns from vast inventories of possible words that best match both what we envision the word to mean and what we seek to communicate to others.

## 3.2 English Nouns and Their Concepts

English nouns are classified into a rather clear-cut system of concepts or mental images:

- things or entities that are **concrete, visible, and tangible**, like *table, chairs, faucet, sink, placemats,* and *sugar*

- things that might be visible or perceivable through other senses but **not tangible or concrete**, like *sunlight*, *aroma*, and *sky*
- notions that **you can imagine and mentally visualize but not concretely see or touch**, like *work*, *collaboration*, and *friendship*
- persons or things or brands or products that **officially name** them like *Mountain Dew*, *Kleenex*, *Hi-Chew*, and *Evian*

How we use nouns in English reflects how we conceptualize and imagine those things and those ideas. Noun choice in English also reflects how we *distinguish* things, ideas, and people from other things, ideas, and people. The following text summarizes the basic categories of nouns in English. In the later sections, we explain each category in detail.

## Basic Distinctions in Noun Types: Concepts and Grammatical Encoding

Common nouns    vs.    Proper nouns
*coffee, water, car, book*      *Starbucks, Evian, Ford, The Martian*

Common nouns can be further categorized into:

### Type 1 nouns

 *apple, table, flower, pencil, eraser, name*

### Type 2 nouns

 *jelly, wood, information, homework, jewelry*

### Type 3 nouns *police, team, staff, faculty*

 Type 3a [conceptualized as a SINGLE UNIT]

 Type 3b [conceptualized as INDIVIDUAL MEMBERS]

## 3.3 Common Nouns vs. Proper Nouns

The most basic categorical distinction that linguists and grammarians make in their discussion and analysis of nouns involves that of the **common noun** and the **proper noun** (see Aarts, 2011; Biber et al., 1999; Givón, 1993; Murphy, 2012; Quirk et al., 1985; Radden & Dirven, 2007; Sloat, 1969; Swan, 2005; Yule, 2010, among others).

A **common noun** is the most frequent and basic type of noun in English. Common nouns denote tangible, concrete objects as well as abstract notions. A common noun labels any entity, thing, person, place, or idea that is **not also its officially designated name**.

Examples of common nouns include fruit, keyboard, light, energy, miniskirt, teacup, rodeo, chopsticks, rice, taco, fingerprint, suitcase, luggage, hair, eye, smile, and television.

**A proper noun** *officially names* the thing, person, language, brand, company, day, month, or place that it designates. A proper noun serves to uniquely and officially identify its referent. Proper nouns are capitalized in English: Antarctica, Saturn, The Beatles, Mick Jagger, Maroon 5, United Colors of Benetton, Kleenex, Heinz Tomato Ketchup, Mandarin, English, and Tagalog.

A proper noun in English is orthographically noticeable because the first letter of every word in a proper noun cluster (except for prepositions such as *of*, *with*, *for*, *in*, *at*, etc. that are not the first word of the cluster) must be a capital letter. *Animal Farm* is a proper noun when it refers to the classic satirical novella by George Orwell. Otherwise, the words *animal* and *farm* would be common nouns.

- *Game of Thrones* is the name of a popular TV series in the US. The words *game* and *thrones* are typically common nouns.
- *Aimée* is a proper noun designating a specific and uniquely identifiable girl.
- The words *girl* and *female* are common nouns.

Table 3.1 lists and categorizes more proper nouns.

*Table 3.1* More proper nouns, according to category

| Category | Proper noun |
| --- | --- |
| People | Marcos, Yi Ting, Ahmed, Maryam, Barack, Courtney |
| Computer manufacturers | IBM, Apple, Acer, and Hewlett-Packard |
| Electronics companies | LG, Samsung, Sony, Nokia, Canon, Ricoh, Hitachi, Xerox, Haier |
| Car manufacturers | Chevrolet, Ford, Hyundai, Honda, Toyota, Fiat, Seat, Maserati, Aston Martin, McLaren, Tesla |
| Planets | Mercury, Venus, Earth, Mars, Jupiter, Saturn, Uranus, Neptune |
| Continents | Europe, Asia, Africa, South America, North America, Antarctica, Australia |
| Day names | Sunday, Monday, Tuesday, Wednesday, Thursday, Friday, Saturday |
| Languages | Mandarin, Tagalog, Korean, Japanese, Arabic, Spanish, French, Hebrew, Celtic, Esperanto, Latin, Greek |

## Mini Review and Practice

### Common nouns and proper nouns

Have a look at the following passage on the history of the Fuji apple in the US, adapted from Wikipedia:

> The **Fuji apple** is an apple hybrid developed by growers at the Tohoku Research Station in Fujisaki, Aomori, Japan, in the late 1930s, and brought to market in 1962. It originated as a cross between two [. . .] apple varieties—the Red Delicious and old Virginia Ralls Genet . . . apples.
>
> ("Fuji apple," n.d.)

Try to locate all of the nouns—both common and proper.

1. What do you notice about **the common nouns**? For example:
   - Two common nouns can appear side-by-side with each other, like <u>apple</u> <u>hybrid</u>, where the **first noun** <u>describes</u> the second noun.
   - A particular decade or century can appear as a pluralized common noun <u>the</u> [late] <u>1930s</u>.

   Any other observations?

   [Note: For now, it might also help to identify common nouns by virtue of words like *the*, *a/an*, and *some* that precede them. We will discuss these types of word combinations in detail in Chapter 4.]

2. What types of entities are named by using **proper nouns** (e.g., people, geographic locations, specific items or groups)?

### Answers: common nouns and proper nouns

<u>Common nouns</u>:

apple, hybrid, growers, the 1930s, market, cross, varieties, apples

<u>Two contiguous common nouns occurring side by side</u>:

apple hybrid, apple varieties

<u>Proper nouns</u>:

Fuji (apple), Tohoku Research Station, Fujisaki, Aomori, Japan, Red Delicious, Virginia Ralls Genet, Rawls Jennet

<u>Proper noun and common nouns occurring side by side</u>:

Fuji apple, Red Delicious apple, Virginia Ralls Genet apple

## 3.4 Common Nouns: Type 1, Type 2, and Type 3 Nouns

In traditional approaches to grammar, common nouns are further distinguished on the basis of one specific criterion: whether the item, idea, person, or entity that is designated by a noun can be counted and made plural or not.

Nouns that can be counted and made plural are often referred to as "count" nouns. And nouns that are typically not countable are often referred to as "non-count" or "mass" nouns (Berry, 2013; Chafe, 1994; Langacker, 1991, 2008; Lee, 2001; Radden & Dirven, 2007; Strauss & Feiz, 2014; Talmy, 2000; Taylor, 1993; Tyler, 2012; Yule, 2010).

As we will illustrate, the notion of "countability" and the strict categorization of individual words as "count" or as "non-count" (or "mass") nouns is not sufficient to account fully for and grasp the range of conceptual meanings of nouns that we find in English discourse.

Note the list of prototypical English "count nouns" in Table 3.2. The singular form is shown in the left-hand column, the plural forms (for both regular plural and irregular plural) are shown in the right-hand column.

While the distinction of "count" and "non-count" nouns for these individual words might seem to work on an extremely basic level, this distinction tends to break down once we use

*Table 3.2* Prototypical "count" nouns: Singular and plural forms

| \<Count nouns with regular plural forms\> | | \<Count nouns with irregular plural forms\> | |
| --- | --- | --- | --- |
| *Singular form* | *Plural form* | *Singular form* | *Plural form* |
| book | books | tooth | teeth |
| key | keys | foot | feet |
| note | notes | goose | geese |
| elephant | elephants | woman | women |
| window | windows | man | men |
| sink | sinks | child | children |
| faucet | faucets | knife | knives |
| placemat | placemats | thief | thieves |
| program | programs | life | lives |
| page | pages | index | indices |
| name | names | appendix | appendices |
| chicken | chickens | addendum | addenda |
| approach | approaches [Note: -*es*, not -*s*] | focus | foci |
| picture frame | picture frames | cactus | cacti |
| apple hybrid | apple hybrids | criterion | criteria |
| | | phenomenon | phenomena |
| | | city | cities |
| | | country | countries |
| | | diary | diaries |
| | | fairy | fairies |

54  *Nouns and Their Meaning in Discourse*

language and grammar in discourse, **because meanings of words do not rest simply at the word level**. That is, we use words and grammar in discourse to imagine and talk about people, things, objects, and ideas and to express our thoughts and perceptions in more complex ways.

Rather than designating nouns as "count" or "non-count" or "mass," we instead categorize nouns according to their conceptual meanings.

### 3.4.1 Common Nouns: Type 1

The Type 1 noun, similar in basic nature to the "count" noun, is illustrated using Figure 3.2.

**Type 1 Nouns**

The Type 1 designation includes a more discerning set of criteria than simply the notion of "countability."

Beyond the notion of "countability," Type 1 nouns can be described as follows:

- **individuated:** with separate, delineated boundaries or edges; the boundaries can be literal/concrete or abstract/metaphorical
- **distinguishable:** from other possibly similar things or concepts, for example, shapes: *triangle, circle, square, diamond, rectangle, octagon*
- **divisible:** that is, they can be broken down into identifiable component parts, like *kitten → whiskers, paws, claws*
- **potentially multiple:** that is, they can be conceptualized as either singular entities or plural entities; this means that **plural forms of the noun are grammatically and conceptually possible**.

Type 1 nouns can occur either in the singular form, denoting ONE instance of an entity (e.g., *a key, the key, her diary, one criterion, that woman, my child*), or in the plural form, denoting MULTIPLE instances of the entity (e.g., *five keys, her diaries, many criteria, those women, my children*).

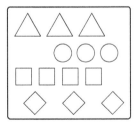

*Figure 3.2* Conceptual meaning—Type 1

## Mini Review and Practice

### Conceptual Meaning—Type 1

1 Look at the following word list. Can you identify all four criteria (or at least three) from our definition of Type 1 nouns? Most importantly, can you individuate each noun, like the diagram shows? Can you think of the noun as a single thing AND as more than one of the same thing, namely, having potential multiples? Does the entity have separate, delineated boundaries or edges? Can you distinguish that entity from other possibly similar things? Can you identify component parts that make up that noun?

> battery
> package
> toy
> wall
> statue
> screen

2 The following lyrics are from the children's song "Head, Shoulders, Knees, and Toes" by Karl-Axel Elmqvist (originally in Swedish):

> Head, shoulders, knees, and toes.
> Head, shoulders, knees, and toes.
> Eyes and ears and mouth and nose
> Head, shoulders, knees, and toes

The song is typically sung and enacted with each person pointing to and touching the noun each time the word is sung. Sometimes, the enactment includes stretching and bending, especially for *knees* and *toes*.

As you read or sing the lyrics, what images of objects and their **quantities** come to mind? The song clearly underscores how Type 1 nouns work and function. Explain this concept using the song lyrics. Be sure to note that three of the nouns are singular. Which ones? Why? What kind of meaning shift would occur in the singing of the song if each of those singular nouns was made plural?

### 3.4.2 Common Nouns: Type 2

Traditionally, "mass" nouns are called "mass" nouns because they often label things that are considered in English to be quantitatively singular and denote substances, materials, liquids, solids, gases, or abstract ideas, as illustrated in Figure 3.3.

Prototypical exemplars of "non-count" or "mass" nouns are listed in Table 3.3. The left column indicates the noun in singular form. The middle and right columns illustrate that non-count/mass nouns do not typically co-occur with determiners that designate singularity or the number "one" (e.g., *one* or *a/an*), nor can they occur with any plural marking (e.g., final *-s*). Ungrammatical words, phrases, and sentences are marked with an asterisk (*) to the left of that word or phrase or sentence.

56  *Nouns and Their Meaning in Discourse*

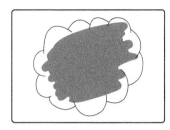

*Figure 3.3* Conceptual meaning—Type 2

*Table 3.3* Prototypical "non-count" or "mass" nouns: No plural forms possible

| *Singular* | *(NO co-occurring one, a/an)* | *Plural (NO co-occurring plural -s)* |
|---|---|---|
| oxygen | *an oxygen | *oxygens |
| stuff | *one stuff | *stuffs |
| junk | *a junk | *junks |
| luggage | *a luggage | *luggages |
| information | *an information | *informations |
| advice | *one advice | *advices |
| homework | *one homework | *homeworks |
| trash | *a trash | *trashes |
| sunshine | *one sunshine | *sunshines |
| luck | *a luck, one luck | *lucks |

Type 2 nouns such as *junk*, *oxygen*, *metal*, *sunshine*, *homework*, and *information* label concepts, matter, ideas, and abstractions that cannot be individuated (by delineated boundaries or edges) or separated into identifiable component parts. Each is conceptualized as unified, amorphous, indivisible, and singular wholes.

*a junk, *one junk, *an oxygen, *many homeworkS, *all my stuffS, *three adviceS

Similarly, gerunds, or nouns derived from verbs using the present participle *-ing* suffix, also typically follow the conceptual meaning pattern for **Type 2** nouns.

Land's End provides free *shipping* on all orders of $50.00 or more.
The nonstop *yelling* and *arguing* by our neighbors kept us up all night.

Note: Some gerunds can indeed be conceptualized as plural entities, since they evoke a repeated cycle of events or multiple instances of an item:
readings, mailings, comings and goings, ramblings, savings, markings, meanings, findings BUT *shippings, *yellings, *arguings

The handful of words that end in *-s* but are predominantly used in the singular, like *news*, *linguistics*, *genetics*, *politics*, *ethics*, *rickets*, *mumps*, and *semiotics*, are characterized as non-count/mass nouns. For example:

No news is good news. [**singular** verb morphology]
(Meaning: If we don't hear anything, we can assume that everything is alright.)

*Nouns and Their Meaning in Discourse* 57

"For Vancouver real estate developer Michael Ching Mo Yeung, politics **is** a family affair." (Young, 2015) [**singular** verb morphology]

"Certain areas of linguistics, such as the study of sounds (phonology) and of sentence construction (syntax) are well defined, but semantics **does** not have such clear limits." (Biggam, 2012, p. 9) [**singular** verb morphology]

**Compare:**

Politics **is** the heart of the issue.   [singular = more preferred]
Politics **are** dividing our nation.   [plural = less preferred but used in discourse]

There is a subtle difference in conceptual meaning between these two sentences.

## Type 2 Nouns

The Type 2 designation includes a more discerning set of criteria than simply the notion of "non-countability" or "massness."

### Type 2 nouns can be described as follows:

- **amorphous:** that is, they have no separate or distinct boundaries
- **indivisible:** that is, they cannot be broken down into smaller parts; any part of this type of noun is just a smaller portion of the whole
- **conceptually a singular whole:** that is, they have no potential multiples and cannot be conceptualized as a plural entity; **plural forms are not grammatically or conceptually possible in English**

Note how the underlined nouns in the following examples express meanings that are of the **Type 2** conceptual category.

- Today's weather: sunshine, followed by some rain, thunder, and lightning.
- You can ask me anything, but, please, not my advice on love or marriage.
- "Human progress is neither automatic nor inevitable. . . . Every step toward the goal of justice requires sacrifice, suffering, and struggle; the tireless exertions and passionate concern of dedicated individuals." (Martin Luther King Jr., 1961)

## Mini Review and Practice

### Type 1 and Type 2 Nouns

Read through the following excerpt from an online advice website for parents of teens. Read the passage at least twice. First, identify the nouns. Then, classify each noun as evoking a Type 1 or Type 2 conceptualization. Try to explain why the Type 1 nouns can be pluralized and why the Type 2 cannot be made plural in these contexts.

**KidsHealth (adapted from "Top 10 homework tips," 2014)**

- **Make sure kids do their own work.** They won't learn if they don't think for themselves and make their own mistakes. Parents can make suggestions and help with directions. But it's a kid's job to do the learning.
- **Set a good example.** Do your kids ever see you diligently balancing your budget or reading a book? Kids are more likely to follow their parents' examples than their advice.
- **If there are constant problems with homework, get help.** Talk about it with your child's teacher.

**Answers**:

Type 1 nouns:
kids, mistakes, parents, suggestions, directions, job, example, budget, book, example, problems, child, teacher

Type 2 nouns:
health, work, learning, advice, homework, help
(*healths, *works, *learnings, *advices, *homeworks, *helps)

Which type of conceptualization pattern (Type 1 or Type 2) is more common in this excerpt? Why do you think this is so? What defining features of Type 1 nouns and Type 2 nouns helped you classify the nouns in this excerpt?

How is the word *job* used here conceptually different from the word *work*? That is, why is *job* a Type 1 concept in this excerpt and *work* a Type 2 concept?

### 3.4.2.1 Why Type 1 and Type 2 Categories Are Clearer Than the Traditional "Count" and "Non-Count"/"Mass" Categories

Traditional approaches to grammar typically illustrate the differences between "count" and "non-count"/"mass" as word lists, where a particular noun is designated as a "count" noun or as a "non-count"/"mass" noun.

Table 3.4 on the next page illustrates this tendency for "non-count"/"mass" nouns, based on classifications like substances, materials, liquids, and so forth.

The problem arises when the distinctions are less straightforward. In fact, there may well be more exceptions to the rule than there are perfect exemplars of "count" nouns and "non-count"/"mass" nouns. Let's take a look at the following words used in different discourse contexts:

**Are the words *wood, oak, maple,* and *bamboo* in the following examples "count" nouns or "non-count"/"mass" nouns?**

First, note the nouns. Underlined nouns are "non-count"/"mass." Nouns in boldface are "count."

- <u>wood</u>: material, therefore "non-count"/"mass" noun
  - Which is the best <u>wood</u> (non-count/mass) for **a cutting board**? (count)
- <u>oak, maple, bamboo</u>: material, therefore "non-count"/ "mass" nouns
  - I have only made **cutting boards** (count) out of <u>oak</u>, <u>maple</u>, and <u>bamboo</u>. (non-count/mass)

But:

- **oaks:** a specific kind of tree (count)
- **maples:** a specific kind of tree (count)
  - Most **oaks** (count) retain their **leaves** throughout the autumn **months**, while **maples** begin to lose theirs quite early.

So, depending on contextual meanings and intended conceptual imageries, many so-called non-count/mass nouns also function as count nouns in actual language use. **It is not the words themselves that constitute the type of noun. It is the concept that each noun conjures up in the discourse.**

The nouns *oak* and *maple* occur easily in plural forms, *oaks* and *maples*.

What about the noun *bamboo*? Do you think the plural form *bamboos* will be as frequent as *oaks* and *maples* in English discourse? Why do you think this is the case?

Thus, rather than listing words as members of "count" and "non-count"/"mass" noun categories, we prefer a system of conceptual imageries for noun meaning in context and discourse, based on our Type 1 and Type 2 classification system.

*Table 3.4* Traditional "non-count"/"mass" nouns denoting substances, materials, liquids, solids, gases, and abstract concepts

| *Examples of the traditional categories of words often termed "non-count"/"mass" nouns:* | |
| --- | --- |
| Substances | gypsum, magma, lava, pulp, slime, marijuana, paraben, glucose, insulin, plasma, clay, silt, cement, asphalt, chlorophyll, cacao, whiskey, wine |
| Materials | wood, mahogany, pine, oak, plastic, paper, cardboard, papyrus, metal, gold, silver, aluminum, copper, drywall, wax, bamboo, glass, lycra, cotton, wool, nylon, concrete, porcelain |
| Liquids | water, soda, pop, juice, alcohol, coffee, tea, broth, soup, bisque |
| Solids | ice, rock, gravel, earth, sand, meat, chicken, beef, flour, salt, pepper, saffron, rice, wheat, bread, chocolate, vanilla |
| Gases | oxygen, carbon dioxide, nitrogen, helium, ozone, neon, steam |
| Abstract concepts | freedom, justice, perfection, health, independence, knowledge, work, homework, cruelty, kindness, common sense |

## Mini Review and Practice

### Identical word—Type 1 or Type 2?

1. Look at Figure 3.1, the cartoon at the beginning of the chapter. Identify the four nouns in the caption. Then list them and determine whether each noun evokes a Type 1 or a Type 2 conceptualization pattern. Explain your responses.

2. The following boxes contain examples of sentence pairs where the same word functions first as a Type 1 noun and then as a Type 2 noun. Think about **conceptual meanings** expressed by the boldface instance of the word (Type 1) and the underlined instance of the same word (Type 2). How does the **meaning** of each instance of the same noun change, depending on the Type 1 conceptual schema or the Type 2 schema?

What are the characteristics of the Type 1 uses of each of the following words? Can you identify boundaries? Physical edges around an object are a boundary. A container constitutes a boundary. A particular *type* of thing or *a kind* or *class* of thing, idea, or substance that can be distinguishable from *other types, other kinds*, and *other classes* also constitutes a **boundary**. What are the characteristics of the Type 2 uses of each noun?

**chocolate:**

| | |
|---|---|
| Type 1 | How does your wife feel if you give her **chocolates** for Valentine's Day? Slow down! **One chocolate** at a time! |
| Type 2 | The Swiss are famous for cheese and chocolate. |

**perfume:**

| | |
|---|---|
| Type 1 | **Perfumes**, scented soaps, and household sprays can be asthma triggers. I'm looking for **a perfume** that doesn't smell fruity. |
| Type 2 | "A woman who doesn't wear perfume has no future" (Coco Chanel). |

**food:**

| | |
|---|---|
| Type 1 | VitaClick: Your best source for vitamins and health **foods** online. Tofu is **a** popular, low-calorie **food** made from soybeans. |
| Type 2 | How long can humans survive without food or water? |

**room:**

| | |
|---|---|
| Type 1 | We loved the place. The **rooms** were clean and each one had a great view. Should we try to heat the entire house or just **one room**? |
| Type 2 | The compact parking space is not enough room for our minivan. |

**metal:**

| | |
|---|---|
| Type 1 | **A metal** is malleable if it can be bent or formed. Not **all metals** are good conductors of electricity. |
| Type 2 | The new findings show that one star in 10,000 might be made entirely of metal. |

**coffee:**

Type 1    We feature a variety of dark roasts. These **coffees** are our signature blends.
Kopi luwak is **a coffee** from Indonesia made from civet droppings.

Type 2    The espresso machine broke, and there was <u>coffee</u> all over the counter.

Now, construct your own sentence pairs using the following nouns, first as a Type 1 noun and then as a Type 2 noun, similar to the examples we provided previously. Try to locate your examples from actual discourse, for example, internet searches, literature, textbooks, essays, and so forth.

**time:**

Type 1: _____
Type 2: _____

**water:**

Type 1: _____
Type 2: _____

**ribbon:**

Type 1: _____
Type 2: _____

**man:**

Type 1: _____
Type 2: _____

**space:**

Type 1: _____
Type 2: _____

Conceptually, how do the nouns that pattern predominantly as Type 1 nouns differ from those that pattern predominantly as Type 2 nouns? What images of those nouns come to mind as Type 1 conceptualizations vs. Type 2 conceptualizations? Explain these differences in your own words and also try to represent them using the same or similar graphics that we provide here for each conceptualization type.

### 3.4.2.2 *Type 1 Nouns and Type 2 Nouns: More Practice With Conceptual Imagery*

In English discourse, prototypical Type 1 nouns can also function as Type 2 nouns, as if the boundary delimitation and the divisible nature of Type 1 nouns has morphed into a shapeless, edgeless material, aroma, flavor, substance, or concept.

## TYPE 1 NOUNS EVOKING TYPE 2 CONCEPTUAL IMAGERY

fruit in a basket, in the fridge (Type 1)   →   flavor, a product made of that fruit (Type 2)

*Figure 3.4*  A *strawberry*/one *strawberry*/red, ripe *strawberries* (Type 1)

*Figure 3.5*  *Strawberry* jam (Type 2)

### OTHER TYPE 1 NOUNS EVOKING TYPE 2 IMAGERY

| Type 1 noun | **EVOKES** → | Type 2 conceptual imagery |
|---|---|---|
| orange, lemon | | It was the sweet scent of <u>orange</u> mixed with <u>lemon</u> that I recall. |
| dog | | Her email subject line was "All things <u>dog</u>." |
| chicken | | Not all exotic meats taste like <u>chicken</u>. |
| man | | He is 10 times more <u>man</u> than I ever expected. |
| cookie | | Here is a napkin. You have <u>cookie</u> on your cheek. |

Type 1 nouns also evoke Type 2 imagery when used as a descriptor before another noun (i.e., NOUN + NOUN, where the first noun serves to describe a second noun, as we observed earlier with *apple* hybrid, *apple* varieties). The first noun becomes Type 2.

| | | |
|---|---|---|
| strawberry jam | strawberry jams but NOT: | *strawberries jam |
| newspaper article | newspaper articles but NOT: | *newspapers articles |
| sunflower seed | sunflower seeds but NOT: | *sunflowers seeds |

## Type 1 nouns as the first noun in a NOUN + NOUN combination: First noun becomes Type 2

picture frame, dog collar, dog food, cat food, whale blubber, mystery novel, car battery, cake decoration, teacher talk, adolescent troubles, group photo, bottle cap, house key, computer screen, market price, printer paper, house paint, city ordinance, hand soap, body wash, dish towel, birthday party, day job

*Nouns and Their Meaning in Discourse* 63

Note that the first noun in these constructions typically occurs in the singular and not the plural form, because what is in focus here is the *symbolic concept or idea* of the thing and *not the thing itself*. The first Type 1 noun now functions as a Type 2 noun.

TYPE 2 NOUNS EVOKING TYPE 1 CONCEPTUAL IMAGERY

amorphous, boundless mass, substance, or → takes on boundaries, limits (Type 1)
concept (Type 2)

*Figure 3.6 Coffee* (Type 2). General term, concept, ingredient, flavor.

*Figure 3.7 Coffees* (Type 1). Coffee in cups, various styles of serving.

The noun *coffee* denoting the substance, liquid, beans, or crop *as* a Type 2 noun morphs into a Type 1, delimited by the cups it is served in for drinking or by the different types of coffee that one can select in terms of preparation style (e.g., cappuccino, espresso, and Americano) or in terms of specialties (e.g., French Roast, Sidamo, and Sumatra).

*Coffee* as a flavor, ingredient, or color typically remains a **Type 2** noun.

We stopped in for ***a coffee*** and a Danish.    [Type 1]
We woke up to the aroma of freshly brewed <u>*coffee*</u>.    [Type 2]

Additional examples of abstract/conceptual boundaries causing Type 2 nouns to take on the Type 1 conceptualization patterns are as follows:

- Containers (glass, cups, bottles):
  - waters, sodas, pops, juices, milks, lemonades
- Varying types or differing kinds:
  - meats, cheeses, breads, waters (e.g., carbonated, flavored), coffees, teas, wines, liqueurs, brandies, whiskeys, rices, flours, gravies

64  *Nouns and Their Meaning in Discourse*

- Recurring events or cycles:
  - winds, rains, snows, fires, mailings, musings
- Non-Type 1 nouns with specific expanses or areas that could be considered as separable by physical, imaginary, or invisible boundaries:
  - waters, skies, fires

    25 vacation spots with the clearest <u>waters</u> in the world
    The forest is ablaze with <u>fires</u> soon approaching the structures.
    Meteorologists are predicting clear, cloudless <u>skies</u> for the eclipse.

### 3.4.3 Common Nouns: Type 3

As you look at the following list, note the primary feature of meaning that the nouns all have in common. Some are proper nouns. Some are common nouns. Some are derived from adjectives (e.g., *the innocent, the wealthy*). This class of nouns exhibits an important characteristic when it comes to grammar, meaning, and conceptual representation.

> the Swiss, the English, the Maya, the Cheyenne, NYPD, Los Angeles City Schools, family, couple, pair, fan base, Brazil, the College, the mafia, the administration, staff, faculty, class, committee, crew, team, audience, jury, the prosecution, the defense, army, navy, corps, division, battalion, congregation, parish, club, union, minority, majority, the Borg, party, the innocent, the guilty, the middle class, the intelligentsia, the wealthy

Each noun designates **a group** of people that are united on the basis of such criteria as follows:

- blood relationships, marriage
- geographic location
- nationality, government
- institutional affiliation/responsibility
- sports
- religious/political/ideological belief system
- employment
- personal interest
- education/socio-economic factors

What sets **Type 3** nouns apart from Type 1 and Type 2 is the **meaning** underlying these nouns. That is, nouns of this type designate a group of persons.

Sometimes the group is referred to in discourse as a SINGLE UNIT (**Type 3a**).

- The lights flicker and *the congregation* **remains** silent.    [verb: SINGULAR]
- *Tesla* **announces** record sales for its Model S.    [verb: SINGULAR]

Sometimes in discourse the group is described with a PLURAL verb, foregrounding the MULTIPLE INDIVIDUAL MEMBERS of that group (**Type 3b**).

- *The wounded* **were** transported to local hospitals.   [verb: PLURAL]
- How **do** *the French* make such good bread?   [verb: PLURAL]

**Conceptual meaning:**

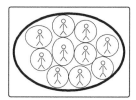

*Figure 3.8* Foregrounds the UNIT as a whole (Type 3a). Takes SINGULAR verb form.

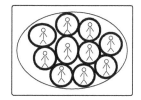

*Figure 3.9* Foregrounds the MEMBERS (Type 3b). Takes PLURAL verb form.

### Type 3 Nouns

The Type 3 nouns designate groups of individual people. Some Type 3 nouns designate the group as an entire UNIT (i.e., Type 3a). The verb is singular.

*The audience* **applauds** as she gracefully completes the double axel.
If *the union* **goes** on strike, what will happen to my job?
*The jury* **does** not decide the defendant's prison term.

Some Type 3 nouns designate the group as MULTIPLE INDIVIDUAL MEMBERS (i.e., Type 3b). The verb is plural.

Who **are** *the working poor* in America?
*The Maya* **have** lived for thousands of years in Mexico and Central America.
*The Borg* **ingest** only energy to drive their technological system via an energy conduit port. (StarTrek.com)

And some Type 3 nouns can foreground EITHER the group as a UNIT or the INDIVIDUAL MEMBERS of that group, where the verb can be singular or plural.

**Type 3a:**

The army **is** closing in.   [verb: SINGULAR]

**Type 3b:**

The army **are** closing in.   [verb: PLURAL]

66  *Nouns and Their Meaning in Discourse*

**Type 3** nouns like *audience, union, congregation, orchestra, band*, and *jury* often pattern with SINGULAR verb morphology (Type 3a), underscoring the group as a UNIT.

**Type 3** nouns like *the Swiss, the French, the Maya, the Lakota*, and even the science fictional cyborg nation *the Borg* pattern with PLURAL verb morphology (Type 3b), underscoring the MULTIPLE INDIVIDUAL MEMBERS of that group.

However, in English, a number of these (and other) nouns can be used with **singular or plural verb forms**, depending how the group and/or its members are being foregrounded. Nouns like *staff, faculty, family, the army*, and *the mafia* pattern in discourse with both types of conceptualization patterns, Type 3a and Type 3b.

*staff* (Type 3a)—with SINGULAR verb—foregrounding the people as a UNIT:

> This hotel is literally a diamond in the rough . . . I didn't expect such a modern, brand new facility right in the heart of the Redwoods. **The staff <u>is</u> amazing** and super friendly.
> ("The staff is . . .", 2015)

*staff* (Type 3b)—with PLURAL verb—foregrounding the people as MULITIPLE INDIVIDUAL MEMBERS:

> TripAdvisor employees all engage in community service. . . . As an added bonus, lunch is provided three times a week—and each week, *staff* **donate** what they would've spent on food to charities.
> (*The Daily Muse Editor*, 2015)

---

### Mini Review and Practice

1  The noun *family*: Type 3a or Type 3b?

**Excerpt 1: Wolf Blitzer interview with Madeleine Albright on The Situation Room**

> Joining us now from New York, Madeleine Albright, the former secretary of state. Madam Secretary, congratulations on writing this book. It really is very personal and moving. I want to get to some of the highlights right now. You begin the book by writing this: "I had no idea that **my family was Jewish** or that 20 of my relatives had died in the Holocaust." Here's the question, why didn't you know that?
> (Blitzer, 2012)

**Excerpt 2: "My Daily Bread"**

> <u>My</u> <u>family</u> <u>were</u> **happy parishioners** in an old, American-Irish Catholicism, when the church and school and social hall of Holy Angels filled our days with lessons, novenas, rosaries, meetings, choir practice, the major sports, pancake breakfasts, spaghetti dinners, bake sales, dances and other activities, and it was not unusual to get there for Mass before eight in the morning and leave after eight at night.
> (Hansen, 2000)

The noun phrase *my family* occurs in both excerpts. How is the verb used in each case? Is it singular? Is it plural? Why? Conceptually, which example uses the noun *family* as a Type 3a noun? Which example uses it as a Type 3b noun? How do the different conceptualizations relate to foregrounding the people (*my family*)? Explain these differences in

*Nouns and Their Meaning in Discourse* 67

your own words and also try to see how the meaning changes if the verb changes from the plural to the singular and vice versa.

2   Conceptual meaning in news headlines: Type 3a or Type 3b?

The following excerpts from newspaper headlines and captions all contain Type 3 nouns. Some refer to the group by foregrounding its status as an INDIVIDUAL UNIT with SINGULAR verb morphology (Type 3a). Some refer to the group by foregrounding the MULTIPLE INDIVIDUAL MEMBERS, with PLURAL verb morphology (Type 3b).

First, locate the full subject of each headline (these have been marked by a double underline to help them stand out). What is the subject?

Then, identify whether the verb in that headline appears with singular morphology (i.e., ending in *-s* in the present tense, *has* [instead of *have*], or *does* [instead of *do*]).

Which noun subjects reflect the Type 3a conceptualization pattern, and which reflect the Type 3b pattern? In cases where singular morphology is used, would plural morphology also be grammatically possible and vice versa?

How are grammar and conceptualization of nouns related?

   *San Francisco Globe*, February 9, 2015

   **Couple Meets Their Adopted Baby Boy**

   *Centre Daily Times*, December 22, 2014

   **State College Friends and Farmers takes** step toward co-op grocery with launch of online market

   *Gothamist*, March 2, 2015

   **NYPD Announce** New Machine Gun-Free Unit to Handle Protesters

   *Telegraph*, January 15, 2015

   Daggers, pistols and blood bonds: **how the Mafia works**
   **How does the real mafia compare** with fictional representations?

   *Guardian*, June 2, 2012

   "I knew **the mafia were accused of crimes**, from murder to racketeering, but I was too young to understand what it meant"

   *New Vision* (Uganda's Leading Daily), August 8, 2014

   **Rwanda appeal CAF (Confederation of African Football) disqualification**

   *USA Today*, August 21, 2014

   **Rwanda appeals African Cup disqualification**
   CAIRO (AP)—The Confederation of African Football says **Rwanda has** appealed against its disqualification from African Cup qualifying for fielding a striker who was using two identities.

> These excerpts underscore all the more the various ways in which grammar and verbal imagery work hand in hand in discourse.
>
> In addition, the last two examples, each with the identical referent *Rwanda* (the country name, but here, specifically referring to the soccer team for that country), also reflect dialectal differences (especially US vs. British English) in representing certain groups using Type 3 nouns (Algeo, 1988; Bauer, 1988; Bock et al., 2006; Depraetere, 2003; Hundt, 2006; Levin, 2001, 2006; Vantellini, 2003). The *USA Today* headline refers to Rwanda as a singular entity: "Rwanda appeals African Cup disqualification" and "Rwanda has appealed against its disqualification." In contrast, the Ugandan newspaper *New Vision*, following the convention of British English, refers to the team with plural verb morphology: "Rwanda appeal CAF disqualification."

*********

## PRACTICE WITH DATA ANALYSIS: PUTTING IT ALL TOGETHER

1 We introduced the concept of the gerund (a noun formed by adding the present participle -*ing* to a verb, e.g., *reading, writing, finding, dining, enjoying, predicting*).

We noted that gerunds tend to function as Type 2 nouns (e.g., *enjoying* → *\*enjoyings*, *predicting* → *\*predictings*, *dining* → *\*dinings*), but that because of the conceptualization patterns for some gerunds as nouns, we can consider those as Type 1 nouns, where they can easily be made plural because of their meanings:

| reading | → | readings |
| writing | → | writings |
| finding | → | findings |
| meaning | → | meanings |

Have a look at the following brief excerpt from the April 3, 2017, press release about Food Bowl, a culinary-based festival scheduled for May 2017 featuring world-class chefs, local chefs, food waste reduction plans, and awareness raising about hunger (the target forms are underlined and appear in boldface type).

> The festival will also support food access, sustainability and waste reduction through charity partners and participating events. The extensive lineup of **dining** events, panel discussions, culinary collaborations, volunteer projects and other food-inspired **happenings** is online now at lafoodbowl.com.

Two gerunds appear in the excerpt. One is functioning as a straightforward Type 2 noun. The second is functioning as a Type 1 noun. Can *dining* function as a Type 1? Why is it possible for *happening* to function as a Type 1? What is the meaning of this noun that allows pluralization and the meaning of *dining* that resists pluralization?

2 As we have illustrated throughout this chapter, nouns are the most frequently used word class or part of speech in English. In fact, every fourth word in English discourse is a noun

(Biber et al., 1999, p. 65). Nouns empower us to name and label, to identify and specify. Nouns enable us to make sense of the world, to organize it, to categorize it, to make our world deliberately ambiguous, or to clarify it with minute precision and accuracy.

According to *The Wit and Wisdom of Mark Twain*:

"The difference between the right word and the almost right word is the difference between **lightning** and **a lightning bug**."

(Twain, 1998)

Explain what Twain meant by this, and provide your own examples to illustrate (examples from personal experience can be compelling).

3   New words and old words used anew. New nouns are constantly entering our dictionaries and lexicons as reflections of how our world is changing. Here is an example of a once outdated noun that has recently reemerged in news discourse: *dotard*

- What does the word mean?
- Why has it recently been used? In what contexts?

4   Proper nouns and common nouns

a   *Red Delicious*, *Golden Delicious*, *Fuji*, and *Gala* are proper nouns that refer to specific varieties of apples. In what sorts of contexts might you hear speakers actually use the proper nouns for the specific apple variety in lieu of the common noun *apple*? Do you think that a speaker's or writer's use of a proper noun to designate an apple variety can serve a means to distinguish and/or specify the flavor or texture of one variety over another? Could the use of such proper nouns reflect a speaker's or writer's expertise and technical knowledge in the field?

- Thinking about *apple* and *Apple* (another proper noun), compare and contrast what you imagine to be the similarities and differences between the following two individuals:

    An apple expert   vs.   An Apple expert.
    What would the responsibilities be for each worker? Who earns more? Why?

- Now, let's change the scenario and topic of discussion from apples to wine, and we can see if anything changes.

    In what sorts of contexts might you hear speakers discussing the topic of wines, specifically *reds* or *whites*? How might the overall impression of a speaker change when using common nouns as opposed to proper nouns such as *Cabernet*, *Malbec*, and *Merlot* for *reds* and *Chardonnay*, *Moscato*, and *Semillon* for *whites*? Explain.

b   What difference do you think it makes whether a noun is a proper noun or a common one? Why is capitalization so important in designating nouns as proper nouns? How is a proper noun for a person or an entity conceptualized? That is, are there *many instances* of that person or entity, or just one, such that the person or referent becomes an *icon* or *symbol* of something far greater than just the referent (i.e., the person or the thing)? Here are a few examples:

| | | |
|---|---|---|
| The Green Arrow | vs. | the green arrow |
| Superman | vs. | super man |
| Milk (Harvey Milk) | vs. | milk (the beverage) |
| Sting (the rock star) | vs. | sting (injury from a biting insect) |
| Rockstar (energy drink) | vs. | rock star |
| The President | vs. | the president |
| Best Buy (the retail store) | vs. | a good buy, a better buy, the best buy |
| Grace (female first name) | vs. | grace: elegance, poise |
| China (east Asian country) | vs. | china: porcelain |

- Can you think of other nouns that occur in English as a proper noun and also as a common noun?
- What are they? Try to find **five more examples** (not already covered in this chapter).
- Write one sentence using one word used as a proper noun.
- Now, write a different sentence with the same word used as a common noun.
- You should have 10 sentences for this exercise in all.
- Conceptually, how do the imageries of each word change in your mind as it appears as a proper noun and then as a common noun?

c   What about the noun *earth*?

Why is *earth* a <u>common noun</u> here?:    but a **proper noun** here?:
The <u>earth</u> rotates around the sun.    The third planet from the sun is **Earth**.

- What are some other ways that *earth* is used as a common noun?
- The following explanation from Dictionary.com discusses when to capitalize *Earth* as a proper noun and when it should remain as a common noun. Read the explanation carefully. Do you notice anything problematic in this advice? (Hint: Look at the entire explanation and then go back and reread the first sentence. Does the author follow his/her own advice?)

**When do I capitalize the word *earth*?**
> "If you are talking about the **Earth** as a proper noun, as a planet or celestial body, then you can capitalize **Earth** and use no article (*the*): How far is **Earth** from the Sun? But it is also fine to leave it as lowercase and use *the* with *earth* if you are talking about it as the planet we live on."
>
> ("When should Earth be capitalized?," n.d.)

d   Have a look at the following headline. Does this mean that a thief is looking forward to playing football for Penn State? How do you know?

*Centre Daily Times*, September 20, 2014

"Penn State football notes: Crook relishes chance to play for Nittany Lions"

5   Common nouns and their meanings

As we know, Type 1 nouns share certain characteristics that distinguish them conceptually from Type 2 nouns.

Nouns and Their Meaning in Discourse 71

Type 1 nouns are individuated, they have boundaries (actual, conceptual, or metaphorical), and they can be used in the SINGULAR and PLURAL FORMS (*a key, one key, seven keys, a cloud, many clouds*).

Type 2 nouns are amorphous, they are indivisible, and they are conceptually SINGULAR. PLURAL forms for Type 2 nouns yield an UNGRAMMATICAL utterance (*attention, \*an attention, \*attentions, advice, \*one advice, \*advices*).

- a  Have a look at Figure 3.10, where an accountant is helping his canine client design an ideal retirement plan. Identify the Type 1 nouns in the accountant's advice. Then, identify the Type 2 nouns. Explain your rationale for why you categorized each noun as Type 1 or Type 2.

- b  Now, draw your own cartoons in which you keep the accountant but switch the recipient of the advice. That is, change the dog to a cat, a circus clown, and a gourmet chef. For each new client, include a list of five things that would make for an ideal retirement plan. Be sure to use both Type 1 and Type 2 nouns. Be creative. If you are taking a class on grammar, you might want to share your drawings and your answers with your classmates.

6  Have a look at the following list of nouns as they appear in singular forms and in plural forms.

- a  Think about *conceptual meaning*. What images are evoked when the noun is in the singular? What images are evoked when the noun is in the plural? Are these nouns patterning conceptually as Type 1 or Type 2? Think through your answers carefully, and explain in as much detail as possible for each word pair.

- b  How does your conceptualization of these words shift as you imagine the plural forms (in the right-hand column)? Can you describe this in conceptual terms? Using just this

"A good retirement fund should include bones, rawhide, beefy treats, a few toys and an assortment of kitchen trash."

*Figure 3.10* "A good retirement fund should include bones, rawhide, beefy treats, a few toys and an assortment of kitchen trash."

© Randy Glasbergen. Reproduced with permission of Glasbergen Cartoon Service.

set of noun pairs, try to articulate an argument in which you illustrate the ways in which grammar shapes our conceptualization of things and the ways in which our conceptualization of things shapes grammar.

| *Singular form* | *Plural form* |
|---|---|
| light | lights |
| service | services |
| shampoo | shampoos |
| weight | weights |
| injustice | injustices |
| ballet | ballets |
| danger | dangers |
| vanilla | vanillas |
| life | lives |
| death | deaths |
| money | monies |

7  What do you think C. S. Lewis in *Letters to Children* meant by "Never use abstract nouns when concrete ones will do. If you mean 'More people died,' don't say 'Mortality rose'"? Do you think this is good advice for writers? Explain in detail and provide examples to illustrate your points.

8  The following list contains nouns that don't look like nouns at first glance:

Items a through e contain examples of nouns that have derived from different communicative functions or different parts of speech.

Look up the etymologies of the expressions in items a and b. Share your findings with your classmates. Is it really possible that *hello*, *good-bye*, *yes*, and *no* can function as nouns? How so? How can you best support your answer?

For the examples in items a through e, try to find additional instances from actual discourse (e.g., the internet, poetry, literature) where words that are not *typically* nouns are used as nouns. Then determine whether each instance is closer to a Type 1 or a Type 2 noun.

Record the results of your discourse-based search for words that do not look like nouns at first glance but that are indeed functioning as nouns. Are there any other categories in addition to those in a through e that you found?

  a  Greeting words:

   hello
   good-bye

  b  Response words:

   yes   In what way can *yes* be used as a noun?
   no    In what way can *no* be used as a noun?

  c  Nouns from verbs:

   run   We went for a long *run* this morning.
   cry   What we all needed was a good *cry*.

| | |
|---|---|
| squeeze | Marco gave Emily a mighty *squeeze*. |
| read | *The Old Man and the Sea* is a relatively easy *read*. |
| laugh | We had so much fun and a lot of *laughs*. |

How does the meaning of *laughs* differ from *laughter*? How is grammar related to this type of conceptualization pattern for English nouns?

d   Nouns from prepositions:

"Find Your Away: AWAY is a place that's not on any map, but you know it when you find it." (adapted from "About Away," n.d.)

e   Nouns from adjectives (see Chapter 13):

All names have been changed to protect *the innocent*.
Blessed are *the meek*.
TAG: Magnet School for *the Talented* and *the Gifted*.
"*The Bold* and *the Beautiful*" [title of a US television soap opera]

9   Extended data excerpts from discourse

Analyze the nouns in the following excerpts from various discourse samples and multiple genres. Are they evoking Type 1 or Type 2 conceptualization patterns? Sometimes a particular word appears as a Type 1 noun and sometimes as a Type 2 noun. What accounts for this variation? Explain in detail using concepts from this chapter to help you articulate your responses.

a   From the *Washington Post*

"**Department of Public Works** hosts a display and demonstration of almost 30 vehicles used to clean and repair streets, change traffic lights, collect refuse, clear snow, provide emergency services, administer mobile health care and more."

(DC Community Calendar, 2012)

b   From *Popular Mechanics* website

"**How Much Snow is Too Much for Your Roof?** You know your roof may need bracing if the rafters are cracked from previous heavy snows or if they've been damaged by fire, termites, or rot."

(Berendsohn, 2012)

c   From *Sunset Magazine*

"Find brown jasmine rice alongside other rices at the grocery store."

(Johnson, 2008)

d   From *Real Simple* website

**Simple Strawberry Ice Cream**
"In the summer when strawberries are in season, a pale pink, creamy ice cream is the perfect way to show them off. For really concentrated flavor, try roasting the fruit before adding it—but if you'd rather keep things easy, simple sliced berries will do the trick."

("Homemade ice cream recipes," n.d.)

e   From *Perfume: The Story of a Murderer*

"Talent means nothing, while experience, acquired in humility and with hard work, means everything."

(Süskind, 2015, p. 74)

f   From *A Long Walk to Water*, "chicken" vs. "chickens"

> Now that Salva was learning more than a few simple words, he found the English language quite confusing.
>
> Like the letters "o-u-g-h."
>
> Rough . . . though . . . fought . . . through . . . bough—the same letters were pronounced so many different ways!
>
> Or how a word had to be changed depending on the sentence. You said "chickens" when you meant the living birds that walked and squawked and laid eggs, but it was "chicken"—with no "s"—when it was on your plate ready to be eaten: "We're having chicken for dinner." That was correct, even if you had cooked a hundred chickens.
>
> (Park, 2010, p. 99)

Salva is a so-called Lost Boy from Sudan. He recounts the story of his new life in the US, and some of his stories have to do with language. In this case, he mentions specifically how confusing nouns can be, especially the noun *chicken*. He is absolutely right in his observation. First, how can you help Salva better understand the rule? Also, can you explain the rule in such a way that it applies to other nouns and not just *chicken*? Give some examples.

## COMMON ERRORS, BUMPS, AND CONFUSIONS

Identify the errors or "bumps" in the following sentences. Use the concepts and terminology that you learned in this and other chapters to articulate what might be grammatically or pragmatically problematic. Suggest ways that each sentence can be rewritten more clearly and more accurately. (Note: While all bumps do involve some element of nouns, they are not limited to only that.)

1. I have a lot of good memory of learning English.
2. I got the feelings that I wanted to be independent from my boyfriend.
3. The special effect of the film is impressive.
4. Their presentation had good imaginations.
5. The bus could not leave because the passengers had too many luggages.
6. They used some good picture to depict important historical event.
7. Two womans and three mens played in string quartet.
8. As we drove through the city we were sad to see trashes and a garbage piling up in the streets.

## SUGGESTED ACTIVITIES

1. Imagine you are given the task of placing recycling signs on the recycling bins in the hallway of your school or office. You create the following signs using the singular form for every possible item. Are there some nouns that should actually appear in the plural? Which ones? Why? Explain your answer using concepts and terminology that you learned in this chapter.

Nouns and Their Meaning in Discourse 75

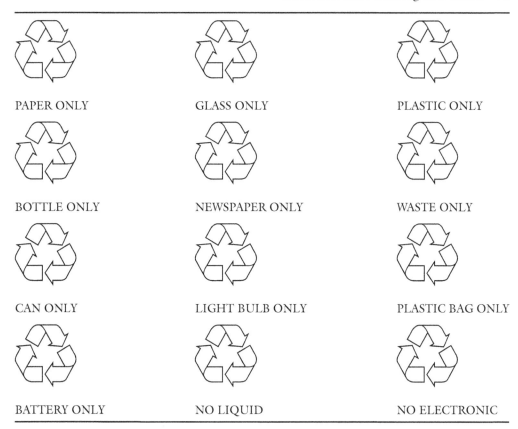

2 The US Department of Agriculture has created the following website for children, students, families, parents, and professionals: www.choosemyplate.gov.

Explore this "Choose My Plate" guide.
There are five food groups mentioned: fruits, vegetables, grains, protein, and dairy.
Classify each food group name as representing a Type 1 or Type 2 conceptualization.
As you navigate through the website, find examples of food items that fit each one of the five categories, and list seven items for each group.
Then, write a short essay that suggests a healthy weekly diet for an infant, a teenager, an adult, or a senior citizen. Write your essay as creatively as possible, providing vivid details and thorough explanations. Be sure to pay attention to the grammar and conceptualization patterns related to Type 1, Type 2, and Type 3 nouns.
You might want to answer some of the following questions:

- What kinds of foods should persons of that age consume every day?
- Why are those food items important?
- Think about contexts outside the US. What kinds of foods might you substitute to fulfill the recommended daily consumption of foods for each food group?

## Academic References

Aarts, B. (2011). *Oxford modern English grammar*. Oxford, UK: Oxford University Press.
Algeo, J. (1988). British and American grammatical differences. *International Journal of Lexicography, 1*, 1–31.
Bauer, L. (1988). Number agreement with collective nouns in New Zealand English. *Australian Journal of Linguistics, 8*, 247–259.
Berry, R. (2013). *English grammar: A resource book for students*. New York: Routledge.
Biber, D., Johansson, S., Leech, G., Conrad, S., Finegan, E., & Quirk, R. (1999). *Longman grammar of spoken and written English*. Boston, MA: MIT Press.
Bock, K., Butterfield, S., Cutler, A., Cutting, J. C., Eberhard, K. M., & Humphreys, K. R. (2006). Number agreement in British and American English: Disagreeing to agree collectively. *Language, 82*(1), 64–113.
Chafe, W. (1994). *Discourse, consciousness and time*. Chicago: University of Chicago Press.
Depraetere, I. (2003). On verbal concord with collective nouns in British English. *English Language and Linguistics, 7*(1), 85–127.
Gentner, D. (1978). On relational meaning: The acquisition of verbs meaning. *Child Development, 49*, 988–998.
Gentner, D. (1982).Why nouns are learned before verbs: Linguistic relativity versus natural positioning. In S. Kouczaj (Ed.), *Language development: Vol. 2. Language, thought and culture*. Hillsdale, NJ: Erlbaum.
Givón, T. (1993). *English grammar: A function-based introduction* (Vol. 1). Amsterdam and Philadelphia: John Benjamins.
Hundt, M. (2006). The committee has/have decided . . . : On concord patterns with collective nouns in inner- and outer-circle varieties of English. *Journal of English Linguistics, 34*(3), 206–232.
Langacker, R. (1991). *Foundations of cognitive grammar: Vol. 2. Descriptive application*. Stanford, CA: Stanford University Press.
Langacker, R. (2008). *Cognitive grammar: A basic introduction*. New York: Oxford University Press.
Lee, D. (2001). *Cognitive linguistics: An introduction*. Oxford: Oxford University Press.
Levin, M. (2001). *Agreement with collective nouns in English*. Lund, Sweden: Lund University Press.
Levin, M. (2006). Collective nouns and language change. *English Language and Linguistics, 10*(2), 321–343.
Macnamara, J. (1972). Cognitive basis of language learning in infants. *Psychological Review, 79*(1), 1–13.
Murphy, R. (2012). *English grammar in use* (4th ed.). Cambridge, UK: Cambridge University Press.
Nelson, K. (1973). Structure and strategy in learning to talk. *Monographs of the Society for Research in Child Development, 38*(1–2), 1–135.
Quirk, R., Greenbaum, S., Leech, J., & Svartvik, J. (1985). *A comprehensive grammar of the English language*. London and New York: Longman.
Radden, G., & Dirven, R. (2007). *Cognitive English grammar*. Amsterdam: John Benjamins Publishing Company.
Sloat, C. (1969). Proper nouns in English. *Language, 45*(1), 26–30.
Strauss, S., & Feiz, P. (2014). *Discourse analysis: Putting our worlds into words*. New York: Routledge University Press.
Swan, M. (2005). *Practical English usage: New international*. Oxford, UK: Oxford University Press.
Talmy, L. (2000). *Toward a cognitive semantics: Vol. 1. Concept structuring systems*. Cambridge, MA: MIT University Press.
Taylor, J. R. (1993). Some pedagogical implications of cognitive linguistics. In R. Geiger & B. Rudzka-Ostyn (Eds.), *Conceptualization and mental processing in language* (pp. 201–224). Berlin and New York: DeGruyter Mouton.
Tyler, A. (2012). *Cognitive linguistics and second language learning: Theoretical basics and experimental evidence*. New York: Routledge.
Vantellini, L. (2003). Agreement with collective nouns in New Zealand English. *NZEJ, 17*, 45–49.
Yule, G. (2010). *Explaining English grammar*. Oxford: Oxford University Press.

## Data References

About Away. (n.d.). GoRVing website. Retrieved September 10, 2016, from http://away.gorving.com/about/

Berendsohn, R. (2012, February 17). How much snow is too much for your roof? *Popular mechanics.* Retrieved August 15, 2014, from www.popularmechanics.com/home/outdoor-projects/how-to/a7333/how-much-snow-is-too-much-for-your-roof/

Biggam, C. (2012). *The semantics of color: A historical approach.* Cambridge: Cambridge University Press.

Blitzer, W. (Interviewer) & Albright, M. (Interviewee). (2012). The situation room [Interview transcript]. CNN. Retrieved August 8, 2014, from http://transcripts.cnn.com/TRANSCRIPTS/1204/25/sitroom.01.html

The Daily Muse Editor. (2014, October 1). 10 companies where you'll be able to do tons of good. *Newsweek.* Retrieved January 15, 2015, from www.newsweek.com/career/10-companies-where-youll-be-able-do-tons-good

DC Community Calendar. (2012, June 15). Retrieved August 15, 2014, from www.washingtonpost.com/local/dc-community-calendar-june-14-21/2012/06/11/gJQAdtpwdV_story.html

Elmqvist, K-.A. (n.d.). Head, shoulders, knees, and toes.

Fuji (apple). (n.d.). Wikipedia. Retrieved August 8, 2014, from https://en.wikipedia.org/wiki/Fuji_%28apple%29.

Hansen, R. (2000). My daily bread. *America: The National Catholic Review, 182*(9), 14–18.

Homemade ice cream recipes. (n.d.) Retrieved October 21, 2014, from www.realsimple.com/food-recipes/recipe-collections-favorites/desserts/homemade-ice-cream-recipes

Johnson, E. (2008). Filipino modern. *Sunset, 221*(4), 144.

King, M. L. The future of integration. Speech delivered on February 10, 1961, at New York University. Information retrieved September 10, 2016, from www.nyu.edu/life/events-traditions/mlk-week.html

Park, L. S. (2010). *A long walk to water.* New York: Clarion Books.

The staff is amazing and super friendly. (2015, April 22). Redwood Hotels and Casino (customer review). Retrieved April 19, 2015, from http://redwoodhotelcasino.com/2015/04/22/staff-amazing-super-friendly/

Süskind, P. (2015). *Perfume: The story of a murderer.* New York: Knopf Doubleday Publishing Group.

Top 10 homework tips. (n.d.). Kids health. Retrieved August 8, 2014, from http://kidshealth.org/en/parents/homework.html

Twain, M. (1998). *The wit and wisdom of Mark Twain: A book of quotations.* North Chelmsford, MA: Courier Corporation.

When should Earth be capitalized? (n.d.). Dictionary.com. Retrieved June 14, 2014, from http://dictionary.reference.com/help/faq/language/s05.html

Young, I. (2015). Politics is all in the family for corruption fugitive Michael Ching Mo. *South China Morning Post.* Retrieved May 15, 2015, from www.scmp.com/news/world/article/1786367/politics-all-family-corruption-fugitive-michael-ching-mo-yeung

# 4 Referring to, Identifying, Specifying, Underspecifying, Possessing, and Quantifying Things, People, and Ideas in Discourse

## Determiners

*Figure 4.1* "Don't slice the pizza. My diet says I'm only allowed to eat one piece!"
© Randy Glasbergen. Reproduced with permission of Glasbergen Cartoon Service.

This chapter extends the discussion of nouns to the topic of determiners. Determiners belong to the class of words that precede nouns to express a narrow and specific type of conceptual meaning. Table 4.1 provides a brief list of English determiners, their basic category types, and a few examples. Every noun in English is preceded by a determiner, even if that determiner is not visible or overt. Covert, non-visible determiners are marked with the symbol ∅.

Here, you'll find the determiners from the opening Glasbergen cartoon.

**Determiners from Figure 4.1:**

"Don't slice **the** pizza.          [definite article *the*]
**My** diet says                     [possessive determiner *my*]
I'm only allowed to eat **one** piece."   [quantifier *one*]

*Table 4.1* Determiner types and examples

| Determiner type | Examples | Phrasal examples |
|---|---|---|
| Articles | | |
| • indefinite article | a/an[1] | **a** moon of Jupiter (Leda) |
| • definite article | the | **the** moon of Earth |
| Demonstratives | that/those | **that** building/**those** bridges |
| | this/these | **this** discovery/**these** facts |
| Possessives | my, your, his, Zhan's | **my** opinion/**Zhan's** work |
| Quantifiers | | |
| • cardinal numbers | one, two, seventeen, 150 | **twenty** people |
| • more than one | some, a few, a number of | **some** scholars/**some** milk |
| • sequence, order | first, next, last, third | **last** winter/**third** quarter |
| • wholes, parts of wholes | all, every, each, some, both | **all** creatures/**both** sides |
| • zero quantity | no, zero, none of | **no** problem/**zero** calories |
| Interrogatives | which? how many? whose? | **how many** languages? |
| Covert determiner | ∅ [no determiner before noun] | ∅ time, ∅ politicians, ∅ ice |

The type of conceptual meanings that all determiners evoke is narrowly and consistently limited to the following:

> **The narrow range of conceptual meanings for English determiners**
> - IDENTIFIABILITY, SPECIFICITY
> - degrees of FOCUS (high, medium, and low)
> - POSSESSION and possession-like concepts
> - GENDER (for third-person singular possessive determiners only)
> - SEQUENCE and order
> - NUMBER and QUANTITY [including part/whole relationships]
> - IRRELEVANCE of ANY OF THE PREVIOUSLY LISTED CONCEPTS [i.e., ∅]

Determiners like *the, our, a, my, every, this, each, two*, and *no* seem like relatively inconsequential words when we view them against larger stretches of discourse. They form a relatively closed class of words and constructions. They are often very short in length, and they can occur side by side with other determiners. Yet, determiners convey **essential meaning** with regard to the nouns that they modify, meaning that relates to the following questions (and more):

> Can my hearer/listener or reader identify the entity that I am naming using a particular noun? Does it matter?
> Do I want my hearer or reader to pay special attention to that noun?
> Is there a quantity related to this noun?
> Is there a possession type of relationship associated with this noun?

Learners of English often mention that the uses and meanings of *the* (definite article) and *a* (indefinite article) are among the most challenging aspects of English grammar. Complicating this issue even more is the fact that sometimes determiners are covert and not visible in the discourse [indicated here and elsewhere in this book with the symbol ∅].

80   *Determiners*

Let's first have a quick look at how determiners pattern in English discourse. The following passage is adapted from Rick Browne's (2013, p. 11) *A Century of Restaurants: Stories and Recipes from 100 of America's Most Historic and Successful Restaurants*. Note how Browne vividly describes his visit to the classic eatery, Jones' Bar-B-Q Diner, in Marianna, Arkansas.

### "Jones' Bar-B-Q Diner/Marianna, Arkansas, EST. 1910"

**The** air was hot and sticky and uncomfortable. There was **no** wind or ∅ breeze to cool **the** Arkansas Delta—only **that** fiery round sun baking me nearly to ∅ death. But I had driven **150** miles to visit **a** local barbecue legend, and **no** blazing sun was going to stop me.

I had heard and read about **the** legendary pulled-pork sandwiches sold at **the** historic Jones' Bar-B-Q Diner in ∅ tiny Marianna, Arkansas—**a** restaurant that had survived more than **a** century in one of **the** poorest counties in **the** state. But **the** Diner, **a** two-story white house, seemed to be losing **its** battle with ∅ time. **The** paint was peeling, **the** windows were so dirty you couldn't see in, and **the** wrought-iron door squealed in ∅ protest as it was opened. . . .

**The** sandwich was good—no, it was damn good. **The** Wonder Bread fought **a** losing battle with **the** sauce and ∅ drippingly moist pork, **the** chunks and ∅ strands, tender and steaming and sopping wet with **a** thin cayenne-paprika-vinegar sauce. **Every** bite was **an** epiphany, **the** mustardy slaw wrapping **its** arms around **the** smoky meat. I hurried through **the second** sandwich, worried that **the** bread and I would both lose **the** battle—me suffering by having **most of my** lunch drop in **my** lap.

(Browne, 2013, p. 11)

As you see, we have marked the overt determiners in bold and have underlined the main nouns that each determiner modifies. Covert determiners are marked with ∅.

**Nouns from the previous passage:**

air, wind, breeze, Arkansas Delta, sun, death, miles, barbecue legend, pulled-pork sandwiches, Jones' Bar-B-Q Diner, Marianna, Arkansas, restaurant, century, counties, state, Diner, house, battle, time, paint, windows, wrought-iron door, protest, sandwich, Wonder Bread, battle, sauce, pork, chunks, strands, cayenne-paprika-vinegar sauce, bite, epiphany, slaw, arms, meat, sandwich, bread, battle, lunch, lap

By isolating just these nouns and their determiners, we can well imagine the primary themes as they progress in the passage, paragraph by paragraph:

**Paragraph 1: the weather, the outside environment**

the air, no wind, (no) ∅ breeze, the Arkansas Delta, ∅ death, that sun, no sun

**Paragraphs 1–2: the restaurant**

a barbecue legend, the Jones' Bar-B-Q Diner, a restaurant, a century, the counties, the state, the Diner, a house, its battle, ∅ time, the paint, the windows, the wrought-iron door, ∅ protest

**Paragraphs 2–3: the food**

the pulled-pork sandwiches, The Wonder Bread, the sauce, pork, the chunks, ∅ strands, a cayenne-paprika-vinegar sauce, every bite, an epiphany, the slaw, its arms, the meat, the second sandwich, the bread, my lunch, my lap

## 4.1 The Linguistic Category of *Reference*

As illustrated in this introductory discussion, determiners are intricately related to the various ways we pick out nouns in discourse. Determiners and nouns belong to the linguistic category of *reference*. The term reflects the everyday verb *to refer*. So, when we mention a person, a thing, or an idea in discourse, we *refer* to that entity. There are an infinite number of ways to refer to entities, people, things, and ideas in discourse, using a variety of different nouns and a selection of one or more determiners.

In any human language, there are countless possible ways to refer to the same entity. Here is one illustrative example: The referent is *our favorite family vacation destination*, and here are a few different ways that we might refer to that destination—that is, Hawaii.

**Overt determiners** are in **bold**, the symbol ∅ designates the covert determiner, and nouns are underlined:

∅ Hawai'i
**the** islands
**a** perfect getaway
**our** beloved Hanauma Bay
∅ paradise
**that** home away from ∅ home      (generally if we are not there)
**this** land of ∅ sun and ∅ sea     (generally if we are there)

Try to extend this list to see how many potential ways one might refer to Hawaii as a favorite vacation place.

Now let's go back to Browne's passage about the diner:

- Which determiners are used in the entire excerpt, and how frequently?
  - **the** [19 tokens—not all listed here]: **the** air, **the** Arkansas Delta, **the** legendary pulled pork sandwiches, **the** historic Jones' Bar-B-Q Diner, **the** paint, **the** windows, **the** wrought-iron door, **The** sandwich, **The** Wonder Bread, **the** smoky meat . . .
  - **a, an** [7 tokens]: **a** local barbecue legend, **a** restaurant, **a** two-story white house, more than **a** century, **a** losing battle, **a** thin cayenne-paprika-vinegar sauce, **an** epiphany
  - ∅ [7 tokens]: no wind or ∅ breeze, to ∅ death, in ∅ tiny Mariana, Arkansas; with ∅ time; in ∅ protest; with the sauce and ∅ drippingly moist pork, the chunks and ∅ strands
  - **no** [2 tokens]: **no** wind, **no** blazing sun
  - **its** [2 tokens]: losing **its** battle with time, wrapping **its** arms around
  - **my** [2 tokens]: **my** lunch, **my** lap
  - **150 (cardinal number)** [1 token]: **150** miles
  - **that** [1 token]: **that** fiery sun
  - **every** [1 token]: **every** bite
  - **most of** [1 token]: **most of** my lunch

- How many different ways is the restaurant referred to in the title and in paragraphs 1 and 2? What if the author simply repeated "a restaurant" or "the restaurant" each time he referred to the place?

- How many different ways does the author refer to the food?
  - How do these reference strategies affect how you envision the setting and the food?

- What effect does the part-whole relationship have on how you envision the building and how you envision the sandwiches?
  - The <u>restaurant/building</u> represents the <u>whole</u>.
    - The *parts* referred to are the paint, the windows, and the wrought-iron door.
  - The <u>pulled pork sandwiches</u> represent the whole.
    - The *parts* referred to are the Wonder Bread, the sauce, ∅ drippingly moist pork, the chunks and ∅ strands, a thin cayenne-paprika-vinegar sauce, the mustardy slaw, its arms, the smoky meat, and the bread.
- Based on the author's choice of determiners, nouns, adjectives, and adverbs, what can you say about his *stance* regarding his trip to this diner? Think about how all of these grammatical elements work together to depict this scene. How does grammar contribute to the author's evaluation of the overall scene and the food?

*Reference*, then, involves the act of labeling and naming the things and people and ideas that fill our lives and our imaginations. It is through the inventories of nouns (Chapter 3), determiners, and pronouns (Chapter 5) that we pick out and refer to these entities from the near-infinite sets of possible choice. Our use of one noun over others, of a particular determiner or determiner type, or of a pronoun instead of a noun depends on how specific we want or need our discourse to be. Our choice depends on what our hearers or readers may know or not know about our topic. And it depends on the degrees of specificity, precision, or vagueness that we want to invoke as we represent our referents in all of our daily discourse.

## 4.2 English Determiners and Their Conceptual Meanings

The meanings of determiners in English all center around the following narrow concepts:

identifiability, specificity
degrees of focus [low, medium, high]
possession and possession-like or affiliative relationships
dender [with third-person singular possessive determiners only]
sequence and order
number and quantity [including part/whole relationships]
irrelevance of any of the foregoing concepts [represented by ∅ as the covert determiner]

To illustrate, compare the possible grammatical variations on the following Virginia Woolf title, *To the Lighthouse*, and see how the conceptual imageries of the nouns change as the determiners change. Think about the narrow range of meanings that determiners evoke.

**ORIGINAL TITLE:** *To The <u>Lighthouse</u>*

Determiner = definite article *the* → the noun is **specific, identifiable**, the author assumes that the reader or addressee knows or can figure out which *lighthouse* is being referred to.

| VARIATIONS *on the title* | *Conceptual imageries of lighthouse* |
|---|---|
| To *A* <u>Lighthouse</u> | author assumes the hearer or reader does not know which one [not specific, not identifiable; number = *one*] |
| To *That* <u>Lighthouse</u> | the hearer or reader knows which one; **higher focus** than *the* [degree of focus] |
| To *My* <u>Lighthouse</u> | my favorite one, the one I built/work at/own/affiliate with [possession, possession-like, or affiliative relationship] |
| To *Scotty's* <u>Lighthouse</u> | the one Scotty built/works at/owns/affiliates with [possession, possession-like, or affiliative relationship] |
| To *Her* <u>Lighthouse</u> | the one that she built/works at/owns/affiliates with [possession, possession-like, or affiliative relationship; gender] |
| To *Either* <u>Lighthouse</u> | there are exactly two lighthouses, and the destination is one of them; it doesn't matter which [not specific; number = two] |
| To *Both* <u>Lighthouses</u> | there are exactly two lighthouses, and the destination is both of them [specific; number = two] |
| To ∅ <u>Lighthouses</u> | all we know about the referent is that there is more than one, by virtue of the *-s*; all other features of determiners are irrelevant in this reference [identifiability, specificity, focus, possession, number, quantity, gender = all are irrelevant] |

## 4.3 Articles: Indefinite Article *a/an*, Definite Article *the*

The English article system functions in such a way that the choice between the indefinite article *a/an* and the definite article *the* is based on three of the broad conceptual features that underlie the meanings of all determiners: identifiability, specificity, and number. We will explain these conceptual features in the following sections.

### 4.3.1 Indefinite Article a/an

The indefinite article *a/an* designates referents that have typically not been previously introduced into the discourse and that are assumed to be unknown to or unidentifiable by the hearer. *A/an* also designates the conceptual meaning of "one."

> **Meaning of *a/an***
>
> The referent is not specific or identifiable; quantity = "one."
>
> *A/an* signals a notion of "previously unfamiliar," "it doesn't matter which," "one," or "one of among others."
>
> - Typically used in discourse that presents "new" information and/or facts, names, or details not assumed to be known by the reader/hearer. That is, *a/an* is typically

84    *Determiners*

used with nouns that indicate people, concepts, things, and ideas that are "new" and unshared with the reader/hearer and are **mentioned for the first time in that spate of discourse**.

- *A/an* is used when the intended conceptual meaning of the referent is "one" or "one of among (many) others."

Because of the conceptual meaning evoked by *a/an*, we can predict some patterns of usage in particular types of discursive contexts and genres—especially in contexts where new things, places, artistic creations, foods, and concepts are introduced:

*4.3.1.1 Discursive contexts/genres*

- **Proverbs, sayings, and quotes about life and people and society:**

    You can't judge **a** <u>book</u> by its cover.
    (no specifically identifiable <u>book</u>; quantity = "one")

    **A** <u>chain</u> is only as strong as its weakest link.
    (no specifically identifiable <u>chain</u>; quantity = "one")

    **A** <u>team</u> is where **a** <u>boy</u> can prove his courage on his own. **A** <u>gang</u> is where **a** <u>coward</u> goes to hide. (Mickey Mantle)

    As long as she thinks of **a** <u>man</u>, nobody objects to **a** <u>woman</u> thinking. (Virginia Woolf, *Orlando*, 1928)

- **Definitions of objects, concepts, places:**

    hammer:     **A** <u>hand tool</u> consisting of **a** <u>handle</u> with **a** <u>head</u> of metal or other heavy rigid material that is attached at **a** <u>right angle</u>, used for striking or pounding. (The Free Dictionary, n.d.)

    waterspout:     **A** <u>whirling column of air and water mist</u>. (National Ocean Service, n.d.)

    hunger:     **A** <u>craving</u> or urgent need for **a** <u>specific nutrient</u>, **an** <u>uneasy sensation</u> occasioned by the lack of food, **a** <u>weakened condition</u> brought about by prolonged lack of food. (Merriam-Webster, n.d.)

    town:     **A** <u>human settlement</u> larger than **a** <u>village</u> but smaller than **a** <u>city.</u> (adapted from Wikipedia, n.d.)

    monument:     **A** <u>building</u> or **a** <u>statue</u> that honors **a** <u>person</u> or **an** <u>event</u>, **a** <u>building</u> or **a** <u>place</u> that is important because of when it was built or because of something that happened there. (adapted from Merriam-Webster, n.d.)

    landmark:     **A** <u>recognizable natural or artificial feature</u> used for navigation, **a** <u>feature</u> that stands out from its environment and is often visible from long distances (adapted from Wikipedia, n.d.)

- **Introductions to types of foods:**

    - Common and everyday things, like *noodle*

        noodle:     **A** <u>narrow, ribbon-like strip of dough</u>, usually made of flour, eggs, and water. (The Free Dictionary, n.d.)

- And less common, less well-known food items like *opakapaka* and *frittata*

  opakapaka:     A <u>deepwater pink snapper</u> that is native to Hawaiian and other tropical waters. (Hawai'i-seafood.org., n.d.)

  frittata:     **An** Italian dish made with eggs and chopped vegetables or meat, resembling **a** <u>flat, thick omelette</u>. (The Free Dictionary, n.d.)

- **Introductions to people:**

  Leonardo William DiCaprio is **an** <u>American actor</u> and film producer. (Wikipedia, n.d.)

- **Introductions to fables, fairy tales, film/storyline settings, some types of jokes, some types of math and science word problems [first mention of referents in narratives, stories, and science/math word problems]:**

  Once upon **a** <u>time</u>, there was **an** <u>old woman</u> who lived near the seashore . . . (fairy tale opener)

  **A** <u>long time ago</u>, in **a** <u>galaxy</u> far, far away . . . ("Star Wars" opening crawl)

  **A** <u>man</u> and **a** <u>giraffe</u> walk into **a** <u>bar</u> . . . (narrative joke opener)

  On **a** <u>summer day</u> . . . **a** <u>Lion</u> and **a** <u>Boar</u> came at the same moment to **a** <u>small well</u> to drink. (Aesop, "The Lion and the Boar")

  **A** <u>person</u> shoots **an** <u>arrow</u> with **a** <u>velocity of 42.5 miles per second</u> toward **a** <u>target</u> that is exactly 35 feet above the archer's head. When will the arrow hit the target? (adapted from Chegg Study, n.d.)

- **Introductions to some news stories:**

  Johanna Turner, **a** <u>sound effects editor for Universal Studios</u>, joined the ranks of citizen scientists years ago, placing remote cameras in the San Gabriel Mountains to record the movements of wildlife. (Groves, 2015)

  **A** <u>new study</u> sheds light on what happens when **a** <u>supervolcano</u> erupts, providing insight on how rivers of hot ash and gas called pyroclastic flows manage to travel huge distances of over 100 miles during supereruptions. (University of Buffalo, 2016)

In addition to introducing "new" information and new ideas and concepts into the discourse, the indefinite article <u>a/an</u> also signals the meaning of "one," as in the following examples:

Need **a** <u>reason</u> to get more sleep at night? Here are three.
(cf. Need **one** <u>reason</u> to get more sleep at night?)

How many courses do students normally take in **a** <u>semester</u>?
(cf. How many courses do students normally take in **one** <u>semester</u>?)

This happened exactly **a** <u>year ago</u>.
(cf. This happened exactly **one** <u>year ago</u>.)

She'll be home in about **a** <u>week</u>.
(cf. She'll be home in about **one** <u>week</u>.)

**A** <u>year later,</u> in 2014, Milonas entered college.
(cf. **One** <u>year later,</u> in 2014, Milonas entered college.)

86  *Determiners*

> **Mini Review and Practice**
>
> 1   Review Type 1 and Type 2 nouns from Chapter 3. Do the nouns that we have used to illustrate the use, function, and meaning of *a/an* pattern like Type 1 nouns, Type 2 nouns, or both? We'll start you off on this process:
>
> Here are some nouns that appear in the first few examples provided previously from discursive contexts/genres used to illustrate the meaning and usages of *a/an*: *book, chain, team, boy, gang, coward, man, woman, hammer, tool, handle, head, angle, waterspout, column.*
> You can continue this list on your own from the underlined words with *a/an* in the discourse/genre-based examples.
>
> Do these nouns function as Type 1 or Type 2 nouns in all of these contexts of use?
>
> Now, find three nouns from Chapter 3 that function with **Type 2** usages:
> List them here:
> _____, _____, _____
>
> Try to use those **Type 2** nouns in a sentence in which the noun is preceded by *a/an*.
>
> Is this grammatically and/or conceptually possible? Why, or why not?
>
> Explain your answer in full detail (using the terminology and concepts introduced in this chapter and in Chapter 3). You might want to use the remaining two Type 2 nouns from your list to provide additional support for your findings.
>
> 2   Locate five new examples of the construction *a/an* + noun in particular genres of discourse (e.g., proverbs, sayings, quotes about life and people; definitions; introductions to famous people, stories, fables, narrative-based jokes, math/physics word problems). Are these nouns functioning as Type 1, Type 2, or Type 3 nouns?
>
> What do you notice about the *referent* that is marked with *a/an* in terms of conceptualization and especially in terms of the *meanings* of identifiability, specificity, and number within the discourse samples that you located? That is, does there seem to be an expectation that the reader or hearer should be able to identify the noun being referred to, or is it being introduced as so-called new information?
> Can you replace the determiner *a*/an with the word "one" in such a way that the intended meanings are similar? In which cases is this possible? In which cases is it not possible?

## 4.3.2 *Definite Article* the

In contrast with the indefinite article *a/an*, which signals "new" information or the quantity of "one" or "one of among many," the definite article *the* signals "assumed familiarity of the referent on the part of the hearer or reader." The definite article *the* evokes a sense of sharedness of knowledge on the part of the hearer or reader, because *the* frames the noun referent as both *identifiable* and *specific*, expressing an underlying concept like "you know the noun I am talking/writing about," or "I am assuming that you know the noun I am talking about." This kind of conceptual sharedness can be established through (a) a mutually experienced event or shared information through common knowledge or prior mention; (b) the logical and natural association of smaller parts that are integral to some familiar, larger whole (e.g., *building* → *the paint, the windows, the door*, *sandwich* → *the bread, the sauce, the meat*); and (c) a meaning of "one and only one" or "the one and only" as it relates to the referent in question—since the use of *the* rules out the notion of other possible referents (e.g., **a good candidate** for the job [i.e., one of among (many) other possible candidates] vs. **the best candidate** for the job [the one and only one]).

To illustrate briefly, note the following two sentences. They differ only in terms of the article used, but the scope of meaning underlying each reference to *birthday party* is significantly different.

> I'm going to **a** birthday party.
> (not specified as to whose party, where it is being held, by whom, etc.)
>    vs.
> I'm going to **the** birthday party.
> (it is assumed that this party has been mentioned before and/or that the hearer or reader shares some degree of familiarity with what the speaker or writer is referring to)

---

**Meaning of *the***

The referent is both specific and identifiable; quantity = "one and only one."
*The* signals the concept of "shared" information or "prior knowledge that the hearer or reader has with respect to the referent."

- *The* is typically used in discourse that presents a noun referent as "shared" information and/or facts, names, and details assumed as shared by the reader/hearer.
- *The* is often used in discourse when the nouns that indicate people, concepts, things, and ideas are mentioned as **"not new to the discourse"** or mentioned **after a prior mention.**
- *The* is often used in fictional and nonfictional writing to frame the referents **as if those referents are already known by or familiar to the reader/hearer (even though they may not really be).**
- *The* is used when the intended conceptual meaning of the referent is "the one and only one."

---

*4.3.2.1 Discursive Contexts/Genres/Parts of Genres*

- In stories, fairy tales, and narratives after a first mention of a referent using *a/an*:

    **Opening lines of the story "The Seven Sneezes" in *A Family Treasure of Little Golden Books***

    There was once **a** bunny, **a** kitten, and **a** dog who lived together in **a** back yard.

    **The** bunny was white, with long fluffy ears. **The** kitten was black, and like all kittens it had teeny ears. **The** dog was **a** great big dog with **a** great big bark. . . .

One day, **a** <u>rag man</u> came along in **an** <u>old wagon</u>. It was **a** <u>chilly day</u>. **The** <u>rag man</u> started to sneeze—A-choo! A-choo! . . .

"Goodness gracious—" **the** <u>bunny</u>, **the** <u>kitten</u>, and **the** <u>dog</u> started to say to each other. And then they saw something strange that had happened to them! **The** <u>black kitten</u> had **the** <u>bunny's long white ears</u>. **The** <u>white bunny</u> had the <u>kitten's teeny black ears</u>.

(Cabral, 1998, p. 85)

FIRST MENTION: a bunny, a kitten, a dog, a back yard, a rag man, a chilly day
SUBSEQUENT MENTION: the b<u>unny</u>, **the** <u>kitten</u>, **the** <u>dog</u>, **the** <u>rag man</u>

- Proverbs, sayings, and quotes about life and people and society:

    **The** <u>time</u> to be happy is now.   **The** <u>place</u> to be happy is here.
    (**the one and only time** = now    **the one and only place** = here)

    Honesty is **the** <u>best policy</u>.
    (the **one and only** way to interact with others)

    **The** <u>only true wisdom</u> is in knowing you know nothing. (Socrates)
    (the **one and only** truth)

    Any fool can know. **The** <u>point</u> is to understand. (Mark Twain)
    (the **one, single specific and identifiable goal or purpose**)

    **The** <u>pen</u> is mightier than **the** <u>sword</u>.
    (**one specific and identifiable means of expressing/defending oneself:** the pen = writing
    compared with:
    **the one specific and identifiable means of expressing/defending oneself:** the sword = fighting)

    **The** <u>squeaky wheel</u> gets the grease.
    (**one specific and identifiable type of individual:** the squeaky wheel = the people who speak up if there is a problem
    **one specific and identifiable positive outcome of speaking up:** grease = the solution to the problem)

- Definitions for very specific types of entities in the world around us:

    hypotenuse: **The** <u>longest side</u> of *a* right triangle; **the** <u>side</u> that is opposite from **the** <u>right angle</u>.

    nucleus: **The** <u>center of an atom</u>, which contains **the** <u>protons</u> and <u>neutrons</u>; in cells, **the** <u>structure</u> that contains **the** <u>cell</u>'s genetic material in **the** <u>form of DNA</u>. (Miller & Levine, 2009)

    lung: **The** <u>essential respiration organ</u> in many air-breathing animals. (adapted from Wikipedia, n.d.)

    ionosphere: **The** <u>region</u> of **the** <u>earth's atmosphere</u> between **the** <u>stratosphere</u> and **the** <u>exosphere</u>, consisting of several ionized layers and extending from about 50 to 250 miles (80 to 400 km) above **the** <u>surface</u> of **the** <u>earth</u>. (Dictionary.com, n.d.)

*Determiners* 89

- Essential descriptions of iconic personages in history:

  George Washington was **the** <u>first President of</u> **the** <u>United States</u>, **the** <u>Commander-in-Chief</u> of **the** <u>Continental Army</u> during **the** <u>American Revolutionary War</u>, and *one of* **the** <u>Founding Fathers of the United States</u>. (Wikipedia, n.d.)

  Abraham Lincoln was **the** <u>16th President of</u> **the** <u>United States</u>, serving from March 1861 until his assassination in April 1865. (Wikipedia, n.d.)

- Designations of iconic landmarks throughout the world:

  **The** <u>Statue of Liberty</u> (New York, New York)
  **The** <u>Great Buddha</u> (Kamakura, Japan)
  **The** <u>Flavian Amphitheater</u>, the Colosseum (Rome, Italy)
  **The** <u>Western Wall</u> (Jerusalem)
  **The** <u>Blue Mosque</u> (Istanbul, Turkey)
  **The** <u>Eiffel Tower</u> (Paris, France)
  **The** <u>Washington Monument</u> (Washington, DC)
  **The** <u>Forbidden City</u> (Beijing, China)

- Expressions where the meanings of the nouns and noun phrases signal "one and only one" instance of something:

  - Mathematical calculations

    To find **the** <u>area of a rectangle</u>, multiply **the** <u>base</u> times **the** <u>height</u>.
    **The** <u>perimeter</u> of a polygon is **the** <u>sum</u> of **the** <u>lengths</u> of all of **the** <u>sides</u>.
    **The** <u>circumference</u> of a circle is calculated by multiplying ϖ (3.14) times **the** <u>diameter</u>.

  - Ordinal numbers (e.g., the first, the second, the 16th)

    **The** 15th Amendment to **the** <u>Constitution</u> guarantees all citizens **the** <u>right</u> to vote.
    When was **the** <u>last time</u> you ate at McDonald's?
    **The** <u>first time</u> I ever saw a Frank Gehry building I was breathless.

  - Superlatives: the best, the worst, the most, the world's _____, the _____ in the world

    Thomson Reuters is **the** <u>world's leading source</u> of intelligent information for businesses and professionals. (Thomson Reuters, n.d.).
    **The** <u>cerebrum</u> is **the** largest part of **the** <u>human brain</u>. (Wikipedia, n.d.).
    **The** <u>safest, fastest-acting, pain reliever</u> you can get . . . Bayer Aspirin. (ad from Life, 1957, p. 22).

  - Words that carry the meaning of "single individuated parts" (e.g., *the beginning, the end, the middle, the pinnacle, the cusp, the peak, the top, the bottom, the identical, the exact same*)

    One episode in **the** <u>TV series "Lost"</u> is called "**The** <u>Beginning</u> of the <u>End</u>."
    Lupita Nyong'o reached **the** <u>pinnacle</u> of her career with **the** film *12 Years A Slave*.
    Why do some wines collect sediment at **the** <u>bottom</u>?

- Associations of smaller units with larger units, parts of wholes (signaling that the existence of the smaller unit is naturally familiar because of our familiarity with the larger unit):

(Note that these nouns all function here as **Type 1**)

| LARGER UNIT | SMALLER UNITS |
|---|---|
| shoe: | the insole, the heel, the laces, the aglets |
| building: | the walls, the paint, the windows, the door, the ceiling |
| circle: | the perimeter, the diameter, the radius, the circumference |
| school: | the principal, the lockers, the gym, the boys' bathroom |
| sandwich: | the bread, the meat, the sauce, the cheese, the pickles |
| park: | the swings, the baseball diamond, the water fountain |
| city/town: | the library, the zoo, the police station, the schools |
| book: | the cover, the spine, the publisher, the illustrations |

**Mini Review and Practice**

1. We illustrated conceptual usages and meanings of the definite article *the* through a number of discourse-based excerpts, from sayings and quotations about people and life to definitions and other types of reference to things, places, people, and ideas. We have repeated three of these examples here:

    **The** time to be happy is now. **The** place to be happy is here.
    **The** pen is mightier than **the** sword.
    **The** squeaky wheel gets **the** grease.

    a  List all of the underlined nouns or noun phrases. Which are more literal in meaning? Which are more figurative, and why?

    b  Is it possible to replace each instance of *the* with *a*? Are there any examples where such a replacement is grammatically and conceptually impossible? Hint: Think about Type 1 and Type 2 nouns. There is one noun in the previously listed sayings that functions strongly as a Type 2 noun. Which one?

    c  For those noun phrases where it is possible to change *the* to *a*, how does the meaning of the saying change? (e.g., 'A pen is mightier than a sword.') Start first with how you conceptualize these objects:

    That is, what happens to your mental picture when you change the saying from *the pen* and *the sword* to *a pen* and *a sword*? What do you imagine in the original saying? What do you imagine in the altered saying?

    d  Do the same thing with *the squeaky wheel* → *a squeaky wheel*.
    What images come to mind in each noun phrase as part of the entire saying?

    e  Now, let's go in the opposite direction. These two sayings were among those introduced in the section for the indefinite article *a/an*:

    You can't judge **a** book by its cover.
    As long as she thinks of **a** man, nobody objects to **a** woman thinking.

    Change each of the underlined noun phrases from *a* + noun to *the* + noun (i.e., 'You can't judge **the** book by its cover'). How does the conceptual meaning of each saying change? Does the revised saying carry the same message as the original version? Why, or why not?

2   Each of the two sections on articles (i.e., indefinite *a/an* and definite *the*) includes **definitions of things and concepts**.

Review the ways in which the definitions of words are presented in each section. How do the types of words listed for each section differ? How do the defined words used to illustrate the indefinite article differ from those used to illustrate the definite article? In what ways does conceptual meaning for determiners come into play here?

Now, review the following list of four new words. Imagine how you might write your own definition of each. Also try to predict whether you would prefer to introduce the term and its definition with indefinite articles or definite articles, or a mixture. Write your own definition for each noun. What types of conceptual meanings are influencing your choice of article between *a/an* and *the*?

> heart
> piano
> museum
> numerator

3   The following discourse is "A Brief Introduction" to the story of Hugo Cabret, as presented by Professor H. Alcofrisbas, from *The Invention of Hugo Cabret* (Selznick, 2007, p. ix).

Fill in the blanks with **either** *a/an* or *the*. Sometimes, either choice is grammatically possible (and other determiners could fit in the blanks as well). But for this exercise, the only possible choices are *a/an* or *the*. As you now know, the determiner changes how the noun is represented in the discourse, so do your best to select the article that you feel best fits the context. Explain your choice(s).

If **both** *a/an* **and** *the* are possible, explain how the meaning changes with each choice and predict which one was actually used by the author and why.

You can find the full text of the original at the end of this chapter.

**"A Brief Introduction" to *The Invention of Hugo Cabret***

> _____ story I am about to share with you takes place in 1931, under _____ roofs of Paris. Here you will meet _____ boy named Hugo Cabret, who once, long ago, discovered _____ mysterious drawing that changed his life forever.
>
> But before you turn _____ page, I want you to picture yourself sitting in _____ darkness, like _____ beginning of _____ movie. On _____ screen, _____ sun will soon rise, and you will find yourself zooming toward _____ train station in _____ middle of _____ city. You will rush through _____ doors into _____ crowded lobby. You will eventually spot _____ boy amid _____ crowd, and he will start to move through _____ train station. Follow him, because this is Hugo Cabret. His head is full of secrets, and he's waiting for his story to begin.
> (Selznick, 2007, p. ix)

## 4.4 Demonstrative Determiners: A System of Conceptual Focus

The demonstrative system of English determiners includes the following forms:

*that* (s.) / *those* (pl.)
*this* (s.) / *these* (pl.)

92  *Determiners*

Traditional linguistic accounts for these forms are typically established on the basis of a binary system whereby the forms *this/these* designate a noun referent that is "near to the speaker," while the forms *that/those* designate a referent that is "far from the speaker." (e.g., Carter & McCarthy, 2006, pp. 178–181; Larsen-Freeman & Celce-Murcia, 2016, p. 316; see also, Dik, 1981; Halliday, 1985; Halliday & Hasan, 1976; Quirk et al., 1985). However, by using discourse-based examples, we will illustrate more precise conceptual meanings for demonstratives.

Demonstrative reference is part of the larger system of reference called *deixis*, which contains the Greek root *deiktikos*, meaning "to point" or "to show." In this case, demonstrative determiners (and demonstrative pronouns; see Chapter 5) work in such a way that they verbally point to a contextualized referent in a number of possible ways (Carter & McCarthy, 2006 pp. 179–181; Garcia, 1975, p. 65; see also Fillmore, 1982, 1971/1997; Hanks, 1992).

Imagine yourself at a Dunkin' Donuts shop. You and a handful of other customers are standing at the counter, looking at the mouth-watering selection of donuts, crullers, and coffee rolls. Within this hypothetical scenario, you overhear the following four ways of ordering a Dunkin' Donuts treat:

| Customer 1: | I'll have **a** <u>donut</u> please. | A DONUT (indefinite article *a*) |
| Customer 2: | May I have **the** <u>donut</u>? | THE DONUT (definite article *the*) |
| Customer 3: | I'll have **that** <u>donut</u>, please. | THAT DONUT (demonstrative *that*) |
| Customer 4: | May I have **this** <u>donut</u>? | THIS DONUT (demonstrative *this*) |

Of these four, which seem to be the most ambiguous and problematic for this particular context and setting? Which seem to be the least ambiguous? Why? What else do you imagine in the scene that is not written here? Maybe a follow-up question is necessary for the server to better understand at least two of the requests, like this one:

Customers 1 and 2:   I'll have **a** <u>donut</u> please./May I have **the** <u>donut</u>?
Server:   **Which** <u>one</u>?
(because neither *a* or *the* is specific enough to designate which item the customer really wants)

And, maybe a pointing gesture is needed by Customers 3 and 4, designating all the more clearly the particular pastry:

Customers 3 and 4, pointing: I'll have **that** <u>donut</u>./May I have **this** <u>donut</u>?
(because even though *that* and *this* are more specific than both *a* and *the*, the determiners alone are not enough to specify precisely which one each customer wants)

We can begin to see a particular type of conceptual hierarchy emerge, a hierarchy that is created by the four determiners, involving degrees of specificity of the noun that each determiner is picking out.

Degrees of specificity:

| Noun phrase | | Meaning |
|---|---|---|
| *a donut* | → | "one," "it doesn't matter which" |
| *the donut* | → | "a particular one that I assume you know, that I assume you can recognize" |
| *that donut* | → | "the one that I am pointing to [gesturally] and that I am designating with **more FOCUS than** *the*" |

*this donut* → "the one that I am pointing to [gesturally] and that I am designating with **EVEN MORE FOCUS than** *that*"

Determiners in English provide speakers and writers with multiple levels of choice concerning how much FOCUS, if any, should be placed on the noun that it modifies (Strauss, 1993, 2002; Strauss & Feiz, 2014). By FOCUS, we simply mean *how much attention the hearer or reader should be paying to the referent in question* (Garcia, 1975; Kirsner, 1979, 1990). If we only include the four determiners we have examined thus far in detail, we can postulate a partial conceptual system for these determiners as follows:

| | |
|---|---|
| *a, the* | LOW FOCUS |
| *that* (s.)/*those* (pl.) | MEDIUM FOCUS |
| *this* (s.)/*these* (pl.) | HIGH FOCUS |

### 4.4.1 Demonstratives That/Those *and* This/These *as Markers of MEDIUM and HIGH FOCUS*

**Meaning of *that/those***

The referent is both specific and identifiable.
MEDIUM FOCUS (and HIGHER FOCUS THAN *the*)

Like *the*, *that* signals the concept of "shared" information or "prior knowledge that the hearer or reader has with respect to the referent," but demonstrative *that/those* places the noun referent in a status of HIGHER IMPORTANCE than *the* does.

*the* = LOW FOCUS                *that/those* = MEDIUM FOCUS

Don't push **the** <u>button</u>!        Don't push **that** <u>button</u>!
Where'd you get **the** <u>hats</u>?   Where'd you get **those** <u>hats</u>?

Do you remember **the** awkward <u>moment</u> when you squirted ketchup on your tie? [LOW]
Do you remember **that** awkward <u>moment</u> when you squirted ketchup on your tie? [MED]
                **those** awkward <u>moments</u> when . . .                    [MED]

**Meaning of *this/these***

The referent is both specific and identifiable.
HIGH FOCUS (and HIGHER FOCUS THAN *that*)

*This* frames a referent as either new or shared information and places that referent in the status of HIGHEST FOCUS, signaling to the hearer or reader to attend strongly to that noun.

94  *Determiners*

*that/those* = MEDIUM FOCUS          *this/these* = HIGH FOCUS

Don't push **that** <u>button!</u>          Don't push **this** <u>button!</u>
Where'd you get **those** <u>hats?</u>          Where'd you get **these** <u>hat</u>s?

And we can extend the HIGH FOCUS meaning associated with *this* to also signal a HIGH FOCUS CONNECTION to the HERE AND NOW, as in expressions of time cycles:

*This* designating the immediate present or the near-immediate future

**this** <u>month</u>, **this** <u>year</u>, **this** <u>semester</u>, **this** <u>quarter</u>, **this** <u>day</u>/**these** <u>days</u>, **this** <u>session</u>, **this** <u>summer</u>, **this** <u>winter</u>, **this** <u>season</u>, **this** <u>cycle</u>, **this** <u>week</u>/**these** <u>weeks</u>, **this** <u>life</u>

### Mini Review and Practice

1   In the cartoon in Figure 4.2, there are two instances of the determiner *this*. In both cases, the referent (i.e., "light") is actually near the hearer and not near the speaker. The traditional "near speaker" interpretation for *this* cannot hold here. Using the concept of FOCUS, try and come up with a better explanation for why *this* is used in each of the two sentences.

2   The Organic Consumers Association produces stickers for consumers to affix onto "bogus organic" products, i.e., products that are falsely labeled as organic, to alert potential buyers of misrepresentations by certain food manufacturers.

"This light warns you that your battery may be critically low. And this light warns you that your conversation may be critically dull."

*Figure 4.2* "This light warns you that your battery may be critically low. And *this* light warns you that your conversation may be critically dull."

© Randy Glasbergen. Reproduced with permission of Glasbergen Cartoon Service.

The labels read:

**Original:**

PANIC! **THIS** PRODUCT IS NOT ORGANIC!
PANIC! **THESE** PRODUCTS ARE NOT ORGANIC!

How would the message change if the determiners shifted to *the*, *that*, or *those*?

**Change the determiners → Change the mental representation/context**

PANIC! **THE** PRODUCT IS NOT ORGANIC!
PANIC! **THE** PRODUCTS ARE NOT ORGANIC!

PANIC! **THAT** PRODUCT IS NOT ORGANIC!
PANIC! **THOSE** PRODUCTS ARE NOT ORGANIC!

How does just this shift in determiner choice affect your conceptualization of the context(s) or scene(s) in which the altered message would appear?

Who do you assume to be the addressee of each of these messages? Does there appear to be a shift in stance on the part of the assumed writer/creator of these labels that comes about as a result of the shift in grammar?

## 4.5 Possessive Determiners: Possession, Affiliation, Connection, and More

Possessive determiners do not only denote "possession" or "ownership." They also indicate such concepts as personal affiliation or connection to a referent; someone's stance of preference or dispreference toward a noun; a product or creation by someone; an offer by someone; a designation of an intended recipient of a product or service; and even products, predictions, or outcomes within a designated time period (e.g., **yesterday's** stock market numbers, **next year's** resolutions).

The forms of possessive determiners fall into two categories:

- personal possessive determiners:

| *singular possessor* | *plural possessors* |
|---|---|
| my brother | our relatives |
| your sisters | your paper |
| his notebook | their equipment |
| her pencils | |
| its colors | |

- noun phrase–based possessive determiners:

| *NOUN + 's (singular possessors)* | *NOUNS + s' (plural possessors)* |
|---|---|
| the cat's whiskers | both cats' whiskers |
| the book's preface | all the books' prefaces |
| Minho's escape | the prisoners' escape |

Here are some examples of possessive determiners in discourse:

> **My sister's** <u>favorite movie</u> of all time is *The Shawshank Redemption*. It is one of **Frank Darabont's** best films.
> Ask not what **your** <u>country</u> can do for you, ask what you can do for **your** <u>country</u>.
> **Today's** <u>Stock Market</u> <u>News</u>
> **Last week's** <u>failure</u> is **this week's** <u>success</u>.
> From Amazon.com: "**March's** greatest **kids'** <u>books</u>"

Here are some examples of possessive determiners in names of brands, products, retail facilities, and websites:

> **Papa John's** <u>Pizza</u>
> **David's** <u>Tea</u>
> **Levi's** <u>501</u> The Original Button Fly Jean
> **Vitello's** <u>Italian Restaurant</u>
> **McDonald's**
> **My**<u>UCLAhealth.com</u>
> **My** <u>Verizon online</u>
> The **My** <u>Hero Project</u> (at MyHero.com)

Note that when some **Type 3** nouns, for example, *the board*, *Chipotle*, *Nintendo*, *the union*, *the committee* (see Chapter 3), occur with possessive determiners, the determiner choice can reflect the noun referent as either a single unit [evoked by the possessive determiner *its*] or as a collective of individual members [evoked by the possessive determiner *their*], as in the following sentences:

> The CFC Board of Trustees will be holding **their** <u>annual election</u> in May 2016.
> [plural]
>
> The Planning Committee will hold **its first** <u>hearing</u> on Monday, June 5.
> [singular]

---

### Mini Review and Practice

1   Think about the brand names, retail facilities, and websites that include possessive determiners (e.g., OurDocuments.gov, Jessee's Barbecue & Market, Gigi's Southern Table, MyAccountingLab.com). How do these business and site names compare to others where no possessive determiners are used? What sort of persuasive effect does this use of grammar seem to create for the consumer? Try to find more such brand names and list them according to category (e.g., health, utilities, learning, retail food/drink, etc.). Are there certain types of businesses or services that tend to use possessive determiners in their names more than other types?

2    Often, "possessive" relationships can be paraphrased into longer constructions, as in the following examples:

   a   Here are three points we learned from **last night's** <u>Democratic debate</u>.

   vs.

   b   Here are three points we learned from <u>the Democratic debate</u> (**of**) **last night**.

   How does the meaning shift between the a version and the b version? Does the temporal reference *last night* seem to be equally connected in the two versions? If so, why? If not, why not? What other similar types of examples with possessive determiners can you find that reflect this same relationship between grammar-meaning-conceptualization?

3    The following passage is from the opening lines of Khaled Hosseini's *And the Mountains Echoed*. Pay close attention to the use of determiners here, and especially to the indefinite article *a*, the definite article *the*, and possessive determiners. Be sure to locate all relevant forms of the possessive determiners.

   Once upon **a time** . . . there lived **a farmer** named Baba Ayub. He lived with <u>his family</u> in **a little village**. . . . Because he had **a large family** to feed, Baba Ayub saw <u>his days</u> consumed by hard work. Every day, he labored from dawn to sundown, plowing <u>his field</u> and turning <u>the soil</u> and tending to <u>his meager pistachio trees</u>. . . .

   Though he loved all of <u>his children</u>, Baba Ayub privately had **a unique fondness** for one among them, Qais, who was three years old. Qais was **a little boy** with dark blue eyes. . . . When he learned to walk, he took such delight in it that he did it all day while he was awake, and then, troublingly, even at night in <u>his sleep</u>. . . . Naturally, <u>his parents</u> worried. What if he fell into **a well**, or got lost. . . . In <u>the end</u>, <u>the solution</u> Baba Ayub found was **a simple one**, as <u>the best solutions</u> often are: He removed **a tiny bell** from around <u>the neck</u> of one of <u>his goats</u> and hung it instead around <u>Quai's neck</u>.
   (Hosseini, 2013, pp. 1–2)

Think about the conceptual meanings of these determiners. Also think about which determiners are the most frequent. Which are the least frequent?

Which noun referents are the indefinite article *a* used with? We will start you off in the process, and you can complete the list:

- Once upon **a time** . . . [formulaic story opening]
- there lived **a farmer** [formulaic story opening; also note subject-verb inversion: *there lived* (verb) *a farmer* (subject/noun) vs. *a farmer lived* . . .]
- in **a little village**
- Because he had **a large family** to feed,

How about the definite article *the*? Are there any more instances?

- turning *the soil*
- *the solution* Baba Ayub found was **a simple one**

- as *the best solutions* often are
- He removed **a tiny bell** from around *the neck* of one of his goats . . .

What are the possessive determiners? You can complete the list:

- He lived with his family . . .
- Baba Ayub saw his days . . .
- plowing his field and turning the soil

How about this sentence:

> "He removed **a tiny bell** from around *the neck* of one of his goats and hung it instead around Quai's neck."

Why is Quai's neck the possessive determiner here instead of his neck? What would happen to your ability to process the referent associated with the question "around *whose* neck"?

What are the meanings of possessive determiners beyond "possession" and "ownership"?

Is it possible to substitute any of these determiners for other determiners?
For example: He removed *the tiny bell* from around ***a*** **neck** (?) of one of the goats.

How does the meaning change, slightly or otherwise, by virtue of the change in determiners?

## 4.6 Quantifiers: Categories of General Quantities or Amounts, Specific Amounts

Quantifiers are the category of determiners that center on number, quantity, and amount. We can sub-categorize quantifiers according to general amounts that signal such concepts as one or more than one; parts and wholes; specific numbers; relative amounts; fractions as parts; measurements; containers; and collectives/collections of objects, insects, and animals. This category of determiners contains the largest number of exemplars. Some grammar books consider a subset of quantifiers as *partitives* (e.g., *a slice of* bread, *a head of* lettuce, *a piece/slice/wedge of* pizza) and *collectives* (e.g., *a gaggle of* geese, *a pride of* lions), essentially as belonging to grammatical categories outside of determiners (Carter & McCarthy, 2006, pp. 343–344; Larsen-Freeman & Celce-Murcia, 2016, pp. 332–334).

However, all constructions that we provide in this section (and the list is not exclusive) fit perfectly within the natural class of determiners, because they function in an identical manner as all other determiners and they designate the identical conceptual meanings of specificity, identifiability, and number in relation to the nouns that they modify.

The categories are as follows:

- **General: signaling part, whole, totality**

  any (of), all (of), any and all, some (of), the entire, the entirety of, the whole, none of, no, not one (of), zero, not a single

- **Specific [specific number preceding a noun, cardinal numbers, fractions]**

  one, two, seventeen, half of, a quarter of, a third of, less than half (of), more than a third (of)

- **Ordinal numbers and sequence**

    first, second, fifth, next, last

- **More than one**

    several, a couple (of), a few (of), some (of), scores (of), both (of), either (of), either one of, neither, neither one of, other, another, each, every

- **Relative amounts**

    much, many, a lot of, a ton of, a little of, a large/small amount (of), a large/small number (of), a bit of, any number of, quite a few (of), enough (of), too much (of), the majority of, a good percentage of, various, a variety of, a range of, an assortment of, less than, more than, almost all (of), almost every, almost every one of, almost any, almost any one of, almost none

- **Individuated parts, units, measurements, and collectives**

    - **individuated parts and/or individuated wholes**

        a slice of, a segment of, a sheet of (*paper*), a head of, a stick of, a stalk of, a pinch of, a ball of, a hunk of, a chunk of, a piece of, a movement of (*a symphony*), a bar of (*music, chocolate, gold*), a ray of, a glimmer of, a tidbit of, a block of

    - **measurement units**

        an inch of, a pound of, a gram of, a kilo of, a bushel of, a peck of, a ream of (*paper*), a row of (*seats, math problems*), a load of, a ton of, a teaspoon of, a cup (i.e., 8 oz) of, a yard of, 6 cubic yards of, 9 square yards of, a bite of, a brick of

    - **containers**

        a bag of, a sack of, a box of, a carton of, a pack of (*cigarettes* cf. *a pack of wolves*), a package of, a truckload of, a backpack full of, a refrigerator full of, a keg of, a barrel of, a vat of, a cup of, a cartridge of

    - **collectives**

        a school of (*fish*), a gaggle of (*geese*), a pod of (*whales, dolphins*), a murmuration of (*starlings*), a swarm of (*bees, insects, wasps, ballerinas*), a herd of (*cattle, horses, college students*), a flock of (*sheep, geese, birds, sparrows*), a pack of (*wolves, dogs, thieves*), a pride of (*lions*), a colony of (*rabbits*), an army of (*ants*), a band of (*jays, brothers, angels*), a fleet of (*ships, cars*), a gang/army (*of people*)

    - **collection, assortment**

        an assortment of, a mix of, a mixture of, a variety of, an amalgamation of, a range of, a spectrum of, a bouquet of, a collection of

Our discussion of **Type 1** and **Type 2** nouns from Chapter 3 becomes relevant with regard to a number of these quantifiers.

That is, some quantifiers can only occur with nouns functioning as **Type 1** (e.g., *book, window, battery, package, toy, statue, screen, raindrop, whisker, kitten*), and some can only occur with nouns functioning as **Type 2** (e.g., *health, work, progress, learning, independence, stuff, trash*). Because nouns that function as **Type 2** cannot occur in the plural form or with any determiner that denotes a specific number (not a fraction), the collocation of the following determiners with **Type 2** nouns yields an ungrammatical phrase:

100  *Determiners*

Type 2 nouns cannot co-occur with:

- determiners that evoke "one or more than one"  *one progress
- cardinal numbers (one, two, twenty-seven)  *seven healths

Type 2 nouns easily co-occur with:

- individuated parts:  * **square of** chocolate, **clove of** garlic, **bead of** caulk

Conversely, **Type 1 nouns** cannot co-occur with:

- much  *much cookies, *much kittens

### 4.6.1 *Quantifiers in discourse*

One of the most obvious and predictable discursive genres that makes wide use of certain types of quantifiers is the recipe. The following recipe for meatballs has been adapted from Rachael Ray's spaghetti and meatballs recipe.

**Meatballs (for Spaghetti and Meatballs)**

1¼ **pounds** ground sirloin
2 **teaspoons** Worcestershire sauce
1 egg
½ **cup** Italian bread crumbs, **a couple of** handfuls
¼ **cup** grated Parmesan cheese
2 **cloves** garlic

(Ray, n.d.)

This recipe contains cardinal numbers (*1, 2*), precise units of measure (*pounds, teaspoons, cup*), an imprecise amount of "more than one" (*a couple of*), and individuated parts (*clove*).

Quantifiers of various types also populate many other genres of discourse and serve a wide variety of functions. Have a look at the following narrative, which includes just the first few lines of a much longer blog entry by a teacher. Think about the author's stance. What happened? How is she reporting the event? What is her tone?

After over **a dozen** years of following the literature regarding online teaching and **several** years of using courseware to supplement face-to-face teaching, this semester I am teaching my **first** fully online class—and there was a surprise. **Half a dozen** names of people who are not students and who were completely unknown to me showed up on the class roster. **Some of those** names I was able to remove from the course, but **other** names I could not.

(Braman, 2004)

What function do the quantifiers seem to fulfill here? What types of quantifiers do you notice? Why are quantifiers so important to the context and to these first few lines of her longer story? What other determiners appear here? Which nouns follow each determiner? How does the variation in determiner choice allow the author to repeat certain nouns effectively, without making the discourse sound heavy or repetitious?

## Mini Review and Practice

1  The following is a brief excerpt from Christopher Knight's October 6, 2016, review of the exhibit "Making Waves: Japanese American Photography, 1920–1940."

   **See how Japanese American photography from 1920 to 1940 is still "making waves."**

   **One** of *the* most fascinating chapters in American art from **the first half of the 20th** century is also among the least known. The details of its efflorescence may never be fully grasped, regardless of how relatively recent the events. But an absorbing, must-see exhibition at the Japanese American National Museum goes far in bringing the episode back into long-awaited view.

   With **103** works, the current show has **two dozen more** photographs than **the last** one. Some haven't been shown since the 1930s. "Making Waves" resonates as the often-impressive **tip of** *a* regrettably lost iceberg.

   (Knight, 2016)

   What is Knight's stance with regard to this exhibit? How does the use of determiners help to construct his stance? Which determiner seems to be the most frequent? In what types of contexts and with which types of grammatical constructions is it used? How many instances of the indefinite article *a/an* occur in the excerpt?

   Which quantifiers are used?

   How do the quantifiers also work to construct the critic's overall stance?

2  The following abridged excerpt is from the opening paragraph of a *Washington Monthly* article by Benjamin Ginsberg, about the rising costs of college tuition in the US.

   **No** statistic about higher education commands **more** attention—and anxiety—among members of the public than the rising price of admission. Since 1980, inflation-adjusted tuition at public universities has tripled; at private universities it has more than doubled. Compared to **all other** goods and services in the American economy, including medical care, only "cigarettes and **other** tobacco products" have seen prices rise faster than the cost of going to college.

   (Ginsberg, 2011)

   Ginsberg opens his article with a strong statement concerning college tuition costs in the US. This entire opening passage is based on a comparison and contrast. What is the issue at hand? What are the comparisons? What is the author's stance (or feeling) with regard to the issue? How does he establish that position and stance through his use of grammar? Focus first on the determiners (*no, more, ∅, the, all other, other*). Then, locate additional instances of discourse (e.g., nouns, verbs, adverbs, sentence structure) that work together to help the author build his argument.

## 4.7 Interrogatives: Question Words That Function as Determiners

The following question words are also determiners in that they signal, in an interrogative way, the concepts of identifiability, specificity, possession (and possession-like concepts), and number.

- What?
- Which? (foregrounds an already established or given set)
- Whose?
- How many? (used with Type 1 nouns)
- How much? (used with Type 2 nouns)

*What?* and *Which?* both establish a query concerning a particular noun. *What?* is more general in terms of its flexibility. It is the more commonly used of the two. *Which?* foregrounds the notion that a set of possible choices has already been established.

> **What** school do you go to?        [indefinite in terms of possible choices]
> **Which** school do you go to?       [assumes a set of possible schools is known, established]
>
> **What** color shirt did you get?
> **Which** color (of these that you see/know) would you like?

*Whose?* is the so-called possessive interrogative determiner:

> **Whose** face is on the $10 bill?
> **Whose** pen is this?

The use of *How many?* and *How much?* depends on whether the inquiry involves a **Type 1** or a **Type 2** noun:

> **How many** M&Ms did Mario eat?         [M&Ms = **Type 1**]
> **How much** candy did Mario eat?        [candy = **Type 2**]

How would the answers to the following questions differ?

> **How many** waters shall I bring?       [water = **Type 1**]
>     Answer: _____
> **How much** water should I use?         [water = **Type 2**]
>     Answer: _____

---

### Mini Review and Practice

1  At the post office, you need stamps to mail an oversized envelope. You ask the clerk:

> How _____ stamps do I need?
> How _____ postage do I need?

2  Some tongue twisters are structured using interrogative quantifier determiners.

Here is a very well-known example, using a Type 2 noun, *wood*.

> **How much** wood would a woodchuck chuck if a woodchuck could chuck wood?

Other tongue twisters play on this quantifier/question-like structure with a parallel scenario of an entity doing something to another entity. One such example has to do with

> the word *cookies* and related word and sound play with the word *cook*, used both as a noun and a verb. It also uses rhyming words *good* and *could*, all with the same vowel sound and alternations of consonants /k/, /g/, and /d/, as well as the interrogative quantifier determiner for Type 1 nouns:
>
> **How many** cookies could a good cook cook, if a good cook could cook cookies?
>
> You can even make up your own tongue twisters using this structure. Here is one that we made up for a Type 1 noun:
>
> **How many** birds could a bird breeder breed with a bread box for a bird box?
>
> Now, try to compose your own tongue twister like the ones listed previously.
>
> Another idea is this: Have a look at Shel Silverstein's (1981, p. 8) poem "How Many, How Much," which starts out like this:
>
> "How many slams in an old screen door?"
> "Depends how loud you shut it."
>
> You can see how Silverstein structures his questions with interrogative quantifier determiners (Type 1 and Type 2 nouns) and how he symbolically answers those questions. None of them is a literal question-answer sequence. His questions and the answers that follow have much deeper meanings.

## 4.8 Covert Determiner ∅: Nouns Preceded by No Apparent Determiner at All

The covert determiner, represented here as ∅, is discussed in textbooks and reference grammars as the *zero* article and the *null* article (Celce-Murcia & Larsen-Freeman, 1999; Master, 1987, 1990, 1997; see also Chesterman, 1991). Master (1997) differentiates the *zero* article from the *null* article (both being a complete absence of any article), calling the *zero* article the "the most generic" (∅ eggs, the diners ate ∅ goulash), and the *null* article "the most definite" (We are traveling to ∅ London ∅ next week). The problem here is that Master (1987, 1990, 1997) and later Celce-Murcia and Larsen-Freeman (1999) indicate that the complete absence of any article means at once "the most generic" of possible references as well as "the most definite." These two concepts are nearly polar opposite.

In contrast, with our conceptualization-based approach to determiners focusing on the narrow semiotic concepts of identifiability, specificity, degrees of focus [low, medium, high], possession and possession-like or affiliative relationships, and number and quantity [including part/whole relationships, sequence, and order], we can now simply say the following with respect to the grammatical concept of no visible determiner:

> **Meaning of the covert determiner ∅**
>
> ∅ precedes nouns in cases where the concepts of identifiability, specificity, possession, gender, and number and quantity are irrelevant to the reference of that noun.

**Overt determiner**

The students need **a** <u>book</u>.
The students need **the** <u>book(s)</u>.
The students need **that/this/those/these** <u>book(s)</u>.
The students need **all seventeen** <u>books.</u>
The students need **what** <u>books</u>? . . . **which** <u>books</u>? . . . **how many** <u>books</u>?

**Covert determiner**

The students need ∅ <u>books.</u>     **[Type 1]**
The room just needs ∅ <u>carpet</u> and ∅ <u>paint</u>. **[Type 2]**

MEANING: No indication of or necessity to mark specificity, identifiablity, or number (beyond the plural marking on **Type 1** nouns).

One of the most obvious and predictable grammatical categories that co-occurs with the covert determiner ∅ is the **proper noun**. See the following examples for individual persons, product names, and school subjects.

∅ Barack Obama, ∅ Gwen, ∅ Mrs. Suzuki, ∅ Yuan, ∅ Dr. Doolittle
∅ Fiat, ∅ LG, ∅ Honda, ∅ KLM, ∅ Thai Airways, ∅ Heinz, ∅ Knorr
∅ Algebra 101, ∅ World Literature, ∅ Media Studies, ∅ Drawing

From the point of view of genre, the most transparent and predictable types of discourse where the covert determiner occurs frequently are as follows:

- **Product item names on labels:**

    Chicken Noodle Soup, ∅ Aspirin, ∅ Shampoo, ∅ Garbanzo Beans, ∅ Chocolate Cupcakes, ∅ Dominoes (game), ∅ Monopoly (game), ∅ Ultra Stomp Rocket (toy), ∅ Mr. Potato Head (toy), ∅ Vitamin C, ∅ Blueberry Muffins, ∅ Cream Soda, ∅ Peanuts

- **News headlines—newspapers and online news**

    - ∅ SUSPECT CAPTURED, ∅ CITY CALLS OFF ∅ SEARCH
    - ∅ NEWBORN DISCOVERED UNDER ∅ RUBBLE RESCUED BY ∅ PASSERSBY
    - ∅ FIRE ENGULFS ∅ VEGAS HOTEL
    - ∅ LONE GUNMAN THEORY DEBUNKED
    - ∅ LAKE MICHIGAN REACHES ∅ HIGHEST LEVEL SINCE 1998

In which other genres do you notice a high frequency of the covert determiner ∅? Why do you think this might be so?

In the following examples adapted from actual discourse, note the nouns and noun phrases that are preceded by covert determiner ∅. The first entry for each example is the original. We then contrast the original discourse with alternatives by switching out some of the determiners.

- Mark Twain essay: "To **the** <u>Person</u> Sitting in Darkness"         [∅ <u>darkness</u>]
    cf. "To **the/that** <u>Person</u> Sitting in **the/This/That** <u>Darkness</u>"

- Website updates  [∅ website updates]
  cf. **Google's** website updates, **our** website updates

- "Introducing Solid Food to Baby"  [∅ solid food]/
  cf. Introducing **All/No** Solid Food to **Your** Baby  [∅ baby]

- "Soda Drinks and Disease"  [∅ soda drinks]/
  cf. **Those/All** Soda Drinks and **Some/Most** Disease  [∅ disease]

- "**Five** Ways to Draw Water From Wells"  [∅ water]/[∅ wells]
  cf. **Five** Ways to Draw **Some/the/That** Water From **Your** Wells

The covert determiner ∅ simply means that the author, writer, or speaker chooses to indicate nothing with respect to specificity, identifiability, possession, or number, either because no such specification is necessary in that particular discourse or because identifiability or specificity is already assumed, as in the case of **proper nouns**.

As you will see later, the use of the covert determiner ∅ is quite frequent and natural in all genres of discourse, each time conveying the same meaning as irrelevance of the essential determiner features of identifiability, specificity, possession, and number.

And as you have seen with the ∅ + **Type 1** examples, number can be made more relevant or salient when the noun appears in the plural form (e.g., ∅ books, ∅ passersby, ∅ website links, ∅ wells, ∅ soda drinks).

---

**Mini Review and Practice**

1. As we have shown, it is not uncommon to find strings of noun phrases modified only by the covert determiner ∅ in a number of specific genres of discourse. Two that we pointed out specifically earlier involve commercial product names on labels and news headlines.

   Note that while the item names themselves may appear with the covert determiner ∅, other references to the product on the label will likely contain overt determiners. Have a look at a few commercial product labels and packages (e.g., food, cosmetics/hygiene, home repair products, toys/games) and compare and contrast the naming and reference practices on those labels and packages, focusing first on just the product name and then on how the product is referred to in other parts of the label. What do you find?

   Similarly, while newspaper and online news headlines frequently make use of the covert determiner ∅, you will likely find variations of this (and really interesting ones at that) on magazine covers and in magazine story headlines.

   Here is one example, adapted from the cover of the January/February 2016 issue of *Men's Health* magazine.

   FLATTEN **YOUR** BELLY
   SCULPT **YOUR** ARMS
   BURN ∅ FAT FASTER

   ∅ AGE ERASERS: **5** QUICK FIXES SHE'LL NOTICE

   What sorts of determiners do you find on various types of magazine covers?

106    *Determiners*

Why do you suppose that magazine covers in general differ so strikingly from newspaper headlines and online news headlines? Think about magazines that are displayed at your local grocery store, convenience store, or bookstore (in checkout lines and in special magazine sections). How do the headlines in these magazine covers use determiners? How does this type of genre differ in terms of determiner use from newspaper headlines (both mainstream news and tabloid news)?

Can you think of other discourse genres where you will find a noticeably high frequency of the covert determiner ∅?

2   The following excerpt, from the Your Amazing Brain website (n.d.), addresses the neurological condition called synaesthesia. The passage contains the determiners *a* [indefinite article], *the* [definite article], *other* [quantifier type], as well as 14 tokens of the covert determiner ∅. We have coded the overt determiners in bold and have underlined the nouns that each modifies. We have not placed the symbol ∅ next to the noun modified by covert determiners.

**What is synaesthesia?**

Synaesthesia is **a** curious condition where there is **a** mingling of **the** senses due to cross-wiring in **the** brain.

Hearing **a** musical note for example might cause **a** person with synaesthesia to see **a** particular colour; C is red, F sharp is blue. Or perhaps **the** number 2 is always green and 5 always blue.

**Other** people may taste spoken words, for example, on hearing **the** word "table" they might taste apricots, whereas "book" tastes like tomato soup and "telephone" tastes like earwax.

(*Your Amazing Brain* website, n.d.)

List all of the noun phrases in the passage, and categorize them according to determiner type. We will start you off:

| with *a/an* [indefinite article] | with *the* [definite article] | with covert determiner ∅ |
|---|---|---|
| a curious condition | the senses | _____ |
| a mingling | _____ | _____ |
| a musical note | _____ | _____ |
| a person with synaesthesia | _____ | _____ |
|  |  | _____ |
|  |  | _____ |
|  |  | _____ |
|  |  | _____ |
|  |  | _____ |
|  |  | _____ |
|  |  | _____ |
|  |  | _____ |
|  |  | _____ |
|  |  | _____ |

> What do you notice about the conceptual meanings expressed by the determiners *a*, *the*, and ∅? Can you try to articulate a "rule" or a description of patterns of uses/meanings for *a*, *the*, and ∅ when used in discourse? Your descriptions should take into account many of the issues we have addressed in this chapter. With regard to ∅, you might also want to consider other factors, such as the sorts of grammatical features that precede ∅, for example, prepositions (e.g., the invention **of** ∅ seatbelts, its battle **with** ∅ time, to be scared **to** ∅ death; see Chapter 12) and perception copular verbs (e.g., tastes **like** ∅ ice cream; see Chapter 6).

## 4.9 Additional Comments and Notes About Determiners

### 4.9.1 Determiners Occurring in Strings

As you have seen in the examples throughout this chapter, determiners can and often do occur in strings, where multiple determiners occur preceding a noun, as shown here:

**The** <u>book</u> chronicles **all the president's** <u>accomplishments</u> since 2012.
She introduced me to **every one of her** cousins at the <u>family reunion</u>.
Clem, **our** <u>dog</u>, jumped onto **the** <u>table</u> and devoured **almost half of Zhan's** <u>steak</u>.
**Most of Europe's** <u>bananas</u> are imported from ∅ Central America.
**The first 10** <u>facts</u> about **the many** <u>hazards of</u> ∅ <u>smoking</u> were enough to convince **my** <u>dad</u> to quit.

### 4.9.2 Determiners Are Not "Adjectives"

Determiners are often referred to as "adjectives" in reference grammars and textbooks. We limit determiners to just those lexical items and constructions that evoke the narrow conceptual meanings of determiners—that is, identifiability, specificity, degrees of focus [low, medium, high], possession and possession-like or affiliative relationships, gender [for third-person singular possessive determiners], and number and quantity [including part/whole relationships, sequence, and order].

| Determiners + Noun | Determiners + ADJECTIVE + Noun |
|---|---|
| <u>all *the President's*</u> **accomplishments** | <u>all *the President's*</u> PURPORTED **accomplishments** |
| <u>every *one of* her</u> **cousins** | <u>every *one of* her</u> TEENAGE **cousins** |
| <u>half of *Janel's*</u> **steak** | <u>half of *Janel's*</u> FIRE-GRILLED **steak** |
| <u>Most of *Europe's*</u> **bananas** | <u>Most of *Europe's*</u> CAVENDISH **bananas** |
| <u>*The first 10*</u> **facts** | <u>*The first 10*</u> SPECIFIC **facts** |

See Chapter 13 for detailed discussions of adjectives and their meanings and functions.

********

### PRACTICE WITH DATA ANALYSIS: PUTTING IT ALL TOGETHER

1   In the sections on article usage (i.e., *a/an*, *the*), we discussed the genres of stories and narratives, where so-called new information is introduced first with the indefinite article *a/an* for first-mention entities and subsequent mention occurs with *the* and other indicators of given

or "shared" information. For example: "There was once **a** <u>bunny</u>, **a** <u>kitten</u>, and **a** <u>dog</u> . . ." or "Once upon a time, there lived **a** <u>beautiful princess</u> . . ."

This is also true for certain categories of discourse built on the structure of a storyline narrative, as in some jokes:

> **A** <u>snail</u> is painting a big letter "S" on his car. His friend, the turtle, sees him and asks why. **The** <u>snail</u> replies, "When people see me drive by, they can say 'Look at that little "S" car go!'" [sounds like: "Look at that little *escargot*," the French word for "snail"]
>
> ("The snail's ride," n.d.)

How is the main character (the snail) introduced as a first-mention character? How is that same character referred to subsequently, with various determiners preceding it? Explain your answer in detail.

How about this one:

> **A** <u>penguin</u> walks into **a** <u>bar</u>, goes to **the** <u>counter</u>, and asks **the** <u>bartender</u>, "Have you seen my brother?" **The** <u>bartender</u> says, "I don't know. What does he look like?"
>
> ("A penguin walks into," n.d.)

The main character is *a penguin*, and he walks into *a bar*. (Note the use of subject NP ellipsis with the verbs.) Then, instead of an actual subsequent mention of either the penguin or the bar, we have *the counter* and *the bartender*. Why is the use of *the* so perfectly natural and fitting here?

However, now that you are familiar with the general concepts of "new/unshared information" and "given/shared information," have a look at the introductory paragraph of novels that you know. Does the introduction of these new characters or of the new setting necessarily follow the same patterns that we have just worked with?

Here is an excerpt from *Treasure Island*, in the Junior Classics for Young Readers collection. These are the exact opening lines of the book. Is the information presented as "new/unshared" or as "given/shared"? Also consider ∅. Explain. What effect does this technique create for you as a reader of the text?

> *The* **Squire** and *the* **Doctor** have asked me to write all I remember of Treasure Island—from *the* **beginning** to *the* **end**. I am to put everything except where *the* **island** is located, for there is still treasure there, *not yet found*. [emphasis original]
>
> I will go back to *the* **beginning**, to *the* **time** when my father owned *the* **Admiral Benbow inn**. It was then that *the* **brown old seaman** with *the* **scar** across his cheek came to stay with us.
>
> (Stevenson, 2014, p. 1)

- Who, exactly, is the narrator/protagonist—the "I," "me," and "my" of the story so far? (We learn later that it is a young man named Jim Hawkins.)
- Who are the Squire and the Doctor? And why have they asked this protagonist to recount everything that he can remember about the island?
- Where and what is Treasure Island?
- Who is the narrator's father?
- What is the Admiral Bengow inn? And what is/was its importance to the story?
- Who is "*the* **brown old seaman** with *the* **scar** across his cheek"?

(Note, too, that this character is not described as "*a* **brown old seaman** with <u>*a scar*</u> across his cheek"—as if newly introducing both the man and his scar.)

How do other novels begin? Using your five all-time favorite novels in English, compare and contrast how the opening paragraphs are structured from the point of view of "new/unshared" and "given/shared" information.

To complexify this, do the same with five book reviews, five movie reviews, and five essays and analyze them from the point of view of "new" vs. "given" information.

2   How do the following two news story starters differ?

> **A ninth** <u>Powerball Lottery winner</u> has been named.
> **The ninth** <u>Powerball Lottery winner</u> has been named.

Just by virtue of the indefinite vs. definite article usage, what kind of information can you glean regarding the number of winners involved in each particular lottery game?

3   The following is an excerpt from the Yelp review for Hot Shots Coffeehouse in Blue Jay, California:

> Excellent breakfast spot. . . . *The* **oatmeal** was creamy and *the* **toppings** fresh and unique. Try *the* **blueberry granola almond oatmeal** . . . *the* **portions** were reasonable and *the* **staff** very friendly and attentive.
>
> (Bernard, 2015)

Identify the nouns and their conceptualization patterns (Type 1, Type 2, or Type 3). What types of ellipses do you find in the segment?

Paying attention to nouns, determiners, and ellipsis, write your own reviews of (a) the best restaurant that you encountered on your last vacation (or your last weekend adventure) and (b) the last product that you purchased online. When do you find yourself using *a/an*, and when do you use *the*? Which other determiners did you use?

4   We have all seen the message "SKIP AD →" when advertisements precede online video clips. We'll show you a few variations on the message "SKIP AD." How does the meaning change, just by changing the determiner from ∅ to an overt determiner?

> SKIP **THIS** AD
> SKIP **EVERY** AD
> SKIP **EACH** AD
> SKIP **ALL** ADS

Are you familiar with the SKIP AD Project? You can find more about it on the Skip Ad Project website (Skipad, n.d.). Describe in your own words what the project is about and explain why it even exists in today's digital world. Again, pay attention to your determiners.

5   Some math word problems are much like narratives. Here is one:

> It takes **a** <u>gardener</u> **one** <u>hour</u> to mow and edge **two** <u>lawns</u> on **a** <u>Beverly Hills residential street</u>.
> **How many** <u>lawns</u> can **the** <u>gardener</u> mow and edge in **three** <u>hours</u> on **that** <u>street</u>?

First, write down how you would solve this math problem, and then solve it (just for fun). Then, analyze the nouns and determiners in this problem and in your answer.

Now, compose two original math problems of your own, paying close attention to how you use nouns and determiners. You can also try this by composing riddles (and even tongue twisters).

6   The April 6, 2015, issue of *Time* magazine has this sentence on the cover:

> CUBA: What will change when the Americans arrive?

What if the question was worded in this way: What will change when Americans arrive?

> What will change when **the** <u>Americans</u> arrive?   [original]
> vs.
> What will change when ∅ <u>Americans</u> arrive?   [re-worded]

What sort of stance difference do you sense, just by virtue of the presence or absence of the definite article *the*?

7   The following excerpt is from the nonfiction book titled *Make Your Bed: Little Things That Can Change Your Life and Maybe the World* by Admiral W. H. McRaven. Admiral McRaven is a retired US Navy officer. The book is an expanded version of what Admiral McRaven presented in his May 2014 commencement speech at the University of Texas, Austin. This is one link to a video of his speech: www.youtube.com/watch?v=U6OoCaGsz94. He begins by saying:

> If you wanna change the world, start off by making your bed. If you make your bed every morning, you will have accomplished the first task of the day. . . . Making your bed will also reinforce the fact that the little things in life matter. If you can't do the little things right, you'll never be able to do the big things right.
>
> (McRaven, 2017)

In both the speech and the book, Admiral McRaven gives advice from his own training as a Navy SEAL (highly trained Sea, Air, and Land special operations teams in the US Navy). The advice is delivered in the form of lessons that include grit, tenacity, teamwork, sensitivity, discipline, and success. The following lines are from the introductory paragraphs of Chapter 1, "Start Your Day With a Task Completed":

> Those mornings that I stayed in the barracks I would roll out of my Navy "rack" [a tiered, bunk-like sleeping compartment] and immediately begin the process of making my bed. It was the first task of the day. . . .
>
> The bed was as simple as the room, nothing but a steel frame and a single mattress. A bottom sheet covered the mattress, and over that was a top sheet. A gray wool blanket tucked tightly under the mattress provided warmth from the cool San Diego evenings. A second blanket was expertly folded into a rectangle at the foot of the bed. A single pillow, made by the Lighthouse for the Blind, was centered at the top of the bed and intersected at a ninety-degree angle with the blanket at the bottom. This was the standard. Any deviation from this exacting requirement would be the cause for me to "hit the surf" and then roll around on the beach until I was covered head to toe with sand—referred to as a "sugar cookie."
>
> (McRaven, 2017, pp. 3–5)

  a   First, read through the text. What is your impression of the writing and the message as you read the passage? Can you imagine the scene that McRaven has set for us? In his descriptions, what kind of information is presented as if it is "shared"? What kind of information is presented as "new"? How does McRaven explain what the requirements are?

  b   Identify the determiner + noun combinations. List them.
      We'll start you off with observations from the first paragraph:

> First paragraph: **Those** <u>mornings</u>, **the** <u>barracks,</u> **my** <u>Navy "rack,"</u> **the** <u>process of making</u> <u>my</u> bed. **the** <u>first task</u> of **the** <u>day</u>

Determiners   111

Second paragraph:
_____
_____
_____

c   Which determiners are used in this passage?
Which is the most frequent? Why?

Explain the meaning/function/usage of the indefinite article *a*.
Explain the meaning/function/usage of the definite article *the*.

As you answer the two questions about *a* and *the*, be sure to draw from the sections in this chapter to help you articulate your responses—that is, think about the concepts of given (shared) vs. new (unshared), including first mention and subsequent mention.

Also think about concepts of identifiability (which is related to given/new), number/quantity, part vs. whole, and so forth. All of these concepts are evoked by the determiners *a* and *the* in this text.

d   How does McRaven use possessive determiners?
Analyze how McRaven both *refers to* and *describes* his bed. What types of nouns does he use? What types of determiners? What kinds of part-whole relationships are described?

e   How does McRaven use the demonstrative determiner *this*? Where is it placed in the discourse?

Note that the first instance of *this* in "*This* was the standard" is being used as a demonstrative **pronoun,** since there is no noun that follows it. It still evokes a meaning of *high focus*, but it is not being used as a determiner here (see Chapter 5). McRaven's use of *this* as a determiner in this passage is important. Why? What is it placing into *high focus*?

f   What is McRaven's stance? What is his purpose in describing this episode in this way so early in the book (and so early in his speech, if you have a chance to view it)?

**Answers for second paragraph:**
the <u>bed</u>, the <u>room</u>, a <u>steel frame</u>, a <u>single mattress</u>, a <u>bottom sheet</u>, the <u>mattress</u>, a <u>top sheet</u>, a <u>gray wool blanket</u>, the <u>mattress</u>, the <u>cool San Diego evenings</u>, a <u>second blanket</u>, a <u>rectangle</u>, the <u>foot of the</u> bed, a <u>single pillow</u>, the <u>Lighthouse for the Blind</u>, the <u>top of the bed</u>, a <u>ninety-degree angle</u>, the <u>blanket</u>, at the <u>bottom</u>, the <u>standard</u>, **any** <u>deviation</u>, **this** <u>exacting requirement</u>, the <u>cause</u>, the <u>surf</u>, the <u>beach</u>, a "<u>sugar cookie</u>"

8   Possessive determiners are interesting in the world of Facebook. Regardless of the gender of the subject, Facebook used to notify us that "David changed **their** profile picture," using the third-person plural possessive determiner.

David (male) CHANGED **THEIR** <u>PROFILE PICTURE</u>
Chloé (female) CHANGED **THEIR** <u>PROFILE PICTURE</u>

But, if David or Chloé commented on a post or liked a photo on his or her own Facebook account, we see the following messages:

David (male) COMMENTED ON **HIS OWN** <u>POST.</u>
Chloé (female) COMMENTED ON **HER OWN** <u>POST.</u>

David (male) LIKED **HIS OWN** <u>PHOTO.</u>
Chloé (female) LIKED **HER OWN** <u>PHOTO.</u>

*Figure 4.3* "Nurses work 12 hours a day: 4 hours caring for patients and 8 hours washing our hands."
© Randy Glasbergen. Reproduced with permission of Glasbergen Cartoon Service.

Why do you think Facebook used the third-person plural possessive determiner (*their*) to announce the change in profile picture and the gender-specific third-person singular possessive determiner (*his/her*) to announce comments on one's prior post or "likes" for a photo that the person himself or herself posted?

Why do you think the adverbial intensifier *own* is used here? What does *own* signal as a possessive determiner intensifier?

What are some other contexts in which you find the construction **possessive determiner + own + *noun*?** What function does *own* serve there? In what ways can the determiner + *own* serve as a stance marker? That is, how does it emphasize or intensify a speaker's or writer's position about something?

9   As we have observed in a number of excerpts in this chapter, reference to singular entities sometimes alternates with plural entities and vice versa. Figure 4.3 above shows a cartoon where a nurse is speaking about some of the daily responsibilities involved in the nursing profession.

Here, the reference shifts from *nurses*, a third-person plural noun subject to the first-person plural possessive determiner (*washing* **our** *hands*). This sort of shift is not at all uncommon in English discourse, and we don't often notice it, unless we are keenly sensitive to grammar.

What does this shift mean? Are there other possible grammatical ways that this bit of information could have been conveyed? Try to paraphrase and then see which version(s) is/are the most effective and why.

**ORIGINAL TEXT (From Mini Review and Exercises, Section 4.3.2)**

**Excerpt from *The Invention of Huge Cabret* (intact)**

> The story I am about to share with you takes place in 1931, under the roofs of Paris. Here you will meet a boy named Hugo Cabret, who once, long ago, discovered a mysterious drawing that changed his life forever.

But before you turn the page, I want you to picture yourself sitting in the darkness, like the beginning of a movie. On screen, the sun will soon rise, and you will find yourself zooming toward a train station in the middle of the city. You will rush through the doors into a crowded lobby. You will eventually spot a boy amid the crowd, and he will start to move through the train station. Follow him, because this is Hugo Cabret. His head is full of secrets, and he's waiting for his story to begin.

(Selznick, 2007, p. ix)

## COMMON ERRORS, BUMPS, AND CONFUSIONS

Identify the errors or "bumps" in the following sentences or paragraphs. Use the concepts and terminology that you learned in this and other chapters to articulate what might be grammatically or pragmatically problematic. Suggest ways that each can be rewritten more clearly and more accurately. (Note: While all bumps do involve some element of determiners, they are not limited to only that.)

1 I usually buy apple, orange, and banana because compared to some fruits this kinds are pretty inexpensive.
2 As a international student, it was difficult to write essay in my second language.
3 In first semester of freshman year, my ESL class was an easiest class to get the A.
4 I learned how to write good summary and how to put critique in my paper. But I still have problem with making essay longer.
5 The advertisement reads: "Do something nice for yourself. Your one in a million. Your the best!"
6 When a staff answered our question about when pool closes, she sounded impatient.
7 It is smartest decision he ever made because from a moment he decided to study the architecture, the perspective of the buildings changed for him.
8 Maybe government is not doing it's job to protect rights and the safety of people because can't see many improvement in how the poors are being treated.

## SUGGESTED ACTIVITIES

1 Stock narrative jokes are a good genre for raising awareness about how grammar works within a limited textual space. The following joke is a stock "bar" joke. The determiners are left blank except the one in the last line, or the punch line. Which determiner would you use in each instance? Why? Think about the role of the determiners in building the narrative. When reflecting on your choices, also think about the subsequent nouns (Type 1 or Type 2).

___ man walked into ___ bar looking sad, and ___ bartender asked him, "What's ___ matter?" ___ man said, "___ wife and I had ___ fight, and she told me she wasn't going to speak to me for ___ month. And *the* month is up today."

Find other samples of joke discourse. Remove the determiners and see which types of determiners can be used to fill in the new spaces. How does the meaning change with each determiner?

2 The following list contains movie titles from 2016 and 2017 ("Best 100 movies of 2016," n.d.).

Take a look at the titles. The determiners are left blank for you to practice. Add the determiners back. Be careful. Some just take ∅.

114  *Determiners*

Which determiner would you use in each case? Why? What other alternatives might there be, and how does the variation change the meaning?

a   *I Don't Feel at ____ Home in _____ World Anymore*

b   ___ *Blackcoat's Daughter*

c   ___*Beauty and ____ Beast*

d   ___ *Guardians of ____ Galaxy V*

e   ____*Alien Covenant*

f   ____*Star Wars: ___ Last Jedi*

g   ____ *Justice League*

h   ____ *Kubo and ____ _____ Strings*

i   ____ *Rogue One: ____ Star Wars Story*

Compare your title lists with the actual film title. Did you get all of them correct? How do your answers compare with the actual movie titles? You can extend this practice by using the top song titles on various music websites.

3   Review the headlines in a local newspaper outlet (e.g., small town, rural region) and then in two other mainstream newspapers (e.g., *Los Angeles Times, New York Times, Chicago Tribune*). Make a list of the front-page headlines and headlines for other articles (including front-page stories that continue on later pages) for each newspaper. Describe how the determiners are used in these headlines. Why those determiners?

4   Also, analyze online news clickbait. Find 10 samples of news clickbait items that attract you and tempt you to click on them for more information. What types of grammatical features tend to pique your curiosity? Make collections of these over the next week. Try to identify patterns in grammar that make the story headlines intriguing.

5   Think about an important concept from your field of study. Define the concept first for readers who are familiar with your field. What types of information do you need to provide for this audience? Then, define the concept for readers who are not at all familiar with your field. How does your presentation of the information change as you shift your readership and intended audience? What role, if any, do determiners play in this activity?

Alternatively, think about a festival or holiday in your culture. Write a three-paragraph essay in which you explain the festival for the benefit of someone who has little to no knowledge of this cultural practice. Now, think about how determiners are used in the presentation of "new" information and "given" information.

## Note

1   *An* is a variant of *a* and is used when the following noun or noun modifier begins with a vowel or vowel sound, as in *a painter* vs. *an artist, a leading figure within an epoch, an important issue; a second* vs. *an hour, an honor* (since the *h* is silent, the word begins with a vowel sound) vs. *a hospital, a hostess* (the *h* is not silent), **an** *FBI agent* (the letter *F* is pronounced with an initial vowel sound "eff"), **an** *MA degree* vs. *a Ph.D. degree.*

## Academic References

Carter, R., & McCarthy, M. (2006). *Cambridge grammar of English: A comprehensive guide; spoken and written English grammar and usage.* Cambridge: Cambridge University Press.
Celce-Murcia, M., & Larsen-Freeman, D. (1999). *The grammar book: An ESL/EFL teacher's course.* Boston, MA: Heinle & Heinle.
Chesterman, A. (1991). *On definiteness: A study with special reference of English and Finnish.* Cambridge: Cambridge University Press.
Dik, S. C. (1981). *Functional grammar.* Dordrecht, The Netherlands: Foris Publications.
Fillmore, C. (1982). Towards a descriptive framework for spatial deixis. In R. Jarvella & W. Klein (Eds.), *Speech, place, and action studies in deixis and related topics* (pp. 31–59). New Jersey: John Wiley & Sons, Ltd.
Fillmore, C. (1971/1997). *Lectures on deixis.* Stanford, CA: CSLI Publications.
Garcia, E. (1975). *The role of theory in linguistic analysis: The Spanish pronoun system.* Amsterdam: North Holland Publishing Company.
Halliday, M. A. K. (1985). *An introduction to functional grammar.* London: Edward Arnold Ltd.
Halliday, M. A. K., & Hasan, R. (1976). *Cohesion in English.* London: Longman.
Hanks, W. F. (1992). The indexical ground of deictic reference. In A. Duranti & C. Goodwin (Eds.), *Rethinking context: Language as an interactive phenomenon* (pp. 46–76). Cambridge: Cambridge University Press.
Hosseini, K. (2013). *And the mountains echoed.* London, UK: Penguin Publishing Group.
Kirsner, R. S. (1979). Deixis in discourse: An exploratory quantitative study of the modern Dutch demonstrative adjectives. In T. Givón (Ed.), *Syntax and semantics: Vol. 12. Discourse and syntax.* New York: Academic Press.
Kirsner, R. S. (1990). From meaning to message in two theories: Cognitive and Saussurian views of the modern Dutch demonstratives. In R. A. Geiger & B. Rudzuka-Ostyn (Eds.), *Conceptualizations and mental processing in language: A collection of papers from the Duisburg symposium on cognitive linguistics (April 1989).* Berlin: Mouton de Gruyter.
Knight, C. (2016). See how Japanese American photography from 1920–1940 is still "making waves." *Los Angeles Times.* Retrieved August 1, 2016, from www.latimes.com/entertainment/arts/la-et-cm-knight-making-waves-review-20160308-column.html
Larsen-Freeman, D. & Celce-Murcia, M. (2016). The *Grammar book: Form, meaning and use for English language teachers.* Boston, MA: Cengage Heinle.
Master, P. (1987). Generic the in scientific American. *English for Specific Purposes*, 6(3), 165–186.
Master, P. (1990). Teaching the English articles as a binary system. *TESOL Quarterly*, 24(3), 461–478.
Master, P. (1997). The English article system: Acquisition, function, and pedagogy. *System*, 25(2), 215–232.
Quirk, R., Greenbaum, S., Leech, G., & Svartvik, J. (1985). *A grammar of contemporary English.* London: Longman Group Limited.
Strauss, S. (1993). Why "this" and "that" are not complete without "it." In K. Beals, G. Cooke, D. Kathman, S. Kita, K. McCullogh, & D. Testen (Eds.), *Papers from the 29th regional meeting of the Chicago linguistic society* (pp. 403–417). Stanford, CA: CSLI.
Strauss, S. (2002). *This, that,* and *it* in spoken American English: A demonstrative system of gradient focus. *Language Sciences*, 24(2), 131–152.
Strauss, S., & Feiz, P. (2014). *Discourse analysis: Putting our worlds into words.* New York and London: Routledge.

## Data References

Aesop. (n.d.). The lion and the boar. Retrieved August 1, 2016, from www.taleswithmorals.com/the-lion-and-the-boar.htm
Bernard, D. (2015). Yelp review of Hot Shots Coffeehouse. Retrieved August 1, 2016, from www.yelp.com/biz/hot-shots-coffeehouse-blue-jay?hrid=q1IWsPaC2nL2X2XO56soUQ
Best 100 movies of 2016. (n.d.). Retrieved November 2, 2016, from www.rottentomatoes.com/top/bestofrt/?year=2016

Braman, S. (2004). Who are all these people and what are they doing in my classroom? *EDUCAUSE Review*, *39*(4), 10–11. Retrieved February 23, 2015, from http://er.educause.edu/articles/2004/1/who-are-all-these-people-and-what-are-they-doing-in-my-classroom

Browne, R. (2013). *A century of restaurants: Stories and recipes from 100 of America's most historic and successful restaurants*. Kansas City, MO: Andrews McMeel Publishing.

Cabral, O. (1998). The seven sneezes. In E. L. Buell (Ed.), *A family treasury of little golden books: 46 best-loved stories* (pp. 85–87). Racine, WI: Golden Books Publishing Company.

Chegg Study. (n.d.). Physics questions and answers. Retrieved May 23, 2016, from www.chegg.com/homework-help/questions-and-answers/archer-shoots-arrow-velocity-30-m-s-angle-20-degrees-respect-horizontal-assistant-standing-q5731927

Dictionary.com. (n.d.). Definition for "ionosphere." Retrieved May 15, 2016, from http://dictionary.reference.com/browse/ionosphere

The Free Dictionary. (n.d.). Definitions for of "frittata." Retrieved May 15, 2016, from www.thefreedictionary.com/frittatas; "hammer." Retrieved from www.thefreedictionary.com/hammer; "noodle." Retrieved from www.thefreedictionary.com/noodle.

Ginsberg, B. (2011, September/October). Administrators ate my tuition. *Washington Monthly*. Retrieved May 15, 2016, from www.washingtonmonthly.com/magazine/septemberoctober_2011/features/administrators_ate_my_tuition031641.php?page=all

Groves, M. (2015, May). Meet the Verdugo Mountains' very own mountain lion. *Los Angeles Times*. Retrieved June 10, 2016, from www.latimes.com/local/california/la-me-verdugo-puma-20150529-story.html

Hawaii-seafood.org (n.d.). Pink snapper (Opakapaka). Retrieved November 16, 2016, from www.hawaii-seafood.org/wild-hawaii-fish/pink-snapper-opakapaka/

Life. (1957, June 22). Bayer Aspirin, p. 22.

McRaven, W. H. (2017). *If you want to change the world, make your bed*. New York: Grand Central Publishing.

Men's Health. (2016). The January issue cover. Retrieved May 1, 2016, from www.menshealth.com/guy-wisdom/reasons-to-buy-mens-health-january-issue

Merriam-Webster. (n.d.). Definitions for "hunger." Retrieved May 15, 2016, from www.merriam-webster.com/dictionary/hunger; "monument." Retrieved from www.merriam-webster.com/dictionary/monument

Miller, K. R., & Levine, J. R. (2009). *Biology*. Upper Saddle Water, NJ: Prentice Hall.

National Ocean Service. (n.d.). What is a waterspout. Retrieved May 15, 2016, from http://oceanservice.noaa.gov/facts/waterspout.html

A penguin walks into… (n.d.). Retrieved August 1, 2016, from www.rd.com/joke/a-penguin-walks-into

Ray, R. (n.d.). Spaghetti and meatballs. Retrieved May 15, 2016, from www.foodnetwork.com/recipes/rachael-ray/spaghetti-and-meatballs-recipe.html

Selznick, B. (2007). *The invention of Hugo Cabret*. New York: Scholastic Press.

Silverstein, S. (1981). *A light in the attic*. New York: Harper Collins.

Skipad. (n.d.). About. Retrieved June 10, 2016, from www.skipad.co/about.html

The snail's ride. (n.d.). Retrieved May 15, 2016, from http://jokes.cc.com/funny-kids/oab0gz/the-snail-s-ride

Stevenson, R. L. (2014). *Treasure island (junior classics for young readers)*. Ashland OH: Bendon Publishing.

Thomson Reuters. (n.d.). What we do. Retrieved May 15, 2016, from http://thomsonreuters.com/en/careers/what-we-do.html

Time. (2015). Cover of April 6, 2015 issue. Retrieved May 15, 2016, from http://time.com/magazine/us/3759615/april-6th-2015-vol-185-no-12-u-s

University at Buffalo. (2016, March 7). How rivers of hot ash and gas move when a super volcano erupts: Study suggests that pyroclastic flows traveled in dense, slow-moving currents during one ancient super eruption. *Science Daily*. Retrieved September 1, 2016, from www.sciencedaily.com/releases/2016/03/160307092311.htm

Wikipedia. (n.d.). Definitions for "town." Retrieved from https://en.wikipedia.org/wiki/Town; "landmark." Retrieved from https://en.wikipedia.org/wiki/Landmark; "lung." Retrieve from https://en.wikipedia.org/wiki/Lung; "cerebrum." Retrieved from https://en.wikipedia.org/wiki/Cerebrum. Description of Leonardo DiCaprio is retrieved from https://en.wikipedia.org/wiki/Leonardo_DiCaprio. Description of George Washington is retrieved from https://en.wikipedia.org/wiki/George_Washington. Description of Abraham Lincoln is retrieved May 15, 2016, from https://en.wikipedia.org/wiki/Abraham_Lincoln

Your Amazing Brain. (n.d.). Synaesthesia. Retrieved May 15, 2016, from www.youramazingbrain.org/brainchanges/synesthesia.htm

# 5 Alternate Ways to Identify, Specify, Underspecify, Focus On, and Quantify Things, People, and Ideas in Discourse

## Pronouns

*Figure 5.1* "IPOD/YOUPOD/WEPOD/THEYPOD"
© Randy Glasbergen. Reproduced with permission of Glasbergen Cartoon Service.

The focus in Chapter 3 is the noun and Chapter 4, the determiner. Nouns and noun phrases (NPs) are central, if not the central element, in all of human communication.

This chapter covers pronouns—words like *we, us, ourselves, they, she, it, I, herself, me, anyone, someone, this, that,* and *nothing*. These are words that replace a noun or other noun-like structures (like noun phrases and noun clauses) as referents in discourse. The noun or noun-like structure replaced by a pronoun is called the **antecedent**.

**Roy** called to say that **he**'s running late.      Roy/he = the same person
[antecedent NP]      [pronoun]

**Your dinner** is on the table. Eat **it** before **it** gets cold.      Your dinner/it = the same thing
[antecedent NP]           [pronoun] [pronoun]

**What I did** was wrong, and I apologized for **it**.      What I did/it = the same thing
[antecedent NP]                [pronoun]

Like determiners, pronouns evoke conceptual meanings—meanings that relate to specificity, identifiability, focus, number, ownership, possession (and possession-like qualities, e.g., preference, affiliation; see Chapter 4). In fact, some of the same forms used for demonstrative, quantifier, and interrogative determiners also function as pronouns in discourse. Pronouns add other powerful features of conceptual meaning in discourse, as we will see in this chapter.

The opening cartoon is a play on words, based on the mini electronic audio/tablet device known as an iPod. The humor derives from the apparent possible (but really impossible) separation of the initial *i* from the second element *pod*, thus yielding a simple and traditional-looking substitution drill switching from *I* as a subject pronoun to *you*, and then to *we* and finally to *they*, as if "pod" were a verb, and the person at the blackboard (or whiteboard) is conjugating it.

I pod, **you** pod, **we** pod, **they** pod[1]

Like:
I write, **you** write, **we** write, **they** write

## 5.1 Pronouns and Their Forms: First-Person, Second-Person, and Third-Person Reference

Nouns, determiners, and pronouns all function together to create an intricate and conceptually rich system of reference—that is, the various ways in which speakers and writers pick out and discuss entities in discourse. We can broadly categorize the forms of pronouns according to *person*, designating the perspective or point of view represented and referred to in the discourse. Table 5.1 encapsulates this notion.

### First-person singular [subject pronoun]: *I*

- Yesterday **I** read a fascinating article about the brain and memory.
- **I** have added you to the listserv.

### First-person plural [subject pronoun]: *we*

- **We** are using this network to chat about team projects.
- It's a good thing that **we** can sleep in tomorrow.

### Second-person singular [subject pronoun]: *you*

- I tried calling your number, but **you** didn't answer.
- Do **you** have a No. 2 pencil for the exam?

*Table 5.1* The referential concept of *person*—encapsulated

| Person | Perspective in the discourse |
| --- | --- |
| First person | The speaker or the writer, the one whose direct perspectives we are hearing or reading |
| Second person | The addressee or reader, the one to whom the discourse is addressed |
| Third person | The entity being discussed, written about, talked about |

### Second-person plural [subject pronoun]: *you*

- My expectations are that **you** (all) will come to class having read the chapters.
- When did **you** (all) visit Mount Rushmore?

### Third-person singular [subject pronouns]: *he, she, it*

- <u>Jongsoo</u> is <u>a good friend of mine</u>. **He** is in my physics class.
- <u>Xinyi</u> watches cooking shows every day. **She** is a creative cook.
- I can't find <u>my ATM card</u>. I may have left **it** at the bank.

### Third-person plural [subject pronouns]: *they*

- Finally, <u>*Star Wars* fans</u> were treated to Episode VII. **They** had waited a decade.
- <u>Tickets</u> sold out soon after **they** went on sale.

Pronouns and their forms that designate first-, second-, and third-person referents will change according to the particular grammatical functions in discourse and according to the meanings intended by the speaker or writer. In the previous examples, the pronouns are used as *subject*s of sentences or clauses (see Chapter 2). How the forms of pronouns change in discourse according to grammatical function (e.g., subject, object, reflexive) is illustrated by the following Maya Angelou quote.

> **We** write for the same reason that **we** walk, talk, climb mountains or swim the oceans—because **we** can. **We** have some impulse within **us** that makes **us** want to explain **ourselves** to other human beings. That's why **we** paint, that's why **we** dare to love someone—because **we** have the impulse to explain who **we** are.
>
> (Angelou, quoted in Shah, 2016)

This quote reflects a perspective and viewpoint concerning the **first-person plural** referent *we*. **We** refers to Angelou herself together with all writers (i.e., *we* = writers). **We** also serves to address all of us, every one of us who reads these words or hears them (i.e., *we* = everyone).

The referent remains constant throughout (*we, us, ourselves* = writers; *we, us, ourselves* = everyone), regardless of the grammatical form/function—that is, **subject pronoun**, **object pronoun**, or **reflexive pronoun**.

**We** is used as the **subject pronoun**, **us** is used as the **object pronoun**, and **ourselves** is the reflexive pronoun.

The **first-person plural** pronouns from the previous passage are as follows:

Subject pronoun: **we**
Object pronoun: **us** ("that makes **us** want . . . ," "within **us**")
Reflexive pronoun: **ourselves**

The various functions of pronouns in grammar and discourse are as follows:

- Subject pronouns
- Object pronouns
- Possessive pronouns

- Reflexive pronouns
- Reciprocal pronouns
- Determiner pronouns
- Indefinite pronouns
- Quantifying pronouns
- Interrogative pronouns
- Relative pronouns

## 5.1.1 Pronoun Types and Their Forms

**Subject pronouns** are used as the subject of the sentence or clause:

| PERSON | SINGULAR | PLURAL |
| --- | --- | --- |
| first | I | we |
| second | you | you (*colloquially*, you all, you guys, y'uns) |
| third | he, she, it | they |

**Object pronouns** appear as direct objects and indirect objects of verbs, and following prepositions (see Chapter 6 for direct and indirect objects and Chapter 12 for prepositions):

| PERSON | SINGULAR | PLURAL |
| --- | --- | --- |
| first | me | us |
| second | you | you (etc.) |
| third | him, her, it | them |

- Did you see **me** on TV?  (direct object)
- Were you speaking to **us**?  (indirect object)
- The story was about **him** and his dog.  (following a preposition)

**Possessive pronouns** replace the possessor together with the possessed entity (e.g., her shoes → hers):

| PERSON | SINGULAR | PLURAL |
| --- | --- | --- |
| first | mine | ours |
| second | yours | yours |
| third | hers, his | theirs |
|  | my father's | my brothers' |

- Where'd you find that sweater? It looks just like **mine**. Jenna had to exchange **hers** because it was too big.
- Here's a photo of the summer cottage we rented last year. It's **Jin's uncle's.**

**Reflexive pronouns** include the word "self"/"selves" and designate that the subject and object of a transitive verb (see Chapter 6) are the same entity, that someone or something accomplished a task alone or without help, or that the speaker or writer is strongly emphasizing that entity.

| PERSON | SINGULAR | PLURAL |
|---|---|---|
| first | myself | ourselves |
| second | yourself | yourselves |
| third | herself, himself, itself | themselves |

- These dishes are so clean. <u>I</u> can see **myself**!
  [the subject and object are the same person]

- <u>He</u> lied to everyone, but in the end, we could see <u>he</u> was only fooling **himself**.
  [the subject and object are the same person]

- No one actually had to do anything. <u>The problem</u> resolved **itself**.
  [it happened on its own, possibly spontaneously]

- <u>They</u> baked the cake all by **themselves**.
  [they did it without help]

- "<u>He</u> brought everything back, all the food for the feast. And <u>he</u>, **he himself**, <u>the Grinch</u> carved the roast beast." (Dr. Seuss, *The Grinch Who Stole Christmas*)
  [the Grinch is emphatically mentioned]

**Reciprocal pronouns** replace the object and designate that the (plural) subject and object of a transitive verb have a mutually corresponding relationship.

| PERSON | PLURAL |
|---|---|
| first, second, third | each other, one another |

- *You and your sister* should always help **each other**.
- Why do some *people* kiss **each other** on the cheek when they first meet?
- Lego *blocks* not only can be stacked on **one another**, they interlock.
  or: Lego *blocks* not only can be stacked upon **each other**, they interlock.

**Demonstrative pronouns** are used to point to or show.

| PERSON | SINGULAR | PLURAL | |
|---|---|---|---|
| third | this | these | HIGH FOCUS |
| | that | those | MEDIUM FOCUS |
| | it | them | LOW FOCUS |

- What's **this**? I have never seen anything like **it** before.
- **Those** are my rain boots! <u>Mine</u> have the yellow and white polka dots.
- Peace. **It** is our greatest hope.

| Compare: | Peace. **This** is our greatest hope. | (HIGH FOCUS) |
|---|---|---|
| | Peace. **That** is our greatest hope. | (MEDIUM FOCUS) |
| | Peace. **It** is our greatest hope. | (LOW FOCUS) |

**Indefinite pronouns** refer to unknown, non-specific, or unspecified entities.

### PERSON   HUMAN

third    everyone, everybody, someone, somebody, anyone, anybody, no one, nobody, whoever, whosoever, whomever

- **Everyone** in the room was quiet. **No one** said a word.
- Getenet was looking for **somebody** to dance with.

### NONHUMAN

what, whichever, everything, something, anything, nothing

- **What** the press needs to do now is remain as neutral and objective as possible.
- The tenant will pay a security deposit of one month's rent or $1,200.00, **whichever** is greater.
- Esteban tried **everything** to get rid of his cat's fleas, but **nothing** worked.

Note the use of **singular verbs** with indefinite pronouns. Here are a few more examples:

| Everything *is* (singular) okay. | Everybody *was* (singular) surprised. |
|---|---|
| Somebody *needs* (singular) to talk to him. | Nothing *matters* (singular) anymore. |

**Quantifying pronouns** provide information about number and amount.

| PERSON | SINGULAR | PLURAL |
|---|---|---|
| third | one, any, each, another, either, neither, none | some, all, many, much, more, others, enough, both, a little, a few, few, three, six, seventeen |

- Is that a 33 rpm record? I still have **a few** at home. My dad has collected more than **50**.
- The cookies were delicious. May I have **another?**
- Who and what are the referents in this passage? How is **each** referred to?

**Interrogative pronouns** appear in questions and replace the unknown information that the question targets:

### PERSON

third    what, which, who, whose, whom

- **What** did you do at the party yesterday? **Who** was there?
- Did SooHee find the person who lost the ring? **Whose** was it?

**Relative pronouns** relate/connect the modified noun to its description:
(See Chapters 2 and 13 for more on relative clauses.)

### PERSON

third    that, which, who, whom, whoever, whomever, whichever

- The vaccine **that** Jonas Salk discovered was never patented.
- I'm looking for a tutor **who** can teach both French and math.

**Remember:** If there is an overt noun following one of these forms, then the grammatical function is that of a determiner and not a pronoun. Compare:

That 33 rpm [determiner + noun] is **my father's** record [determiner + noun].
That [pronoun] is **my father's** [pronoun].

**Whose** ring [determiner + noun] did SooHee find?
**Whose** [pronoun] is it?

**Which** class [determiner + noun] is the hardest for you?
**Which** [pronoun] is the hardest for you?

I'll have **some** pistachios [determiner + noun].
I'll have **some** [pronoun].

---

### Mini Review and Practice

Think about nominal reference (i.e., referring to people, ideas, concepts, places, and things using nouns and pronouns) in the following passage from the opening paragraphs from an abridged version of L. M. Montgomery's *Anne of Green Gables* (adapted by K. Olmstead, 2005). Who and what are being referred to and how?

One day in early June, as Mrs. Rachel Lynde looked out her window, **she** saw Matthew Cuthbert ride by. **He** was wearing a white collar and his best suit of clothes—a sure sign **he** was leaving Avonlea. And his horse and buggy looked newly cleaned. Where could **he** be going?

Mrs. Lynde knew that Matthew was a quiet man **who** rarely went far from home. Although **she** thought long and hard, **she** did not know what to make of what **she** had just seen. "I'll just step over to Green Gables and ask his sister Marilla where **he's** gone and why after tea," **she** told **herself**.

(Olmstead, 2005)

This is also a good place to review what we have covered in Chapter 3 for nouns, especially common nouns and proper nouns, and in Chapter 4 for determiner + noun combinations and their meanings:

Green Gables was built far back from the main road, by Marilla and Matthew's father—a man as quiet and shy as his son. **It** sat far back from the main road, surrounded by orchards. "No wonder Marilla and Matthew are so set in their ways, with only trees and **each other** to talk to," Mrs. Lynde said. . . .

Marilla had expected **her**. **She** knew that Matthew would drive right past Mrs. Lynde's window, making **her** curious. Despite their differences—or perhaps because of **them**—**they** were friends. **She** tried not to smile at Rachel Lynde's attempt to discover more information.

(Olmstead, 2005)

Who and what are the referents in the full passage? Note the various ways that each is actually named or mentioned:

| *Character/place name* | *Proper nouns, common nouns* | *Pronouns* | *Determiner + noun [not including ∅]* |
|---|---|---|---|
| Rachel Lynde | Mrs. Rachel Lynde, Mrs. Lynde, Rachel Lynde | she, her, herself | Mrs. Lynde's window, Rachel Lynde's attempt |
| Matthew Cuthbert | Matthew | he, who | a quiet man who rarely went far from home, his best suit of clothes, his horse and buggy, his sister Marilla, his (father's) son |
| Marilla Cuthbert | Marilla | | his sister Marilla |
| Marilla and Matthew Cuthbert | Marilla and Matthew | they, each other | Marilla and Matthew's father, so set in their ways |
| Green Gables | | it | |
| Rachel Lynde and Marilla Cuthbert | | they | their differences |
| Rachel's and Marilla's differences | | them | |

From the four quoted paragraphs, find the clauses or phrases that contain the following pronoun types and write them in the spaces provided or on a separate sheet of paper. Underline or highlight the pronoun for that type, as we have done for the **relative pronoun** category at the end of the list. With the exception of relative pronouns, there may be more than one answer for each category.

Subject: _____
Object: _____
Reflexive: _____
Reciprocal: _____
Relative: Matthew was a quiet man **who** rarely went far from home

Note the various ways in which each character (or place) is introduced and then developed in the text. What does this suggest about potential variety in reference terms in written discourse? Are there any pronouns or determiners that appear in this passage that refer to *different* entities (e.g., *his, they, them, their*)? How can you tell which of these pronouns or determiners refers back to which antecedents in the discourse?

## 5.2 More on Pronouns and Reference: Conceptual Meanings and Assumptions

As with all aspects of grammar, there are a number of broader assumptions that underlie the use of pronouns, especially with regard to **conceptual meanings** and **referential scope**.

### 5.2.1 The Use of Pronouns Assumes Shared or Given Information Regarding Referents

Readers and hearers assume that the referents marked by a pronoun (rather than a full noun phrase or a proper noun) are sufficiently recognizable—either through prior mention, common knowledge, or upcoming future mention. Sometimes, it is not immediately clear what the pronoun is actually referring to, as the following examples 1 and 2 illustrate:

**Examples:**

1  "And all of a sudden, **he** came out of nowhere."

   Q: "Who?" [→ the pronoun alone is an insufficient referent]
   A: "The driver who hit my car." [antecedent not mentioned yet]

2  "Before you Replace **it,** Shake **it**"

   Q: "What is **it**?" [→ You need to keep reading to find out.]

   > "The next time your printer displays a 'change *toner cartridge*' message, you might want to give it a shake instead. . . . *Those toner cartridges* . . . may contain as much as 60 percent of the original toner." ("Customer service newsletter," n.d.)

   A: **it** = your toner cartridge [antecedent assumed to be known by reader]

   [Note in 2 that **it** ("you might want to give it a shake instead") could technically also refer to "the printer," but it would be harder and more awkward to shake that.]

3  "Morphological differences are among the most obvious divergences between languages, and linguistic science has been aware of **them** since the Spanish encountered Aztec and other polysynthetic languages in sixteenth-century Mexico." (Evans & Levinson, 2009, p. 432)

   **them** = morphological differences [antecedent mentioned in prior clause]

### 5.2.2 You, Yours, Yourself, *and* Yourselves *Mean More Than "You" as "Direct Addressee"*

Second-person references **you**, **yours**, **yourself**, and **yourselves** can denote an actual addressee or readership of one person or more than one person, including an entire audience (at any point in time). However, the referential scope of **you** (including **yours**, **yourself**, and **yourselves**) can actually extend well beyond an addressed person or a group of addressees, evoking a far more general and generic set of unspecified addressees (i.e., everyone and anyone). The meaning of **you** can evoke a stronger sense of inclusiveness, meaning **"we"** (as if first-person plural), as well as a sense of genericness and non-specificity of the referent meaning **"one"** or **"anyone."**

**Examples:**

1 **you:** referring to groups of designated recipients of the discourse

    a   **John F. Kennedy:**

>And so, <u>my fellow Americans</u>: ask not what *your* country can do for **you,** ask what **you** can do for *your* country. <u>My fellow citizens of the world</u>: ask not what America will do for **you,** but what together *we* can do for the freedom of *man*.
>
>(Kennedy, 1961)

[Addressees = all Americans, and then everyone/anyone hearing or reading the speech: **you** = Americans as a group, *you* as an individual → **we** as a united group of Americans and then extending to all of humanity]

2 **you:** ambiguous between specific addressee or reader or generic use

    a   If **you** smoke, **you** are more likely to have cavities and tooth problems.

[you = designated addressee]
OR
[you = non-specific addressee = "one," "anyone"]

If **one** smokes, **one** is more likely to have cavities and tooth problems.
If **anyone** smokes, **he/she/(they)** is (are) more likely to have cavities and tooth problems.

    b   **You** have to have a key to open this door.

[you = designated addressee]
OR
[you = non-specific addressee = "one," "anyone," "anybody"]

**One/Anyone/Anybody** has to have a key to open this door.
A key is necessary (for anyone/anybody) to open this door.

In the previous examples, imagine the scope of reference in terms of who exactly is being addressed and how. What is the message conveyed by each utterance? Who is that message intended for? How does the shift from generic "you" to "one" in 2 and 3 change the tone of the message and/or the degree of speaker involvement with regard to the topic and/or the intended addressees? Think about the notion of a speaker's or writer's "proximity" or closeness to vs. distance from an addressee. The sense of proximity is stronger with "you" than it is with "one." Also, think about the speaker's or writer's stance shifts in 3: *You have to have a key to open this door* vs. *One has to have a key to open this door* vs. *Anyone has to have a key to open this door.* What sorts of stance shifts do you sense simply by virtue of the shift in pronouns?

Also, because **you** is ambiguous with regard to number (i.e., **you** can designate a single addressee [singular] or multiple addressees at once [plural]), variations of this form in English have developed that designate unambiguously plural addressees. Such variations differ in terms of register and regional dialects.

Alternative forms for **you** when addressing more than one person:

    **You all, all of you**                      [more formal]
    *I expect that **you all** have done the readings before class today.*

    **You guys**                                   [more informal and predominantly gender neutral]
    *Are **you guys** ready?*

128  *Pronouns*

    **Y'all**                                    [regional variant: southern states, approximately from
    Can *y'all* hear me?                      Texas to North Carolina]

    **Youse, Yuns, Yinz**                  [regional variant: Ohio and Pennsylvania]
    *Yinz* goin' downtown? = 'Are you all going downtown?'
    [*Yinz* = an example of Pittsburghese second-person plural (Johnstone, 2013)]

### 5.2.3 We, Ours, and Ourselves *Mean More Than Just "You and I"*

In addition to designating first-person plural viewpoints, **we**, **ours**, and **ourselves** (and *us*, *our*, etc.) also function powerfully in discourse to signal the *inclusion* of the addressee or reader with the speaker or writer or the *exclusion* of the addressee or reader from the speaker or writer (i.e., *inclusive* **we** vs. *exclusive* **we**).

    Pronoun **we** (**ours, ourselves**) can also carry a *generic* meaning, similar in function to generic **you**, **one**, **anyone**, **anybody**, and even **someone** or **somebody**.

### Examples:

1. Just $ell it. **We** sell *your* things on eBay.
   [→ **We** = the company, and not the addressee 'you' = exclusive]

2. *I* hope *you*'re in *my* class next year. **We**'ll have so much fun.
   [→ **We** = the speaker and the addressee 'you' (and possibly others) = inclusive]

3. When **we** bake chicken, **we** want to be sure that it's cooked well, but not overdone.
   [→ **We** = anyone who cooks = generic, **you, one, anyone, someone**]
   [could also be interpreted as inclusive and exclusive]

4. If **we** drop things of different weights from the same height, which objects will fall first?
   [→ **We** = anyone at all = generic, **you, one, anyone, someone**]
   [could also be interpreted as inclusive and exclusive]

As we observed in Section 5.2.2 with generic **you**, think about how the speaker's or writer's stance changes with respect to the information and/or the addressee with the shifts between **we, you, one, anyone**, or **someone**.

### 5.2.4 Third-Person Pronouns in English: Gender and Stance

**Third-person singular** entities referred to as **he** or **she** assume an understood gender distinction, whereby **he** typically marks masculine gender and **she** marks feminine gender.

### Examples:

1. Should <u>a student</u> tell a professor that **he** or **she** needs an A in the course?

   Alternate wording—substituting **he** or **she** with genderless **they**:
   [→ Should <u>a student</u> tell a professor that **they** need an A in the course?]

2. "He Says Goodbye, She Says Hello"

   The *Vanity Fair* headline highlighting a 2015 story by Buzz Bissinger refers to Olympic gold medal decathlete Bruce Jenner, who underwent a gender transition and publicly changed from male identity to female identity in June 2015.

   (Vanity Fair Staff, 2014)

3   "What pronoun should you use for Caitlin Jenner?"

> "When Caitlyn Jenner came out as a transgender woman to ABC News's Diane Sawyer, **she** asked to be referred to with male pronouns for the time being. But in a new Vanity Fair cover story by Buzz Bissinger, Jenner is referred to as '**she.**' The reason is simple: Jenner is now publicly referring to **herself** that way."
>
> (Lopez, 2015)

In these examples, gender is a crucial determining factor in terms of choosing between **he/him** and **she/her**.[2]

Sometimes third-person **singular** entities can be referred to not only as **he/him** or **she/her** but also as **it**. That is, beyond the gender distinction separating **he/him** and **she/her**, there is an additional assumed distinction between human/sentient beings (**he/him**, **she/her**, **they/them**) and non-human/non-sentient beings (**it**).

As you will find in everyday conversation, news reports, blogs, novels, journals, and essays, pets and other animals are often endearingly referred to through their gender—**he/him/his** or **she/her/hers**—instead of or in addition to genderless/non-sentient **it**. Similarly, cars, ships, motorcycles, and even countries are sometimes affiliatively referred to as third-person singular entities: **she**, **her**, **hers**.

## Examples:

1   Ship referred to variably as **she** and **it**

   **From "The sinking of the *Titanic*, 1912" (n.d.)**

   **She** was touted as the safest ship ever built, so safe that **she** carried only 20 lifeboats. . . . John Thayer witnessed the sinking from a lifeboat. "We could see groups of the almost fifteen hundred people still aboard . . . as the great after part of the ship . . . rose into the sky, till **it** reached a sixty-five degree angle."

   ("The sinking of the *Titanic*, 1912," n.d.)

   [→ pronouns for the ship, *Titanic* = **she**, **it**]

2   Pet pig referred to variably as **he/him** and **it**

   **From *Charlotte's Web***

   [the story is about a little girl named Fern; her pet pig, Wilbur; and a barn spider named Charlotte]

   Fern couldn't take her eyes off <u>the tiny pig</u>. "Oh," she whispered. "Oh *look* at **him**! **He's** absolutely perfect." . . . Then she opened the lid again, lifted <u>the pig out</u>, and held **it** against her cheek. . . . Fern had named her pet, selecting the most beautiful name she could think of.

   "<u>Its</u> name is Wilbur," she whispered to herself. . . . Fern loved <u>Wilbur</u> more than anything. She loved to stroke **him**, to feed **him**, to put **him** to bed.

   (White, 1952, p. 4–6)

   [→ pronouns for Wilbur the pig = **him**, **he**, **it**]

The choice between third-person plural **they** and third-person singular **it** can also evoke the same type of distinction between human/sentient (**they**) and non-human/

non-sentient (**it**). **They** also evokes a generic and indefinite meaning that points to a non-specific referent.

**Examples:**

1 Type 3a nouns referred to as singular **it**

> <u>Facebook</u> is conducting an all-out assault on Google. **It** just launched embeddable videos and a new ad network. <u>Google</u> looks like **it** is basically helpless to stop Facebook. **It** doesn't have an answer to Facebook.
>
> (Yarrow, 2015)

[→ Facebook and Google are both used as Type 3a nouns, referred to as **it**. **They** is also both grammatical and possible.]

2 Type 3b noun referred to as plural **they**

> Despite all the damage **they** have done to US workers and communities, a 2007 study found that, as of that date, <u>Walmart</u> had received more than $1.2 billion in tax breaks.
>
> ("WalMart strikes . . .," 2014)

[→ Walmart is used as a Type 3b noun, referred to as **they**. **It** is also both grammatical and possible.]

3 **They** denoting a *generic*, non-specific, and indefinite entity that can be replaced with the word "**people**"

  a  Why do **they** say that elephants never forget?
     cf. "Why do **people say** that elephants never forget?"

  b  **They** say that one dog year is equal to seven human years. Is that really true?
     cf. "**People say** that one dog year is equal to seven human years."

**Singular they**[3] is often used in discourse to avoid designating gender, especially where gender is contextually irrelevant. We often find such instances in discourse when the subject or object in question is designated with the singular indefinite pronoun **someone** or **somebody**.

> How do you diplomatically let **someone** know **they** have hurt you?
> What is the best way to tell **somebody they** are awesome?

**Compare:**

> How do you diplomatically let **someone** know that **he or she** has hurt you?
> What is the best way to tell **somebody** that **he or she** is awesome?

These two versions, with **they** vs. **he or she**, evoke differences in both stance and register. One salient difference is that the versions with *he or she* are slightly more formal. That said, what sort of stance (e.g., position, feeling) on the part of the speaker or writer is evoked by this?

### 5.2.5 Pronouns This, That, *and* It *Designate a FOCUS Continuum*

FOCUS as we discussed in Chapter 4 pertains to the degree of attention that hearer or readers are asked to attend to a particular referent. HIGH FOCUS (**this/these**) is typically associated with a referent that is important, often introduced as (if) new information. MEDIUM FOCUS (**that/those**) is associated with a referent that is important but less so than the referent marked with HIGH FOCUS. MEDIUM FOCUS pronouns are often introduced as (if) given/shared information. LOW FOCUS (**it/they/them**) is associated with a referent that requires the least amount of attention to it, mostly introduced as (if) highly shared information (Strauss, 2002).

> **this/these**   HIGH FOCUS (pay strong attention to this referent)
> **that/those**   MEDIUM FOCUS (pay medium attention to this referent
> **it/they/them**   LOW FOCUS (pay low attention to this referent)

Examples:

1   Q: What is **this** on my screen?
    ((photo shows a phone screen with the letter *N* in an orange star hanging from an orange thread))

   R₁: **It** may have something to do with NFC. (NFC = Near Field Communication).
   R₂: Does **it** do anything if you tap on **it**?
   R₃: The first reply was right. I turned **that** off and **it**'s gone.
                                                   (Android Central Forums, n.d.)

2   Book title:

   *Eat **This**, Not **That**: The No-Diet Weight Loss Solution!* (Zinczenko, 2008)
   [→ cf. *Eat It*—presupposes that we already know what **it** refers to, or that we will soon find out in the upcoming discourse]

### 5.2.6 LOW FOCUS It: *Referential and Non-Referential* It

Referential *it* designates the use of this pronoun to refer to a known and identifiable antecedent as in the following excerpt from an online educational entry on genetics:

> <u>Genetics</u> is probably one of the most exciting lessons in biology. But at the same time, **it** can be a bit confusing. . . . Genetics is the science of studying how living things pass on characteristics or traits . . . in their cell make-up from one generation to the other. Simply, **it** is the study of how living things inherit features like eye-color, nose shape. . .
>                                                   (Genetics, n.d.)

The antecedent is the noun *genetics*. This noun phrase is replaced with the pronoun **it** in two instances in subsequent sentences. In each instance, we can associate the meaning of **it** with the noun phrase *genetics*. Note also that even though *genetics* ends with an *s*, it is not plural (see Chapter 3).

However, because the pronoun *it* occupies the lowest level on the referential scale, this pronoun is a perfect candidate for the so-called dummy subject placeholder in temporal and climatic expressions that have no true full referent or antecedent for *it*:

- Non-referential *it* for time and weather:

   *It's* 8:30. *It's* finally spring. *It's* June! *It's* my birthday. *It's* New Year's Eve. *It's* cold out today. *It's* raining. *It's* cloudy in Seattle for a good part of the year.

- Other expressions of non-referential *it*:

- Idiomatic expressions:
    Don't be so hard on her. She can't **help** *it*.
    Let's **call** *it* **a day**.
    I'm feeling sort of **out of** *it* this afternoon.
    —Why don't you call her?   —I just don't **feel like** *it*.
    Can you **find** *it* **in your heart** to apologize to them?

- Cleft constructions: Cleft constructions with *it* bring focus to a particular construction (a noun, noun phrase, or noun clause) in a sentence. They typically follow this formula:

    It + be + (not) + FOCUSED ENTITY + (who, that) . . . (adapted from Larsen-Freeman & Celce-Murcia, 2016, p. 661).

The focused constructions following the *it*-clefts are underlined in the following sentences.

*It's* not <u>that I don't want to go to summer camp</u>. I'm just afraid of being homesick.
*It* <u>was</u> <u>Sungtae</u> who took care of everything for us.
*It's* <u>because of daylight saving time</u> that the days feel longer.
*It's* <u>the healthy food selection at Nature's Table</u> that keeps us coming back.

---

### Mini Review and Practice

Solidify your understanding of the concept of reference in general, with a focus on first-person, second-person, and third-person reference types:

1  We noted that the most common first-person singular reference term is **I, me, myself**. Often, though, we find many variations to this in actual discourse. Here are a few examples:

| | |
|---|---|
| *Give <u>me</u> a big hug!* | *I want a big hug!* |
| *Give <u>Mommy</u> a big hug!* | *Mommy wants a big hug!* |
| *Give <u>us</u> a big hug!* (meaning "me") | *We* (meaning "I") *want a big hug!* |

How does this shift in the pronoun reference term change the stance of the speaker? Explain.

Can you find similar examples of first-person referential variation in actual discourse (e.g., from interactions that you have experienced, TV dramas, movies, commercials, books)? Also, think about how referring to one's self (or a family member) by using third-person names or kinship terms (e.g., "Mommy," "Daddy," "brother") in lieu of first-person reference terms is done in other languages such as Japanese, Korean, Arabic, Spanish, Chinese, and French.

We also find the use of first-person plural forms **we** and **us** intended as second-person address terms. For example:

*How are **we** doing today?*       Meaning: *How are **you** doing today?*

Have you heard this expression in service encounters (e.g., at the post office, in the grocery store checkout line, at restaurants by your waitstaff)? How about at the doctor's office?

How do you react when you hear this use of **we** or **us** meaning **you**? It is a marked usage (see Chapter 2 for markedness) of this pronoun.

Listen for these types of expressions in your daily interactions. Is the first-person plural option (i.e., *we*, *us*) also possible in other languages addressing someone?

2   Object pronouns vs. subject pronouns

Which is correct—a or b?

1   a The plumber recommended to Chun and **me** that we not use Drano anymore.
    b The plumber recommended to Chun and **I** that we not use Drano anymore.

[a is correct, because **me** follows the preposition *to*—the pronoun should be an object pronoun.]
[b is ungrammatical * . . . to Chun and **I** ← this is a subject pronoun, but the object pronoun should used because of the preceding preposition *to*.]

2   a Hello, it's **me**.
    b Hello, it is **I**.
    [Both are correct. a is more commonly used; b is correct but stilted—higher and more formal register; its use is rare in American English.]

3   a These are the photos that my family and **I** took on our trip to Jamaica.
    b These are the photos that my family and **me** took on our trip to Jamaica.

[a is correct—**I** is the proper subject pronoun; **me** is an object pronoun.]

4   a Kokob traveled with Mateus and **I** throughout central Ethiopia.
    b Kokob traveled with Mateus and **me** throughout central Ethiopia.

What about this one? Explain which is correct and why.

3   "**No one** can be authentically human while **he** prevents **others** from being so."
(Paolo Freire)

What does this quote mean? What sorts of reference terms (especially pronouns) does it contain? What other nouns or pronouns do you need to explain the meaning of this statement in your own words? Paraphrase the meaning of this expression in at least three different ways. Pay attention to the nouns and pronouns that you use in the process.

4   Similar to the exercise we just did in number 3, have a look at the following proverb. This saying carries a generalizable message using the very specific example of cooking.

"**You** can't make <u>an</u> <u>omelet</u> without breaking <u>a few</u> <u>eggs</u>."

The proverb contains the pronoun **you**, as well as the **determiner + noun** construction with items that are particular to cooking. However, the message that it is intended to convey is actually very general. What is the message? Try to paraphrase the meaning in your own words. What sorts of pronouns do you need in order to explain what the proverb means? Which words would you substitute for **you** as you paraphrase this? What other analogies could you use to express a similar idea, beyond *omelet/eggs*?

**134** *Pronouns*

> How about this one?
>
> "Don't count your chickens before they hatch."
>
> While this proverb also has to do with eggs, it is not at all related to the earlier one. Who is being addressed here? That is, who is "you"? How do you know? Try to explain the meaning of this proverb in your own words. Then, invent two or three more proverbs that carry the same meaning but use different imagery (i.e., not chickens, eggs, or hatching). Pay attention to noun types (Type 1, Type 2, or Type 3), determiners, and pronouns.

\* \* \* \* \* \* \* \*

## PRACTICE WITH DATA ANALYSIS: PUTTING IT ALL TOGETHER

1   What is the difference between these two evaluative sentences?

    a   I know a fine restaurant when I see **it**.
    b   I know a fine restaurant when I see **one**.

These differ only by virtue of the pronoun. The meanings in the two sentences are subtly different. What does each version mean? Some of the conceptual categories that we have discussed in this chapter and in Chapter 4 may help you articulate the distinction.

How about this pair?

    a   I have a feeling that **someone** has read my private emails.
    b   In auditing Siyu's records, we found that **somebody** made a withdrawal without her knowledge or consent.

Can you articulate a preliminary analysis or impression that could account for the difference (albeit a subtle one) between *someone* and *somebody*? What accounts for this impression? Try to find more discourse-based examples to better determine the conceptual differences between *someone* and *somebody*.

Here is one more:

*Teacher ((to the class))*:   Who can tell me what a contract is?
*Student 1:*   Something that a person signs.
*Teacher:*   Close. Let's keep trying.
    **Anyone** else?  vs.  **Someone** else?

What is the difference in meaning between the teacher's follow-up questions:
    **Anyone** else?
    **Someone** else?

As a student, which of the two would you prefer to hear? Why?

2   The following is an excerpt from a news story about the aquatic amusement park known as SeaWorld.

**From "SeaWorld Says Current Generation of Killer Whales at Parks Will Be Its Last"**

> The killer whales currently in SeaWorld's care will be the last generation of the mammals enclosed at the water parks, according to a company announcement posted on its website.
>
> "Why the big news? SeaWorld has been listening and we're changing. Society is changing and we're changing with it," the company said. "SeaWorld is finding new ways to continue to deliver on our purpose to inspire all our guest(s) to take action to protect wild animals and wild places."
>
> (CNN, 2016)

We discuss the concept of *person*—that is, first-, second-, and third-person reference—in terms of *perspective* or *point of view*. What happens in the SeaWorld corporate quote in the second paragraph? Does the *person* reference remain constant throughout this quotation, or are there variations from one perspective to another? How can you recognize the shift in *person* reference? Explain. Why do you feel the corporate viewpoint is being represented in this way?

3   The following news story includes a brief interview with Tom Teves, a man who lost his son Alex (age 24) in the tragic 2012 shooting in Aurora, Colorado (during a midnight screening of the "The Dark Knight Rises"). In this clip, Teves is referring to the convicted killer, James Holmes (on 24 counts of murder and 140 counts of attempted murder).

**From *Voices of Aurora: Coping With Grief***

> The thing . . . responsible for **this** is still just sitting in a jail cell enjoying **itself**. . . . **We** need to say "the defendant" and not **its** *name*, because **they** want **their** fifteen minutes of fame.
>
> (Edwards et al., 2015)

Describe the ways in which grammar and grammatical choice are intricately related to stance, position, and emotion toward Holmes. Can you find other similar media-based examples of grammatical variations that express extreme stances of the writer or speaker?

4   Here is a message the Facebook Help Team sent immediately after Susan removed a friend from a Facebook account:

> Here's **what** happens when you unfriend **someone**:

> Susan, **we** noticed you recently unfriended **someone**. **This** means that **they**'ll no longer be able to see the posts **you** share only with your friends, and **you** won't be able to see **theirs**. Don't worry, **we** won't tell **them** that **you**'ve unfriended **them**.
>
> (Facebook, n.d.)

First, locate all of the pronouns in the text. You'll find the list at the end of this exercise. As you work though the list, try and identify possible full antecedent referents that each pronoun refers to.

The following example will start you off:

> Here's **what** happens when **you** unfriend **someone**:

Full referents:

> Here is the outcome of an action [what happens] when a Facebook member [you] unfriends another Facebook member [someone]

Go through the remaining lines in the same way to more deeply understand how pronouns take the place of larger bits of referential information. Then, where possible, replace the pronouns with other pronouns and determine how those substitutions affect the meaning:

We noticed you recently unfriended **someone**.
cf. We noticed you recently unfriended **somebody**.

Which other pronouns can replace the following pronouns in bold?

**This** means that **they**'ll no longer be able to see the posts . . .

As you work through these examples, think about the functions of pronouns from the multiple points of view of: economy of words, emphasis, focus, clarity or vagueness, specificity/identifiability of referent, gender, number (singularity/plurality), and so forth.

[Prounouns: what, someone, this, they, you, theirs, we, them]

5   Explain the caption in Figure 5.2 by focusing on the meaning of pronoun **that**. What is being depicted? What is the argument being put forward? How does pronoun **that** serve to support the child's argument? What if she used pronoun **this** instead: ". . . and **this** is why you need to raise my allowance"? How does her stance shift with regard to her argument? Does her position sound slightly weaker or slightly stronger? Why?

6   We note that the demonstrative determiners and pronouns are part of what we call a gradient system of FOCUS, whereby referents are afforded varying degrees of attention and emphasis through language choice. These variables are based on such concepts as the perceived sharedness/givenness or perceived newness of the referent in question, such that highly important (and assumed new) referents are marked by demonstrative/pronoun **this** and highly unimportant (and assumed given/shared/known) referents are marked by **the** and **it**.

Such gradience lends itself well to certain types of discourse, for example, argumentative discourse (exhibiting a preponderance of tokens of **this** and **that**) and advertising discourse, in which demonstratives tend to be used in strikingly persuasive ways.

First, have a look at the following advertisements that use HIGH FOCUS **this**:

a   Partnership for a Drug-Free America (classic 1987 public service announcement)

((man in a kitchen in front of a stove with a hot frying pan on it))

Is there anyone out there who still isn't clear about what doing drugs does? Okay. (This is the) last time (I'm going to try to explain).

((picking up a raw egg)) **This** is your brain.

((pointing to the hot frying pan)) **This** is drugs.

((cracks egg onto hot frying pan)) **This** is your brain on drugs. ((sizzles))

Any questions?

b   Microsoft Cloud

**This** is Titanfall. The first multi-player game for Xbox One, built and run on Microsoft Azure, letting gamers around the world interact in ways they never thought possible. **This** cloud turns data into excitement. **This** is the Microsoft Cloud.

*Figure 5.2* "... and *that's* why you need to raise my allowance!"
© Randy Glasbergen. Reproduced with permission of Glasbergen Cartoon Service.

Why do you feel that **this** is the chosen demonstrative for these ads? Find other ads on TV and in magazines that use **this** as a pronoun and/or a determiner. You can isolate the product type (e.g., cars, chocolate, perfumes/cosmetics, food products, restaurants) as you work on your analysis of demonstrative determiners and pronouns. What sort of persuasive effect are these FOCUS-based grammatical items intended to produce?

Now, have a look at these advertising slogans that use LOW FOCUS **it**:

| | |
|---|---|
| Just do **it**. | Nike |
| Whatever **it** is. | eBay |
| Maybe she's born with **it**. | Maybelline |
| Because you're worth **it**. | L'Oreal |
| I'm lovin' **it**. | McDonald's |
| You can do **it** all on TripAdvisor. | TripAdvisor |

What does **it** refer to in the slogans, if anything? Do you find instances of non-referential **it**? From the point of view of conceptual meaning, why does **it** seem to be a good choice of pronoun in this type of advertising? Explain. Locate more examples and see whether you note similar patterns of reference, suggestion, and persuasion as you do in the previously listed slogans.

7   Much of our discussion in this chapter has centered on *person* reference as *point of view* or *perspective* and how these perspectives and points of view pattern in discourse, as a means of both conveying information and expressing stances of the writer/speaker, vis-à-vis the topic, their readers, and so forth.

In this section, we present two excerpts of discourse on a similar topic: inherent challenges in cultural communication. The first excerpt, "Negotiation Across Cultures" is from the Skills You Need website. The second is from "Tips for Successful Cross Cultural Communication" by A. J. Schuler, Psy.D.

Read both excerpts carefully. What informational elements do they have in common? In what ways do they differ?

**Text 1: "Negotiation Across Cultures" [excerpt]**

Negotiations are rarely easy, mainly because **they** tend to consist of two sides trying to "beat" the **other**.

**Everything** from language barriers to body language to how **you** meet-and-greet can have an impact on your negotiations.

*The Difficulties of Language*

Of course, the most obvious problem with negotiating between cultures is the language barrier. In many cases, **you** won't be able to directly understand the person across from you and **they** won't be able to understand **you**. **You** will have to communicate through interpreters, **which** can be a laborious process to say the least. It's important to see your interpreter as an extension of **yourself** or your team—**they** need to be on your side and work to help **you** overcome cultural challenges.

Where a common language is spoken, usually English, **this** doesn't necessarily mean **you** won't have problems. People speak different types of English, with differences in vocabulary and, if **they** are not native speakers, **they** tend to struggle to understand **everything**. It's imperative **you** stay well away from colloquialisms or technical jargon as **this** can confuse people.

("Negotiation Across Cultures," n.d)

**Text 2: "Tips for Successful Cross Cultural Communication" [excerpt]**

In today's global business environment, more and more of **us** are required to understand people who come from countries and cultures different from **our own**. While there is no short and easy way to learn about a given culture in any depth, there are some general principles that lead to success in communicating and conducting business with people of backgrounds unlike **our own**.

**No one** likes to feel like a stranger, and feeling unable to communicate or to decipher aspects of behavior that don't fit with our own habitual experiences can make any of **us** feel alone.

*Potential Hot Spots in Cross Cultural Communication*

**This** is not meant to be an exhaustive list, but when working with other people, or traveling abroad for work or pleasure, **it** may pay to ask some experts about the following communication styles of the area **you** plan to visit. . . .

Use of Humor: In the West, **we** often try to build immediate rapport through humor, but of course, this is not universally seen to be appropriate in all contexts. The use of laughter can be experienced as a sign of disrespect by **some**, and so **it** is important to understand that **this** is another area where misunderstandings can be very likely to occur.

(Schuler, 2003)

The purpose of each of these writings is similar—that is, to present information that a certain group of people may need if or when they engage in intercultural interactions, for business, pleasure, travel, study, and so forth.

What pronouns are used the most frequently in text 1? Do you find any instances of singular **they**? What pronouns are used the most frequently in text 2? Who is being addressed in each text? Who is being referred to by each pronoun? Is the referent the same for each instance of the pronouns *other, you, us, we, they, them, no one, it*, and so forth, or does the actual referent shift in the discourse? How do you know? How does the use of pronouns create a sense of inclusion within a group of addresses/referents or exclusion from a group of addressee/referents? Explain by focusing on the subject and object pronouns and their shifts in reference within the discourse.

As you work through your analysis of the two texts, be sure to focus on all aspects of reference: nouns (proper, common), determiners, and pronouns. Also, pay special attention to the use of the demonstratives (**this/these, that/those, the/it**) and note their relevance to the way the information is being conveyed in each text as well as to the stance of each writer.

## COMMON ERRORS, BUMPS, AND CONFUSIONS

Identify the errors or "bumps" in the following sentences or paragraphs. Use the concepts and terminology that you learned in this and other chapters to articulate what might be grammatically or pragmatically problematic. Suggest ways that each can be re-written more clearly and more accurately. (Note: While all bumps do involve some element of pronouns, they are not limited to only that.)

1   A real lover cares about feelings and emotions but it does not deny the importance of understanding and respect.

2   Each of these guidebooks have helped me in a different way.

3   Me and her used to play basketball together in high school.

4   I was interested in the English language from childhood. I found this language to be a really interesting and easy language as compared to mine own mother tongue.

5   We seriously hurt ourself during the game, but Hayden and them said, "Keep playing!"

## SUGGESTED ACTIVITIES

1   The following quotes are from some well-known people. Fill in the blanks with the pronouns that you think best fit the sentence. We provide a list of the possible pronouns to complete each saying. Note that pronouns can be used more than once. If you are still unsure, you can look up the quotes online. How can you tell which pronoun works best in the respective blanks?

[Pronouns: everything, we, who, you, nothing, it, all, anybody, yourself, none, ourselves]

a   If there is a book that ___ want to read, but ___ hasn't been written yet, ___ must be the one to write ___. (Toni Morrison)

b   A friend to ___ is a friend to _____. (Aristotle)

c   The most dangerous creation of any society is the man _____ has _____ to lose. (James Baldwin)

d   You, _____, as much as _____ in the entire universe, deserve your love and affection. (Buddha)

e   Perhaps when ___ find _____ wanting _____, ___ is because ___ are dangerously close to wanting _____. (Sylvia Plath)

2   Conduct an informal research project on a new company that you have recently heard about. It can be a technology company, a food manufacturer, an auto manufacturer, a cosmetics line, sporting equipment products, a retail store, and so on. Write a two- to three-paragraph report on your findings. Pay attention to how you refer to that company, using proper nouns, common nouns, determiner + noun combinations, and pronouns. Also pay special attention to how you use Type 3 nouns.

3   a   Analyze the use of pronouns in an academic article from your field of study. What types of pronouns are more common? Which ones are less common? Think about why pronoun use might pattern this way.

For example, you can consider the following questions:

- What are the subject pronouns? Who/what do they refer to?
- What are the object pronouns? Who/what do they refer to?
- Do you find instances where the antecedent referents are overtly stated prior to the use of a pronoun?
- Do you find many instances of *this*, *that*, or *it*? Between *that* and *this*, which is more common?

You may also want to compare and contrast the previous grammar points as they pattern within articles from different areas of study.

b   Using the same criteria in A, analyze argumentative essays from *The New York Times*, *Time* magazine, or *The Washington Post*. Focus on nouns, determiners, and pronouns. What sorts of patterns in reference terms do you find? Do the same thing with online or televised debates, where two parties are arguing an issue from polar opposite sides. Analyze the reference terms and stance marking within this context as well. What sorts of patterns do you find when speakers are affiliating with other speakers? What types of patterns do you find when speakers are in conflict with other speakers?

## Notes

1 This same grammatical play on words is reminiscent of the 1927 song "I Scream, You Scream, We All Scream for Ice Cream," by Billy Moll, Robert King, and Howard Johnson. The wordplay is still used in lighthearted interactions in today's popular culture. Many people who use this saying are unaware of its musical origin.
2 In recent news, ze has been proposed as a genderless alternate pronoun to **he/him** and **she/her** (Benett, 2016; McWhorter, 2015), but it is not yet commonly used in discourse.
3 Singular they was selected as the 2015 Word of Year by the American Dialect Society. Singular *they* was discussed as the "most sensible" choice for a gender-neutral pronoun in English, by the New Words Committee of the American Dialect Society, since "it has the advantage of already being a part of the language" (see "2015 word of the year is singular 'they,'" on americandialect.org). For more on singular **they** and gender-neutral pronouns in English, see Abbott (1984). Bodine (1975), Cameron (1992), Gastil (1990), MacKay (1980), Martyna (1980), and Meyers (1993).

## Academic References

Abbott, G. (1984). Unisex they. *ELT Journal*, 38(1), 45–48.
Bodine, A. (1975). Androcentrism in prescriptive grammar: Singular "they," sex-indefinite "he" and "he or she." *Language in Society*, 4(2), 129–146.
Cameron, D. (1992). *Feminism and linguistic theory*. London: The MacMillan Press Ltd.

Gastil, J. (1990). Generic pronouns and sexist language: The oxymoronic character of masculine generics. *Sex Roles, 23*(11/12), 629–640.

Johnstone, B. (2013). *Yinz: Speaking Pittsburghese: The story of a dialect*. Oxford: Oxford University Press.

Larsen-Freeman, D., & Celce-Murcia, M. (2016). *The grammar book: Form, meaning, and use for English language teachers*. Boston, MA: National Geographic and Heinle.

MacKay, D. J. (1980). On the goals, principles and procedures for prescriptive grammar: Singular they. *Language in Society, 9*(3), 349–367.

Martyna, W. (1980). Beyond the "he/man" approach: The case for non-sexist language. *Signs, 5*(3), 482–493.

McWhorter, J. (October, 2015). Goodbye to "he" and "she" and hello to "ze"? CNN. Retrieved January 3, 2016, from www.cnn.com/2015/10/14/opinions/mcwhorter-pronouns-gender-neutral/

Meyers, M. W. (1993). Forms of they with singular noun phrase antecedents: Evidence from current educated English usage. *Word, 44*(2), 181–192.

Strauss, S. (2002). This, that, and it in spoken American English: A demonstrative system of gradient focus. *Language Sciences, 24*(2), 131–152.

## Data References

Android Central Forums. (n.d.) Retrieved August 5, 2015 from https://forums.androidcentral.com/

Benett, J. (2016, January). He, she, ze? What's in a gender pronoun? *New York Times*. Retrieved February 3, 2016, from www.nytimes.com/2016/01/31/fashion/pronoun-confusion-sexual-fluidity.html?_r=0

Customer service newsletter. (n.d.). The official website of South Carolina. Retrieved August 11, 2015, from www.state.sc.us/newsletter/ciocs/200781453300700.125.html

Edwards, M., Scott, N., & Ramsey, K. (2015). Voices of aurora: Coping with grief, conquering life. CNN. Retrieved May 10, 2015, from www.cnn.com/2015/04/26/us/voices-of-aurora/index.html

Evans, N., & Levinson, S. C. (2009). The myth of language universals: Language diversity and its importance for cognitive science. *Behavioral and Brain Sciences, 32*(5), 429–448.

Genetics. (n.d.). Your cool tips on genetics. Retrieved November 22, 2016, from www.eschooltoday.com/science/genetics/what-is-genetics-for-kids.html

Lopez, G. (2015). What pronoun should you use for Caitlin Jenner? *Vox Identities*. Retrieved August 5, 2015, from www.vox.com/2015/6/1/8700273/transgender-pronouns

Montgomery, L. M. (2005). *Classic starts: Anne of Green Gables*. Adapted by K. Olmstead. New York: Sterling.

Negotiation across cultures. (n.d.). Skills you need. Retrieved March 5, 2016, from www.skillsyouneed.com/rhubarb/negotiation-across-cultures.html#ixzz446qDEZjw

SeaWorld says current generation of killer whales at parks will be its last. (2016, March 3). Channel 16 WNEP, ABC. Retrieved March 5, 2016, from http://wnep.com/2016/03/17/seaworld-says-current-generation-of-killer-whales-at-parks-will-be-its-last/

Schuler, A. J. (n.d.). Tips for successful cross-cultural communication. Retrieved March 10, 2016, from http://wenku.baidu.com/view/3e9371906bec0975f465e2d2.html

Shah, V. (2016, December 7). Why we write. Thought economics. Retrieved August 10, 2015, from https://thoughteconomics.com/why-we-write/

The sinking of the *Titanic*, 1912. (n.d.). Eyewitness to history. Retrieved September 1, 2015, from www.eyewitnesstohistory.com/titanic.htm

Vanity Fair Staff. (2015). He says goodbye, she says hello. *Vanity Fair*. Retrieved August 5, 2015, from www.vanityfair.com/hollywood/2015/06/caitlyn-jenner-bruce-cover-annie-leibovitz

WalMart strikes boycotts govt welfare for 1% Walton family. (2014). Retrieved August 5, 2015, from http://oppermanreport.blogspot.com/2014/11/walmart-strikes-boycotts-govt-welfare.html

White, E. B. (1952). *Charlotte's web*. New York: Harper Brothers.

Yarrow, J. (2015). Google should be terrified right now. *Business Insider*. Retrieved April 2, 2015, from www.businessinsider.com/google-should-be-terrified-right-now-2015-3

Zinczenko, D. (2008). *Eat this, not that: The no-diet weight loss solution!* New York: Rodale Books.

# 6 The Grammar of Events, States, Identities, Actions, Power, Control, and Spontaneity in Discourse
Verbs

"I love you and enjoy our time together, but I'm still young and I've decided to start seeing other bears."

*Figure 6.1* "I love you and enjoy our time together, but I'm still young and I've decided to start seeing other bears."

© Randy Glasbergen. Reproduced with permission of Glasbergen Cartoon Service.

Chapters 3, 4, and 5 centered on nouns, determiners, and pronouns—the very parts of speech that enable us to initiate and maintain communication about ideas, concepts, people, places, and objects. Here, we introduce verbs—those words that give life to nouns, that situate them, activate them, animate them, and act on them. Verbs express actions and movement in addition to states and existence. Verbs even help us express what we know and how we know it.

Every clause contains a verb. Every sentence contains a verb. The verb is the essential part of speech that we use to depict and describe events and conditions (Croft, 1994), to evoke characteristics of people and objects, to make comparisons and contrasts, and to assert and claim and deny (Bowerman & Brown, 2008). Through verbs and their meanings, we establish our positions and convey our perspectives and stances. Verbs allow us not only to objectively depict and describe but also to emphasize, exaggerate, diminish, and downplay.

In this chapter, we will examine English verbs and the robust scopes of meanings that verbs evoke. Basic categories of verb meanings begin with the most primary of verbal distinctions: **dynamic verbs** (i.e., force, energy, action, movement, process; e.g., *play, decide, sleep, breathe,*

144   *Verbs*

*happen, transmit, post, circulate*), **stative verbs** (i.e., emotion, cognition, existence, containment, possession, stable location, stable condition; e.g., *love, like, know, weigh, remember, resemble, contain, belong, own, possess, exist, there is/are*), and **linking verbs** (i.e., identity, characteristics, comparisons, relationships; e.g., *be, become, remain, seem*) (Allerton, 1978; Comrie, 1976; Goldberg, 2006; Halliday, 1967; Hopper & Thompson, 1980; Huddleston & Pullum, 2002; Lakoff, 1987, 1990; Langacker, 1991; Leech, 1971; Levin, 1993; Michaelis, 2011; Palmer, 1988; Quirk et al., 1985; Schleppegrell et al., 2004; Slobin, 1996; Talmy, 1985, 1991, 2000; Vendler, 1967; Wierzbicka, 1988).

Within the categories of **dynamicity** and **stativity** we make a further distinction involving the notion of **transitivity**. We will examine **transitive verbs, ditransitive verbs, complex transitive verbs,** and **intransitive verbs,** and explore the ways in which stance and perspective may be expressed through the choice of verbs and the accompanying subjects and objects (i.e., affected entities from the action) (Hopper & Thompson, 1980; Lakoff, 1977; Langacker, 1991).

## 6.1 Dynamic Verbs, Stative Verbs, and Linking (Copular) Verbs

### 6.1.1 Dynamic Verbs

**Dynamic verbs** evoke the following basic conceptual imageries:

- **Movement** (progressively along a path, or while in one place)
  *go, run, walk, jump, climb, push, pull, spin, rotate, shiver, tremble*

- **Activity/process**
  *read, speak, eat, prepare, start, scare, terrify, happen, construct*

**Dynamic verbs** can evoke more fine-grained meanings:

- **specificity of actions:** actions that differ in terms of specificity, manner, degree, or register (e.g., *eat* → *nibble, gnaw at, devour, gobble up* [lower register, aspectual meaning—see Chapter 12], *chow down* [lower register, aspectual meaning—see Chapter 12]; *read* → *glance, peruse, skim, study, examine; start* → *activate, initiate, found, institute, take the plunge* [lower register]; *cook* → *bake, broil, boil, fry, sauté, whip up* [informal way to say 'to prepare,' 'to put something together quickly']; *write* → *compose, author, document, scribble, jot down*)
- **motion and manner of motion** (because not all motion verbs encode manner, e.g., *come* and *go*): concepts and meanings in verbs that express **how** someone or something moves from one place to another (e.g., *run, skip, dance, twirl, sashay, spin, tumble, somersault*) (Lakoff, 1987; Slobin, 2004, 1996; Talmy, 1985, 1991, 2000)
- **reporting:** actions that relate to the manifold ways in which information is relayed, either through our own words/ideas or the words/ideas of others (e.g., *say, claim, tell, report, assert, indicate, mention, comment, suggest, admit, argue, propose*) (Li, 1986; Lucy, 1993; Silverstein, 1985; Yule et al., 1992)

The subject of a clause or sentence with a dynamic verb is typically the *doer* of the action. The subject can be virtually any NP (noun phrase = modifier [determiner/adj.] + noun) or pronoun. In the following examples, *the dynamic verb* appears in *italics* and the **subject** is marked in **bold**.

Do **you** *walk* to school, or do **you** *ride* your bike?
    [movement]                [movement]

**We** usually *eat* scrambled eggs for breakfast on Sundays.
    [activity]

When **the neighbors** upstairs *play* their music too loud, **we** can't *sleep*.
                [activity]                  [activity]

**The moon** *orbits* the earth every 27 days.
    [movement]

The majority of verbs in English are dynamic. Words like *occur, happen, take, bring, say, look, destroy, build, re-create, untangle, disavow, worry, walk, run, scamper, flee, protect, proclaim,* and *ponder* are all dynamic verbs.

Note the following excerpt. All of the verbs are in italics. The subjects (either NPs or pronouns) are in bold. Try to imagine the scene depicted here, focusing on the combination of nouns, pronouns, and verbs, and especially the actions described through the dynamic verbs.

> **Adapted from *Polar Bears Past Bedtime***
>
> "Whoo." **The strange sound** *came* from outside the open window. **Jack** *opened* his eyes in the dark. **The sound** *came* again. "Whoo." **Jack** *sat up* and *turned on* his light. **He** *put on* his glasses. Then **he** *grabbed* the flashlight from his table and *shone* it out the window. **He** *saw* a white snowy owl on a tree branch. "Whoo," **the owl** *said* again. **Its large yellow eyes** *looked* right into Jack's. . . . **Jack** *jumped* out of bed and *hurried* to Annie's room. **She** *was* asleep.
>
> (Osborne & Murdocca, 1998, pp. 1–2)

What is happening as the story opens? How does the imagery progress from Jack's initial reaction of confusion and not knowing to his ultimate understanding of what the strange sound was and how he figured it out? It is the author's use of nouns, pronouns, and verbs that portrays this progression.

> **nouns, noun phrases, and pronouns**: the strange sound, the open window, Jack, his eyes, the dark, the sound, his light, he [pn—Jack], his glasses, the flashlight, his table, it [pn—the flashight] the window, a white snowy owl, a tree branch, the owl, its large yellow eyes, Jack's [pn—eyes], bed, Annie's room, she [pn—Annie]

146  *Verbs*

**verbs**: came, opened, sat up, turned on, put on, grabbed, shone, saw, said, looked, jumped, hurried, was

Pay attention to the meanings of the verbs in the passage and think about the difference between all the verbs in the passage in contrast with the last verb, noted in italics and also underlined:

She *was* asleep.

How does the last line differ in terms of the depiction of the entire scene? What sorts of actions do you imagine in this opening paragraph? Is there any real action related to Annie in this last line? [compare with *she was sleeping*]

The verb form *was* is a past tense form of the verb *to be*. It is used here as a linking verb that simply linked Annie with the adjective *asleep* ('She was asleep.'). **Linking verbs** (Section 6.1.3) and **stative verbs** (Section 6.1.2) do not evoke dynamic meaning. The verb *sleep* in *she was sleeping* evokes a dynamic meaning, in contrast with *she was asleep*.

## 6.1.2 Stative Verbs

In contrast with dynamic verbs, **stative verbs** express no movement, action, or process. They express essentially stable and unchanging states. Verbs that can function **statively** evoke the following basic conceptual imageries:

- **stable and unchanging physical states**
  have, own, possess, contain, resemble, occupy, involve, weigh, live, lie, exist

- **states of cognition, preference, and emotion**
  know, understand, believe, remember, like, love, hate

- **existence**
  exist, live, there is/are, remain

  **An orange** *has* more potassium than an apple.
  [contains—stable physical state]

  *There is* **more potassium** in oranges than in apples.
  [existence—stable state]

  Do **you** *know* how **most Americans** *like* their steaks? (i.e., rare, medium, well-done)
  [stable cognitive state]     [stable state of emotion]

  I *think* that **many Americans** *prefer* their meat medium—not well-done, not rare.
  [stable cognitive state]     [stable state of emotion]

Note the use of stative verbs in the following passage about Antarctica [Note: Here, the verb *do* is a pro-verb that stands in for *live*.]:

> The coldest, windiest, and driest continent, **Antarctica** *contains* 90 percent of all of the ice on the planet in an area just under one and a half times the size of the United States. . . . **Antarctica** *has* no trees or bushes. . . . **Penguins, whales, and seals** *live* in

and around Antarctica, as **do fish and krill**. . . . Today, **human habitation** *exists* at a variety of science research stations placed by a number of countries.

(Redd, 2012)

Just as illustrated in the previous passage, **stative verbs** (*contains, has, live, exists*) can be found in discourse genres that describe characteristics, traits, or properties of places, people, things, and concepts. The same observation holds for linking verbs.

### 6.1.3 Linking Verbs (Copular Verbs)

**Linking** verbs are also referred to as *copular* verbs. The word *copula* comes from the Latin meaning 'link.' Linking verbs in English are an exceptionally limited and rather CLOSED class of words.

The following verbs can serve as **linking** or **copular verbs**:

be, become, turn, feel, get, grow, smell, sound, taste, appear, seem, look, stay, remain

These function in discourse in a very narrow way to *link* or *equate* a subject (NP or pronoun) of the clause or sentence to another NP, a pronoun, an adjective (or an adjective phrase), or a prepositional phrase, as in the following examples:

**NP SUBJECT is LINKED to another NP, noun, or pronoun:**

Biming *is* my brother.
SUBJ COP NP

**NP SUBJECT is LINKED to a preposition + NP or pronoun**

Biming *is* like my brother.
SUBJ COP + PREP NP

**NP SUBJECT is LINKED to an adjective:**

Biming *is* tall.
SUBJ COP ADJ

Linking verbs typically express

- what or who something or someone is, was, or will be;
- how something or someone is, looks, sounds, tastes, appears, or seems;
- comparisons of someone/something to someone/something else; or
- a change from one condition or state of being to another.

Building on this linking or equating relationship as illustrated in the previous examples with the verb *be* (present tense forms: I *am*, you *are*, it/he/she *is*, we *are*, they *are*) and the Jack and Annie excerpt that preceded this discussion [She *was* asleep], we can see how some of the other **linking verbs** also evoke the same type of **verbal equation**:

- **immovable state linking verbs + adj:** *stand, stay, remain*
    We *remain* excited about the future proposals.
    SUBJ COP ADJ

**The president** *stands* firm on the issue of equal rights.
    SUBJ          COP        ADJ

There are many ways for **alumni** to *stay* connected and involved.
                         SUBJ     COP ADJ         ADJ

- **change of state linking verbs:** *become, turn, turn into, get*

    Our goal: for **all children** to *become* readers.
                      SUBJ         COP **NP**

    Did you actually see **your tadpole** *turn into* a frog?
                      SUBJ       COP       **NP**

    Come in out of the rain before **you** *get* wet.
                                  SUBJ COP **ADJ**

- **verbs of perception (perception copula):** denote sensory details about what something looks like, smells like, tastes like, feels like, and so forth (e.g., *smell, taste, sound, feel, appear, look, seem, look like*)

    **Tofu ice cream** *tastes* exactly like regular ice cream.
    SUBJ            COP        PREP    **NP**

    **The judges** *appear* divided on the travel ban.
    SUBJ        COP   ADJ

    **That shrimp scampi** really *smells* delicious!
    SUBJ                       COP **ADJ**

It is important to remember that these categories of dynamic, stative, and linking verbs refer to the functions of the verbs and not the verbs themselves. This means that the verbs listed under certain categories can and do function as verbs from other categories, and that such function is dependent on the *meanings* of the verbs in context.

# Examples:

- The verb *occupy* can function as a **stative verb** and as a **dynamic verb**.

    Union Bank *occupies* the entire first floor of the Kaufman & Broad building downtown.
        OCCUPY [stable location] = STATIVE VERB

    Squatters try to *occupy* land or buildings in the hopes of eventually gaining ownership.
        OCCUPY [take possession of = activity] = DYNAMIC VERB

- The verb *remain* can function either as a **copula** or as a **stative verb**.

    **The plan** for our senior picnic *remains* unchanged, even with the threat of rain.
        REMAIN [be = immovable state] = COPULA

    Our **luggage** *remained* on the tour bus for hours before they finally unloaded it.
        REMAIN [sit, be located = stable physical state] = STATIVE VERB

- Perception copulas like *smell, taste, look,* and *feel* can also function as dynamic verbs.

    **Brigitte** *tasted* all of the appetizers and liked the stuffed cherry tomatoes the best.
        TASTE [activity] =DYNAMIC VERB

    The broiled brie *tasted* salty.
        TASTE [perception] = COPULA

# Mini Review and Practice

Think about the conceptual differences between **dynamic, stative,** and **linking verbs** (or copulas). All three types of verbs are used often in discourse, but each serves a different communicative function in terms of

- representing and describing oneself and one's own actions and
- representing and describing others and the actions of others.

As you read and hear discourse, think about these questions:

- By focusing only on the subject NPs and the verbs, think about in what ways speakers and writers describe or represent themselves and their actions. What sorts of verbs do they use? For what purpose?
- How do speakers and writers represent other people or things, concepts, and ideas? How do they describe actions and states related to others? What sorts of verbs do they use? For what purpose?

1  The following two passages include a mixture of **dynamic** verbs, **stative** verbs, and **linking** verbs. We have marked all **NP subjects** in **bold** and all *verbs* in *italics*. The *linking verbs* are also underlined.

First, read the passages to get a sense of what is being described. Then, list the dynamic verbs. And list the linking verbs. What sorts of actions are depicted by the dynamic verbs (e.g., movement, activity, process, reporting, specificity of actions)? How would you characterize each linking verb (e.g., sensory perception, change of state)?

a  **Butterier butter!**

"The first thing **I** *ate* in Sweden *was* butter," **Harrington** *tells* me. "And **I** *remember being* amazed at how much butterier **it** *tasted* than the butter I'd *had* at home."

. . . **He** *shows* me a tray of fermented cream. **It** already *looks* buttery and *smells* like a kind of mild soft cheese.

(Derry, 2016)

Note also the verb *had*: It tasted butterier than the butter I'd *had* at home. Is it being used here as a stative verb, like the verb *have* in the following sentence?

Octavia *had* more experience than Clarke, which is why she got the job.

How is the use of *had* in excerpt A different in meaning of *had* in the previous sentence? What verbs can you substitute for *had* to capture meanings of each instance?

**Answers:**

Dynamic verbs: ate, tells, had, shows
Stative verb: remember
Copular/linking: was, being, tasted, looks, smells

150  Verbs

b **Ah Tuscany!**

**Tuscany *looks*, *smells* like heaven**
*Is* there really such a place as heaven on earth? If so, you can *find* it in the central region of Italy, known as Tuscany. . . . Finally, nothing *sounds* better than the thick Italian accent of the friendly small town inhabitants as they *welcome* visitors and *tell* them all about the region.
(adapted from "Tuscany looks, smells like heaven," 2001)

**Answers:**

Dynamic verbs: find, welcome, tell
Stative verb: there is (is there. . . ?)
Copular/linking: sounds

2   Let's have a look at another passage to more deeply analyze some of the conceptual differences between **dynamic** verbs, **stative** verbs, and **linking** verbs.

When dynamic verbs are used to depict a subject's (or the *doer* of the action's) ability to control or change things or situations, it can be said that these verbs express **agency** (i.e., the potential of a person, thing, concept, idea, or force to move itself or others willfully, to influence deliberately, to exert control, or to cause something to happen). **Agency** reveals itself in discourse on a continuum ranging from low agency (e.g., linking verbs, some intransitive verbs) to high agency (e.g., transitive verbs, some intransitive verbs) (Hopper & Thompson, 1980; Langacker, 1990; Tsunoda, 1985).

**Linking verbs** express **very low agency**, if any agency at all.

**Compare:**

Linking verb         *be* = is (linking verb)
DNA *is* a molecule.                                              [low agency]

Linking verb         *turn into*, *become* (linking verbs)   [low agency]
DNA *turns into* RNA and *becomes* a protein.

Dynamic verb:        *determine*
DNA *determines* the unique genetic makeup of organisms. [high agency]

a   Have a look at the following description from the Tinker Crate website. By focusing only on the subject NPs and the verbs, think about the ways in which this online retail sales company is depicted. In particular, look at the dynamic verbs and their meanings and the linking verbs and their meanings. There is also one stative verb in the discourse.

First, identify the verbs as dynamic, stative, and copular (linking). Then, as you work through the text, think about what/who the subjects of the sentences or clauses are. What are the verbs that are used with the subjects?

STEM (Science, Technology, Engineering, and Math) *is* a key to creative problem solving, a foundation for critical thinkers and a pipeline to innovation. **Our mission** in creating Tinker Crate *is* to *help* **kids** *gain* these crucial skills through **hands-on activities** that *are* also seriously fun. . . . **We** *are* not just another science kit. **We** *create* "low threshold, high ceiling" projects, so **they** *are* accessible and fun for all types of learners. **This** *means* **we** *make sure* **it** *is* easy for **kids** to *dive into* the activity and *get* excited about it, without *getting* bogged down in technical terms.

(Tinker Crate, n.d.)

**Answers:**

Dynamic verbs: help, gain, create, make sure, dive into
Stative verb: means
Copular/linking: STEM *is* a key, we *are* not just another science kit;
so they *are* accessible and fun, . . . for kids to *get* excited. . . ,
without *getting* bogged down . . .

Do you notice any variations in how much control or intentionality is expressed in the dynamic verbs vs. how much control or intentionality comes through in the stative or copular verbs? How do the dynamic verbs in this excerpt reflect the author's or company's stance? That is, in which types of descriptions do you find more dynamic verbs? Who are the subjects of the verbs? Why do you think the text reads this way? What is the purpose of the discourse?

Note how the verb *get* here is used twice as a <u>change of state</u> **linking verb**.

What other meanings does *get* have? When it means "to receive," it is **dynamic**.

b    Now, have a look at the description of the Isle of Navaro that is advertised on the Private Islands Online website.

**"Isle of Navaro"**

Located in front of beautiful Dolphin Bay near Bocas del Toro in Panama, Isle of Navaro *offers* 9 acres of dry island for you to *enjoy*. The island *includes* a 2800 sq ft house built over the water as well as an 18 x 20 caretaker's residence. The island *comes equipped with* a 26 ft boat with a motor as well as 2 generators. . . . The lush island *has* approximately 900 pineapple plants, 700 coconut palms, bananas and papaya trees as well as a wide verity of orchids and other native flowers.

(adapted from Private Islands Online, n.d.)

Identify the verbs in this passage, according to their functions as dynamic, stative, or copular. How do the verbs in this passage differ from those in the Tinker Crate excerpt from the point of view of verb type (i.e., dynamic, stative, and copular)? How do the authors'/websites' stances differ between the A and B passages? Why do you think this is so?

152  *Verbs*

> **Answers:**
> Dynamic verbs: offers, enjoy
> Stative verbs: includes, comes equipped with, has
> Copular/linking: NONE

## 6.2 Transitivity and Verb Meaning

**Transitivity** refers to the grammatical and conceptual property of meaning that combines *three* crucial elements: **the subject** of the verb (or the *doer* of the action), **the verb itself**, and the ability of that subject + verb combination to move, create, destroy, or otherwise affect a **third entity**, often referred to as a direct object. We refer to the direct object here as the ***affected entity*** (Hopper & Thompson, 1980).

Verbs in English function either **transitively**, when the previously mentioned three entities are all involved in the conceptual scene, or **intransitively**. Verbs that function **intransitively** involve only TWO elements: the subject of the verb and the action or state expressed by that verb. **Intransitively** functioning verbs have no possibility of affecting any additional element in the discourse.

**Transitivity** in discourse is related to **agency**.

> **Agency** refers to the potential of a person, thing, concept, idea, or force to move itself or others willfully, to influence deliberately, to exert control, or to cause something to happen.
> Verbs like *eat, devour, destroy, create, build, help, push, pull, bend*, and *cut* all encode a high degree of agency.

Imagine a scene in which you can invent a sentence or clause that uses any one of these verbs. What is happening in that scene? That is, who is the subject, and what is the subject doing? Does anything in the scene change in form, color, shape, size, or ability as a result of the subject and the action of the verb? In what way does that change take place?

### 6.2.1 Transitive Verbs

Verbs functioning **transitively** in discourse involve the essential combination of THREE factors: (1) *the doer* of the action (which is the subject NP of the clause or sentence), (2) the action depicted by the verb that affects something or someone, and (3) someone or something that is affected by or otherwise involved in that action—that is, the affected entity (often referred to as the "direct object") as in *Yumi heats the ramen* [direct object or affected entity: *ramen*] or *Chaoxing designs* skyscrapers [direct object or affected entity: *skyscrapers*]. In each case, there is an affected entity: the ramen; skyscrapers.

In the sentence *Chaoxing designs* skyscrapers, we see that the verb *design* relates both to the subject *Chaoxing* and what it is that she designs (i.e., skyscrapers). If a sentence were written \**Chaoxing designs*, it would not make sense, because the conceptual meaning of the verb *design* absolutely requires another entity in the image—what it is that Chaoxing designs (e.g., skyscrapers, women's fashions, computer programs, video games).

The following list contains verbs that commonly function transitively. You can fill in possible subjects and possible affected entities (direct objects). We completed the first string of subject +

verb + affected entity for you. Try constructing at least one full clause or sentence for each verb, by filling in both a subject and an affected entity.

**Chaoxing** *designs* **skyscrapers.**
SUBJ    V    affected entity    [three components]

| Verb: | Subject | + | Verb | + | Affected Entity [DIRECT OBJECT] |
|---|---|---|---|---|---|
| eat | Johanna | | eats | | hamburgers |
| build | _____ | | _____ | | _____ |
| create | _____ | | _____ | | _____ |
| hit | _____ | | _____ | | _____ |
| see | _____ | | _____ | | _____ |
| touch | _____ | | _____ | | _____ |
| hear | _____ | | _____ | | _____ |
| like | _____ | | _____ | | _____ |
| love | _____ | | _____ | | _____ |
| hate | _____ | | _____ | | _____ |
| remove | _____ | | _____ | | _____ |
| cut | _____ | | _____ | | _____ |
| include | _____ | | _____ | | _____ |
| complete | _____ | | _____ | | _____ |

It is important to keep in mind that even if an affected entity is not overtly mentioned in the discourse, if the meaning of the verb is not complete without the assumption or imagination of an affected entity, the verb is still transitive. The meaning of transitive verbs incorporates an affected entity, whether it is actually mentioned in the discourse or not. Remember, there are THREE components involved in transitivity: the subject, the action of the verb, and the affected entity.

**Example:**

*Eat* is a **transitive verb.**

    **Johanna** *eats* hamburgers.
        [hamburgers = affected entity (direct object)]

But: Did you *eat* today?
[*today* is NOT the direct object; it is an adverb, situating the time]

Did you *eat* [breakfast, lunch, anything] today?
        [affected entity = direct object—whether or not it is mentioned]

*Eat* is still transitive. One has to *eat* SOMETHING.

There is some object/affected entity in the conceptualization of the verb.

*Read* is a **transitive verb.**

    **Ikue** *reads* poetry.
        [affected entity = direct object]

But:  Q: What is Nina doing?
      A: She's *reading* in the library.
        [*in the library* is NOT the direct object; it is an adverbial, situating the place]

154  *Verbs*

She is *reading* [poetry, a book, the newspaper] in her room.
  [affected entity = direct object—whether or not it is mentioned]

*Read* is still transitive. One has to *read* SOMETHING.

There is some object/affected entity in the conceptualization of the verb.

### 6.2.2 Ditransitive Verbs

The meaning of this sub-category of transitive verbs involves a total of FOUR components: (1) the doer of the action (which is the subject of the clause or sentence), (2) the action depicted by the verb, (3) the affected entity, and (4) **the recipient** of **that affected entity** (often referred to as the "indirect object").

| **My brother** | *handed* | his credit card | *to me.* |           |
|----------------|----------|-----------------|----------|-----------|
| SUBJ           | V        | affected entity | recipient | [four components] |

Examples of ditransitive verbs include:

**Verb:**

**Subject  +  Verb  +  Affected Entity + Recipient of That Entity**
                     [DIRECT OBJECT] [INDIRECT OBJECT]

| give | Marla       | gives | chocolate | **to** the children. |
| buy  | Mia and Ken | buy   | gifts     | **for** the teachers. |
| pass | _____      | _____ | _____   | _____ |
| ask  | _____      | _____ | _____   | _____ |
| send | _____      | _____ | _____   | _____ |
| tell | _____      | _____ | _____   | _____ |
| mail | _____      | _____ | _____   | _____ |

Typically, ditransitive expressions involve some sort of *transfer* of the affected entity (i.e., direct object) to a recipient (i.e., an indirect object). Such expressions therefore often include the prepositions *to* or *for* designating the intended recipient of the entity being transferred.

### 6.2.2.1 Ditransitive Verbs: Changing the Order of Affected Entity and Recipient

With **ditransitive verbs** or **verbs of transfer**, we can often change the order of the affected entity and the recipient. (See Thompson [1995] and others for more on dative alternation.)

Marla *gives* chocolate        to the children.
      [affected entity]        [recipient]

**Changed order:**

Marla *gives* the children chocolate
      [recipient] [affected entity]

- What does Marla give?      chocolate [affected entity]
- To whom?                    the children [recipient]

Mia and Ken *buy* gifts       for the tour guides.
            [affected entity] [recipient]

## Changed order:

Mia and Ken *buy* the tour guides gifts.
 [recipient] [affected entity]

- What do Mia and Ken buy?    gifts [affected entity]
- For whom? the tour guides    [recipient]

This can also be done using pronouns for either the affected entities or the recipients, as in the following examples:

Marla *gives* chocolate    to the children.
 [affected entity]    [recipient]

Marla *gives* chocolate    to them (pronoun, replacing "the children").
 [affected entity]    [recipient]

**Changed order—with pronoun for recipient:**

Marla *gives* them    chocolate.
 [recipient]    [affected entity]

Mia and Ken *buy* them    gifts.
 [recipient]    [affected entity]

Here, the form of the pronoun would be the **object pronoun** (*me, us, you, her, him, it, them*). (See Chapter 5.)

Change the order of the affected entity and recipients in the following sentences:

Juan *handed* the document to me. → Juan handed _____    _____
 [affected entity] [recipient]    [recipient]    [affected entity]

Sungho *mailed* the bill to her. → Sungho mailed _____    _____
 [affected entity] [recipient]    [recipient]    [affected entity]

Now, change the orders of the affected entities and the recipients for the sentences or clauses that you designed for Section 6.2.2, using the verbs *pass, ask, send, tell,* and *mail*.

- First, write the original sentence or clause for each verb.
- Identify the affected entity.
- Identify the recipient.
- Change the recipient into an object pronoun.
- Change the order of the affected entity and recipient in the sentence or clause.

### 6.2.3 Complex Transitive Verbs

Like the **ditransitive verb** construction, this sub-category of transitivity also involves FOUR components.

In the **complex transitive verb** construction, the four components are (1) the doer of the action (or subject), (2) the action of the verb as affecting something, (3) the affected entity, and (4) MORE about the affected entity—either in the form of an adjective (ADJ)/adjective phrase or a noun phrase (NP). This added information provides more detail about how that affected entity changed.

**Example**:

*Paint* is a **transitive verb.**

| We | *painted* | the house. | | [three components] |
|---|---|---|---|---|
| SUBJ | V | affected entity | | |

| We | *painted* | the house | white. | [four components] |
|---|---|---|---|---|
| SUBJ | V | affected entity | MORE about the affected entity | (ADJ or NP) |

156 *Verbs*

*Take* is a **transitive verb.**

**The warriors** were going to *take* him.  [three components]
SUBJ                            V    affected entity

**The warriors** were going to *take* him          prisoner.  [four components]
SUBJ                            V    affected entity  MORE about the affected entity (ADJ or NP)

Here are a few more examples to illustrate:

**The students** *elected* Max.     **The students** *elected* Max           president.
SUBJ    V    affected entity     SUBJ        V    affected entity     MORE

**The parents** *call* their children.   **The parents** *call*   their children   gifts from heaven.
SUBJ         V    affected entity    SUBJ         V    affected entity      MORE

**The suspect** *held* the bank employees.  **The suspect** *held* the bank employees   hostage.
SUBJ        V    affected entity        SUBJ        V    affected entity       MORE

Note that in all of the previous examples, the sentences with four components are more specific and more complex than their counterparts with three components.

Typical expressions using **complex transitives**:

To *find* someone guilty or innocent
To *declare* someone or oneself free
To *name* someone X (i.e., a name or title)
To *call* someone, something, or one's self X (i.e., a name or title)
To *make* someone or something a partner, a hero, happy, sad, worried, famous
To *leave* someone or something upset, reeling, elated, perplexed, concerned, speechless
To *make* something easy, hard, difficult, impossible, possible
To *make* someone or oneself comfortable, better, at home
To *get* someone or oneself healthy, help, better
To *hold* someone or something hostage, responsible, accountable, dear
To *keep* someone or something safe, warm, fresh

You can practice this construction by completing the four components in the following strings.

| **Verb:** | **Subject** | **+ Verb** | **+ Affected Entity +** | **MORE** |
|---|---|---|---|---|
|  |  |  | [DIRECT OBJECT] | [ABOUT THE AE = ADJ or NP] |
| paint | _____ | _____ | _____ | _____ |
| call | _____ | _____ | _____ | _____ |
| name | _____ | _____ | _____ | _____ |
| take | _____ | _____ | _____ | _____ |
| elect | _____ | _____ | _____ | _____ |
| make | _____ | _____ | _____ | _____ |
| leave | _____ | _____ | _____ | _____ |
| hold | _____ | _____ | _____ | _____ |
| keep | _____ | _____ | _____ | _____ |

### 6.2.4 Intransitive Verbs

In contrast with **transitive, ditransitive,** and **complex transitive** expressions, the conceptual imagery of **intransitive verbs** involves only TWO components: (1) the doer of the action (which is

*Verbs* 157

the subject or the clause or sentence) and (2) the action, movement, or state depicted by the verb itself. In this case, **the action, movement, or state conceptually cannot affect another entity**. In other words, the subjects of intransitive verbs do the action, animate the movement, or exist in a state—entirely and completely on their own. There is no possible way to construe an affected entity (i.e., no possible "direct object") (Hopper & Thompson, 1980; Levin & Rappaport Hovav, 1995).

Prototypical intransitive verbs include *sleep*, *arrive*, *exist*, and *happen*, as in the following examples:

**We** *arrive* at 6:00 p.m. [two components]
SUBJ V

Do you think **Bigfoot** *exists?* [two components]
SUBJ V

**Birds** *fly* south for the winter. [two components]
SUBJ V
[south is NOT a direct object; it is an adverb denoting direction]

You can practice this construction by filling in subjects and verb forms for the following strings:

| Verb: | Subject | + | Verb |
|---|---|---|---|
| sleep | _____ | | _____ |
| happen | _____ | | _____ |
| exist | _____ | | _____ |
| occur | _____ | | _____ |
| arrive | _____ | | _____ |
| go | _____ | | _____ |
| come | _____ | | _____ |
| lie | _____ | | _____ |
| die | _____ | | _____ |
| arise | _____ | | _____ |
| be | _____ | | _____ |

So, the crucial concept here is that there is **no conceptual possibility of an affected entity** in the intransitive scene:

**Jinna** *sleeps* late on Sundays.
   ['late on Sundays' is not an affected entity; it is an adverbial of time]

**Their plane** *arrives* at 6:00
   ['at 6:00' is not an affected entity; it is an adverbial of time]

**Mistakes** *happen*
   [no affected entity (and also no person identified as responsible for those mistakes)]

In contrast, remember, in the sentences *Nina is reading* and *Did you eat?* even though the affected entities or direct objects are not explicitly mentioned, the verbs are still **transitive**.

## 6.3 Transitive or Intransitive?

Some verbs function in **inherently and unchangeably <u>transitive</u>** ways. This means that there must be an affected entity in the conceptual scene:

hit, eat, read, include, complete, cut, remove, trim

Some verbs function in **inherently and unchangeably** intransitive ways. This means that there CANNOT be an affected entity in the conceptual scene:

> go, come, lie, die, rise, happen, arrive, occur, be, sleep

And some verbs have contrasting pairs, where one verb form is transitive and the other form is intransitive. Common pairs like these are *lay* vs. *lie*, *set* vs. *sit*, and *raise* vs. *rise*.

| Transitive | Intransitive |
|---|---|
| lay ['to place,' 'to set down'] | lie ['to rest in a horizontal position'] |
| Can **you** *lay* <u>the carpet</u> right there?<br>   SUBJ V affected entity | Did **you** *lie* on the carpet?<br>   SUBJ V |
| set ['to place'] | sit ['to adopt an upright position, with weight on buttocks'] |
| Can **you** *set* <u>the pieces</u> right here?<br>   SUBJ V affected entity | **You** may *sit* now.<br>SUBJ    V |
| raise ['to move something upward']<br>raise ['to lift s.t. up'] | rise ['for something to move upward']<br>rise ['to move in an upward direction'] |
| Did **you** *raise* <u>your hand</u>?<br>   SUBJ V affected entity | I watched **the balloon** *rise* into the sky.<br>   SUBJ    V |

Finally, some verbs can function **either transitively** or **intransitively**. As you read through the following examples, think about why the verb is functioning transitively in the first version and intransitively in the second.

Try and articulate the conceptual features of a transitively functioning verb and the conceptual features of an intransitively functioning verb.

*walk*
**We** *walk* <u>our dog</u> twice a day.         [<u>three</u> components]      transitive
**We** *walk* to school.                          [<u>two</u> components]        intransitive

*change*
Did **you** *change* <u>your hairstyle</u>?       [<u>three</u> components]      transitive
**Your hairstyle** *changed*.                     [<u>two</u> components]        intransitive

*move*
**You** can *move* <u>your chess piece</u> here.  [<u>three</u> components]      transitive
**The Ouija board planchette** *moved* all by itself!   [<u>two</u> components]  intransitive

*fly*
**I** have always wanted to *fly* <u>a kite</u>.  [<u>three</u> components]      transitive
**That kite** *flew* over those treetops?         [<u>two</u> components]        intransitive

*smoke*
**Yasmin** has never *smoked* <u>cigarettes</u>.  [<u>three</u> components]      transitive
Why is **your engine** *smoking*?                 [<u>two</u> components]        intransitive

*mount*
Joy watched Jongsoo as **he** *mounted* <u>the stairs</u>.   [<u>three</u> components]   transitive
We were nervous. **The tension** was *mounting*.  [<u>two</u> components]        intransitive

*run*

| | | |
|---|---|---|
| **Myongsoo** *ran* <u>the experiment</u> with precision. | [<u>three</u> components] | transitive |
| For exercise **we** *run* every day. | [<u>two</u> components] | intransitive |

*rush*

| | | |
|---|---|---|
| **They** *rushed* <u>the patient</u> to the ambulance. | [<u>three</u> components] | transitive |
| **The concertgoers** *rushed* into the auditorium. | [<u>two</u> components] | intransitive |

How about this pair?

| | | |
|---|---|---|
| Do **you** *smoke*? [cigarettes, cigars, pipes?] | [<u>three</u> components] | transitive |
| **The furnace** is *smoking*. It needs to be fixed. | [<u>two</u> components] | intransitive |

Why is the verb *smoke* transitive in the first sentence, even though there is no overt direct object or affected entity? Is there a direct object or affected entity that is understood as part of the meaning of the verb? Imagine a human smoking. Now imagine a furnace smoking. How does the action of "smoking" differ in the two scenes? Who or what is smoking? Is there something in the scene that is being smoked (i.e., an affected entity)?

The imageries created by these contrasting transitive/intransitive scenes should help solidify the concept of **transitivity** more generally. **Transitive** scenes involve a force or action whereby another object, person, or entity is created, changed, destroyed, or in any way acted upon by the subject of the sentence in conjunction with the meaning of the verb itself. **Intransitive** scenes involve only the subject and the action or movement or state expressed by the verb. **Transitive** scenes are often **agentive** (e.g., *Myongsoo ran* <u>the experiment</u>; *DNA determines* <u>the unique genetic makeup of organisms</u>). **Intransitive** scenes can range from **low agency** (e.g., *sleep, happen, occur, smoke, disappear*) to **high agency** (e.g., *walk away, get out, run, hurry, rush*), as in the following examples:

| | | |
|---|---|---|
| Harry *disappeared* as soon as he saw his boss. | intransitive | [lower agency] |
| Harry *walked away* as soon as he saw his boss. | intransitive | [higher agency] |
| Harry *scurried away* as soon as he saw his boss. | intransitive | [even higher agency] |

---

### Mini Review and Practice

1   The following excerpt is from Diane Setterfield's novel *The Thirteenth Tale*:

> There is something about words. In expert hands, manipulated deftly, they take you prisoner, wind themselves around your limbs like spider silk, and when you are so enthralled you cannot move, they pierce your skin, enter your blood, numb your thoughts. Inside you they work their magic.
>
> (Setterfield, 2009, p. 8)

Think about the conceptual scenes depicted here. The passage contains a robust and vivid use of verbs.

Read the passage again and think about its meaning. Try to imagine the scene as depicted by the author. How do you think she feels about words and language?

Next, identify the **subject NPs** [both as pronouns and as NP antecedents] and the *verbs*. Then, try to classify the verbs according to the following functional categories:

**Dynamic verbs**, **stative verbs**, or **linking verbs**?

For dynamic verbs, further classify them according to

- verbs functioning transitively,
- verbs functioning ditransitively,
- verbs functioning as complex transitives, and
- verbs functioning intransitively.

Does your understanding of verbs from these various conceptual perspectives help you better understand how language can be used creatively to depict scenes and express ideas, stances, and feelings? Explain.

**Answers:**

| | |
|---|---|
| transitive | they *pierce* your skin, *enter* your blood, *numb* your thoughts, they *work* their magic |
| ditransitive | NONE |
| complex transitive | they *take* you prisoner |
| intransitive | they *wind* themselves, you cannot *move* |
| stative | *there is* |
| linking | you *are* so enthralled |

2   Reviewing ditransitive and complex transitive verbs

Recall that both ditransitive and complex transitive verbs involve FOUR components in the verbal scene, not THREE as in the typical transitive construction or TWO as in the typical intransitive construction.

**Ditransitive verbs** typically involve some type of transfer of one thing (i.e., the affected agent) to another entity (i.e., the recipient). In this way, the verb *to email* could easily be used in a ditransitive scene.

May I *email* the paper to you?
**Ditransitive:** Why?

What are some other verbs of transfer that involve new types of technology that can be used in a ditransitive scene?

**Complex transitive scenes** involve verbs that naturally add MORE to the description of the affected entity—verbs like *call*, *elect*, *name*, *find*, and *leave*.

What is the difference in meaning between these two sentences?

They *found* the defendant.
**Transitive:** What is the affected entity? Where did they find him?

> They *found* <u>the defendant</u> innocent.
> **Complex transitive:** Why?
>
> What is the affected entity? What MORE information is provided about the affected entity?
>
> How about this example?:
>
> Can **you** *call* <u>a taxi</u> for me?
> What is the subject? What is the verb? What is the affected entity? Who or what is the recipient?
>
> Now, change the order of the affected entity and the recipient.
>
> Can **you** *call* <u>a taxi</u> for me? → Can you call me a taxi?
> Affected entity: _____
> Recipient: _____
>
> In response to the question, *Can you call me a taxi?* someone might answer:
>
> "Sure. Hey, Taxi!"
> OR
> "Okay, you're a taxi! Ha-ha!"
>
> Using the concepts you have learned from this section, explain the ambiguity of the question that makes at least the previous two responses possible.
>
> How about this one? Explain the ambiguity in the two responses provided to the following question, using grammatical terms.
>
> *Can you make me a chocolate cake?*
>
> - "Of course. I'll make it for your birthday."
> - "Abracadabra! Poof! You are a chocolate cake!"
>
> And lastly, here is a final joke:
>
> I met the kindest cannibal yesterday.
> He said he wanted to make me dinner. Should I go?
>
> What is the source of humor here? Explain the ambiguity using the concepts in this chapter.

## 6.4 Verbs and More Meanings

### 6.4.1 Verbs Derived From Nouns: Proper Nouns and Common Nouns

Like the category of nouns, the grammatical category of verbs is also constantly in flux and growing. Dynamic verbs represent an OPEN class of words.

Some verbs in English are derived from common nouns (see Chapter 2), as in the following list:

| **Nouns** | **Verbs and meanings** |
|---|---|
| water | *to water* (to pour water onto) |
| butter | *to butter* (to put butter on) |

162  *Verbs*

| | |
|---|---|
| eye | *to eye* (to look at) |
| powder | *to powder* (to put powder on) |
| shell | *to shell* (to remove the shell from) |
| can | *to can* (to place in cans) |
| shelf | *to shelve* (to put onto shelves) |
| roof | *to roof* (to install a roof onto) |
| paint | *to paint* (to apply paint) |
| hammer | *to hammer* (to pound with a hammer) |
| saw | *to saw* (to cut with a saw) |
| medal | *to medal* (to earn an athletic medal) |
| circle | *to circle* (to move in a circle) |
| weed | *to weed* (to remove weeds from a place) |

The meanings of dynamic verbs derived from nouns typically incorporate that noun into the action, as in to add that noun to something (e.g., *to water* plants, *to butter* bread, *to grease* a pan) or to take away that noun from something (e.g., *to shell* peanuts, *to skin* an animal, *to dust* furniture). Some verbs derived from nouns mean to use that noun to accomplish an action (*to hammer* a nail, *to saw* a board). Also verbs derived from nouns of body parts evoke actions that use those body parts (e.g., *to eye* the suspects) or more figuratively (e.g., *to shoulder* the burden).

For the verbs in the previous list, think about whether they typically function **transitively or intransitively**, or **both ways**.

New verbs continue to populate our dictionaries and increase our verbal lexicons as new concepts emerge in our daily lives. The following list of neologisms influenced by social media, technology, news, politics, retail commercialism, and film reflect this phenomenon:

| **Nouns (common and proper)** | **Verbs and meanings** |
|---|---|
| Google | *to Google* (to look up using Google) |
| Skype | *to Skype* (to contact via Skype) |
| fax | *to fax* (to send via fax) |
| email | *to email* (to send via email) |
| friend | *to friend* (to add someone on Facebook) |
| unlike | *to unlike* (to change an original positive evaluation on social media to no evaluation or to a negative evaluation) |
| Bork | *to bork* (to reject due to negative publicity) |
| Walmart | *to walmart* (to drive a competitor out of business) |

For verbs derived from proper nouns (like Google, Skype, Bork, Walmart), try to find the history behind the emergence of those verbs in discourse. What do these verbs mean? How did these new meanings come about?

And once again, think about whether the verbs derived from nouns in general typically function **transitively or intransitively**, or **both ways**. For the transitive verbs, can any of the previously listed verbs function as **ditransitive** verbs? Which ones? Why do you think this is so?

### 6.4.2 *More Precise Meanings Evoked in the Actions of Dynamic Verbs*

Now that we have a solid sense of the meanings evoked by English verbs, we can expand on and explore verb meanings in more depth by examining other categories that relate to verb meanings.

### 6.4.2.1 Motion and Manner of Motion

**Manner of motion** verbs is one such category. This type of verb specifies details concerning **how an entity moves or is caused to move** through space. Let's look at one example, and we can expand the concepts from there.

| Motion verb | Meaning |
|---|---|
| *go* | to move from one place to another (no manner encoded) **intransitive** |

**Manner of motion verbs**

| | |
|---|---|
| *walk* | to move from one place to another—How? **on foot** |
| *run* | to move from one place to another—How? **on foot, quickly** |

**Other manner of motion verbs:** moving across expanses of land or water. HOW?

> trot, gallop, canter
> zigzag, meander, sashay, twirl, spin, pirouette
> glide, slide, climb, dance, waltz, bunny hop, crawl, tumble, somersault, hop, jump
> swim, paddle, canoe, kayak, raft, float, wade

Note that some of these verbs are also derived from nouns (e.g., *pirouette, waltz, somersault, paddle, canoe, kayak, bunny hop*).

As you consider these verbs and the sorts of motions they express, also think about whether they might function **transitively**, **intransitively**, or **both ways**.

Understanding how these verbs function and pattern in discourse can aid significantly in both understanding and producing figurative and creative uses of language.

If the entity is represented as *moving on its own*, then it is **intransitive.**

If the subject *causes an entity to move*, then it is **transitive.**

**Examples:**

*spin*

| | |
|---|---|
| The ping-pong ball *spun* right off the table. | intransitive [spontaneous motion] |
| Xu Xin *spins* the ball in many different directions. | transitive [caused motion] |

*slide*

| | |
|---|---|
| Why do glasses *slide* across the counter when they are wet? | intransitive [spontaneous motion] |
| If I am not in my office, please *slide* your paper under the door. | transitive [caused motion] |

### 6.4.2.2 Verbs of Cognition and Perception

This category of meaning relates to the processes by which we come to understand or know things. What follows is an inventory of some verbs that fit within this category. Meaning distinctions for

164  *Verbs*

such verbs might involve certainty vs. uncertainty (e.g., *know* or *believe* vs. *guess, surmise, theorize*, or *assume*), various stages that unfold in the process of knowing or coming to know (e.g., *understand, realize, solve, identify, synthesize, differentiate, predict*), the particular perspectives or stances on the part of the speaker or writer (e.g., *contrast, evaluate, criticize, argue*), and ways of knowing through sensory perception (e.g., *perceive, feel, see, hear, smell*, and *taste*).

*6.4.2.3 Reporting Verbs*

This category of meaning relates to the process by which information is conveyed through one's own words or the words of others, be it orally or in writing. Meaning distinctions here involve modalities or mediums through which communication takes place (e.g., *say, write, text, email, post, blog, broadcast*), processes of discovery and communication (e.g., *depict, illustrate, explore, observe, investigate*), and particular perspectives or stances of the speaker or writer (e.g., *suggest, state, claim, hypothesize, oppose, question, ask, argue, reject, call into question, doubt, wonder, declare* (Celce-Murcia & Larsen-Freeman, 1999, pp. 702–709; Quirk et al., 1985, p. 1181).

Here are some more examples of reporting verbs:

> say, tell, write, text, describe, depict, declare, insist, doubt wonder, ask, oppose, support, call into question, refute, reject, challenge, define, posit, assume, explore, observe, investigate, inform, point out, discuss, broadcast, announce, email, post, blog.

Reporting verbs are crucial to academic writing. They are required in contexts of citations and references to other scholars' work (Hyland, 1999, 2002, 2014). Hyland (2014, p. 118) categorizes reporting verbs commonly used in academic articles into three main (but not watertight) groups, based on the activity they refer to:

1  Research (real-world) acts: Verbs that represent experimental activities carried out in the real world, e.g., *observe, discover, notice, analyze*.
2  Cognition acts: Verbs that represent the researcher's mental processes, e.g., *believe, suspect, assume, view*.
3  Discourse acts: Verbs that focus on the verbal expression of the previous two acts, e.g., *report, describe, ascribe, hypothesize*.

Some reporting verbs are unique to informal oral narratives; for example, *go* and *be like* are used in a variety of English dialects, including American English (Blyth et al., 1990), Glasgow English (Macauley, 2001); British English (Tagliamonte & Hudson, 1999), and Canadian English (Tagliamonte & D'Arcy, 2004).

**Example:**

> At the beach the other day, this really cute lifeguard comes up to us. Outa nowhere and **he goes**, "Have you girls seen a miniature white poodle anywhere? She got away from her owner and ran this way." And we **were** *like*: "No, but if we do see the poodle, we will be sure to call you. Can you give us your cell phone number?"

*6.4.2.4 Similarities of Action: Differences by Degree, by Specialized Activities*

This final category of verb meaning that we address here involves similarities of actions that are distinguished based on degree of intensity (typically following a general continuum of intensity, from low to high or manner of action) and verbs that belong to specialized activities, from cooking to lawn care. As you work through the following list, try to imagine how the more specific verbs in the right-hand column enhance the meanings of the very general verbs in the left-hand column.

| General | Degree of intensity: low → high; manner |
|---|---|
| eat: | nibble, bite, taste, peck at, gobble, devour, inhale |
| drink: | sip, nip, nurse, swallow, slurp, down, guzzle, inhale |
| laugh: | chuckle, giggle, snicker, guffaw, whoop, scream, shriek |
| cry: | weep, tear up, snivel, whimper, sob, lament, howl, wail |
| sing: | hum, chant, serenade, croon, warble, belt out |
| write: | jot down, note, scribble, scrawl, author, compose, record |
| read: | peruse, glance, scan, see, study, devour |
| break: | crack, chip, splinter, tear, fracture, burst, shatter, smash, demolish |
| put: | lay, place, apply, insert, inlay, install, plant, stack, pile, nail, rivet, deposit |
| speak: | tell, express, describe, opine, whisper, blurt out, bark, growl, gab, yak, gossip |

**Specialized**

| Activities | Verbs |
|---|---|
| cook: | boil, parboil, bake, broil, fry, panfry, sauté, grill, barbecue |
| cut: | [for food] dice, chop, slice, julienne, mince, cube, quarter, half |
| draw: | sketch, copy, paint, illustrate, caricature, design, outline, pencil, draft |
| build: | construct, erect, manufacture, produce, fabricate, assemble, manufacture |
| say: | [figurative] bark, meow, chirp, tweet, snort, chortle, giggle, roar |
| perform: | act, mime, impersonate, portray, emote, parody, characterize, enact, play |
| lawn care: | cut, mow, trim, edge, fertilize, mulch |

\*\*\*\*\*\*\*\*

## PRACTICE WITH DATA ANALYSIS: PUTTING IT ALL TOGETHER

1  The opening cartoon for this chapter depicts a girl having a heart-to-heart talk with her teddy bear. The text goes like this: "I love you and enjoy our time together, but I'm still young and I've decided to start seeing other bears."

Are the verbs used in the caption transitive or intransitive verbs—*love, enjoy, see*? How do you know? Explain your answer using the concepts we have provided in this chapter.

Think about the meaning of the verb *see*. Conduct an internet- and/or dictionary-based study of the scope of meaning of the verb *see*.

How many different meanings for this verb do you find? Are they dynamic? Transitive? Intransitive? Can you find a common semantic thread that connects most, if not all, of the meanings associated with the verb *see*? Explain.

2  This next cartoon (Figure 6.2) involves the use of the verb *sound* in its caption:

One goldfish says to another goldfish in their fishbowl, "What cellphone service are you using? It *sounds* like you're talking under water."

166  *Verbs*

"What cellphone service are you using?
It sounds like you're talking under water!"

*Figure 6.2* "What cellphone service are you using? It sounds like you're talking under water!"
© Randy Glasbergen. Reproduced with permission of Glasbergen Cartoon Service.

What is the source of humor?

Which category does this use of the verb *sound* belong to? Be specific and explain your answer in detail.

Here are some other uses of the same verb *to sound*. Determine whether each use of the verb belongs to the same category as in the cartoon or different categories. Explain.

- "Erin Brockovich *Sounded* the Alarm on Flint a Year Ago. Why Didn't' Anyone Listen?" (Stuart, 2016)
- "The shot swished through the [basketball] hoop just as the buzzer *sounded*." (McCluskey, 2016)

Think about this verb *sound*. Similar to your study on *see*, conduct an internet- and/or dictionary-based analysis of *sound*, as it occurs in English as a *noun*, a *verb*, and an *adjective*. Are all of the instances of the word *sound* related? If so, how? If not, why not? You'll need to investigate the etymology of the words patterning separately as nouns, verbs, and adjectives.

3. Have a look at **perception verbs** used in context as **perception copulas (i.e., linking verbs), dynamic verbs**, or **stative verbs**. For dynamic and stative verbs, also determine whether they are used **transitively** or **intransitively**.

    *Taste*

    **Perception copula**
    I bought a new brand of coffee today, and it <u>*tastes*</u> stronger than my regular brand.

    **Transitive**
    *Taste* <u>our pretzels</u>. We are giving out free samples.

    *Smell*
    [now you make up your own example sentences for this verb based on the following categories]

    **Perception copula** with the verb *smell* (write your example in the line below)

    _____

**Transitive** use of the verb *smell* (your example)

___

**Intransitive** use of the verb *smell* (We provide an example here.)
You need to change your socks everyday or **your feet** might *smell*.

*Feel*
[now you make up your own example sentences for this verb based on the following categories]

**Perception copula** with the verb *feel* (your example)

___

**Transitive** use of the verb *feel* (your example)

___

**Intransitive** use of the verb *feel* (We provide an example here.)
Are you *feeling* well? You look a little pale.

4   Read the following opening lines of the essay "The Renegade" by Charles Simic (2007).

> As **the curtain** *goes up*, **I**'m *sitting* naked on the potty in my grandfather's backyard in a little village in Serbia. **The year** *is* 1940. **I** *look* happy. **It**'s a nice summer day full of sunlight, although **Hitler** *had* already *occupied* most of Europe. **I** *have* no idea, of course, that **he and Stalin** *are hatching* an elaborate plot to *make* me an American poet. **I** *love* the neighbor's dog, whose name *is* Toza. **I** *run after* him *carrying* my potty in my hand, wanting to *pull* his tail, but **he** won't *let* me.
>
> (Simic, 2007)

The verbs are marked in italics, though this time, the linking verbs are not underlined. The NP subjects (noun phrases and pronouns) are marked in bold. Make a list of the following constructions:

- NP subject + linking verb + noun/adjective
- NP subject + verb (for intransitive verbs)
- NP subject + verb + affected entity (for transitive verbs)
- NP subject + verb + affected entity + MORE (for complex transitives)

Of these, which do you feel encode lower agency? Which do you feel encode higher agency? How does this affect the imagery portrayed in these opening lines? What sort of information or detail is backgrounded? What is foregrounded? How is this backgrounding/foregrounding achieved through the grammar of verbs?

Think about the use of the verb *hatch* in the Simic quote above. In what contexts do you typically see the verb? That is, what is a common subject for the verb *hatch*?

In Chapter 5, we asked you to think about this proverb:
   DON'T COUNT YOUR CHICKENS BEFORE THEY *HATCH*.
Is *hatch* used **transitively** or **intransitively** in this proverb? How do you know?

168  *Verbs*

Here is how *hatch* was used in the Simic (2007) excerpt:

> I have no idea, of course, that he and Stalin are *hatching* an elaborate plot to make me an American poet.

What does *hatch* mean here? Is it used **transitively** or **intransitively**?

5   Look at the following three quotes about music from Brainyquote.com (Music Quotes, n.d.). *Music* (or the pronoun *it* referring to music) is the NP subject of all sentences in these quotations:

- Plato:

    **Music** *is* a moral law. It *gives* soul to the universe, wings to the mind, flight to the imagination, and charm and gaiety to life and to everything.

- Hand Christian Andersen:

    Where words fail, **music** *speaks*.

- Bono:

    **Music** can *change* the world because **it** can *change* people.

How is music described in each? Which of the three quotations do you like the best or do you relate to the most? Why?

Now, let's look at the verbs. Are they appearing as **linking** verbs, **stative** verbs, or **dynamic** verbs? Make a list of the verbs, and categorize them according to this initial broad distinction. As always, be sure to include the subject, the affected entity (if there is one), and the recipient (if there is one) as you work with each verb.

For the dynamic verbs, indicate which are used **transitively**. Are any verbs **ditransitive verbs**? Which? Which are used **intransitively**?

Do you detect any difference from the point of view of **agency** and in how music is described in the three quotations? Does the concept of **agency** seem to affect how you interpret these quotations?

6   As we know, many verbs can be used both **transitively** and **intransitively**. Some motion verbs only function **intransitively** (e.g., *come*, *go*). Most can function both **transitively** (evoking caused motion) and **intransitively** (evoking spontaneous motion). The meanings of the verbs and how one imagines the actions depicted by those verbs used transitively or intransitively change significantly. **Intransitive** scenes with motion verbs typically evoke a type of self-propelled motion across or through an expanse of concrete space, air, or water.

### Motion verbs — Intransitive uses — two components (NP SUBJ + verb)

| | |
|---|---|
| *swim* | We *swim* every day in the summer. |
| *jump* | Forty-five-year-old Sergio Perez *jumped* into the fire to save his son. |
| *run* | If you *run* fast, you can still catch your bus. |
| *walk* | People say it is bad luck if you *walk* under a ladder. |

*Figure 6.3* Icon meaning "Walk Your Bike"

## Motion verbs — Transitive uses — three components (NP SUBJ + verb + affected entity)

| | |
|---|---|
| *swim* | **Gertrude Ederle** *swam* the English Channel in 1926. |
| *jump* | In checkers, **you** can *jump* your opponent and take the piece. |
| *run* | Do you know **who** *is running* the Environmental Protection Agency? |
| *walk* | This icon (Figure 6.3) means WALK YOUR BIKE. |

In the following excerpt from the *Tampa Bay News*, you'll learn about how to avoid getting stung by a stingray. This passage contains a number of **manner of motion verbs** (e.g., *sprint, slow down, shuffle*).

> You might *sprint* to the beach, but be sure to *slow down* and start *shuffling* as soon as your feet *hit* the water.

> The warm currents of the Gulf of Mexico *attract* more than tourists to the beaches of Pinellas County. Summer *is* stingray season, which means it*'s* time to *do* the stingray shuffle. The venomous barbs in their whiplike tails *are* painful if an unsuspecting beachgoer *kicks* or *steps on* one.
> (Carroll, 2013)

Which verbs are **linking verbs**? Which are **dynamic**?
Are the **dynamic verbs** being used **transitively** or **intransitively**? How do you know?
How about the manner of motion verbs? Are *sprint, slow down,* and *shuffle* being used **transitively** or **intransitively**? How do you know?

Look at Figure 6.4 on the next page. Is *shuffle* being used **transitively** or **intransitively**?

7 Verbs from nouns

 a In this chapter, we introduced a number of nouns that now function as verbs—from common nouns like *to shell, to water,* and *to hammer*. The proper noun Bork has evolved into a verb, *bork*, just like Bogart has evolved into *bogart*. There are many other instances of how nouns become verbs in English public discourse. We will give you a few examples:

 • Read the article by Jon Hird "Do You Salad or Sandwich? The Verbing of English" (Hird, 2013).

170  *Verbs*

*Figure 6.4* Sign, "Shuffle Your Feet for Stingrays."

Photograph taken by jlwelsh. © 2008 by jlwelsh. Retrieved from www.flickr.com/photos/jlwelsh/3310386903 on July 10, 2017, and reproduced under the Creative Commons Attribution Generic 2.0 license.

- There is an advertising slogan for Geico Insurance that goes like this:
  ANYONE CAN GEICO
- What do you think this slogan means?

Can you find other examples of this noun-to-verb phenomenon in your readings and/or internet searches?

  b  Investigate the origin of the verbs *macgyver* (from the TV show) and *bogart* (from classic films). What were the background issues that caused these proper nouns to become verbs? Do you know of any other proper nouns (referring to people) that have also become verbs in English? Have you found the use of the name Steve Harvey as a verb in any of your searches? What does this verb mean, and what was the situational background that led to its becoming a verb?

  c  The following passage is from the children's book *Amelia Bedelia* (Parish & Siebel, 1963, pp. 6–22). Amelia Bedelia is starting her first day of work as a housekeeper, employed by the wealthy couple Mr. and Mrs. Rogers. On her first day, Mrs. Rogers was not able to be there, so she left a note with a list of things for Amelia Bedelia to do while she was gone. Here is a snippet from this part of the book:

  "Now let's see what this list says," Amelia Bedelia read,

  *Change the towels in the green bathroom.*

  Amelia Bedelia found the green bathroom. "Those towels are very nice. Why *change* them?" she thought. . . . Amelia Bedelia got some scissors. She snipped a little here and a little there. And she *changed* those towels. . . .

  She looked at her list again.

  *Dust the furniture.*

  "Did you ever hear tell of such a silly thing. At my house, we undust the furniture. But to each his own way." Amelia Bedelia took one last look at the bathroom. She saw a big box with the words *Dusting Powder* on it.

"Well, look at that. A special powder to dust with!"

So Amelia Bedelia dusted the furniture. [The illustration shows Amelia Bedelia sprinkling white powder all over the furniture.] "That should be dusty enough. My, how nice it smells."

(Parish & Siebel, 1963, pp. 6–22)

What happened? What did Mrs. Rogers *really* mean for Amelia Bedelia to do with the towels and the furniture? How did Amelia Bedelia interpret the instructions? Try and articulate why this sweet misunderstanding occurred, using the terms and concepts that we covered in this chapter.

8   Here is an excerpt from the website of the University of Texas MD Anderson Cancer Center.

   a   The MD Anderson Cancer Center's slogan is this: "Making Cancer History"

   What is the play on words here? How can you describe the wordplay and the multiple meanings behind this slogan using the concepts about nouns and verbs that you have learned throughout these chapters so far?

   b   The home page includes a testimonial by a cancer survivor:

   "I knew I would be in the very best hands, because I was going to MD Anderson. I'll never be able to repay my team for beating my cancer and for the life that it gave me and my family."

   Identify the verbs in the testimonial. Also identify the determiners and the pronouns. Does anything strike you about the uses of grammar here? For example, what verb types and meanings are used—transitive, intransitive, ditransitive? What does the verb *go* mean in this excerpt? What nouns are preceded by the determiner *my*? Which pronoun other than *I* is used here to designate a human referent or group of referents?

   Taking into account the entire home page of this medical facility, think about how grammar works to draw readers (and prospective clients/patients) in and make them want to learn more about their practices, their services, and their success stories?

   Also, think about how determiners work to describe various illnesses (e.g., the flu, the chicken pox, my cancer). Note in particular how the cancer survivor quoted previously refers to the issue of *beating my cancer* rather than *beating cancer*. How does the reference to this disease change by virtue of the possessive determiner *my*?

## COMMON ERRORS, BUMPS, AND CONFUSIONS

Identify the errors or "bumps" in the following sentences or paragraphs. Use the concepts and terminology that you learned in this and other chapters to articulate what might be grammatically or pragmatically problematic. Suggest ways that each can be re-written more clearly and more accurately. (Note: While all bumps do involve some element of verbs and verb meanings, they are not limited to only that.)

1   Today, I want to talk something about the global warning.

2   The author argues in this essay.

3   My manager at work means really good to me.

4   We write because we need to express ourselves and influence to others.

5   In my opinion, the internet could occur a big dispute. It might not happened, but the internet could occur a conflict between some groups.

6   My ideas no had supporting information, I took out.

7   I became realize there's a big gap between my father's thoughts and mines.

8   My parents never impacted to me in a negative way.

## SUGGESTED ACTIVITIES

1   Have you ever heard the following saying?

> "Rosa sat so that Martin could walk; Martin walked so that Obama could run; Obama ran so that our children could fly."

The subject in each clause is the first or last name of an important figure in US history. Who is each person—what is their full name?

> [We will start you off: Rosa = Rosa Parks]

Also think about the conceptual meanings of each of the verbs (*sit, walk, run, fly*). Are they transitive or intransitive?

How do these verbs evoke the historical importance associated with each individual? Are the verbs used figuratively or literally? Do they involve agency?

Once you've determined who the referents are and what each historical figure did, explain the meaning of this saying in full detail.

2   Let's think about some helpful household tips. For example, how do you keep a peeled apple fresh to be used later in a salad? Or, if you accidentally spilled coffee on a white cotton shirt, how do you remove the stain? What kinds of advice would you give for these situations?

The following example is from Epicurious.com about how to keep peeled apples fresh. Using the list after the excerpt, fill in the blanks with the most fitting verb. Compare your choice with the original piece using this link:

www.epicurious.com/expert-advice/how-to-keep-apples-from-turning-brown-article.

### "How to Prevent An Apple from Turning Brown"

> _____ 1/8 teaspoon of salt into one cup of water, ____ your apple slices, ___ them ___ for a few minutes, then ___ them. ___ the slices a quick rinse in fresh water after you ___ them, so your fruit won't ___ salty.
>
> (Prakash, 2015)

[Verbs: drain, let, give, dissolve, soak, drain, taste, add]

As you work through this exercise, think about verbs like *drain*, *soak*, and *dissolve*. Can each be used both transitively and intransitively? Give additional examples to illustrate.

How is the verb *give* used in this passage? How would you characterize the construction that includes the verb *give*? Give _____ _____.

Do you have a household tip or hack?

Prepare a presentation in which you demonstrate the tip or hack to your classmates.

Think about the vocabulary that you'll need to describe your tip, especially nouns, determiners, pronouns, and verbs. Try to use accurate word choices throughout.

Here are a few more suggestions that you can use as you work with this exercise:

- www.wikihow.com/Separate-an-Egg
- www.wikihow.com/Remove-a-Coffee-Stain-from-a-Cotton-Shirt
- www.youtube.com/playlist?list=PLrIRP14xXUYBx66hYaegHH17WcEGQH-HM

3  My kind of hero

Do you have a favorite superhero character? Who is it? What is his/her everyday identity vs. the superhero identity? How did the person become a superhero? What is the superpower?

For starters, we've provided the following sample, leaving the verbs blank for practice. After you've written your own superhero description, you can design a follow-up exercise for other members in your class by leaving the verbs blank. You can provide options for your classmates, as we have done, or you can leave the possibilities open.

> Doctor Strange ___ a talented neurosurgeon who ____ pride in his hands that can _____ the most delicate brain surgery. One day, a car accident completely _____ his hands. He no longer can perform surgery. He ___ in despair and ____ the world over, hoping for an impossible cure. By a series of strange events, he _____ he can _____ his inner energy and turn it magically into a superpower.

[Verbs: searches, perform, discovers, destroys, is, control, finds himself, takes]
(Of course, many other verbs are also possible.)

As you work with this passage, also think about collocations and pay attention to verbs and nouns that typically occur together—for example, *take pride in*, *perform surgery*, *search the world over*. Pay attention to these kinds of collocations in your daily reading and language study. Because they occur so commonly, we often take these for granted as actual collocations.

4  Work with the transcripts (and audio recordings) in the Michigan Corpus of American Spoken English (MICASE): http://quod.lib.umich.edu/cgi/c/corpus/corpus?c=micase;page=simple

Pay attention to the opening segments in which the individual teachers and/or assistants introduce themselves. Transcribe five segments of self-introduction discourse.

Analyze the self-introduction discourse with a particular focus on the types of verbs each speaker is using (copular verbs, dynamic verbs, stative verbs/transitive, intransitive, ditransitive, complex transitive).

How does each speaker describe him/herself? What sorts of personal accomplishments does each speaker highlight in their self-introductions beyond a stative description of who they are?

Write your own self-introduction. Imagine that you will be introducing yourself to new colleagues, classmates, co-workers, or fellow club members. Provide information about yourself in a way that is relevant to your group of addressees as well as engaging, grammatically accurate, and pragmatically appropriate Be sure to indicate who you are and relevant details concerning why you are there, as well as indicating a few personal accomplishments that your audience will be able to relate to.

## Academic References

Allerton, D. J. (1978). The notion of "givenness" and its relation to presupposition and theme. *Lingua, 44,* 133–168.

Blyth, C., Recktenwald, Jr., S., & Wang, J. (1990). I'm like, "Say what?!": A new quotative in American oral narrative. *American Speech,* 65, 215–227.

Bowerman, M., & Brown, P. (Eds.). (2008). *Crosslinguistic perspectives on argument structure: Implications for learnability.* New York and London: Erlbaum.

Celce-Murcia, M., & Larsen-Freeman, D. (1999). *The grammar book: An ESL/EFL teacher's course.* Boston, MA: Heinle & Heinle.

Comrie, B. (1976). *Aspect: An introduction to the study of verbal aspect and related problems* (Cambridge textbooks in linguistics). Cambridge: Cambridge University Press.

Croft, W. (1994). Voice: Beyond control and affectedness. In B.A. Fox & P.J. Hopper (Eds.) *Voice: Form and function* (pp. 89–118). Amsterdam and Philadelphia: John Benjamins.

Goldberg, A. E. (2006). *Constructions at work: The nature of generalization in language.* Oxford: Oxford University Press.

Halliday, M. (1967). Notes on transitivity and theme in English, Part I. *Journal of Linguistics, 3,* 37–81.

Hopper, P. J., & Thompson, S. A. (1980). Transitivity in grammar and discourse. *Language,* 56(2), 251–299.

Huddleston, R. & Pullum, G. K. (2002). *The Cambridge grammar of the English language.* New York: Cambridge University Press.

Hyland, K. (1999). Academic attribution: Citation and the construction of disciplinary knowledge. *Applied Linguistics,* 20(3), 341–367.

Hyland, K. (2002). Authority and invisibility: Authorial identity in academic writing. *Journal of Pragmatics,* 34(8), 1091–1112.

Hyland, K. (2014). Activity and evaluation: Reporting practices in academic writing. In J. Flowerdew (Ed.), *Academic discourse.* New York: Routledge.

Lakoff, G. (1977). Linguistic Gestalts. In *Papers from the thirteenth regional meeting of the Chicago Linguistics Society 13* (pp. 236–287). Chicago, IL.

Lakoff, G. (1987). *Women, fire, and dangerous things: What categories reveal about the mind.* Chicago: University of Chicago Press.

Lakoff. G. (1990). *Concept, image, and symbol: The cognitive basis of grammar.* Berlin and New York: Mouton de Gruyter.

Langacker, R.W. (1990). Subjectification. *Cognitive Linguistics,* 1(1), 5–38.

Langacker, R.W. (1991). *Foundations of cognitive grammar: Vol. 2. Descriptive application.* Stanford, CA: Stanford University Press.

Leech, G. N. (1971). *Meaning and the English verb.* London: Longman.

Levin, B. (1993). *English verb classes and alternations.* Chicago: University of Chicago Press.

Levin, B., & Rappaport Hovav, M. (1995). *Unaccusativity: At the syntax-lexical semantics interface.* Cambridge, MA: The MIT Press.

Li, C. N. (1986). Direct and indirect speech: A functional study. In F. Coulmas (Ed.), *Direct and indirect speech* (pp. 29–45). New York: Mouton de Gruyter.

Lucy, J. A. (1993). *Reflexive language: Reported speech and metapragmatics.* New York and Cambridge: Cambridge University Press

Macauley, R. (2001). You're like "Why not?" The quotative expressions of Glasgow adolescents. *Journal of Sociolinguistics,* 5(10), 3–21.

Michaelis, L. A. (2011). Stative by construction. *Linguistics,* 49, 1359–1400.

Palmer, F. R. (1988). *The English verb.* London: Longman.

Quirk, R., Greenbaum, S., Leech, G., & Svartvik, J. (1985). *A comprehensive grammar of the English language.* London and New York: Longman.

Schleppegrell, M. J., Achugar, M., & Oteíza, T. (2004). The grammar of history: enhancing content-based instruction through a functional focus on language. *TESOL Quarterly,* 38(1), 67–93.

Silverstein, M. (1985). The culture of language in Chinookan narrative texts; or, on saying that . . . in Chinook. In J. Nichols & A. Woodbury (Eds.), *Grammar inside and outside the clause: Some approaches to theory from the field* (pp. 132–171). Cambridge: Cambridge University Press.

Slobin, D. I. (1996). Two ways to travel: Verbs of motion in English and Spanish. In M. Shibatani & S. A. Thompson (Eds.), *Grammatical constructions: Their form and meaning* (pp. 195–220). Oxford: Clarendon Press.
Slobin, D. I. (2004). The many ways to search for a frog: Linguistic typology and the expression of motion events. In S. Strömqvist & L. Verhoeven (Eds.), *Relating events in narrative: Typological and contextual perspectives* (pp. 219–257). Mahwah, NJ: Lawrence Erlbaum Associates.
Tagliamonte, S. A., & D'arcy, A. (2004). He's like, she's like: The quotative system in Canadian Youth. *Journal of Sociolinguistics, 8*, 493–514.
Tagliamonte, S., & Hudson, R. (1999). Be like et al. beyond America: The quotative system in British and Canadian youth. *Journal of Sociolinguistics, 3*, 147–172.
Talmy, L. (1985). Lexicalization patterns: Semantic structure in lexical forms. In T. Shopen (Ed.), *Language typology and lexical description: Vol. 3. Grammatical categories and the lexicon* (pp. 36–149). Cambridge: Cambridge University Press.
Talmy, L. (1991). Path to realization: A typology of event conflation. *Proceedings of the Berkeley Linguistics Society, 17*, 480–519.
Talmy, L. (2000). *Toward a cognitive semantics: Vol. II. Typology and process in concept structuring.* Cambridge, MA: MIT Press.
Thompson, S. (1995). The iconicity of "dative shift" in English: Considerations from information flow in discourse. In M. E. Landsberg (Ed.), *Syntactic iconicity and linguistic freezes* (pp. 155–176). Berlin: Mouton de Gruyter.
Tsunoda, T. (1985). Remarks on transitivity. *Journal of Linguistics, 21*, 385–396.
Vendler, Z. (1967). *Linguistics in philosophy.* Ithaca, NY: Cornell University Press.
Wierzbicka, A. (1988). *The semantics of grammar.* Amsterdam: John Benjamins.
Yule, G., Mathis, T., & Hopkins, M. (1992). On reporting what was said. *ELT Journal, 46*(3).

## Data References

Carroll, L. (2013, June 7). Do the stingray shuffle to avoid nasty stings. *Tampa Bay Times.* Retrieved April 30, 2016, from www.tampabay.com/news/publicsafety/do-the-stingray-shuffle-to-avoid-nasty-stings/2125433
Derry, J. (2016, April 27). This guy figured out how to make butter taste more buttery [Web post]. Retrieved April 30, 2016, from https://munchies.vice.com/en/articles/this-guy-figured-out-how-to-make-butter-taste-more-buttery
Hird, J. (2013, March 5). Do you salad or sandwich? The verbing of English [Web post]. Oxford University Press English language teaching global blog. Retrieved April 30, 2016, from https://oupeltglobalblog.com/2013/03/05/do-you-salad-or-sandwich-the-verbing-of-english/
McCluskey, M. (2016, February, 24). Vanderbilt player sinks 80-foot buzzer-beater without even jumping. *Time.* Retrieved April 30, 2016, from http://time.com/4235860/vanderbilt-80-foot-buzzer-beater/
Music Quotes. (n.d.). Brainyquote.com. Retrieved April 30, 2016, from www.brainyquote.com/quotes/topics/topic_music.html
Osborne, M. P., & Murdocca, S. (1998). *Polar bears past bedtime (Magic tree house, no. 1).* New York: Random House Books for Young Readers.
Parish, P., & Siebel, F. (1963). *Amelia Bedelia.* New York: Harper & Row.
Prakash, S. (2015, February 29). The easiest ways to keep your apples from browning [Web post]. Retrieved November 1, 2016, from www.epicurious.com/expert-advice/how-to-keep-apples-from-turning-brown-article
Private Islands Online. (n.d.). Isle of Navaro. Retrieved May 6, 2017, from www.privateislandsonline.com/central-america/panama/isle-of-navaro
Redd, N. T. (2012). Antarctica: Facts about the coldest continent. Live science. Retrieved May 6, 2017, from www.livescience.com/21677-antarctica-facts.html
Setterfield, D. (2009). *The thirteenth tale.* New York: Double Day.
Simic, C. (2007, December 20). The renegade. *The New York Review of Books.* Retrieved April 30, 2016, from www.nybooks.com/articles/2007/12/20/the-renegade/

Stuart, T. (2016, February 1). Erin Brockovich sounded the alarm on Flint a year ago—Why didn't anyone listen? *Rolling Stone*. Retrieved April 30, 2016, from www.rollingstone.com/politics/news/erin-brockovich-sounded-the-alarm-on-flint-a-year-ago-why-didnt-anyone-listen-20160201

Tinker Crate. (n.d.). About us. Kiwi Crate. Retrieved April 30, 2016, from http://tinker.kiwicrate.com/about-us/

Tuscany looks, smells like heaven. (2001). *The Cedartown Standard*, *1*(4). Retrieved April 30, 2016, from https://news.google.com/newspapers?nid=365&dat=20010313&id=4qUkAAAAIBAJ&sjid=oD4DAAAAIBAJ&pg=3417,872145&hl=en

# 7 The Grammar of Time, Fact, Habit, Changeability, Permanence, Sequence, and Relevance in Discourse

Tense and Aspect

*Figure 7.1* "When you're trying to fall asleep, does it ever feel like your thumbs are still texting?"
© Randy Glasbergen. Reproduced with permission of Glasbergen Cartoon Service.

In Chapter 6, we discussed verbs and their functions and power in discourse. In this chapter, we introduce tense and aspect as features of grammar that infuse verbs with time reference and perspectival detail about states and events that verbs express.

Tense relates to the *time* of a situation or event. In English, there are three categories of grammar that establish a broad frame of basic time reference—present tense, past tense, and future—but only present tense and past tense are formed with morphological inflections (see Chapter 2). Future time is expressed with the modal *will* (see Chapter 8).

Aspect works within these temporal frames of time to provide additional detail revealing perspectives and viewpoints with respect to how those events, processes, and actions unfold; what relationship they have with their time of unfolding; and what relationship they have with other events and times within discourse (Bybee, 2008; Bybee et al., 1994; Comrie, 1976, 1985; Fenn, 1987; Hirtle, 1967; Hopper, 1982; Langacker, 2008; Leech, 1971; Radden & Dirven, 2007).

There are four grammaticalized aspects in English: simple, progressive, perfect, and perfect progressive. These four aspects interact with the three tenses to create 12 combinations of tense and aspect forms. That is, grammatical aspect and tense are inextricably interrelated. Later, we will discuss the 12 possible tense and aspect categories for English in more detail.

As you work through the various discussions of tense and aspect, also pay attention to the verbs and functional verb types from Chapter 6 (e.g., dynamic, stative, copular, transitive, intransitive, ditransitive, complex transitive).

## 7.1 Simple Aspect

**Conceptual meaning:** The event, condition, or situation is conceptualized as a complete whole, a bounded entity. The event is stable and not expected to change.

### 7.1.1 Simple Present Tense

**Simple present tense** indicates the following types of events:

- An event or situation that takes places in the here and now (or at the time of speaking/writing)
- An event or situation that is true now or is always true
- An event or situation that is characterized by **timelessness** (e.g., factual information)
- An event that occurs consistently (e.g., a habit)

#### 7.1.1.1 Simple Present Tense: Uses and Meanings (verbs are in italics)

SELF-INTRODUCTIONS

My name *is* Tina. I *come* from Barcelona, Spain. I *am* a physics teacher. I *am* married, and my husband and I *have* three sons. We *travel* to the US every summer, and we always *choose* a new city to visit.

DEFINITIONS

An escalator *is* a mechanized moving stairway. An escalator *is* similar to a conveyor belt, but *differs* in that it *is* on an incline and *has* a surface of stairs rather than a flat belt. Most escalators also *include* a handrail that *moves* in conjunction with the stairs.

("Abstract (hydraulic escalator)," 2016)

PHYSICAL PROPERTIES, TYPICAL CHARACTERISTICS

Protons *have* a positive charge, electrons *have* a negative charge.
Objects that *are* denser than water *sink*.
Pomegranates *contain* hundreds of edible seeds.
Water *boils* at 212°F or 100°C.
Some fraternal twins *look* identical.

EXPRESSIONS RELATING TO HABITUAL OCCURRENCES

The cuckoo *comes* out when the clock *strikes* 12:00.
When the pizza delivery *is* late, *are* the pizzas free?
Every time I *call* Apple Support, they only *keep* me on hold for a few minutes.

EXPRESSIONS DEPICTING FUTURE OCCURRENCES

> The opera production *moves* to Pittsburgh in June.
> Our exam *is* on Friday of next week.
> Tonight's fireworks show *begins* just after sunset.

CITATIONS WITH REPORTING VERBS IN ACADEMIC PAPERS (TARGET VERBS IN ITALICS AND UNDERLINED)

> As Du Bois (2007, p. 163) *notes*, "In taking a stance, the stancetaker (1) *evaluates* an object, (2) *positions* a subject (usually the self), and (3) *aligns* with other subjects."
> (Moore & Podesva, 2009, p. 448)

> As Scollon and Scollon *explain*, "When we are communicating with people who *are* very different from us, it *is* very difficult to know how to draw inferences about what they *mean*."
> (Kaur, 2011, p. 94)

BOOK REVIEWS: REPORTING VERBS AND SUMMARY VERBS (TARGET VERBS IN ITALICS AND UNDERLINED)

**Review of *Swing Time* by Zadie Smith**

> With *Swing Time*, Zadie Smith *identifies* the impossible contradiction all adults *are* asked to maintain—be true to yourself . . . be proud of your heritage, but don't be defined by it. She *frays* the cords that *keep* us tied to our ideas of who we *are*, to our careful self-mythologies. Some writers *name*, *organize*, and *contain*; Smith *lets* contradictions bloom, in all their frightening, uneasy splendor.
> (Quinn, 2016)

*7.1.1.2 Simple Present Tense: Forms*

REGULAR VERBS

The majority of English verbs are regular in the present tense. Note that the present tense is very sensitive to the notion of singularity and plurality in the third person, because only the third-person singular form is marked with a different morpheme, *-s*. The rest of the forms do not change.

|  | **singular** | **plural** |
|---|---|---|
| first person | I walk | we walk |
| second person | you walk | you walk |
| third person | he, she, it **walks** | they walk |

For third-person singular, if the verb ends with *o*, *sh*, *ch*, *zz*, *ss*, or *x*, instead of just adding *-s*, **add** *-es*.

| go | → | goes |
| flash | → | flashes |
| hatch | → | hatches |

| fizz | → | fizzes |
| gas | → | gasses (add another *s*) |
| bless | → | blesses |
| box | → | boxes |

If the verb ends with <u>consonant + y</u>, **change the *y* to an *i* and add -*es*.**

| try | → | tries |
| fly | → | flies |
| testify | → | testifies |

BUT <u>vowel + y</u> **does not change to *i*.**

| play | → | plays |
| buy | → | buys |

IRREGULAR VERBS: *BE* AND *HAVE*

*be*

|  | <u>singular</u> | <u>plural</u> |
| --- | --- | --- |
| first person | I **am** | we are |
| second person | you **are** | you are |
| third person | he, she, it **is** | they are |

*have*

|  | <u>singular</u> | <u>plural</u> |
| --- | --- | --- |
| first person | I **have** | we have |
| second person | you **have** | you have |
| third person | he, she, it **has** | they have |

## 7.1.2 Simple Past Tense

**Simple past tense indicates the following types of events or situations:**

- An event or situation that took place before now (or before the time of speech/writing), one time, multiple times, or as a regular cycle.
- An event, condition, or situation that has passed and is over and done with.
- A situation that was true in the past but is no longer true.

### 7.1.2.1 Simple Past Tense: Uses and Meanings

Note the following examples of **simple past tense** within discourse. Pay special attention to the verb types—for example, transitive/intransitive, dynamic/stative, agency—and how grammar is tied to genre, stance, position, and perspectives. (Verbs in the past tense are in italics.)

*Tense and Aspect* 181

EVENTS THAT OCCURRED IN THE PAST AND THAT ARE REPRESENTED AS BEING OVER

When you *called* Apple Support, how long *were* you on hold?
We *placed* heavy objects in the water and they *sank*.
The woman's name *was* Tina. She *came* from Barcelona, Spain.

OPENINGS OF STORIES, FOLK TALES, SCENE SETTINGS

**From the first paragraph of "The Happy Prince" by Oscar Wilde (1909):**

High above the city, on a tall column, *stood* the statue of the Happy Prince. He *was* gilded all over with thin leaves of fine gold. For eyes he *had* two bright sapphires, and a large red ruby *glowed* on his swordhilt.

(Wilde, 1909)

HISTORICAL DESCRIPTIONS, BIOGRAPHICAL INFORMATION FOR DECEASED PERSONS

**From "The 1994 Northridge Earthquake,"** *Los Angeles Daily News:*

The 1994 Northridge Earthquake on Jan. 17 *ripped* across the region and *rattled* 10 million Angelenos in what would be the costliest temblor in U.S. history. For roughly 10 horrifying seconds, the Southland *shuddered* into widespread urban collapse and chaos. It *took* years to rebuild from the nation's first earthquake that *struck* from directly beneath a metropolitan area.

(Bartholomew, 2014)

**From Walt Disney:**

Walter Elias "Walt" Disney *was* born on December 5, 1901, in Hermosa, Illinois. He and his brother Roy *co-founded* Walt Disney Productions, which *became* one of the best-known motion-picture production companies in the world. Disney *was* an innovative animator and *created* the cartoon character Mickey Mouse. He *won* 22 Academy Awards during his lifetime, and *was* the founder of theme parks Disneyland and Walt Disney World.

(Disney, n.d.)

NARRATIVES DESCRIBING PROCEDURAL EVENTS, STEPS TAKEN TO ACCOMPLISH SOMETHING

**"Narrative: Visiting a New School"**

As soon as we *arrived* at the school, we *met* the principal and office staff and *requested* a tour. One teacher, Mrs. Kostas, *came* to greet us. She *introduced* herself, *told* us a little more about the school, and *proceeded* to show us around. We *started* on the first floor and *visited* the science and language classrooms. Then, we *went* upstairs to the art and music rooms.

SCIENCE EXPERIMENT (E.G., LAB REPORTS): WHICH ICE CUBE MELTS FASTER?

**"Describing the Procedures to Answer This Question"**

First, we *put* one ice cube into two separate containers. We then *sprinkled* one teaspoon of table salt over the ice cube in one container. We *watched* as the ice cube with the salt on it

182  *Tense and Aspect*

*began* to melt. Using a thermometer, we *measured* the temperature in each container and *compared* the two results.

*7.1.2.2 Simple Past Tense: Forms*

REGULAR VERBS

Add the past tense inflectional morpheme *-ed* to change a verb into the past tense. Regardless of subject (first, second, or third person) or number (singular or plural), there is just one paste-tense form: **verb + -ed**.

|  | singular | plural |
|---|---|---|
| first person | I walked | we walked |
| second person | you walked | you walked |
| third person | he, she, it walked | they walked |
| want | → | wanted |
| call | → | called |
| need | → | needed |

If the verb ends with an *e*, then **simply add -d** for the past tense.

| receive | → | received |
|---|---|---|
| finalize | → | finalized |
| opine | → | opined |

If the verb ends with a *y*, **change the *y* to *i*** and then **add –ed**.

| try | → | tried |
|---|---|---|
| modify | → | modified |
| identify | → | identified |

IRREGULAR VERBS

There are many, as follows:

**Irregular verb *be***

|  | singular | plural |
|---|---|---|
| first person | I **was** | we **were** |
| second person | you **were** | you **were** |
| third person | he, she, it **was** | they **were** |

**Other Irregular Verbs**

Unlike the irregular verb be, the forms are all the same for first-, second-, and third-person plural and singular subjects.

Verbs relating to communication

| say | → | said |
|---|---|---|
| speak | → | spoke |

| | | |
|---|---|---|
| tell | → | told |
| read | → | read |
| write | → | wrote |
| teach | → | taught |

Verbs relating to cognition and thinking

| | | |
|---|---|---|
| think | → | thought |
| know | → | knew |
| understand | → | understood |
| find out | → | found out |

Verbs relating to motion

| | | |
|---|---|---|
| go | → | went |
| come | → | came |
| swim | → | swam |
| wind | → | wound |
| leave | → | left |
| run | → | ran |
| drive | → | drove |
| fall | → | fell |
| rise | → | rose |
| sit | → | sat |
| grind | → | ground |
| spin | → | spun |
| sink | → | sank |
| swing | → | swung |

Verbs relating to having and transporting

| | | |
|---|---|---|
| have | → | had |
| get | → | got |
| give | → | gave |
| hold | → | held |
| keep | → | kept |
| take | → | took |
| bring | → | brought |
| buy | → | bought |
| sell | → | sold |
| pay | → | paid |
| find | → | found |
| lose | → | lost |
| win | → | won |

Verbs relating to ingestion

| | | |
|---|---|---|
| eat | → | ate |
| drink | → | drank |

184  *Tense and Aspect*

Verbs relating to change of state

become → became
grow → grew
get → got

Verbs relating to creation and destruction

make → made
draw → drew
build → built
break → broke
tear → tore

Verbs relating to perception

see → saw
hear → heard
feel → felt

## 7.1.3 Simple Future Time (With Will)

**Simple future time (with *will*) points to the following types of events or stances:**

- An event or situation that has not yet taken place but is *expected* to.
- A stance of strong prediction/determination/intended outcome.

Note: English has a **present tense** and a **past tense** where verbal morphology will overtly indicate tense (i.e., third-person singular inflection -*s* for regular present tense verbs and past tense inflection -*ed* for regular past tense verbs). English does not have a formal or morphologically marked future tense. English marks future time using the modal *will* and other constructions (Biber et al., 1999; Declerck, 2006; Givón, 1993; Larsen-Freeman & Celce-Murcia, 2016; Quirk et al., 1985; Yule, 1998). As we have noted and will see later in more detail, *present tense* can also be used to talk about the future. (For other markers of future time, see Chapter 8 on modality.)

### 7.1.3.1 Simple Future Time: Uses and Meanings

Here are a number of examples of how **simple future time** reference (with *will*) is used within discourse (*will* + <u>*Verb*</u> constructions are in italics—the main verb is underlined):

**Future plans:**

We *will <u>discuss</u>* the budget at our next meeting.
*Will* you <u>*be*</u> home in the morning?

I'*ll email* you the questionnaire as soon as it's ready.

## Predictions:

That sweater *will* probably not *be* enough to keep you warm.
The storm *will move* across the region later this afternoon.
Here are 25 tips that *will make* you a better graphic designer.

## Requests, commands, requirements:

| | |
|---|---|
| *Will* you *read* my essay and let me know how it sounds? | [request] |
| *Will* you *tell* Abella that I stopped by? | [request] |
| Students *will* complete all assignments before the due date. | [command, requirement] |

## Official promises, oaths, commitments to future actions:

### "Hippocratic Oath" (promises to maintain proper conduct for physicians) (excerpt)

I *will prevent* disease whenever I can, for prevention is preferable to cure. I *will remember* that I remain a member of society, with special obligations to all my fellow human beings, those sound of mind and body as well as the infirm.

("Bioethics," n.d.)

### "The US Presidential Oath of Office" (excerpt)

I do solemnly swear that I *will* faithfully *execute* the Office of President of the United States, and *will* to the best of my ability, *preserve, protect* and *defend* the Constitution of the United States.

### 7.1.3.2 Simple Future Time: Forms

English uses the modal *will* + Verb as one of many possible forms to express future time:

### Verb: *walk*

| | singular | plural |
|---|---|---|
| first person | I *will* walk | we *will* walk |
| second person | you *will* walk | you *will* walk |
| third person | he, she, it *will* walk | they *will* walk |

### Verb: *practice*

| | singular | plural |
|---|---|---|
| first person | I *will* practice | we *will* practice |
| second person | you *will* practice | you *will* practice |
| third person | he, she, it *will* practice | they *will* practice |

*7.1.4 Special Uses of Simple Present Tense: Marking the Future and the Past*

*7.1.4.1 Present Tense Marking Future Events*

**Simple present tense** is also used to discuss **future events**, particularly events or situations that will take place or hold in the near future (as long as the future time reference is implicitly or explicitly clear in the discourse). In the following examples, simple present is used with expressions relating to scheduled events in a designated future time:

> Our train *leaves* Paris at 7:49 a.m. this morning, and we *arrive* in Lyon at 9:56.
> The Planning Committee *meets* again next Thursday in Sparks 200.
> Let's have lunch tomorrow when your classes *are* over.
> Old Navy's sale *ends* today at 8:00 p.m.

*7.1.4.2 Present Tense Marking Past Events: The Historical Present/The Dramatic Present*

In addition to expressing present and future time, present tense is also used to indicate past events. The present tense evokes a sense of timelessness, whereby speakers and writers depict entities and events that are typically unchangeable and always (or almost always) "true." In this sense, the present tense can be used in **historical descriptions or representations of fact that essentially hold true**.

The **historical present** is exemplified in the following extract:

**From "This Day in History"**

> This Day in History (June 10): On this day in 1752, Benjamin Franklin *flies* a kite during a thunderstorm and *collects* a charge in a Leyden jar when the kite *is* struck by lightning.
>
> (history.com, n.d.)

[verbs: *flies, collects, is*—present tense]

The very next sentence and all sentences that follow this introductory discourse about Franklin's kite event of June 10, 1752, are in the past tense:

> Franklin b*ecame* interested in electricity in the mid-1740s, a time when much *was* still unknown on the topic, and *spent* almost a decade conducting electrical experiments.
>
> (history.com, n.d.)

[verbs: *became, was, spent*—past tense]

The historical present is also known as **dramatic present**, since it can serve to *dramatize* a past experience. It can take a past event and bring it into the forefront of the speaker's or writer's discourse. The historical present highlights the event, episode, or description and imbues it with a here-and-now-like vividness for the hearers and readers to relate to or envision as if it is currently unfolding (Declerck, 2006; Fludernik, 1991; Schlenker, 2004; Wolfson, 1979, 1982).

The **dramatic present** is exemplified in the following extract:

**Narrative of personal experience:**

**From "Horrible customer service"**

> I *booked* this place on Expedia with a $50.00 credit toward spa services. I *called* the day I *booked* . . . to confirm the spa credit and schedule [a massage] in advance. It

*was* confirmed. The place *looked* very nice in the pictures online at [the] website . . . and the reviews *seemed* good as well. However, when we *drove* up, we *were* shocked at the appearance outside. . . . We *went* to check in. The front desk lady *was* very nice, but **tells** me as I *check in* that they *moved* my massage [time]. Then I **ask** about the [$50.00] credit to double check. She *says* she *has* no knowledge of any such credit. . . . She ***proceeds*** to walk us to our hotel room and we ***run*** into the manager. <u>This is where it went all downhill.</u>

("Horrible customer service," n.d.)

[past tense: booked, called, was, looked, seemed, drove, were, went, was, went]
[present tense: tells, ask, says, has, proceeds, run, is]

**Narrative of personal experience:**

**Movie excerpt, "Happy Birthday, Darling," from *City Slickers***

((Every year, on September 8 at 5:15 a.m., Mitch receives a phone call from his mother as she recounts the details of when she gave birth to him. In the film, on the morning of Mitch's 40th birthday, we see the digital alarm clock change from 5:14 to 5:15. The phone rings, and here begins the narrative)).
((telephone rings))

Mitch: Hi Mom.

Mom: Ha ha ha ha. It*'s* September eighth, nineteen fifty two. We*'re driving* back from your Aunt Marsha. My water ***breaks***. Your father ***jumps*** the divider of the Sawmill River Parkway and ***races*** me to Doctors' Hospital. <u>And, ha ha ha ha at five sixteen out you came</u>. Ah . . . Happy Birthday darling.

(Ganz & Mandel, 1991)

[present tense: is → 's, are → 're, breaks, jumps, races]
[past tense: *came*]

In each of these personal narrative excerpts, there is a shift in tense, either from past to present and back to past again ("Horrible Customer Service") or from present to past ("Happy Birthday, Darling"). What effect do these tense shifts create in the telling of the events in question? At what point(s) in the stories do the shifts in tense occur? Accompanying these shifts in tense marking, do you sense any shifts in **stance** or varying degrees of emotional responses that the author is conveying at the very moment of the tense shift in each episode?

### 7.1.5 Subject-Verb Agreement

Subject-verb agreement refers to the basic grammatical rule that the form of the verb must match the subject of its clause or sentence. Subject-verb agreement is often abbreviated as SVA.

SVA is only grammatically obvious in English with present tense forms for all verbs and with past tense forms of only the verb *be* (*was* vs. *were*). SVA is especially noticeable in the following cases:

**Present tense**

- Third-person singular regular verbs—requiring *-s* (or *-es*, *-ies*)
- **Irregular verbs** *be* (*am*, *is*, *are*) and *have* (*have*, *has*)

**Past tense**

- *be* (*was, were*)

The following examples illustrate the concept of SVA within a number of sentences about birds. We have highlighted the subject NPs and verbs so that they stand out.

**Regular verbs**

| | |
|---|---|
| **A bird** *uses* its beak to eat. | [third-person singular *-s* on the verb] |
| **Birds** *use* their beaks to eat. | [third-person plural, no *-s* on the verb] |
| **A seagull** *catches* fish with its beak. | [third-person singular *-es*] |
| **Seagulls** *catch* insects when they fly. | [third-person plural, no *-s*] |
| **The Canada goose** *flies* up to 55 mph. | [third-person singular *-s*] |
| **Canada geese** *fly* in V formation. | [third-person plural, no *-s*] |
| **The barn swallow** *migrates* to South America. | [third-person singular *-s*] |
| **Barn swallows** *migrate* back to San Juan Capistrano. | [third-person plural, no *-s*] |

**Irregular verbs (*have* and *be*)**

| | |
|---|---|
| **The duck** *has* a bill instead of a beak. | [third-person singular *has*] |
| **Ducks** also *have* nostrils in **their** bills. | [third-person plural *have*] |
| **A hummingbird's** beak *is* longer than other birds' beaks. | [third-person singular *is*] |
| **Hummingbirds'** beaks *are* sharp. | [third-person plural *are*] |

Examples of SVA with third-person singular/plural be (was/were) in the past tense

**Irregular verb (*be*)**

| | |
|---|---|
| **The northern mockingbird** *was* the North Carolina state bird. | [third-person singular *was*] |
| **Northern mockingbirds** *were* high up in the branches. | [third-person plural *were*] |
| There *was* just **one dodo bird** left in 1681. | [third-person singular *was*]<br>Subject: one dodo bird—singular |
| There *were* still **some dodos** found near Mauritius. | [third-person plural *were*]<br>Subject: some dodos—plural |

Typically, SVA rules assume that a clause or sentence is grammatical or ungrammatical based on the appropriate choice of the verb form.

---

**Mini Review and Practice**

1. Read the following passages. The first is an excerpt from the biography *Who Was Rosa Parks?* The second is excerpted from the Troy University website about its Rosa Parks Museum in Montgomery, Alabama. Compare and contrast the ways in which grammar helps advance the discourse. That is, the verbs have been indicated in italics (the verb *be* is also underlined). Note the tense of the italicized verbs. Are they past

or present? Why do you think that one document is written predominantly using past tense forms, while the other predominantly uses present tense forms?

Hint: Think about the concept of *genre*. What is the genre of the first excerpt [predominantly past tense]? What is the genre of the second excerpt [predominantly present tense]?

a   Past tense [the verb *be* is also underlined]

**"Who Was Rosa Parks?"**

> Every morning, Rosa Parks *walked* to school. Every afternoon, she *walked* back home again. There <u>*was*</u> no school bus to her school. . . . Often she *saw* a big, yellow school bus roll past her, but the bus never *stopped* for her. All the children inside <u>*were*</u> white. . . . Rosa <u>*was*</u> black.
>
> Rosa *grew up* in Pine Level, Alabama. At that time in the South, black people and white people *led* separate lives. All of Rosa's friends and family <u>*were*</u> black. She hardly *knew* any white people. . . .
>
> The school for the white children <u>*was*</u> nicer, too. It *had* real glass panes in the windows. At Rosa's school, there <u>*was*</u> no glass, only shutters. Still, Rosa *knew* inside that she <u>*was*</u> as good as any white child. She <u>*was*</u> as good as anyone, and one day she would prove it.
>
> (McDonough, 2010, pp. 1–4)

b   Present tense [the verb *be* is also underlined]

**"Rosa Parks Museum"** (See www.youtube.com/watch?v=Ep2jUJklJ2Q for a video tour of this impressive historical museum.)

> The purpose of the Rosa Parks Museum <u>*is*</u> to uphold and interpret . . . materials related to the events and accomplishments of individuals associated with [the] Montgomery Bus Boycott. The Museum *includes* a permanent exhibit, a time machine, temporary exhibit space, archives . . . and [a] conference room. . . .
>
> The Museum <u>*is*</u> a major landmark in the revitalization of downtown Montgomery. . . . In the Rosa Parks Library & Museum Children's Wing, visitors *go* back in time . . . to discover that things don't just *happen*—people *make* things happen. . . .
>
> As visitors *enter* the Cleveland Avenue Time Machine, they *see* what they *think* <u>*is*</u> a standard 1955 Montgomery city bus. On closer inspection, they *discover* the vehicle *has* no wheels and indeed *appears* to be floating above a layer of violet-colored light.
>
> (Rosa Parks Museum, n.d.)

In addition to the verbs and the tenses used in each excerpt, also review what you have learned so far about the following parts of speech:

- Nouns (Chapter 3), NPs (Chapter 2), and pronouns (Chapter 5): How are the subjects of the sentences first mentioned? How are they referred to again later?

**Examples:**

    Rosa Parks → she → Rosa → she
    As **visitors** enter the Cleveland Avenue Time Machine, **they** see what **they** think is. . .

What other NP/pronoun could be possible in the second example above?

**Possible answers:**

    cf. 'As **you** *enter* the Cleveland Avenue Time Machine, **you** *see* . . .'
    cf. 'As **one** *enters* the Cleveland Avenue Time Machine, **one** *sees* . . .'

How might the stance of the author shift by virtue of these variations in pronouns?

    they → you → one

What effect does each choice of reference marker create? The differences from one choice of words or names to another may be subtle, but there clearly *is* a difference. In order to conceptualize these distinctions, it might help to think about grammatical choice in terms of a continuum:

| **you** | | **they** | **one** |
|---|---|---|---|
| more connected to addressee | → | | less connected to addressee |
| more welcoming | → | | less welcoming |
| more subjective | → | | more objective |

Verbs and verb types (Chapter 6): Try to identify the verb types used in the two passages. Start with the broad distinction of **dynamic**, **stative**, and **copular** (or linking verbs).

- Identify the **linking verbs**.
- Identify the **stative verbs**.
- For **dynamic verbs**, are they verbs of motion, inclusion/containment, or activity/process?
- Which verbal expressions are transitive, ditransitive, complex transitive, and intransitive?
- Do you notice how the concept of **agency** figures into the two passages? How? Where do you notice **lower agency**? Where do you notice **higher agency**? (See Chapter 6.)

2    Present tense and past tense: Is it just a matter of adding *-ed*?

To illustrate the meaning and use of **present tense** as evoking timelessness, or unchanging physical properties or typical characteristics of an entity or situation, we used the following example:

    Present tense:    Water *boils* at 212°F [=100° C].

We also indicated that the general grammatical rule for changing a present tense form into a past tense form involves the addition of the past tense inflectional marker *-ed*.

Can you change this sentence then to past tense just by adding *-ed*?

    Past tense:    ?Water *boiled* at 212°F.

[Note: In contrast with * placed directly preceding a word, phrase, clause, or sentence to indicates an "ungrammatical" utterance, the designation of ? placed directly preceding a word phrase, clause, or sentence indicates that the utterance is *odd* but not necessarily ungrammatical.]

The sentence as it appears in the past tense does follow the grammatical rule: Add *-ed* to form past tense of a regular verb. But, from the point of view of meaning, the sentence is odd. Why?

Think about this carefully, because it may not be straightforwardly obvious if you just think in terms of grammatical form.

?*Water boiled at 212°F.*

The sentence is odd because the past tense implies that the action or change of state *actually took place*. It made the event *REAL*, different from the present tense counterpart Water *boils* at 212°F as a statement that is generally true.

By virtue of the past tense in this statement, what is missing now is some additional information pertaining to the noun phrase *water* that fits this NOW REAL event.

One change could be this:

    Add **the:**    →    **The** water *boiled* at 212°F.

Another change could be this:

    Add **context:** →    Water *boiled* at 212°F, even though we were in Denver, where it typically boils at 202°F.

So, changing declarative statements from present tense to past tense also changes the conceptual scene. In many cases, all that is required is a simple morphological shift: Just change present to past by adding *-ed*, thus transforming a present tense sentence into a past tense one.

In other cases, though, as we have just illustrated, the conceptual representation or the speaker's or writer's stance might shift noticeably.

Here is another example:

    **Some fraternal twins** *look* identical.     [present tense]
    (a generally true statement about fraternal twins in general)

    **Some fraternal twins** *looked* identical.     [past tense]
    (a statement about an **actual** designated set of fraternal twins. The impression was REAL.)

So, even though the words in the previously listed NPs are the exact same words, the referents picked out by the NPs are not—and we can see this just by virtue of the shift in tense from present to past. Why?

In the following example, the subject's (Caspian's) feeling toward the speaker or writer (me) may or may not still hold true:

    **Caspian** said he *loves* me     [present tense]
    **Caspian** said he *loved* me.     [past tense]

By virtue of the past tense of *loved*, it is unclear whether Caspian still feels the same way.

What is it about **the past tense** that changes our conceptualizations of some types of situations?

3    Subject-verb agreement (SVA)

In the following questions (and answers), why do you think the choice of a singular verb works, even though the question seeks an answer that would inevitably contain plural verb morphology?

**Questions with singular morphology and plural referents:**

Who **thinks** faster? Machines or humans?
[cf. Who *think* faster, machines or humans?]

Who's ahead in the race? The Democrats or the Republicans?
[cf. Who *are* ahead in the race, the Democrats or the Republicans?]

Who's more popular?    The Beatles or The Rolling Stones?
[cf. Who *are* more popular, The Beatles or The Rolling Stones?]

Regardless of which side you choose (e.g., machines or humans; Democrats or Republicans, The Beatles or The Rolling Stones), if your ***answer*** to the question contains parallel **singular morphology** in the **verbs**, it will become a crashingly ungrammatical utterance:

**Some possible answers to the previous questions:**

| Singular morphology: <u>Ungrammatical</u> | Plural morphology: <u>Grammatical</u> |
|---|---|
| *Machines *thinks* faster. | Machines *think* faster. |
| *Machines *does*. | Machines *do*. |
| *(The) Democrats *is* ahead. | (The) Democrats *are ahead*. |
| *(The) Democrats *is*. | (The) Democrats *are*. |
| *The Beatles *is* more popular. | The Beatles *are* more popular. |
| *The Beatles *is*. | The Beatles *are*. |

Now, have a look at the following sets of sentence pairs. These types of constructions using variations on SVA appear all throughout natural discourse.

a    There's 22 students in my grammar class this semester.
b    There **are** 22 students in my grammar class this semester.

a    There's six dollars in my drawer.
b    There **are** six dollars in my drawer.

a    There's 12 apple trees in bloom already.
b    There **are** 12 apple trees in bloom already.

Both do occur in natural native discourse, and both are "right." Think about the conceptual pattern that the a versions evoke and the conceptual patterns that the b versions evoke. Think about the *there is/there are* construction and how it affects grammar. Will you find the same distribution pattern with other verbs? For example, "I see that 22 students *are/*is* in my grammar class this semester."

How can you articulate this phenomenon of grammatical flexibility?

How are the subjects in the a versions conceptualized? How are the subjects in the b versions conceptualized?

## 7.2 Progressive Aspect

**Conceptual meaning:** The event, condition, or situation is not stable, not bounded, and is, was, or will be ongoing. Progressive aspect evokes the concept of possible past, present, or future **change**.

**Progressive aspect** is used to express the following types of actions or conditions:

- An action or condition that is (was or will be) underway or ongoing at a specific time
- A condition that is (was or will be) temporary, changing, and/or changeable

### 7.2.1 Progressive Aspect: Forms

**Progressive verb *forms*:** Auxiliary verb *be* + present participle (*V-ing*)

    **Present** progressive: *am, is, are* + V-ing
    **Past** progressive: *was, were* + V-ing
    **Future** progressive: *will be* + V-ing

**Present participle:**

| V | + | -*ing* |
|---|---|---|
| walk | → | I am, you are, s/he is, it is, we are, they are walking |
| speak | → | speaking |
| tell | → | telling |

If the verb ends with *e*, drop the -*e* and then add –ing.

| bake | → | baking |
|---|---|---|
| smile | → | smiling |
| write | → | writing |

If the verb ends in vowel + *d, g, m, n, p, r, t, b, f, s,* or *z*, double the final letter and then add -*ing*.[1]

| skid | → | skidding |
|---|---|---|
| bag | → | bagging |

194  *Tense and Aspect*

| | | |
|---|---|---|
| swim | → | swimming |
| spin | → | spinning |
| skip | → | skipping |
| star | → | starring |
| get | → | getting |
| bat | → | batting |
| rub | → | rubbing |
| quiz | → | quizzing |

### 7.2.2 Progressive Aspect: Uses and Meanings

#### 7.2.2.1 Uses and Meanings of the Present Progressive

**Temporary situations, results of a recent change**

Meheret *is running* a 5K race almost every week now. (This was not the case before.)
We*'re living* in Yokohama. (This will likely change; it's temporary.)

**Descriptions of immediate and ongoing situations**

I feel like something awful *is happening*.
I *am writing* a memoir about my life in Tibet.

#### 7.2.2.2 Uses and Meanings of the Past Progressive

**Temporary situations in the past, recent developments (at a particular time) in the past**

That spring, I *was working* at a café in downtown Boise.
[temporarily and at that specific time period]

My wife *was calling* her mother every day.
[a recent change at a specific time period in the past]

**An ongoing action that coincided with another action in the past; background information for other events**

Later that night, as they *were walking* home, Danica pulled up in her black truck.
[two events coincided; past progressive provides background]

We *were having* a nice conversation, and he just loudly interrupted everyone.
[an ongoing event coincided with another one in the past; past progressive as background]

#### 7.2.2.3 Uses and Meanings of the FUTURE Progressive

**An action or condition that will be underway or ongoing at a certain time or time period in the future**

A car *will be waiting* for you at the train station.
They *will be watching* the games from home.

Strong plans for future actions

He *will be voting* Liberal Democrat in the elections.
I *will be going* out shortly, but I do have a few minutes, if you'd like to chat.

### 7.2.3 Present Progressive vs. Simple Present

The essential difference between the conceptual meanings of simple present tense and progressive aspect has to do with *stability* vs. *the expectation of change*.

For the **simple present**, the conceptual meaning is that an event, condition, or *situation is stable and not expected to change*. For the **progressive aspect**, the basic conceptual meaning is that *an event, situation, or condition is not stable and is expected to change*.

| | |
|---|---|
| Soulayma *wears* glasses. | [simple present] stable, typical characteristic |
| Soulayma *is wearing* glasses. | [present progressive] a change from the ordinary, not typical |

The following discourse from job placement ads is a good illustration of how grammar functions to express stance or position. Both examples are taken from actual discourse of job ads in which an active search is underway. The first example (with simple present tense) can be ambiguous, expressing one of these two possibilities: (1) the company is simply stating its general preferences for the types of employees they hire, or (2) there is an active search under way. In the case of the second example, the search is unambiguously under way.

a   We *seek* personable and polite customer service representatives.
    [**simple present**]

b   We *are seeking* personable and polite customer service representatives.
    [**present progressive**]

In the b example, the present perfect creates an impression of *changeability* in the sense of *immediacy*, *urgency*, and possibly *vividness*.

For most verbs, the choice between simple present tense and progressive aspect is based on these conceptual distinctions:

| | | |
|---|---|---|
| timelessness, stable, non-changeable, typical | → | simple present |
| ongoing, immediate, changeable, not usual | → | present progressive |

Some stative verbs do not pattern well with the present progressive, because they mean that the situation or condition is inherently constant and non-changeable.

For example, the stative verb *know* indicates an inherently stable cognitive state. Someone either knows something or does not know something. There are no "progressive stages of knowing" typically associated with this type of mental process in English.

| | |
|---|---|
| Sara *knows* what the capital of Texas is. | [simple present] |
| Sara *knew* what the capital of Texas is. | [simple past] |

but:

*Sara *is knowing* what the capital of Texas is. [present progressive]
*Sara *was knowing* what the capital of Texas is. [past progressive]

In contrast, while the verbs of cognition like *believe*, *understand*, and *realize* are also essentially stative verbs, they can evoke various incremental stages in the process and are, at times, used with the progressive aspect, as illustrated by the following classic example by McCawley (1998, p. 227):

*I'm understanding* the problem less and less the more I think about it.

### 7.2.4 Multiple Meanings of Verbs: Inherently Stable and Possibly Also Changeable

As we know, all words have multiple meanings. As we mentioned in Chapter 6, the multiple meanings associated with verbs affect grammar. Stative verbs like *contain, have, occupy, weigh, cost, love,* and *like* are "defined" as verbs that resist the progressive aspect because of the seemingly inherent stable states that they evoke. So, sentences like the following are ungrammatical:

**Present progressive: Ungrammatical**

*Sodas are *containing* much sugar.
*Cristobal *is having* one brother.
*The camera *is costing* $325.00.
?Jenny *is weighing* 120 pounds.
?Children *are loving* chocolate.
?David *is liking* sci-fi movies.

**Simple tense: Grammatical**

Sodas *contain* much sugar.
Cristobal *has* one brother.
The camera *costs* $325.00.
Jenny *weighs* 120 pounds.
Children *love* chocolate.
David *likes* sci-fi movies.

However, these verbs also evoke other meanings, where the progressive aspect may in fact be possible. The following brief definitions that involve stable, non-changing conditions or situations are noted in italics, and it is these meanings that typically resist co-occurring with the progressive aspect. The meanings in standard font will typically not resist the co-occurrence with the progressive aspect.

| Verb | Meanings |
|---|---|
| contain | *to hold, to include* |
|  | to keep something from spreading (e.g., a fire) |
| have | *to possess, to own* |
|  | to host a party |
|  | to experience, to undergo (e.g., a test) |
|  | to give birth to a baby |
|  | to eat or drink (e.g., at home, at a restaurant |
|  | 'We're having baked cod for dinner') |
| weigh | *intransitive: to be a certain heaviness* |
|  | transitive: to determine how heavy someone or something is |
| cost | *to be valued at, requiring payment for* |
|  | to take a toll on someone or something |

| | |
|---|---|
| love | *to feel a strong positive emotion toward or to experience a strong preference for s.o. or s.t.* (stable) |
| | to have the same feeling as above, only changeable |
| like | *to feel a positive emotion toward or preference for s.o. or s.t.* (stable) |
| | to have the same feeling as above, only changeable |
| | to express positive reactions on social media |

We illustrate briefly:

Yogurt *contains/*is containing* more sugar and calories than milk.
Firefighters *are containing* the huge fire in the Colorado forest.

| | |
|---|---|
| Marisol *has/*is having* a cold. | [stable] |
| Women *have/are having* more dental issues than men. | [stable/changeable] |
| Peng *has* a party in his apartment (every Friday). | [typical, stable] |
| Peng *is having* a party upstairs, and I can't sleep. | [dynamic, ongoing right now] |
| The salmon that Salamon caught *weighs/*is weighing* 26.5 pounds. | [stable] |
| Noriko *is* now *weighing* 99 pounds. Her doctor is pleased. | [ongoing, changeable] |
| Iowa State's football recruit is still *weighing* his options. | [transitive, changeable, figurative] |
| Abdul-Aziz *likes* his new job. | [stable] |
| Abdul-Aziz *is liking* his new job more and more. | [changeable] |

## 7.3 Perfect Aspect

> **Conceptual meaning:** The event, condition, or situation happened *prior* to a reference point (e.g., another event, a particular point in time).
>
> Some **core features** of **perfect aspect**:
>
> - It indicates an action, condition, or situation that occurred or was held *prior* to some other time.
> - Through the use of perfect aspect, the ***priorness* of the action**, situation, or condition is enhanced in the discourse.
> - It signals that the ***importance of that prior*** action is **connected to another time**.

### 7.3.1 Perfect Aspect: Forms

**Perfect verb forms:** Auxiliary verb *have* + past participle (*V-en*)

    **Present** perfect:   *have, has* + *V-en*
    **Past** perfect:   *had* + *V-en*
    **Future** perfect:   *will have* + *V-en*

198    *Tense and Aspect*

**Past participle:** V + *-en*

Many of the past-participle forms look like the simple past. In cases where the past-participle form *differs* from the simple past, we indicate those forms with italics.

**For regular verbs,** add *-ed*. (But, if the verb ends with *-e*, just add *-d*.)

| | | |
|---|---|---|
| walk | → | I *have/had*, you *have/had*, s/he *has/had*, it *has/had*, we *have/had*, they *have/had* <u>walked</u> |
| cook | → | cooked |
| spoil | → | spoiled |
| wait | → | waited |
| live | → | lived |
| notice | → | noticed |

**Irregular verbs**

| | | |
|---|---|---|
| be | → | *been* |
| say | → | said |
| speak | → | *spoken* |
| tell | → | told |
| read | → | read |
| write | → | *written* |
| teach | → | taught |

Verbs relating to cognition and thinking

| | | |
|---|---|---|
| think | → | thought |
| know | → | *known* |
| understand | → | understood |
| find out | → | found out |

Verbs relating to motion

| | | |
|---|---|---|
| go | → | *gone* |
| come | → | *come* |
| swim | → | *swum* |
| wind | → | wound |
| leave | → | left |
| run | → | *run* |
| drive | → | *driven* |
| fall | → | *fallen* |
| rise | → | *risen* |
| sit | → | sat |
| grind | → | ground |
| spin | → | spun |
| sink | → | *sunk* |
| swing | → | swung |

Verbs relating to having and transporting

| | | |
|---|---|---|
| have | → | had |
| get | → | *gotten* |

| | | |
|---|---|---|
| give | → | *given* |
| hold | → | held |
| keep | → | kept |
| take | → | *taken* |
| bring | → | brought |
| buy | → | bought |
| sell | → | sold |
| pay | → | paid |
| find | → | found |
| lose | → | lost |
| win | → | won |

Verbs relating to ingestion

| | | |
|---|---|---|
| eat | → | *eaten* |
| drink | → | *drunk* |

Verbs relating to change of state

| | | |
|---|---|---|
| become | → | *become* |
| grow | → | *grown* |

Verbs relating to creation and destruction

| | | |
|---|---|---|
| make | → | made |
| draw | → | *drawn* |
| build | → | built |
| break | → | *broken* |
| tear | → | *torn* |

Verbs relating to perception

| | | |
|---|---|---|
| see | → | *seen* |
| hear | → | heard |
| feel | → | felt |

### 7.3.2 Perfect Aspect: Uses and Meanings

#### 7.3.2.1 Uses and Meanings of the Present Perfect

The present perfect depicts an event, experience, or situation that occurred or started prior to now; it has some relevance or importance to the current time. It may still be in effect or has just ended:

> This *has been* an incredibly productive conversation, and we thank you for your input.
> [The conversation has just ended; it has implicit present relevance.]
>
> They *have known* each other for a long time.
> [They knew each other prior to now, and this fact is implicitly important to the current time.]

200  *Tense and Aspect*

> **Compare:** They *knew* each other for a long time → it is considered over and done with; not implicitly relevant to now.

You *have changed* a lot.
[The change began prior to now, and this fact is important to the current time.]

> **Compare:** You *changed* a lot → the change is final and done with; not implicitly relevant to now.

The present perfect depicts an event or situation that happened **prior to now**, but the **actual time** of occurrence **is not important** to the discourse:

> I *have eaten* silkworm larva before.
> [It doesn't matter when, but the issue is important now.]
>
> *Have* you *contacted* Maryam's agent?
> [It doesn't matter when, but the issue is important now.] You've all *worked* so hard on this campaign.
> [It doesn't matter when, but the issue is important now.]

### 7.3.2.2 Uses and Meanings of the Past Perfect

The past perfect depicts an event, experience, or situation that occurred prior to a past event; the event in past perfect is linked to a subsequent event/time. (Note: As you will see in the following examples, the order of the two clauses is flexible. That is, the clause that evokes the prior event does not to be expressed first).

> Lily *was* upset last night because of what Novak *had told* her at the meeting.
> [simple past, reference point]  [**past perfect**, happened prior to the reference point]
> [Lily's bad mood happened as a *result of* Novak's earlier comments.]
>
> Alain *had decided* on his major one year before he *entered* college.
> [**past perfect**, happened prior to the reference point]  [simple past, reference point]
> [Alain's earlier decision is linked to the subsequent event → entering college.]
>
> They *invited* me to stay for dinner, but I *had eaten* earlier with my boss.
> [simple past, reference point] [**past perfect**, prior to past]
> [My decision not to have dinner with them was related to a prior event—that is, having already eaten.]

### 7.3.2.3 Uses and Meanings of the FUTURE PERFECT

The future perfect depicts future expectation for the completion of an event or the end point of a situation **prior to** the occurrence of another event (or a specific time) in the future.

> <u>By the end of this academic year</u>, we *will have read* 16 historical fiction novels.
>                         [future expectation]
>
> <u>In 2020</u>, it is predicted that the company *will have reached* maximum efficiency.
>                         [future expectation]
>
> <u>By next summer</u>, I *will have competed* in 26 Pokémon tournaments.
>                 [future expectation]

Expressions using the future perfect aspect typically include a temporal expression with the prepositions *by* and *in* (e.g., *by next year, by tomorrow, by the time . . . in 2025, in seven months*) or

### 7.3.2.4 Uses and meanings of the PERFECT with modals other than will

When modals other than *will* precede the perfect construction, they express **counterfactual thinking** (see Chapters 8 and 15 on modals and counterfactuals), as in the following example:

> By the end of this academic year, we *WOULD have read*
> 16 historical fiction novels, if the flood **hadn't happened**. [past perfect/counter to fact]
> [The facts: The flood did happen, and we did not read 16 novels.]

Chapters 8 and 15 provide a more detailed discussion of modals and hypothetical/counterfactual thinking and grammatical expressions.

## 7.4 Perfect Progressive Aspect

> The **conceptual meaning** combines the core features of the progressive and perfect aspects. The **progressive aspect** means the event is *ongoing* or *changeable*; the **perfect aspect** means the event is *relative and prior to a reference point*.

### 7.4.1 Perfect Progressive Aspect: Forms

**Perfect progressive** verb forms: Auxiliary verb *have been* + *V-ing*

> **Present** perfect progressive:   *have/has been* + *V-ing*
> **Past** perfect progressive:   *had been* + *V-ing*
> **Future** perfect progressive:   *will have been* + *V-ing*

### 7.4.2 Perfect Progressive Aspect: Uses and Meanings

#### 7.4.2.1 Present Perfect Progressive: Uses and Meanings

The present perfect progressive depicts an *event, experience, or situation that was ongoing prior to now and is still ongoing*, typically designating (explicitly or implicitly) the duration of that action or condition (e.g., for 6 hours, during the lesson, throughout the ceremony, ever since, all these years).

> That infant *has been screaming* throughout the entire flight.
> Massoud *has been searching* for hotels on the internet for the past 3 days.
> Sofia and Lucas *have been fighting* on and off ever since they got married.

#### 7.4.2.2 Past Perfect Progressive: Uses and Meanings

The past perfect progressive depicts an event, experience, or situation that was ongoing or underway prior to or simultaneous with another past event; typically designating (explicitly or

202  *Tense and Aspect*

implicitly) the duration of that action or condition (e.g., for years, for decades, for hours, all those years)

> After she *had been working* at Macy's <u>for years</u>, Aisha *decided* to start her own business.
> [had been] + [*V-ing*] ← ongoing past prior to past reference point] [simple past, reference point]
>
> We *forgot* to ask for a student discount because we'*d been waiting* in line <u>for so long</u>.
> [simple past]   [had been] + [*V-ing*] ← ongoing past prior to past reference point]
>
> Ian *had been playing* tennis <u>for 4 hours</u> when he *fainted* from exhaustion.
> [had been] + [*V-ing*] ← ongoing past prior to past reference point] [simple past]

### 7.4.2.3 Future Perfect Progressive: Uses and Meanings

The future perfect progressive expresses the prediction of an on-ongoing event prior to or simultaneous with another situation in the future, typically designating (explicitly or implicitly) the time that the events will overlap or that the second event will begin (e.g., by April, by then, by next year, when + future time event, for + future time period).

> The troupe *will have been performing Tosca* <u>for 2 years</u>, when the theater *closes* in May.
> [will have been] + [*V-ing*] ← future prediction of continuousness    [simple present]
>
> By the time we *reach* Arizona, we will *have been driving* <u>for 6 full weeks</u>.
> [simple present]         [will have been] + [*V-ing*] ← future prediction of continuousness
>
> If Mari *continues*, she *will have been sneezing* constantly <u>for one full hour by 3:15</u>
> [simple present]         [will have been] + [*V-ing*] ← future prediction of continuousness

---

### Mini Review and Practice

1   Let's review the cartoon that we used at the beginning of this chapter, Figure 7.1. The cartoon shows a married couple in their bed, ready to go to sleep. The woman asks her husband this question:

**Original text:**

"When **you**'*re trying* to fall asleep,    [present progressive]
does it ever feel like
**your thumbs** *are* still *texting*?"    [present progressive]

What is the meaning of the present progressive here? What if we changed it to the simple present tense, as follows?

**Modified version—present progressive → simple present:**

"When **you** *try* to fall asleep,    [simple present]
does it ever feel like
**your thumbs** still *text*?"    [simple present]

Both the original text and the modified version are grammatical from a syntactic or structural perspective. Does the modified version, with both target verbs in the present tense (in italics), make sense? Are both verbs in the present tense (*try* and *text*) equally acceptable or equally problematic? Which is more problematic in the present tense? Why? How does your conceptualization of the two scenes change, just by virtue of the choice of present progressive aspect (original text) and simple present (modified version)?

2   Practice the forms and review the meanings.

**Tense and Aspect: 12 Possible Combinations**

Using lines from the well-known children's song "The Wheels on the Bus," let's review the forms and meanings of all tense and aspect combinations in English.

Recall that the **perfect aspect** is relative, in that it **connects events and situations** that hold/held or take place/took place at one time **to other events or situations in another time**.

So, as you proceed down the list, when you arrive at the perfect and the perfect progressive, you'll need to add more contextual information in order for the grammatical forms to make conceptual sense.

Song line:
  "The wheels on the bus go round and round, all through the town."

**Simple Aspect (x3):**

| | |
|---|---|
| Simple Present | The wheels on the bus *go* round and round, all through the town. |
| Simple Past | The wheels on the bus **went** round and round, all through the town. |
| Simple Future | The wheels on the bus **will** *go* round and round, all through the town. |

| **Progressive Aspect (x3):** | *be + V-ing* |
|---|---|
| Present Progressive | The wheels on the bus **are going** round and round, all through the town. |
| Past Progressive | The wheels on the bus **were going** round and round, all through the town. |
| Future Progressive | The wheels on the bus **will be going** round and round, all through the town. |

| **Perfect Aspect (x3):** | *have + V-en* |
|---|---|
| Present Perfect | The wheels on the bus **have gone** round and round, all through the town, (**and now** _____). |
| Past Perfect | The wheels on the bus **had gone** round and round, all through the town, **when** _____. |

204  *Tense and Aspect*

Future Perfect    The wheels on the bus *will have gone* round and round, all through the town, **by the time** _____.

**Perfect Progressive (x3):**    *have been + V-ing*

Present Perfect Progressive

The wheels on the bus *have been going* round and round, all through the town, **and now** _____.

Past Perfect Progressive

The wheels on the bus *had been going* round and round, all through the town, **when** _____.

Future Perfect Progressive

The wheels on the bus *will have been going* round and round, all through the town, **by** _____.

Now, you can try filling in the blanks, with a different line from the same song:

"The driver on the bus *says* 'Move on back!' "

**Simple Tense (x3)**

| | |
|---|---|
| Simple Present | The driver on the bus *SAYS* "Move on back!" |
| Simple Past | The driver on the bus _____ "Move on back!" |
| Simple Future | The driver on the bus ____ ____ "Move on back!" |

**Progressive Aspect (x3):**    *be + V-ing*

| | |
|---|---|
| Present Progressive | The driver on the bus ___ _____ "Move on back!" |
| Past Progressive | The driver on the bus ___ _____ "Move on back!" |
| Future Progressive | The driver on the bus ___ ____ _____ "Move on back!" |

**Perfect Aspect (x3):**    *have + V-en*

Present Perfect    The driver on the bus ___ _____ "Move on back!" (**and now** _____).

Past Perfect    The driver on the bus ___ _____ "Move on back!" **when** _____.

Future Perfect    The driver on the bus ___ ____ _____ "Move on back!" **to 88 children by** _____.

**Perfect Progressive (x3):**    *have been + V-ing*

Present Perfect Progressive

The driver on the bus ___ ____ _____ "Move on back!" **all morning, and now** _____.

Past Perfect Progressive

The driver on the bus ___ ____ _____ "Move on back!" **all morning, and then** _____.

Future Perfect Progressive

The driver on the bus ___ ____ ____ _____ "**Move on back!**" **all morning, by** _____.

[**Answers:** says, said, will say, is saying, was saying, will be saying, has said, had said, will have said, has been saying, had been saying, will have been saying]

3   Progressive and perfect aspects vs. simple aspect

The following pairs of sentences provide subtle contrasts in conceptual meaning between simple tense and progressive or perfect aspect. All versions of these utterances are grammatical. The meanings change because of the tense and aspect choices:

a   Are you okay?

  1   You look like you *have* (just) *seen* a ghost. [**present perfect—connects to now**]

  2   You look like you (just) *saw* a ghost.   [**simple past—over and done with**; separation from now; adverb *just* serves to connect the expression to now]

How do utterances 1 and 2 differ from each other? Of the two, which feels *more empathetic* on the part of the speaker vis à vis the addressee? Why?

b   <u>actual email</u> sent by Susan to a student (the student's name has been changed):

  1   Hi Jackie,
      Thanks so much for sending this.
      **I** *am looking forward* [**present progressive**] to reading your work and to hearing how **your topic** *has developed* [**present perfect**].

  2   Variation on 1, by changing the present progressive and the present perfect to simple present and simple past, respectively:

      cf. Hi Jackie,
      Thanks so much for sending this.
      **I** *look forward* [**simple present**] to reading your work and to hearing how **your topic** *developed* [**simple past**].

Again, how do these two messages differ? The content is almost identical. What is different is *the stance* of the writer. In one version, the writer sounds *more engaged* or *more connected* to the addressee and to the topic.

In the other, the writer sounds *more neutral* or *a bit more distant* with regard to the topic and to the addressee. Given the meanings of the present progressive and the present perfect aspects vs. those of the simple present and simple past, what accounts for the change in the writer's stance from the original email in version 1 to the variation in version 2? How would you describe the change in the writer's stance toward the addressee and/or the topic?

4   Here is the text of another email. It is a request by a university for a letter of recommendation for someone who has applied for a faculty position there.

**The applicant referenced below** *has applied* for a position at The University of North Carolina at Greensboro and *has* also *requested* a recommendation from you for the job to which **they** *are applying*. Please click on the link below and fill out the information and/or upload the documents requested. Thank you and have a wonderful day.

The text has three target verb forms: two instances of the present perfect and one instance of the present progressive. Indicate the subjects and the verb forms here. (You'll also need to think about ellipsis.)

_____     _____
subject              present perfect

_____     _____
subject              present perfect

_____     _____
subject              present progressive

First, what strikes you about the subject of the verbs in each case? Do you notice anything interesting with regard to the pronoun that serves as the subject of the verb in the present progressive? What is it?

What function does each use of aspect marking serve here? That is, why is the **present perfect** used and not the **simple past**?

> cf. The applicant referenced previously *applied* for a position and also *requested* a recommendation from you.

How does the use of the simple past change the nature of this request? Comparing the simple past form with the present perfect, why is the present perfect both more appropriate and more polite sounding?

5   The following is the text of an announcement that appeared on the Weather Channel website (www.weather.com) for the first time on May 6, 2016. We have indicated the target verbs and tense and aspect verb forms with italics. You will find one instance each of present perfect, present perfect progressive, and simple present. Be sure to pay attention to not only the verbs and the tense and aspect marking but also to the subjects of the sentences (we have highlighted the subjects in bold).

> WE'*VE MADE* SOME IMPROVEMENTS
>
> **We**'*ve been listening* to your feedback. **You** now *have* immediate access to radar, constant access to your locations, and your pollen, farming and other forecasts to plan your day.
>
> ("We've made some improvements," n.d.)

Match the correct forms to the correct category:

   Present perfect:              _____
   Present perfect progressive:  _____
   Simple present:               _____

How would the message change (even if slightly) if the two markers of perfect aspect (present perfect and present perfect progressive) were changed to simple past? Explain.

> **We** *listened* to your feedback.
> **We** *made* some improvements.

6   What is the difference between these two greeting-type questions? They differ only by virtue of their tense and aspect marking.

   a   How *are* you?           [simple present]
   b   How *have* you *been*?   [present perfect]

In what contexts would the a version be used? In what contexts would the b version be used? What sort of information regarding the speaker and addressee is implied simply by virtue of the use of the present perfect?

7   When you apply for services online, there is often a box to check indicating your agreement to abide by certain contractual terms. Here are two examples:

   a   I *have read* and I *accept* the terms and conditions of this payment plan.
   b   I *confirm* that I *have read* the Student Handbook.

What are the subjects of each clause? What types of tense and aspect marking do you find here? Why these? Can you substitute these choices of tense and aspect marking for other seemingly similar forms (e.g., simple past tense)? If so, how will that substitution affect the meaning? That is, see the following variations (i.e., a¹ and b¹) and discuss how the meaning of the statements change with the shift in tense.

   cf. a¹ I *read* and *accepted* the terms and conditions of this payment plan.
       b¹ I confirmed that I read the Student Handbook.

8   What is the difference between the following two descriptions?

   Markus *is acting* like an intellectual.
   Markus *acts* like an intellectual.

What can we assume about Markus and his personality on the basis of the grammar in each description? That is, which sentence describes his personality as more "usual" and "general"? Which describes this personality trait as more temporary? Why?

* * * * * * * *

## PRACTICE WITH DATA ANALYSIS: PUTTING IT ALL TOGETHER

1   Have a look at the following quote by Brigid Gorry-Hines:

   Life has a way of going in circles. Ideally, it would be a straight path forward—we'd always know where we were going, we'd always be able to move on and leave everything else behind. There would be nothing but the present and the future.

   Instead, we always find ourselves where we started. When we try to move ahead, we end up taking a step back. . . . But however we remember it—or choose to remember it—the past is the foundation that holds our lives in place. . . . What defines us isn't where we're going, but where we've been.

   (Gorry-Hines, n.d.)

In the first half of the quote, Gorry-Hines sets up an ideal, unreal world such that life and time are not circular or cyclical, but run in a straight line—a single path where "before" is behind us, "now" is right where we are, and "later" is in front of us. That linear path *would* allow us to see precisely where we are, where we have been, and where we will be going. (You can revisit this

208   *Tense and Aspect*

first part of the quote in the next chapter (Chapter 8) as it discusses the modal *would* and its relationship to unreal or hypothetical situations.)

"Instead," she tells us in the second part that the world is not like that. Time is not like that. Our lives are not like that. Time and life and experience, she says, run in a circular, cyclical pattern.

Think about the meaning of this second part of her quote. How does grammar (especially the tense and aspect system of English) help us understand time in the way that Gorry-Hines discusses here?

Hints for you to think about as you respond:

    a    Hint 1: simple present → simple past:

        Water *boils* at 212°F. → ?Water *boiled* at 212°F.
        Some fraternal twins *look* identical. → Some fraternal twins *looked* identical.

        What does the use of the past tense do to the concepts in these two sentences?

    b    Hint 2: the conceptual meanings of the progressive, perfect, and perfect progressive aspect

    c    Hint 3: anything else that strikes you from this chapter or related chapters

2    In this chapter, we observed that in most instances of English grammar, subject-verb agreement (SVA) is not particularly noticeable. The forms of regular present tense verbs do not change according to person or number (i.e., singular vs. plural), except for third-person singular. The forms of regular past tense verbs do not change at all according to person or number.

Think about the following examples from actual discourse in which SVA does become noticeable. For excerpts A and B, remember that with *there is* and *here is* types of constructions, the subject of the verb is the NP that comes directly after the copula *be*.

For all examples, we have indicated the **NP subjects** in **bold** and the *verbs* in *italics*. In all cases, both the original versions and the variations are considered to be "grammatical" by descriptive linguists, because these constructions do occur frequently in discourse. They are considered to be "ungrammatical" by prescriptive linguists. Their meanings shift in terms of how the entities are being conceptualized.

    a    "Samsung Galaxy S7—Consumer feedback"

        **Original:**

            Here'*s* **two pieces of bad news** about the Samsung Galaxy S7.
            (answers.com)

        **Variation:**

            cf. Here *are* **two pieces of bad news** . . .

    b    **Commentary on human nature by David Della Rocco**

        **Original:**

            There'*s* **two kinds of people in this world** when you boil it all down. You got your talkers and you got your doers. Most people are just talkers, all they do is talk. But when it is all said and done, it's the doers that change this world.

                                                                                    (goodreads.com, n.d.)

**Variation:**

cf. There *are* two kinds of people in this world . . .

c   "Larry King Live" (2000) ((King is interviewing Dr. Klippel, a specialist in rheumatoid arthritis.))

**Original:**

*King*: We're back with our panel [. . .] Dr. Klippel, how is arthritis preventable?
*Klippel*: Well, Larry, three-ways: being overweight increases one's risk of osteoarthritis; being unfit, that is staying fit protects you from osteoarthritis; and number three, we believe the first sign that you get of joint pain you should see a doctor [. . .] So **there** *is* **three important ways** we can think about prevention.

(adapted from Davies, 2008–)

**Variation:**

So **there** *are* **three important ways** we can think about prevention.

d   Discourse from multiple versions of an older TV commercial about using prunes as a safe and effective children's laxative (Product: Fletchers Castoria—the medication provides a perfect dose for children and removes the worry that parents may have about giving their children too many prunes or too few as a natural laxative)

"Fletcher's Castoria" (1967)

**Original:**

The Problem With Prunes: *Is* **Three** Enough, *Is* **Six** Too Many?

**Variation:**

cf. The Problem With Prunes: *Are* **Three** Enough, *Are* **Six** Too Many?

e   From the film *Meet Joe Black* (Brest, 1998): "Who **IS** you?"

**Relevant synopsis of the plot:**

Bill Parrish (Anthony Hopkins) is a wealthy businessman. He will soon be celebrating his 65th birthday. The film reveals how Parrish needs to come to terms with his life, his business, and his family, when he meets the character, Joe Black (Brad Pitt), who is actually "death" disguised in the body of a handsome young man. Joe enters the family, interacts with Parrish and his daughters, and falls in love with Parrish's youngest daughter, Susan. Susan has fallen in love with him as well.

(Brest, 1998)

The film excerpt, which is a conversation between Joe Black and Bill Parrish, appears just as Joe Black (the personification of "death") reveals his love for Susan (Bill's daughter) and his intent to take Susan with him when he leaves.

**Transcribed from the film:**

**JOE ((to Bill Parrish)):**
I love her, Bill. She is all that I ever wanted, and I've never wanted for anything because I've never wanted anything before, if you can understand. . . .

Susan wants to come. She says she's in love with me.

**PARRISH:**
→ With <u>you</u>?! Who *is* "you"? Did you tell her who you *are*?

**JOE:**
No.

**PARRISH:**
Does she know where she's going?
((Joe doesn't answer.))

<u>Variation—to highlight the grammar:</u>

**PARRISH:**
cf. With you?! **Who** *are* **"you"?** Did you tell her who you *are*?

Review and analyze all of the original discourse excerpts in A through E and compare and contrast them with the variations.

How does the conceptual representation change between the two versions? What might be some of the motivations for using the seemingly "less correct" forms in each of these excerpts? Be sure to provide sufficient detail as you discuss all of the excerpts in A through E.

3   Explicate the ambiguity in the following humorous statement made famous by linguist and computer scientist Anthony Oettinger (1966):

"Time flies like an arrow; fruit flies like a banana."

Use your knowledge of SVA, noun types, and determiners to provide a detailed explication for this intentional linguistic joke and its ambiguity.

4   The following two excerpts are the exact headlines that appeared online on May 7, 2016. Neither contains a grammatical error. How do you account for the grammatical differences exhibited here? What is the subject of each headline?

   a   **CNN News headline, May 7, 2016:**

   **Swarm** of earthquakes *strikes* Mt. St. Helens

   b   **MSN News headline, May 7, 2016:**

   Swarm of **earthquakes** *strike* Mount St. Helens

5   Identify the categories of tense and aspect in the following excerpt from the four opening paragraphs of Steinbeck's *Of Mice and Men* (1937/1993, p. 3) listed as paragraphs a-d below.

In order to do this thoroughly, you'll also need to attend to the NP subjects in each clause. We have marked the NP (noun and pronoun) subjects with boldface type, and we have indicated the target verb forms in italics.

Read the first two paragraphs. What do you notice about the verb tense? What is the predominant tense used?

   a   A few miles south of Soledad, **the Salinas River** *drops in* close to the hillside bank and *runs* deep and green. The water *is* warm too, for **it** *has slipped* twinkling over the yellow sands in the sunlight before reaching the narrow pool. . . . On the sandy bank under the threes **the leaves** *lie* deep and so crisp that **a lizard** *makes* a great skittering if **he** *runs* among them.

(Steinbeck, 1937/1993, p. 3)

b   There *is* **a path** through the willows and among the sycamores, a path beaten hard by boys coming down from the ranches to swim in the deep pool, and beaten hard by **tramps** who *come* wearily down from the highway in the evening to jungle-up near water.

(Steinbeck, 1937/1993, p. 3)

Start your analysis by first listing the verbs. Then identify the categories of tense and aspect for each verb that you find. Also, note the subjects of the verbs. You'll see that some subjects are overt, and some are ellipted (e.g., **the Salinas River** *drops in* close to the hillside bank and [the Salinas River] *runs* deep and green—see Chapter 2 for ellipsis). In the case of overt subjects, be careful to note the noun antecedent as well as the pronoun that replaces it in a subsequent clause or sentence.

Now, read the second two paragraphs. Do you notice anything different with regard to tense and aspect marking?

c   **Evening of a hot day** *started* the little wind to moving among the leaves. **The shade** *climbed* up the hills toward the top. On the sand banks **the rabbits** *sat* as quietly as little gray, sculptured stones. And then from the direction of the state highway *came* **the sound of footsteps** on crisp sycamore leaves. **The rabbits** *hurried* noiselessly for cover. **A stilted heron** *labored* up into the air and *pounded* down river. For a moment **the place** *was* lifeless, and then **two men** *emerged* from the path and *came* into the opening by the green pool.

(Steinbeck, 1937/1993, p. 3)

d   **They** *had walked* in single file down the path, and even in the open **one** *stayed* behind the other. . . . **Both** *wore* black, shapeless hats and **both** *carried* tight blanket rolls slung over their shoulders.

(Steinbeck, 1937/1993, p. 3)

Continue to list the verbs and identify the tense and aspect categories. Also note the subjects. Are they full noun phrases? Pronouns? Is there any ellipsis? For example, in "**A stilted heron** *labored* up into the air and *pounded* down river," the subject of both clauses is "a stilted heron."

What sorts of observations can you make with regard to tense/aspect marking in the first two paragraphs in contrast with tense/aspect marking in the second two paragraphs? Why do you think this is so?

What types of **dynamic verbs** and **stative verbs** are used in these four paragraphs? As you identify the verb types, try also to determine whether they are being used **transitively or intransitively**. Which category is more frequent in the passage? Why do you think this is so in these introductory lines of the novel? How is the landscape depicted as the background for the emergence of the men whom we meet in the last two lines of paragraph c?

Which **copular verbs** are used in these four paragraphs? Where do they appear?

What other sorts of contrasts do you observe? In addition to the contrasts in tense and aspect marking, think about the descriptions of the scenes and detailed movement and motion vs. less detailed movement and motion. How do these features of description all combine to help Steinbeck set the scene for this novel?

6   The previous excerpt from *Of Mice and Men* illustrates artistic uses of tense and aspect and verbs/verb types in depicting the scenes and characters of a novel. Now, let's have a quick look at an excerpt from nonfiction discourse, Eva Hoffman's (1989, p. 3) *Lost in Translation*.

It *is* April, 1959, I*'m standing* at the railing of the *BATORY's* (the ship's name) upper deck and I *feel* that **my life** *is ending*. I*'m looking* out at **the crowd** that *has gathered* on the shore to see the ship's departure from Gdynia—**a crowd** that, all of a sudden, *is* irrevocably on the other side—and **I** *want* to break out, run back, run toward the familiar excitement, the waving hands, the exclamations. . . **I** *am* thirteen years old, and **we** *are emigrating*.

212  *Tense and Aspect*

> **My sister**, four years younger than I, *is clutching* my hand wordlessly; **she** hardly *understands* where **we** *are*, or **what** *is happening* to us. **My parents** *are* highly agitated; **they** *had* just [*had*] a body search by the customs police, probably as the farewell gesture of anti-Jewish harassment. Still, **the officials** *weren't* clever enough, or suspicious enough, to check my sister and me—lucky for us, since **we** *are* both *carrying* some silverware **we** *were* not allowed to take out of Poland.
>
> (Hoffman, 1989, p. 3)

Re-read the passage. List the verbs. Identify the categories of tense and aspect. Indicate the subjects of the verbs (overt or ellipted, full NP or pronoun, for pronoun **it**—what are the actual referents?).

We will start you off in this process:

> It *is* April, 1959.
> subject = *it* (non-referential), verb = *be* copula, simple present tense
>
> I'*m standing* at the railing.
> subject = *I*, verb = *stand* = dynamic/intransitive, aspect = present progressive
>
> I *feel* that . . .
> subject = *I*, verb = *feel* = stative, aspect = simple present
>
> . . . my life is ending
> subject = *my life*, verb = *end* = dynamic/intransitive, aspect = present progressive
>
> I'*m looking* out *at* the crowd . . .
> subject = *I*, verb = *look at* = dynamic/transitive, aspect = present progressive
>
> . . . that *has gathered* on the shore
> subject = the crowd, verb = *gather* = dynamic/intransitive, aspect = present perfect

*Lost in Translation* was published in 1989, exactly 30 years after the opening episode where Hoffman was aboard the *BATORY*. We know that the book is recounting nonfictional events from the past.

What is the predominant type of tense and aspect marking used here? The tense and aspect marking that is illustrated in the opening paragraphs is quite consistent throughout Hoffman's entire autobiographical account. What sort of effect does this create? In which places in this excerpt do you find tense shifts? Why do you think these shifts occur where they do?

7 The excerpts in numbers 5 and 6 exhibit a variety of tense and aspect markers used effectively and deliberately within relatively short spates of discourse. The following two excerpts use only the simple past.

a  "The Boston Tea Party"

> This famed act of American colonial defiance *served* as a protest against taxation. Seeking to boost the troubled East India Company, British Parliament *adjusted* import duties with the passage of the Tea Act in 1773. While consignees in Charleston, New York, and Philadelphia *rejected* tea shipments, merchants in Boston *refused* to concede to Patriot pressure. On the night of December 16, 1773, Samuel Adams and the Sons of Liberty *boarded* three ships in the Boston harbor and *threw* 342 chests of tea overboard. This *resulted* in the passage of the punitive Coercive Acts in 1774 and *pushed* the two sides closer to war.
>
> ("Boston Tea Party," n.d.)

## Tense and Aspect    213

b  **"Biography of Louis Daniel Armstrong"**

Louis Armstrong *was* born in New Orleans in the Storyville District known as "the Battlefield" on August 4, 1901. He *left* school [in] the 5th grade to help support his family. He *sang* on street corners, *sold* newspapers and *delivered* coal.

He *went* to the Colored Waif's Home for shooting a gun to celebrate New Year's Eve on December 31, 1912. He *learned* to play the bugle cornet and to read music from Peter Davis at the Waif's Home. After 18 months, he *left* the Waif's Home [and *decided*] to become a musician.

("Biography of Louis Daniel Armstrong," n.d.)

Compare and contrast the four excerpts (i.e., 5 [*Of Mice and Men*], 6 [*Lost in Translation*], 7a ["The Boston Tea Party"], and 7b ["Biography of Louis Daniel Armstrong"]) for their uses of tense and aspect marking. Why do you think there is little variation in tense and aspect marking in 7a and 7b in comparison to the excerpts from 5 and 6?

8    Tense, time, agency: references to future events

We have observed a number of references to future time through the use of various types of tense and aspect markers:

Simple present:       scheduled events in a designated future time
Future time:          predictions, strong commitment, determination
Future progressive:   strong plan for the future

The following sets of sentence triplets illustrate how future time can be and is expressed in discourse. Think about the meanings of each utterance. Compare and contrast the utterances in the simple present to those in the simple future and also in the future progressive. Based on what you know about the meanings of the simple present, the simple future, and the future progressive, try and articulate what conceptual features underlie the utterances in each version. Is there a continuum that comes to mind as you attempt to do this? Do you notice any differences that are related to agency, whereby the subjects in one of the three versions sound the least (implicitly) agentive and the subjects in another version sound the most (implicitly) agentive? How about issues of urgency and immediacy as captured and contrasted by tense and aspect marking?

a    The sale *ends* tonight            [simple present]
b    The sale *will* <u>end</u> tonight.        [future time]
c    The sale *will be* <u>ending</u> tonight.     [future progressive]

a    On Tuesday, we *choose* partners for our projects.              [simple present]
b    On Tuesday, we *will choose* partners for our projects.         [simple future]
c    On Tuesday, we *will be choosing* partners for our projects.    [future progressive]

a    Homerun cure for cancer starts now (tomorrow, at midnight . . .)
     (*The Cure Starts Now Foundation*)
b    cf. Homerun cure for cancer *will <u>start</u>* now (tomorrow, at midnight . . .)
c    cf. Homerun cure for cancer *will be <u>starting</u>* now (tomorrow, at midnight . . .)

Now, consider the following text. It is an actual email sent by an elementary school teacher to the parents of the children in her class to let them know about the plans for the last few weeks of the school year. The text contains three instances of the future progressive, marked in italics.

Hi everyone,

Today we introduced End of Year Projects. Students *will be choosing* topics that interest them to research and plan presentations around. They *will be creating* research questions, interactive introductions and conclusions, and presentations that will engage and entertain their audiences. We started by brainstorming ideas. Students *will be completing* proposals and research throughout the rest of the week.

First, is it grammatically possible to change any of the three sentences with the future progressive into the **simple present** to indicate future meaning? Why, or why not? That is, **what meaning** does the **future progressive carry here** that the simple present does not? The concept of **agency** may shed light on this.

Next, is it grammatically possible to change any of the same three sentences into the simple future? What sort of meaning change would accompany the grammatical change? The change might involve such concepts as stance, determination, and so forth.

Articulate your answers in full detail.

9   Present perfect progressive

The excerpts in this section all reflect discourse-based uses of the present perfect progressive:

a   "You've been cutting watermelon all wrong (all this time)!"

> Angurello is a stainless steel cutting tool designed to cut watermelon in such a way that it slices a whole watermelon uniformly and also lifts the pieces out efficiently and neatly, without having to switch tools. It looks and functions like a knife and tongs at the same time.
>
> (Angurello, n.d.)

One of the ads for this product opens like this:

"You'*ve been cutting* watermelon all wrong!"
(implied time periods: all your life, all this time, all summer)

Why is the use of the present progressive so fitting for the ad? Can you find other uses of the present perfect progressive to express similar types of situations?

**Example:**

Other ads for similar products?

> Tips on how to do things better?
> Advice about what you have been doing wrong or right—all this time, all your life, and so on

Some of these examples include the following:

> You've been washing your hands all wrong.
> You've been peeling hard-boiled eggs all wrong.
> 15 Things You've Been Doing All Wrong

Try and locate more examples of this construction. Do you find a balance of positive stances, or do you predominantly tend to find this type of expression in more negative constructions? Why do you think this is the case?

b   Here is another example of present perfect progressive used in a magazine article called "Homemade Herbal Medicines," in *Essence*.

> The reason I don't take even one prescription pharmaceutical every day is mostly due to my lifestyle—primarily because of my reliance on herbal medicines. I **have been**

**using** homemade herbal remedies as my primary health care for about 30 years. I've successfully treated everything from minor colds, flus, cuts and scrapes, which we all encounter on our journey through life, to irritable bowel syndrome and staph.

(Davies, 2008–)

How does the choice of the present perfect progressive in this example help establish the author's level of certainty and expertise? Which other bits of discourse help the author establish this level of expertise and certainty?

## COMMON ERRORS, BUMPS, AND CONFUSIONS

Identify the errors or "bumps" in the following sentences. Use the concepts and terminology that you learned in this and other chapters to articulate what might be grammatically or pragmatically problematic. Suggest ways that each can be re-written more clearly and more accurately. (Note: While all bumps do involve some element of tense and aspect marking, they are not limited to only that.)

1. According to Lifehacks website I been cooking artichokes a wrong way.
2. We seen that movie trailer in our social study class.
3. Have you ever dreamed of becoming astronaut when you were young?
4. Some TV advertisement is containing dangerous messages to teenager.
5. (This involves a multiple-choice question.)

    Which of the following is true of gravity?

    a  It is man-maid.
    b  It affects everythings on the Earth.
    c  It's range is infinite.
    d  a and b only
    e  all of the above
    d  b and c only

6. Not only this essay but all the essays I had wrote in the class teached me how to think.
7. Mo have been surprised that Nan was knowing his name. They did not meet each other before that time.
8. Did you runned in marathon at the middle school?

## SUGGESTED ACTIVITIES

1. The following are some classic song titles and lyrics. In each of the excerpts, the main verb is missing. Can you guess what the missing verb is? Be sure to use the correct tense and aspect. The bare verbs from the song titles are provided after the set of excerpts.

    a  I'___ ___ _____ for a girl like you to come into my life.
    b  Here _____ Santa Claus!
    c  You'__ _____ That Lovin' Feeling
    d  I _____ My Heart in San Francisco
    e  It's raining, it's _____, the old man is _____.
    f  I'm _____ of a white Christmas.
    g  A baby was _____, its mother was _____.
    h  Happy Days _____ Here Again

    [bare verbs: dream, snore, be, leave, lose, weep, come, pour, sleep, wait]

You can continue this same activity and find other song lyrics and titles. Design a competitive game in which class members are asked to provide possible and/or correct words to fill in the blanks.

2   Newspaper headlines, tense, and time

Have a look at the most recent headlines in your local and national news (newspapers, online news). Often, the headlines of the latest stories—just as they are happening—appear in the **present tense**, even though the events have truly already happened in the past.

The following headlines are from three major news stories in the US—two recent ones and one from long ago. Note the tenses used in these headlines.

### April 21, 2016

| | |
|---|---|
| "Prince Dies at 57: How the news unfolded" | *The Telegraph* |
| "Prince Dead: Singer Dies at 57" | *Billboard* |
| "Prince, singer and superstar, dies aged 57" | *BBC News* |

### May 9, 2017

| | |
|---|---|
| "President Donald Trump Fired FBI Director James Comey" | *Chicago Sun Times* |
| "Trump fires FBI Chief, citing handling of Clinton email investigation" | *Los Angeles Times* |
| "Trump fires FBI Director James Comey" | *Washington Post* |

These are some of the **November 23, 1963**, headlines on JFK's assassination:

| | |
|---|---|
| "Assassin Kills Kennedy" | *Chicago Tribune* |
| "Kennedy Is Killed by Sniper As He Rides In Car In Dallas" | *New York Times* |
| (For more on present tense and passive voice, see Chapter 9) | |

What effect does the use of the present tense create in the previously listed headlines, especially in contrast with past tense?

Scan current newspapers (both local and national) and collect 10 headlines from each paper. What kinds of tense and aspect marking do you find?

How is tense and aspect marking used in news headlines? Is there a correlation between importance, impact, or immediacy of the story and the use of tense in the headlines? How is future tense represented in news headlines?

In addition to tense and aspect, note the use of nouns (common and proper), determiners, pronouns, verbs (e.g., transitivity, agency), and voice (see Chapter 9, active, passive, middle).

Conduct a similar study with tabloid news headlines. Does the discourse change at all when you analyze tabloid news headlines? (Hint: In addition to tense and aspect, also pay attention to nouns, determiners, pronouns, verbs, and verb types.)

3   Find a sporting event on TV or on the internet. Pay attention to how the commentating is done, with a special focus on tense and aspect. Take notes on—or better yet, transcribe—five minutes of play-by-play sports discourse and analyze the nouns, determiners, pronouns, verb types, tense and aspect, and register. What types of patterns of tense and aspect marking do you find? Compare notes with students working on commentating for other sports. How do these discursive patterns of reporting differ for different sports? In what ways are they similar?

Learn about sports commentating and find out what the roles of each type of reporter are: play-by-play announcing, analyst/color commentator, sidelines reporter, sports presenter, or studio host. Use video clips of sports events and have students take on these various roles as they provide commentary for a sports event.

Try another activity: Take a 3-minute segment of a sporting event. Turn off the volume. Write the commentary and/or play-by-play discourse to describe what you are viewing on the screen.

## Note

1 Exceptions include verbs that end with long vowel + *b*, *m*, *n*, *t*, or *p*—for example, *pining* (vs. *pinning*), *taping* (vs. *tapping*), *fusing* (vs. *fussing*), *biting*, *tubing*, *plating*, and *roping*.

## Academic References

Biber, D., Johansson, S., Leech, G., Conrad, S., Finegan, E., & Quirk, R. (1999). *Longman grammar of spoken and written English*. Boston, MA: MIT Press.

Bioethics. (n.d.). Retrieved September 23, 2017, from http://dal.ca.libguides.com/c.php?g=256990&p=1717826.

Bybee, J. (2008). Usage-based grammar and second language acquisition. In P. Robinson & N. Ellis (Eds.), *Handbook of cognitive linguistics and second language acquisition* (pp. 216–236). New York: Routledge.

Bybee, J., Perkins, R., & Pagliuca, W. (1994). *The evolution of grammar: Tense, aspect, and modality in the languages of the world*. Chicago: University of Chicago Press.

Comrie, B. (1976). *Aspect: An introduction to the study of verbal aspect and related problems*. Cambridge: Cambridge University Press.

Comrie, B. (1985). *Tense*. Cambridge: Cambridge University Press.

Declerck, R. (2006). *The grammar of the English verb phrase: The grammar of the English tense system: Vol. 1*. Berlin: Walter de Gruyter.

Fenn, P. (1987). *A semantic and pragmatic examination of the English perfect*. Germany: Gunter Narr Verlag.

Fludernik, M. (1991). The historical present tense yet again: Tense switching and narrative dynamics in oral and quasi-oral storytelling. *Text-Interdisciplinary Journal for the Study of Discourse*, 11(3), 365–398.

Givón, T. (1993). *English grammar: A function-based introduction: Vol. 2*. Amsterdam and Philadelphia: John Benjamins Publishing.

Hirtle, W. H. (1967). *The simple and progressive forms: An analytical approach*. Paris: PUF.

Hopper, P. (1982). *Tense-aspect: Between semantics & pragmatics: Containing the contributions to a symposium on tense and aspect, held at UCLA, May 1979*. Amsterdam: John Benjamins Publishing.

Langacker, R. (2008). *Cognitive grammar: A basic introduction*. New York: Oxford University Press.

Larsen-Freeman, D., & Celce-Murcia, M. (2016). *The grammar book: Form meaning and use for English language teachers*. Boston, MA: National Geographic.

Leech, J. (1971). *Meaning and the English verb*. London: Longman.

McCawley, J. D. (1998). *The syntactic phenomena of English*. Chicago: Chicago University Press.

Quirk, R., Greenbaum, S., Leech, G., Svartvik, J., & Crystal, D. (1985). *A comprehensive grammar of the English language*. London: Longman.

Radden, G., & Dirven, R. (2007). *Cognitive English grammar*. Amsterdam: John Benjamins Publishing.

Schlenker, P. (2004). Context of thought and context of utterance: A note on free indirect discourse and the historical present. *Mind & Language*, 19(3), 279–304.

Wolfson, N. (1979). The conversational historical present alternation. *Language*, 168–182.

Wolfson, N. (1982). *CHP: The conversational historical present in American English narrative*. Berlin: Walter de Gruyter.

Yule, G. (1998). *Explaining English grammar*. Oxford: Oxford University Press.

## Data References

Abstract (hydraulic escalator). (2016, February 28). Retrieved August 15, 2016, from www.project-topics.info/Mechanical/Hydraulic_Escalator.php

Bartholomew, D. (2014). The 1994 Northridge earthquake. *Los Angeles Daily News*. Retrieved January 8, 2016, from www.dailynews.com/general-news/20140111/northridge-earthquake-1994-disaster-still-fresh-in-los-angeles-minds-after-20-years

Biography of Louis Daniel Armstrong. (n.d.). Louis Armstrong educational foundation. Retrieved April 5, 2016, from www.louisarmstrongfoundation.org/louis.php

The Boston Tea Party. (n.d.). History. Retrieved March 10, 2016, from www.history.com/this-day-in-history/the-boston-tea-party

Brest, M. (1998). *Meet Joe Black* [Motion Picture]. United States: Universal Pictures.

Davies, M. (2008–). *The corpus of contemporary American English: 520 million words, 1990–present*. Retrieved from http://corpus.byu.edu/coca/

Ganz, L. & Mandel, B. (1991). Script for *City Slickers*. Retrieved August 15, 2016 from www.cswap.com/1991/City_Slickers/cap/en/25fps/a/00_08

Gorry-Hines, B. (n.d.). Good reads. Retrieved December 2, 2016, from www.goodreads.com/quotes/312075-life-has-a-way-of-going-in-circles-ideally-it

Horrible customer service. (n.d.). Retrieved March 5, 2015, from www.tripadvisor.com.

Hoffman, E. (1989). *Lost in translation*. New York: Penguin.

Kaur, J. (2011). Intercultural communication in English as a lingua franca: Some sources of misunderstanding. *Intercultural Pragmatics, 8*, 93–116.

McDonough, Y. (2010). *Who was Rosa Parks?* New York: Penguin.

Moore, E., & Podesva, R. (2009). Style, indexicality and the social meaning of tag questions. *Language in Society, 38*, 447–485.

Oettinger, A.G. (1966). The uses of computers in science. *Scientific American 215*(3), 160–175.

Quinn, A. (2016). Know thyself? 'Swing Time' says it's complicated. NPR.org. Retrieved November 20, 2016, from www.npr.org/2016/11/16/501484095/know-thyself-swing-time-says-it-cant-be-done

Rosa Parks Museum. (n.d.).Retrieved September 23, 2017, from www.smitshonianmag.com/museumday/venues/museum/rosa-parks-museum/

Steinbeck, J. (1993). *Of mice and men*. New York: Penguin.

Walt Disney. (n.d.) Retrieved August 15, 2016 from www.biography.com/people/walt-disney-9275533

We've made some improvements. (n.d.). The weather channel. Retrieved December 2, 2015, from https://weather.com.

Wilde, O. (1909). The star child. In O. Wilde, *A house of pomegranates: Vol. 4*. Leipzig: B Tauchnitz.

You've been cutting watermelon all wrong (n.d.). Retrieved March 10, 2016, from www.youtube.com/watch?v=9mZ51AXsz4M.

# 8 The Grammar of Directives, Permissions, Obligations, Opinions, and Mitigations

Imperatives and Modals

*Figure 8.1* "Employees must wash hands"
© Randy Glasbergen. Reproduced with permission of Glasbergen Cartoon Service.

In Chapter 7, we observed the robust ways in which tense and aspect interrelate with verbs and enhance our ability to depict and envision events, actions, and conditions in discourse. We observed how inflectional morphemes designate present and past tense, both in **simple tenses** as well as in **complex markings of aspect**, in addition to signaling concepts of singularity and plurality for a handful of reference types. Most importantly, we examined the conceptual meanings of tense, time, and aspect and observed the ways in which grammatical features of tense and aspect evoke meaning well beyond the simple notion of time, including stance-related meanings.

In this chapter, we focus on the grammar of giving orders and directions; granting permission; expressing obligation; putting forth offers and invitations; encouraging; giving information; and communicating suggestions, advice, and opinions.

We introduce the categories of **mood** (especially **imperative mood**) and **modality** (especially **deontic modality**, **epistemic modality**, and **dynamic modality**) that serve to fulfill these and other functions in discourse (Blakemore, 1994; Bybee et al., 1994; Chung & Timberlake, 1985; Nuyts & van der Auwera, 2016; Palmer, 2001; Portner, 2009; Quirk et al., 1985; Sweetser, 1982). Beyond the interactional and conceptual meanings, the categories of **imperatives** and **simple modals** take **no overt inflectional morphology** for tense or number in English.

**Imperatives** belong to the category of grammar typically associated with the **communicative functions** (or **speech acts**)[1] of orders, offers, commands, requests, invitations, suggestions, cheers, challenges, wishes, and dares (e.g., *Keep* calm, *Pay* here, *Be* a good boy, *Stop!*, *Hit* a home run!, *Eat* your vegetables, *Try* this, *Come* to my party, *Join* us for tea, *Go* Bruins!, *Have a good day! Enjoy!*). Imperatives also express prohibitions, negative suggestions/requests, and encouragements (i.e., *Don't* litter, *Don't* waste food, *Don't* play with matches, *Don't* drink and drive, *Don't* worry, *Don't* give up). Imperatives appear throughout discourse: in face-to-face interaction involving strangers, acquaintances, friends, family members, bosses, teachers, and coaches; in the discourse of procedures, policies, instructions, advertising, public signage, and warning labels; and in the discourse of ethics, morality, and religion.

**Modals** are also associated with communicating offers, suggestions, and requests, and some modals are found in many of the same discursive environments as imperatives. However, the functions and meanings of modals are much broader than those related to imperatives. Modals are divided into three basic categories of function and meaning: (1) **deontic modality**, expressing the notions of permission and obligation; (2) **epistemic modality**, expressing the speaker's or writer's evaluative stance or belief about something—on a continuum ranging from being very certain to being entirely unsure; and (3) **dynamic modality**, expressing ability—typically with modals *can* and *could*. We will explain these three types of modality in detail in Section 8.2.

## 8.1 Imperatives: Asking, Requesting, Commanding, Urging, or Nudging the Addressee to Do or Not Do Something

Imperatives essentially function to directly tell someone to do something or not do something. Imperatives are found in objective instructions or directions for the accomplishment of a task or procedure, in gentle nudges, in direct commands and in warnings or threats. The **form** of the imperative is simple in that it can be a one-word utterance. There is **no added morphology** and, therefore, **no subject-verb agreement**. The time expressed by an imperative encompasses both present tense (i.e., now) or future time (i.e., later than now). The subject of an imperative is typically the second person, i.e., **you**, intended as a specific and identifiable addressee, a group of specific addressees; or a set of non-specific, generic addressees or overhearers. The **subject pronoun 'you'** (denoting a singular addressee or a plural addressee) is **not typically overt** (e.g., *Proceed with caution* vs. ?*You proceed with caution*).

Imperatives also express inclusiveness with the speaker. Inclusive imperatives appear in formal and informal forms, typically using *Let's*, *Let us*, or *Let*: "*Let's go*" (informal) or "*Let us all unite*" (formal). The so-called *Let* imperatives can also be used without the inclusive first-person plural pronoun (*us*), to express a desire to bring about a particular outcome: *Let the games begin! Let there be peace on earth*. These types of imperatives are called **exhortative imperatives**.

The following encapsulate the main features of imperatives:

- Bare verb, no tense marking or SVA. The time implied is present or future.
- Addressee is second-person 'you' (implied or overt): singular, plural, and generic (see Chapter 5).

*Imperatives and Modals* 221

- Pronoun 'you' is typically not mentioned in the imperative.
- Affirmative imperatives include commands, orders, suggestions, requests, offers, and invitations.
- Negative imperatives (*don't, do not, never, don't ever*) include prohibitions, negative suggestions/requests, and expressions of encouragement.
- The exhortative imperatives (*let's, let us, let*-something-happen) express a desire to bring about a particular outcome: *Let the games begin! Let there be peace on earth and let it begin with me.*

## *8.1.1 Imperatives: Forms and Conceptual Meaning*

An addressee or recipient of an imperative is directly ordered, urged, requested, encouraged, invited, persuaded, warned, advised, or threatened to do or not do something. Such expressions can be delivered in the following ways:

- Objectively for the addressee to follow a procedure or accomplish a task (e.g., *Turn left.*)
- Urgently, to forewarn the addressee or to advise the addressee of danger (e.g., *Get out! Stay down!*)
- To show closeness, solidarity, or intimacy (e.g., *Stay warm.*)
- To exhibit authority over someone (e.g., *Put your pencils down.*)
- To imply that the addressee would benefit from the action or from not performing the action (e.g., *Exercise and eat more vegetables. Don't listen to the rumors.*)
- In a mitigated way with *please* to seemingly decrease the burden or intrusiveness of a directive (e.g., *Please take your seats.*)
- In an intensified way with *please* to implore or emphasize a request (e.g., *Please respond. Please stop sending us junk mail.*)

## Forms of Imperatives

**Unmitigated, bald imperative** (no "please" or other mitigation):

| Affirmative | Negative |
| --- | --- |
| *Read* Chapter 1 for tomorrow. | *Don't answer* the questions on p. 20. |
| *Do* your own work. | *Don't call* after 9:00 p.m. |
| *Wash* your dishes after you eat. | *Don't run* in the house. |

**Imperative mitigated/softened with please:**

| Affirmative | Negative |
| --- | --- |
| *Please provide* your full name. | *Please don't use* pencil. |
| *Please put* your trash in plastic bags. | *Please don't tell* Mom! |

**Uncontracted negative imperatives:** *Don't* becomes *do not*—used both with and without *please*. Uncontracted negative imperatives are emphatic and strong. They are also more formal, which accounts for why this form is more commonly seen in public notices and signs.

*Do not insult* the deaf or *cause* the blind to stumble. (Leviticus 19:14)
DO NOT ENTER                          [traffic sign]
Silica gel. *Do not* eat.                 [sachets of silica gel enclosed in retail packaging]
(*Please*) *Do not* disturb.             [doorknob placards in hotels, etc.]
*Do not use* physical force when disciplining children.
A representative will be with you shortly. *Please do not* hang up.

**Exhortatives** (three types: Let's, Let us, Let . . .)²:

a   *Let's* type of inclusive imperative: let us → contracted to *let's*
    informal; adding *please* is possible

    *Let's analyze* this chemical compound.    *Let's not compare* it to the prior one.
    (Please) *Let's leave* now so we're not late.   (Please) *Let's not be* late again.

b   *Let us* type of inclusive imperative: no contraction
    formal; adding *please* is possible

    *Let us celebrate* his life and memory.    *Let us not forget* his accomplishments.
    *Let us observe* the failures of the past.   (Please) *let us not make* the same mistakes.

c   *Let*-something-happen type of imperative
    not inclusive; formal; adding *please* is possible but extremely marked

    *Let* the good times roll.
    *Let* there *be* light.
    *Let* bygones *be* bygones.


### 8.1.2 Objective Imperatives in a Procedure or a Task (Instructional/Procedural Discourse, No Mitigation)

Unmitigated imperatives are typical in instructional or procedural discourse (e.g., recipes, step-by-step instruction, website navigational buttons, and how-to demonstrations). We also commonly find unmitigated imperatives in public signs and product labels (often uncontracted, e.g. "Do not . . ."). These are essentially neutral, objective-sounding instructions that addressees are expected to or directed to follow. Such imperatives are designed to be information-based and not intended to offend or to sound overly direct. In other words, these types of imperatives are not particularly "face threatening"[3] from a pragmatic perspective. These are designed for generic readers/hearers, and not addressed to any individual in particular. What follows are more specific examples of the types of genres in which these types of pragmatically neutral imperatives appear:

- Recipes

    *Pre-heat* oven to 450°F.
    *Beat* eggs until fluffy.
    *Pour* mixture into medium-sized bowl.
    *Season* with salt and pepper,
    *Place* mixture into greased baking dish.

    Typical imperatives: *bake, broil, panfry, whip, whisk, fold, stir, combine, knead*

- **Procedural instructions**

    *Sign* here.
    *Make* checks payable to Chase Card Services.
    *Wait* here for next available representative.

    Typical imperatives: *use, write, provide, complete, fill in, respond, submit*

- **Procedural instructions: electronic technology-mediated**

    For more information, *go* to www.moreinformationaboutgrammar.com.
    *Click* "submit" to complete this application.
    *Copy* and *paste* your résumé into the space provided.
    *Enter* your work history, one field at a time.

    Typical imperatives: *submit, browse, log in, log out, attach, delete, upload, edit*

- **Signage**

    *Stop*
    *Yield*
    *Proceed With Caution*
    *Push*
    *Pull*
    *Do Not Enter*
    *Keep Off the Grass*

    Typical imperatives: *keep, stop, avoid, reduce, beware of, pitch in*

- **Product labels**

    | | |
    |---|---|
    | *Lather. Rinse. Repeat.* | [shampoo] |
    | *Turn* nozzle to spray position. | [liquid cleaning spray] |
    | *Pre-treat* tough stains. | [laundry detergent] |
    | *Ask* your doctor . . . | [medicine] |
    | *Use* as directed. | [medicine] |

    Typical imperatives: *apply, pour, peel, tear, spray, fold, snip, take, wash, dry, remove*

## 8.1.3 Unmitigated Imperatives: Not Objective

In contrast, in certain contexts or situations, unmitigated imperatives can indicate subjective speaker stances such as urgency and critical timing; social or emotional distance, especially when imperatives are used for the regulation of others' behaviors; and social or emotional closeness between friends or family. These imperatives also indicate persuasive stances, as in advertising discourse. In advertising, imperatives seem to draw recipients into an emotional space where they may anticipate a benefit from a product or service.

The use of unmitigated imperatives in this way can indeed be face threatening, depending on the context and the relationship between the participants.

- **For the sake of urgency or safety**

    *Evacuate* the building! There's a fire!
    *Watch out!* That truck is changing lanes.

224  *Imperatives and Modals*

*Duck!* The ball's coming right toward you.
*Do not use* if you have ever had an allergic reaction to this product.
*Walk faster!* Those people are following us.

- **To regulate another person's behavior**

   *Eat* your vegetables.
   *Don't talk* with your mouth full.
   *Clean* your room.
   *Show* your work.
   *Leave* package on doorstep.
   *Show* me your license.

- **To signal emotional and/or social closeness between speaker and addressee**

   *Call* me.   *Text* me.   *Message* me.
   *Send* us a postcard when you arrive.
   *Try* that tea I sent you. You'll feel better.
   *Take* a seat.
   *Make* yourself at home.
   *Help yourself* to a snack.
   *Go* Pirates! *Hit* a home run!
   *Sleep* well.

- **To promote a product or service to benefit the recipient or addressee, where the imperative sounds more like an invitation**

   *Request* your free catalog.
   *Learn* more.
   *Create* your own sundae.
   *Find* hundreds of giveaways.
   *Get* 6 months free.

### 8.1.4 *Mitigating or Intensifying Stance: Adverbs* Please, Just, Already, Never

Adverbs such as *please*, *just*, *already*, and *never* can affect the overall meanings of imperatives in discourse, sometimes mitigating the imperatives and sometimes intensifying them.

### 8.1.4.1 *Mitigated and Intensifying Imperatives: With* Please

One common way of mitigating imperatives involves the addition of the adverb *please*, commonly just before the verb, but not always. *Please* is often considered a "politeness marker," used to soften the intrusion of a more direct, non-objective imperative (Allen, 1995; Celce-Murcia & Larsen-Freeman, 1999, pp. 234–235; House, 1989; Ogiermann, 2009; Wichmann, 2004).

As you'll see later, *please* does occur quite formulaically as a single adverb preceding the verb, and it does create the impression of making the imperative sound "more polite," by seemingly decreasing the burden of what is being directed.

   *Please make* checks payable to State Farm Insurance.
   For information about this account, *please see* our Current Report on 9-K.
   *Please read* this notice carefully.
   If you have a disability and need this letter in large print, *please call* our help line.

*Please join* me in welcoming our special guest, Dr. Reynaldo Batista.
Our website is under construction. *Please pardon* our dust.
*Please see* important safety information below and full pharmaceutical details.
*Please write* legibly.
*Please use* ink.
*Please use* the envelope provided.

While the adverb *please* may serve to tone down a request or directive, it's important to note that adding *please* does not always reduce the strength of the message. In spoken discourse, speakers can change their tone of voice to emphatically express stances that actually intensify the communicative intent (e.g., begging, insistence, or sternness). *Please* can be reduplicated or repeated ("please, please, please"), or embellished with highly marked formulaic expressions like "pretty please" or "pretty please with sugar on top." These latter variations of *please* are very marked and only used in limited contexts.

## Imperatives intensified with *please*

*Pleeease* give me another cookie!  [tone of voice—imploring]
*Oh please*. Tell us more.  [tone of voice—hyper-eliciting, affiliative]
*Oh please*. Don't bother.  [tone of voice—ironic, disaffiliative]
*Please, please* give me another chance.  [reduplication—imploring]

## Embellished request

*Let* me stay up until 11:00 . . . *pretty please?* (*with sugar on top.*)  [embellished—imploring, childlike]

### 8.1.4.2 Imperatives + Just

Similar to *please*, the adverb *just* can both mitigate and intensify an imperative. Due to its original meaning that involves restriction, *just* can either downplay a request, making the task sound simpler, or intensify the request, making the utterance sound more harsh (Aijmer, 2002, pp. 153–174; Brown & Levinson, 1987, p. 147; Holmes, 1984, p. 364).

## Just: Restrictiveness, limited in quantity or scope

*Just play* the opening part of the piece.  [not the entire sonata]
  cf. *Play* the opening part of the piece.

*Just give* us the facts, no added details, please.
  cf. *Give* us the facts, no added details, please.

*Just eat* the meat. You can leave the bread and the pickles.
  cf. *Eat* the meat.

## Just: Making an action sound easier to accomplish

*Just pretend* you're having a good time.
  cf. *Pretend* you're having a good time.

*Just shred* and *discard* the old policy documents.
  cf. *Shred* and *discard* the old policy documents.

226  *Imperatives and Modals*

*Just add* hot water.
   cf. *Add* hot water.

*Just do it.*
   cf. *Do it.*

*Just* may also co-occur with the adverb *already* in imperatives. The adverb *already* expresses a strong stance of impatience. Expressions with adverb *already* can be highly face threatening in most contexts.

| *Do* it. | Just do it already. |
| *Add* hot water. | Just add hot water already. |

Adding *please*—intensifies the stance of impatience all the more:

Please just do it already.
Please just add the hot water already.

### 8.1.5 Negative Imperatives—Continuum of Message Strength: Don't, Never, Don't Ever

We introduced *don't* and its uncontracted form *do not* as typical forms to express the negative imperative as a prohibition or negative suggestion. Adverbs *never* and *ever* can be added to this continuum of stance marking.

Negative imperatives: *Don't* → *Do not* → *Never* → *Don't ever*

| **Neutral** | **Emphatic** | **Stronger** | **Strongest** |
|---|---|---|---|
| Don't try this at home. | Do not try this at home. | Never try this at home. | Don't ever try this at home. |
| Don't forget. | Do not forget. | Never forget. | Don't ever forget. |
| Don't give up. | Do not give up. | Never give up. | Don't ever give up. |

"Lesson 1: Don't spend more than you earn.
Lesson 2: Don't spend more than you earn.
Lesson 3: Don't spend more than you earn.
Lesson 4: Don't spend more than you earn.
Lesson 5: Don't spend more than you earn."

*Figure 8.2* "Don't spend more than you earn"

© Randy Glasbergen. Reproduced with permission of Glasbergen Cartoon Service.

*Don't* share your password with anyone.
*Do not* share your password with anyone.
*Never* share your password with anyone.
*Don't ever* share your password with anyone.
*Don't* share your password with anyone, *ever*.
*Never* share your password with anyone, *ever*.

### Mini Review and Practice

1  We have observed that the form of imperatives is simple. It involves just the bare verb with no added morphology and typically no overt subject *you*. The essential meaning of the imperative fulfills a number of different types of **communicative functions** or **speech acts** such as the following:

- orders
- commands
- requests
- giving assignments
- designating steps in a procedure
- advice giving
- invitations
- suggestions
- offers
- encouragements

*Context* is key to understanding imperatives: We need to consider the following questions: In what context is the imperative used? Who is producing the imperative? To whom? And for what purpose? If spoken, what is the tone of voice?

Let's compare and contrast some examples:

a   www.Apple.com    iPhoneSE

*Watch the keynote* > (hyperlinked) > *Learn* more (hyperlinked)

(iPhoneSE, n.d.)

Within the previous context, the imperatives "*Watch* the keynote" and "*Learn* more" are perfectly objective and neutral. How would you identify these two directives as speech acts? Are they closer in function to orders/commands or to invitations/offers?

Now, let's change the context (face-to-face) and the participants:

**Student to teacher**
"*Watch* the film." "*Learn* more."

What happens when the near identical words are used in a different context, involving different participants, and especially participants of unequal social status?

How would you characterize the speech acts in the new context? Do the speech acts have the same communicative functions?

Part of the puzzle also involves the meaning of the verb *learn*. In the context of the iPhone description or an online link for added information about an advertised product, what does *learn* mean? In the context of a student speaking to his or her teacher, what would *learn* mean there? Is it the identical meaning? Is it polite or pragmatically acceptable to tell someone simply to "learn more" with just these two words and no other surrounding context, especially when it is a student speaking to a teacher?

How does the context of the Apple.com website make this imperative perfectly acceptable and, in fact, inviting?

    b    From the cover of the May 16, 2016, *Woman's World* magazine:

        *CUT* YOUR GROCERY BILL IN HALF
        *EAT* WHAT YOU WANT WITHOUT GAINING WEIGHT
        *GET* A BETTER MEMORY in just three weeks
                                                      (*Woman's World*, 2016)

Who is being addressed? How do you know? What is the **communicative function** of each imperative-based utterance? Is it a request, an order, or a suggestion? Think about context: Why do these types of sentences appear on the cover of a women's supermarket weekly magazine? Can these imperatives seem offensive or face threatening in any way?

Now, let's change the context:

| | |
|---|---|
| Mother to son: | *Cut* your grocery bill in half. |
| Waiter to restaurant customer: | *Eat* what you want without gaining weight. |
| Teacher to student: | *Get* a better memory in just three weeks. |

When we change the context, what happens to the message? The words are identical, but the meanings of each imperative sentence are not. What might the communicative functions be in the changed contexts? Would they be offensive or face threatening? Why? How does the power relationship between the speaker and the addressee affect our understanding of these speech acts?

2    As we have seen, most imperatives do not include the pronoun *you* in the utterance. When *you* is included, the utterance may sound more harsh and more direct, as in the following examples:

    a    Imperatives with overt *you*—intensified harshness

        *Be quiet. / Come here.*        bald imperative, strong intention
        *You be quiet! / You come here!*    imperative with *you*, intensified harshness

    However, overt *you* can be used with imperatives in a variety of other ways:

    b    Imperatives with overt *you*—no intensified harshness

        *Have* a great weekend.
        Thanks. *You* have a great weekend, too.

Do you want to flip a coin, or do you want me to?
*You* do it.

((boarding a bus—two people reach the bus door at the same time))
*You go ahead.*     or     *You go first.*

((a teacher is distributing work assignments for the class))
Patricia and Fabian, *you read* the first two chapters, and *this team here* ((pointing out two more students)), *you read* the next two chapters.

((an individual takes charge at a crowded shopping mall as the fire alarm sounds and the sprinklers go off))
*You, call* 911! ((with pointing gesture)). *You three, spread out* and *lead* people out of the building! *Somebody, anybody, find* mall security and *get* them to help! *Everyone else, exit* the building quickly and *stay* out of the way of the fire trucks.

How do the types of imperatives listed under b differ from those that we have examined throughout this chapter that involve no overt addressee or subject pronoun *you*?

Does the inclusion of *you* with the imperative in these examples make the utterances sound especially harsh, like the examples in a (*You be quiet!* or *You come here!*)? If not, why not?

What do you sense the pronoun *you* is doing in all of the b examples? What function does the overt pronoun fulfill that makes this type of imperative slightly different in meaning from the common type with no overt *you*?

In the last example, we include *you* vs. *you three* in addition to other pronouns that can be and are used with imperatives (e.g., *everyone, everyone else, someone, somebody, anyone, anybody*).

How does the delivery of the message change with these variations in overt pronouns? What is the difference between the following imperatives? Can you rank these according to strength in terms of which will get the job done the most efficiently and which the least efficiently? Why is that the case?

*You, find* mall security! ((using a pointing gesture))
*Somebody, find* mall security!
*Anybody, find* mall security!

3   Same words, different tone of voice, different communicative function

As we work with imperatives, especially in oral discourse, it is important to keep in mind that both context and tone of voice are critical.

**Compare:**

| | |
|---|---|
| Go ((rising intonation)), Makoto! | uttered as a cheer |
| Go ((falling intonation)), Makoto! | uttered as a strong order for Makoto to leave |
| Go ahead, make my day! | uttered as an encouragement |
| Go ahead, make my day! | uttered with ironic tone, as a dare[4] |

Think about the various types of communicative functions the following utterance might carry. Vary the context, the participants (who says this and to whom?), and the delivery style (e.g., tone of voice, gestures) to construe multiple possible meanings for this one utterance.

How does the speech act change when the context, participants, and delivery style change?

*Come on. Take* **one more step.**

Context: _____
Participants: _____
Communicative function/speech act: _____

Context: _____
Participants: _____
Communicative function/speech act: _____

Context: _____
Participants: _____
Communicative function/speech act: _____

4   The following quote by William Arthur Ward contains an interesting collection of imperatives.

*Do* more than belong: *participate. Do* more than care: *help. Do* more than believe: *practice. Do* more than *be* fair: *be* kind. *Do* more than forgive: *forget. Do* more than dream: *work.*

(Ward, as cited in Gilliland, 2015, p. 84; emphasis added)

The imperative forms appear in italics. First, what does this message really mean? What do you notice about the way the message is constructed?

The entire quote is essentially a series of six pieces of advice. Each piece of advice is structured with a longer sentence, followed by a colon and then a one-word imperative. There are a total of 12 imperative utterances in the passage. Each piece of advice contains a contrast involving verb meanings. How does this systematic set of contrasts enable Ward to construct his message the way he does in this quote?

The five pieces of advice are all expressed in the form of affirmative imperatives. By virtue of the contrast and how it is presented, it is also possible to construe a similar (but clearly not identical) message using negative imperatives:

Affirmative imperative: *Do* **more than belong**: *participate.*
Negative imperative:   *Don't just belong: participate.*

Continue this pattern for the remaining five pieces of advice. How does the strength of the overall message of the text change as we alter the structure throughout from an affirmative imperative to a negative one? Explain your answer in detail.

## 8.2 Modality: Giving/Asking Permission, Suggesting, Prohibiting, Guessing, Assuming, Conjecturing, Inferring, and Expressing Ability

**Modals** provide speakers and writers a wide range of choice with regard to pragmatics and stance marking. The inventory of modals that we use in English naturally evokes a continuum of stance-related notions such as *authoritative strength*, *certainty*, *possibility*, *evaluative judgment concerning social expectations*, and the cognitive-affective psychological mechanism of *flipping from actuality to the unreal* or *hypothetical*. Modals are also closely associated with politeness.

Modals are typically categorized into three basic groups, according to their functions (Nuyts, 2016; Palmer, 2001, among others).

- **Deontic modality (D):** Expressing permission, obligation, advice, suggestions, promises, prohibitions, and social judgment.
    - Permission: You *may use* pencil for this exam. / *Can* I *go* now?
    - Obligation: Passengers *must wait* behind the yellow line. / Paid workers *must file* a tax return if their income is above a certain level.
    - Advice and suggestions: You *should study* harder. / Jeremy *should consult* with his boss first.
    - Promises: We *will* always *support* each other. / Our company *will replace* your damaged merchandise at no cost to you.
    - Prohibitions: Permit holders under the age of 16 *may not drive* without an adult in the car. / The auditor *must not be* an employee of the company.
- **Epistemic modality (E):** Evoking a **range of positions with varying degrees of uncertainty to certainty**. Note that a stance of absolute certainty typically requires no modal with the verb *be*. Modal *will* also indicates certainty with future time reference.

    It's 3:30, so the children *must be* home from school.   [strong speculation: *must*]
    cf. The children *are* home now.   [absolute certainty: no modal]
    Joan *might receive* a scholarship to Joffrey next year.   [speculation, uncertainty: *might*]
    cf. Joan *will receive* a scholarship to Joffrey next year.   [certainty/future: *will*]

- **Dynamic modality (Dy):** Expressing ability (or lack of ability), typically with the modals *can* and *could*.

    I *can recite* the alphabet in three seconds, *can* you?   [ability = dynamic]
    They *couldn't open* the door, even though they had the key.   [ability = dynamic]

**Modals** are structurally similar to imperatives in that there is no added verbal morphology to denote tense or subject, and no SVA is possible.

### 8.2.1 Modals: Forms and Conceptual Meaning

Modals express the speaker's or writer's stance, ranging from authoritative strength to non-assertiveness, strong to weak evaluative judgment, high certainty to low certainty, high degree of possibility and/or likelihood to low degree of possibility and/or likelihood, and ability of an entity to carry something out.

### Forms of modals: Simple modals

Simple modals are one-word modals.
They have no verbal morphology: no tense, **no SVA**.
They typically occur as auxiliaries **preceding the main verb** of the clause or sentence.

### Forms:

shall[5] (very limited usage in discourse)
will
must
should
could
can
might
may
would

All can be used deontically (D) or epistemically (E).

*Can/could* can be used deontically (D), epistemically (E), or dynamically (Dy).

### Examples:

**Zahara** <u>might</u> *graduate* this fall.  [speculation, uncertainty] **E**
[subj]  [modal]  [verb]

Here are seven questions **you** <u>should</u> *ask* yourself each day. [suggestion, advice] **D**
 [subj][modal] [verb]

**Hurricane Fred** <u>will</u> *hit* Cabo Verde on Friday.  [strong prediction, certainty] **E**
 [subj]   [modal]  [verb]

Meteorologists say **the storm** <u>should</u> *weaken* by Sunday.  [speculation, medium certainty] **E**
 [subj]  [modal]  [verb]

**Winnie** <u>can</u> *read* almost 1,000 Chinese characters already. [ability] **Dy**
[subj]  [modal][verb]

My vegan husband says he loves how my beef curry smells.
**It** <u>must</u> *be* the spices. Meat never smells good to him.  [speculation, high certainty] **E**

**You** *must stop* smoking, and soon.  [strong suggestion, command] **D**

### 8.2.1.1 Deontic Modality (D)

**Deontic modality** is related to **imperatives** in that both grammatical categories involve the general communicative function of the directive. Their use in discourse and interaction is associated with social expectations; personal, social, and legal obligations; and permission. Deontic modals, like imperatives, function to ask, urge, order, command, offer, permit, or encourage someone to do something (or not do something), as well as to prohibit someone from some action. Deontic modals and first-person references (e.g., *I*, *we*) express promises, plans, and self-judgments regarding social/personal expectations concerning one's own behavior (e.g., *I should leave now*; *We must accept responsibility for this outcome*).

The nine modals—*shall, will, must, should, could, can, might, may, would*—typically express a gradience in stance from a strong legal or moral obligation, strong will, and high agency (e.g., *shall*) to hypothetical scenarios of obligation or expectedness (e.g., *could*, *would*), as in Figure 8.3. The interpretations in brackets to the right of each example are general ideas illustrating the overall scale of meaning and do not represent fixed categories or a rigid hierarchy.

**shall:**      [legal requirement, obligation, strong will/high agency]
             The tenants <u>shall</u> *maintain* the premises in a neat and orderly fashion.
             But of the tree of knowledge of good and evil, you <u>shall</u> *not eat* . . .
             "We <u>Shall</u> *Overcome*" (song title)

**will:**        [absolute obligation, promise, commitment]
             The team <u>will</u> *work* collaboratively for the good of the corporation.
             We <u>will</u> *notify* as soon as we receive your application.
             "I <u>Will</u> Always *Love* You" (song title)

---

Gradience: From legal requirement, obligation/high agency to permission, possibility, and hypothetical

Topic: Child passenger safety in automobiles

| | |
|---|---|
| **Children under 26 pounds** <u>shall</u> *use* a rear-facing car seat. | [legal requirement, obligation] |
| **Children under 26 pounds** <u>will</u> *use* a rear-facing car seat. | [absolute obligation/ expectation] |
| **Children under 26 pounds** <u>must</u> *use* a rear-facing car seat. | [strong obligation] |
| **Children under 26 pounds** <u>should</u> *use* a rear-facing car seat. | [strong suggestion, expectation] |
| **Children under 26 pounds** <u>can</u> *use* a rear-facing car seat. | [possibility, permission] |
| **Children under 26 pounds** <u>might</u> *use* a rear-facing car seat. | [possibility, weak suggestion] |
| **Children under 26 pounds** <u>may</u> *use* a rear-facing car seat. | [permission, it is optional] |
| **Children under 26 pounds** <u>could</u> *use* a rear-facing car seat. | [hypothetical possibility] |
| **Children under 26 pounds** <u>would</u> *use* a rear-facing car seat. | [hypothetical expectation] |

*Figure 8.3* Gradience in meanings for deontic modals

234  *Imperatives and Modals*

**must:** [strong obligation]
Students <u>must</u> *come* to class prepared.
We <u>must</u> *be sure* to send a thank-you note to Yosef.
You <u>must</u> *look* both ways (i.e., to the left and the right) before you cross the street.

**should:** [strong suggestion, social/moral expectation]
In peer review sessions, your peer <u>should</u> *read* your essay aloud to you.
The babysitter <u>should</u> *call* you if anything at all happens.
Administrators <u>should</u> *treat* all employees fairly and with respect.

**could:** [possibility, permission, suggestion; hypothetical/counter-to-fact]
We <u>could</u> *call* his parents and find out about his family history.
You <u>could</u> *take* a day trip to Catalina Island, if you want to take a boat ride somewhere.
Teachers <u>could</u> *provide* a more detailed study guide for their students.

**can:** [possibility, permission, weak suggestion]
Following the seminar, participants <u>can</u> *remain* in contact with the organizers.
At the Creamery, you <u>can</u> *sample* any flavor of ice cream that you want.
You <u>can</u> *use* your class notes for the final exam.

**might:** [weak possibility, weak suggestion; hypothetical suggestion]
To make a homemade drum set, children <u>might</u> *use* empty coffee cans and pencils.
Next, the teacher <u>might</u> *ask* the students to write an essay on freedom.
To cut costs, we <u>might</u> *re-evaluate* the floor plan and not use mahogany trim.

**may:** [possibility, permission, suggestion; hypothetical prediction]
Buyers <u>may</u> *approach* the sellers to discuss more details about the property.
If you roll a one or a six, you <u>may</u> *advance* to the next square.
You <u>may</u> *substitute* whole milk with skim or non-fat milk.

**would:** [possibility, permission, suggestion; hypothetical/counter-to-fact]
Since it failed the first time, I <u>would</u> *change* the design.
What <u>would</u> Patria *do* in a case like this one?
Heidi directed the show so that everyone <u>would</u> *have* a singing part.
What would you have done if you saw that? [but you didn't see it = counter-to-fact]. (Is this deontic reading in any way ambiguous with an epistemic modality interpretation? See Section 8.2.1.2 for Epistemic Modality).

### 8.2.1.2 Epistemic Modality (E)

**Epistemic modality** expresses the speaker's or writer's belief, judgment, or evaluation of an issue as grounded within a particular system of knowledge. This sub-category of modality evokes a gradience in stance, ranging from strong certainty to weak belief, uncertainty, hypotheticality, and counterfactuality.

The same nine modals—*shall, will, must, should, could, can, might, may, would*—used epistemically express predictions, guesses, inferences, suppositions, and conjectures, as illustrated in Figure 8.4. Again, the meanings are not fixed, and the hierarchy is not rigid.

*Imperatives and Modals* 235

> Gradience: From strong certainty and predictions to weak belief, low possibility, strong certainty to strong uncertainty
>
> Topic: Oil prices
>
> *Oil prices <u>shall</u> *rebound* next month.  [ungrammatical: *shall* requires high agency, commitment, duty]
>
> Oil prices <u>will</u> *rebound* next month.  [strong certainty, future prediction]
>
> Oil prices <u>must</u> *rebound* next month.  [strong belief, high expectation]
>
> Oil prices <u>should</u> *rebound* next month.  [strong belief, medium expectation]
>
> Oil prices <u>could</u> *rebound* next month.  [medium belief or likelihood]
>
> Oil prices <u>can</u> *rebound* next month.  [medium belief or likelihood]
>
> Oil prices <u>might</u> *rebound* next month.  [weak belief, uncertain, low likelihood]
>
> Oil prices <u>may</u> *rebound* next month.  [weak belief, uncertain, low likelihood]
>
> Oil prices <u>would</u> *rebound* next month.  [hypothetical prediction for future]

*Figure 8.4* Gradience in meanings for epistemic modals

**shall:** [usage is rare—high register, future prediction evoking *deontic overtones*]
No one can predict the outcome, but we <u>shall</u> soon *see*.
All further treatment <u>shall</u> *be determined* by the health care professional.
Boeing <u>shall</u> *complete* its plans for the redesigned 787 by March 2019.

**will:** [strong certainty, future prediction]
Your video <u>will</u> *be* available in less than 3 minutes.
Smoking cigarettes <u>will</u> *make* your fingertips yellow.
A thunderstorm <u>will</u> *move* into the area later this evening.

**must:** [strong belief, high certainty, high expectation]
The bookshelf <u>must</u> *have* a center support bracket. It's not sagging in the middle.
The sign said "Las Vegas, 25 miles." We <u>must</u> *be* in Nevada already.
Fido keeps whimpering. He <u>must</u> *know* that Whiskers is hiding in the closet.

**should:** [strong belief, medium certainty, medium expectation]
Lady Gaga's new song <u>should</u> *make* the top 10 list in the first week. It's so good!
The play <u>should</u> *start* soon. The lights are flickering.
At this rate, we <u>should</u> *arrive* at Niagara-on-the-Lake by morning.

**can:** [medium belief, low certainty, less hypothetical]
If you don't take care of yourself, your cold <u>can</u> *get* much worse.
That <u>can</u> *be* a viable solution, but I'd rather not try it at this point.
If you haven't heard from Avis yet, that <u>can</u> *mean* that they don't have a car for you (to rent).

**could:** [medium belief, low certainty, more hypothetical]
Be careful when you receive strange emails. They <u>could</u> *be* scams.
They say that babies born today <u>could</u> *live* to 116 years old.
Here is a realistic scenario that <u>could</u> actually *happen*: . . .

**might:** [weak belief, low certainty]
That reddish light in the sky <u>might</u> *be* Venus.
Please put your key on a key chain. You <u>might</u> *lose* it.
Mario and Favio <u>might</u> *join* us for dinner later. Is that okay with you?

**may:** [weak belief, low certainty]
　　　　We <u>may</u> *be able to* visit Paris this summer.
　　　　Stocks <u>may</u> *rise* for the third week in a row.
　　　　That humming sound <u>may</u> *indicate* that you need a new refrigerator.

**would:** [prediction for future; hypothetical (possible)/counter-to-fact (impossible, did not happen)]
　　　　The sale of Cravate's painting <u>would</u> *raise* lots of money for the foundation.
　　　　I wanted you to join the group that <u>would</u> best *fit* your interests. [hypothetical]
　　　　The grass <u>would</u> *have grown* faster if you watered it more often. [ . . . *but you didn't* = counter-to-fact]

### 8.2.1.3 Dynamic Modality (Dy)

Dynamic modality is related to ability associated with things and people. It is this concept of natural, internal, spontaneous, physical, and mechanical ability that separates dynamic modality from deontic (permission, obligation, social expectation, authority) and epistemic (belief, degrees of uncertainty) modality.

The forms that typically express dynamic modality are *can* and *could*, as follows:

**can:** [ability—unchanging, present tense, future time]
　　　　Biniyam <u>can</u> *run* faster than Samuel.
　　　　Some fish <u>can</u> *swim* backward.
　　　　A jigsaw <u>can</u> *cut* almost any shape in many different types of materials.
　　　　Superglue <u>can</u> *fix* the soles of some shoes.

**could:** [ability—lower certainty, past time, hypothetical/counter-to-fact]
　　　　I wasn't sure whether he <u>could</u> *finish* the marathon race.
　　　　Naomi wished she <u>could</u> *talk* to her deceased mother again.
　　　　Did you see how high that kangaroo <u>could</u> *jump*?
　　　　Fiona had a parrot that <u>could</u> *mimic* sounds in any language.

---

### Mini Review and Practice

We have examined the basic categories of meanings of modals in English.

　　**Deontic (D):** permission, obligation, and social expectation
　　**Epistemic (E):** belief and degrees of uncertainty
　　**Dynamic (Dy):** natural, spontaneous, physical, and mechanical ability

1　Imperatives and deontic modality

　　We observed how imperatives and some aspects of deontic modality are associated with having other people perform certain actions:

**Imperative:**

| | |
|---|---|
| <u>Make</u> your check payable to Liberty Mutual. | [unmarked] |
| <u>Please</u> *make* your check payable to Liberty Mutual. | [unmarked] |
| <u>Just</u> *make* your check payable to Liberty Mutual. | [marked] |
| *Make* your check payable to Liberty Mutual <u>already</u>. | [marked, face threatening] |

**Deontic modality:**

You <u>must</u> *make* your check payable to Liberty Mutual.
You <u>may</u> *make* your check payable to Liberty Mutual.
You <u>can</u> . . .
You <u>should</u> . . .

How do these individual messages differ from one another? First, think about the four exemplars in the imperative category and then the four exemplars in the deontic modality category. How might you rank them within each category in terms of stance (e.g., degree of authoritative strength, objective, impatient, urgent)?

For the deontic modals, how much *choice* do you feel is implied for the addressee in each of the modals? Can you also rank the four messages according to the category of *choice afforded to addressee*? Also think about the role that context might play in these messages: Is the discourse oral/spoken or written? Where is the interaction taking place? Who are the participants? What is their relationship?

2   Let's revisit the opening cartoon for this chapter, Figure 8.1. It features a man at a restroom sink, above which is a series of four signs, stacked vertically with the largest sign on top and the smallest one on the bottom. These are the words in the signs:

> EMPLOYEES MUST WASH HANDS
> . . . then take a polygraph test to prove that you actually washed them.
> Yes, we are really serious about this.
> No kidding.

The cartoon serves as a parody and commentary on hand-washing and hygiene requirements in public places to prevent the spread of diseases. Signs (with varying types of wording) are now required to be posted in a number of different public locations. You can find the state-by-state laws as well as answers to FAQs here: www.signs.com/blog/handwashing-laws-for-all-50-states/.

Compare the wording of the parodied sign in the cartoon to the actual signs from the New Jersey and Kansas Departments of Health in Figures 8.5 and 8.6.

Think about how the directives are expressed through imperatives (affirmative and negative) and other grammatical means. What other written text accompanies these directives? How do the visuals complement the meaning in these signs? Explain your answers in detail.

Knowing this background, what makes the cartoon funny?

3   *Can* and *could*: **deontic, epistemic,** or **dynamic**?

The three basic categories for modals are useful guidelines for the understanding of the meanings of modals. As you see, all nine modals can function both deontically and

*Figure 8.5* Sign by New Jersey Department of Health

*Figure 8.6* Sign by Kansas Department of Health and Environment

*Imperatives and Modals* 239

epistemically. *Can* and *could* function in three ways: deontically, epistemically, and dynamically. These overlapping functions for the modal *can* can also be the source of ambiguity in discourse, as in the following classic jokes:

| Student to teacher: | <u>Can</u> I go to the bathroom? | (D) or (Dy) |
| Teacher: | I don't know. <u>Can</u> you? | (Dy) |
| Student: | Okay. <u>May</u> I go to the bathroom? | (D) |

And:

| Bobby: | Teacher, <u>can</u> I go to the bathroom? | (D) or (Dy) |
| Mrs. Jones: | <u>May</u> I go to the bathroom? | (D) |
| Bobby: | But Mrs. Jones, *I* asked you **first**! |  |

The following use of *can* will illustrate further:

We <u>can</u> *walk* to school. (D), (E), (Dy)

Meaning:

We are allowed to. (D)
It's a possible option, as opposed to taking the bus, but we're not sure. (E)
We have the physical ability, and the school is within walking distance. (Dy)

4   One more cartoon (Figure 8.7):

Who is uttering these words?
Why is it humorous?
What does the modal *might* mean in this context, and how does it contribute to the joke?

"Did you hear? They might make us wear uniforms to school next year!"

*Figure 8.7* "Did you hear? They <u>might</u> *make* us wear uniforms to school next year!"
© Randy Glasbergen. Reproduced with permission of Glasbergen Cartoon Service.

## 5 Modals in academic discourse

In academic writing, writers use modals to build rhetorical moves (Salager-Meyer, 1992). The modals *may, might, could,* and *would* evoke stances of lower certainty and hypotheticality when reporting on experimental procedures and/or outcomes of studies. The modal *can*, used dynamically, sometimes underscores potential dangers or risks associated with entities under investigation. The specific subjective stances that modals help convey are essential tools for writing in the scientific discourse community (Gledhill, 2000; Salager-Meyer, 1992; Swales, 1990).

The following excerpt is from an article titled "New Crop Pest Takes Africa at Lightning Speed," published in the May 5, 2017, issue of *Science*. It is a scientific news article under the heading "Food Security," and it reports on the mounting threat of the fall armyworm, a pest that has only recently come to Africa (Nigeria) in January 2016 and could have a devastating impact on maize, a primary crop of the continent.

Pay special attention to the modals used in the extract. List the sentences that contain them. What types of modals are they: epistemic, deontic, or dynamic? What other discourse features work together with the modals to express modality?

Hint: Look for conditional constructions with *if* (see Chapter 15) and other constructions that express necessity, possibility, doubt, urgency, and so forth that are not modals.

What meanings and stances do the modals in this excerpt express?

The larval stage of a small gray moth, the fall armyworm, <u>can</u> devastate maize, a staple, and <u>could</u> well attack almost every major African crop. One research group estimates that the damage to maize <u>could</u> total $3 billion in the next 12 months. . . .

Brazil has released parasitoid wasps to devour caterpillars; they <u>could</u> be imported to Africa, if regulators approve. Another approach <u>could</u> be to rear and release African predators of the fall armyworm, but they <u>would</u> first need to be identified. . . . Crop management <u>may</u> help, too.

[R]esearchers in Kenya <u>will</u> test nontransgenic maize with partial resistance against fall armyworm, but . . . it <u>could</u> take 4 to 5 years before new varieties are ready for farmers. . . .

If the species reaches Asia, says entomologist Ramasamy Srinivasan of the World Vegetable Center in Taiwan, "its introduction <u>might</u> have a huge economic impact."

(Stokstad, 2017)

## 8.3 Modals: Gradient Scale of Meaning From Strong Obligation/Certainty to Weak Suggestion/Low Likelihood—Establishing the Domain of the Unreal

Because the meanings of modals are associated with scalar stance-related notions of authoritative strength and social judgment on the one hand (deontic modality) and uncertainty, conjecture, and guessing on the other (epistemic modality), modals are found in discourse in which speakers

*Imperatives and Modals* 241

and writers express the unreal. That is, modals are used to express the hypothetical (what could *possibly be*) and the counterfactual (what could *never possibly be*).

### 8.3.1 Modals: Expressing the Hypothetical

Modals can express the hypothetical where the speaker or writer describes an event/situation in a tentative tone, portraying it as a "possible" but admittedly not real scenario. That is, there is a perceptual distance between the actual world and the imagined, hypothesized world. The modals most often used to construct these scenarios are *would*, *could*, and *might*. The following examples illustrate:

**Examples:**

a    How do you think you would/might/could *look* with red hair? [hypothetical:possible, but not the case now]

Question: Is can possible here? Why, or why not?

b    This history lesson is designed to help students understand whether a Great Depression could *happen* again and what might cause it.    [hypothetical]

c    **"This Woman Changed Her Name Just So She Could Log In to Facebook"**

You might *change* your name as a spy. Or adopt a new moniker to elude the law. But would you *change* your name for Facebook?

Jemma Rogers did. The holistic therapist from Lewisham, southeast London, changed her name to match her Facebook pseudonym, Jemmaroid Von Laalaa, after she was locked out of her account, according to the *Telegraph*.

(Time Staff, 2015)

d    **"The Golden Gate Bridge"**

Once called "the bridge that couldn't *be built*," today it (The Golden Gate Bridge) is one of the seven wonders of the modern world. This magnificent span, perhaps San Francisco's most famous landmark, opened in 1937 after four years of struggle against winds, fog, rock and treacherous tides.

(adapted from Golden Gate Bridge, n.d.)

### 8.3.2 Distancing From Realis: Expressing Politeness

As we have seen, modals depict the departure from the domain of the real and the factual to that of the unreal, imaginative, and hypothetical. They create a perceptual distance. In the same way, modals also serve to create a social distance and help speakers and writers express deference in certain types of deontically motivated communicative functions (e.g., in making requests, making suggestions, and giving advice), and as we saw in the discussion of imperatives, context is crucial.

**In close relationships, in urgent situations—bald imperative (no deference):**

Help me hang this picture.

**Mitigated requests, with modals (deference possible):**

<u>Can</u> you help me hang this picture?
<u>Could</u> you help hang this picture?
<u>Would</u> you help hang this picture?

**In close relationships, in urgent situations—bald imperative:**

Call him back on his cell phone!            [no deference]
Try calling him back on his cell phone.   [slight deference possible]

**Mitigated suggestions, with modals (more deference possible):**

You <u>can</u> try calling him back on his cell phone.
You <u>should</u> try calling him back on his cell phone.
You <u>could</u> try calling him back on his cell phone.
You <u>might</u> try calling him back on his cell phone

### 8.3.3 Flipping Reality: Modals for Counterfactual Thinking

Speakers and writers appeal to counterfactual thinking as a way of *flipping reality* from the domain of *realis*—what is or was true and factual to the domain of *irrealis* to juxtapose what *did not*, *would not*, or *could never happen now* but *could have*, *might have*, or *should have happened* in the transformed light of wishes, hopes, relief, and regrets.

Modal constructions coupled with perfect aspect (<u>modal</u> + *have* + *V-en*—see Chapter 7) evoke just these types of feelings of regret, disappointment, and even relief, by counterfactually flipping our understanding of the real and what did happen with an imagined scenario of what <u>could</u> *have*, <u>might</u> *have*, <u>would</u> *have*, or <u>should</u> *have happened*. In this way, modals indicate the conceptual domain of *irrealis*.

**Examples of flipped reality, from the realis domain of the real and actual to irrealis—counterfactual thinking:**

We heard that rain was expected today.
We <u>should</u> *have brought* our umbrellas.
   *irrealis*                              real → We did not bring umbrellas.

Malihe <u>could</u> *have told* me that her mom was sick.
   *irrealis*                              real → She did not tell me her mom was sick.

The soup is bland. I <u>should</u> *have used* more salt.
      *irrealis*                         real → I did not use enough salt for the soup.

"Deena Barselah, holistic wellness coach, on giving in to cravings"

> How many times have you eaten something and felt bad about yourself afterwards? You grab that second piece of cake, wing of fried chicken, donut, half of a bagel, scoop of ice cream, etc. and within minutes you say to yourself or the person next to you, "I really <u>shouldn't</u> *have eaten* that."
>
> (Barselah, 2014)

In oral discourse, the modal + perfect construction (<u>modal</u> + *have* + *V-en*) is often produced quickly, making the words run together and sound like "could of," "should of," and "would of" instead of "could/should/would have." This variant (i.e., replacing *have* with *of*) is not an acceptable one. It is entirely ungrammatical. *\*I should OF called first*. This is clearly ungrammatical because *of* should be *have*.

One variant that is acceptable in highly limited contexts is the phonologically reduced versions of these constructions: *woulda, coulda, shoulda*. These colloquialized expressions are often heard and seen in informal discourse to flip reality and express regret/disappointment for mistakes, missteps, and misdeeds. Used together in variable order, the set of three words "*Woulda, coulda, shoulda*" formulaically appear in article titles (e.g., Taylor, 2012), blogs (http://wouldashoulda.com), poems (Shel Silverstein's "Woulda-Coulda-Shoulda"), and songs ("Coulda Woulda Shoulda" by Céline Dion; "Shoulda Woulda Coulda" by Beverley Knight).

## 8.4 Multi-Word Modal Expressions

Other expressions in English also evoke similar meanings and stances as those expressed by the simple one-word modals. **Multi-word modals** are referred to elsewhere as phrasal modals (Celce-Murcia & Larsen-Freeman, 1999; Larsen-Freeman & Celce-Murcia, 2016), periphrastic modals (Yule, 1998, 2010), semi-modals (Biber et al., 1999), or quasi-modals (Quirk et al., 1985). They differ from simple one-word modals in terms of scope of meaning, stance, and SVA. That is, these multi-word modals and other expressions not in the list (e.g., be set to, be fixing to, be required to, be obliged to) that might also fulfill the same communicative function are sensitive to time-marking (present/past tense, future time) as well as SVA. Note that the multi-word modals also express the three categories of modality: deontic, epistemic, and dynamic.

| General meaning overlap | Simple modal | Multi-word modal |
| --- | --- | --- |
| future time | will | be going to, be about to |
| social expectation | should | be supposed to, be expected to, *ought to* |
| ability, permission | can | be able to, be permitted to, be allowed to |
| past ability, permission | could | was able to, was permitted/allowed to |
| permission | may | be allowed to, be permitted to |
| obligation, strong conjecture | must | have to, have got to, need to, had better |
| past time narrative | would | *used to* |

Of the multi-word modals, *ought to* and *used to* are not inflected for tense or SVA.

### 8.4.1 Simple Modal Will and Multi-Word Modal Be Going To

In Chapter 7, we observed that the modal *will* is typically used to express future time. It is used to discuss a situation that has not yet happened but is likely to happen. We indicated that *will* is also used to express a stance of strong prediction, determination, or intended outcome.

244   *Imperatives and Modals*

Most of the instances of *will* that we discussed as markers of future time are in fact (a) **deontic modals** of promises, oaths, requests, and expressions of future plans and (b) **epistemic modals** of prediction.

| | |
|---|---|
| I <u>will</u> *prevent* disease whenever I can . . . | (D) |
| <u>Will</u> Trevor *fix* the leak? | (D) |
| <u>Will</u> this sweater *be* enough to keep you warm? | (E) |
| Esso stock prices <u>will</u> *rise* in the near future. | (E) |

The multi-word modal *be going to* can also be used to express future time and situations that have not happened as yet but are indeed likely to happen.

**Compare:**

| | |
|---|---|
| I <u>will</u> *prevent* disease whenever I can. | **will (D)** |
| I <u>am going to</u> *prevent* disease whenever I can. | **be going to (D)** |
| <u>Will</u> Trevor *fix* the leak? | **will (D)** |
| <u>Is</u> Trevor <u>going to</u> *fix* the leak? | **be going to (D)** |
| Esso stock prices <u>will</u> *rise* in the near future. | **will (E)** |
| Esso stock prices <u>are going</u> *to rise* in the near future. | **be going to (E)** |

The multi-word modal *be going to* indeed expresses future time. However, unlike *will*, *be going to*[6] signals the following:

- a slightly lower register (according to Davies [2008], *be going to* is twice as frequent in spoken vs. written registers)
- a higher degree of interpersonal closeness
- stronger affect/emotion
- a more time-immediate/imminent action
- a stance evoking stronger certainty

The simple modal *will*, in contrast, signals the following:

- higher register
- a lower degree of interpersonal closeness/higher degree of interpersonal distance
- less strong affect/emotion
- a less time-immediate or time-specific action
- a stance evoking a higher degree of predictive force

These differences account for why official oaths or promises are expressed with *will* and not with *be going to*.

The following excerpt is from the naturalization oath that is taken by all immigrants who become US citizens. Note the strings of promises expressed by *will* (deontic modality). We have underlined the instances of <u>will</u> + *verb* and have italicized the verbs that co-occur with *will*:

"Naturalization Oath of Allegiance to the United States of America"

> I hereby declare, on oath, that I absolutely and entirely renounce and abjure all allegiance and fidelity to any foreign prince, potentate, state, or sovereignty, of whom or which I have heretofore been a subject or citizen; that I <u>will</u> *support* and *defend* the Constitution and laws of the United States of America against all enemies, foreign and domestic; that I <u>will</u> *bear* true faith and allegiance to the same; . . . that I <u>will</u> *perform* work of national importance under civilian direction when required by the law; and that I take this obligation freely, without any mental reservation or purpose of evasion; so help me God.
>
> (The Department of Homeland Security, n.d.)

Now, let's examine these same expressions, altered by exchanging *be going to* (deontic modality) with *will*:

> ?I hereby declare, on oath, . . . that <u>I am going to</u> *support* and *defend* the Constitution, that <u>I am going to</u> *bear* true faith and allegiance, . . . that I am going to perform work of national importance.

### 8.4.1.1 Multi-Word Modal Be Going To *vs.* Be About To: *Both Indicate "Later Than Now or Time of Speech"—The Difference Is an Aspectual One*

| | |
|---|---|
| My mom looks like she's <u>going to</u> *cry*. | very soon |
| My mom looks like she's <u>about to</u> *cry*. | very very soon, immediately |

Message printed on hot beverage cup sleeves:

| | |
|---|---|
| Caution: The beverage you are <u>about to</u> *enjoy* is extremely hot. | very very soon, immediately |

    cf. ?Caution: The beverage you <u>are going to</u> *enjoy* is extremely hot.
    ?Caution: The beverage you <u>will</u> *enjoy* is extremely hot.

## 8.4.2 Simple Modal Must *and Multi-Word Modals* Have to, Have Got to, Need To

*Must, have to, have got to,* and *need to* appear to be synonymous, expressing strong obligation (deontic modality). However, these modal expressions differ both in terms of register and the speaker's or writer's stance toward the expressed information. Here we will elaborate their differences in discourse and usage.

The differences between simple modal *must* vs. *have to/have got to* and *need to* are summarized as follows and then exemplified in the following extracts:

Simple modal *must* signals the following:

- a much higher register (common in formal discourse)
- rigid stipulations or conditions in institutional discourse
- little or no room for options or deviations
- a strong authoritative stance

Multi-word modals *have to, have got to,* and *need to*, in contrast, signal the following:

- lower register (common in conversation and informal discourse)
- room for options or deviations
- a less strong authoritative stance

*8.4.2.1 Modal* Must: *Obligation, Requirement*

**Deontic**

1. Data excerpt: restroom signage

    Employees <u>must</u> *wash* hands.   (D)   [obligation]

2. Data excerpt: Actual note to students regarding school camping trip: Modals: ***must, can, should***

    You <u>must</u> *bring* a backpack to carry on the hikes. This <u>can</u> *be* your school book bag. In your backpack you <u>should</u> *have* these things, labeled with your name: rain gear, a reusable water bottle, pencils/pens, extra clothing layer like a sweatshirt.

    You **must** *bring* a backpack.   (D)   [obligation]
    This <u>can</u> *be* your school book bag   (D)   [permission]
    . . . you <u>should</u> have these things   (D)   [strong suggestion, expectation]

3. Data excerpt: Requirements for becoming an FBI Special Agent

    To qualify for a position as an FBI Special Agent:
    Candidates <u>must</u> *be* at least 23 years old, but younger than 37 . . .   (D) [requirement]
    Candidates <u>must</u> *hold* a four-year degree from a college . . .   (D) [requirement]
    ("FBI requirements," n.d.)

**Epistemic**

The driveway is wet. It <u>must</u> *have rained* last night.   (E)   [strong belief, inference based on evidence]

Those kids are too young to see this film.
They <u>must</u> *be* only about 12 years old.   (E)   [strong belief, inference based on evidence]

Excerpt from journal article on close reading (Fisher & Frey, 2014):
((a middle school class is discussing the identity of the author of the poem they are reading and the students are trying to guess who the author is))

> . . . After this third reading, [the teacher] asked them to think about who the author was and what his role might be. Balaji said, "Maybe he was a slave and wanted his rights . . ." . . . The teacher asked the class to look at the date the poem was first published, . . . saying, "Place this text in history . . ."
>
> . . . Jovan [said] "Look, Martin Luther King did his speech in 1963.
>
> → So this is way before.
>
> → So he ***must*** *have been a slave*. . ." [emphasis added]   (E)   [strong belief, inference based on evidence]
> (Fisher & Frey, 2014)

*8.4.2.2 Multi-Word Modals* Have to, Have Got to, Need to: *Obligation, Requirement, Strong Suggestion, Stipulation, Strong Belief*

**Deontic**

***Have to*** **as a modal** (forms: *have, has* [third-person singular present tense], *had* [past tense])

Commentary on class assignment for freshman composition:

Anita <u>has to</u> *write* a 1,000-word essay every week.   (D)   [obligation]

Advice on good study habits:

> Make someone test you on the study guide. Talking about the information out loud [makes it] a lot easier to retain than going over the same stuff in your brain over and over.
>
> → When you <u>have to</u> *explain* it to someone else, it forces you to understand it, not just know it.   (D)   [obligation]
>
> (Wikihow Staff, n.d.)

***Have got to* as a modal** (forms: *have*, *has* [third-person singular present tense], *had* [past tense])

Friend to friend:

> You <u>have got to</u> *call* home and let them know you're okay. (D) [urging, strong suggestion]
>
> Slightly more emphatic than:
> cf. You <u>have to</u> *call* home and let them know you're okay.
> cf. You <u>need to</u> *call* home and let them know you're okay.

Senator Chris Coons interview on CBS:

> It's not about moving to *common* ground ((in the political/ideological sense)), we're beyond that. We <u>have got to</u> move to *higher* ground, because this <u>has got to</u> be a win-win for everybody.   (D) [urging, strong suggestion]
>
> (Davies, 2008–; emphasis added)

***Need to* as a modal** (forms: *need*, *needs* [third-person singular present tense]), *needed* [past tense])

Friend to friend:

> We really <u>need to</u> *get* together the next time I'm in town. (D) [strong suggestion]

General commentary, instruction:

> This absolutely <u>needs</u> *to be* said.   (D) [obligation/strong opinion]
> That work <u>needs</u> to get done.   (D) [obligation/ strong suggestion]

Parent commentary about school administration:
> The principal <u>needs to</u> *step in* on that issue.   (D) [strong opinion/obligation]

**Epistemic**

***Have to, have got to need to*** [*need to* is not often used epistemically]

Friend to friend:

> That <u>has got to</u> *be* Jacob's brother. He looks just like him.   (E)   [strong belief]
> slightly more emphatic than:
> cf. That <u>has to</u> *be* Jacob's brother. He looks just like him.
>
> Hiruni's answer <u>has got to</u> be right. She checked it many times.   (E)   [strong belief]
> slightly more emphatic than:
> cf. Hiruni's <u>has to</u> *be* right. She checked it many times.

PBS *NewsHour* interview on November 9, 2012, about David Petraeus's resignation as CIA director due to scandal and the discovery of his extramarital affair:

> And, you know, he built his entire career on public service to the nation. . . .
> This <u>has got to</u> be a severe blow to General Petreaeus. And our thoughts and prayer goes (*sic*) out to him and his family in this time of healing.
>
> (Davies, 2008–)

248  *Imperatives and Modals*

*8.4.2.3 Negating Deontic* Must *and* Have To

*Must* and *have to* used deontically become significantly different in meaning when they are negated. While *must* expresses an obligation, *must **not*** expresses a negative prohibition ("Don't do X"). In order to negate the obligation, we would need to switch to the multi-word modal *have to*:

**Compare:**

>Employees <u>must</u> *wash* their hands. (D)

>This does not negate the sign—it is a negative prohibition:
>Employees <u>must</u> **not** wash their hands. → Don't wash your hands.

>This does negate the sign:
>Employees **do not** <u>have to</u> wash their hands. (D)
>Employees **do not** <u>need to</u> wash their hands. (D)

## 8.5 Other Ways of Expressing Modality: Adverbs, Adjectives, Verbs of Cognition, Verbs of Obligation, Perception Copula

It is important to note that there are many features of grammar and discourse that also express gradient notions of certainty/uncertainty, speculation, reservation of opinion, necessity, obligation, permission, and so forth.

These can be expressed in the following ways:

- Adverbs and adverbial expressions (see Chapter 15): *maybe, perhaps, possibly, probably, it is likely that, in the unlikely event that,* and so on
- Verbs of cognition and reporting: *think, know, don't/doesn't know, surmise, assume, predict, assert, maintain, ascertain*
- Verbs of obligation, urging, and invitation: *require, insist, expect, urge, encourage, invite, permit, prohibit, allow*
- Perception verbs: *seem, seem like, appear, look, look like, taste like, give/create an impression of*
- Adjectives: *it is possible, likely, probable, certain, doubtful, unlikely*

## 8.6 *Would* vs. *Used to*—in Past Time Narratives: Not Necessarily a Contrastive Pair

Some approaches to grammar frame the simple modal *would* and the multi-word modal *used to* as indicators of "repeated action in the past," such that *used to* establishes the frame for such repeated action and *would* "elaborates on" and provides the specific details with regard to the event (Suh, 1992, 1993). Also, according to Carter and McCarthy (2006, p. 663), Swan (2005, p. 634), and Swan and Walter (2011, p. 73), *would* in this use within past time narratives requires that a specific past time frame be established or known.

And while a number of discursive samples do seem to indicate that these modals fulfill such descriptive functions, we propose an analysis whereby *used to* expresses an action, habit, or condition that once held in the past but *no longer holds*, and *would* serves as to foreground, spotlight, or highlight elements within a past time event, whether or not that action or condition was repeated and habitual.

*used to*: actions, habits, or conditions that once held in the past *but no longer hold*

*would*: foregrounds, spotlights, or highlights elements in the narration of past time events that stand out as salient in the speaker's or writer's mind in juxtaposition with the simple past

Also, while both do seem to occur in past time narratives evoking these meanings, they do not necessarily function as a pair. Each can and does occur independently of the other.

### 8.6.1 Discourse-Based Examples of Used to Indicating Time in the Past

1   Past active practice: *used to travel*

> "The Way We Used to *Travel*: 12 Ways Travel Has Changed in the Digital Age"
> (Huffingtonpost Staff, 2014)

The article juxtaposes pre-technology travel practices with current ones:

> **Then:** There were no smartphones, tablets, or GPS devices.
> → We used to *need* international calling cards, physical maps, guidebooks, and so on.

> sub-text: *NOW this is no longer the case*. We don't need those things.

2   Past state: *used to be*

> *That Used to Be Us: How America Fell Behind in the World It Invented and How We Can Come Back*

((The book lays out four areas in which America must improve and regain its strength as a world power. It juxtaposes prior decades with now.))

> Our optimism about America's future still rests on America's past. We, as a nation, have risen to challenges even more formidable than the ones we face now. We have succeeded at tasks even more daunting than striking the bargains on which our national well-being depends. The America that recognized, confronted, and mastered those challenges is *the country that used to be us*. We still believe that it can be again.
> (Friedman & Mandelbaum, 2011, p. xix)

Each excerpt establishes juxtapositions between the past and now. The second excerpt builds on that juxtaposition by contrasting other elements within the discourse, for example, third-person singular pronouns (*that* and *it*) vs. first-person plural pronouns (*us, we*), the verbs *fall behind* vs. *come back*, America's *future* vs. America's *past*, and the ways of referring to America—*that; it; we as a nation; the America that recognized, confronted, and mastered those challenges; the country that used to be us*. Also note how tense and aspect work to create the overall meanings of past vs. present time.

### 8.6.2 Discourse-Based Examples of Would (and Could) in Past Time Narrative

> "Lives on the Boundary"
>
> I *was* aware of my parents watching their money and *got* the sense from their conversations that things could quickly *take a turn* for the worse. I *started* taping pennies to the bottom of a shelf in the kitchen.

250   *Imperatives and Modals*

> My father's health *was* bad and he *had* few readily marketable skills. Poker and pinochle *brought* in a little money, and he *tried out* an idea that *had worked* in Altoona during the war: He *started* a "suit club." The few customers he could scare up would pay two dollars a week on a tailor-made suit. He would take the measurements and send them to a shop back East and hope for the best. My mother *took* a job at a café in downtown Los Angeles, a split shift, 9:00–12:00 and 5:00 to 9:00, but her tips *were totaling* sixty cents a day, so she *quit* for a night shift at Coffee Dan's.... In a couple of years, Coffee Dan's would award her a day job at the counter. Once every few weeks, my father and I would take a bus downtown and visit with her, sitting at stools by the window, watching the animated, but silent mix of faces beyond the glass.
>
> (Rose, 2005, pp. 12–13)

**Modals:**

*could*: the first instance is epistemic; the second is dynamic

*would*: past emphatic, past highlight—repeated action in the past that the author wants to make more salient in the narrative in juxtaposition with the simple past

In this example with the modal *would*, what is being juxtaposed are actions in the past, depicted with a variety of tense and aspect marking, e.g., simple past [*was, got, had, brought, tried, started, took, quit*], past perfect [*had worked*], past progressive [*were totaling*] vs. actions that the author chose to **make salient**, **highlight**, or **spotlight** through the use of the modal *would*.

\*\*\*\*\*\*\*\*

## PRACTICE WITH DATA ANALYSIS: PUTTING IT ALL TOGETHER

1   Throughout this chapter we have investigated imperatives and modals. We have also examined a number of discursive contexts in which imperatives and modals are often found.

Modals and imperatives are especially frequent in the discourse of legal and institutional requirements and regulations, policy documents, and contracts.

   a   The following excerpt from the California State Department of Motor Vehicles website itemizes some of the requirements for a California driver's license.

Read the excerpt for its basic content, and pay attention to the imperatives and modals. We have italicized the imperatives and have indicated the modals + *Verb* construction through underline (modals) and *italics (verbs)*.

> **"Applying for a California Driver's License"**
>
> How to apply for a driver license if you are over 18.
>
> If you are a visitor in California over 18 and have a valid driver license from your home state or country, you may *drive* in this state without getting a California driver license as long as your home state license remains valid.
>
> If you become a California resident, you must *get* a California driver license within 10 days. Residency is established by voting in a California election, paying resident tuition, filing for a homeowner's property tax exemption, or any other privilege or benefit not ordinarily extended to nonresidents.
>
> To apply for an original driver license if you are over 18, you will *need* to do the following:
>
> - *Make* an appointment before visiting a DMV office...
> - *Complete* application form DL44

- Give a thumb print
- *Have* your picture taken
- *Provide* your social security number. It <u>will</u> be verified with the Social Security Administration while you are in the office.
- *Provide* your true full name.
- *Pay* the application fee.
- *Pass* a vision exam.
- *Pass* a traffic laws and sign test.

When you practice, you <u>must</u> *have* an accompanying adult who is 18 years of age or older, with a valid California license. This person *must be* close enough to you to take control of the vehicle if necessary. It is illegal for you to drive alone.

(State of California Department of Motor Vehicles, n.d.)

Now, think about the kinds of requirements that are indicated through imperatives. How do these compare and contrast with the instructions and information represented through modals *may*, *must*, and *will*? How does the use of the modal *may* differ from the modal *must*? Are the uses of *may* and *must* deontic or epistemic? How do you know?

b  The next document is from the website on the placement policy for Penn State foreign language courses. Do you find any imperatives here? Why do you think this is so?

Read the document, first for overall content. Then read it a second time and attend to how the modals are used. Which modals do you find? Which is the most frequent? Why? Think about epistemic and deontic meanings. Which instances of *must*, *may*, and *should* are deontic? Which are epistemic?

### "Placement Policy for Penn State Foreign Language Courses"

All students interested in studying a foreign language at Penn State <u>may</u> *choose* either to continue the language studied previously or to begin a new one. To continue with a language, students <u>must</u> *follow* the placement policy as outlined below.

Placement Policy—Students who have studied a foreign language within four years immediately before admission to Penn State <u>may</u> *enroll* in that language for credit based on the number of Carnegie units prior to admission. . . . If a period of four or more years has elapsed between a student's graduation from high school and admission to college, he/she <u>may</u> *be* eligible to enroll in level 1 of the language studied in high school.

Students <u>may</u> *choose* to audit a lower-level course but <u>may</u> <u>not</u> *receive* credit for it. Students who feel they are qualified for a more advanced course, or students seeking proficiency certification or credit by examination, if available, <u>should</u> *contact* the appropriate language department for details. . . .

Non-Course Work Knowledge of Foreign Languages—Students who have acquired a knowledge of a foreign language by means other than course work (e.g., family background, travel or study in a foreign country, participation in noncredit summer language programs, etc.) <u>may</u> *enroll* in elementary and intermediate courses in that language only with permission of the course coordinator or department head. Once students have been placed in a skills course, they <u>may</u> <u>not</u> *receive* credit for a lower-level skills course.

Students whose native language is not English <u>may</u> <u>not</u> *receive* credit (through course work or examination) for elementary and intermediate courses in their native language.

Enrollment in skills courses beyond intermediate level (e.g., conversation, composition) <u>must</u> *be approved* by the department head.

(Penn State University Bulletin, n.d.)

In what sorts of statements do you find the modal *must*? In what sorts of statements do you find the modal *may*? How does the information with *must* differ from the information with *may*? Which of the two is more frequent? Why do you think this is so?

Are there any instances of modal usage in which there could be an ambiguous reading, where the message could be interpreted in one way in an epistemic sense and a second way in a deontic sense? Hint: In this document, some modals with *may* can be interpreted as expressing deontic meaning or epistemic meaning, which would render ambiguous at least one of the provisions in the text.

If you did locate any ambiguities in terms of deontic and epistemic readings, how would such ambiguity change the intended meaning of the messages? What sort of advice might you provide to the writers of this policy to disambiguate the few instances of modal usage?

2  Often in internet-based communication, we find messages like the following that provide recommendations for similar items, products, commentary, and so forth.

If you liked this, you <u>might</u> also *like* . . .

What does *might* mean in the second clause? How would the meaning change if you substituted *might* with *will, must, could, can, are going to, are supposed to* . . . ? Once you go through this list (and include other modals as well), try to come up with your own articulation of how these various modals differ in meaning.

3  This excerpt from London's Metropolitan Police Service contains lots of useful information and tips concerning how to stay safe on the internet. You'll find a number of negative imperatives, affirmative imperatives, simple modals, and multi-word modals.

For the imperatives, which are more frequent: the negative imperatives or the affirmative ones? Why? What forms do these negative imperatives take? (There is more than one form used here.) How do the forms differ from each other in terms of intended message?

What about the modals? List all the modals that appear in the text. How is the modal *would* used in this discourse? How might you characterize the meaning of all five instances of *would*?

How would you characterize the various communicative functions (speech acts) in the text? Some are warnings, some are prohibitions, and some involve giving affirmative advice. Also, some are very direct and some more indirect. Analyze the discourse from the point of view of communicative functions of imperatives and modals.

### "Metropolitan Police Service: Some Golden Rules"

Don't give your personal information such as your address or phone number.
Don't send pictures of yourself to anyone, especially indecent pictures.
Don't open emails or attachments from people you don't know.
Don't become online "friends" with people you don't know.
Never arrange to meet someone in person who you've met online.
If anything you see or read online worries you, tell someone about it.

*Social networking*

Social networking websites and apps, such as Facebook, MySpace, Instagram, Viber, Tumblr, SnapChat, Ask.fm and Twitter have become incredibly popular in recent years.

Most users are genuine, but because it is so easy to hide your real identity, it is possible to come into contact with people you <u>would</u> normally *avoid*.

*The risks: privacy*

The internet offers you a lot of freedom and this *can lead* some people to behave in ways they <u>would</u> <u>not</u> behave in public.

They <u>might</u>:

- say things on a status update/*post/tweet* they <u>would</u> <u>never</u> say face to face
- give out personal information about themselves or others (including photos) that they <u>would</u> normally keep private

*A common example*

A young person tries to let their friends know about their birthday party by posting the information about when and where on their social networking site. This means hundreds of people end up knowing about the party and turn up uninvited. The party <u>could</u> turn into chaos with people getting angry and even refusing to leave. The police <u>would</u> <u>have</u> <u>to</u> get involved to turn people away.

(Metropolitan Police Service, n.d.)

List all of the imperatives in the document (affirmative and negative). List all of the modals (simple and multi-word). What are the functions of the modals (deontic, epistemic, or dynamic)? Do you notice any overlap in categories? (If so, this is normal and expected. Just as we observed in the Penn State foreign language placement policy document, and as we will see in number 4, some meanings of modals are indeed ambiguous and crosscut the three functional categories.) Do you find any instances of hypothetical meanings? How does the appeal to hypothetical situations help frame the "warning" nature of this document? Do you find any other words (e.g., adverbs, adjectives, verbs of obligation, expressions of possibility) that also express epistemic or deontic modal meanings?

4    Smucker's is the brand name of a good number of jellies, jams, syrups, and even peanut butter sold in the US. Its advertising slogan goes like this:

"WITH A NAME LIKE SMUCKER'S, IT <u>HAS TO</u> *BE* GOOD" (emphasis added)

Also, Purina makes a dog food product called Puppy Chow. The Puppy Chow TV ads often show puppies in exaggerated scenes accomplishing feats like carrying an entire newspaper-dispensing machine into the owner's living room after being told to "go get the paper," or just running happily through an open field. At the end of the commercial, we hear a male voiceover saying this:

"IT<u>'S</u> *<u>GOTTA</u> BE* THE PUPPY CHOW" (emphasis added)
[reduced form, informal form for *it has got to*]

Think about the two multi-word modals in these advertising slogans, *has to* and *has got to* (reduced to *'s gotta*). What do these two modals mean? Are they used epistemically, deontically, or both ways?

If there are ambiguous readings, how do they enhance the advertised message in each ad?

5   We observed how *used to* and *would* are used in discourse. We examined some similarities and differences in their meanings and functions. One common feature that each form seems to share has to do with the narration of events or situations that took place in the past.

Clearly, *used to* expresses some aspect of a past situation that no longer holds. *Would* highlights bits of past time narratives in ways that make those particular events or situations more salient with regard to the surrounding discourse.

According to some traditional approaches to English grammar, both *used to* and *would* are said to express "repeated actions in the past."

The following two literary excerpts are autobiographical accounts that serve as memoirs. The first one, by Lucy Grealy, contains a number of tokens of <u>would</u> + *Verb*, a number of tokens of simple past tense, and one token of <u>used to</u>. The second one, by Anwar F. Accawi, contains a mixture of tense and aspect markers like simple past, past progressive, and past perfect.

Both nonfictional excerpts depict "repeated actions in the past," yet the second one ("The Telephone") contains not a single instance of *used to* or *would* in the snippet selected.

Read each text carefully and try to imagine the scenes that the authors are depicting. What sorts of regular and irregular occurrences are depicted?

   a   From Autobiography of a Face (Grealy, 1994)

   **"Prologue: Pony Party"**

   My Friend Stephen and I <u>used to</u> *do* pony parties . . .

   As **we** *drove* by the houses, **I** *gazed* into the windows. . . . Somewhere nearby, **a wife** in a coordinated outfit *chatted* on the phone . . . while **their children** *set* the dinner table. As **they** *ate* their home-cooked food . . . **they**'*d casually* ask each other about the day. Perhaps **someone** <u>would</u> *mention* the unusual sight of a horse trailer going past the house. . . .

   Once **we** *reached* the party, there *was* **a great rush of excitement. The children**, realizing that the ponies had arrived, <u>would</u> *come* running . . . **their now forgotten balloons** . . . <u>would</u> *fly off* in search of some tree or telephone wire. **The ponies**, reacting to the excitement of new sounds, <u>would</u> promptly *take* a crap in the driveway, to a chorus of disgusted groans.

   **My pleasure** at the sight of the children *didn't last* long, however. **I** *knew* **what** *was coming*. As soon as **they** *got over* the thrill of being near the ponies, **they**'*d notice* me. **Half my jaw** *was missing*, **which** *gave* my face a strange triangular shape, accentuated by the fact that **I** *was* unable to keep my mouth completely closed. When **I** first *started* doing pony parties, **my hair** *was* still short and wispy, still growing in from the chemo.

   (Grealy, 1994)

   b   From "The Telephone"

   When **I** *was growing up* in Magdaluna, a small Lebanese village in the terraced, rocky mountains east of Sidon, **time** *didn't mean* much to anybody, except maybe to **those** who *were dying* or **those** [who *were*] *waiting* to appear in court because they *had tampered* with the boundary markers on their land. In those days, there *was* **no real need** for a calendar or a watch to keep track of the hours, days, months, and years. **We** *knew* what to do and when to do it, just as the **Iraqi geese** *knew* when to fly north, driven by **the hot winds** that *blew in* from the desert. . . . The only timepiece that **we** *had* need of then was the sun. **It** *rose* and *set*, and **the seasons** *rolled by*, and **we** *sowed* seed and *harvested* and *ate* and *played* and *married* our cousins and **had babies** who *got* whooping cough and chickenpox—and **those children** who survived *grew up* and *married* their cousins and *had* **babies** who *got* whooping cough and chickenpox. **We** *lived* and *loved* and *toiled* and *died* without ever needing to know what **year** it *was* or even the time of day.

(Accawi, 2006)

How do the scenes differ between Grealy's viewpoint in her narrative and Accawi's in his? How do *used to* and *would* in Grealy's narrative add to the description of the scene? Conversely, how does the use of the simple past add to the regularity of the occurrences in Accawi's description?

Conduct an in-depth analysis of the use of tense and aspect markers as well as modals *would* and *used to* in each excerpt. Compare and contrast the temporal descriptions in A with those in B. In addition to modality, also look at the authors' use of tense and aspect, nouns (common and proper, Type 1, Type 2), pronouns, determiners, and verbs to see how these might also play into the setting of the scenes for each introductory segment.

We provide a few ideas here to start you off:

Grealy's narrative opens with the multi-word modal *used to*, as a way of setting the scene for her story to come. It is a past time narrative of a lived personal experience, and one that took place regularly, for some time, at least.

*Used to* opens up the story and sets the scene that depicts her regularly repeated activities.

Her use of past tense indicates the regularity of her activities with vivid detail—some of which were actual and some imagined: *I gazed into the windows, a wife ... chatted on the phone, their children set the table; As they ate their home-cooked food ... they'd casually* **ask** *each other about the day. Perhaps someone* **would mention** *the unusual sight of a horse trailer.* Here, we find our first two instances of the modal *would* in this past time narrative.

How do the remaining uses of *would* highlight the key elements in the narrative that Grealy wants to highlight in terms of their importance to the story and how that regularity of her activities came to an abrupt end, especially in contrast with her use of past tense? Think about the other grammatical elements in her description that help you envision this scene—for example, her choice of nouns, determiners, adjectives (see Chapter 13), and adverbials (see Chapter 15).

Now, do the same with "The Telephone." Here, Accawi sets the scene of his personal reminiscences with the use of the past progressive: *When I* **was growing up** *in Magdaluna* ...

You will find two more instances of the past progressive, and one instance of the past perfect (*because they* **had tampered** *with the boundary markers*).

The rest of the tense and aspect marking in Accawi's autobiographical narrative is the simple past tense: *We* **knew** *what to do and when to do it, just as the Iraqi geese* **knew** *when to fly north; It [the sun]* **rose and set** ... *the seasons* **rolled by** ... *we* **sowed** *seed*. And there are more instances of these in the excerpt.

How does "The Telephone" compare and contrast with *Autobiography of a Face* in regard to scene setting, descriptions, depictions of regular occurrences, and instances of past time events that are highlighted or spotlighted in the discourse? Be sure to provide concrete examples to thoroughly analyze the discourse and support your examples.

6   Have a look at the following jokes. All are funny because of different features of grammar. All contain some instances of imperatives and/or modals. Some of the sources of humor are related to these very features of grammar (i.e., imperatives and modals, nouns, verbs, and ellipsis). Others are funny because of word meanings and punctuation.

First, read through the jokes to appreciate the humor. Then, try to articulate why each is funny. Which one(s) do you like the best, and why?

**In the Restroom:**       "Toilet out of order. Please *use* floor below."
**In a Laundromat:**       "Automatic Washing Machines:
                           Please *remove* all your clothes when the light goes out."

| | |
|---|---|
| **In an Office:** | "<u>Would</u> the person who took the stepladder yesterday <u>please</u> *bring it back*? Otherwise, further steps will be taken." |
| **In an Office:** | "After coffee break, staff <u>should</u> *empty* the coffee pot and stand upside down on the draining board." |
| **Spotted in a Safari Park:** | "Elephants *please stay* in your car." |
| **On a Repair Shop Door:** | "We can repair anything. (<u>Please</u> *knock* hard on the door—the bell doesn't work)" |

(Kathleen, 2014)

## COMMON ERRORS, BUMPS, AND CONFUSIONS

Identify the errors or "bumps" in the following sentences. Use the concepts and terminology that you learned in this and other chapters to articulate what might be grammatically or pragmatically problematic. Suggest ways that each can be re-written more clearly and more accurately. (Note: While all bumps do involve some element of modals or imperatives, they are not limited to only that.)

1. Ariel mights know the answer.
2. When the computer system was down, we was have to do everything the old way.
3. Tadaaki coach say Tadaaki to runs one miles every day.
4. Zainai may saved the file.
5. Don't you forget to sign the form.
6. Starbucks barista cannot to helped us yesterday.
7. They should of responded to you by now. What could of happened?

## SUGGESTED ACTIVITIES

1. Hall's brand cough lozenges come in individually wrapped pieces. Each wrapper contains printed uplifting sayings, representing their slogan, "A pep talk in every drop." The message is that even if you are not feeling well, you can always have one of their cough lozenges to help you push through your illness.

   Here are a few examples:

   > "Flex your 'can do' muscles."
   > "Impress yourself today."
   > "Tough is your middle name."
   > "Get back in there, champ!"
   > "Bet on yourself."
   > "High-five yourself."

   Most of the "pep talk" messages are structured with imperatives. Some imperative structures also include the reflexive pronoun *yourself*.

   Some messages only imply an imperative message (e.g., "Tough is your middle name [so push through. . .]").

   Think of another product that would work well accompanied by this type of "message to self" that serves to encourage or support, especially in challenging situations. What is that product?

Invent a set of 10 pep talk messages that fit the product and the challenge it is designed to help you overcome.

2   Explain the humor in the following pun:

   DOGS CAN'T OPERATE MRI MACHINES, BUT CATS CAN.

3   a   Provide five examples from actual discourse of five different simple modals used deontically.

   b   Provide five examples from actual discourse of five different simple modals used epistemically. (They can be the same modals as you used for A or different modals).

   c   Write five sentence pairs. Write the first sentence using a simple modal (e.g. *will*). Write the second sentence with identical (or near identical) wording, only using a corresponding multi-word modal (e.g., *be going to*) instead of the simple modal.

How do the meanings change as you move from the simple modal to the multi-word modal in each case? Think about each sentence pair carefully and respond in as much detail as necessary to account for the differences in meaning.

4   Simple modals and multi-word modals can occur very naturally in discourse side by side. For example, "Tova has a friend who might be able to help." Or, "Only British journalists will be allowed to ask questions at the press conference."

Think about which simple modals can and do naturally co-occur with multi-word modals. Which cannot? Why? Find a variety of examples from actual discourse that reflect the natural co-occurrence of simple modals with multi-word modals.

5   The following excerpt is from actual discourse that expresses multiple instances of the speech act of *request*. The letter comes from an international, non-English corporation.

The document contains imperatives, *please*, and modals, as well as other grammatical means of conveying the request. Analyze this text from the point of view of pragmatics. What is the message of the overall request? How is the overall request broken down into smaller parts to convey the request? How does the writer use modals and *please*? Does *please* function as a mitigator in all of its uses here? Which parts are particularly well done? Which parts might benefit from some revision?

Suggest for the writer or the organization a revised version of this document that might have a somewhat different pragmatic (and grammatical) appeal. You can address all features of grammar that you area familiar with so far. For grammatical terms not covered yet, just explain using your own intuition.

   Dear Sir/Madam:

   On behalf of the Partnership International Foundation (pseudonym), we sent questionnaires to your E-mail address (janedoe@myuni.edu] requesting an update of information about database of ex-fellows at 12 jan. 2016.

   But we have not received your reply yet.

   Could you please send us back the questionnaire as soon as possible?

You can use response form on webpages of the Partnership International Foundation.

Your ID Number for this survey is jdmyuni.

(I hope you will enter this number in the form on the webpage.
But you can fill in the form without this number.)

In the case of no response to this email until a few days after,
I will send by fax to:

> Professor Jane Doe
> 1(222) 555–2222
> Dept. of English Language Instruction

If you are not an Ex-fellow, or if these data are incorrect, please let us know.

If you have any questions about this survey, please access our webpage and contact us immediately.

We really expect your understanding and kind cooperation and we are looking forward to hearing from you.

Very truly yours,

Mr. Charles Basso. (Project Head)
22222 Avenue des Etoiles
44000 Nantes, France

6. Should you or should you not intervene? Read this report by the *New York Times* titled "Should You Intervene When a Parent Harshly Disciplines a Child in Public?" (www.nytimes.com/2016/09/29/us/should-you-intervene-when-a-parent-harshly-disciplines-a-child-in-public.html).

What is the dilemma in this reported incident? Find the two polar positions in the article. For each position, make a list of supporting points and a list of potential oppositions based on how the piece is written. Find the various stance markers used by the author to support certain points and to refute others.

Also, consider these questions: Could any of the issues reported in the essay be cultural specific? That is, do the same arguments apply outside of the US? Are expectations concerning parent-child interaction the same in every culture?

Think about these issues and develop them further in the form of an essay in which you express your opinions and support them with this article and additional readings/research, a debate, a panel discussion, and so forth.

7. Advice giving in public discourse: The advice column in newspapers

Many newspapers have an advice column for readers to share their experiences, usually in the form of a letter that voices a complaint or a question about social norms and expectations. Sometimes the experiences are highly personal and focus on a spouse, a girlfriend or boyfriend, a child, friends, friends of spouses, and so on.

Examples of these columns in US newspapers include Dear Abby, Ask Amy, and Ask Ann Landers. Various magazines also have advice columns.

Find five examples of these types of letters with the responses by the advice columnists.

How do the letters open? Do they all start with a personal narrative? At what point in the letter does the writer state the problem, dilemma, or question? How does the writer ask for advice? How does the writer sign his or her name at the bottom of the letter? Typically, the writers do not use their own names but descriptions of how they feel, often linked to the town or city they live in (e.g., Frustrated in Fresno, Blue in Erie, Confused and Wondering).

Now, look at the responses by the advice columnist. How are those responses worded? Do you find modals (both simple and multi-word) and imperatives? Do you find most of the responses in the affirmative or in the negative (with *not, don't, never, don't ever*)?

Conduct an analysis of the five responses by the advice columnist. Address the kinds of verb forms that appear in the responses. Does the advice columnist side with or against the writer? How is the advice columnist's stance expressed?

Write your own letters to an advice column—for fun. As a class activity, the class can be divided in half, with half of the class writing the questions or complaints and the other half of the class writing the advice.

8  Have you ever traveled outside your country? If so, where did you go? When was it? How old were you at the time?

Was there ever an occasion when you felt uncomfortable or awkward because you were unaware of the social/cultural norms of the country that you visited? Describe how you felt. In what sorts of contexts did the country's social/cultural norms emerge (e.g., shopping; riding public transportation; visiting homes of friends, family, or acquaintances; at the dinner table at a private home or in a restaurant; in a classroom; at a movie theater)?

Recall the precise events, and think about why you may have had those feelings.

Then, write a list of helpful advice that other people might be able to use in the same or similar situations. Write full sentences and use modals (both simple and multi-word) and imperatives to articulate your advice. Also, provide a rationale for why each piece of advice might be helpful or necessary.

| What to do | What to avoid |
| --- | --- |
| _____ | _____ |
| _____ | _____ |
| _____ | _____ |
| _____ | _____ |

## Notes

1  *Speech act* is the technical term for the type of communicative function an utterance serves. Speech acts can range from a simple declarative statement ("The sky is so blue today") to apologies ("It was all my fault," "I'm sorry"), invitations ("Would you like to have dinner with me tomorrow?"), and compliments ("Nice car!" or "You did a great job on your kitchen remodel"). See Austin (1962), Bach (1994), Grice (1989), and Searle (1969) for the classic literature on speech acts and speech act theory. See Bardovi-Harlig and Hartford (2005), Cohen (2005), Judd (1999), Kasper and Blum-Kulka (1993), Kasper and Rose (2002), and Rose and Kasper (2001) for more recent

work on speech acts and pragmatics in second language teaching and interaction. One utterance can express/contain multiple speech acts (e.g., an apology as well as a request, a complaint as well as a scolding, etc.)
2 It is important to note that not all tokens of *let* involve this type of imperative. The verb *let* also carries meaning similar to *allow* or *permit*, e.g., The city did not *let* my grandfather build his garage. An example of a typical imperative with *let*, which is not the exhortative c type: (Please) *Let* my grandfather build his garage → (Please) *Permit/allow my grandfather to build his garage*.
3 Face-threatening acts, or FTAs, are those types of language- and discourse-based interactions that can feel harsh, intrusive, embarrassing, insulting, disrespectful, and so on. See Brown and Levinson (1987), Foley (1997), Goffman (1955), and Yule (1996).
4 This line, as a dare, was made famous by the character Dirty Harry (Clint Eastwood) in the film *Sudden Impact* (Eastwood et al., 1983).
5 *Shall* is the least frequent and the least commonly used modal of the list. As of May 2017, there were 18,752 tokens of *shall* in the COCA Corpus, compared to *can* and *will*, with more than 1,000,000 tokens, respectively. The other six modals each have more than 40,000 tokens. *Shall* in US discourse is most commonly used in legal or religious discourse and other high-register and/or technical discourse genres. It is also rather frequent in invitations or suggestions—*Shall we. . . ? Shall I. . . ?*—in both formal and informal discourse. *Shall* patterns differently in British English.
6 Bybee (2003) suggests that *be going to* as, a marker of future time, developed from the motion verb construction *going to + location*. This spatial movement involves an agentive instance of motion whereby an entity is moving toward a location or goal. The combined notion of agentivity and *goal* construal gave rise to the pragmatic interpretation of "intentionality" (see also Bybee et al., 1991, 1994). This may also account for why *be going to* evokes a higher degree of certainty when used as an epistemic modal.

## Academic References

Aijmer, K. (2002). The interpersonal particle just. In *English discourse particles: Evidence from a corpus* (pp. 153–174). Philadelphia: John Benjamins.
Allen, C. L. (1995). On doing as you please. In A. H. Jucker (Ed.), *Historical pragmatics: Pragmatic developments in the history of English* (pp. 275–309). Amsterdam and Philadelphia: John Benjamins.
Austin, J. L. (1962). *How to do things with words*. Cambridge, MA: Harvard University Press.
Bach, K. (1994). Conversational implicature. *Mind & Language*, 9, 124–162.
Bardovi-Harlig, K., & Hartford, B. (2005). Institutional discourse and interlanguage pragmatics research. In K. Bardovi-Harlig & B. Hartford (Eds.), *Interlanguage pragmatics: Exploring institutional talk* (pp. 7–36). Mahwah, NJ: Erlbaum.
Biber, D., Johansson, S., Leech, G., Conrad, S., & Finegan, E. (1999). *Longman grammar of spoken and written English*. London: Longman.
Blakemore, D. (1994). Evidence and modality. In R. E. Asher (Ed.), *The encyclopedia of language and linguistics* (pp. 1183–1186). Oxford: Pergamon Press.
Brown, P., & Levinson, S. C. (1987). *Politeness: Some universals in language usage*. Cambridge: Cambridge University Press.
Bybee, J. (2003). Cognitive processes in grammaticalization. In M. Tomasello (Ed.), *The New psychology of language: Vol. II* (pp. 145–167). Mahwah, NJ: Lawrence Erlbaum Associates Inc.
Bybee, J. L., & Pagliuca, W. (1987). The evolution of future meaning. In A. G. Ramat, O. Carruba, & G. Bernini (Eds.), *Papers from the VIIth international conference on historical linguistics* (pp. 109–122). Amsterdam: John Benjamins.
Bybee, J., Pagliuca, W., & Perkins, R. (1991). Back to the future. In E. C. Traugott & B. Heine (Eds.), *Approaches to grammaticalization* (pp. 17–58). Amsterdam: John Benjamins.
Bybee, J., Perkins, R., & Pagliuca, W. (1994). *The evolution of grammar: Tense, aspect, and modality in the languages of the world*. Chicago: University of Chicago Press.
Carter, R., & McCarthy, M. (2006). *Cambridge grammar of English: A comprehensive guide. Spoken and written English grammar and usage* [Cambridge International Corpus]. Cambridge: Cambridge University Press.

Celce-Murcia, M., & Larsen-Freeman, D. (1999). *The grammar book: An ESL/EFL teacher's course*. Boston, MA: Heinle & Heinle.

Chung, S., & Timberlake, A. (1985). Tense, aspect and mood. In T. Shopen (Ed.), *Language typology and syntactic description: Grammatical categories and the lexicon: Vol. 3* (pp. 202–258). Cambridge: Cambridge University Press.

Cohen, A. (2005). Strategies for learning and performing L2 speech acts. *International Pragmatics*, 2(3), 275–301.

Foley, W. (1997). *Anthropological linguistics: An introduction*. Oxford: Blackwell.

Gledhill, C. J. (2000). *Collocations in science writing*. Tübingen: Gunter Narr Verlag.

Goffman, E. (1955). On face-work: An analysis of ritual elements in social interaction. *Psychiatry: Journal of Interpersonal Relations*, 18(3), 213–231.

Grice, H. P. (1989). *Studies in the way of words*. Cambridge, MA: Harvard University Press.

Holmes, J. (1984). Modifying illocutionary force. *Journal of Pragmatics*, 8(3), 345–365.

House, J. (1989). Politeness in English and German: The functions of please and bitte. In S. BlumKulka, J. House, & G. Kasper (Eds.), *Cross-cultural pragmatics: Requests and apologies* (pp. 96–119). Norwood, NJ: Ablex.

Judd, E. L.(1999). Some issues in the teaching of pragmatic competence. In E. Hinkel (Ed.), *Culture in second language teaching and learning* (pp. 152–166). Cambridge: Cambridge University Press.

Kasper, G., & Blum-Kulka, S. (1993). *Interlanguage pragmatics*. New York and Oxford: Oxford University Press.

Kasper, G., & Rose, K. (2002). *Pragmatic development in a second language*. Oxford: Blackwell Publishing, Inc.

Larsen-Freeman, D., & Celce-Murcia, M. (2016). *The grammar book: Form, meaning, and use for English language teachers*. Boston, MA: National Geographic and Heinle.

Nuyts, J. (2016). Surveying modality and mood: An introduction. In J. Nuyts & J. van der Auwera (Eds.), *The Oxford handbook of modality and mood* (pp. 1–8). Oxford: Oxford University Press.

Nuyts, J., & van der Auwera, J. (Eds.). (2016). *The Oxford handbook of modality and mood*. Oxford: Oxford University Press.

Ogiermann, E. (2009). Politeness and in-directness across cultures: A comparison of English, German, Polish and Russian requests. *Journal of Politeness Research*, 5(2), 189–216.

Palmer, F. R. (2001). *Mood and modality* (2nd ed). Cambridge Textbooks in Linguistics. New York: Cambridge University Press.

Portner, P. (2009). *Modality*. Oxford: Oxford University Press.

Quirk, R., Greenbaum, S., Leech, G., & Svartvik, J. (1985). *A comprehensive grammar of the English language*. London: Longman.

Rose, K. R., & Kasper, G. (2001). *Pragmatics in language teaching*. Cambridge: Cambridge University Press.

Salager-Meyer, F. (1992). A text-type and move analysis of verb tense and modality distribution in medical English abstracts. *English for Specific Purposes*, 11(2), 93–115.

Searle, J. (1969). *Speech acts: An essay in the philosophy of language*. Cambridge, UK: Cambridge University Press.

Suh, K. (1992, December). Past habituality in English discourse: Used to and would. *Ohak Yonku/Language Research*, 28(4), 857–884.

Suh, K. (1993). *A discourse analysis of the English tense-aspect-modality system*. Unpublished dissertation, University of California, Los Angeles, CA.

Swales, J. M. (1990). *Genre analysis: English in academic and research settings*. Cambridge: Cambridge University Press.

Swan, M. (2005). *Practical English usage: New international*. Oxford: Oxford University Press.

Swan, M., & Walter, C. (2011). *Oxford English grammar course: Advanced*. Oxford: Oxford University Press.

Sweetser, E. E. (1982). Root and epistemic modality: Causality in two worlds. Berkeley *Linguistic Papers*, 8, 484–507.

Wichmann, A. (2004). The intonation of please-requests: A corpus-based study. *Journal of Pragmatics*, 36(9), 1521–1549.
Yule, G. (1996). *Pragmatics*. Oxford: Oxford University Press.
Yule, G. (1998). *Explaining English grammar*. Oxford and New York: Oxford University Press.
Yule, G. (2010). *The study of language*. New York: Cambridge University Press.

## Data References

Accawi, A. F. (2006). The telephone. In R. Atwan & L. Slater (Eds.), *Best American essays* (pp. 1–8). Boston, MA: Mariner Books.
Barselah, D. (2014, January 2). I shouldn't have eaten that [Web log post]. Retrieved May 15, 2016, from http://deenabarselah.com/shouldn/
The Department of Homeland Security. (n.d.). Naturalization oath of allegiance to the United States of America. Retrieved May 1, 2016, from www.uscis.gov/us-citizenship/naturalization-test/naturalization-oath-allegiance-united-states-america
Davies, M. (2008–). *The corpus of contemporary American Englsih (COCA): 560 million words, 1990–present*. Available online at https://corpus.byu.edu/coca/
Eastwood, C., Manes, F., & Perry, S. (Producers) & Eastwood, C. (Director). (1983). *Sudden impact* [Motion Picture]. Warner Bros, USA.
Friedman, T. & Mandelbaum, M (2011). *That used to be us: How America fell behind in the world it invented and how we can come back*. New York: Farrar, Strauss, and Giroux.
FBI requirements. (n.d.) Retrieved May 15, 2016, from www.fbiagentedu.org/fbi-requirements/
Fisher, D., & Frey, N. (2014, February). Close reading as an intervention for struggling middle school readers. *Journal of Adolescent & Adult Literacy*, 57(5), 367–376.
Gilliland, S. (2015). *Detour: Developing the mindset to navigate life's turns*. Charleston, SC: Advantage-Media Group.
Golden Gate Bridge. (n.d.). San Francisco travel. Retrieved March 6, 2016, from www.sftravel.com/golden-gate-bridge
Grealy, L. (1994). *Autobiography of a face*. New York: Mariner Books.
Huffingtonpost Staff. (2014, February 22). The way we used to travel. Retrieved from www.huffingtonpost.com/2014/02/22/the-way-we-used-to-travel_n_4818247.html
iPhoneSE. (n.d.). Apple.com. Retrieved September 10, 2016, from www.apple.com/iphone-se/?afid=p238%7CsWC69zut5-dc_mtid_20925d2q39172_pcrid_104710526586_&cid=wwa-uskwgo-iphone-slid-;
Kansas Department of Health and Environment. (n.d.). Don't forget to wash them. Kansas Department of Health and Environment. Retrieved September 10, 2016, from www.kdheks.gov/flu/download/Handwashing_Signs_1.pdf
Kathleen, L. (2014). Did I read the sign right? Retrieved September 10, 2016, from http://yes-23.com/lighterside/did-i-read-that-sign-right/
Metropolitan Police Service. (n.d.). Internet safety. Retrieved September 10, 2016, from http://safe.met.police.uk/internet_safety/get_the_facts.html
New Jersey Department of Health. (n.d.). Wash your hands. State of New Jersey Department of Health. Retrieved September 10, 2016, from www.nj.gov/health/cd/documents/wash_your_hands_flyer_eng.pdf
Penn State University Bulletin. (n.d.). Placement policy for Penn State world language courses. Retrieved May 1, 2016, from http://bulletins.psu.edu/undergrad/generalinformation/Placement2
Rose, M. (2005). *Lives on the boundary: A moving account of the struggles and achievements of America's educationally underprepared*. New York: Penguin Books.
State of California Department of Motor Vehicles. (n.d.). Retrieved May 1, 2016, from www.dmv.ca.gov/portal/dmv/detail/dl/dl_info#two500
Stokstad, E. (2017, May). New crop pest takes Africa at lightning speed. *Science*, 356(6337), 473–474.
Taylor, J. (2012). Personal growth: Woulda, coulda, shoulda. What's the worst emotion you could experience? [Web log post]. Retrieved May 1, 2016, from www.psychologytoday.com/blog/the-power-prime/201205/personal-growth-woulda-coulda-shoulda

Time Staff. (2015, July 13). This woman changed her name just so she could log in to Facebook. *TIME*. Retrieved May 1, 2016, from http://time.com/3955056/facebook-social-media-jemma-rogers-uk/

Woman's World. (2016, May 16). Cover of May 16, 2016, issue. Bauer Media Group.

Wikihow Staff. (n.d.). How to get good grades. Retrieved May 15, 2016, from www.wikihow.com/Get-Good-Grades.

# 9 The Grammar of Agency, Control, Responsibility, Passivity, Non-Agency, and Non-Accountability
## Voice

*Figure 9.1* "Conspiracy theorists say Humpty Dumpty was pushed."
© Randy Glasbergen. Reproduced with permission of Glasbergen Cartoon Service.

In Chapters 6 and 7, we worked with the conceptual meanings underlying verbs and the relationship of those conceptual meanings to grammar. In Chapter 6, we examined the basic categories of verb conceptualizations (i.e., **dynamic**, **stative**, and **copular or linking** verbs) in addition to the crucial notions of **transitivity** and **intransitivity**. In Chapter 7, we observed the interrelationships between tense and aspect and categories of verbal meaning, especially noting that progressive aspect resists occurring with verbs signaling stative characteristics because of the essential semantic clash between progressive aspect (evoking change and non-stability) and stative (evoking stability and unchanging characteristics or qualities). And in Chapter 8, we worked with imperatives and modals and observed the various ways in which directives, permission, obligation, suggestions, possibility, and conjecture pattern in discourse. The concepts from the three preceding chapters, as well as that of **voice** from this chapter, are all interrelated in discourse.

As introduced in Chapter 6, **transitivity** is the grammatical and conceptual feature of verbal meaning that combines three crucial elements: the subject of the verb, the verb itself, and the ability of that subject + verb combination to move, create, destroy, or otherwise affect a third entity—that is, the *affected entity*.

Transitivity, then, involves

1  the *doer* of the action (i.e., the agent),
2  the *action* depicted by the verb, and
3  who or what is *affected* by *the agent* and the *action of the verb*.

Examples of verbs that typically pattern as transitive verbs include: alter, deliver, require, honor, forget, select, build, create, destroy, hit, see, touch, hear, like, love, hate, remove, cut, include, complete, beat, win, lose, throw, kick, maintain, propose, plan, read, write, eat, drink, smoke, consume, drive, control, rent, lease, own, push, follow, pull, water, butter, powder, report, communicate, mail, Google, and Skype.

In each case, and taking context into consideration,

- we can imagine what the action of the verb is depicting;
- we can imagine an entity (a person, a thing, an idea, or a force) *doing* that action (i.e., the agent);
- we can imagine an entity that is affected, acted upon, or changed by that agent and action, whether the entity is specifically mentioned in the phrase, clause, or sentence or not.

**Example:**

What's Teodoro doing right now?
He's *eating*. (transitive)
[imagined or implied affected entity: *dinner, ice cream, fries, rice, something*, etc.]

Conversely, intransitive verbs are those that conceptually do not and cannot involve an affected entity. Intransitive verbs involve only two elements:

1  The *entity* (a person, a thing, an idea, or a force) involved in or doing the action
2  The *action* depicted by the verb

**Example:**

What's Teodoro doing right now?
He's *sleeping*. (intransitive)
[no possible affected entity]

Examples of verbs that typically pattern as intransitive verbs include be, sleep, happen, occur, appear, vanish, arise, come, go, arrive, die, lie, disappear, be, exist, become, live, laugh, appear, occur, emerge, fall, vanish, and belong. Examples of verbs that can function both transitively and intransitively include walk, run, sneeze, change, smoke, rush, move, start, end, finish, begin, freeze, transform, sell, drive, ship, and many others.

We also pointed out in Chapter 6 that transitivity is related to **agency**—that is, the potential of a person, thing, concept, idea, or force to move itself or others willfully, to influence deliberately, to exert control, or to cause something to happen.

Throughout this chapter, we will explore both transitivity and agency in more depth through our discussion of **voice**.

## 9.1 Voice in Grammar: Forms and Meanings of Active Voice and Passive Voice

The term **voice** as it is used in grammar is interrelated with three basic concepts: (1) **verbs** and their meanings, (2) **doers** of the action (as agents [active voice], non-agents [passive voice], and pseudo-agents [middle voice—see Section 9.7]), and (3) the **affected entities**.

Typically, we think of voice from two basic perspectives: **active voice**, on the one hand, and **passive voice**, on the other. The distinction between **active** and **passive** voice is only possible with regard to **transitive** verbs, since only transitive verbs can appear in passive voice.

In the **active voice**, we recognize the typical three components of transitive verbs: **the doer of the action** (the subject—agent), **the action** of the verb, and the **affected entity**:

| An architect | *designs* | buildings. | **Active Voice** |
|---|---|---|---|
| [SUBJ—agent] | V—third-person singular present | [affected entity] | three components of a transitive expression |

In the **passive voice** (involving only transitive expressions), at least two things change: (1) the affected entity becomes the **non-agentive subject** of the expression, and (2) the form of the verb now transforms to **a compound expression with auxiliary *be* + the past participle of the main verb** (*be* + **V-en**). Then, optionally, and where relevant, (3) the subject—agent may be overtly mentioned in the utterance with the preposition *by*.

**Form: Basic steps for converting active voice to passive voice**

1. Make the affected entity the new non-agentive subject; that is, replace the subject with the affected entity.
2. Add *be* auxiliary.
3. Match the tense and aspect in auxiliary *be* to the tense and aspect of the V from the active voice.
4. Subject-verb agreement (SVA): Match *be* to the non-agentive subject (i.e., the new subject).
5. Change the V to past participle (*V-en*—see Chapters 2 and 7).
6. Optionally mention *by* + *agent*—where relevant.

| **An architect** | *designs* | buildings. | active voice—present tense |
|---|---|---|---|
| [SUBJ—agent] | V—present | [affected entity] | |

1. Affected entity → subject — buildings → new, non-agentive
2. Add *be*
3. Match tense of auxiliary *be* to that of the main verb — present tense → are *or* is
4. SVA: *buildings* = plural (verb must be plural) — be → *are*
5. Change main verb to past participle — *designs* → *designed*
6. Optionally indicate agent — (by an architect)

**Result:**

| Buildings | *are designed* (by an architect). | **passive voice—present tense** |
|---|---|---|
| [non-agentive SUBJ] | PASSIVE [former SUBJ—agent] | |

| **Roger Bannister** | *breaks* | the 4-minute mile. | active voice—present tense |
|---|---|---|---|
| [SUBJ—agent] | V—present | [affected entity] | |

1. Affected entity = subject — the 4-minute mile → new, non-agentive
2. Add *be*
3. Match tense of auxiliary *be* to that of the main verb — present tense → are *or* is

4   SVA: *the 4-minute mile* = singular  
    (verb must be singular)          *be* → *is*  
5   Change main verb to past participle      *breaks* → *broken*  
6   Optionally indicate agent          (by Roger Bannister)

**Result:**

    The 4-minute mile    *is broken*    (by Roger Bannister).    **passive voice—present tense**  
    [non-agentive SUBJ] PASSIVE    [former SUBJ—agent]

A few other examples:

**Active voice:**    **White Star Line**    builds    the Titanic.  
                  [SUBJ—agent] V—third-person singular present    [affected entity]

                 the Titanic → new non-agentive subject  
                 add *be*  
                 tense of verb *builds* = present  
                 SVA *be* → *is* (new non-agentive subject is singular)  
                 verb *build*—change to past-participle form → *built*  
                 optionally mention *by* + *agent*—where relevant

**Tense:**

| | | | |
|---|---|---|---|
| present | **The Titanic** | *is built* | (by White Star Line). |
| | [non-agentive SUBJ] | PASSIVE | [former SUBJ—agent] |
| past | **The Titanic** *was built* (by White Star Line). | | |
| future | **The Titanic** will *be built* (by White Star Line). | | |

The six steps mentioned previously can be easily applied to sentences in simple aspect (i.e., where there is no auxiliary). However, the process changes slightly when V is in progressive, perfect, or perfect progressive form. Here are some examples:

**Progressive (*be* + *V-ing*)**

| | |
|---|---|
| present progressive | **The Titanic** *is being built* (by White Star Line). |
| past progressive | **The Titanic** *was being built* (by White Star Line). |
| future progressive | *****The Titanic** *will be being built* (by White Star Line). |
| | (This is ungrammatical. The combination of future progressive and passive causes a semantic, syntactic, and pragmatic clash.) |

**Perfect (*have* + *V-en*)**

| | |
|---|---|
| present perfect | **The Titanic** *has been built* (by White Star Line). |
| past perfect | **The Titanic** *had been built* (by White Star Line). |
| future perfect | **The Titanic** *will have been built* (by White Star Line) |

268  *Voice*

**Perfect progressive (*have* + *been* V-*ing*) IMPOSSIBLE WITH PASSIVE VOICE**
These are all ungrammatical. The combination of perfect progressive and passive causes a syntactic, semantic, and pragmatic clash.

| | |
|---|---|
| present perfect progressive | *The Titanic *has been being built* (by White Star Line). |
| past perfect progressive | *The Titanic *had been being built* (by White Star Line). |
| future perfect progressive | *The Titanic *will have been being built* (by White Star Line). |

**Forms of passives with simple modals, multi-word modals:**

| | |
|---|---|
| The 4-minute mile will *be broken*. | future: will *be broken* |
| Buildings will *be designed*. | future: will *be designed* |
| The Titanic will *have been built*. | future perfect: will *have been built* |
| Buildings will *have been designed*. | future perfect: will *have been designed* |

Now, substitute will in the previous sentences ((4-minute mile, letters, The Titanic) with any other simple modal or any multi-word modal, as follows:

| | |
|---|---|
| The Titanic | must *be built*. |
| | may *be built*. |
| | might *be built*. |
| Buildings | can *be designed*. |
| | should *be designed*. |
| | would *be designed*. |
| The 4-minute mile | is going *to be broken*. |
| | ought to *be broken*. |
| | has to *be broken*. |

## 9.2 Active Voice and Passive Voice in Discourse: What Is Conceptually in Focus?

The following four pairs of sentences describe specific events. In each pair, the first viewpoint is expressed in the **active voice**, with a clear **subject agent**. The second sentences **transform the affected entity into a non-agentive subject** using **passive voice**.

### Teaching excellence awards

a    active voice—simple present: honors                      SUBJ: Duke
      Duke *honors* two professors with awards for teaching excellence.

b    passive voice—present, past: are/were honored           SUBJ: Two professors
      **Two professors** *are honored* for teaching excellence by Duke University.    [present]
      **Two professors** *were honored* for teaching excellence by Duke University.    [past]

### Construction materials and rain

a    active voice—simple past: forgot, left [note subject ellipsis]    SUBJ: Contractors
      **Contractors** *forgot* eight bags of cement and left them outside in the rain.

b    passive voice—past: were forgotten, [were] left   [note auxiliary ellipsis] SUBJ: Five bags of cement
     **Eight bags of cement** *were forgotten and left* outside in the rain (by the contractors).

**Walmart employees (actual February 2011 news item)**

a    active voice—simple past: fired                        SUBJ: Wal-Mart
     **Walmart** *fired* <u>four employees</u> for disarming a gunman.

b    passive voice—past: were fired                         SUBJ: Four employees
     **Four employees** *were fired* (<u>by Walmart</u>) for disarming a gunman.
     **Gymnastics team member** (actual November 2014 news item)

a    active voice—simple past: selected                     SUBJ: USA Gymnastics
     **USA Gymnastics** *selected* <u>9-year-old Kira Fredericson</u> for its 50-member TOPS A Team.

b    passive voice—past: was selected                       SUBJ: 9-year-old Kira Fredericson
     **Nine-year-old Kira Fredericson** *was selected* (<u>by USA Gymnastics</u>) . . .

In the previous sentence pairs, how does the event change conceptually as we shift from the a versions in the active voice to the b versions in the passive voice? What or who is the entity in focus in the a versions for each pair? What or who is the entity in focus in the b versions?

As you have noticed, the sentences in the active voice evoke a far stronger sense of **agency** on the part of the *doer* of the action. That is, in each of the four cases, it is clear that the subject of the action exerts some degree of **agentive control** over another person, thing, concept, or idea, and consequently causes something to happen. In contrast, in the **passive voice counterparts**, the outcome of the event is evoked from a clearly **non-agentive perspective** (Shibatani, 1985). The focus in the b versions is on the outcome itself and not on the three-way interconnectedness between the subject—agent + the action + the affected entity.

## 9.3 Passive Voice With Ditransitive Verbs

Ditransitive verbs can also be used in the passive voice. Recall from Chapter 6 that ditransitive verbs involve <u>four</u> components, not three: (1) the doer of the action or the agent, (2) the action depicted by the verb, (3) the affected entity (direct object), and (4) the recipient of that affected entity (indirect object). Examples of ditransitive verbs include *give, buy, pass, hand, send, tell, allow, mail, toss, throw*, and *promise*. In the case of these ditransitive verbs, it can be either the **affected entity** or the **recipient of the affected entity** that becomes the non-agentive subject in the passive voice.

**Examples: Active voice to passive voice**

1   **Researchers**   *gave*   participants   <u>samples of the tested product</u>.   **active**
    [SUBJ—agent] V—past [recipient]        [affected entity]

    **Participants**   *were given* <u>samples of the tested product</u> (by researchers).   **passive**
    [non-agentive SUBJ] PASSIVE    [affected entity]

    **Samples of the tested product** *were given* to participants (by researchers).   **passive**
    [non-agentive SUBJ]         PASSIVE   [recipient]

270　*Voice*

2　**The college** *promised* incoming freshman <u>free medical insurance</u>.　　　**active**
　　[SUBJ—agent]　V—past　　　[recipient]　　　　[affected entity]

　　**Incoming freshman** *were promised*　　<u>free medical insurance</u> (by the college).　**passive**
　　[non-agentive SUBJ] PASSIVE—past pl. [affected entity]

　　**Free medical insurance** *was promised*　　to incoming freshman (by the college).　**passive**
　　[non-agentive SUBJ]　PASSIVE—past s. [recipient]

However, the previously stated rule does not always apply in cases **where the recipient of the affected entity (indirect object) occurs after a preposition**. Here is an example: *They donated $5,000* [the affected entity] *to the Diabetes Foundation* [recipient of the affected entity]. In this case, only *one* passive form is possible: ***Five thousand dollars** was donated to the Diabetes Foundation*. But <u>not</u>: *\*The Diabetes Foundation** was donated $5,000*.

## 9.4 Optional Addition of *by* + *Overt Agent* in Passivized Expressions

As noted, the addition of *by* + *overt agent* is optional. In some cases, however, explicit mention of the agent is necessary for clarity and precision, as in the following two excerpts:

**Teens who are at least 16** *are being hired* <u>by Dunkin' Donuts.</u>　　　**passive**
[affected entity SUBJ] PASSIVE—pres. progressive [former SUBJ]

**"Black Bears in Yosemite"** (n.d.)

　　Visitors who encounter a bear should keep their distance for
　　safety and respect for themselves and the animal. . . .
　　If visitors see a black bear in undeveloped areas,
　　they should remain at least 50 yards from it. Attacks are rare,
　　and **no one** *has been killed* or *seriously injured* <u>by a black bear</u> in Yosemite.　**passive**

In both cases, the explicit mention of the agent is crucial to the overall message of the utterance. That is, if the agent is not mentioned in the immediate or prior discourse, the utterance would either be so vague as not to make sense, as in the first example:

**Teens who are at least 16** *are being hired*. (By whom? Where?)

Or it would <u>be untrue</u>, as in the second example:

**No one** *has been killed* or *seriously injured* in Yosemite.

Often, the *by* + *agent* component is <u>not mentioned</u> in passive expressions, if

- it is clear from the context or prior mention who or what the *agent* is;
- it is impossible to impute an agent in the scene (e.g., **travelers** *were stranded*);
- the agent is either too general or too obvious;
- the agent is irrelevant or unknown; or
- the agent may be relevant, but mentioning it is avoided deliberately.

The caption for Figure 9.2 actually contains TWO instances of the passive voice in one sentence. For either instance, is there an overt agent in the caption? How about an implied agent?

*Figure 9.2* "The world's greatest hoax was exposed today when it was revealed that algebra will *never* be useful to you later in life."

© Randy Glasbergen. Reproduced with permission of Glasbergen Cartoon Service.

Is an agent (implied or explicit) even necessary in either clause? How would the thrust of the message change if there were an agent (or agents) associated with this issue?

**No explicit mention of agent: Other examples**

1  "3 men rescued from Fanadik Island"

> **Three men** *were rescued* Thursday from the Pacific Ocean island where **they** *had been stranded* for three days. . . . **The men** *were* first *located* about 8 a.m. local time Thursday.
>
> (Carlson, 2016)

<u>NO *by + agent*</u>

| | | |
|---|---|---|
| **Three men** *were rescued* | passive | past |
| **they** *had been stranded* for three days | passive | past perfect |
| **The men** *were* first *located* about 8 a.m. | passive | past |

The focus is on the result, the outcome of the rescue, and not on the individual or group who actively saved the stranded people.

The next example involves telling alternations between active voice and passive voice in the presentation of an unfortunate event and in framing the responsibility (or non-responsibility) associated with that event.

2  "**Yale Doctors** *Remove <u>Wrong Body Part</u>*" (article headline; Cohen, 2016)

**Active voice:** (second paragraph)

> Deborah Craven, 60, had surgery last year to remove part of her eighth rib because of a precancerous lesion—but instead, **doctors** *removed* <u>part of her seventh rib</u>.

**Passive voice:** (third paragraph)

> "We recognized that **an error** *was made*, we informed and apologized to the patient, and we immediately reported it to the Connecticut Department of Health," according to the statement Yale issued last week.

**Active voice:** (fourth paragraph)

> But Craven's lawyer said **she [Craven]** never *received* such an apology and said **one of her surgeons** *tried to cover up* the mistake.

Here, the event is introduced in the headline, as well as in the third and fourth paragraphs, as a mistake. Essentially, **surgeons** at Yale *removed* the wrong part (active voice), and later, **one of her surgeons** *tried to cover up* the mistake (active voice).

However, in the direct quote by the hospital spokesperson (second paragraph), the error is presented in the passive voice: "**an error** *was made*" rather than a version in the active voice, such as "**Dr. Quarrie/our surgical team/we** *made* an error."

---

### Mini Review and Practice

1   In Chapter 6, we examined transitive and intransitive verb meanings that express varying degrees of agency from high agency to low agency. Voice involves a similar type of continuum, which becomes especially evident in discourse. The discursive use of active and passive voices evokes stances and perceptions of agency, power, control, and responsibility on the one hand and lack of agency, power, and control or avoidance of responsibility on the other. This is achieved through the foregrounding of the various elements in the sentences (e.g., subject as active agent OR affected entity as non-agentive subject).

Have a look at the following two brief news story excerpts. The first one is about shark sightings off the coast of Southern California. The second story is about the death of thousands of fish in the Colorado River.

### "Sunset Beach closed after several large sharks spotted in the water"

> HUNTINGTON BEACH—**Authorities** *closed down* Sunset Beach after **several large sharks** *were seen* in the water Sunday afternoon.
>
> At around 2 p.m., the Orange County Sheriff's Department contacted the Huntington Beach Fire Department to report **its helicopter crew** *saw* "multiple sharks" that were more than 8 feet long off Anderson Street near Sunset Beach Tower 26, said Claude Panis, a marine safety lieutenant for the fire department.
>
> (Kwong, 2016)

Sentence 1: **several large sharks** *were seen* in the water   passive
Sentence 2: **its helicopter crew** *saw* "multiple sharks..."   active

### "Chemical runoff *kills* 5,600 fish in Colorado"

> FORT COLLINS, Colo. — **More than 5,600 fish** *were killed* last month in a Colorado river, the result of a chemical runoff from a bridge reconstruction project, according to state parks and wildlife officials.

The agency announced Tuesday that **the fish**, including rainbow and brown trout, suckers and dace, *died* March 7 in the Big Thompson River and its North Fork, in an 8.3-mile section of the river, in the northern part of the state.

(Myers, 2016)

Headline: **Chemical runoff** *kills* 5,600 fish in Colorado     **active**
Sentence 1: **More than 5,600 fish** *were killed*     **passive**
Sentence 2: **the fish** . . . *died* March 7     **intransitive** (active voice)

Think about the concept of a continuum of agency, power, control, and responsibility, and the ways in which entities are framed in discourse, through transitive verbs in the active and passive voices and intransitive verbs. Just based on these bits of extracted discourse, how could you preliminarily describe the meaning continuum of agency? In addition to the *by* + agent construction, how else can "responsibility" or "cause" be framed?

As you'll see in the discourse, there are also other ways to "point fingers" at responsible entities or to designate cause or reason—*the result of, due to, stemming from*, and so forth.

Try to find other discourse-based examples (e.g., in the news, popular magazines, research articles, TV drama/movie dialogue) that capture this continuum by virtue of the alternations in grammatical voice as we observed in these excerpts.

2    Passives in the discourse of policy statements, requests, and requirements:

    a    Review the following excerpt from the Visitor Information page of the website for Garrett Regional Medical Center in Oakland, Maryland. Here, you'll find a good number of passive expressions.

Isolate each occurrence of passive voice. We have marked the target instances in the following ways: **boldface type** for the non-agent subjects and *italics* for the passive elements.

What function is each of these instances of passive voice fulfilling? To start thinking about this question, paraphrase the discourse so that it takes a different form (e.g., active form with overt agent, imperative—with or without "please," deontic modals, etc.; see Chapter 8). How do the messages and the intent of those messages change with the change in structure and grammatical choice?

### "Garrett Regional Medical Center"—Visitor Information

PARKING
**All visitors** *are asked* to park in lots specifically designated for visitors. **Parking** *is provided* free of charge.

TELEPHONES
**The use of cellular phones** *is* only *permitted* in approved areas of the hospital.

VENDORS
All sales representatives must have appointments to visit with any department personnel. **Appointments** *are accepted* Monday through Friday 8 a.m. to 4 p.m. by calling (301) 533-4020 or (301) 533-4021. Click **HERE** to login/register.

VISITING HOURS

Visitors of Garrett Regional Medical Center shall enjoy equal visitation privileges consistent with the patient's preferences and are subject to the hospitals' justification of clinical restriction. . . . **Children under the age of 12** *are* not *encouraged* to visit.

(Garrett Regional Medical Center, n.d.)

Now, also compare and contrast the ways in which the forms of deontic modals (*must*, *shall*) and imperatives (*click HERE*) are used.

How does the strength of the message change in contrast with the passive voice? Why? As you consider these questions, think about the concept of agency with respect to (a) the subjects of the passive expressions (as non-agentive subjects) and (b) the subjects of the deontic modals and the imperative. (See Chapter 8.) Which subjects are framed as more highly agentive?

    b   Do the same with the following excerpt from the University of Illinois policy guidelines for student-athlete admissions. What is the main point of this message? Analyze how the passive voice is used to establish the points. Are there instances of overt *by* + *agent* constructions? Why are the agents explicitly mentioned? Are there any modals? Which ones? Do you note any ambiguity between a deontic or an epistemic reading for the modal *may*? How does the use of passive voice and modality combine to construct the message in this paragraph?

### "Student-Athlete Admissions" at the University of Illinois, Urbana-Champaign

**Applicants** [who *are*] *recruited* to participate in varsity sports **who** *are* not *admitted* through the regular admissions process, or whose application becomes complete after the published deadlines, <u>may</u> *be considered* for admission by the Committee for the Admission of Student Athletes (CASA). **This committee** *was created* by the Chancellor in 1983 under the authority [that *was*] *granted* by the Board of Trustees. Through the CASA review process, **potential student-athletes** <u>will</u> *be evaluated* by a committee of senior admissions officers from each of the undergraduate admitting units.

(Student-Athlete Admissions, n.d.)

In what ways is the tone of the University of Illinois policy statement different from the Garrett Regional Medical Center visitor information statement excerpted previously? Does each excerpt belong to the same genre of discourse?

To determine whether multiple instances of discourse belong to the same genre, consider the following elements:

- shared basic content
- same purpose
- same audience

Who is the intended reader/audience for the visitor information discourse? Who is the intended reader/audience for the University of Illinois discourse? What is the purpose of each statement?

3   Have a look at the following quote by Anaïs Nin. As you read through the passage, pay attention to the use of passive voice. Also attend to the verbs in general, especially transitive verbs.

> What we call our destiny is truly our character and **that character** <u>can</u> *be altered*. The knowledge that we are responsible for our actions and attitudes does not need to be discouraging, because it also means that we are free to change this destiny. One is not in bondage to the past, which has shaped our feelings, to race, inheritance, background. **All this** <u>can</u> *be altered* if we have the courage to examine how it formed us. **We** <u>can</u> *alter* the chemistry provided we have the courage to dissect the elements.
>
> (Nin, 1966)
>
> What is Nin's message? What does she say about destiny? How does she feel about it? Who is Nin addressing? What subject pronouns does she predominantly use? Which determiners does she use?
>
> Conduct a micro-level analysis of this passage to better reveal the structure and the meaning behind this message. That is, analyze all nouns (Type 1, Type 2), determiners, pronouns, verbs, tense and aspect, and voice. Pay close attention to her use of nouns (observe her use of Type 1 and Type 2 nouns—which are pluralized?) and demonstratives (both determiners and pronouns—see Chapters 4 and 6). Discuss how these various "parts of speech" combine into this compact passage to create her message.
>
> And finally, what analogies does she establish? How does the active voice in the last sentence ("**We** <u>can</u> *alter the chemistry*") help Nin depict her ideas in juxtaposition with the two earlier uses of the passive voice (**that character** <u>can</u> *be altered*; **All this** <u>can</u> *be altered*)? In her analogy, what does the NP "the elements" refer to?

## 9.5 *Be*-Passive vs. *Get*-Passive

In addition to the traditional *be*-passive (*be* + *V-en*) construction, English also uses a *get*-passive (*get* + *V-en*) where the auxiliary *be* is replaced by the auxiliary *get* (Carter & McCarthy, 1999; Chappell, 1980; Fleisher, 2005, 2006; Givón, 2015; Givón & Yang, 1994; Lakoff, 1971; Mitkovska & Bužarovska, 2011; Quirk et al., 1985; Sussex, 1982).

The primary difference between the *be*-passive and the *get*-passive is one of **aspect** (see Chapter 7). That is, *be*-passive constructions express a more stative or durative situation. In contrast, *get*-passives express more punctual situations or situations *that focus on both a process as well as the end point of that process*.

As a lexical verb, *get* is complexly polysemous (see Chapters 1 and 6). It can evoke meanings similar to such transitive verbs as *receive, fetch, catch, support,* and *apprehend* and such intransitive verbs as *become* [change of state copula], *arrive* [motion verb], and *come* [change of state/process].

| receive, fetch, catch, support, apprehend | *get* (transitive) |
|---|---|
| Saul *received* a gift from Greta. | Saul *got* a gift from Greta. |
| Duke, our pit bull, *fetched/caught* the ball. | Duke, our pit bull, *got* the ball. |
| Caffeine *helps* me through the morning. | Caffeine *gets* me through the morning. |

| become, arrive, come | *get* (intransitive) |
|---|---|
| Laptops *became* popular very fast. | Laptops *got* popular very fast. |
| Please do call when you *arrive* there. | Please do call when you *get* there. |
| Oda *is coming* to know her students better. | Oda *is getting* to know her students better. |

In each case, the transitive and intransitive versions with *get* evoke the following four basic differences:

- lower register
- **process** of transfer, transporting, or transformation (change of state)
- less specific conceptualization of the action than the counterparts (cf. *receive/get, become/get, fetch/get*)
- focus on the end point or result of that transfer, transporting, or transformation (**Telic aspect** is the aspectual category that focuses on the goal of the action or change of state.)

In contrast with the copula *be*, *get* as a lexical verb inherently marks a change of state, whereas *be* marks a state of being, as in the following examples:

*be* [copula] vs. *get* [change of state copula]

| | |
|---|---|
| Bounyang's face *is* red. | current state |
| Bounyang's face *was* red. | past state |
| Bounyang's face *gets* red (when he is embarrassed). | change of state/process to end point |

Think about the difference between *get* and *be* functioning as passive auxiliaries:

I don't want *to **be** involved* in their argument.   stative

vs.

I don't want *to **get** involved* in their argument.   process to end point

[*be*-passive]
   I *was locked out* of my office.   **aspect:** durative
                                         Start point and end point are not relevant.
                                         *Be* is stative.

[*get*-passive]
   I *got locked out* of my office.   **aspect:** telic
                                         It could have happened all of a sudden.
                                         End point is in focus.
                                         *Get* is telic.

Here is an example of the *get*-passive from discourse. This excerpt is taken from the beginning of a CBS News report:

### "Like Something Out of Ocean's Eleven" (*CBS This Morning*)

> The gang planned this heist down to every last detail, except apparently disabling the security cameras. . . .
>
> You're watching CBS THIS MORNING: SATURDAY. And I'm Vinita Nair. Coming up this half hour, the heist was right out of a Hollywood thriller and the thieves got away with millions. But they also **got caught** on video.

(Davies, 2008–)

Because of this aspectual difference, *be*-passives tend to evoke a more neutral or objective stance. *Get*-passives tend to evoke a subjective stance, typically carrying affective undertones of surprise, excitement, disappointment, guilt, counter-to-expectation, and so forth.

| | |
|---|---|
| Aamil *was accepted* to MIT. | **stance:** objective |
| Aamil *got accepted* to MIT. | **stance:** subjective |
| | surprise, pride, envy, etc. |
| | End point of the process is in focus. |
| | |
| Franco *was* not *scolded* for coming home late. | **stance:** objective |
| Franco *did* not *get scolded* for coming home late. | **stance:** subjective |
| | End point is in focus. |

Here is a message that used to appear when users logged on to Penn State's webmail system. The message contains two contiguous sentences. The first one uses *be*-passive, and the second *get*-passive.

**Penn State Webmail Message:**

You <u>will</u> *be re-directed* to your inbox in 5 seconds.
If **you** <u>do not</u> *get redirected* click here.

This message is perfectly clear and perfectly grammatical. How do the two meanings differ? That is, what does one version of the passive expression highlight or emphasize aspectually that the other does not, and vice versa?

Also, because *get* is a less formal (lower register) counterpart of the intransitive change of state copula *become* (see Chapter 6), as well as a less formal (lower register) counterpart of the transitive verb *receive*, it can (though not always) also evoke a less formal register as the *get*-passive auxiliary.

## 9.6 *Have* and *Get* as "Causative Passives"

Other uses of passives occur in causative-like constructions with auxiliary verbs *have* and *get*. For example: We <u>had</u> the kitchen <u>remodeled</u> last summer and We finally <u>got</u> our refrigerator <u>fixed</u>.

In causative-passives, the subject (or doer of the action) causes something to be done, either for his or her own benefit or for someone else. Causative-passives can also express an idea that a *negative* outcome happened to a non-agentive subject, but not all instances of *get* used as a passive auxiliary are negative.

While both *have* and *get* function as auxiliaries for the causative-passive, *have* is the more objective of the two. With the *get* auxiliary placing focus on the end point of a process, the *get*-causative-passive lends itself to a more subjective reading—expressing concepts like the subject is more affected by the action, the subject benefits more directly from the action, the subject has more control over the action, and so forth. *Have* is the less marked of the two auxiliaries.

Both *have*- and *get*- can express causative passive:

**Javier** *had* <u>his car</u> *washed* on Saturday.
   **Javier** *got* <u>his car</u> *washed* on Saturday.
**Monica** <u>will</u> *have* <u>her eyes</u> *checked* by an ophthalmologist.
   **Monica** <u>will</u> *get* <u>her eyes</u> *checked* by an ophthalmologist.
**The kids** <u>need to</u> *have* <u>their hair</u> *cut* before we leave on vacation.
   **The kids** <u>need to</u> *get* <u>their hair</u> *cut* before we leave on vacation.

Abdul-Aziz *had* his passport *stolen* at Disney World.
Abdul-Aziz *got* his passport *stolen* at Disney World.

**Jolan** *had* the pizza delivery person *fired* because of her mistake.
**Jolan** *got* the pizza delivery person *fired* because of her mistake.

Let's look at an example from actual discourse. The excerpt is the final line of a news story about two hunters who killed an 800-pound alligator in Florida.

**"Hunters Kill 800-Pound Florida Alligator They Say Was Eating Cattle"**

**The hunters** plan to *have* the alligator *stuffed* for display, but will donate the meat to charity.

(Bever, 2016)

cf. The hunters plan to *get* the alligator *stuffed* for display.
[*get*: focus on end point of the process, more informal register, stronger focus on subject's deliberate action]

In this excerpt from actual discourse, one of the main characters (Ricky Underwood) from the TV series "The Secret Life of the American Teenager" is introduced:

Ricky is the son of Nora and Bob Underwood.
Both of his parents were drug addicts and in prison.
**Ricky** *got* his father *sent to prison* for sexually and physically abusing him.

[*got:* more subjective: focus on the end point; more control; more highly deliberate act; Ricky benefits from the outcome]

(From secretlife.wikia.com, n.d.)

cf. **Ricky** *had* his father *sent to prison*.
   [*had:* more objective]

## 9.7 Middle Voice: Defocusing the Agent Entirely—The Affected Entity Becomes a Pseudo-Agentive Subject

Throughout this chapter we have examined the interrelationships between **voice and agency**, through the following encapsulation:

Active       **Subject agent** *does the action of the verb* involving an affected entity.

Passive      **Affected entity** (that conceptually receives the action of the verb in the active voice) becomes the subject but is non-agentive. **Agent is assumed.** The agent may or may not be overt in the discourse.

There is a third category of voice: **middle voice**. In middle voice constructions, the conceptual affected entity remains the subject (as with passive voice), but two conceptual shifts occur: (1) its essential feature of non-agency is replaced by what we call a **pseudo-agentive** function, and (2) **no actual agent is assumed** or even conceptually possible. That is, the scene is construed as "The event involving the affected entity occurs through its own force acting upon itself." Syntactically, the verb takes on the appearance of the active form (Davidse & Heyvaert, 2007; Halliday, 1985; Kemmer, 1993; Lyons, 1969).

> Middle    **Affected entity** (that conceptually receives the action of the verb in the active voice) becomes the **PSEUDO-agentive subject**. An **actual agent is conceptually impossible**. These verbs resemble intransitive verbs in that there are only TWO components: (1) the doer and (2) the action, depicted by the verb.

Examples:

| | | |
|---|---|---|
| **Amazon** *shipped* my package yesterday. [SUBJ—agent] V—past [affected entity] | | active |
| **My package** *was shipped* (by Amazon) yesterday. [non-agentive SUBJ] PASSIVE—past [former SUBJ—agent] | | passive |
| **My package** *shipped* yesterday. [PSEUDO-agentive SUBJ] MIDDLE—past [like intransitive] | | middle |
| **The doorman** *opened* the door. [SUBJ—agent] V—past [affected entity] | | active |
| **The door** *was opened* (by the doorman). [non-agentive SUBJ] PASSIVE—past [former SUBJ—agent] | | passive |
| **The door** *opened*. [PSEUDO-agentive SUBJ] MIDDLE—past [like intransitive] | | middle |

The **agency continuum** associated with **voice** is distributed in a variety of ways in discourse. Active voice underscores or emphasizes an agentive entity acting on an affected entity; passive voice underscores an affected entity that is non-agentive; and middle voice underscores that a **transitive event** happened—but we don't exactly know how it happened or who or what was responsible for it happening. Sinclair (1990) refers to English verbs that can function in this three-way voice patterning as *ergative* verbs. Sinclair defines the ergative verb as a "verb which can be either transitive or intransitive in the same meaning. To use the verb intransitively, you use the object of the transitive verb as the subject of the transitive verb as the subject of the intransitive verb" (p. 10).

The following examples will illustrate further:

| | |
|---|---|
| **Our new picture window** *cracked*. | [middle voice] |
| vs. | |
| Someone *cracked* our new picture window. | [active] |
| or | |
| Our new picture window *was cracked* (by . . .). | [passive] |
| **The turkey** *is defrosting* on the counter. | [middle voice] |
| **Harvard** *ranks* number one in at least 10 subjects. | [middle voice] |
| **Chili** should *cook* slowly and for a long time. | [middle voice] |

280  *Voice*

**Middle voice on signage**

What do the two signs in Figures 9.3 and 9.4 mean?
How can you re-word each one using the active voice? Then, re-word with the passive voice. How do the meanings change? Is re-wording (i.e., middle to active, active to passive) actually possible for both sentences? Why, or why not?

Most of the commonly used so-called ergative verbs can be categorized as (a) verbs that involve some type of change from one state to another, for example, *break, shatter, bleach, burn, burst, change, crack, darken, freeze, dissolve,* and *soak*; (b) verbs that relate to food and cooking, for example, *bake, boil, fry, cook, simmer, thicken,* and *roast*; or (c) verbs that relate to motion or movement [contrasting caused motion = transitive verbs, and spontaneous motion = intransitive verbs—see Chapter 6]. Verbs that evoke both caused motion and spontaneous motion include: *swing, balance, drop, glide, rock, stand, turn, run, walk, drive, sail, fly,* and *ship*. There are a number of other ergative verbs that do not fit into the previously listed categories, for example, *perform, rank, sell, wear, process, distribute,* and *dispense*.

Because **voice** evokes varying degrees of agency, control, responsibility, passivity, non-agency, and non-accountability, we prefer to use the concept of **middle voice** for constructions using the previously listed verbs with pseudo-agents as subjects rather than "ergativity."

*Figure 9.3* Sign in front of a café in State College, Pennsylvania: "**Bikes** *Park* Free"

*Figure 9.4* Road sign in the northeast US: **Bridge** *Ices* Before Road

## PRACTICE WITH DATA ANALYSIS: PUTTING IT ALL TOGETHER

1   The cartoon that opens this chapter, Figure 9.1, depicts a father reading a bedtime story to his son. He adds, "Conspiracy theorists say Humpty Dumpty *was pushed*."

The nursery rhyme about Humpty Dumpty tells the story of an egg (Humpty Dumpty) who was sitting on a wall and then fell. ("Humpty Dumpty sat on a wall. Humpty Dumpty had a great fall."). The poor egg's injuries were so severe he could not *be mended*.

In this cartoon, we see a different version of the story:

| | |
|---|---|
| The joke is that **Humpty Dumpty** did not simply *fall*. | intransitive |
| Instead, some people think **he** *was pushed*. | passive |
| If this is the case, **who** *pushed* <u>Humpty Dumpty</u> and why? | active |

Think about this continuum of agency as it pertains to transitivity (and intransitivity) and voice in the previous discussion about the nursery rhyme. Now, have a look at the headline and two sub-heads, adapted from the *Daily Mail*:

| | |
|---|---|
| "Humpty Dumpty didn't *get bumped* . . . because he *bungee jumped*: How our nursery rhymes *have been sanitized*" | headline |
| New push to *save* traditional British rhymes and songs. . . | sub-head 1 |
| Classics including Humpty Dumpty (*are being*) *re-written* with happier endings | sub-head 2 |

(Conway, 2012)

The verbs are indicated in italics. Within each context, think about transitive and intransitive verbs. There is one intransitive verb in the data. What is it? [Hint: It is a "compound verb" composed of two words.]

The remaining verbs are transitive. One is in active voice, and the rest are in passive voice.

Analyze the use of transitivity and voice in this discourse (i.e., the cartoon caption and the news excerpt). For passive voice, what are the auxiliaries that are used (i.e., *be, get*)? How do the meanings differ in this context? As you work with the discourse, don't just focus on the verbs. Also attend to nouns, determiners, and pronouns, as well as tense and aspect.

Just based on this small snippet of data, what do you think the *Daily Mail* news story is about? Why do you think it was written?

Think about stance and perspective taking. How can you alter some of these event descriptions to evoke a different stance and a different perspective on the issue?

2   What is the difference in conceptual meaning and stance between the a and b versions of the following sentences? The a versions all involve the *get*-passive; the b versions are the identical sentences, only with the *be*-passive. How can you articulate the differences between these two passive forms using the following sentence pairs? It helps to imagine possible scenarios for each example.

   a   Indra used food coloring for the cookies, and her fingers *got stained*.
   b   Indra used food coloring for the cookies, and her fingers *were stained*.

   a   Usami will *get promoted* to section chief next month
   b   Usami will *be promoted* to section chief next month.

a   Unlike most aspiring actors, you *got noticed* quite early in your career.
b   Unlike most aspiring actors, you were noticed quite early in your career.

a   The investors *get excited* by sudden spikes in sales.
b   The investors *are excited* by sudden spikes in sales.

a   It's difficult because everything he ever had *got destroyed*.
b   It's difficult because everything he ever had *was destroyed*.

The best way to analyze data like these is to work with the examples and take notes about your observations. Then, try to find *common threads* that apply to your data and *articulate a generalization* that accounts for most, if not all, of the exemplars.

3   Perspective taking, voice, and transitivity in sports reporting

Have a look at the following headlines from a historic football loss involving two rival Pennsylvania teams: Penn State (Nittany Lions) and Temple University (Owls). The game took place on September 5, 2015, and the underdog team, Temple University, won.

The first two headlines presented here are from national sports websites. The third is from a Pennsylvania-based news outlet. The last two are from each university's respective college newspapers.

*NBC Sports*

Temple *sacks* Penn State, *ends* 39-game winless streak

*SB Nation*

Temple *beats* Penn State for first time since 1941, ending 39-game winless streak

*TribLive* (PA newspaper)

Penn State *(is) beaten* by Temple for first time since 1941

*The Temple News* (Temple University's newspaper)

Owls *beat* Penn State: The Owls *defeated* their in-state rival 27–10, for the first time since 1941 in front of a sellout crowd at Lincoln Financial Field Saturday

*The Daily Collegian* (Penn State's newspaper)

Temple *upsets* Penn State in season opener

Analyze the discourse in these headlines from the point of view of stance and perspective taking. How is each team referred to in the various papers? How is the event described in each headline? As you work with the discourse, don't just focus on verbs, voice, and transitivity. Also attend to other bits of discursive descriptive detail contained in the headlines, for example, tense and aspect, nouns (proper and common), determiners, dates, numbers, and so forth.

Does anything stand out to you in terms of how each university frames its own situation? How do the university newspaper headlines compare and contrast with the headlines from other news outlets?

4   Middle voice and discourse

Here a few more instances of middle voice constructions in discourse. You'll find expressions like these all throughout discourse, from scientific writing to real estate websites, in blogs, in the news, and even in advertising slogans.

- "Don McLean's 'American Pie' Manuscript *Sells* for $1.2 Million" (Lewis, 2015)
- "10 salads that *eat* like a meal"
- "My car *drives* like a boat on the highway" (LS1tech)
- "When it rains, it *pours*" (Morton Salt motto)
  [The first "it" here is the non-referential "it" that co-occurs as the subject with the verb *rain* (see Chapter 5). The second "it" refers to the salt. This means that when the weather is damp or humid, the salt will still pour out freely and not get clumped.]
- "It *melts* in your mouth, not in your hand." (M&Ms)

Middle voice constructions are lexically economical. That is, they convey a lot of meaning with few words. The best way to test this is as follows:

Use the verb in:

Active voice:
**Christie's** *Sells* Don McLean's "American Pie" manuscript for $1.2 million

Passive voice:
**Don McLean's "American Pie"** *is/was sold* for $1.2 million (to. . . /by. . .)

Middle voice:
**Don McLean's "American Pie"** *sells* for $1.2 million. . .

In each case, a slightly different construal of the scene takes place in one's imagination. Crucially, with middle voice constructions, there is no focus on an agentive-subject/affected entity (active voice) or non-agentive subject that was once the affected entity (passive voice)—just an emphasis on the event itself, with a pseudo-subject.

Follow the same procedure with the other examples listed previously. That is, try to convert the clauses into active and passive voice to get a more solid sense of how middle voice functions conceptually in discourse.

Then, look for other examples of middle voice usages in specific types of discourse (e.g., news, advertising, science), and test to see whether your selections of transitive verbs actually meet the criteria of being able to be expressed in all three voices.

5   *Get-* and *be-*passive used creatively: *Got Starbucked, Got Trumped, You've Just Been Wal-Marted*

In Chapters 3 and 6, we introduced proper nouns and the various ways in which proper nouns enter our lexicons transformed into other parts of speech, like verbs. The following three examples provide a small glimpse into this phenomenon. In each case, a persistent and iconic figure in society and the news is further iconized and characterized through creative textual analogies.

Why do you think these three entities have emerged in the discourse in this way? What, specifically, is meant by each of these verbs as used in the passive voice?

> Pizza *is getting Starbucked*; there's a pizza joint on every corner, and there's no end in sight.
> (Davies, 2008–)

> How We *Got Trumped* by the Media: They're so obsessed with "The Donald" that they can barely be bothered to cover the other candidates, much less the important issues.
> (Nichols, 2016)

> Boxed Out: You've Just *Been Wal-Marted*
> The competition in personal lines just got a whole lot stiffer: Wal-Mart, the biggest and most cutthroat competitor in America, is now hawking car insurance.
> (Banham, 2014)

> Note: The author of "Boxed Out" is referring to the Big Box approach to retail sales and marketing. You can read more about this phenomenon online.

How do the first two instances with *get*-passive contrast in meaning with the third example with *be*-passive?

Have you run across other such instances of proper nouns becoming creatively expressive verbs in discourse? How do the previous examples compare?

6   The following passage contains the opening words from Mitch Albom's book *Tuesdays With Morrie*.

### "The Curriculum"

> The last class of my old professor's life took place once a week in his house, by a window in the study where he could watch a small hibiscus plant shed its pink leaves. The class met on Tuesdays. It began after breakfast. The subject was The Meaning of Life. It was taught from experience.
>
> No grades were given, but there were oral exams each week. You were expected to respond to questions, and you were expected to pose questions of your own. You were also required to perform physical tasks now and then, such as lifting the professor's head to a comfortable spot on the pillow or placing his glasses on the bridge of his nose. Kissing him good-bye earned you extra credit.
>
> No books were required, yet many topics were covered, including love, work, community, family, aging, forgiveness, and, finally, death. The last lecture was brief, only a few words.
>
> A funeral was held in lieu of graduation.
>
> Although no final exam was given, you were expected to produce one long paper on what was learned. That paper is presented here.
>
> The last class of my old professor's life had only one student.
>
> I was the student.
> (Albom, 1997, pp. 1–2)

The entire book is as beautifully written as its opening words. This chapter is written predominantly in the passive voice. Why? Are all instances of the passive *be*-passive, or do you also find tokens of *get*-passive? Why do you think this is so?

This excerpt opens as Albom sets the scene of his last "class" with his beloved professor. Albom uses the past tense of the dynamic/intransitive verb *took place*: *The last class of my old professor's life **took place** once a week in his house.*

As we observed in Chapter 7, the past tense captures the notion of regular occurrences (see *Autobiography of a Face* and "The Telephone").

Here are a few examples of how Albom uses passive voice in this narrative:

*The subject was The Meaning of Life. It **was taught** from experience.*
*No grades **were given**. . . . You **were expected** to respond to questions, and you **were expected** to pose questions of your own. You **were also required** to perform physical tasks now and then.*

What were those physical tasks?
You can continue the list of instances of passive voice.

Now, analyze the power of these introductory remarks by focusing on the progression of the scenes that Albom describes and the relevant analogies that he establishes. Here are some items to focus on:

- sentence structure and sentence length—how does the variety of sentence length enhance the flow of the narrative?
- instances of active voice
- pronouns
- non-agentive subjects of passive expressions
- copula *be* (or *was* for past tense), as opposed to auxiliary *be* for passive
- determiners: articles *the*, *a*; possessive determiners; quantifiers; negative determiner *no*; demonstrative *that*

How does Albom make use of these combined features of grammar to depict the scene, depict the people in that scene, and evoke his stance with regard to his experience?

Running through this entire discourse is a set of contrasts or juxtapositions. What are those contrasts? How does Albom set them up?

Consider these issues in as much detail as possible, using examples from the text (and possibly from the entire book, should you choose to read it—and we very much hope you do).

## COMMON ERRORS, BUMPS, AND CONFUSIONS

Identify the errors or "bumps" in the following sentences or paragraphs. Use the concepts and terminology that you learned in this and other chapters to articulate what might be grammatically or pragmatically problematic. Suggest ways that each can be re-written more clearly and more accurately. (Note: While all bumps do involve some element of voice, they are not limited to only that.)

1. My family been investigating because we was immigrated to US before two months.
2. Korean War was happened after North Korea tanks was crossed the 38th parallel.
3. Are barbecue grill got heated too much and burgers were burned by the fire.
4. People get changed from hearing talks. I listened Brené Brown talked about vulnerability and empathy. People gotta be understood by us.
5. Melania's gown got sewed special by a tailor.
6. It very very hard to see when sun go down. One car hit three deers in road. One was died.

## SUGGESTED ACTIVITIES

1. Think about the game/sport of bowling. How do you play? What kind of equipment do you need for a game (e.g., lanes, bowling shoes, balls, pins, score card)? What do you do with the equipment? Provide a step-by-step description of how to bowl. Think about how you would use elements of active, passive, and middle voice. Other features of grammar in addition to voice (active, passive, and middle) that will also be helpful in this activity include imperatives, modals, multi-word modals, pronouns, nouns, determiners, verbs (dynamic/stative/copular, transitive/intransitive), and agency.

   Now, think about the history of video games. How have video games changed from *Pong* to the most current ones? How is or was *Pong* played? What is the premise of the game? How do you collect points? Is it played individually or in competition with others.

   Prepare a poster or slide show that discusses the history of video games. What were the oldest games like? What are the current games like? (You an also compare and contrast the histories of popular games in the US and outside the US.) To do this, you'll need to work with at least all of the features of grammar, as in the previous bowling description, in addition to tense and aspect (an important category of grammar for this task) and negation (and others as well, but these will be key).

2. Research the lives of famous outlaws and lawmen in the US—for example, Butch Cassidy, "Wild Bill" Hickok, John Henry "Doc" Holliday, and Wyatt Earp. What were they known for? What is each person's history? What did they do? What are some of the details of their lives? How did they die? Were the outlaws captured? By whom? Did the lawmen capture any famous outlaws? What are some of the details behind those stories? Write a brief bio for each individual, making sure to attend to active, passive, and middle voice, in addition to nouns, determiners, pronouns, ellipsis, verbs, tense and aspect, and modals.

3. Find five current mainstream news stories that center on celebrity couples. Why are their stories in the news? What happened? In each news story, locate all instances of active, passive, and middle voice. Then, re-write each story as if you were writing it for a tabloid gossip column (typically exaggerated and sensationalized). How does grammatical voice affect some of the details in your story?

4. Research the history of the Bhopal disaster of 1984, the Exxon Valdez oil spill of 1989, and other environmental disasters. Use mainstream news stories from various sources about each event. Then, compare and contrast the news stories and narratives of each event to the company's own description of what happened. As you work through the texts, focus on active, passive, and middle voice, as well as the following grammatical features: nouns, determiners, verbs, negation, and other relevant descriptors. How is responsibility/accountability framed in these publications and/or websites?

5. Re-read the excerpt of the article "**Yale Doctors** Remove Wrong Body Part," in Section 9.4. If you can find the original article online, you should read the full text to get a more detailed view of what happened.

   Now, imagine that you are a close family member of Deborah Craven. Write a one- to two-page letter to the surgeon(s) responsible for the error, letting them know how Ms. Craven's life was affected by their actions.

   Then, imagine that you are the surgeon(s) responding to Ms. Craven's family member's letter. What will you say? Write a one- to two-page letter in response.

As you work through both letters, think about register (how formal/informal will you be? How emotional, passionate/composed, phlegmatic will you be in each case?), sentence structure, and word choice. Each side should reflect different perspectives, stances, and tones.

## Academic References

Carter, R., & McCarthy, M. (1999). The English get-passive in spoken discourse: Description and implications for an interpersonal grammar. *English Language and Linguistics, 3*(1), 41–58.
Chappell, H. (1980). Is the get-passive adversative? *Research on Language and Social Interaction, 13*(3), 411–452.
Davidse, K., & Heyvaert, L. (2007). On the middle voice: An interpersonal analysis of the English middle. *Linguistics, 45*(1), 37–83.
Fleisher, N. (2005). Passive get, causative get, and the phasehood of passive VP. *Proceedings From the Annual Meeting of the Chicago Linguistic Society, 41*(1), pp. 59–67.
Fleisher, N. (2006). The origin of passive get. *English Language and Linguistics, 10*(2), 225–252.
Givón, T. (2015). *The diachrony of grammar*. Amsterdam: John Benjamins.
Givón, T., & Yang, L. (1994). The rise of the English GET-passive. In B. Fox & P. Hopper (Eds.), *Voice: Form and function*. Amsterdam: John Benjamins.
Halliday, M. A. K. (1985). *An introduction to functional grammar*. London: Arnold.
Kemmer, S. (1993). *The middle voice*. Amsterdam: John Benjamins Publishing.
Lakoff, R. (1971). Passive resistance. *CLS 7*. Chicago: University of Chicago, Chicago Linguistics Society.
Lyons, J. (1969). *Introduction to theoretical linguistics*. Cambridge: Cambridge University Press.
Mitkovska, L., & Bužarovska, E. (2011). An alternative analysis of the English get-past participle constructions: Is get all that passive? *Journal of English Linguistics, 40*(2), 196–215.
Quirk, R., Greenbaum, S., Leech, G., Svartvik, J., & Crystal, D. (1985). *A comprehensive grammar of the English language*. London: Longman.
Shibatani, M. (1985). Passives and related constructions: A prototype analysis. *Language*, 821–848.
Sinclair, J. (1990). *Collins COBUILD English grammar*. London: Harper Collins.
Sussex, R. (1982). A note on the get-passive construction. *Australian Journal of Linguistics, 2*, 83–95.

## Data References

Albom, M. (1997). *Tuesdays with Morrie: An old man, a young man, and life's greatest lesson*. New York: Walker Publishing Company.
Banham, R. (2014). Boxed out: You've just been Wal-Marted. *i.a. Magazine*. Retrieved June 21, 2016, from www.iamagazine.com/magazine/read/2014/08/01/boxed-out-you've-just-been-wal-marted
Bever, L. (2016). Hunters kill 800-pound Florida alligator they say was eating cattle. *Chicago Tribune*. Retrieved June 1, 2016, from www.chicagotribune.com/news/nationworld/ct-florida-alligator-20160406-story.html
Black bears in Yosemite. (n.d.). National Park Service. Retrieved June 15, 2015, from www.nps.gov/yose/learn/nature/bears.htm
Carlson, A. (2016). 3 men, stranded on Pacific island for days, rescued after spelling out "HELP" in leaves on the beach. *People Magazine*. Retrieved June 16, 2016 from, http://people.com/celebrity/3-men-rescued-on-pacific-island-after-spelling-out-help/
Cohen, E. (2016). Patient accuses Yale doctors of cover-up. CNN. Retrieved June 18, from www.cnn.com/2016/03/23/health/yale-doctor-lawsuit/
Conway, L. (2012). Humpty Dumpty didn't get bumped . . . because he bungee jumped: How our nursery rhymes have been sanitized. *Daily Mail*. Retrieved June 20, 2016, from www.dailymail.co.uk/news/article-2157108/Humpty-dumpty-didnt-bumped—bungee-jumped-How-nursery-rhymes-sanitised.html
Davies, M. (2008–). *The corpus of contemporary American English: 520 million words, 1990–present*. Retrieved from http://corpus.byu.edu/coca/

Garret Regional Medical Center: Visitor information.(n.d.). Retrieved June 16, 2016, from www.gcmh.com/visitor-information/

Kwong, J. (2016). Sunset Beach closed after several large sharks spotted in the water. *The OC Register*. Retrieved August 8, 2016, from www.ocregister.com/articles/beach-718328-water-closed.html

Lewis, R. (2015). Don McLean's "American Pie" manuscript sells for $1.2 million. *LA Times*. Retrieved June 20, 2016, from www.latimes.com/entertainment/music/posts/la-et-ms-don-mclean-american-pie-manuscript-auction-20150407-story.html

Meyers, S. (2016). Chemical runoff kills 5,600 fish in Colorado. *USA Today*. Retrieved June 16, 2016, from www.usatoday.com/story/news/nation-now/2016/04/28/chemical-runoff-kills-5600-fish-colorado/83667854/

Nichols, J. (2016). How we got Trumped by the media. *The Nation*. Retrieved June 19, 2016, from www.thenation.com/article/how-we-got-trumped-by-the-media/

Nin, A. (1966). *The diary of Anais Nin: Vol. 1. 1931–1934*. New York: Houghton Mifflin Harcourt Publishing.

Student-Athlete Admissions. (n.d.). University of Illinois, Urbana-Champaign. Retrieved June 20, 2016, from www.admissions.illinois.edu/policies

# 10 The Grammar of Juxtaposing, Contrasting, Denying, Excluding, Contradicting, and Reversing

Negation

*Figure 10.1* "Your brain *is* like a sponge that absorbs knowledge, but that's not exactly how it's done."

© Randy Glasbergen. Reproduced with permission of Glasbergen Cartoon Service.

Negation is not necessarily the simple equivalent of the concept of negative as opposed to positive. That is, just because an utterance, a clause, or a phrase may be expressed using negative morphology and negative words, it might not, in and of itself, convey a negative idea as opposed to a positive one. Further, most approaches to grammar assume that the affirmative form is the default form and the corresponding negative form is simply that, i.e., the negative form of an affirmative expression. Such approaches do not adequately address conceptualization and stance as they relate to negation in discourse.

As we will observe, negation in discourse is quite closely associated with the communicative functions of juxtaposing, contrasting, denying, excluding, contradicting, and reversing rather than just "negating."

## 10.1 Grammatical Forms of Negation

Let's begin with a brief overview of the prototypical grammatical forms of negation, i.e., negating the verbal message of an expression and negating other elements of the utterance (e.g., nouns, basic verb meaning, adjectives, adverbs).

*Negating the verbal message of an expression is achieved by adverbs such as* **not**, **n't**, **never**, *and* **not ever**

| | |
|---|---|
| MOMA (the Museum of Modern Art) opens at 8:00 a.m. | [affirmative] |
| MOMA **does** **not** open at 8:00 a.m. | [negative—*does not*] |
| MOMA **does**n't open at 8:00 a.m. | [negative—*doesn't*] |
| MOMA **never** opens at 8:00 a.m. | [negative—*never*] |
| MOMA does **not ever** open at 8:00 a.m. | [negative—*not ever*] |
| MOMA **does**n't **ever** open at 8:00 a.m. | [negative—*n't ever*] |
| They are concerned about their finances. | [affirmative] |
| They are **not** concerned about their finances. | [negative—*not*] |
| They are**n't** concerned about their finances. | [negative—*n't*] |
| They are **never** concerned about their finances. | [negative—*never*] |
| They are **not ever** concerned about their finances. | [negative—*not ever*] |
| They are**n't ever** concerned about their finances. | [negative—*n't ever*] |

*Negating other elements of the utterance—nouns, noun phrases, adverbs, and adjectives*

| | | |
|---|---|---|
| Sofia leads a *healthy* lifestyle. [adjective] | → | an **un**healthy lifestyle [adjective] |
| The bookstore is *conveniently* located. [adverb] | → | **in**conveniently located [adverb] |
| Existing policies are *adequate*. [adjective] | → | policies are **in**adequate [adjective] |
| Kyle prefers candy made *with sugar*. [adverb/adjective] | → | **sugar-free** or **sugarless** candy [adjective] [adjective] |
| There was just one *truth* in the story. [noun/noun phrase] | → | the rest were **falsehoods** [noun/noun phrase] |

Even with just these few illustrative examples, it becomes clear that the *meaning* of negation in discourse is not just a simple shift in grammar that turns an affirmative sentence, clause, phrase, or word into a negative one.

Let's have a quick look at the following quote by fashion and portrait photographer Richard Avedon (1993):

> A portrait is not a likeness. The moment an emotion or fact is transformed into a photograph it is no longer a fact but an opinion. There is no such thing as inaccuracy in a photograph. All photographs are accurate. None of them is the truth.
>
> (Avedon, 1993)

The statement that "a portrait is **not** a likeness" juxtaposes the difference between a person's physical face and the evaluative, artistic representation of the same face through photography. The sentence is designed to refute a commonly held assumption that a portrait *is* a likeness. And Avedon goes on to explain his position in the next few lines of the quote.

The same perspective of negation is true in the text of the opening cartoon, Figure 10.1, where the teacher says to the student: "Your brain <u>is</u> like a sponge that absorbs knowledge, but that's <u>not</u> exactly how it's done." The teacher's use of negation here serves to counter the boy's literal interpretation of the simile; that is, a brain is like a sponge, so it can soak up just about anything it comes into contact with, which is also the source of humor. How easy would it be to learn everything from a book, just by laying it on your head?

### 10.1.1 FORMS: *Negating the Verbal Message of an Expression Using* Not, n't, Never, *and* Not Ever

We can negate the verb within a clause in the following five basic ways: with *not*, the contracted form *n't*, *never*, *not ever*, and *n't ever*.

> Marla **was not** a suspect.
> Marla **wasn't** a suspect.
> Marla was **never** a suspect.
> Marla was **not ever** a suspect.
> Marla **wasn't ever** a suspect.

All of these negated sentences oppose an assumption that Marla <u>was</u> a suspect in a crime. Each version of the sentence carries this same overall message, one that opposes the assumption. However, they differ in terms of their strength, intention, and stance.

The full form *Marla was **not** a suspect* can be considered the unmarked form in formal written discourse. And the contracted form *Marla wasn't a suspect* can be considered the unmarked form in casual spoken or written discourse. As we have noted in Chapter 2, contractions in formal or academic writing (e.g., *wouldn't, doesn't, he's, I'm*) are not the preferred style unless the writer is intentionally creating a register shift from formal to slightly less formal discourse.

Also, uncontracted *not* can evoke a stronger stance for a writer or speaker to emphasize a point, an opinion, or a position; or to dny one. Uncontracted *not* establishes a stronger basis for contrast, denial, or exclusion (e.g., what <u>is</u> and what <u>is</u> <u>*not*</u> at issue; Marla was <u>not</u> a suspect, contrary to what the media had reported; Morrie did <u>*not*</u> teach at Princeton—he taught at Yale). In spoken discourse, such emphasis can also be heard in a speaker's higher pitch, increased volume, and/or hyperarticulation of the consonants /n/ and /t/.

The adverbs *never* and *not ever* express an even stronger and more emphatic stance than *not*. They express an absolute negation of an event or an absolute absence of a requirement, experience, and so forth. As such, the conceptual contrast established by *never* and *not ever* is very strong:

> I had**n't** been to Peru, but I did visit Chile.      [unmarked]
> I had **not** been to Peru, but I did visit Chile.      [slightly emphatic]
> I had **never** been to Peru, but I did visit Chile.      [more emphatic]
> I had**n't ever** been to Peru, but I did visit Chile.      [more emphatic]
> I had **not ever** been to Peru, but I did visit Chile.      [most emphatic]

A quick search in *The Corpus of Contemporary American English* (COCA; Davies, 2008–) reveals that negations with *not* are considerably more frequent (almost four times) in discourse than negations with *never* and that the most frequent form of verbal negation is the contracted form *n't*.

Why might this be the case? It is probably due to the strength of negation or contrast conveyed by each form. In clauses with *not* and *never*, the negated component is magnified, accentuating the contradiction, juxtaposition, or contrast embedded within the message.

About 100 years ago, Otto Jespersen (1917) had a similar observation concerning contracted and non-contracted forms of negation:

> The negative adverb [*not*] very often is rather weakly stressed, because some other word in the same sentence receives the strong stress of contrast—the chief use of a negative sentence being to contradict and to point to a contrast. The negative notion, which is logically very important, is thus made to be accentually subordinate to some other notion; and as this happens constantly, the negative gradually becomes a mere proclitic syllable (or even less than a syllable) [*n't*] prefixed to some other word.
>
> (Jespersen, 1917, pp. 4–5)

Jespersen's idea essentially says this: Negation is predominantly used to signal contradiction or contrast. The negative adverb *not* in its full form is less common than contracted *n't* because the contrast, denial, or contradiction is captured by other words in the discourse.

**Compare:**

| | |
|---|---|
| She did*n't* write the article on her own. It was edited by someone. | [weaker contrast/stance] |
| I knew immediately that Marie did *not* write that letter. | [stronger contrast/stance] |
| Quinn sent the letter, but her uncle *never* wrote back. | [strongest contrast/stance] |

The contracted version—that is, the *n't* form—is more typical in speech and informal register than in writing and more formal register. Its high frequency could also be due to its being an informal register marker. This is discussed in Quirk et al. (1985, p. 123) and Biber (1988, p. 243).

---

### Mini Review and Practice

Now let's take a look at some examples from actual discourse. All three excerpts are from COCA (Davies, 2008–). Compare the meaning, strength, and stance encoded in the statements with negation in each excerpt. Take into account the context in which the statements appear. As you work with the excerpts, it will be helpful if you try replacing one negated form with another (e.g., replace "*didn't see*" with "*did not see*" and then "*never saw*," respectively in the three cases) and then think about how the meaning of each utterance changes in terms of the stance of the speaker or writer.

### Example 1: Contracted verbal negation *n't*: "The Life and Death of Robin Williams"

His (Robin Williams's) wife, Susan Schneider, told police <u>she last saw</u> her husband around 10:30 Sunday night. But that the couple had slept in separate beds. . . . Mr. Williams was last seen alive by his wife at approximately 10:30 PM on August 10, 2014, when she retired for the evening in a room in the home. . . . And when she woke up the next morning, she **didn't see him**. . . . At approximately 10:30 AM, on August 11, 2014, Mr. Williams's wife left the home, believing Mr. Williams to still be asleep.

(American Broadcasting Company, 2015)

### Example 2: Uncontracted verbal negation *not*: "George Mendonsa and Greta Friedman, Reunited"

((Mendonsa and Friedman are the sailor and the nurse, respectively, in Eisenstaedt's world-famous photo "Kissing Sailor." In this photo, a sailor who has just returned from World War II is caught on film kissing a stranger, a female nurse, in Times Square, New York City.))

Times Square. . .

Michelle Miller (CBS host): Eighty-nine-year-old George Mendonsa says he's the sailor in the photograph that would come to symbolize the end of World War II; and Greta Friedman, the nurse in white. World famous photographer, Alfred Eisenstaedt, snapped four pictures; ten seconds was all it took. We reunited George and Greta at the spot of their kiss for just the second time since that day in 1945.

Greta Friedman: I **did not see him** approaching. And before I knew it, I was in this tight grip.

(Columbia Broadcasting System, 2012)

### Example 3: Verbal negation with *never*: *Thunder at Dawn*, a novel

((Jack, the little boy described in the following excerpt, had a cleft in his palate and upper lip that the surgeon agreed to correct.))

These imaginings [Jack's feeling that he was handsome and that he could speak as well and as clearly as any other child his age] also came to pass, though they might not have if not for the ministrations of an itinerant surgeon, who saw six-year-old Jack on the street in Harrisonville and told his mother he would correct the fissure in return for a home-cooked meal of fried chicken, mashed potatoes, and apple pie with cream. His mother agreed. On the day of the operation, Jack was alarmed when he detected the smell of whiskey on the surgeon's breath, but despite this he did a fine job. Jack healed quickly and without complications, and he was deeply grateful to the physician though he **never saw him** again after that day. By the time he was old enough to grow a mustache, the scar was hardly visible.

(Salzer, 2015, p. 11; taken from Davies, 2008–)

Think about the gradation in stance and emphasis with "I didn't see him," "I did not see him," and "he never saw him again" in the light of the contexts of each scenario.

## 10.2 FORM: Negating the Main Verb or the Auxiliary With *Not* or *n't*

### 10.2.1 Not *and* n't *Negation for all Main Verbs, Except* Be

- Find the main verb.
- Add *do* as an auxiliary + *not* before the main verb.
- Match the tense of the auxiliary *do* with the tense of the original verb.
- SVA: If the original verb encodes third-person singular present tense, make sure that the auxiliary *do* becomes *does*.
- Use the main verb in its base form (i.e., no morphology for tense or number).

**Here is how it works:**

- Lucy loves Charlie Brown.                    [main verb: *love*]

Find the main verb [*loves*—third-person singular present tense]. Add *do* + **not** before the verb. Put *do* in present tense and use third-person singular → *does*. Use the base form of the main verb [*love*].

|   |   |
|---|---|
| Lucy loves Charlie Brown. | [affirmative] |
| Lucy *does* not love Charlie Brown. | [negative—full form] |
| Lucy *doesn't* love Charlie Brown. | [negative—contracted] |

- Amazon purchased Zappos.                    [main verb: *purchase*]

Find the main verb [*purchased*—past tense]. Add *do* + **not** before the verb. Put *do* in past tense → *did*. Use the base form of the main verb [*purchase*].

|   |   |
|---|---|
| Amazon purchased Zappos. | [affirmative] |
| Amazon did not purchase Zappos. | [negative—full form] |
| Amazon didn't purchase Zappos. | [negative—contracted] |

- This year, February *has* 29 days.           [main verb: *has*]

Find the main verb [*have*—third-person singular present tense = *has*]. Add *do* + **not** before the verb. Put *do* in present tense. Use third-person singular → *does*. Use the base form of the main verb [*have*].

|   |   |
|---|---|
| This year, February has 29 days. | [affirmative] |
| This year, February *does* not have 29 days. | [negative—full form] |
| This year, February *doesn't* have 29 days. | [negative—contracted] |

- The first player has to spin to start the game. [main verb: *has to*—multi-word modal]

Find the main verb. Here the main verb is *have* from the **multi-word modal** *have to* (see Chapter 8). [Main verb: *have*—third-person singular present tense = *has*.] Add *do* + *not* before the verb. Put *do* in present tense. Use third-person singular → *does*. Use the base form of the main verb [*have*].

| | |
|---|---|
| The first player <u>has to</u> spin to start the game. | [affirmative] |
| The first player *does **not*** <u>have to</u> spin to start the game. | [negative—full form] |
| The first player *doesn't* <u>have to</u> spin to start the game. | [negative—contracted] |

Note: The verbs in multi-word modals are generally treated as main verbs for negation, except *ought to* and *used to* (e.g., *be* going to, *have* to, be allowed to, etc.; see Chapter 8).

## 10.2.2 Not, n't *Negation for Copula* Be *as a Main Verb*

Simply add *not* after the main verb *be*.

- The Beatles <u>are</u> on Spotify.  [main verb: *be*]

    Find the main verb = a form of *be*. Add *not* after the main verb.

    | | |
    |---|---|
    | The Beatles <u>are</u> ***not*** on Spotify. | [negative—full form] |
    | The Beatles <u>are</u>*n't* on Spotify. | [negative—contracted] |

- Japanese <u>is</u> an easy language to learn.  [main verb: *be*]

    Find the main verb = a form of *be*. Add *not* after the main verb.

    | | |
    |---|---|
    | Japanese <u>is</u> ***not*** an easy language to learn. | [full form] |
    | Japanese <u>is</u>*n't* an easy language to learn. | [contracted] |

Note: First-person singular *am* cannot be used with the contracted *n't* form:

- I am a linguistics major.

    Find the main verb = a form of *be*. Add *not* after the main verb.

    | | |
    |---|---|
    | I <u>am</u> **not** a linguistics major. | [full form] |
    | I'm **not** a linguistics major. | [contracted—pronoun *I* with *am*] |
    | *I <u>am</u>n't a linguistics major. | [incorrect form—*am not* cannot be contracted] |

## 10.2.3 Not *Negation With Auxiliary Verbs*

Auxiliary verbs could be simple modals: *can, may, might, must, will, should, could, would,* and *shall*, as well as the auxiliary verbs for perfect aspect (*have* + *-en*), progressive aspect (*be* + *-ing*), and passive voice (*be* + *-en*).

*Not* negation with auxiliary verbs has the following forms:

- Add *not* after the auxiliary verb.
- If there is more than one auxiliary, just add *not* <u>after the first auxiliary verb</u> and leave the rest as is.

Note: If the first auxiliary in the sentence is *will*, the negation will either be *will not* or, if contracted, → *won't*.

- The DMV **will** <u>issue</u> you a driver's license in one day.

Find the main verb [*issue*]. Identify the auxiliary [simple modal *will*]. Add *not* after the auxiliary verb, but if the modal is *will*, it needs to be contracted to *won't*.

| | |
|---|---|
| The DMV **will not** <u>issue</u> you a driver's license in one day. | [full form] |
| The DMV **won't** <u>issue</u> you a driver's license in one day. | [contracted] |

- Engin Akyürek **may** <u>be</u> the most handsome man of the year.

Find the main verb [*be*]. Identify the auxiliary [simple modal *may*]. Add *not* after the auxiliary verb.

Engin Akyürek **may** *not* <u>be</u> the most handsome man of the year.   [full form]

Note: **May not** is not typically contracted in English → ?**mayn't**.
?Engin Akyürek **mayn't** <u>be</u> the most handsome man of the year.
[The contraction is possible, but it is rarely used in modern discourse.]

- Congress **should** <u>pass</u> stronger gun laws.

Find the main verb [*pass*]. Identify the auxiliary [simple modal *should*]. Add *not* after the auxiliary verb.

| | |
|---|---|
| Congress **should not** <u>pass</u> stronger gun laws. | [full form] |
| Congress **shouldn't** <u>pass</u> stronger gun laws. | [contraction] |

- Kindergartners are taking naps every day.

Find the main verb [*take*]. Identify the auxiliary [progressive *be + -ing*]. Add *not* after the auxiliary verb.

| | |
|---|---|
| Kindergartners **are not** <u>taking</u> naps every day. | [full form] |
| Kindergartners **aren't** <u>taking</u> naps every day. | [contraction] |

- The customer **has been** <u>waiting</u> for a long time.

Find the main verb [*wait*]. Identify the first auxiliary [perfect *have + -en* third-person singular = *has*]. Add *not* after the auxiliary verb.

| | |
|---|---|
| The customer **has not been** <u>waiting</u> for a long time. | [full form] |
| The customer **hasn't been** <u>waiting</u> for a long time. | [contraction] |

---

### Mini Review and Practice

#### Forms of negation with *not* [full form] and *n't* [contracted]

1. Here is a suggestion from a co-worker with regard to how to edit a students' instruction manual for dusting crime scenes in order to find fingerprints:

    Use fingerprint powder to dust surfaces where fingerprints are visible.
    Firmly press a piece of clear tape to the now enhanced fingerprint.
    Remove the tape and adhere it to paper that contrasts with the print.

See Willow's photo as a sample.
→ Should Willow's photograph not be included? (as a clarification request)

How do you interpret the meaning of this question? Is there any ambiguity? If so, where, and what causes it?

If you receive such commentary from your co-worker, what would be your own first questions in response to this? How can you resolve the issue?

Dear _____,
Did you mean _____?
Or _____?

2   Using the explanations from the first part of this chapter, negate the following 15 sentences using both full form of *not* and the contracted *n't* form.

**Remember:**

*will not*, when contracted becomes *won't*
*can not*, when contracted becomes *can't*
*am, may, might,* and *shall* should not be contracted
*must not* is only contracted to *mustn't* when it is used deontically (see Chapter 8)
*have* in the multi-word modal *have to* should be treated as a main verb

a   Newly certified teachers find jobs immediately upon graduation.

\_\_\_\_\_full sentence\_\_\_\_***do not find** jobs*\_\_... _____ [full form]
\_\_\_\_\_ full sentence\_\_\_\_***don't find** jobs* \_\_... _____ [contracted]

b   Some restaurants in our town can stay open later than 10:00 p.m.
c   We are used to the new ticket vending machines in the NYC subways.
d   Hemingway won the Nobel Prize in Literature for his "art of narrative."
e   Baltimore could be the largest city in Maryland.
f   Our family will be making a road trip to visit Ascaya, Nevada, next summer.
g   Carl Clauberg must have been tried for war crimes in the Soviet Union in 1948.
h   You are going to need a bigger boat for Saturday's fishing trip in the Banana River.
i   Sasuke might have been better off alone.
j   Permits will be required for special events at Mount Rushmore.
k   Taiwan's Wei-Chung Wang pitches for the Milwaukee Brewers (baseball team).
l   I am planning to join the Peace Corps in 2 years.
m   Six Flags Great Adventure in Jackson, New Jersey, must have closed because of the floods.
n   The cafeteria supervisor has to interview the new applicants for this job.
o   Omaha has one of the best zoos in the Midwest.

## 10.3 Form: Negating Utterances With *Never* and *Not Ever/n't Ever*

### 10.3.1 Never *With All Main Verbs, Except* Be

- Be sure that the meaning of the clause or sentence is semantically and pragmatically compatible with the absolute meaning expressed by *never*. That is, is it conceptually possible to

express the absolute negation of an event or the absolute absence of a requirement, experience, and so forth?
- Then add *never* before the main verb.

| | |
|---|---|
| Lucy <u>loves</u> Charlie Brown. | [affirmative] |
| ?Lucy **never** <u>loves</u> Charlie Brown. | [negative—never = odd] |
| BUT: | |
| Lucy **never** <u>loved</u> Charlie Brown. | [negative—never] |
| Talia's boss <u>asked</u> her to lie. | [affirmative] |
| Talia's boss **never** <u>asked</u> her to lie. | [negative—never] |
| Students <u>have to</u> show their work for math. | [affirmative] |
| Students **never** <u>have to</u> show their work for math. | [negative—never] |
| Courteney Cox <u>won</u> an Emmy. | [affirmative] |
| Courteney Cox **never** <u>won</u> an Emmy. | [negative—never] |
| cf. I don't think Courteney Cox **ever** <u>won</u> an Emmy. | [variation] |
| I don't think Courteney Cox <u>has</u> **ever** <u>won</u> an Emmy. | [variation] |

### 10.3.2 Never With Be *as a Main Verb and With All Auxiliaries (i.e., Simple Modal; Perfect, Passive, and Progressive)*

- Check for conceptual compatibility of the absolute meaning of *never* with the event, state, or experience being negated.
- Simply add *never* after the main verb *be* or after the first auxiliary.

| | |
|---|---|
| Dr. Oz <u>was</u> a guest on Oprah's show. | main verb: *be* [affirmative] |
| Dr. Oz <u>was</u> **never** a guest on Oprah's show. | [negative—never] |
| The children **would have** <u>put</u> a frog in Maria's pocket. | [affirmative] |
| The children **would never have** <u>put</u> a frog in Maria's pocket. | [negative—never] |
| Our family **has** <u>been</u> to Kazakhstan. | [affirmative] |
| Our family **has never** <u>been</u> to Kazakhstan. | [negative—never] |
| cf. I don't think our family **has ever** <u>been</u> to Kazakhstan. | [variation] |

### 10.3.3 Not Ever, n't Ever *With Main Verbs, With Be as a Main Verb, and With All Auxiliaries*

- Check for conceptual compatibility of the absolute meaning of *not ever*, *n't ever* with the event, state, or experience being negated.
- Follow the steps from Section 10.2 for *not* and *n't*.

| | |
|---|---|
| Amazon purchased Zappos. | [affirmative] |
| Amazon **did *not ever* <u>purchase</u>** Zappos. | [*did not ever*] |
| Amazon **did*n't* *ever* <u>purchase</u>** Zappos. | [*didn't ever*] |
| The DMV will issue you a driver's license in one day. | [affirmative] |
| The DMV **will *not ever* <u>issue</u>** you a driver's license in one day. | [*will not ever*] |
| The DMV **wo*n't ever* <u>issue</u>** you a driver's license in one day. | [*won't ever*] |
| cf. I don't think the DMV **will ever <u>issue</u>** you a driver's license in one day. | [variation] |

---

**Mini Review and Practice**

1   **Negation and contradiction:** The famous surrealist painting by Magritte called *La trahison des images* (*The Treachery of Images*) shows a lovely wooden pipe, and below it appear these words, in the original French:

  *Ceci n'est pas une pipe.* ('This is not a pipe.') (Magritte, 1928–1929)

The translated sentence has become quite famous in English:

  This is not a pipe.

And whether in French or in English, Magritte's intent, in simplified terms, was to establish that paintings are representations of things and not the things themselves, **contradicting** our tendency to equate the representation of an entity with the reality of that thing.

What would happen to the message in English if "*is not*" were contracted to "*isn't*?"

  This is not a pipe. → This isn't a pipe.

The two utterances are not identical in meaning. In what ways do the two forms differ?

At first, the difference may not seem obvious to you, but the more you work with negation and contraction vs. full form, the more you will begin to notice about the relationships between grammar, meaning, intent, and stance. The denial is constructed much more strongly with uncontracted *not*. Why?

2   **Negation and contrast:** Have a look at the following quote by Barack Obama about the notion of "change."

  "Change <u>*will*</u> **not** <u>come</u> if we wait for some other person or some other time. We are the ones we've been waiting for. We are the change that we seek." (Obama, 2008)

Paraphrase the meaning of Obama's quote. What elements is Obama contrasting, excluding, or juxtaposing?
The general issues here are *change, wait, we, some other person, some other time.*
How does negation figure into the contrasts being established here?

Hint: Think about the concept of **hope for change** (which is the theme of Obama's February 5, 2008 speech).

>     **Who** should enact that change ["We" vs. "some other person"]?
>     **When** should that change happen ['now' vs. 'some other time']?
>     **How** are the previous two concepts of **who?** and **when?** built into Obama's quote?

How would Obama's stance regarding this issue shift (even slightly) if he contracted *will not* → *won't*? Explain.

>     cf. Change wo*n't* <u>come</u> if we wait for some other person.

And how would his stance shift if he used *never, not ever,* or *n't ever*?

>     Change will **not** <u>come</u> if we wait for some other person.     [original]
>     cf.   Change will ***never*** <u>come</u> if we wait for some other person.
>           Change will ***not ever*** <u>come</u> if we wait for some other person.
>           Change ***won't ever*** <u>come</u> if we wait for some other person.

Also think about **agency** in Obama's quote. Do these utterances sound like they would rank high on an agency scale or low? Why? How does the notion of agency play into the overall message being delivered? Read the entire text of Obama's February 5, 2008 speech for added background in terms of the contrasts and juxtapositions he establishes.

3   **Negation and juxtaposition:** Here is the quote from *To Kill a Mockingbird* that explains the significance of the title of the novel as well as the significance of other crucial events that take place in the storyline. Scout, the main character (and Jem's sister), is narrating her recollection of this conversation:

>     Atticus said to Jem one day, "I'd rather you shoot at tin cans in the backyard, but I know you'll go after birds. Shoot all the blue jays you want, if you can hit 'em, but remember it's a sin to kill a mockingbird." That was the only time I ever heard Atticus say it was a sin to do something, and I asked Miss Maudie about it. "Your father's right," she said. "Mockingbirds **don't** do [anything] except make music for us to enjoy. They **don't** eat up people's gardens, **don't** nest in corn cribs, they **don't** do [anything] but sing their hearts out for us. *That's* why it's a sin to kill a mockingbird."
>
>                                                                                                     (Lee, 1960, p. 49)

What is crucial here is the use of verbal negation in the discourse to establish the philosophies of Atticus Finch (Jem and Scout's father) and Miss Maudie Atkinson's (the Finches' neighbor) on moral judgment and justice.

As you read through the text, try to discern the precise types of contrasts and juxtapositions that are being established in the passage. How is verbal negation used for establishing contrasts? How does negation help establish certain moral values that Miss Maudie and Atticus uphold? Also, as you work through this passage, you should attend to the use of imperatives and modals, as well as the **middle focus** pronoun *that* in the last line of the quote, as they combine together to create this intricately woven combination establishment of ideas, philosophies, and stances.

Some juxtapositions that you will find in this excerpt are as follows:

>    ***Shoot*** *at* <u>*tin cans*</u> *in the backyard,* ***but*** *. . . you'll go after* <u>*birds*</u>*.*
>    ***Shoot*** <u>*all the blue jays*</u> *you want . . .* ***but****, it's a sin to* ***kill*** *a* <u>*mockingbird*</u>*.*

*<u>Mockingbirds</u>* **don't** *do anything, except make music . . .*
*They* **don't** *eat up people's gardens,* **don't** *nest in corn cribs, they* **don't** *do*
*[anything] but sing their hearts out for us.*

First, think about how Lee sets up the argument about shooting things, both non-living and living. Then, think about how she sets up the issue about shooting at birds. Which birds, according to Miss Maudie, are acceptable as targets? Which are not? Why? How does the concept of negation work to establish these perspectives and juxtapositions?

Now, what does the title of the novel mean? Paraphrase the rationale and symbolism in Scout's description.

4  **Absolute negation with *never, not ever,* or *n't*:** As we have indicated, negation with *never, not ever,* or *n't ever* expresses an emphatic stance toward an issue. The emphasis can express an extremely positive position or an extremely negative position. And such expressions can be used to urge people strongly to *not do something*.

Mardy Grothe wrote a creatively witty book called *Neverisms: A Quotation Lover's Guide to Things You Should Never Do, Never Say, or Never Forget*. The following is an excerpt from the preface (2011, p. 4).

> When we exhort people, we're encouraging them to do something; we're trying to spur them on. It's a form of persuasion. When we dehort people, on the other hand, we're trying to convince people that they should *not do* something, or maybe even *never* do it. Dehortation is a form of discouragement or negative persuasion.
> (Grothe, 2011)

Here are a few examples of the chapter titles from Grothe's book:
"Never Answer an Anonymous Letter"
"Never Judge a Book by Its Movie"
"Never Go to a Doctor Whose Office Plants Have Died"

Grothe also compares these *never*-based sayings to those that are constructed with *don't* or *do not*:

"Do not blame anybody for your mistakes and failures." (Bernard M. Baruch)
"Don't overestimate your own merits." (Bertrand Russell)

How do Grothe's witty *never*-based "dehortations" compare and contrast with the *do-not*- or *don't*-based "dehortations"? There are multiple angles you can view these difference from. Explain in detail.

5  **Negation, rejection, and opposition:** In the longer stretch of discourse that follows, you will find verbal negation used in conjunction with a number of other grammatical constructions within the context of advice giving. The excerpt comes from a blog post titled "@ISSUE: Should You Snoop on Your Kids' Text Messages?" by Dyrness-Olsen (2014).

As you read through the passage, think about the following: What is the purpose of verbal negation? How, through the use of negation, does the writer respond or react to certain ways of parenting? What are those (implied) parental styles that the author rejects or opposes? How do you account for some contractions of *not* and some full forms of *not*? If contrasts are being established, how? That is, through which types of real-world examples and illustrations and which grammatical features are they established?

What is the stance of the author concerning the issue of parents reading their kids' text messages? How do you know? Which word choices and grammatical structures reveal this to you?

> Parents ask me all of the time in counseling if they should or should **not** read their child's text messages. Kids are growing up way too fast today. . . . Many parents say that they **don't** want to invade their child's privacy. Smart parents will check up to see what their kids are really doing. . . . If you *really* want to know who your kid is and what they are doing, then read their text messages. . . . Passwords should **not** be allowed on their phones or other electronic devices. You should have full access 24/7. If they have **nothing** to hide, then they should **not** care. . . .
>
> **Don't** be afraid to make your child mad. It is much more important to make sure that they are on the right road. . . .
>
> Kids should **not** have and do **not** need a cellphone before middle school.
> (Dyrness-Olsen, 2014)

Finally, this passage also contains one instance of negation that is not negating the message conveyed by the verb. Instead, it is a pronoun that carries the meaning of negation: "If they have **nothing** to hide . . ." This message can be re-structured to negate the verbal part of it—that is, "If they **don't** have **anything** to hide."

The original clause "If they have **nothing** to hide" is structured with affirmative verb morphology. It's the object pronoun that is negated, not the verb. Our focus now shifts toward *the thing* being negated ("**nothing** to hide") and away from the *verbal action* ("they **don't** have **anything** to hide"). We can see here how the grammar serves to emphasize, albeit very subtly, the writer's stance with regard to this issue of parenting.

We will look more closely at *negation beyond the verb* in the next section.

## 10.4 Negating Other Elements in the Discourse Beyond the Verb: Determiners, Pronouns, Prefixes, and Suffixes

Negation of ideas and concepts is not limited to using negative forms like *not*, *n't*, *never*, and so forth with verbs. When verb forms appear with these markers, it is the entire sentence that is negated, because the verbs are negated with negative morphology.

In this section, we will examine other means of expressing negation that extend beyond the verb: We begin with markers of negation that form a relatively closed class of words, like determiners (see Chapter 4) and pronouns (see Chapter 5). We then move to prefixes and suffixes (see Chapter 2) that are attached to nouns, verbs, adverbs, and adjectives that also signal various elements of negation.

The notion of *sentential negation* involves the negation of the verb, as in sentence a. The concept of *lexical negation* involves the negation of a word in the sentence (but not the verb), as in sentence b.

a   Donka *was* **not** *usually* late.   [the verb is negated = the entire sentence is negated]
b   Donka was *unusually* late.   [**only** the adverb is negated]

These meaning differences can be thought about in terms of the concept of *scope of negation* (Biber et al., 1999; Larsen-Freeman & Celce-Murcia, 2016; Quirk et al., 1985). The scope of negation has to do with determining exactly what part of the utterance is being negated. If it is the verb, then it is said that the entire sentence is negated, like the a version.

If it is only part of the sentence that is negated—that is, a determiner, a noun, an adjective, or an adverb—then the scope of negation changes and is *more limited* and *more local* (Biber et al., 1999, p. 175), as in the b version (*usually* → *unusually*).

Actually, the local scope of negation may not even occur lexically, but phonologically as in "Amazon didn't purchase Zappos in 200*6* (*emphatic vocal stress*); the purchase took place in 200*9* (*emphatic vocal stress*)."

The notion of scope of negation becomes especially clear when verbal negation (*not, n't, never, not ever*) is used with variations of *any-* (e.g., *anything, anyone, anybody, anywhere*) in contrast to the more local and limited lexical (word-based) negation:

a   Ina *did*n't say **anything** to him.   [the verb is negated = sentential negation]
b   Ina said **nothing** to him.   [only the pronoun is negated]

a   We *didn't find* **anyone** to help.   [the verb is negated = sentential negation]
b   We found **no one** to help.   [only the pronoun is negated]

a   My family *did* not *go* **anywhere** this summer.   [verb is negated = sentential negation]
b   My family went **nowhere** this summer.   [only the adverb is negated]

a   Latin *isn't* offered in high school **anymore**.   [verb is negated = sentential negation]
b   Latin *is* **no longer** offered in high school.   [only the adverb is negated]

Now, think about the difference in stance, position, or strength of the speaker or writer between the a and b versions listed previously. Which do you sense is stronger? Is it the a versions, with verbal negation, or the b versions, with the more local and limited lexical negation involving determiners, pronouns, and adverbs formed with *any-*? Because of the more limited and local scope of negation in the b versions, the meaning is grammatically and conceptually more intensified. The b versions express a stronger stance or position.

### 10.4.1 Lexical Negation: Determiners, Pronouns, Adverbs, and Prepositions

In this section you will find the common types of lexical negation for determiners, pronouns, adverbs, and prepositions. These types of negations typically occur with forms like *no, no-, not,* and *none*.

#### A   Negative determiners

| | |
|---|---|
| no + NP (including gerunds): | **no** smoking, **no** left turn, **no** way, **no** idea, **no** evidence, **no** sign of, **no** reason |
| **not** + determiners of quantity: | **not** one, **not** a single, **not** every, **not** all |
| **few** + NP: | **few** errors, **few** interviewees agreed |
| | [Note: This is very different in meaning from **a few** + NP.] |

### B Negative pronouns

| | |
|---|---|
| none | There was **none** left./I like **none** of the choices. |
| nothing | **Nothing** was visible because of the fog. |
| no one | **No one** told me you'd be here. |
| nobody | **Nobody** should have to go through that. |
| nowhere | There is **nowhere** better than home. |
| (not) anybody | There is **not anybody** in the world who agrees. |
| (not) anything | There was **nothing**, **not anything**, that he enjoys. |
| neither | Both were good answers, but **neither** was right. |

### C Negative adverbs

| | |
|---|---|
| nowhere | That business idea was going **nowhere**, fast. |
| (not) anywhere | I could**n't** find those notes **anywhere**. |
| (not) anymore | They do**n't** use 35 mm film anymore. |
| no longer | Miles is **no longer** employed with Delta Airlines. |
| hardly | The statue was **hardly** visible because of the fog. |
| seldom | Manu **seldom** laughed or smiled. |
| rarely | ATMs **rarely** break down. |
| barely | Bellamy **barely** passed physics with a 61%. |

### D Negative prepositions

| | |
|---|---|
| without | Tristan left **without** saying goodbye to us. |

### E Negative conjunctions

| | |
|---|---|
| neither . . . nor | **Neither** the fruits **nor** the meats were fresh. |
| (not) either | They don't speak French. They don't speak English **either**. |

## 10.4.2 Prefixes un-, non-, in-, im-, ir-, de-, dis-, mis-, and a-

Negative prefixes like *un-*, *non-*, *in-*, *im*, *ir*, *il-*, *de-*, *dis-*, *mis-*, and *a-* convey a variety of negative-related meanings. These prefixes indicate the following concepts:

- reversal of a process
- subjective or objective negation of an affirmative quality
- removal of something, to rid something of an element
- wrong, incorrect
- complete absence of

### 1 Un- with verbs

Meaning of *un*-verb: to reverse a process

The formation is productive, meaning that *un*- can be added to many verbs to express the notion of "to reverse a process."

| | |
|---|---|
| do | undo |
| tie | untie |

| | |
|---|---|
| dress | undress |
| cover | uncover |
| friend | unfriend (social media usage only) |
| like | unlike (social media usage only) |

## 2 Un- with adjectives and adverbs

Meaning of *un*-adjective or *un*-adverb: subjective negation of an affirmative quality, subjectively indicating the opposite or inverse of a quality

The formation of *un*-adjective is very productive.

**adjectives:** → **adverbs:**

*affirmative → negative*

| | | | |
|---|---|---|---|
| selfish | unselfish | unselfishly | [the meaning here is positive] |
| helpful | unhelpful | unhelpfully | |
| happy | unhappy | unhappily | |
| usual | unusual | unusually | |
| professional | unprofessional | unprofessionally | |
| planned | unplanned | | |
| seen | unseen | | |
| able | unable | | |
| holy | unholy | | |

"I'm reading an updated version of Romeo and Juliet. This time their relationship comes to a tragic end when she unfriends him on Facebook."

*Figure 10.2* "I'm reading an updated version of *Romeo and Juliet*. This time their relationship comes to a tragic end when she unfriends him on Facebook."

© Randy Glasbergen. Reproduced with permission of Glasbergen Cartoon Service.

## 3  Un- with nouns

Meaning of *un*-noun: subjective negation of an affirmative entity or concept, subjectively indicating the opposite or inverse of an entity or concept

The formation of *un*-noun is moderately productive.

> unselfishness
> unusefulness
> unhelpfulness
> unhappiness
> unprofessionalism
> unconcern
> unrest (not exactly the opposite of 'rest,' but still negative)

## 4  Non- with adjectives or nouns

Meaning of *non*-adjectives or nouns: objective negation of a quality, entity, or concept, objectively indicating the opposite or inverse of that quality, entity, or concept

The formation of *non*-adjectives or nouns is extremely productive.

### adjectives

#### *affirmative → negative*

| | |
|---|---|
| ceramic | nonceramic |
| lethal | nonlethal |
| practicing | nonpracticing |
| taxable | nontaxable |
| judgmental | nonjudgmental |
| porous | nonporous |
| dairy | nondairy |

### nouns

| | |
|---|---|
| issue | nonissue |
| compliance | noncompliance |
| specialist | nonspecialist |
| action | nonaction |
| landowner | nonlandowner |
| swimmer | nonswimmer |
| math class | non-math class |

## 5  *in-, il-, im-, ir-* with adjectives, adverbs, and nouns

Meaning of *in-, il-, im-, ir-* + adjectives, adverbs, and nouns: subjective negation of an affirmative quality, subjectively indicating the opposite or inverse of a quality.

The formation of these prefixes is very productive. (The use of *in-*, *-im*, or *ir-* depends on the sound in the original word that is being negated. See the following examples.)

adjectives: →   adverbs:   nouns:

*affirmative* → *negative*

| | | | |
|---|---|---|---|
| sincere | insincere | insincerely | insincerity |
| adequate | inadequate | inadequately | inadequacy |
| animate | inanimate | inanimate | inanimacy |
| complete | incomplete | incompletely | incompleteness |
| conclusive | inconclusive | inconclusively | inconclusiveness |
| visible | invisible | invisibly | invisibility |
| possible | impossible | impossibly | impossibility |
| probable | improbable | improbably | improbability |
| moral | immoral | immorally | immorality |
| partial | impartial | impartially | impartiality |
| movable | immovable | immovably | immovability |
| proper | improper | improperly | impropriety |
| regular | irregular | irregularly | irregularity |
| rational | irrational | irrationally | irrationality |
| refutable | irrefutable | irrefutably | irrefutability |
| reparable | irreparable | irreparably | irreparability |
| resistible | irresistible | irresistibly | irresistibility |
| reverent | irreverent | irreverently | irreverence |

Beligon (n.d.) cites Ferris's (1993) analysis for prefix *non-* denoting "associative adjectives," while *in-*, *un-*, and so forth denote "ascriptive adjectives." According to Beligon, *non-* types actually classify the entity *as not something*, whereas the *un-* and *in-* types *characterize the entities*. This could account for why *non-* prefixed lexical items sound more objective than the *in-*, *un-*, and so on prefixed lexical items.

Also, note that the negative prefixes are influenced orthographically and phonologically by the first letter of the word that is being negated (e.g., sensitive → *insensitive*; perfect → *imperfect*; regular → *irregular*).

## 6   De- with verbs

Meaning of *de*-verb: to remove, to rid of, to make less

The formation is productive.

| | |
|---|---|
| emphasize | de-emphasize |
| glamorize | deglamorize |
| oxidize | deoxidize |
| populate | depopulate |
| louse (n.) | delouse |
| frizz | de-frizz |
| ice | de-ice |

## 7 Dis- with verbs

Meaning of *dis*-**verb:** to do the opposite of that verb

The formation is productive.

| | |
|---|---|
| credit | discredit |
| agree | disagree |
| hearten | dishearten |
| please | displease |

## 8 Mis- with verbs and nouns

Meaning of *mis*-**verb** or *mis*-**noun:** wrong(ly), incorrect(ly)

The formation is productive.

**verbs**

| | |
|---|---|
| understand | misunderstand |
| hear | mishear |
| speak | misspeak |
| interpret | misinterpret |
| spell | misspell |
| diagnose | misdiagnose |

**nouns**

misdeed
misstep
mistake
mishap

## 9 A- or an- with adjectives, nouns

Meaning of *a*-**adjective,** *a*-**adverb, or** *a*-**noun:** complete absence of

The formation is not very productive. It also signals a specialized register. Words formed with this prefix are typically academic, scientific, or technical. The words *anonymous, anecdote, apathy,* and *anarchy* are exceptions.

**nouns**

apathy
aphasia
anecdote
anarchy
anemia

| adjectives: → | adverbs: |
|---|---|
| asocial | asocially |
| atheoretical | atheoretically |
| apolitical | apolitically |
| asexual | asexually |
| amoral | amorally |
| anonymous | anonymously |
| abiotic | abiotically |

## 10.4.3 Negative Suffixes: -less and -free

English has two productive suffixes that also express negation. Typically, these suffixes attach to nouns and become adjectives that mean essentially "without that noun."

- **Forms:** Negative suffixes *-less* and *-free*, conveying meanings of "without that **noun**" or "does not contain that **noun**."

noun + *-less* → adjective meaning "without that noun"
noun + *-free* → adjective meaning "without that noun"

These two suffixes appear on the surface to be quite similar in meaning:

**Examples:**

**on gum or candy wrappers:**

| sugar**less** gum or candy | gum or candy that **contains no sugar** |
| sugar-**free** gum or candy | gum or candy that **contains no sugar** |

**on vitamins/food supplements labels:**

| odor**less** garlic (gel caps) | garlic supplements that **have no odor** |
| odor-**free** garlic (gel caps) | garlic supplements that **have no odor** |


**Noun + *-less* → adjective:**

Meaning of **noun**-*less* → **adjective** "without that noun, does not contain that noun, does not exhibit that noun, does not cause that noun"

The formation is very productive.

| *noun* | → | *adjective* |
|---|---|---|
| sugar | | sugarless |
| odor | | odorless |
| salt | | saltless |
| end | | endless |
| wire | | wireless |
| color | | colorless |

310  *Negation*

| | |
|---|---|
| point | pointless |
| pain | painless |
| fear | fearless |
| cloud | cloudless |
| worth | worthless |
| hope | hopeless |
| help | helpless |
| | relentless |
| | countless |

### Noun-free → adjective:

Meaning of **noun**-*free* → **adjective** "without that noun, does not contain that noun, does not exhibit that noun, does not cause that noun"

| *noun* | → | *adjective* |
|---|---|---|
| sugar | | sugar-free |
| odor | | odor-free |
| crime | | crime-free |
| dairy | | dairy-free |
| trouble | | trouble-free |
| salt | | salt-free |
| error | | error-free |
| tax | | tax-free |
| toll | | toll-free |
| hands | | hands-free |
| stress | | stress-free |
| pain | | pain-free |

*Figure 10.3a* Odorless garlic supplement label

*Figure 10.3b* Odor-free garlic supplement label

So, if the general meanings for each suffix are the same, how do the two suffixes actually differ in meaning? Beyond "without that noun" or "does not contain/have/cause/exhibit that noun," what other kinds of meanings do **noun**-*less* and **noun**-*free* evoke?

Let's start with a look at both suffixes that can share the *same nouns*:

| **noun-less** | **noun-free** |
|---|---|
| sugarless | sugar-free |
| odorless | odor-free |
| saltless | salt-free |
| stressless | stress-free |
| painless | pain-free |
| seamless | seam-free |

In each pair there is a slightly different conceptualization of what it is that is "missing" and why. Let's examine this a bit more closely:

### Other words that co-occur with noun-less

furniture: armless sofa, armless loveseat, armless office chair

"This **armless** loveseat is covered in a fun and elegant print upholstery." ("Armless," n.d.)

animals: hairless dogs, whiskerless cats

"The Chinese Crested (dog) is believed to have evolved from the African **hairless** dogs." ("Hairless," n.d.)

clothing: fingerless gloves, laceless shoes, buttonless shirts

"I've had an obsession with **buttonless** shirts for a while now. They are somewhat uncommon and non-existent in N. America, so I do eye for them whenever I happen to shop." ("Buttonless," n.d.)

So, what additional meanings does **noun**-*less* evoke?
   **Noun**-*less* means not simply the lack of something; it is the lack of something that is assumed to be an inherent or integral part of that thing, idea, or concept to begin with.
   That is, sofas are assumed to have arms, mammals are assumed to have hair, and shirts are assumed to have buttons, just as cats are assumed to have whiskers (whiskerless cat) and gloves are assumed to have fingers (fingerless gloves).

### Now, let's look at other words that co-occur with noun-free

substances: lead-free, acetone-free, alcohol-free, MSG-free, additive-free, fat-free, gluten-free

312  *Negation*

environment and health:   smog-free, ozone-free, lint-free, vermin-free, disease-free, smoke-free, pain-free, guilt-free, gluten-free, illness-free, caffeine-free, saccharin-free, dirt-free

What more does **noun**-*free* mean?

**Noun**-*free* means not simply the lack of something. It is the lack of something **that is assumed to be unwanted, a burden, a disadvantage (e.g., debt-free)**, but not something that is assumed to have been an integral part of the head noun.

The speaker's or writer's stance is stronger with adjectives formed with the **noun**-*free* construction. When a city is described as smog-free or paint is described as lead-free, the adjective choice evokes that very sense of having rid the noun entity of something unwanted or of a negatively viewed element.

## 10.5 *Not, Never* Phrases With Infinitives and Gerunds

### 10.5.1 Not, Never *Phrases With Infinitives*

In addition to sentence-level negation that involves negating the verbs in a clause and the local lexical types of negation involving individual words like determiners, pronouns, nouns, verbs, adjectives, adverbs, and prepositions, it is also possible to negate phrasal parts of utterances that occur with infinitives and gerunds (see Chapter 2).

*not, never* **with infinitives:**

   *to + V:*   *to go, to hide, to eat, to drink, to read, to cheat*

      Isabella had decided **not** <u>to go</u> to the meeting yesterday.
      It's preferable **not** <u>to hide</u> your peanut allergy from your teacher.
      Mom asked us **never** <u>to cheat</u> on any exam in school.
      Patients are advised **not** <u>to eat</u> or <u>drink</u> anything 8 hours prior to surgery.
      Tenants must remember **not** <u>to make</u> excessive noise after 10:00 p.m.

**splitting infinitives:**

   *to + (not, never, please) V: to **not** eat*

      Isabella had decided <u>to</u> **not** <u>go</u> to the meeting yesterday.
      It's preferable <u>to</u> **not** <u>hide</u> your peanut allergy from your teacher.
      Mom asked us <u>to</u> **please never** <u>cheat</u> on any exam in school.
      Patients are advised <u>to</u> **not** <u>eat</u> or <u>drink</u> anything 8 hours prior to surgery.
      Tenants must remember <u>to</u> **not** <u>make</u> excessive noise after 10:00 p.m.

Moving the position of *not* or *never* effects a change (sometimes strong, sometimes subtle) in stance. In the case of the split infinitives, the emphasis evoked by the negative element falls more strongly on the verb that is separated from *to*.

**Compare: Intact infinitive vs. split infinitive**

a  **Intact Infinitive**          **Split Infinitive**

   5 foods **never** <u>to eat</u>          5 foods <u>to</u> **never** <u>eat</u>
   Top 10 reasons **not** <u>to diet</u>    Top 10 reasons <u>to</u> **not** <u>diet</u>

b  **Intact Infinitive**

   "My hope was **never** *to build* a company. I wanted to have an impact."
   (original line from Mark Zuckerberg's Harvard commencement speech on May 25, 2017)

   vs.

   **Split Infinitive**

   My hope was <u>to</u> **never** <u>build</u> a company.

There is a significant difference in meaning in the b example.

Here are a few more excerpts from discourse to illustrate the difference between the stances evoked by each construct (intact infinitive vs. split infinitive):

a  From the website donttextdrive.com **[split] [original version]**

   Here's a scary statistic:
   If you text and drive, you're 23 times more likely to have a car crash.
   Please, take 30 seconds to see why the choice <u>to</u> **not** <u>text</u> *and* <u>drive</u> can save some lives.
   ("Don't text and drive," n.d.)

Compare that statement to: **[intact] [adapted from original]**
   Please, take 30 seconds to see why the choice **not** <u>to text and drive</u> can save some lives.

b  From CNN.com:    **[intact] [original version]**

   City pays kids **not** <u>to kill</u>

   (Drash & Sambou, 2016)

Compare to: **[split] [adapted from original]**

   City pays kids <u>to</u> **not** <u>kill</u>

c  From the website Guns.com **[split] [original version]**

   [The city of Richmond is] dealing with the violence in the right way:

   teaching these kids basic life skills and how <u>to</u> **not** <u>resort</u> to a gun and operate in a civil society.

   (Cruz, 2016)

Compare to: **[intact] [adapted from original]**

   teaching these kids . . . how **not** <u>to resort</u> to a gun. . .

314  *Negation*

"My doctor told me to increase my exercise program, so I switched from not exercising three times a week to not exercising six times a week."

*Figure 10.4* "My doctor told me to increase my exercise program, so I switched from not exercising three times a week to not exercising six times a week."

© Randy Glasbergen. Reproduced with permission of Glasbergen Cartoon Service.

Carter and McCarthy (2006, p. 736) acknowledge that the split infinitive with negation is common, but they also note that it is perceived as "bad style." They do not address speaker or writer stance, position, emphasis, and so forth.

### 10.5.2 Not, Never *Phrases With Gerunds*

**Not** teaching kids basic life skills can be a direct path to failure.
How **never** dieting may be the key to weight loss
What is the difference between lying and **not** telling the whole truth?

"**Not** admitting a mistake is a bigger mistake." (Robert Half, cited in Crisolia, 2002)

"**Living** with integrity means: **Not** settling for less than what you know you deserve in your relationships." (Barbara De Angelis, 2013)

As we have been emphasizing throughout this book, shifts in grammar do evoke shifts in speakers' and writers' perspectives and stances. In the case of the two constructions *not, never* with infinitives (split or intact) and *not, never* with gerunds, we can see that that gerunds are essentially more subjectless than the infinitive-based constructions. While both types of phrases can suggest subjectless generalizations as well as directly implied subjects, the gerund construction conveys a far more general type of statement. This is because gerunds are more "noun-like" in meaning and function than infinitives, which are more verb-like (Yule, 1998, p. 219).

\*\*\*\*\*\*\*\*

## PRACTICE WITH DATA ANALYSIS: PUTTING IT ALL TOGETHER

1  Have another look at the Avedon quote:

> A portrait is not a likeness. The moment an emotion or fact is transformed into a photograph it is no longer a fact but an opinion. There is no such thing as inaccuracy in a photograph. All photographs are accurate. None of them is the truth.
> (Richard Avedon, as cited in Phelan, 1993)

It contains a number of forms associated with negation, from verbal negation to negation involving negative determiners, negative prefixes, negative adverbs, and negative pronouns.

First, locate all forms of negation in the quote. What are they?

What is the meaning of this quotation? How is that meaning constructed through the use of word choice, contrast/juxtaposition, and grammar?

How does the message of this text compare and contrast with Magritte's *Ceci n'est pas une pipe* ('This is not a pipe')?

If you took this same passage and change some of the **negated** forms (e.g., "A portrait is **not** a likeness . . ." → "A portrait is**n't** a likeness. . . ," or ". . . it is **no longer** a fact but an opinion → it is **not** (is**n't**) a fact **anymore** but an opinion," etc.), how would the message change? Be as specific and detailed as you can in your responses.

Now, follow the same pattern of analysis with the following quote by Carlos Barrabes:

> If you don't fail it's because you did not risk enough, and if you didn't risk enough it's because you didn't put your whole self out there.
> (Carlos Barrabes, as quoted in Budinich, 2016)

Find the forms of negation. What is the meaning of the quote? How is it constructed? What are the contrasts/juxtapositions? Are they established only through negation? What effects would changing the forms of negation create in terms of the overall meaning? Think about stance, register, and the overall intended message. Try to paraphrase the message. How does the meaning shift when you change the original words to the paraphrased words?

2   We introduced a rather robust collection of prefixes and suffixes that work to express various features of negation (and contrast, juxtaposition, reversal, opposition, etc.) in many different parts of speech: nouns, verbs, adjectives, adverbs, and so forth. Here are a few questions to consider with regard to lexical (i.e., word-based) negation and meaning:

   a   The word *regardless* is often misused in English, appearing in discourse as \*irregardless. Why is \*irregardless a mistake? Try to locate actual examples of the use of \*irregardless in discourse.

   b   Among the lists of negative prefixes (e.g., *non-*, *in-*, and *un-*), we indicated generally whether these negative affixes tended to take on "objective" or "subjective" meanings. We characterized the prefix *non-* as more "objective" and more highly productive and *in-* and *un-* as more subjective and somewhat less highly productive.

Let's have a quick look at a few more exemplars to see why this may be the case:

| action | → | **in**action vs. **non**-action |
| professional | → | **un**professional vs. **non**-professional |
| believer | → | **un**believer vs. **non**-believer |
| married | → | **un**married vs. **non**-married |
| harmonious | → | **in**harmonious vs. **non**-harmonious |

Other nouns and adjectives that can be prefixed with *non-*:

> non-specialist, non-medical, non-degree, non-violence, non-citizen, non-existence, non-animated, non-partisan, and even non-pizza.

What are the differences between the words that we listed previously with prefixes *in-* and *un-* in contrast with those prefixed with *non-*, as in *inaction* vs. *non-action*; *unprofessional* vs. *non-professional*, and so on? Work through the entire list and try to find discourse-based examples of each word—online, using a corpus, or both.

316  *Negation*

What does prefix *non-* mean that is different from the other negative prefixes that we introduced in this chapter? What do you think accounts for (a) its more neutral and objective meaning and (b) its high productivity in English?

c  The following text is an internet clickbait headline that appeared on Boston.com on September 26, 2014:

   12 PASSENGER SHAMING PHOTOS YOU CAN'T UNSEE

What does this headline mean? How does the verb *unsee* contribute to the power of the message? What do you imagine to be included as content in those 12 photos? What do you think the *purpose* of this online story or collection of photographs is?

Note: As of October 2017, COCA (Davies, 2008–) contains 20 tokens of the verb *unsee* and zero (0) tokens of the verb *unhear*. *Unhear* does occur in discourse, often in the context of courtroom testimony and juries, where juries are asked to disregard certain bits of testimony, which they can never truly *unhear*.

d  The following excerpt is from a Forbes.com blog by Kashmir Hill. The topic is about a courier delivery service (UPS = United Parcel Service, an independent delivery service that is not affiliated with the US mail system). Specifically, the blogger talks about what happened when a package was delivered to the wrong address.

### "If You Get a Misdelivered Package, UPS Will Give a Stranger Your Home Address"

> Last week, UPS dropped off a package on the porch of Jay Friedman's home in Plano, Texas. But the delivery man had made a mistake. The medium-sized cardboard box that looked like it might contain a shirt was addressed to the right house number, but to a different (similar-sounding) street and a different zip code. Misdeliveries happen. No big deal. But two hours later, a stranger showed up at Friedman's door. "He was like, 'I'm here to get my package,'" says Friedman, who later posted about the episode on Facebook and tweeted at UPS about it.
>
> UPS spokesperson Dan Cardillo emphasized that the service delivers 15 million letters and packages daily and that misdeliveries are incredibly rare, but that when they do happen, the policy is to give out the address to which the package was misdelivered to a caller with the package's tracking number. "We never suggest that a customer go to someone's house and pick up the package," emphasized Cardillo. "We reassure them that we will fix the misdelivery."

(Hill, 2014)

Read through the excerpt carefully. What does the author's point seem to be? Why do you feel she wrote the blog post in the first place? Is it simply to tell a story? Does she have a particular stance? Is it positive (i.e., complimentary, celebratory)? Is it negative (i.e., critical, judgmental, complaining)? Who do you imagine her audience to be? Attend to such grammatical features as verb properties (transitive/intransitive; dynamic/stative; perception verbs; reporting verbs), voice (active, passive), and agency. What does the expression "Misdeliveries happen" mean? Who is taking the responsibility here?

How are contrasts, denials, or juxtapositions expressed? How are these created through grammar and/or word choice? Identify all instances of verbal negation and lexical negation. Do you find any instances of grammar or word choice that appear to evoke negation but have no negative morphology (e.g., *different, a stranger*)? How do these grammatical constructions and word choices all work together to convey the author's point and express the author's stance?

Also, analyze the title of the blog post. How does the title relate to the message? What sort of verb construction do you notice in the second clause: "UPS Will Give a Stranger Your Home Address"? Hint: Look for modals/tense and verb type (*ditransitive*—which is the *affected entity* and which is the *recipient*?). (See Chapters 6, 7, and 8.)

e    Analyze the following debate topic from the point of view of its meaning, as it is built through negation. It has two examples of lexical negation: *inaction* and *injustice*. Each falls into the category of "subjective negation," in that there is a judgment associated with each. What is *inaction* as opposed to *action*? What is *injustice* as opposed to *justice*?

"**Inaction** in the face of **injustice** makes an individual morally culpable."

What does the quote mean? How do these instances of negation make the quote more powerful in terms of its meaning? Try to paraphrase the meaning. Does the message gain strength through paraphrase, or does it lose strength?

f    Now, let's look at the concepts of *action*, *inaction*, and *non-action* in Western and Eastern worldviews. The following excerpt, also from Forbes.com, is from a larger piece entitled "The Tao of Leadership: Beyond Action and Non-Action." Read the excerpt to get a sense of what the main points are.

**"The Tao of Leadership: Beyond Action and Non-Action"**

*Working Smart, Not Hard*

As the catchphrase goes, we want to work smarter rather than harder. Yet frantic busyness is commonplace in the association workplace. . . .

Some of this busyness is a sheer waste of time: reports that don't really need to be written; . . . endless e-mails that have no substance; numerous phone messages that do not advance understanding, and so on.

Wu-wei: *Action and Non-action*

The Chinese concept. . . *Wu* refers to action; to the state of movement, decisiveness, even force. *Wei* refers to non-action. . . .

Non-action is not just not doing something; it is an active state of choice. . . .

In non-action, no movement is needed; no thought is needed. . . . Even physical exercise or playing the piano or anything that brings about an inner stillness can be considered non-action.

(The Forbes Group Writing Staff, n.d.)

How does the author juxtapose Western worldviews with Eastern worldviews? What do you see as an essential difference between the two, according to this article? What other types of juxtapositions are established in this excerpt? Identify all of the forms of negation that you can find. Highlight them. Do you find any instances of "double negation"—that is, where multiple forms of negation are used in the same sentence? Often, the occurrence of double negation results in an affirmative meaning. Do you find any instances of that? How does the grammar of negation work in conjunction with other means of establishing contrasts or comparisons in the excerpt? How does the author use grammar and word choice to establish his position in the article? Who do you feel is the audience for this article? Is it the same or different from the audience in the blog post about UPS deliveries? Is it the same genre of discourse? Why, or why not?

3   The following passage is an excerpt from Marianne Williamson's (1992) *A Return to Love: Reflections on the Principles of a Course in Miracles*.

> Our deepest fear is not that we are inadequate. Our deepest fear is that we are powerful beyond measure. It is our light, not our darkness that most frightens us. We ask ourselves, Who am I to be brilliant, gorgeous, talented, fabulous? Actually, who are you *not* to be?
>
> (Williamson, 1992, p. 190)

Analyze the passage first for the use of negation. Find all forms of negation and articulate how Williamson masterfully crafts this argument. What is the contrast that she is establishing?

Have a look at the grammatical features in this short snippet: nouns, pronouns verbs, and verb types (dynamic—transitive/intransitive; copular), as well as adjectives (see Chapter 13).

4   Double negatives

  a   What does this sentence mean? Where are the instances of negation?

> "It's not that I don't like you. It's just that I need to have a little 'alone time.'"

Now, substitute "I don't like" with "I dislike."

> "It's not that **I don't like** sweet corn, it's just that it's hard to eat it in public."
> "It's not that **I dislike** sweet corn . . ."

Do you sense the higher register with *dislike* as opposed to *don't like*?
There is also a stronger stance evoked by *dislike*:

> "Ofra <u>doesn't</u> <u>like</u> writing postcards when she travels."
> "Ofra <u>dislikes</u> writing postcards when she travels."

  b   The following passage is taken from an article whose headline reads "Viral Story of Boy Who Died in Santa's Arms Unravels" (Grinberg & Kudt, 2016). The story emerged because, during the Christmas season of 2016, a man dressed up as Santa Claus (Mr. Schmitt-Matzen) made a video about the event. The video went viral on the internet. Schmitt-Matzen narrated a heartrending account of a terminally ill child who died while in his (Santa's) arms. Within 24 hours of the story being released, people began to question its authenticity. (The story may not have been true).

  There are multiple usages of double negation in this short passage. Identify those instances. Now, think about alternative ways in which the authors could have worded their statements—that is, ways that did not involve double negation. What does this use of double negation accomplish in the context of this news story?

> The *News Sentinel* cannot establish that Schmitt-Matzen's account is inaccurate, but more importantly, ongoing reporting cannot establish that it is accurate," McElroy and Venable wrote. "Therefore, because the story does not meet the

newspaper's standards of verification, we are no longer standing by the veracity of Schmitt-Matzen's account.

(Grinberg & Kudt, 2016)

5   According to Lewis Carroll (1871/1999), in *Through the Looking Glass*, a person has a birthday on one day of the year. The other 364 days are *un-birthdays*. In the Disney (Walt Disney Productions, 1951) version of *Alice in Wonderland*, the Mad Hatter and the March Hare sing the song "A Very Merry Unbirthday to You! (Yes, you)".

Alice comes and wishes the two a happy birthday. The March Hare quickly corrects her, saying:

"My dear child, this is *not* a birthday party." And the Mad Hatter says, "*This* is an un̲birthday party."

(Disney, 1951)

What is the prefix *un-* doing in this construction (e.g., contrast, juxtaposition, denial, reversal)?

Can you think of other creative ways to reverse a concept with negative morphology and then build on the theme so that it is parallel to this grammatical/humorous phenomenon?

## COMMON ERRORS, BUMPS, AND CONFUSIONS

Identify the errors or "bumps" in the following sentences. Use the concepts and terminology that you learned in this and other chapters to articulate what might be grammatically or pragmatically problematic. Suggest ways that each can be re-written more clearly and more accurately. (Note: While all bumps do involve some element of negation they are not limited to only that.)

1   The researchers did not discussed the real-world implications of their study.

2   We no see each other yesterday.

3   Angelique was liking to play in mazes as a child. Children didn't afraid to get lost.

4   I no understand. The examples don't make no sense.

5   That books no helpful. It don't told me how spanish america war start.

6   Death penalty is backwards. Not any other major countries is using death penalty.

7   I never seen Mandy without no makeup.

## SUGGESTED ACTIVITIES

1   Rules and regulations: The discourse of public signage

Signs that express prohibitions (e.g., No Parking, No Smoking) do so in multiple ways:

NO ENTRY
NO THRU TRAFFIC (*thru* is an abbreviated version of *through*)
NO SMOKING
NO PARKING ANY TIME
PLEASE DO NOT DISTURB
PLEASE DO NOT HANDLE MERCHANDISE

Look around your neighborhood, your school, or your workplace. What kinds of signs do you notice? Traffic signs, parking signs, room use signs, grocery store signs, department store signs, and so on. Take notes regarding how the prohibition signs (essentially those that say or suggest "Don't do ____" or "No _____-ing") are worded. Make a collection of at least 10 of those prohibition signs. Try to select examples that have varied structures. Some may have symbols that express prohibition (Figure 10.5)

As you work through this task, do you notice any signs that merely *suggest* prohibition, without any type of negative morphology in the wording of the sign itself? Some signs provide explicit reasons for prohibiting the actions, some only hint at the reasons, and some are just straight prohibitions.

Figures 10.6 and 10.7 show two more examples. What are the messages that these signs are intended to convey? Paraphrase the meanings. As you do, be sure to incorporate a phrase or clause that includes negation.

Try to find 10 more signs like Figures 10.5, 10.6, and 10.7 that include *implicit negation* rather than *explicit negation*. How does the message change in terms of strength when it is *implicit*? Paraphrase the signs with implicit negation. What does the revised message sound like? Stronger? Weaker? More specific? Less specific? Why do you think this is so?

2   The past decade has seen important campaigns against the use of any type of tobacco in the US. A recent new development is the campaign against smokeless tobacco. Smokeless tobacco is like chewing tobacco or "dip." Sometimes you see athletes chewing tobacco and spitting parts out. Here is one campaign that targets smokeless tobacco (i.e., chewing tobacco).

>   SMOKELESS DOESN'T MEAN HARMLESS
>   (What types of misconceptions is this slogan designed to debunk?)

Find at least three websites that discuss the dangers of tobacco use: cigarettes, e-cigarettes, or chewing tobacco or "dip."

What might the possible risks be of using any sort of tobacco? What types of instances of negation do you find on the websites? In your opinion, are the negative aspects of smoking portrayed strongly enough? Are they portrayed too strongly? Why, or why not? [Note: There is no right or wrong answer here. It is just your opinion, and you are entitled to express any opinion you like with respect to the issue.]

3   The internet is full of "list" types of advice-giving articles, like, "5 Things You Should Never Say to Your Professor" (http://college.usatoday.com/2013/01/10/5-things-you-should-never-say-to-yourprofessor/) or "5 Things You Should Never Put in a Cover Letter for a Job."

*Figure 10.5* "Young Lungs at Play" sign

*Figure 10.6* "One Way" sign         *Figure 10.7* "Warning: Pesticide" sign

List the five things that the College USA Today website recommends, regarding those five things one should never say to one's professor. Why do you think the site specifies those five things?

Now, write your own blog posts for the following topics:

    5 things you should never wear to a fancy restaurant
    5 things brothers should never say to their sisters
    5 things customers should never do in a high-end coffee store
    List the 5 things for each category in order of importance. And be sure to provide sufficient reasons to justify your choices.

4   Animal guessing game—using all negative descriptors

This is a game that can be played in pairs, small groups, or in large groups in a classroom. One student will be in charge of giving clues that relate to an animal. The clues must all be expressed using negation, as in the following example:

This animal does not have feathers. It is not a reptile or a fish. It does not have colorful markings. This animal cannot survive on land. It does not see color. It does not drink water. It is not a shark. What is it? [Answer: a dolphin]

    giraffe
    orangutan
    seahorse
    silver fox
    rhinoceros
    puppy
    lobster
    jellyfish
    gecko
    poison dart frog
    walrus
    ladybug
    puffer fish
    mole
    skunk
    bat
    meerkat
    flounder

5   Conduct an internet-based search of songs (popular, folk, blues) whose titles and lyrics include negation. Here are just a few examples:

> "It's Impossible"
> "I'm Not Over You"
> "Misery" (Maroon 5)
> "Nothing but Flowers"

List 20 titles and then find the lyrics for five of those songs that you like the best. Copy the lyrics and conduct a data-based grammatical analysis of the negation in those song lyrics. For each song, introduce your analysis first by answering the following questions:

What is the song about? Who is singing it to whom? Why the use of negation?

Do you find more instances of sentential negation, where the verb is negated, or of lexical negation? Explain how these forms of grammatical negation work to build the content of the song lyrics

6   The following text is for the famous "Think Different" television ad campaign that restored the Mac computer brand upon Steve Jobs's 1996 dramatic return to Apple. Watch the video: https://youtu.be/cFEarBzelBs

> Here's to the crazy ones. The misfits. The rebels. The troublemakers. The round pegs in the square holes. The ones who see things differently. They're not fond of rules. And they have no respect for the status quo. You can quote them, disagree with them, glorify or vilify them. About the only thing you can't do is ignore them. Because they change things. They push the human race forward. And while some may see them as the crazy ones, we see genius. Because the people who are crazy enough to think they can change the world, are the ones who do.
>
> (Jobs, 1996)

The text centers around the notion of contrast. How would you characterize that contrast? How is it established? Note especially the types of nouns, pronouns (*the ones, they, you, them, we*, etc.), verbs, and negative constructions throughout the text.

Who is represented as the positive side of the contrast? What is the status quo?

Now, imagine that you have just been hired to write commercial copy for a service or product that is innovative (e.g., a special app, a food delivery service, lawn care, a shopping service, party planners, singing telegrams). Write an ad for that company emphasizing the innovative nature of the service or product in such a way that establishes a contrast like the Apple ad campaign.

## Academic References

Beligon, S. (n.d.). Lexical negation in English: The case of un- and in- (pp. 1–9). Retrieved from fitcat.uab.at/cit/XXIFALJ/Interlinguistics

Biber, D. (1988). *Variation across speech and writing*. Cambridge, UK: Cambridge University Press.

Biber, D., Johansson, S., Leech, G., Conrad, S., Finegan, E., & Quirk, R. (1999). *Longman grammar of spoken and written English*. Boston, MA: MIT Press.

Carter, R., & McCarthy, M. (2006). *Cambridge grammar of English: A comprehensive guide; spoken and written English grammar and usage*. Cambridge: Cambridge University Press.

Davies, M. (2008–). *The corpus of contemporary American English: 520 million words, 1990–present*. Retrieved from http://corpus.byu.edu/coca.

Ferris, D. C. (1993). *The meaning of syntax*. London and New York: Longman.

Jespersen, O. (1917). *Negation in English and other languages*. Copenhagen: Høst.

Larsen-Freeman, D., & Celce-Murcia, M. (2016). *The grammar book: An ESL/EFL teacher's course*. New York: Heinle and Heinle Publishers.

Quirk, R., Greenbaum, S., Leech, G., & Svartvik, J. (1985). *A comprehensive grammar of the English language*. New York: Longman.

Yule, G. (1998). *Explaining English grammar*. Oxford: Oxford University Press.

## Data References

American Broadcasting Company. (2015, August 12). The life and death of Robin Williams [Video]. *20/20*. Retrieved November 1, 2016, from http://abc.go.com/shows/2020/episode-guide/2014-08/12-2020-0812-the-life-death-of-robin-williams.

Armless. (n.d.). Kingsbury home Corrine medallion floral fabric armless loveseat. Retrieved June 14, 2016, from www.amazon.com/Kingsbury-Home-Corrine-Medallion-Loveseat/dp/B00I4OZ180/ref=sr_1_3?s=home-garden&ie=UTF8&qid=1464445834&sr=1-3&keywords=armless+sofa

Avedon, R., as quoted in Phelan, P. (1993). *Unmarked: The politics of performance* (pp. 35–36). New York: Routledge.

Budinich, V. (2016). Carlos Barrabes' leadership lessons learned from second life. Retrieved August 1, 2016, from www.forbes.com/sites/ashoka/2016/05/24/carlos-barrabes-on-why-leadership-must-change-to-meet-the-future/#1b3d3f0e1d0f

Buttonless. (n.d.). Buttonless shirts, anyone? Retrieved August 1, 2016, from www.styleforum.net/t/118154/buttonless-shirts-anyone

Carroll, L. (1871/1999). *Through the looking glass*. Mineola, NY: Dover publications.

Columbia Broadcasting System. (2012, August 11). Sailor, nurse from iconic VJ Day photo reunited. Retrieved November 1, 2016, from www.cbsnews.com/news/sailor-nurse-from-iconic-vj-day-photo-reunited/.

Crisolia, P. A. (2002). *Wise words: 1,001 truths to inspire, enlighten and enrich everyday life*. Bloomington, IN: Xlibris Corporation.

Cruz, J. (2016). CA city pays criminals $1,000 not to shoot people. Retrieved August 1, 2016, from www.guns.com/2016/03/28/ca-city-pays-criminals-1k-not-to-shoot-people/.

De Angelis, B. (2013). *Real moments: Discover the secret for true happiness*. New York: Random House Publishing Group.

Don't text and drive: Let's save some lives. (n.d.). Don't text and drive. Retrieved August 1, 2016, from www.donttextdrive.com/.

Drash, W., & Sambou, T. (2016, May 19). Paying kids not to kill. Retrieved August 1, 2016, from www.cnn.com/2016/05/19/health/cash-for-criminals-richmond-california/

Dyrness-Olsen, D. (2014). Snoop. Even good kids make some bad choices. *Asbury Park Press*. Retrieved August 1, 2016, from www.app.com/story/opinion/columnists/2014/12/12/issue-snoop-kids-text-messages/20302023/.

The Forbes Group Writing Staff. (n.d.). The tao of leadership: Beyond action and non-action. Retrieved August 1, 2016, from www.forbesgroup.com/inner2.iml?mdl=articles.mdl&ArticleID=41&ArticleCat=2

Grinberg, E. & Kudt, T. (2016, December 14). Viral story of boy who dies in Santa's arms unravels. Retrieved March 6, 2017, from www.cnn.com/2016/12/14/us/knoxville-santa-story-in-question-trnd/index.html

Grothe, M. (2011). *Neverisms: A quotation lover's guide to things you should never do, never say, or never forget*. New York: Collins Reference.

Hairless. (n.d). Did you know? Retrieved August 1, 2016, from www.akc.org/dog-breeds/chinese-crested/detail/#didyouknow.

Hill, K. (2014, April 25). If you get a misdelivered package, UPS will give a stranger your home address. Retrieved from www.forbes.com/sites/kashmirhill/2014/04/25/if-you-get-a-misdelivered-package-ups-will-give-a-stranger-your-home-address/#4540b8b270b2

Lee, H. (1960). *To kill a mockingbird*. Philadelphia, PA: Lippincott.

Obama, B. (2008). Barack Obama's Feb. 5 speech. Retrieved August 1, 2016, from www.nytimes.com/2008/02/05/us/politics/05text-obama.html

Salzer, S. S. (2015). *Thunder at dawn*. New York: Pinnacle.

Walt Disney Productions, Armstrong, S. & Carroll, L. (1951). *Walt Disney's Alice in Wonderland*. Racine, WI: Whitman's.

Williamson, M. (1992). *A return to love: Reflections on the principles of a course in miracles*. New York: Harper Collins.

# 11 The Grammar of Inquiry and Apparent Inquiry in Discourse

Yes-No Questions, *Wh-* Questions, Alternative or Choice Questions, and Tag Questions

*Figure 11.1* "For my Current Events class, I'm supposed to read a newspaper every day. What's a newspaper?"

© Randy Glasbergen. Reproduced with permission of Glasbergen Cartoon Service.

Questions in discourse and interaction are typically thought of as the primary means through which speakers and writers request information. The question "What's a newspaper?" in Figure 11.1 is a perfect illustration. In the cartoon, TVs, smartphones, and tablets are depicted as the family's preferred way of receiving information. The boy uses a *wh-* question to both seek clarification and indicate his lack of familiarity with that seemingly antiquated medium of communication.

Questions indeed serve to elicit information that is not known, to seek clarification, and to request confirmation. In addition, questions can also do much more:

- establish rapport with addressees (e.g., Heritage & Robinson, 2006; Nguyen, 2007; Raymond & Heritage, 2006)
- advance conversation in face-to-face and technology-mediated interaction (e.g., text, Skype, chat, discussion boards) (e.g., Jiang & Ramsay, 2005; Jordan et al., 2014; Licoppe et al., 2014)
- elicit information-central responses in the form of knowledge displays in classroom interaction and testing environments (e.g., Mehan, 1979; Rymes, 2015; Seedhouse, 2004; Sinclair & Coulthard, 1975; Walsh, 2011)

- elicit information-central responses for true inquiry in institutional discourse like classroom settings, legal contexts, medical interactions, business encounters, and research activities (e.g., Heritage & Robinson, 2006; Heritage & Roth, 1995; Heritage & Sorjonen, 1994; Lane, 1985; Waring, 2009;)
- stimulate deeper thinking about issues and topics (e.g., Hinkel, 2002; Hyland, 2002; White, 2003)
- influence ways in which information is presented and intended to be understood (e.g., Ainsworth-Vaughn, 1994; Lauerbach, 2010; Linell et al., 2003)
- express various stances, perspectives, and emotions of speakers' and writers' stances, such as agreement, surprise, disdain, empathy, and criticism (e.g., Lauerbach, 2010; Stivers & Enfield, 2010)
- request action and/or behavioral compliance

Questions in English take four basic forms:

- yes-no questions
- *wh-* questions
- alternative questions
- tag questions

Each form seeks a particular type of information and fulfills a specific range of functions.

## 11.1 *Yes-No* Questions

The yes-no question delivers an inquiry in the form of a complete proposition, designed to ascertain whether the response to such an inquiry is an affirmative one or a negative one, as in the following example:

> In order to complete this survey, you must be 18 years of age or older, and agree to submit your opinion voluntarily. Are you at least 18 years of age?
>
> ☐ YES
> ☐ NO
>
> Do you agree to participate in this survey?
>
> ☐ YES
> ☐ NO

However, beyond this questionnaire type of highly scripted and institutionalized discourse context (survey, questionnaire, courtroom cross-examinations), the yes-no question does much more than simply seek an affirmative or negative response. It occurs in a variety of forms to carry out myriad discourse and communicative functions. We will examine the various forms of yes-no questions and then move to their discursive and communicative functions.

- **Forms of *Yes-No* Questions**
    a **Main verbs other than *be***

### Simple present

Declarative statement:  Disneyland closes at 11:00 p.m.
[subject]  [V-third-person singular present]

Add *do*
Match tense and SVA of V
Remove tense and SVA from V  **Does  Disneyland close at 11:00 p.m.?**
[V-third-person singular present] [subject] [V]

### Simple past

Declarative statement:  Salvador ate lunch with Felipe.
[subject]  [V-past]

Add *do*
Match tense and SVA of V
Remove tense and SVA from V  **Did  Salvador eat lunch with Felipe?**
[V-past]  [subject] [V]

b  *Be* as main verb or auxiliary, *have* as auxiliary, simple modals

### *Be* as a main verb

Declarative statement:  You are my best friend.
[subject]  [V *be*—second-person present]

Reverse order of subject and verb:  **Are you my best friend?**
[V *be*—second-person present]  [subject]

### *Have, be,* simple modal as auxiliary

Declarative statement:  The semester has already started.
[subject]  [*have-aux*]  [V-en.]

Reverse order of subject and auxiliary:  **Has the semester already started?**
[*have-aux*] [subject]  [V-en.]

Declarative statement:  I should send Genevieve a gift.
[subject] [simple modal] [V]

Reverse order of subject and auxiliary:  **Should I send Genevieve a gift?**
[simple modal] [subject] [V]

c  **Affirmative yes-no questions and negative yes-no questions**

### Affirmative

Does the M bus stop here?
Is Sofia the capital of Bulgaria?
Will this be on the test?

### Negative

Doesn't the M bus stop here?
Isn't Sofia the capital of Bulgaria?
Won't this be on the test?

These examples, contrasting affirmative and negative yes-no questions, suggest that there are markedly different speaker assumptions underlying each basic category.

Both affirmative and negative yes-no questions can be designed either as true queries for information or as confirmation requests, but the negative yes-no questions signal that the speaker or writer already has a particular assumption in mind, while at the same time evoking a stance of evaluative judgment, expertise, confidence, uncertainty, surprise, disbelief, and so forth vis-à-vis an interlocutor/addressee or a specific issue at hand (Givón, 2005, p. 372; Quirk et al., 1985, pp. 387–390).

- **The Functions of Yes-No Questions and Answering Yes-No Questions**

Yes-no questions are used in a variety of social and institutional contexts for a wide range of purposes. Yes-no questions seek unknown information, confirm conjectures, register news, request compliance and actions, elicit stories and personal accounts, and even challenge or dispute propositional content. Yes-no questions also constitute essential components of various social activities. They are common in courtroom proceedings (e.g., direct and cross-examination of witnesses); medical discourse (exams, blood donor questionnaires); airport security questions at flight check-in; political, celebrity, and academic interviews; and even just as casual small talk.

Because yes-no questions occur in interactively built activities, most interactive uses do not intend to elicit either a simple yes or no response OR a near-verbatim repetition of the content in the question (e.g., Heritage & Raymond, 2012; Raymond, 2003; Raymond & Heritage, 2013; Steensig & Heinemann, 2013). Here are some examples:

a    Have you ever been to Southeast Asia?

        ?Yes.   or   ?Yes, I have been to Southeast Asia.
        ?No.   or   ?No, I have not/never been to Southeast Asia.

        Yes, once, when I graduated from high school. . .
        (and then elaborate on the trip)

OR

        No, why (do you ask)?

OR

        No. How about you?

b    Did you have a good time at Disneyland?
        ?Yes./?No.

        Oh my gosh, we all had a great time! We went on almost every ride, and it wasn't even that crowded.

c    May I see your passport and boarding pass, please?

        ?Yes. (You may).
        Yes, (here (they are)). ((handing the documents to the agent))

From the standpoint of pragmatics, none of the previous examples is intended to elicit a simple yes or no response. Here, they function as an invitation for narrative, as in small talk for rapport building (examples a and b; Schegloff, 1988) or as part of an institutional procedure requesting action and behavioral compliance (example c).

328    *Inquiry and Apparent Inquiry in Discourse*

Sometimes responding to yes-no questions can be tricky, especially in the case of negative yes-no questions. Negative yes-no questions serve the dual purpose of expressing a proposition that seeks confirmation by the addressee and displaying a stance-laden underlying assumption related to that proposition. For interactants unfamiliar with the structural properties of English yes-no questions, responding to yes-no questions can be confusing.

| Question: | Answer: |
|---|---|
| yes-no type | |
| **Haven't** you read the chapter? | No, I haven't. I'm so sorry. |
| | But NOT typically: |
| | *Yes (you are right), I haven't read it. |

The answer could also be tricky if the yes-no question is designed as a request for consent or permission such that the answer is expected to affirm or reject the request itself.

Questions such as "Do you mind if. . . ?" and "Is it okay if. . . ?" are often confused by speakers whose first language is not English.

"Do you mind if. . . ?" typically prefers a **negative response**.
"Is it okay if. . . ?" Typically prefers an **affirmative response**.

Also, it is not pragmatically sufficient to respond to such questions with just a "yes" or a "no," or to respond as if it were a literal information-seeking question:

Do you mind if I smoke? [negative response preferred]

→ No, I don't mind. Go ahead.

   Yes, (I do mind). I'd rather you didn't.

      But NOT:
      ?Yes, (I mind). or ?Yes, go ahead.
      ((grammatically "correct" but pragmatically face threatening))

Is it okay if I write a check? [positive response preferred]

→ Yes, we accept checks.

   No, we only accept cash or credit cards.

      BUT NOT:
      ?No, it's not okay.
      ((grammatically "correct" but pragmatically face threatening))

## 11.2  *Wh-* Questions

*Wh-* questions start with a *wh-* word, which isolates the content of the unknown element. *Wh-* questions involve the following question words (**in bold**):

**Who**'s your favorite character in the show?
**Whose** gloves are these?/**Whose** father was born in Kenya?
**What** are you looking for?
**When** did she get back home?
**Where** are your parents?

**How** old is Donald?
**How** did you bake those cookies so perfectly?
**Which** is yours?
**Why** did you call him?

In contrast, with yes-no questions, *wh-* questions query specific bits of information about events, people, time, location, cause, manner, or reason.

Sometimes, the relationship between the *wh-* question and its response is complex, particularly in conversation. That is, the speaker asking the *wh-* question might also provide a suggestion for the answer "in the form of an elliptic *yes-no* question" (Biber et al., 1999), as in the following examples:

1   A: **Who** drove? **Karen?**

    B: No, she can't drive...

2   A: **When's** that? **in the afternoon?**

    B: Yeah.

(Biber et al., 1999, p. 205)

*Wh-* questions can also be posed querying the following information by combining *wh-* question words with other lexical items, as in the following examples:

**How much** (money) did you pay?    [For Type 2 nouns]
**How many** (kids) do they have?    [For Type 1 nouns]
**How long** did you stay?
**How far** is the hospital from your house?
**What time** is it?

Sometimes, a preposition precedes the *wh-* word (preposition + *wh-* word). This type of construction is unmarked in more formal registers of discourse—for example, academic discourse, technical discourse, news reports, lectures—but marked in informal registers.

**For what purpose** did you rehire him?
**In which** country was he born?
**To what degree** are these propositions accurate?
**At what age** can children eat solid food?
?**At what time** does the movie start? (stilted, hyper-formal)
?**To whom** did you talk yesterday? (stilted, hyper-formal)

- Forms of *Wh-* Questions

The following examples illustrate the various forms of *wh-* questions:

<u>With Question Word (QW) Replacing Information in the **Subject Position**</u>

| | |
|---|---|
| <u>*Wh-* [subject] with any verb</u> | **Jianjun** should have studied harder. |
| Replace Information with QW | **Who** should have studied harder? |
| | **This** assignment was the easiest. |
| | **Which** assignment was the easiest? |

330  *Inquiry and Apparent Inquiry in Discourse*

<u>With Question Word (QW) Replacing Information in **Other Syntactic Positions**</u>

a  **With copula *be* as main verb:** Reverse order of V and subject

   **Where** was today's homework posted?
   **When** are income taxes due?
   **How** is the weather today?
   **Why** is Hannah sad?

b  **With main verb other than copula be and no auxiliary:** Onyedi arrives at 9:00 a.m.

- Find the main verb.
   V = *arrives* [third-person singular present tense]
- Add *do* as the auxiliary before the main verb.
   do
- Match the tense of the auxiliary *do* with the tense of the original verb.
   Onyedi **does** [third-person singular present tense] arrive [at 9:00 a.m.]
- SVA: If the original verb encodes third-person singular present tense, make sure that the auxiliary *do* becomes *does*.
- Use the main verb in its base form (i.e., no morphology for tense or number). (i.e., remove tense and SVA from V) = arrive
   Onyedi **does** [third-person singular present tense] arrive [at 9:00 a.m.]
- Reverse the order of the auxiliary *do* and the subject.
   **Does** Onyedi arrive [when]?
- Add QW.
   **When** does Onyedi arrive?
   **What time** does Onyedi arrive?

Try the same with the following subject verb combinations:

**SUBJ V**

You exercise    →    **How often** *do* you exercise?
                     **How many times a week** *do* you exercise?
                     **Where** *do* you exercise?
                     **When** *do* you exercise?

**SUBJ V**

Fuhua needs [more pencils].    →    **What** *does* Fuhua need?
                                    **Why** *does* Fuhua need more pencils?
                                    **For what purpose** *does* Fuhua need more pencils?
                                    **What** *does* Fuhua need more pencils **for**?

c  **With main verb (V) [other than be] PLUS auxiliary:**

   <u>AUX (Auxiliaries)</u>
   *have* (perfect aspect)

*be* (progressive aspect, passive voice)
simple modals (e.g., *should, will, can, could*)

Reverse order of AUX and subject:

| Aaron | is | leaving for Paris tomorrow. |
| [subject] | [AUX] | |

| **When** is | Aaron leaving for Paris? |
| [AUX] | [subject] |

| **Where** is | Aaron going? |
| [AUX] | [subject] |

| We | should make guacamole for the party. |
| [subject] | [AUX] |

| **What** | should we make for the party? |
| | [AUX] [subject] |

| **How** | should we make it? |
| | [AUX] [subject] |

| Parisa | hasn't heard the news yet. |
| [subject] | [AUX] |

| **What** | hasn't Parisa heard yet? |
| | [AUX] [subject] |

| **When** | will she find out? |
| | [AUX] [subject] |

## 11.3 Alternative Questions or Choice Questions

Alternative questions, also known as choice questions, resemble yes-no questions in terms of structure, but they typically involve an "either/or" choice, and the potential answer is limited.

Would you like paper **or** plastic? ((at a grocery store))
Did you want soup **or** salad? ((at a restaurant))
Is this for here **or** to go? ((at a café, bakery, or fast-food restaurant))
Shall we spend the day at the beach **or** the park?
Are you thinking of attending a private college **or** a public university?

In certain contexts, these types of questions are reduced to just the items offered as choices:

| at the grocery store: | paper or plastic? |
| in a restaurant: | soup or salad? |
| fast-food restaurant: | for here or to go? |
| ice cream store: | cup or cone? |
| retail store: | receipt in your wallet or in the bag? |
| | paper receipt, email, or both? |

## 11.3.1 Answering Alternative Questions

In alternative questions, the nouns being queried are context-based and very limited in terms of possible choices. Unlike unmarked yes-no questions with rising intonation at the end, these alternate questions exhibit alternating intonation patterns, with the noun as the first choice made vocally salient with rising intonation and the second noun with falling intonation (see Quirk et al., 1985, pp. 399–340, among others) as in this example:

Would you like **paper** ↑ or **plastic**↓? ((at a grocery store))

With rising pitch on the first element of choice and falling pitch on the second element at the end of the question, the speaker signals that the two options are alternative choices in a closed set (i.e., either paper or plastic, which one?). Because the alternative questions typically signal choices between two or three specific items, the expected answer is typically one of the given choices:

| | |
|---|---|
| Would you like soup or salad? | Soup (please). |
| | Or, Salad (please). |
| | But NOT: |
| | *Yes ('both'/'one of the two'). |
| | */?No, thank you. (The * reading would depend on the context) |
| Cup or cone? | Cup, please. |
| | But NOT: |
| | *Yes ('both'/'one of the two'). (Both choices together could be possible, but the request would have to be worded very specifically). |
| | *No, thank you. |

The alternative questions may, however, end with a rising intonation, in which case the noun phrases are intended as suggestions and there are more than two options, as given:

<u>When there are more than two possible options:</u>

| | |
|---|---|
| Would you like cream or sugar↑? | Yes, both please. |
| | Just cream, please. |
| | No, thank you. I take it black. |
| | But NOT: |
| | *Yes, please. |

## 11.4 Tag Questions

Tag questions are markers that are appended to declarative statements that make the entire statement actually sound like a question. Tag questions typically have three types of forms:

a   Actual tag that reverses the polarity of the declarative (i.e., an **affirmative declarative** takes a **negative tag** and vice versa)

**affirmative declarative + negative tag:**

Today is Thursday,               isn't it?
[affirmative declarative]        [negative tag—always contracted]

You're Graciela's brother,       aren't you?
[affirmative declarative]        [negative tag—always contracted]

Baar will be traveling with us,  won't he?
[affirmative declarative]        [negative tag—always contracted]

**negative declarative + affirmative tag:**

It's **not** going to rain, is it?
[negative declarative] [affirmative tag]

They're **not** in China yet, are they?
[negative declarative]    [affirmative tag]

b   Discourse particles with rising intonation to seek confirmation or agreement

   It's actually pretty easy, **right?**
   It's delicious, **huh?**
   The best way to begin is by learning the vocabulary first, **okay?**
   It's a better idea to get the easy things out of the way, **yeah?**
   Let's start by dusting the bedroom furniture, **alright?**

c   Tag questions added to imperative sentences, in which case they generally start with a modal, for example, *will, shall, can, would* (Biber et al., 1999); modal-marked tags tend to signal a higher register and sometimes a stronger sense of urging

   Tell them I said hello, **will** you?
   Let's go, **shall** we?
   Call me when you get there, **would** you?

Note that all tag expressions, whether in full form or discourse particles like *right?*, *okay?*, and *yeah?* are highly interactive. Moore and Podesva (2009) characterize tags in general as *conducive* "because they encourage the hearer to agree with a proposition, in the sense that it is easier to agree with an established proposition than to construct dissent against it" (p. 458). Tags also take on language/culture-specific forms and interactional functions within a number of varieties of English—for example, Hawaiian pidgin ("It's tasty, *yeah?*"), Canadian English (*Eh?*), some dialects of British English (*Innit?*), and Maori English (*Eh?*; Bell, 2001). British English in general tends to use tag questions more frequently and with slightly differing communicative patterns and meanings.

## 11.4.1 Answering Tag Questions

Answering tag questions can be tricky because full-form tag questions contain two polarities, one in the declarative statement and the other, often the opposite polarity, in the tag. The answer expresses polarity that is consistent with either affirming or negating the propositional content, and not commentary on whether the full tag-marked question is correct:

You've never met my kids, have you?   No, I haven't yet. I hope I can soon.

                                      But NOT:
                                      *Yes (you are right), I haven't met them yet.

You're not Brian, are you?  Yes, I am. It's so good to see you again.
No, I'm Bob. Brian is my brother.

But NOT:
*Yes (you are right), I'm Abdul.

---

**Mini Review and Practice**

1  The following is an excerpt from Chapter 4 of *The Little Prince*.

> Grown-ups love figures. When you tell them that you have made a new friend, they never ask you any questions about essential matters. They never say to you: "What does his voice sound like?" "What games does he love best?" "Does he collect butterflies?" Instead, they demand: "How old is he?" "How many brothers has he?" "How much does he weigh?" "How much money does his father make?" Only then do they think they know him.
>
> If you were to say to grown-ups, "I saw a beautiful house made of rosy brick, with geraniums in the windows and doves on the roof," they would not be able to get any idea of that house at all. You would have to say to them: "I saw a house that cost $20,000.00." Then they would exclaim: "Oh, what a pretty house that is!"
>
> (Saint-Exupéry, 1943/1971)

The Little Prince indicates a set of questions that he'd prefer that "grown-ups" ask about new friends vs. a set of questions that he feels grown-ups typically ask:

**Preferred types of questions:** "What does his voice sound like?" "What games does he love best?" "Does he collect butterflies?"

vs.

**Typically asked, but less preferred types of questions:** "How old is he?" "How many brothers has he?" "How much does he weigh?" "How much money does his father make?"

The contrasts in question sets include (among other issues) a focus on truly getting to know a new child friend, especially his likes and dislikes rather than a focus on numbers, quantities, size, and money.

Note how the Little Prince uses negation in the following sentence:

> "When you tell them that you have made a new friend, they **never** ask you **any** questions about essential matters." [ORIGINAL]

How does this use of negation underscore his point? How would the sentence change if it were written in the following way?

> "When you tell them that you have made a new friend, they **don't** ask you questions about essential matters?" [VARIATION]

How does this use of negation reflect the speaker's stance with respect to grown-ups and their questions?

According to the Little Prince, what would prompt grown-ups to exclaim, "Oh, what a pretty house that is"?

What does this sort of commentary reflect about our own questioning practices to get to know people better? Explain your answer in detail. Think about the various contexts in which questions help advance conversation.

**Contexts:**

"small talk" with strangers or acquaintances at a wedding reception
dinner table conversations with family
business lunches/power lunches
contract negotiation meetings

Consider these issues as you work through this task:

When you meet someone for the first time, what sorts of questions do you typically ask in order to get to know the person better? Why those questions? Which of the four forms do your questions typically take (yes-no, *wh-*, alternate, tag)? Also think about pragmatics and what sort of information is acceptable to ask at a first meeting and what sorts of questions might be less appropriate in the social-cultural context of the interaction.

2   Often, in discourse and interaction, we find that polite requests, directives, and offers actually take the form of yes-no questions, and often these include deontic modals, such as *would*, *could*, and *can*.

request: boss to staff member:
**Could** you put that in my appointment book, please?
[meaning: Please put that in my appointment book.]

directive: ophthalmologist to patient:
Mrs. Brewer, **can** you read the eye chart for me?
[meaning: Please read the eye chart.]

directive: receptionist to client:
**Would** you like to have a seat in the waiting room?
[meaning: Please have a seat in the waiting room.]

offer: host to guest:
**Would** you like to try Molly's cheesecake?
[meaning: Please have some cheesecake.]

Why does the use of modals make these communicative functions or speech acts of offers, directives, and requests sound more polite? (See Chapter 8.) Explain your answer in detail. Try to find other instances of such questions used as a directive, a request, or an offer in actual discourse.

3   As we have observed, *wh-* questions isolate more specific bits of information than do yes-no questions. Two versions of a question from actual institutional discourse are provided here. The dispatcher from a bus operator's office has just learned of an accident in the vicinity of the bus route; she needs to determine whether the bus should alter its normal route to avoid the scene.

Each of these questions appears to seek the identical information.

   a   Bus dispatcher to bus driver ((via radio)): Bus 309, *what is your location?*
   b   Bus dispatcher to bus driver ((via radio)): Bus 309, *where are you?*

However, by virtue of the wording, one is designedly more specific. Why would this be important in a context such as this? Think about potential responses to the a version and potential responses to the b version. What is it about the grammar and the wording of each question that makes the possible responses so potentially different? Think about question words (QWs), nouns, determiners, and pronouns and how their use might engender greater specificity in the possible responses.

## 11.5 Other Question-Like Structures

In addition to the four basic question forms, other constructions can also serve as question-like markers. Question-formulated sentences and utterances do not necessarily expect an answer but function as rhetorical devices to help advance the discourse in particular directions. The following three sections elaborate on these question-like structures.

### 11.5.1 Statements With Rising Intonation as Questions: Declarative Questions and Echo Questions

Without any additional formal markers, rising intonation alone can express a yes-no type of inquiry—that is, uninverted or "declarative questions" (Quirk et al., 1985, p. 382–393, among others) This type of question typically occurs in ongoing oral or informal written discourse where an addressee interprets a just-produced utterance for the sake of confirming his or her understanding, advancing the discourse further, and so forth, as in the following examples:

**Yes-no question with no subject-aux reversal**

We were in Japan from June until early August.
→ So, you spent your whole summer vacation in Yokohama?  [yes-no question in meaning, but no *DO* and no reversal of subject and auxiliary]

Another question-like structure is the "echo" question. Sharply rising intonation with a declarative statement following an identical or near-identical declarative statement also functions to confirm the addressee's understanding of a just-produced utterance, or to express an affective reaction such as surprise, disappointment, approval, disbelief, and so forth. This type of construction is sometimes called an echo question because it repeats the words and structure of an interlocutor's prior utterance in a near-verbatim way but with a different communicative function than the original utterance.

**Echo question with no subject-aux reversal:**

    I just saw my first *Harry Potter* movie.     [declarative statement—giving news]
    →You just saw your first *Harry Potter* movie. ?(!)     [echo, registering news]

In ordinary conversation, echo questions can also assume an elliptical form of the initial utterance—for example, "Your first *Harry Potter* movie?"

Other forms of elliptical questions can be constructed using the inflected copular verb *be* or the inflected *do* auxiliary to replace the queried proposition. Elliptical question forms also use simple news-receipt discourse markers (e.g., *really?*). These are common ways of responding to interlocutors in ongoing conversation in American English (Norrick, 2012), as in the following examples:

**Elliptical echo questions and "news-receipt" markers**

    You did?/You are?/He was?/She is?
    Really?/For real?/Are you kidding?/Is he serious?

Other types of elliptical echo questions repeat parts of the just-heard utterance but isolate the uncertain or surprising bits of content with a question word:

    Our cat just swallowed a rubber band.
    → (Your cat) (just) swallowed **(a) what?**

    You don't have to worry. Sharks generally only hunt at dusk, at dawn, and at night.
    → Wait. Sharks hunt **when?**

    We're going to Llanfairpwllgwyngyll in Wales this summer.
    → You're going **where?**

### 11.5.2 Exclamations Using Question Words

Some exclamations in English use either question words (QWs) or inversion, reversing the order of the subject and the auxiliary or main verb, thus resembling the syntax of yes-no questions (e.g., Biber et al., 1999; Larsen-Freeman & Celce-Murcia, 2016; McCawley, 1973):

| | |
|---|---|
| **What** a long day I had! It took us fifteen hours door to door! | [QW: what] |
| **What** a great job you did! | [QW: what] |
| **What** a pretty house that is! | [QW: what] |
| **How** cool is    that! <br>     [V *be*] [subject] | [QW: how, reverse subject and V *be*] |
| **Did** Avigail do an outstanding job! <br> [Aux] [subject] [V] | [reverse subject and V] |
| Wow, **was** Six Flags exciting! <br>     [V *be*] [subject] | [reverse subject and aux] |
| **Isn't** it gorgeous! | [reverse subject and negated be verb] |

Despite the structural resemblance in form to questions, these constructions are intended, read, and heard as exclamations. When produced orally, they end with a declarative final intonation, and not rising intonation, as canonical yes-no questions do (Quirk et al., 1985, pp. 400–401).

### 11.5.3 Rhetorical Questions

Rhetorical questions as a communicative device serve the following basic functions:

- to engage the hearer or reader emotionally and/or logically;
- to "forcefully" evoke a certain line of reasoning or argument (Quirk et al., 1985, p. 401);
- to present alternative views and engage readers or audiences in dialogical reasoning (White, 2003);
- to express the writer's/speaker's stance or position in argumentative discourse.

Typically, rhetorical questions are posed to stimulate deeper thinking among readers or addressees or to express a strong position in favor of or in opposition to an issue at hand. Rhetorical questions are designed to remain unanswered such that the expected response may actually be known but remains unspoken.

| | |
|---|---|
| Who knows? | [QW: who; unspoken answer: no one knows] |
| Why should it matter? | [QW: why; unspoken answer: it shouldn't] |
| Shouldn't the decision be an easy one? | [negative yes-no question; rhetorical effect: the decision should be an easy one). |

Not surprisingly, rhetorical questions are common in academic and professional writing. Although academic writing is typically considered non-interactive, rhetorical questions can be effective devices through which the writer addresses an imagined audience directly, "inviting engagement and bringing the interlocutor into a discourse arena where they can be led to the writer's viewpoint" (Hyland, 2002, p. 530).

One example is from McLoone's (2013) "Is There Any Point to the 12 Times Tables?" from the Wolfram Blog. Here is the opening line to the blog essay:

> My government (UK) . . . recently said that children here should learn up to their 12 times tables by the age of 9.

The essay also poses these questions, in this order, peppered within the first one-third of the piece:

> Exactly why do we use times tables at all?
> What's so special about multiplying 1 to 12?
> Why stop at the 12 times table?
> Why not learn 13, 14, 15, 16, and 17?
> Why not learn your 39 times table?

The essay's title is a rhetorical yes-no question that serves as the basis for McLoone's argument. The *wh-* questions in the third paragraph continue to push the logic, which he convincingly builds until we reach the conclusion of the essay.

In that conclusion, do you predict that the essay puts forward a "yes" response to the title question or a "no" response?

His conclusion is this, and note that he also uses another rhetorical question in the penultimate line of his piece, which he then immediately qualifies with the final line.

> I can only conclude that the logic behind this priority is simply, "If learning tables up to 10 is good, then learning them up to 12 is better." And when you want to raise standards in math, then **who could argue with that**? Unless you actually apply some math to the question.
> (McLoone, 2013)

So, his answer to the title question is unequivocally "no."

A second example is by Leith (2014), from the *Financial Times*: "Is it worth asking a rhetorical question?" The articles begins like this, with a tag question—also intended as a rhetorical question:

> Everyone **knows** about rhetorical questions, **don't they**? Don't answer that. This figure of speech—a question that does not anticipate an answer but implies one—peppers everything from the highest-flown oratory to everyday conversational exchanges.
> (Leith, 2014)

Both McLoone (2013) and Leith (2014) pose affirmative questions that are designed to be gradually dismantled through their essays. So, *is there really any point to teaching the 12 times tables?* Read the essay and you'll see that there isn't. And *is it really worth asking a rhetorical question?* You can guess from the outset that this answer will also be "no." The arguments are so strongly built that the answer is more like, "Of course there/it isn't."

Rhetorical questions do not appear only in academic and professional writing. The following example is from another genre of discourse, a television ad for Geico, a nationwide insurance company:

> Does switching to Geico really save you 15% or more on car insurance?
> Does Elmer Fudd have trouble with the letter *r*?
> Elmer Fudd: Shhh! Be vewy quiet. I'm hunting wabbits.

This humorous Geico commercial poses a yes-no question regarding the competitiveness of its rates: Will it really save you money to switch? The answer this time is "Of course it will!"

In the commercial, the response is implied through a secondary question-answer response sequence: *Does Elmer Fudd* (the Looney Toons cartoon character with an idiosyncratic way of pronouncing his *r*'s) *have trouble saying the letter r properly?* And we immediately hear Elmer Fudd speaking, with his signature pronunciation of the letter *r*: *Be vewy quiet, I'm hunting wabbits* (= Be very quiet. I'm hunting rabbits). Implication: "Of course he has trouble saying the letter *r*." This now leads us back to the initial question with an even stronger implication: "Of course switching to Geico saves you money."

340  *Inquiry and Apparent Inquiry in Discourse*

Rhetorical questions also appear in oral argumentative discourse, from interviews to everyday conversations, often structured in the following formats:

"But is that *really* what is going on?" [expected response: no]
"Is that the most effective way to study for an exam?" [expected response: no]
"Isn't that why we pay taxes?" [expected response: yes]
"Didn't the senator just say the same thing?" [expected response: yes]

\*\*\*\*\*\*\*\*

## PRACTICE WITH DATA ANALYSIS: PUTTING IT ALL TOGETHER

1. As we have seen, rhetorical questions can indeed serve to effectively engage the reader in academic or professional prose. However, among less expert writers, rhetorical questions tend to be overused, especially when they are designed to replace more complex prose.

The following excerpts are actual pieces written by students in a freshman composition course. Each contains a string of at least two contiguous rhetorical questions. How effective is the use of these questions? Think about the rhetorical questions in general in addition to repetition and how each hypothetical argument is established. Also, consider other bits of discourse including pronouns, determiners, nouns, and verbs that might be re-worked to strengthen these arguments. Re-write each paragraph so that the arguments are presented in a more compelling way.

### Student 1:

On the other hand, when it comes to identity, such as your personal information, social security number, and password, **what if** someone get your credit card and pin number and spend all the money without you knowing it? **What if** they use your identity to commit illegal activities and get you into trouble? **What if** they use your identity and then commit a crime?

### Student 2:

In one paragraph they mentioned that cloning animal is ethical as long as the animals are treated in accordance with the rules set up by Institutional Animal Care and Use Committee, said Dick Frisque, professor of molecular virology. However, **could cloning be ethical** as long as the regulations were followed? **Does it mean** that if the whole process was done according to the book then cloning would be perfectly ethical? This is an incorrect concept.

2. News titles, essay titles—real questions, rhetorical questions?

Sometimes, titles of news stories look like rhetorical questions, but are they? Here are three that you might wonder about:

"**Why** does everyone call Donald Trump 'The Donald'?
It's an interesting story" (Argetsinger, 2015)

"**Why** are small banks disappearing?" (Nichols, 2017)
"**Why** do billionaires care so much about charter schools?" (Meyerson, 2017)

Do these titles fit the category of rhetorical questions? Why, or why not?

Now, have a look at the following titles or hypothetical titles:

> Why thinking outside the box isn't always a good thing.
> How managers treat late-arriving employees.
> What theater owners say about popcorn and soda spilled on theater floors.

These titles contain typical question words *why*, *how*, and *what*, but are these titles actually questions? Why, or why not?

Look for rhetorical questions in news story titles and headlines, on magazine covers, and even as titles of academic articles. Do the rhetorical questions appear to be mostly worded affirmatively or negatively? Is the first line of the article or story also a rhetorical question?

Can you anticipate what the answer to each rhetorical question might be? Can you anticipate where the author may be going in his/her line of argumentation just by virtue of the rhetorical questions?

3   Figure 11.2 on the next page is a parody of some forms of American TV advertising. Let's try and uncover the sources of humor here. First, how is the yes-no question structured? What is missing from the question? Why? What is the answer to the yes-no question? Is it explicitly stated? Why, or why not? What is the expected answer? How does the text of this TV commercial and its use of a yes-no question compare and contrast to actual ads, either in print or on TV? Provide examples.

4   The chapter focuses on forms of questions, on discursive contexts where we often find questions, and on the various functions of questions. When we think about classroom discourse, we typically imagine the two canonical types of questions: those that seek information (referential questions) and those that test information (display questions) (Rymes, 2015; Seedhouse, 2004; Sinclair & Coulthard, 1975; Walsh, 2011; among others).

The following transcript comes from the initial class meeting of Integrative Biology 131, taught by Professor Marianne Diamond at UC Berkeley. We include here just the first few minutes of the interaction as Professor Diamond opens her class and introduces the subject matter.

Have a look at how and for what purpose Professor Diamond uses questions. How are the questions formed? Where are they placed? What interactional purpose do they serve—request information, seek confirmation or clarification, establish rapport? How do these questions connect to the subject matter of the class?

### "Professor Marianne Diamond—Integrative Biology 131"

> Alright. I often ask **who is more excited the first day of class, the students or the teacher? Who do you think? Do you get excited coming to class?** I get excited coming to class.
>
> **Do you start by saying "hi," do you start by saying "hello," or do you start by saying "good morning"?** I usually like "good morning." **And why?** Because it

342  *Inquiry and Apparent Inquiry in Discourse*

conveys a positive thought to open the thalamic gates to the cortex. **What do you think of that?** You'll learn more about the thalamic gates when we study the nervous system. But that's an introduction to them.

**How many of you have studied anatomy before?** ((Looks around the room)) Just a few of you. Alright. **And when you studied anatomy, did you introspect?** Because that's the way we study this course. You're gonna look at each other differently from now on. Introspect. Learn who you are beneath the surface, because the knowledge that you'll gain here in Wheeler auditorium in the Fall of 2005 can last you your full one hundred years. **By then will geneticists extend that to one hundred and twenty years? Who knows?** But you will always have your anatomy with you wherever you are. So, learn it well while you're here. So you can take care of yourself, so we'll cut those big health care bills, the latter quarter of those one hundred years. Be healthy for the whole time. . . .

**How many know the structural and functional unit of compact bone?** ((Looks around the room; one person raised her hand)) **We do need a class, don't we?** One person doesn't. ((Laughs)). Alright.

(UC Berkeley, 2007)

How does Professor Diamond use questions to establish rapport with her students while at the same time introducing the content of the course and holding students' interest? Would you like to be a student in a class like this one? (If the video is still available, please do try and watch it.) Explain your answer in detail, first, by categorizing the questions according to their types, functions, and placement within this discourse, and then by explicating how these questions enhance her course introduction.

5   We have seen that questions do so much more than just query information. Questions display stances and assumptions of speakers and writers. That said, think about the following

"Want to settle your case FAST? Call the law firm of Rock, Paper & Scissors!"

*Figure 11.2* "Want to settle your case FAST? Call the law firm of Rock, Paper & Scissors!"
© Randy Glasbergen. Reproduced with permission of Glasbergen Cartoon Service.

question types and try to determine how they differ, from the point of view of the speaker's stance:

Affirmative: It's going to rain tomorrow, isn't it?   It was my fault, wasn't it?
Negative:    It's **not** going to rain tomorrow, is it?   It was**n't** my fault, was it?

Which of the four sentences are more neutral and objective?
Which sound stronger in terms of the speaker's hope or preference?
Why do you think this is the case?

6   Have a look at the question in Figure 11.3 on the next page. What is happening in the scene? Who is speaking? To whom? What is the question? If you were to name a communicative function or speech act that this question is expressing, what might that be? That is, is the spouse really just *asking a question* or is he or she doing something else? What kind of question is this, then?

7   The following two TED Talk excerpts illustrate how speakers use questions and related structures to help them explain their ideas to their respective audiences. The first is from Amy Cuddy's (2012) talk titled "Body Language Shapes Who You Are." The second is from Denis Dutton's (2010) talk "A Darwinian Theory of Beauty." These segments are merely fractions of the full talk, but the question structures as used here seem to work quite effectively. Read through the segments, and think about the questions and question structures in bold.

   a   **Amy Cuddy: "Body Language Shapes Who You Are"**

   8:57 So what we find is that high-power alpha males in primate hierarchies have high testosterone and low cortisol, and powerful and effective leaders also have high testosterone and low cortisol. **So what does that mean?** When you think about power, people tended to think only about testosterone, because that was about dominance. But really, power is also about how you react to stress. **So do you want the high-power leader that's dominant, high on testosterone, but really stress reactive? Probably not, right?** You want the person who's powerful and assertive and dominant, but not very stress reactive, the person who's laid back.

   (Cuddy, 2012)

   b   **Denis Dutton: "A Darwinian Theory of Beauty"**

   6:51 Consider briefly an important source of aesthetic pleasure, the magnetic pull of beautiful landscapes. People in very different cultures all over the world tend to like a particular kind of landscape, a landscape that just happens to be similar to the pleistocene savannas where we evolved. This landscape shows up today on calendars, on postcards, in the design of golf courses and public parks and in gold-framed pictures that hang in living rooms from New York to New Zealand. . . . This landscape type is regarded as beautiful, even by people in countries that don't have it. . . .

   But, someone might argue, that's natural beauty. **How about artistic beauty? Isn't that exhaustively cultural? No, I don't think it is.** And once again, I'd like to look back to prehistory to say something about it.

   (Dutton, 2010)

344  *Inquiry and Apparent Inquiry in Discourse*

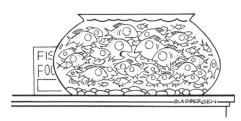

*Figure 11.3* "Why didn't you tell me your relatives were coming for the holidays?!"
© Randy Glasbergen. Reproduced with permission of Glasbergen Cartoon Service.

What types of question structures did you locate in the two segments? What discursive function do these question structures serve in the context of the two TED Talks? How are the two speakers' use of questions similar? How are they different?

9  Questions serve multiple purposes in various types of discourse. Some genres of discourse make use of questions almost exclusively, like courtroom proceedings, hospital intake interviews, celebrity/political interviews, American Red Cross blood donation questionnaires, customer satisfaction surveys, airport check-in and TSA (Transportation Security Administration) screenings, and so on.

Watch for these specific types of discourse, and pay attention to how questions are used. In what order do the questions appear? Are they yes-no, *wh-*, alternative, or statements that are designed to function as questions? Is one type the predominant type? Why do you think that would be the case for that specific type of discourse?

The following excerpt is from the actual courtroom trial of one of the most controversial high-profile murder cases of the past decade. The case involved George Zimmerman, a 28-year old bi-racial man (Hispanic, Caucasian), and Trayvon Martin, a 17-year-old African American young man who was walking around the gated community where Zimmerman lived. The community had had a recent history of burglaries and break-ins, and residents were on edge. On the evening of February 26, 2012, Zimmerman spotted Martin and designated him as a "suspicious" individual in his call to the police, saying that Trayvon Martin began to run. While the details at this point are sketchy and filled with controversy, the essence of the story is this: A fight ensued between Zimmerman and Martin. Zimmerman had a gun and shot Martin dead. Martin was unarmed. There were some eyewitnesses, but their accounts were vague. The verdict: George Zimmerman was found to be not guilty in the murder of Trayvon Martin.

You can read more about this case online or in the numerous books that have been published about it. This landmark murder case inspired the Black Lives Matter movement in the US.

The data provided here come from the June 28, 2013, portion of the trial involving Jonathan Good, Witness No. 6, and lead prosecutor for the State of Florida, Bernie de la Rionda.

As you work with the transcript, first identify the question types posed by Mr. de la Rionda. Think about the structure of the question and the kind of information that each question is designed to seek. Also analyze the answers provided by the witness.

Think about how questions in legal discourse are posed sequentially (the order of question types, answer types, follow-up questions, etc.) so that attorneys can better draw out and establish for the record the specific information they are seeking. As always, also pay attention to other relevant bits of grammar, for example, nouns and noun types (i.e., *noise vs. noises*), determiners, tense and aspect, and modals, as they relate to this interaction.

We have started the analytic process by identifying the first few question types to the right of the transcript line. See the table directly following the transcript and fill in the blank lines:

June 28, 2013
Witness #6 Testimony in State of Florida v. George Zimmerman

ATTORNEY: Good morning, sir. Could you state your name for the record?
GOOD: Jonathon Good.
ATTORNEY: Your last name is spelled G-O-O-D. Is that correct?
GOOD: Correct.
. . .
((Focusing on the night of February 26, 2012))

ATTORNEY: Did you hear **some noise** outside?
GOOD: Yes.
ATTORNEY: And was **the noise you heard** outside such that you were able to hear it inside? In other words, was it loud, or do you recall in terms of how you described it to the jury when you first heard it?
GOOD: It was faint.
. . .
ATTORNEY: Did you then hear **further noises?**
GOOD: Yes.
ATTORNEY: Okay.
. . .
ATTORNEY: . . . What **was the noise you heard** later?
GOOD: **The same noise**, just louder. It seemed like it was getting closer.
ATTORNEY: Okay.
ATTORNEY: At that time, the second time **you heard noise**, could you tell-, could you make out **any words?**
GOOD: No.
. . .
ATTORNEY: And when you looked out, tell us what you saw from your vantage point inside the residence.
GOOD: I couldn't really see anything except it looked like someone or something was out there.
ATTORNEY: Okay.
. . .
ATTORNEY: What **do you see** when **you look out there** at that time?
GOOD: It looked like a tussle. I could really only see one person, and I think I described it as possibly being some kind of dog attack, because there are a lot of dogs that walk in that back area.

| | |
|---|---|
| Could you state your name for the record? | structured as a yes-no question but not requesting a "yes" or a "no" answer |
| Your last name is spelled G-O-O-D. Is that correct? | tag-like construction |
| Did you hear some noise outside? | yes-no question |
| And was the noise you heard outside such that you were able to hear it inside? In other words, was it loud, or do you recall in terms of how you described it to eh jury when you first heard it? | |
| Did you then hear further noises? | |
| What was the noise you heard later? | |
| At that time, the second time you heard noise, could you tell-, could you make out any words? | |
| And when you looked out, tell us what you saw from your vantage point inside the residence. | directive, not a question |
| What do you see when you look out there at that time? | |

Fill in the remaining question types in the right-hand column. What does a close analysis of discourse and specific grammatical features reveal about the intricacies in how information is requested and provided in the previous question-and-answer interchange? Explain in detail, focusing on question types (yes-no, negative/affirmative, *wh*-, echo, etc.) and on the responses that follow each question.

## COMMON ERRORS, BUMPS, AND CONFUSIONS

Identify the errors or "bumps" in the following sentences or paragraphs. Use the concepts and terminology that you learned in this and other chapters to articulate what might be grammatically or pragmatically problematic. Suggest ways that each can be re-written more clearly and more accurately. (Note: While all bumps do involve some element of questions, they are not limited to only that.)

1. Can you imagine how critical would the consequences be due to the divulgence of personal information? It must be awful.

2. However, most significant fault death penalty conducts is that human shortens other's life. To prevent other murder, do we have to put a murderer to death for an example? Although capital punishment can be regarded as a punishment not murder, it is still putting one to death. Isn't there other way to make him realize his fault?

3. Have your mother frequently made you to engage in doing study? Japanese parents, especially Japanese mothers are extremely enthusiastic about education. They have a goal for their sons or daughters to make successful person by concentrating on education.

4. How your opinion different from writer opinion?

5. What means this question?

6. "You haven't met Sunjun, right?" ((introducing friends))
   "Yes, I haven't."

7   "What size—small, medium, or large?" ((ordering coffee))
    "Yes, please."

8   How you make data sharing easier?

## SUGGESTED ACTIVITIES

1   Jokes and riddles are ideal genres for practicing questions.

    Q: What can't you trust an atom?
    A: Because they make up literally everything.

    Q: Why don't teddy bears ever order dessert?
    A: Because they are always stuffed.

These and other jokes and riddles are based on wordplay. What is the source of humor of each joke?

Conduct a small-scale internet study of these types of two-line jokes and riddles based on wordplay. Make a collection of 10 that you like the best. There can be a classroom activity in which one student shares his/her jokes and asks others to try and answer. Be sure that you work through the sources of humor in each wordplay example. Then try to write your own jokes in this style.

2   Lost and found—imaginary scenario. Work in pairs.

Imagine you are staff at the Lost and Found desk at your local library. Your classmate is a hypothetical library patron who approaches the desk and tells you that he/she has lost his/her wallet. You need to be sure that this person is really the owner of the item. You'll need to come up with sets of questions that will help you determine that the library patron is in fact the rightful owner of that item. You can continue the role play with hypothetical patrons having lost their backpacks, glasses cases, computer bags, lunch bags, and so on.

3   Service encounters—learning by listening

This activity is modeled after a language activity proposed in Williams (2009). Go to your favorite coffee shop, music store, clothing store, art supplies store, or a place where you can overhear interactions between clerks and customers at service encounters.

Listen to how individual customers initiate and word their questions. If it is convenient and inconspicuous for you to write, you can take notes on what you hear, or just remember the words and jot them down later. As you overhear and observe, see how each customer is responded to by the clerk. Compare and contrast the styles of each customer, and determine which types of wording seem to be the most pragmatically smooth and successful. Are there any communicative bumps in the interactions? What do you think has caused those bumps?

Based on your observations, make a small corpus for service-encounter questions and responses. Share your corpus with your classmates and compare notes on the various interactional styles.

4   TV or radio interviews—talk shows, morning shows, news interviews

Locate a TV or radio show that is known for interviewing celebrity guests, sports figures, or politicians. Find an interview with a person whom you particularly like or admire. Transcribe the first five minutes of that interview, and see how it opens and how it progresses.

What kinds of question words does the interviewer use? How are these responded to by the interviewee? You can compare and contrast late-night talk show interviews with daytime talk show interviews where the same celebrity is interviewed on different shows and by different people. Which types of questions (think about both content and structure) tend to elicit longer stretches of discourse by the interviewee in response?

5   Story Corps interview

Story Corps is an organization that provides a physical "recording booth" in which friends and families can interview each other and make their life stories known to the world and become part of the society's oral history. You can read more about the organization at https://storycorps.org.

Browse the Story Corps archive (e.g., https://storycorps.org) and listen to a recording that interests you. Who recorded the story? Who asked the first question? How was it formulated? What were the rest of the questions that made an impression on you? Did the questions follow a theme? Did they relate to each other in some way?

Think about creating a Story Corps interview of a friend or a family member. Ask a family member or friend to do this activity with you and be your guest for the interview. You can record the story by using the Story Corps app, or if the recording booth will be in your town soon, perhaps you can schedule a recording session. Or you can simply follow the Story Corps format and create the interview without developing it into a publicly broadcast piece.

6   "It's beautiful, isn't it? The moon." "Had ourselves a little late-night snack, did we?" (Kloves, 2009)

Watch the following clip of the film *Harry Potter and the Half-Blood Prince*: https://youtu.be/3mGqky3VORs.

The scene is where Ron confesses his love for Romilda Vane to Harry Potter. The excerpt contains many of the structures that we introduced in the chapter, in addition to a few variations, including a tag question with no reversal of polarity (both clauses are in the affirmative). Transcribe the segment, and then go through the turns to identify the question types and see whether and how each is responded to. What is the function of each question type? Are they all "real" questions (or so-called referential questions), or are they fulfilling some interactional functions that can only be accomplished in this way with question-like structures?

7   Designing writing prompts

Piccadilly (2015) has published a book called *300 Writing Prompts*. Many of the prompts appear in the form of questions. There are 300 blank pages, at the top of which is a one- or two-line prompt.

Here are a few samples:

> What is your favorite way to spend a lazy day?
> How do you strive to be similar to or different from your parents?
> Is there anything that you are ever a snob about?
> How do you respond when someone compliments you?

Make your own set of writing prompts—either for your own journaling or to be used in a class. Think about how the quality and wording of the question in the prompts affect how you might answer them.

As you work with this topic, also think about writing prompts that are used in your own classes—either by you as a teacher or by your teachers for you as a student to respond to. Evaluate those prompts for clarity, creativity, imagination, and their ability to challenge writers to think beyond the simple task of writing for writing's sake.

## Academic References

Ainsworth-Vaughn, N. (1994). Claiming power in the medical encounter: The Whirlpool discourse. *Qualitative Health Research*, 5(3), 270–291.

Bell, A. (2001). Back in style: Re-working audience design. In P. Eckert & J. R. Rickford (Eds.), *Style and sociolinguistic variation* (pp.139–169). New York: Cambridge University Press.

Biber, D., Johansson, S., Leech, G., Conrad, S., & Finegan, E. (1999). *Longman grammar of spoken and written English*. Halow: Pearson Education.

Givón, T. (2005). *Context as other minds: The pragmatics of sociality, cognition, and communication*. Amsterdam and Philadelphia: John Benjamins.

Heritage, J. C., & Raymond, G. (2012). Navigating epistemic landscapes: Acquiescence, agency and resistance in responses to polar questions. In J-P. De Ruiter (Ed.), *Questions: Formal, functional and interactional perspectives* (pp. 179–192). Cambridge: Cambridge University Press.

Heritage, J. C., & Robinson, J. D. (2006). The structure of patients' presenting concerns: Physicians' opening questions. *Health Communication*, 19(2), 89–102.

Heritage, J. C., & Roth, A. L. (1995). Grammar and institution: Questions and questioning in the broadcast news interview. *Research on Language and Social Interaction*, 28(1).

Heritage, J. C., & Sorjonen, M-L. (1994). Constituting and maintaining activities across sequences: And-prefacing as a feature of question design. *Language in Society*, 23, 1–29.

Hinkel, E. (2002). *Second language writers' text: Linguistic and rhetorical features*. Mahwah, NJ: Lawrence Erlbaum.

Hyland, K. (2002). *Teaching and researching writing*. Harlow: Pearson Education.

Jiang, W. Y., & Ramsay, G. (2005). Rapport-building through call in teaching Chinese as a foreign language: An exploratory study. *Language Learning & Technology*, 9(2), 47–63.

Jordan, M. E., Cheng, A. C. J., Schallert, D., Song, K., Lee, S. A., & Park, Y. (2014). "I guess my question is": What is the co-occurrence of uncertainty and learning in computer-mediated discourse? *International Journal of Computer-Supported Collaborative Learning*, 9(4), 451–475.

Lane, C. (1985). Mis-communication in cross-examinations. In J. B. Pride (Ed.), *Cross-cultural encounters: Communication and mis-communication* (pp. 196–211). Melbourne: River Seine Publications.

Larsen-Freeman, D., & Celce-Murcia, M. (2016). *The grammar book: Form, meaning, and use for English language teachers*. Boston, MA: National Geographic and Heinle.

Lauerbach, G. E. (2010). Maneuvering between the political, the personal, and the private: Talk, image and rhythm in TV dialog. *Discourse and Communication*, 4(2), 125–159.

Licoppe, C., Cudicio, R., & Proulx, S. (2014). Instant messaging requests in connected organizations: "Quick questions" and the moral economy of contribution. *Discourse Studies*, 16(4), 488–513.

Linell, P., Hofvendahl, J., & Lindholm, C. (2003). Multi-unit questions in institutional interactions: Sequential organizations and communicative functions. *Text—Interdisciplinary Journal for the Study of Discourse*, 23(4), 539–572.

McCawley, N. (1973). Boy! Is syntax easy. *Proceedings of the Ninth Regional Meeting of the Chicago Linguistic Society*, 369–377.

Mehan, H. (1979). *Learning lessons*. Cambridge, MA: Harvard University Press.

Moore, E., & Podesva, R. (2009). Style, indexicality, and the meaning of tag questions. *Language and Society*, 38, 477–485.

Nguyen, H. T. (2007). Rapport building in language instruction: A microanalysis of the multiple resources in teacher talk. *Language and Education*, 21(4), 284–303.

Norrick, N. R. (2012). Listening practices in English conversation: The responses responses elicit. *Journal of Pragmatics, 44*(5), 566–576.

Quirk, R., Greenbaum, S., Leech, G., & Svartvik, J. (1985). *A comprehensive grammar of the English language*. New York: Longman.

Raymond, G. (2003). Grammar and social organization: Yes-no type interrogatives and the structure of responding. *American Sociological Review, 68*, 939–967.

Raymond, G., & Heritage, J. (2006). The epistemics of social relations. *Language in Society, 35*, 677–705.

Raymond, G., & Heritage, J. (2013). One question after another: Same-turn-repair in the formation of yes/no type initiating actions. In M. Hyashi, G. Raymond, & J. Sidnell (Eds.), *Conversational repair and human understanding* (pp. 213–272). Cambridge: Cambridge University Press.

Rymes, B. (2015). *Classroom discourse analysis: A tool for critical reflection* (2nd ed.). London: Routledge.

Schegloff, E. A. (1988). Presequences and indirection: Applying speech act theory to ordinary conversation. *Journal of Pragmatics, 12*, 55–62.

Seedhouse, P. (2004). *The interactional architecture of the language classroom: A conversation analysis perspective*. Malden, MA: Blackwell.

Sinclair, J., & Coulthard, M. (1975). *Towards an analysis of discourse: The English used by teachers and pupils*. Oxford: Oxford University Press.

Steensig, J., & Heinemann, T. (2013). When "yes" is not enough—as an answer to a yes/no question. In B. Szczepek Reed & G. Raymond (Eds.), *Units of talk: Units of action* (pp. 207–241). Amsterdam, Philadelphia: Benjamins.

Stivers, T., & Enfield, N. J. (2010). A coding scheme for question—response sequences in conversation. *Journal of Pragmatics, 42*(10), 2620–2626.

Walsh, S. (2011). *Exploring classroom discourse: Language in action*. London: Routledge.

Waring, H. Z. (2009). Moving out of IRF (initiation-response-feedback): A single case analysis. *Language Learning, 59*(4), 796–824.

White, P. R. R. (2003). Beyond modality and hedging: A dialogic view of the language of intersubjective stance. *Text, 23*(2), 259–284.

Williams, J. (2009). Beyond the practicum experience. *ELT Journal*, 68–77.

## Data References

Argetsinger, A. (2015, September 1). Why does everyone call Donald Trump "The Donald?" *The Washington Post*. Retrieved August 11, 2016, from www.washingtonpost.com/news/arts-and-entertainment/wp/2015/09/01/why-does-everyone-call-donald-trump-the-donald-its-an-interesting-story/?utm_term=.56d8400b35b0

Cuddy, A. (2012). Your body language shapes who you are [Video]. Retrieved November 1, 2016, from www.ted.com/talks/amy_cuddy_your_body_language_shapes_who_you_are

Dutton, D. (2010). A Darwinian theory of beauty [Video]. Retrieved November 1, 2016, from www.ted.com/talks/denis_dutton_a_darwinian_theory_of_beauty

Kloves, S. (2009). Screenplay for *Harry Potter and the Half-Blood Prince*. Retrieved from https://youtu.be/3mGqky3VORs.

Leith, S. (2014, September 1). Is it worth asking a rhetorical question? Retrieved August 10, 2017, from www.ft.com/content/560c21cc-2eaf-11e4-afe4-00144feabdc0

McLoone, J. (2013, June 26). Is there any point to the 12 times table? Wolfram blog. Retrieved October 15, 2017, from http://blog.wolfram.com/2013/06/26/is-there-any-point-to-the-12-times-table/

Myerson, H. (2017, May 22). Why do billionaires care so much about charter schools? *Los Angeles Times*. Retrieved August 14, 2017, from www.latimes.com/opinion/op-ed/la-oe-meyerson-billionaire-charters-20170526-story.html

Nichols, R. (2017, May 29). Why are small banks disappearing? *Los Angeles Times*. Retrieved August 14, 2017, from www.latimes.com/opinion/op-ed/la-oe-nichols-dodd-frank-reforms-banks-20170529-story.html

Piccadilly. (2015). *300 writing prompts*. Picadilly.
Saint-Exupéry, A. de. (1943/1971). *Le petit prince* [The little prince]. K. Woods (Trans.). Irvine, CA: Harvest House Publishers.
UCBerkeley. (2007, August 20). Integrative biology 131—Lecture 01: Organization of body [Video]. Retrieved November 1, 2016, from www.youtube.com/watch?v=S9WtBRNydso

# 12 The Grammar of Situating Entities in Space, Time, and Abstractness, Hanging On, Burning Up, and Cooling Down

Prepositions and Phrasal Verbs

*Figure 12.1* "They're adding fluoride to the drinking water in Washington to help fight truth decay."
© Randy Glasbergen. Reproduced with permission of Glasbergen Cartoon Service.

Prepositions are those smaller bits of language and shorter words that function to situate things, people, and ideas in concrete space, as well as to locate events and occurrences in time (Carter & McCarthy, 2006, pp. 462–469; Larsen-Freeman & Celce-Murcia, 2016, pp. 415–440; Quirk et al., 1985, pp. 297–338; Radden & Dirven, 2007, pp. 303–334). Some very common prepositions in English are

from, of, in, to, into, inside, out, outside, for, on, off, onto, at, by, around, about, as, like, through, after, before, over, under, with, without, up, down, toward, below, against, along, behind, above, next to, near, across, opposite, as well as per, than, during, and since.

The prepositions in the caption from Figure 12.1 are *to* and *in*.

They're adding fluoride **to** <u>the drinking water</u> **in** <u>Washington</u>.
                         PREP    NP          PREP      NP

From the point of view of structure, prepositions are followed by nouns, NPs, pronouns, and gerunds, which are also nouns.

These greeting cards *are made* **from** <u>recycled paper products</u>.
                            PREP    NP

Recycled paper pulp *is made* **by** <u>mixing discarded or shredded paper with water</u>.
                        PREP   GERUND

Prepositions can be used to locate items in **concrete space** or designate the occurrence of an event in **time**:

    Agapito *left* the keys **on** <u>my desk</u>.      [concrete space]
    Mansoor *arrived* **on** <u>Friday</u>.          [time]

    Let's meet **at** <u>the museum entrance</u>.    [concrete space]
    The movie starts **at** <u>6:00 p.m</u>.         [time]

Beyond the domains of the physical space and time, the meanings of prepositions extend into the domain of the figurative and metaphorical to designate even more abstract concepts and relationships, as in the following examples:

<u>**on** used figuratively</u>
(i.e., not concrete space or specific period/point in time)

In late 2014, there were almost 50 million Americans *living* **on** <u>food stamps</u>.   [abstract]
For our assignment, Ms. Jun is asking us to *write an essay* **on** <u>bystander apathy</u>.   [abstract]
If you need help, you can *count* **on** <u>me and my family</u>.   [abstract]
He *sobbed* uncontrollably **on** <u>seeing his baby</u> for the first time.   [abstract]
            [**on** + gerund]
We are going to *keep* ***on*** <u>trying</u>, until we get it right.   [abstract]
            [keep **on** + gerund]
            [*keep on* = phrasal verb = '*continue*']

<u>**at** used figuratively</u>
(i.e., not concrete space or specific period/point in time)

The best way to accomplish many things *is to finish* <u>one thing</u> **at** <u>a time</u>.   [abstract]
**At** <u>first</u> we were just friends. Now we are engaged to be married.   [abstract]
You are becoming quite *good* **at** <u>tennis</u>.   [abstract]
How did Javier *arrive* **at** <u>that conclusion</u> when he had such little information?   [abstract]
Aya *is good* **at** <u>playing tennis</u>.   [abstract]
    [**at** + gerund]

The fact that the meanings of prepositions begin in the domain of the concrete and then stretch outward into the domain of time and then even further into that of the figurative and metaphorical is an example of *polysemy* (Lakoff, 1987; Lakoff & Johnson, 1980; Langacker, 1987, 2002; Talmy, 2000; Tyler & Evans, 2001, 2003; Radden & Dirven, 2007). As you will see in this chapter, the meanings of all prepositions are highly polysemous, and those that we address here all follow the same basic trajectory: concrete→ time → abstract/figurative/metaphorical.

## 12.1 Meanings of Prepositions: From Concrete Space to Time to More Abstract and Metaphorical Usages

The meanings of prepositions in English all progress similarly from the domain of concrete, visible, or physical space to the more abstract and figurative notions of time, experience, and condition (Carter & McCarthy, 2006, p. 465; Larsen-Freeman & Celce-Murcia, 2016, pp. 419–439; Lindstromberg, 2010; Quirk et al., 1985, pp. 307–333; Tyler & Evans, 2001, 2003). Table 12.1 lists 25 prepositions in English, the majority of which are listed as the most frequent prepositions from COCA (*from, of, in, to, into, for, on, at, by, about, as, like, through, after, over, with*) (Davies, 2008–). The right-hand column indicates the essential *core meaning* for each preposition.

*Table 12.1* Core meanings of select prepositions

| Preposition | Core meaning (starting from concrete/space to time and abstraction) |
|---|---|
| from | movement—part of a whole, leaving a source |
| of | part of a whole |
| in | enclosure |
| to | in the direction of a goal, end point, or target |
| into | entering an enclosure from a source location |
| inside | enclosure within defined boundaries |
| out | beyond an enclosure |
| outside | beyond an enclosure with defined boundaries |
| for | purpose related to intention, recipient, stand-in, duration |
| on | contact with surface |
| off | disconnect from surface |
| onto | movement resulting in contact with a surface from a source location |
| at | a point |
| by | connection of place/entity to place/entity, action to time, action to agent |
| around | motion that outlines the perimeter of something |
| about | non-specific motion in any direction except not one that designates a perimeter |
| as | in the capacity of equaling in total identity |
| like | similarity |
| through | movement traversing an entire trajectory within an enclosure (or partial enclosure) |
| after | sequentially next, following |
| before | a. sequentially preceding<br>b. in physical space: facing, in front of something greater, larger, more important |
| over | arched trajectory at a higher vertical point (and any point on that trajectory) |
| under | at a lower vertical point |
| with | link |
| without | linkless |

## 12.2 Prepositions: Core Meanings Start in Concrete Space

### 12.2.1 From: *Movement, Part of a Whole, Leaving a Source*

*From* is a good preposition to start with, because its conceptual meaning within concrete space remains straightforwardly transparent as its use progresses from the domain of the concrete to more abstract domains of time, condition, experience, and so forth. Figure 12.2 illustrates the core meaning of *from* as **part of a whole, movement that involves leaving a Source**.

Here, the notion of Source refers to a starting location, a starting time, a starting event, or a starting condition. In the diagram, the large box represents the Source or starting location. The small box indicates that the action or state involved in the conceptual scene was at one point **connected to** or **part of that source**. The arrow indicates movement related to leaving the Source or starting point.

The following examples illustrate the range of meaning and use for the preposition *from*. In each case, *from* evokes movement that involves leaving a starting point (location, time, or condition) or Source.

For the preposition *from* and the remaining prepositions that we present here, we indicate relative categories of conceptual representation, for example, [concrete], [less concrete], [time], [abstract], and so forth. "Concrete" typically means that one can see the noun, touch it, and/or otherwise perceive it in reality. The categories, then, move along a continuum to "less concrete," "time," and then "abstract." Just like word meaning in general, the categories are not intended to be rigid classifications, and some, as you will notice, can and do cross-cut each other.

Why do leaves fall **from** <u>trees</u>?     [concrete space]
 starting location = source = trees

Our flight departs **from** <u>Rome</u>.     [concrete space]
 starting location = source = Rome

Even on national holidays, the mall is open **from** <u>10</u> to 6.     [time]
 starting time = source = 10:00 a.m.

Innovation comes **from** <u>a desire to create something different</u>.     [abstract condition]
 starting condition = source = a desire to create something different

Linguists draw inferences **from** <u>patterns in language</u>.     [abstract condition]
 starting condition = source = patterns in language

How did the US economy recover **from** <u>the Great Depression</u>?     [abstract condition]
 starting condition = source = the Great Depression

Put flour on the rolling pin to *stop the dough* **from** <u>sticking to it</u>.     [abstract condition]
 starting condition = source = dough sticking to rolling pin

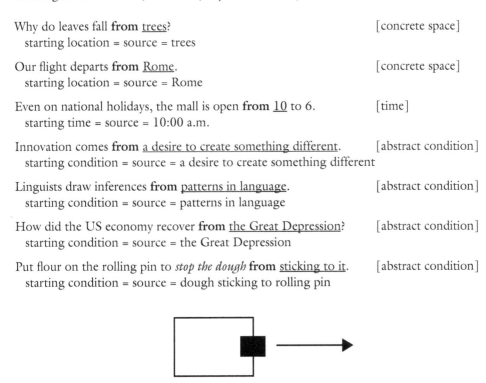

*Figure 12.2 from:* movement—part of a whole—leaving a source

356  *Prepositions and Phrasal Verbs*

Words that tend to co-occur with *from* include:

**Verbs** (V + *from*) of the copular *be*: (*was, is, be, are*), *come, go, fall, take, obtain, get, draw, start, depart, separate, remove, release, open, make, emerge, rise, recover, benefit, suffer, derive*, and *result* (adapted from Davies, 2008–).

### 12.2.2 Of: *Part of a Whole*

The conceptual meaning of the preposition *of* (Figure 12.3) is similar to *from* in that both evoke an essential meaning of **part of a whole**. In the case of *from*, the preposition evokes the movement of leaving the source, as denoted by the arrow. In the case of *of*, there is no movement. Thus, there is also no arrow in the diagram.

<u>One</u> **of** <u>our five puppies</u> is not housebroken.   [concrete space, portion]
part of whole

Let's add <u>a teaspoon</u> **of** <u>salt</u> to the broth.   [concrete space, measurement]
    measurement of whole

Today is <u>the first day</u> **of** <u>Diwali</u>.   [time]
     portion of whole

California is serving as a model for <u>the rest</u> **of** <u>the nation</u>.   [abstract condition]
                    portion of whole

They appeal to <u>a variety</u> **of** <u>instructional approaches</u>.   [abstract condition, assortment]
       variation of whole

Mustafa had just a <u>slight chance</u> **of** <u>reaching home by dusk</u>.   [abstract condition, possibility]
          possibility

Words that tend to precede *of* include:

**Verbs** (V + *of*): *think, consist, know, hear, make, accuse, speak, compose* (be composed of), *comprise* (be comprised of)

**Determiners, nouns, and other prepositions:** *one, out, kind, (a) lot, part, some, all, (a) number, most, many, rest, percent, end, sort, university, front, side, much, a couple, (a) piece, member, director, amount, president, because, outside, inside* (adapted from Davies, 2008–)

### 12.2.3 In: *Enclosure*

The conceptual meaning of the preposition *in* is simply **enclosure** (Figure 12.4). The meaning holds for the domains of the physical and concrete as well as those of time and abstractness (i.e., figurative and metaphorical).

*Figure 12.3 of:* part of a whole        *Figure 12.4 in:* enclosure

*Prepositions and Phrasal Verbs* 357

| | |
|---|---|
| Hanne still had half of her soda left **in** <u>the bottle</u>. | [concrete space] |
| The children had to stay **in** <u>the house</u> until the rain stopped. | [concrete space] |
| Sebi and Farshid have been living **in** <u>Georgia</u> for a year. | [geographical space] |
| Yelena can complete one crossword puzzle **in** <u>19 minutes</u>. | [time] |
| Pablo Picasso died **in** <u>1973</u>. He was 91. | [time] |
| You can go for years without having any goals **in** <u>mind</u>. | [abstract enclosure] |
| Has Bernie ever been **in** <u>trouble</u> with the law before? | [abstract enclosure] |
| Let's take an extra blanket, just **in** <u>case</u> we need it. | [abstract enclosure] |
| Neighborhood Watch <u>believes</u> **in** <u>uniting neighbors for safety</u>. | [abstract enclosure] |

Words that tend to co-occur with *in* include:

**Nouns:** *in* + noun: *fact, place, time, mind, turn, school, court, prison, town, effect, college, the world*

**Verbs** (V + *in*): forms of the copular verb *be* (*was, is, be, are*), *live, find, use, come, say, get, put, believe, participate, see, stay, remain, include, contain*

(adapted from Davies, 2008–)

Other common expressions with <u>in</u> evoking an abstract, metaphorical enclosure:

> in the event that. . .
> in fact
> in contrast
> in sum
> in conclusion
> in advance
> in life
> in love
> in history
> to be in charge of something
> to be in the right/in the wrong

### 12.2.4 To: *In the Direction of a Goal, End Point, or Target*

The preposition *to* evokes a core, essential meaning of *in the direction of a GOAL*, as represented by the diagram in Figure 12.5.

*Figure 12.5 to:* movement in the direction of a goal, end point, or target

## 358  Prepositions and Phrasal Verbs

The arrow in the diagram signifies the directionality of movement toward the GOAL, end point, or target, represented here iconically as a TARGET.

Typically, what follows the preposition *to* in English is a noun, a noun phrase, or a pronoun designating a person, place, or object as the GOAL or TARGET of the preposition. Like most other prepositions, *to* can also be followed by a gerund (*be committed* **to** doing something, *be used* **to** doing something, *look forward* **to** doing something, etc.).[1]

| | |
|---|---|
| Please *hand* your ticket **to** the usher. | [concrete space] |
| You must *go* **to** the Lincoln Memorial when you visit DC. | [concrete space] |
| The board meeting *will have to be postponed* **to** a later date. | [time] |
| Dr. Kildare holds her office hours *from* noon **to** 2:00 on Mondays. | [time] |
| Have you read Hesse's *Journey* **to** the East? | [abstract space, direction] |
| Montevideo, Uruguay, *is home* **to** the first-ever World Cup Final. | [abstract space, location] |
| How does your idea *relate* **to** our discussion? | [abstract] |
| Why *are leafy greens so important* **to** one's daily diet? | [abstract] |
| I promise to *fulfill my duties* **to** the best of my ability. | [abstract] |
| We *look forward* **to** seeing you next week. | [abstract] |
| The company Eat Limmo is dedicated **to** making foods healthier. | [abstract] |

Words that tend to co-occur with *to* include:

**Verbs** (V + *to*): *go, come, get* (as verb of motion—e.g., "How do you *get* **to** San Diego from here?"), *add, give, hand, send, return, talk, dedicate, compare, move, postpone, respond, contribute, refer, turn, relate, look forward* (adapted from Davies, 2008–)

### 12.2.5 Into: *Entering an Enclosure From a Source Location*

The conceptual meaning of the preposition *into* designates entering an enclosure from a source location (Figure 12.6). That enclosure could involve a solid obstacle (e.g., *walk into a wall*) as well as a change of state (*a chrysalis turns into a butterfly*; *divide/cut the brownies into pieces*), such that the collision with the obstacle or the newly transformed state constitutes a metaphorical enclosure. Preposition *into* profiles the motion from a source location into an enclosure, be that enclosure within concrete or physical space, time, or a metaphorical domain.

| | |
|---|---|
| When it's this hot outside, all we think about is *jumping* **into** the pool. | [concrete] |
| The recipe says to *fold* the fresh blueberries **into** the batter. | [concrete] |
| Tommasso worked hard to *get* **into** Duke Medical School. | [less concrete] |
| How did that small town transform **into** a metropolis? | [abstract, change of state] |
| The best way to read a long word is to *divide* it **into** syllables. | [abstract, change of state] |
| Larissa had trouble *logging* **into** the File Manager website. | [abstract] |
| You cannot succeed if you don't *put more effort* **into** your work. | [abstract] |
| Cory *talked himself* **into** climbing Nevada's Mount Charleston. | [abstract] |

*Figure 12.6 into:* entering an enclosure from a source location

*Figure 12.7 inside:* enclosure with defined boundaries

Words that tend to co-occur with *into* include:
**Verbs** (V + *into*): *get, go, log, come, move, drive, walk, run, step, divide, cut, put, fall, look, transform*
**Nouns**: <u>noun + *into*</u>: *way* (*into*), *insight, investigation, entry, research, inquiry*
<u>*into* + noun</u>: *place, effect, trouble, consideration, account*

(adapted from Davies, 2008–)

### 12.2.6 Inside: *Enclosure With Defined Boundaries*

Conceptually, the difference between *in* and *inside* is related to emphasis. *In* and *inside* both evoke the meaning of *enclosure*. The meaning and graphic representation for *inside* signal that the defined boundary is made more conceptually salient (Figure 12.7).

| | |
|---|---|
| Have you ever played the game "What's **Inside** <u>the Box</u>"? | [concrete] |
| Q: What do you *find* **inside** <u>a matryoshka doll</u>? | [concrete] |
| A: A smaller matryoshka doll that looks just like the larger one | |
| "Two nights before the war ended, our family *cuddled* **inside** <u>a Navy ship</u> . . ." (Lai, 2017) | [concrete] |
| One never knows what *goes on* **inside** <u>the mind of a teenager</u>. | [abstract] |
| "Big Mac: **Inside** <u>the McDonald's Empire</u>" (Quintanilla & CNBC, 2007) | [abstract] |

Words that tend to co-occur with *inside* include:
**Verbs** (V + *inside*): *be, go, get, step, come, trap, look, stay, run, walk, remain, fit, find, reach, hide, tuck, live, lock* (adapted from Davies, 2008–)

Note that preposition *in* is also grammatically possible in each of the previously listed examples. However, it does not capture the same sense of *enclosure* **with defined boundary** that *inside* evokes.

**Compare:**

What's *in* the box?
What do you find *in* a matryoshka doll?
Our family cuddled *in* a Navy ship. . .
What goes on *in* the mind of a teenager?
*In* the McDonald's Empire

### 12.2.7 Out: *Beyond an Enclosure*

Just as *in* conceptually designates an enclosure, *out* designates the polar opposite—that is, beyond an enclosure (Figure 12.8).

| | |
|---|---|
| It's the kids' job to *take* **out** the trash on Monday nights. | [concrete] |
| Nachum fainted and had to be *carried* **out** of the room. | [concrete] |
| Then the magician *pulled* **out** a rabbit from his hat. | [concrete] |
| The project *grew* **out** of my earlier work on French grammar. | [abstract] |
| My father always encouraged us to *stay* **out** of politics. | [abstract] |
| I saw that movie and was *scared* **out** of my wits. | [abstract] |
| Raise your hand when the teacher *calls* **out** your name. | [abstract] |

*Out* often co-occurs with the preposition *of*, designating *part of a whole* and *from*, designating *movement leaving a source*.
**Verbs** that tend to co-occur with *out* include (V + *out*) *be, come, go, grow, point, take, pull, run, walk, send, stay, call* (adapted from Davies, 2008–).

### 12.2.8 Outside: *Beyond an Enclosure With Defined Boundaries*

Where *inside* conceptually evokes *enclosure within a defined boundary*, *outside* evokes the polar opposite, *beyond an enclosure with defined boundaries* (Figure 12.9).

| | |
|---|---|
| The carolers *stood* **outside** the front door and sang holiday songs. | [concrete] |
| Dr. Fanoush asked Yafa's cousin to *wait* **outside** the exam room. | [concrete] |
| Luciano's teacher told him not to *color* **outside** the lines. | [concrete] |
| It is important to *make* lasting social connections **outside** the family. | [less concrete] |
| *Stepping* **outside** (of) your comfort zone isn't always the answer. | [abstract] |
| Professors **outside** (of) philosophy may not have the same views. | [abstract] |

Words that tend to co-occur with *outside* include:
**Verbs** (V + *outside*): *get, draw, color, think, stand, walk, wait, work, step, gather*

(adapted from Davies, 2008–)

Figure 12.8 *out:* beyond an enclosure

Figure 12.9 *outside:* beyond an enclosure with defined boundaries

Figure 12.10 *for:* connection to a purpose, intention, recipient, destination, stand-in, or continuous duration

### 12.2.9 For: *Connection to a Purpose*

The preposition *for* evokes an actual or imagined connection of something to a purpose. The purpose can be conceptually realized as an actual purpose, an intention, a recipient, a destination, a stand-in, or the continuous duration of a situation (whether that duration involves past, present, or future time) (Figure 12.10 on the previous page).

The present *is* **for** <u>my sister</u>.  [concrete]
    intended recipient = my sister

We saw that the little girl *was using a plastic bag* **for** <u>a rain hat</u>.  [concrete]
    stand-in = a rain hat

You should *hold the door open* **for** <u>people entering the building</u>.
    stand-in = people entering the building [b/c they cannot do it themselves]  [concrete]
    OR
    intended recipient of a favor = people entering the building [and they
    benefit from it]  [less concrete]

Can you please *call Mr. Marley* **for** <u>me</u>?
    stand-in = me [because I cannot do it myself]  [concrete]
    OR
    intended recipient of a favor = me [and I benefit from it]  [less concrete]

We are *having spaghetti* **for** <u>dinner</u>.  [less concrete]
    stand-in or purpose = dinner

The TV program *is designed* **for** <u>teens</u>.  [less concrete]
    intended recipient = teens

David Blaine, the illusionist, *stayed within a block of ice* **for** <u>66 hours</u>.  [time, duration]
    duration = 66 hours

We'll *be staying in Tokyo* **for** <u>two more weeks</u>.  [time, duration]
    duration = two more weeks

Here are three signs that <u>America</u> *is headed* **for** <u>another recession</u>.  [abstract]
    destination = another recession

Jack Andraka *has developed* <u>a promising test</u> **for** <u>pancreatic cancer</u>.  [abstract]
    intended purpose = pancreatic cancer

Ricky Gervais *apologiz*ed **for** <u>mispronouncing Quvenzhané Wallis's name</u>  [abstract]
    intended purpose = mispronouncing Quvenzhané Wallis's name

Words that tend to co-occur with *for* include:

**Nouns:** noun + *for*: *reason, purpose, explanation, implication, preference, rationale, justification, appetite, advancement, endowment, knack, groundwork, catalyst, blueprint, spokesperson, fondness, impetus, lookout, affinity, distain*

**Verbs** (V + *for*): *account, run, prepare, use, hope, stand, wait, hold, search, request, qualify, care, compensate, opt, yearn, look, check, pay, work, stay, ask, go, vote, long, root, apologize*

**Adjectives (and past particles):** copula (*be, become*) + adj./past part. + *for*: *responsible, eligible, suitable, reserved, accountable, penchant, destined, thankful, liable, known, headed, designed, needed, required, made* (adapted from Davies, 2008–)

### 12.2.10 On: *Contact With a Surface*

The core conceptual meaning of the preposition *on* is contact with a surface (Figure 12.11).

| | |
|---|---|
| Manhattan's 13th Avenue *was built* on <u>a landfill</u> in 1837. | [concrete] |
| Do you *put* whipped cream on <u>your waffles</u>? | [concrete] |
| The gift shop *is* on <u>the first floor</u> of the hospital. | [concrete] |
| Elias always forgets to *write* his name on <u>his papers</u>. | [concrete] |
| Aneta always *wears* a lapel pin on <u>her jacket</u>. | [concrete] |
| What is the best way to *hide* a water stain on <u>the ceiling</u>? | [concrete] |
| The bathroom is down the hall. It'*s* the first door on <u>the left</u>. | [less concrete] |
| Austin and Allie *are getting married* on <u>Saturday</u>. | [time] |
| What do you *do* on <u>weekends</u>? | [time] |
| I'm so sorry you have to *work* on <u>Christmas Eve</u>. | [time] |
| Please *arrive* on <u>time</u> for your first appointment. | [time, abstract] |
| Our class is going to *be* on <u>TV</u> tomorrow. | [transmission waves, abstract] |
| Nestor *posted* some new photos on <u>Instagram</u>. | [transmission waves, abstract] |
| We could only *follow* the game on <u>the radio</u>. | [transmission waves, abstract] |
| Remember to *focus* on <u>the positive aspects</u> for your review. | [abstract] |
| I need to *rely* on <u>my notes</u> for tomorrow's talk. | [abstract] |
| Dr. Zakarian *had a strong influence* on <u>my career</u>. | [abstract] |
| Daishon *published an article* on <u>protecting the elderly in the US</u>. | [abstract] |

**Verbs of support with on**

count on
rest on
depend on
live on

**Verbs of thinking with on**

reflect on
concentrate on
insist on
plan on

*Figure 12.11* *on:* contact with a surface
From Strauss, Chang, and Yoon (forthcoming)

### Verbs of acting/doing with on

embark on
set out on
start off on
get off on the wrong foot/on the right foot
work on

### *on* + nouns or NPs designating a temporary state

on fire
on edge
on the cusp of senility
on the verge of bankruptcy
on cloud 9 [Note: If you don't know this expression, it will make for interesting research.]
on sale (now being sold)
on sale (price is reduced from the normal price)
on hold
on mute
on record
on tap
on a three-year cycle
on the right track
on the road to

### 12.2.11 Off: *Disconnect From Surface*

The core conceptual meaning for *off* is disconnect from a surface, as illustrated in Figure 12.12.

We can express the binary opposition between *on* and *off* with the following metaphor of an electrical circuit. The meaning of *on* evokes *contact* (see Figure 12.12a).[2] The meaning of *off* evokes a *separation from a surface* or *no contact* (see Figure 12.12b).

| | |
|---|---|
| The chimps at the Bronx Zoo *picked bugs* **off** each other's shoulders. | [concrete] |
| Zain *pulled the quilt* **off** the bed and straightened the sheets. | [concrete] |
| The best way to open the glue bottle is to *snip* **off** the very tip. | [concrete] |
| An echo is where sound waves *bounce* **off** (of) a smooth, hard surface. | [concrete] |
| What causes an airplane to *veer* **off** (of) the runway? | [concrete] |
| Do you know how to *keep a cat* **off** (of) the kitchen counter? | [concrete] |
| Rachel is *taking a year* **off** college to join a dance troupe in Barcelona. | [abstract] |
| Little Connor is so scared that he won't *take his eyes* **off** (of) his mom. | [abstract] |
| *Get 50%* **off** (of) the regular subscription price. | [abstract] |
| The pit crew's readiness *shaved 3 minutes* **off** Dale's race time. | [abstract] |

Words that tend to co-occur with *off* include:
**Verbs** (V + *off*): *take, keep, pick, pull, cut, snip, shave, turn, go, veer, fall, pay, show, keep, bounce*
(adapted from Davies, 2008–)

364  *Prepositions and Phrasal Verbs*

*Figure 12.12 off:* disconnect from surface
From Strauss, Chang, and Yoon (forthcoming)

*Figure 12.12a* Electrical circuit metaphor—*on*
From Strauss, Chang, and Yoon (forthcoming)

*Figure 12.12b* Electrical circuit metaphor—*off*
From Strauss, Chang, and Yoon (forthcoming)

### 12.2.12 Onto: *Movement Resulting in Contact With a Surface From a Source Location*

The core conceptual meaning of *onto* entails a movement from one source location to contact with another surface (Figure 12.13 on the next page). Like the preposition *into*, *onto* also profiles that trajectory and not simply the new location.

Tanechka stepped **onto** <u>the balcony</u> and took a photo of the city. [concrete]
Watch as the containers are lifted and then *loaded* **onto** <u>trucks</u>. [concrete]
A splotch of bright yellow mustard *fell* right **onto** <u>his white shirt</u>. [concrete]
*Hold* **onto** <u>that thought</u>. We'll come back to it in a second. [abstract]
Advertisers keep pushing junk foods **onto** <u>small children</u>. [abstract]
After you shoot your film, you should *upload* it **onto** <u>Vimeo</u>. [abstract]

Words that tend to co-occur with *onto* include:
**Verbs** (V + *onto*): *step, turn, hang, load, climb, roll, open, project, stumble, latch, burst, jump, move, push, settle, get, climb, graft, log, upload, grab, hold* (adapted from Davies, 2008–)

### 12.2.13 At: *A Point in Space*

The essential, core conceptual meaning of the preposition *at* designates the concept of a point (Figure 12.14 on the next page).

The couple met for the first time **at** <u>the Roxy</u> (an LA nightclub). [concrete]
The *x* and *y* axes on a coordinate plane intersect **at** <u>the origin</u>. [concrete]
I had no idea why everyone was staring **at** <u>me</u>. [concrete]

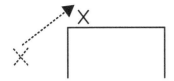

*Figure 12.13 onto:* movement resulting in contact with a surface from a source location

*Figure 12.14 at:* a point that is located in space[3]

| | |
|---|---|
| The police were called to the scene **at** <u>12:30 a.m.</u> | [time as a point] |
| Why is the sky dark **at** <u>night?</u> | [abstract: point in expanse of time] |
| In 1807, France and Britain were **at** <u>war.</u> | [abstract: point in metaphorical space] |
| No one ever *laughs* **at** <u>my jokes</u>. I wonder why. | [abstract: point in metaphorical space] |
| You can contact me **at** <u>this email address</u>. | [abstract: point in metaphorical space] |
| We have to be sure to *look* **at** <u>the bigger picture</u>. | [abstract: point in metaphorical space] |
| Our mayor *needs to work harder* **at** <u>rebuilding the city</u>. [gerund] | [abstract: point in metaphorical space] |
| Prosthetic Leg Gives Abused Dog Second Chance **At** <u>Life</u> (news headline) | [abstract: point in metaphorical space] |

**Common nouns** that tend to co-occur with *at* in prepositional phrases in English include:

*at* home, *at* school, *at* sea, *at* night     [expanse of space or time]
*at* work, *at* play, *at* lunch, *at* war, *at* odds, *at* ease     [abstract state or condition]
*at* stake, *at* risk, *at* a pace of, *at* the rate of, *at* odds     [metaphorical space]
[designating a point in space, time, or abstract/metaphorical state or condition]

**Verbs** that tend to co-occur with *at* include (V + *at*): look *at*, stare *at*, glance *at*, smile *at*, aim *at*, arrive *at* [designating a point in space, time, or abstract/metaphorical state or condition]

---

### Mini Review and Practice

1   Have a look at the following quote by Carl Sagan about books, reading, and writing. In it, you will find the following eight prepositions: *from, with, on, of, at, inside, for, across,* and *to*

Which is the most frequent? Why do you think this is the case?

> What an astonishing thing a book is. It's a flat object made from a tree with flexible parts on which are imprinted lots of funny dark squiggles. But one glance at it and you're inside the mind of another person, maybe somebody dead for thousands of years. Across the millennia, an author is speaking clearly and silently inside your head, directly to you. Writing is perhaps the greatest

of human inventions, binding together people who never knew each other, citizens of distant epochs. Books break the shackles of time. A book is proof that humans are capable of working magic.

(Sagan et al., 1980)

Re-read the quote and highlight all the prepositions. Identify the core conceptual meaning of each. Also think about the nouns and verbs that co-occur with each preposition in this text. How do these co-occurring words relate to the core conceptual meaning of each preposition?

2. Based on the core conceptual meanings of prepositions *in/into* and *on/onto*, discuss why the a versions in the sentence pairs are ambiguous in meaning, while the b versions are not. In order to fully consider these issues, you'll need to imagine a plausible context for each scenario. Explain your answers in detail using the concepts that we covered in the first part of this chapter.

    a    Jana and Petra *jumped* **in** the back of the van.
    b    Jana and Petra *jumped* **into** the back of the van.

    a    Miloje *pirouetted* **on** the stage as his name was called for the award.
    b    Miloje *pirouetted* **onto** the stage as his name was called for the award.

3. Think of various scenarios that help expand the meaning of preposition *at* to encompass its basic meaning of **a point in space**.

| | |
|---|---|
| Three employees are now working *at* _____. | [concrete] |
| Aurora has been asked to work *at* _____. | [concrete] |
| We go to work *at* _____. | [time] |
| Hyo only works *at* _____. | [time] |
| Our CEO is committed to working harder *at* _____ _____. | [abstract] |

4. What is the conceptual difference that affects the meanings in each sentence pair? Try to imagine the contexts in which each sentence might be uttered in order to get at the various meanings of these expressions.

Kleminis *is tired* **from** lifting weights.
Kleminis *is tired* **of** lifting weights.
The outdoor carpet *is made* **from** recycled plastic bottles.
The bubbles in Lady Gaga's costume *are made* **of** heavy gauge plastic.
Why do leaves *fall* **off** trees?
Why do leaves *fall* **from** trees?
The gaming console we saw at Best Buy *was not* **for** sale.
The gaming console we saw at Best Buy *was not* **on** sale.
Kora *wrote a letter* **to** her best friend.
Kora *wrote a letter* **for** her best friend.

5   An eye doctor is examining her patient's vision and says,

> "Can you *read the eye chart* **for** <u>me</u>, please?"

Given what you know about the meaning of the preposition *for*, why is this potentially funny? What are the possible scenarios that can be construed by this request? How does the meaning of the modal *can* (see Chapter 8) play into the humor of this utterance?

For the most unmarked of interpretations, start with the notion of pragmatics (see Chapter 2) and the speech act that is being expressed through this seeming yes-no question (see Chapter 11). What function does the phrase "for me" fulfill with regard to the speech act?

Then, think about other possible ways of interpreting the sentence that might tend toward the humorous.

Do the same with the following:

> A doctor during an office visit places her fingers lightly on her patient's throat to check for thyroid health and says, "Can you *swallow* **for** <u>me</u>, please?"

Given the range of meanings of the preposition *for*, think about how this utterance, too, can take on a humorous interpretation.

6   The verb *take* is highly polysemous. Make a list of the various meanings that it carries. Feel free to use a dictionary or an online source to complete this task.

Now, think about the various meanings of the preposition *for*.

How do you account for the following two expressions that have the identical structure but are very different in meaning?

> Nour took Daniel **for** a walk/a drive/a run.
> Nour took Daniel **for** a farmer/a chemist/a fool.

7   What does the expression "Think outside the box" mean? Describe the meaning in your own words. Do you feel that the message might have culture-specific values associated with it? Explain. That is, do you think this practice is valued in all cultures universally?

How would the message change if it were worded this way: "Think outside **of** the box"? What are some other variations of this expression that might use the same metaphor of "thinking in (or inside/outside) (of) a/the) box"?

8   Have a look at the following travel blog from about a family's trip throughout South America. Read the passage carefully.

### "*In* the Spirit of Adventure: Peru *Into* Chile"

> Cusco and the Sacred Valley had us **in** her mystical clutch for nearly 6 weeks. **In** that time, we held a 24 Hour Bazaar, shipped it all out, spent days diagnosing and sorting a mysterious electrical issue with the van . . . and worked on a

368  *Prepositions and Phrasal Verbs*

hush hush project. . . . Our canvas tent has great breathability, much enjoyed **in** humid environs . . . but we knew it was going to be a cold night. . . . *Hola? Hooolaa?* Ugh- our least favorite way to awaken, we peered through the pixelated windows. . . . The glass was covered **in** a thin layer of frost. . . . Off **in** the distance, a curious alpaca-herder waved and hollered *buenos días*. . . . Gathered **in** corrals at night, by day the packs of 200–300 camelids graze on the wild grasses. . . . [T]he battery slowly drained the whole night, leaving us without enough juice to get going. . . . With the charge controller set to the battery and our high altitude putting us virtually next to the beaming sun—the battery charged **in** 10 short minutes.

(OurOpenRoad, n.d.)

Now, analyze the instances of the preposition *in* from the point of view of its core meaning of *enclosure*. What are the various concrete, temporal, and abstract meanings that you discern for *in* in this text? Also contrast the meaning of *in* with *into* in the blog title. How are *in* and *into* different?

9  This next exercise contains two excerpts from actual discourse. The first is from the autobiographical account of Martin Pistorius's exceptional life from *Ghost Boy: The Miraculous Escape of a Misdiagnosed Boy Trapped Inside His Own Body*. The second is from a tourist publication about Southern California, focusing on Manhattan Beach.

In each case, we have removed the prepositions. Try to fill in the blanks from the list of missing prepositions given after each excerpt. There will be cases where more than one preposition is possible. The actual texts can be found at the end of this section. Compare and contrast your answers with the actual text. In the cases where more than one preposition is possible, explain how the meaning changes by virtue of the core conceptual meaning of each preposition.

There may be other prepositions used in the passages, but we have only left blank those that we have covered through this section of the chapter.

a. *Ghost Boy*

Martin opens the entire book from his perspective as a child treated as if he could not think or respond to reality. He was conscious of everything around him, but he was trapped in a body that could not respond to outside stimuli. He eventually learned to communicate through technology, re-connect with people, and ultimately resumed a normal life after having been institutionalized for 14 years. He fell in love and is now married.

**Chapter 1. Counting Time**

I spend each day ___ a care home ___ the suburbs ___ a large South African city. Just a few hours away are hills covered ___ yellow scrub where lions roam looking ___ a kill. ___ their wake come hyenas that scavenge ___ leftovers and finally there are vultures hoping *to* peck the last shreds ___ flesh ___ the bones. Nothing is wasted. The animal kingdom is a perfect cycle ___ life and death, **as** endless **as** time itself.

I've come *to* understand the infinity ___ time so well that I've learned to lose myself ___ it. Days, if not weeks, can go **by** as I close myself down and become entirely black within—a nothingness that is washed and fed, lifted ___ wheelchair ___ bed—or as I immerse myself ___ the tiny specks ___ life I see **around** me. Ants crawling ___ the floor exist ___ a world ___ wars and skirmishes, battles being fought and lost, **with** me the only witness ___ a history **as** bloody and terrible **as** that of any people.

(Pistorius, 2013, p. 1)

[Prepositions: from, for, on, to, of, off, in (Note: in *to* peck, *to* understand, the word *to* is used as an infinitive, not a preposition).]

b. **"Exploring South Bay: Manhattan Beach"**

Nineteen miles southwest ___ downtown Los Angeles, Manhattan Beach boasts 2 miles ___ beaches **with** sand so fine that developers ___ Waikiki Beach ___ Honolulu imported it ___ the 1920s. This laid-back city is home ___ many professional athletes. You may spot an L.A. Kings player as you walk **along** the Strand, the pedestrian promenade sandwiched **between** multimillion dollar homes and the beachfront bike trail. ___ the end ___ the city's picturesque pier, the Roundhouse Aquarium delights **with** touch tanks. The pier features plaques commemorating winners___ the Manhattan Beach Open—the south Bay is die-hard beach volleyball-country. It's also a playground___ water sports enthusiasts, including bodyboarders and surfers.

("Exploring SOUTH BAY," 2016, p. 46)

[Prepositions: in, at, to, for, from, of]

## Original texts

### *Ghost Boy:*

I spend each day **in** a care home **in** the suburbs **of** a large South African city. Just a few hours away are hills covered **in** yellow scrub where lions roam looking **for** a kill. **In** their wake come hyenas that scavenge **for** leftovers and finally there are vultures hoping to peck the last shreds **of** flesh **off** the bones. Nothings is wasted. The animal kingdom is a perfect cycle **of** life and death, as endless **as** time itself.

I've come to understand the infinity **of** time so well that I've learned to lose myself **in** it. Days, if not weeks, can go by as I close myself down and become entirely black within—a nothingness that is washed and fed, lifted **from** wheelchair **to** bed—or as I immerse myself **in** the tiny specks **of** life I see **around** me. Ants crawling **on** the floor exist **in** a world **of** wars and skirmishes, battles being fought and lost, **with** me the only witness **to** a history as bloody and terrible **as** that of any people.

**Manhattan Beach:**

Nineteen miles southwest **of** downtown Los Angeles, Manhattan Beach boasts 2 miles **of** beaches **with** sand so fine that developers **from** Waikiki Beach **in** Honolulu imported it **in** the 1920s. This laid-back city is home **to** many professional athletes. You may spot an L.A. Kings player as you walk **along** the Strand, the pedestrian promenade sandwiched **between** multimillion dollar homes and the beachfront bike trail. **At** the end **of** the city's picturesque pier, the Roundhouse Aquarium delights **with** touch tanks. The pier features plaques commemorating winners **of** the Manhattan Beach Open—the south Bay is die-hard beach volleyball-country. It's also a playground **for** water sports enthusiasts, including bodyboarders and surfers.

10  Look at Figure 12.1, the cartoon we used to open the chapter. What is the source of humor?

The caption contains two instances of *to*. One is a preposition, and the other is part of the infinitive of a verb. Which is which? What verb does the preposition follow, and what noun phrase does it precede? What verb is used in the infinitive form? What is the core conceptual meaning of *to* used as a preposition or with an infinitive?

### 12.2.14  By: *Connection of a Place or Entity to a Place or Entity, an Action to a Time, a Result to a Process, an Action to an Agent, a Unit to an Equal Unit, an Action to a Supported Position or Gauge*

The core meaning of the preposition *by* involves the notion of *connection* of a place or entity to another place or entity (*The university is located on a hill* **by** *the highway*) in the domain of the physical and concrete. The senses of *by* extend to the more abstract domains of time, action, process, and so forth, according to the following: an action to a time (*Reports are due today* **by** *5:00 p.m.*), a result to a process (*You can succeed* **by** *persevering*), an action to an agent (*"Immortality" was sung* **by** *Céline Dion*), a unit to an equal unit (*He gave a play-***by***-play description of the game*), or an action or state to a supported position or gauge (*Citizens must abide* **by** *the laws of the land* [supported position], *The window measurements are 36 inches* **by** *48 inches* [dimension, gauge]) (Figure 12.15).

| | |
|---|---|
| Have you seen the film *Manchester* **by** <u>the Sea</u>? | [concrete, place] |
| I'd rather *sit* **by** <u>the window</u> instead of in the middle. | [concrete, place] |
| The RSVP asks guests to *respond* **by** <u>May 22</u>. | [time, action] |
| Jot your notes down on a <u>3-inch</u>-**by**-<u>5-inch</u> <u>index card</u>. | [abstract, gauge] |
| A person's success cannot *be measured* **by** <u>his or her wealth</u>. | [abstract, gauge] |
| *Judging* **by** <u>his reaction</u>, I'd say he was really angry. | [abstract, gauge] |
| The applications *were reviewed* **by** <u>the full committee</u>. | [abstract, agent] |

*Prepositions and Phrasal Verbs* 371

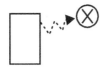

*Figure 12.15 by:* connection of a place to a place, an action to a time, a result to a process, an action to an agent, a unit to an equal unit, an action to a supported position

| | |
|---|---|
| Romance For Men (fragrance name) **by** <u>Ralph Lauren</u> (designer) | [abstract, agent] |
| Dorotea *sewed the dress* **by** <u>herself</u>. | [abstract, agent, emphatic] |
| Let's take this a bit more slowly, <u>step</u>-**by**-<u>step</u>. | [abstract, unit] |
| Zoey's situation worsened **by** <u>the day</u>. | [abstract, unit] |
| Murphy *found the answer* **by** <u>Googling the first word</u>. | [abstract, process] |
| Unity happens **by** <u>building solidarity</u>, not walls. | [abstract, process] |
| Everyone can *help* **by** just <u>remaining calm</u>. | [abstract, process] |

Words that tend to co-occur with *by* include:
**Verbs** (V+ *by*): *sit, respond, measure, judge, play, do, follow, lead, surround, support, create, write, follow, inspire*
**Nouns:** noun + *by* + noun: *side by side, step by step, day by day, little by little;*
   *by* + noun: *law, hand, telephone, email, fax, comparison, definition, nature, accident, surprise*

(adapted from Davies, 2008–)

### 12.2.15 Around: *Motion That Outlines the Perimeter of Something*

The core conceptual meaning underlying *around* involves motion that outlines the inside or outside perimeter of something (Figure 12.16).

| | |
|---|---|
| How fast can a professional ball player *run* **around** <u>the bases</u>? | [concrete] |
| Poppy and Mrs. Pepper *waltzed* gracefully **around** <u>the ballroom</u>. | [concrete] |
| The board members *sat* **around** <u>a large conference table</u>. | [concrete] |
| Princess Anne *wore a pearl necklace* **around** <u>her neck</u>. | [concrete] |
| Lucita *pushed her baby stroller* **around** <u>the playground</u>. | [concrete] |
| The light that you *see* **around** <u>the sun or moon</u> is called a halo. | [less concrete] |
| Everyone **around** <u>the president</u> agrees that the issue is dire. | [less concrete] |
| Mike Wong's map *points out the hot spots* **around** <u>the world</u>. | [less concrete] |
| **Around** <u>the mid-17th century</u>, men started to wear cravats. | [time] |
| We usually *have lunch* **around** <u>noon</u>. | [time] |
| Politicians *are constructing new narratives* **around** <u>food stamps</u>. | [abstract] |
| Collaborate and *build community* **around** <u>your shared interests</u>. | [abstract] |
| The meeting topics *centered* **around** <u>reducing production costs</u>. | [abstract] |

Words that tend to co-occur with *around* include:
**Verbs** (V + *around*): *be, come, go, get, walk, run, wear, wrap, see, look, build, gather*

(adapted from Davies, 2008–)

*Figure 12.16 around:* motion that follows the perimeter of something

### 12.2.16 About: *Non-Specific Motion in Any Direction But That Which Designates a Perimeter*

In contrast with *around*, the core conceptual meaning of *about* designates non-specific motion in any direction except the direction that follows an inside or outside perimeter of something (Figure 12.17 on the next page). It is in this very conceptualization schema that *about* contrasts with *around*.

| | |
|---|---|
| We can't keep cats because raccoons *wander* **about** our yard at night. | [concrete] |
| At dawn the seabirds *hover* **about** the shore looking for food. | [concrete] |
| Mr. Faro *displays his kids' drawings* **about** the room every year. | [concrete] |
| Everyone *left the party* **about** the same time. | [time] |
| The accident *happened* on or **about** May 14. | [time] |
| Kamal *is learning* **about** the Roman Empire in his history class. | [abstract] |
| What part did you *like the most* **about** the film? | [abstract] |
| Do you *know the joke* **about** the chicken and the egg? | [abstract] |
| I don't enjoy talking to Warren anymore. It *is* always just **about** him. | [abstract] |
| Success *is* all **about** working hard and keeping your eye on the prize. | [abstract] |

Words that tend to co-occur with *about* include:
**Verbs** (V + *about*): *be, know, think, like, worry, wonder, care, say, hear, ask, joke, feel, learn, wander, hover*
**Nouns** (noun + *about*): *information, question, story, concern, idea, decision, truth, doubt, assumption, feeling*

(adapted from Davies, 2008–)

### 12.2.17 As: *In the Capacity of, Equaling in Total Identity To*

The core conceptual meaning of *as* is *in the capacity of*, such that a referent is equal in total identity to something (Figure 12.18 on the next page).

| | |
|---|---|
| Even **as** a child, Enrico Fermi was studying theoretical mechanics. | [concrete] |
| This is my 22nd year **as** a professional singer. | [concrete] |
| Dolan plans to *work* **as** a volunteer for the Thirst Project in Africa. | [concrete] |
| You need no prescription for such over-the-counter medicines **as** aspirin. | [less concrete] |
| **As** a developing country, Costa Rica sets a fine example for the world. | [geographical space] |
| Let's cite Twitter **as** an example of a company with high morale. | [abstract] |

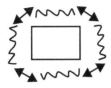

*Figure 12.17 about:* non-specific motion in any direction but that which designates a perimeter

*Figure 12.18 as:* in the capacity of, equaling in total identity to

Words that tend to co-occur with *as* include:
**Verbs** (V + *as*): *work, use, know, see, think, regard, cite, state, serve, describe, define, identify, recognize, perceive, treat*
**Nouns** (noun + *as*): *job, career, role, duty, reputation, status, fame, credibility, prominence, designation, certification, identity, function, clue, debut*

(adapted from Davies, 2008–)

## 12.2.18 Like: *Similarity*

In contrast to *as*, which establishes the equal identity of a referent to another entity, *like* establishes *similarity* between a referent and another entity (Figure 12.19 on the next page).

| | |
|---|---|
| Bora Bora for us *was* **like** paradise. | [concrete] |
| Polina *acts* **like** my own mother. | [concrete] |
| **Like** good educators, we must teach how to think, not what to think. | [concrete] |
| Caves are **like** time capsules because they contain bones and fossils. | [concrete] |
| The entire night *seemed* **like** fantasy to me. It *felt* **like** a dream. | [abstract] |
| "*Be* **like** Bill" is a humorous meme circulating on social media. | [abstract] |
| Abbreviations **like** lol, ttyl, cul8r [see you later] can be confusing. | [abstract] |
| For busy teachers **like** me, printable worksheets come in handy. | [abstract] |

Words that tend to co-occur with *like* include:
**Verbs** (V + *like*): *be, act, seem, feel, look, sound, smell, (be) shaped, dress, work, think, walk,* talk

(adapted from Davies, 2008–)

## 12.2.19 Through: *Movement Traversing an Entire Trajectory Within an Enclosure or Partial Enclosure*

The core conceptual meaning of *through* is movement traversing an entire trajectory within an enclosure or partial enclosure (Figure 12.20 on the next page).

| | |
|---|---|
| Radley's milkshake was so thick he could not *drink it* **through** the straw. | [concrete] |
| I cannot *pull the thread* **through** the eye of the needle. | [concrete] |
| My children always hold their breath when we *drive* **through** tunnels. | [concrete] |
| Dana *biked* **through** the neighborhood three times looking for Kitty. | [less concrete] |

374  *Prepositions and Phrasal Verbs*

*Figure 12.19* like*:* similarity

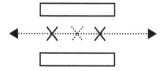

*Figure 12.20* through*:* movement traversing an entire trajectory within an enclosure or partial enclosure

| | |
|---|---|
| Come to the festival and watch colorful balloons *fly* **through** the clouds. | [less concrete] |
| On our last road trip, we *passed* right **through** Memphis without stopping. | [less concrete] |
| Art school in our area starts in March and *runs* **through** the end of June. | [time] |
| Buy One Get One. Offer (*is*) good **through** July 4. | [time] |
| Ramiro was so tired that he *slept* **through** the entire movie. | [abstract] |
| The device *tracks students' progress* **through** all stages of the exercise. | [abstract] |
| One good way to *learn new techniques* is **through** observation. | [abstract] |
| **Through** his dedication to UNICEF, Iker helped hundreds of children. | [abstract] |
| The only way *to make sense of this* is **through** logic and critical thinking. | [abstract] |
| United **Through** Reading is a non-profit literacy organization. | [abstract] |
| We *gained insights about our pasts* **through** searching Ancestry.com. | [abstract] |

Words that tend to co-occur with *through* include:
**Verbs** (V + *through*): *be, go, drive, run, walk, move, pass, sleep, see, look*
**Nouns:** noun + *through: way, journey, trip, path, passage, hole, ride, tour, stroll*; (*through* + noun): *translator, interpreter, time, life, college, space*

(adapted from Davies, 2008–)

### 12.2.20 After: *Sequentially Next, Following*

The core conceptual meaning of the preposition *after* profiles the concept of sequentially *next* or sequentially following in a physical setting (Figure 12.21 on the next page). The meaning then extends to more abstract domains of time and events.

| | |
|---|---|
| We *are in line* **after** the white-haired man. | [concrete] |
| **After** you, please *go* ahead. | [concrete] |
| Declan typically likes to go first. Who will *read* **after** him? | [less concrete] |
| I usually *wake up* **after** three cups of coffee. | [less concrete] |
| Parking in this lot *is free* **after** 5:00 p.m. | [time] |
| **After** 4 years of college, Constanza *landed an excellent job*. | [time] |
| Scientists are *predicting a rise in population* **after** 2020. | [time] |

*Figure 12.21 after:* sequentially next, following    *Figure 12.22 before:* sequentially preceding, prior

| | |
|---|---|
| <u>Day</u> **after** <u>day</u>, <u>week</u> **after** <u>week</u>, he *tried hard* to kick his habit. | [time] |
| What letter *comes* **after** <u>q</u>? | [abstract] |
| Math riddle: What numbers *come* **after** the sequence <u>2, 4, 8</u>? | [abstract] |
| Some people *brush their teeth* **after** <u>every meal</u>. | [abstract] |
| The couple *got married* shortly **after** <u>their engagement</u>. | [abstract] |
| Maja *consulted* <u>doctor</u> **after** <u>doctor</u>. No one had a clue what it was. | [abstract] |
| **After** <u>hearing that song</u>, all I could do was think of him. | [abstract] |

Words that tend to co-occur with *after* include:
**Verbs** (V + *after*): *be, go, come, happen, occur, do, leave, call, read, make, run, seek, chase, name*
**Nouns:** *after* + noun: *breakfast, lunch, dinner,* determiner + *meal(s), sunrise, sunset, midnight, birth, college, graduation, engagement, work, surgery, treatment*

(adapted from Davies, 2008–)

### 12.2.21 Before: *Sequentially Preceding, Prior*

In contrast with *after*, the core conceptual meaning of *before* profiles the concept of sequentially *prior* or sequentially preceding in a physical setting (Figure 12.22). As with all prepositions, the more abstract meanings of *before* in the domains of time, events, and stance all derive from the core meaning in the physical, concrete world.

| | |
|---|---|
| There are only *three people in line* **before** <u>me</u>. | [concrete] |
| What does the saying "*Age* **before** <u>beauty</u>" mean? | [less concrete] |
| What does your family *do on the night* **before** <u>Christmas</u>? | [time] |
| Bautista and I went to the mall *the day* **before** <u>yesterday</u>. | [time] |
| *Take one tablet* **before** <u>bedtime</u>. | [time] |
| *American art* as we know it *emerged* decades **before** <u>the Civil War</u>. | [time] |
| I am grateful to *those administrators* who *have come* **before** <u>us</u>. | [abstract] |
| Always *write out a plan* even **before** <u>the pre-writing activity</u>. | [abstract] |
| *Sketching lightly* **before** <u>painting</u> will make your work easier. | [abstract] |
| *Check your light meter* **before** <u>going on a long photo shoot</u>. | [abstract] |

Words that tend to co-occur with *before* include:
**Verbs** (V + *before*): *be, go, come, say, do, pass, look, happen, occur, check, exist, emerge*
**Nouns** (*before* + noun): *dawn, breakfast, lunch, dinner, sunrise, sunset, noon, bedtime, school, college, surgery, work, graduation, marriage*

(adapted from Davies, 2008–)

### 12.2.20.1 Before: *Pertaining to Physical Space: Facing, in Front of Something Relatively Greater, Larger, or More Important*

In discourse, the preposition *before* is used with generally the same core conceptual meaning of *sequentially prior or preceding*. *Before* is used with a handful of verbs such as *stand, appear, kneel, come*, and *go* where the referent is positioned as smaller than, less powerful than, or less greater than the entity designated by *before* (Figure 12.23).

| | |
|---|---|
| Each claimant that is *called* **before** the committee will provide testimony. | [concrete] |
| Witnesses *appeared* **before** the grand jury for the case. | [concrete] |
| In some religions, men are not supposed *to kneel* **before** kings or idols. | [concrete] |
| We *stood* **before** Van Gogh's painting *Sunflowers* and wept. | [concrete] |
| Elijah *went* **before** the people and said: "How long will you waver . . ." | [concrete] |
| (Psalms 18:21, New King James Version) | |

Words that tend to co-occur with *before* [spatially] include:
**Verbs** (V + *before*): *be, go, get, come, stand, sit, testify, appear, speak, perform*
**Nouns:** *people, public, committee, jury, panel, board, judge, audience, court, council, hearing, painting, sculpture*

(adapted from Davies, 2008–)

### 12.2.22 Over: *Arched Trajectory and Any Point on That Trajectory*

The core conceptual meaning of *over* evokes an arched trajectory, and the meaning can include any point on that trajectory or the entire trajectory (Figure 12.24). See Tyler and Evans (2004) for an extensive discussion and analysis of *over*.

| | |
|---|---|
| The *Times* reported that a Chinese jet *had flown* **over** a US Air Force jet. | [concrete] |
| Ivana *glanced* **over** her shoulder and caught sight of Ariana Grande. | [concrete] |
| Barb *tripped* **over** the curb in the parking lot. | [concrete] |
| The kingfisher hunts by *hovering* **over** water. | [concrete] |
| The table will have a classier look if you *drape the cloth* **over** the edges. | [concrete] |
| Romina got a flat tire because she *drove* **over** a nail. | [concrete] |
| We haven't *seen each other* in **over** three years. | [time] |

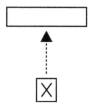

*Figure 12.23 before:* in physical space only, with a limited inventory of verbs, such as *stand before, appear before, kneel before, come before, go before*

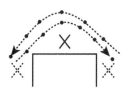

*Figure 12.24 over:* arched trajectory and any point on that trajectory

| | |
|---|---|
| Monte called Walmart and was *kept on hold* for **over** <u>30 minutes</u>. | [time] |
| You might get a speeding ticket if you *drive* **over** <u>the speed limit</u>. | [abstract] |
| What movie is the song "Somewhere **Over** <u>the Rainbow</u>" from? | [abstract] |
| The details of the bank robbery *were broadcast* **over** <u>the radio</u> yesterday. | [abstract] |
| We *have little control* **over** <u>many things in life</u>, including traffic. | [abstract] |
| Some drugs *give athletes an unfair advantage* **over** <u>their opponents</u>. | [abstract] |
| We sometimes erroneously *favor natural talent* **over** <u>hard work</u>. | [abstract] |
| John McCardell *was embroiled* in the debate **over** <u>the minimum drinking age</u>. | [abstract] |

Words that tend to co-occur with *over* include:
**Verbs** (V + *over*): *turn, bend, lean, roll, reach, drape, fly, hover, trip, run, glance*
**Nouns** (noun + *over*): *control, power, authority, win, influence, debate, controversy, battle, concern, dispute, fight, struggle, improvement, advantage, jurisdiction*

(adapted from Davies, 2008–)

### 12.2.23 Under: *At a Lower Vertical Point*

In contrast with *over*, the core conceptual meaning of *under* denotes a physical orientation at a lower vertical point (Figure 12.25). Also, unlike *over*, the core meaning of *under* does not evoke a trajectory or points on that trajectory. It simply designates the relative orientation of the referent vis-à-vis a lower vertical point, either concrete or abstract.

| | |
|---|---|
| We *found two quarters and a dime* **under** <u>the sofa cushions</u>. | [concrete] |
| In the movie "Toy Story," Woody *ran and hid* **under** <u>a milk crate</u>. | [concrete] |
| Lincoln couldn't find his keys because they *were* **under** <u>his briefcase</u> | [concrete] |
| There is a kind of TB test that *is done with a needle* **under** <u>the top layer of skin</u>. | [concrete] |
| Chris Solinsky is the largest man to *run the 10K* in **under** <u>27 minutes</u>. | [time] |
| You can also get a ticket if you *drive* **under** <u>the speed limit</u>. | [abstract] |
| Mr. Henning told students to *list all adjectives* **under** <u>the heading "descriptors."</u> | [abstract] |
| *No one* **under** <u>21</u> is allowed to sit at a bar in the US. | [abstract] |
| Seventy percent of *Iran's population* was **under** <u>the age of 35</u> in 2013. | [abstract] |
| *Smith and Carter were* both **under** <u>suspicion for burglary</u>. | [abstract] |
| *When a patient* is **under** <u>general anesthesia</u>, he or she is unable to feel pain. | [abstract] |

Other common expressions with under:
    under threat of
    under extreme stress

*Figure 12.25 under:* at a lower vertical point

under certain circumstances
under a storm warning
under surveillance
under the weight of
under the oppression of
under the assumption that
under specific conditions
under the impression that
under the influence of

Words that tend to co-occur with *under* include:
**Verbs** (V + *under*): *be, fall, place, tuck, hide, keep, find, drive*
**Nouns** (*under* + noun): *control, pressure, oath, investigation, consideration, development, construction, stress*

(adapted from Davies, 2008–)

### 12.2.24 With: *Link*

The core conceptual meaning of *with* is simply that of *link* (Figure 12.26). The concept relates to accompaniment (to do something, to go somewhere *with* someone), instrument (to perform a task *with* something), mutual communication (to speak *with* someone), parts of a string or sequence (start *with*, end *with*), and so forth, all of which can be subsumed under the concept of *link*.

| | |
|---|---|
| Henri de Toulouse-Lautrec *walked* with a cane. | [concrete] |
| He *walked* to school **with** his sister. | [concrete] |
| Oscar loved *playing* **with** bugs as a child. | [concrete] |
| Tonight we *are having pork chops* **with** raspberry sauce. | [concrete] |
| *Stay in touch* **with** your family and friends. | [less concrete] |
| I was unable to *speak* **with** him to confirm his statement. | [less concrete] |
| Even **with** the strongest detergent, you'll never *get that stain out*. | [less concrete] |
| The agent needs an actress **with** a high-pitched voice. | [less concrete] |
| *Xanthosis starts* an **with** x, and *psalm* starts with a p. | [abstract] |
| Can you ever *start a sentence* **with** and or but? | [abstract] |
| What letter does the word *lamb* end **with**? Do you say the *b*? | [abstract] |
| We *left the meeting* **with** a far deeper understanding of the problem. | [abstract] |
| *Advertise* **with** us. | [abstract] |
| Lipton and Knorr cannot *compete* **with** Nissin in the soup business. | [abstract] |
| What's *wrong* **with** Finn? He seems a bit edgy today. | [abstract] |
| What's *going on* **with** Firefox? It hasn't responded all morning. | [abstract] |

*Figure 12.26 with:* link

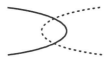

*Figure 12.27 without:* linkless

Words that tend to co-occur with *with* include:
**Verbs** (V + *with*): *mix, combine, do, associate, deal, fill, work, agree, disagree, compare, charge, start, end, stay, live, meet, go, cover, begin, come, compete, play, speak, work*

(adapted from Davies, 2008–)

*12.2.25 Without: Linkless*

Where *with* signals a link that connects two or more entities or concepts, *without* signals the absence of that link, or *linkless* (Figure 12.27).

| | |
|---|---|
| I *have never seen Marvin* **without** <u>a toupee</u> or *Marilyn* **without** <u>makeup</u>. | [concrete] |
| Camping is a good way *to spend time* **without** <u>electronic devices</u>. | [concrete] |
| *Don't go to the beach* **without** <u>your sunscreen</u>. | [concrete] |
| No one *will be allowed in the country* **without** <u>a valid passport</u>. | [concrete] |
| Olive Oatman *disappeared* **without** <u>a trace</u> in 1851 and was later found. | [concrete] |
| Balance is key to *being able to ride a bike* **without** <u>hands</u>. | [concrete] |
| **Without** <u>a sound</u>, *Cima tiptoed across the room* and then left. | [less concrete] |
| **Without** <u>your help</u>, *I never would have been able to finish this*. | [abstract] |
| Can capitalism *exist* **without** <u>democracy</u>? | [abstract] |
| Sign: NO ENTRY **WITHOUT** <u>PERMISSION</u> | [abstract] |
| I *can write my name in cursive* **without** <u>looking</u>. | [abstract] |

Words that tend to co-occur with *without* include:
**Verbs** (V + *without*): *do, live, be, go, leave, work, survive, make, pass, exist, happen*
**Nouns** (*without* + noun): *warning, question, fear, regard, hesitation, disabilities, thinking, power, parole, permission, exception, success, incident, food, pay, water, comments*

(adapted from Davies, 2008–)

## 12.3 Multi-Word Prepositions

Prepositions also occur naturally in English in two- and three-word sequences. Quirk et al. (1985, pp. 669–671) refer to these as *complex prepositions*.

We indicate later a handful of multi-word prepositions, and we will revisit them again as conjunctions, connecting phrases, or logical connectors (see Chapter 14) and adverbials (see Chapter 15). As you will see, even within these longer strings of words, the core conceptual meaning of each preposition is still discernible in the abstract uses of each preposition in the string.

**Connecting phrases that contain prepositions:**

*of* preceding the noun or NP: **because of** <u>illness</u>, **by means of** <u>physical force</u>, **in the hope(s) of** <u>reducing costs</u>

Examples: because of, in the hope(s) of, instead of, by means of, on account of, on the basis of, with the exception of

*to* preceding the noun or NP: **in reference to** <u>your memo</u>, **in addition to** <u>the company's assets</u>

Examples: in addition to, according to, with respect to, due to

**Adverbial phrases that contain prepositions:**

as logical connectors and stance markers with *in* or *on*
Examples: **in** other words, **in** fact, **in** any case, **on** the contrary
as adverbs of time with *in*, *before*, *by*, *until*, *around*
Examples: **in** less than a week, **before** sunrise, **until** noon, **around** dusk

---

## Mini Review and Practice

1   As we have observed, the meaning of prepositions extends outward from the domain of the physical and concrete to more abstract conceptual domains. Here you'll find two sets of sentence pairs or triplets. Using the basic graphic for the core conceptual meanings of *over* and *under*, explain the process of meaning shift in each sentence pair:

   a   Bennett *drove* **over** <u>broken glass</u> and got a flat tire.
   b   Bennett *drove* **over** <u>the speed limit</u> and got a ticket.

   a   Nathan *drove* **under** <u>a canopy of elm trees</u> to get to Molly's house.
   b   Nathan *drove* **under** <u>the speed limit</u> because of road construction.
   c   If you *drive* **under** <u>the influence of alcohol</u>, you can be fined up to $1,000.00.

2   What is the ambiguity in the meaning of these two sentences with preposition *as*? That is, there are at least two ways to understand them. Describe the possible interpretations of each.

   Lisa had been stubborn **as** <u>a teenager</u>.
   Hunter was stubborn **as** <u>a child</u>.

Why does the preposition *as* lend itself to this type of ambiguity? Who are the possible referents of the NPs "a teenager" and "a child"?

3   Describe the differences in meaning between *like* and *as* using the following sentence pair:

   **Like** <u>good educators</u>, we must teach students how to think, not what to think.
   **As** <u>good educators</u>, we must teach students how to think, not what to think.

Is there a major difference in meaning?

Now, think about the advertising slogan or tagline for State Farm insurance company:

   LIKE A GOOD NEIGHBOR, STATE FARM IS THERE.

How would the meaning change if the tagline read:

**AS** A GOOD NEIGHBOR, STATE FARM IS THERE.

4 Think about the meanings of the prepositions *as*, *for*, and *like*. The meanings of these prepositions can all be related to either the identity of something or the purpose of something.

How do the following scenarios differ, simply by virtue of preposition choice?

We just bought a lovely lace piece at Claeys in Belgium.

a   Wafa wants to use it **as** a table runner.
b   Wafa wants to use it **for** a table runner.
c   Wafa wants to use it **like** a table runner.

5 Because of the range of meanings that prepositions evoke, they can also serve as stance indicators.

How would a speaker's or writer's stance differ with respect to an interactional scene just by virtue of a shift in prepositions?

To talk **to** someone
To talk **with** someone
To talk **at** someone
To bring an issue up **to** someone
To bring an issue up **with** someone

6 Meanings of *with* and *without*

The prepositions *with* and *without* form a natural pair, whereby one signals the concept of *link* and the other *linkless*. These two prepositions appear to express *polar opposite* notions. And in some ways, they do. But in other ways, especially in terms of some of the assumptions underlying their meanings, they are not exact polar opposites of each other.

The words that tend to co-occur with each are listed again here:

With: (V + *with*)
**Verbs:** *mix, combine, do, associate, deal, fill, work, agree, disagree, compare, charge, start, end, stay, live, meet, go, cover, begin, come, compete, play, speak, work* (adapted from Davies, 2008–)

Without:
**Verbs** (V + *without*): *do, live, be, go, leave, work, survive, make, pass, exist, happen*
**Nouns** (*without* + noun): *warning, question, fear, regard, hesitation, disabilities, thinking, power, parole, permission, exception, success, incident, food, pay, water, comments* (adapted from Davies, 2008–)

By virtue of these simplified collocation patterns, think about some of the assumptions underlying the meanings of the prepositions *with* and *without*. That is, analyze the verbs that typically co-occur with each. Do the verb patterns for *with* seem to be similar to those for *without*?

Let's start with some recipe data to help stimulate your thinking. In the A versions, we provide various recipe titles that contain the preposition *with*:

### A1. Recipe titles with *with*

Pork chops **with** collard greens
Marinara sauce **with** basil
Blueberry waffles **with** blueberry sauce

### A2. More recipe titles with *with*

Waffles **with** ham and cheese
Tacos **with** pineapple
Vanilla ice cream **with** chili powder

### B1. Recipe titles with *without*

Chili **without** beans
Refried beans **without** the refry
Pizza **without** the red source
Tomato salsa **without** onions
Black bean hummus **without** tahini

(Allrecipes.com, n.d.)

### B2. More examples with *without*

Of course we can live **without** our cell phones or the internet, but it's not easy.
Residents are not permitted to have guests in their dorm rooms **without** prior permission.
"A day **without** _____ is like a day **without** sunshine."

(You can fill in the blank)

So, while *with* means *link* and *without* means *linkless*, what do you see as the assumption underlying *without* that does not seem to hold for *with*? (Use the set of recipes in A2 with the preposition *with* as a clue. Do you normally expect chili powder in an ice cream recipe? How about pineapples in tacos?)

7  Art Beyond Sight (Rojas-Sebesta & Axel, n.d.) is a website designed for persons who are visually impaired. Among other features, it provides audio materials that describe famous paintings, sculptures, architecture, and historical sites, for public use as well as for art museums and other institutions.

Describing the designs in paintings, photographs, buildings, and sculptures is also an excellent way to work linguistically with spatial orientations.

The following excerpt is from Art Beyond Sight's Verbal Description Database for *The Red Studio* by Henri Matisse (The Red Studio, n.d.), followed by an excerpt from the description of the Hans Christian Andersen sculpture that can be found in Central Park in New York City.

### *The Red Studio*—painting by Henri Matisse

Paintings and frames are propped **against** the walls, sculptures rest **on** stools, and compositions hang **at** various heights **throughout** the room. Most striking is the color. Matisse floods the canvas **with** red: a deep, rich red, **like** tomato soup. The walls are red; the floor is red. Even the furniture appears just **as** outlines **against** the red background.

(The Red Studio, n.d.)

### Central Park bronze sculpture of Hans Christian Andersen by sculptor, George Lober

The setting: . . . You'll find the sculpture **of** Hans Christian Andersen **on** the West side **of** the conservatory pond. That's a small-like pond **for** ducks and sailboats **with** children pulling them. . . . The sculpture is set **within** a half-circle **of** space carved **out of** the trees and the green **of** the park. . . . **Near** the back **of** the half-circle, Hans Christian Andersen sits **on** a rose marble bench facing the pond. There are benches **for** visitors **along** the sides **of** the sculpture.

(Hans Christian Anderson sculpture, n.d.)

Analyze all of the prepositions in the two excerpts. Some we have covered here. You will find that there are also a number of prepositions that we did not cover in this chapter (i.e., *throughout, against, within, near, along*). Try to determine a core conceptual meaning for each. Then, draw a diagram that captures the basic conceptual meaning that you propose. Find discourse-based examples that illustrate the uses of these prepositions that begin first within the domain of concrete space and then extend beyond the physical domain into the more abstract domains of time and metaphor.

Find a photo of each piece of art and continue to describe each in more detail, paying special attention to prepositions and adjectives. For the Hans Christian Andersen statue, you will see that he is reading a book and there is a bronze duck next to him. What is the significance of the duck? (You may need to do some research about the stories that Andersen wrote in order to better understand the details surrounding this piece of art.)

8  Similar to the previous exercise, here we provide excerpts from two pieces of writing. The first is from *The House on Mango Street* (Cisneros, 1984), and the second from a non-fiction book, *Curious Behavior* (Provine, 2012), on the phenomenon of yawning. Robert Provine is a professor of psychology and neuroscience at the University of Maryland, Baltimore County.

**384** *Prepositions and Phrasal Verbs*

We have removed the prepositions. Fill in the blanks from the list of missing prepositions given after each excerpt. Again, there may be cases where more than one preposition is possible. The actual texts can be found at the end of this section. Compare and contrast your answers with the actual text. In the cases where more than one preposition is possible, explain how the meaning changes by virtue of the core conceptual meaning of each preposition.

a  *The House on Mango Street*

*Mamacita* is the . . . mama ___ the man ___ the street. . . .
The man saved his money to bring her here. He saved and saved because she was alone _____ the baby boy _____ that country.
Then one day *Mamacita* and the baby boy arrived _____ a yellow taxi. . . .
Out stepped a little pink shoe, a foot soft _____ a rabbit's ear. . . .
All ___ once she bloomed. Huge, enormous, beautiful . . . _____ the salmon-pink feather _____ the tip _____ her hat down _____ the little rosebuds ___ her toes.
I couldn't take my eyes ___ her tiny shoes. . . .
Whatever her reasons, whether . . . she can't climb the stairs . . . or is afraid ____ English, she won't come down. She sits all day _____ the window and plays the Spanish radio show and sings all the homesick songs _____ her country ___ a voice that sounds _____ a seagull.

(Cisneros, 1984, pp. 76–77)

[Prepositions: as, by, off, on, from, at, across, with, like, about, to, in, of]

b  *Curious Behavior*

We steer our body ____ life's straits and shoals, walking, working, talking, speeding up and slowing down, avoiding obstacles. We are captains ___ our ship, alert, confident, and rational. That is the illusion. But what if we are deceived ___ our brain's subtle whispers, its effort, as ___ dreams, to weave a coherent sometimes faulty narrative ___ irrational events? Are we instead unthinking herd animals, driven ___ subconscious instincts, acting ___ our species' ancient biological script? Pursuit___ this theme requires rethinking the human condition and turning history ___ its head, immodest goals ___ a chapter ___ yawning. We will settle instead ___ revealing chinks ___ our neurologically generated, virtual edifice ___ daily life. Turning history ___ its head must wait ___another day.

Imagine the face ___ a yawning person, ___ gaping jaws, squinting eyes, and long inhalation followed ___ a shorter outward breath. Ahh. This visual stimulus hijacks your body and induces you to replicate the observed behavior. As many readers have noticed, the contagiousness ___ yawns is so potent that simply discussing yawns triggers yawns. Contagious yawns occur automatically, ___ any desire to imitate a yawner. When you see someone yawn, do you think, "I want to yawn just ___ that person?"

(Provine, 2012, pp. 13–14)

[Prepositions: for, like, of, from, on, out, with, without, through, about, in, by]

As you work through these texts, what kinds of imageries come to mind as you attempt to fill in the blanks with prepositions? Do you find any instances where prepositions other than the ones that were actually used are also possible? How does the meaning change?

For example, from the Cisenros descriptive excerpt:

"He saved and saved because she was alone ____ (1) the baby boy ____ (2) that country." For the first preposition, *with* is a likely choice.

It is the blank for the second preposition that has the potential to significantly change the meaning:

Original: She was alone *with* the baby boy *in* that country.
Variations: . . . the baby boy *from* that country, *of* that country

The preposition *in* portrays the two as being together there for a long time, if not forever. It modifies **the living situation** of *Mamacita* having been living alone *with* just her baby (and no other family) in their country. As we can see, the phrase *in that country* functions as an adverbial (see Chapter 15).

She **was alone** *with* the baby boy *in* **that country**. [adverbial]

In contrast, the proposition *from*, in *the baby boy from that country*, now modifies **the baby boy**: *the baby boy [who was] from that country*. The phrase *from that country* in this example is functioning as an adjective (see Chapter 13).

This seemingly simple change in preposition also evokes a significant change in the relationship between the two people. Explain why this is so.

She was alone *with* the baby boy *from* **that country**. [adjective]

Other blanks in the excerpt can be filled with prepositions beyond those used in the original, including the following (though there are many more):

. . . a foot soft _____ a rabbit's ear. (*as, like*)
She sits all day _____ the window. (*by, near, next to, across from, in front of*)

Think about how the conceptual meanings of prepositions change the imagery of the story, either with significant shifts in meaning as in *She was alone with the baby boy* **in/from** *that country* or more subtle ones as in . . . *a foot soft* **as/like** *a rabbit's ear*.

Do this for all of the prepositions in both passages (i.e., *The House on Mango Street* and *Curious Behavior*). In some cases, only one preposition is possible, for example, the formulaic metaphorical expression of time: *All* **at** *once* and *she . . . is afraid* **of** *English*. In other cases, multiple selections are possible.

Think about conceptual imageries of prepositions and how they create and shape meaning in discourse.

9 Here you will find a quote by Norman Maclean, from his beautifully written autobiography (and later a movie of the same title) *A River Runs Through It*. The quote, an extended metaphor, sums up Maclean's life and appears as the final two paragraphs of the piece.

Read the quote. Without having read the novel or watched the film, it will be difficult to sense the true power of these words as they relate to Maclean's life, but you can still draw out the main ideas, or you can consider it as a snippet of poetry.

> Eventually, all things merge into one, and a river runs through it. The river was cut by the world's great flood and runs over rocks from the basement of time. On some of the rocks are timeless raindrops. Under the rocks are the words, and some of the words are theirs.
> I am haunted by waters.
>
> (Maclean, 1976)

What are the main images in the quote? How does Maclean establish those images? You can examine his use of nouns (including repetitions of nouns), determiners, pronouns, verbs (transitive/intransitive), voice (where is passive voice used?), and prepositions as you think about how he constructed this final commentary on life in general and on his life in particular.

From the standpoint of grammar and conceptualization, what do you notice about his use of transitive and intransitive verbs (which are transitive, and which are intransitive?) and nouns, especially repetitions of nouns and the final noun *waters*? Explain his use of *waters* using the concepts from Chapter 3. How does he use the pronouns *one*, *it*, and *theirs*?

**Original Text:** *The House on Mango Street*

> *Mamacita* is the . . . mama of the man across the street. . . .
>
> The man saved his money to bring her here. He saved and saved because she was alone with the baby boy in that country.
>
> Then one day *Mamacita* and the baby boy arrived in a yellow taxi. . . .
>
> Out stepped a little pink shoe, a foot soft as a rabbit's ear. . . .
>
> All at once she bloomed. Huge, enormous, beautiful . . . from the salmon-pink feather on the tip of her hat down to the little rosebuds of her toes. I couldn't take my eyes off her tiny shoes. . . .
>
> Whatever her reasons, whether . . . she can't climb the stairs . . . or is afraid of English, she won't come down. She sits all day by the window and plays the Spanish radio show and sings all the homesick songs about her country in a voice that sounds like a seagull.
>
> (Cisneros, 1984)

**Original Text:** *Curious Behavior*

> We steer our body through life's straits and shoals, walking, working, talking, speeding up and slowing down, avoiding obstacles. We are captains of our ship, alert, confident,

and rational. That is the illusion. But what if we are deceived by our brain's subtle whispers, its effort, as in dreams, to weave a coherent sometimes faulty narrative from irrational events? Are we instead unthinking herd animals, driven by subconscious instincts, acting out our species' ancient biological script? Pursuit of this theme requires rethinking the human condition and turning history on its head, immodest goals for a chapter about yawning. We will settle instead for revealing chinks in our neurologically generated, virtual edifice of daily life. Turning history on its head must wait for another day.

Imagine the face of a yawning person, with gaping jaws, squinting eyes, and long inhalation followed by a shorter outward breath. Ahh. This visual stimulus hijacks your body and induces you to replicate the observed behavior. As many readers have noticed, the contagiousness of yawns is so potent that simply discussing yawns triggers yawns. Contagious yawns occur automatically, without any desire to imitate a yawner. When you see someone yawn, do you think, "I want to yawn just like that person?"

(Provine, 2012)

## 12.4 From Prepositions to Phrasal Verbs

Phrasal verbs look very much like a verb + preposition (or adverb) construction. Phrasal verbs differ from the verb + preposition (or adverb) construction in a number of ways:

- The meanings of phrasal verbs cannot be broken down into the literal meaning of the verb plus the literal meaning of the preposition (or adverb) (Jackendoff, 1997).
- This meaning shift is due to the more abstract/figurative meanings taken on by both the verb and the particle (so-called, because it is no longer a preposition or an adverb).
- Phrasal verbs indicate such concepts as *directionality, aspect* (e.g., *completive, continuative*), *register* (i.e., *more informal, typically less technical*) (Biber et al., 1999; Gardner & Davies, 2007; Liu, 2011).

Phrasal verbs are said to be "idiomatic" (Boers, 2004), which is true, on the one hand, and somewhat untrue, on the other.

While phrasal verbs do indeed express actions that cannot be expressed through a literal description of the verb plus the particle with which it co-occurs, their meanings are not at all as arbitrary and possibly not as "idiomatic" as they are said to be in the literature and reference grammars. That is, for every phrasal verb particle that was once a preposition or adverb, its abstract, figurative meaning is still traceable to the core conceptual meaning of that word as represented in concrete space.

Here are a few examples to illustrate, using *on*:

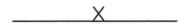

*Figure 12.28 on*: contact with a surface

From Strauss, Chang, and Yoon (forthcoming)

### Verb (carry) + Preposition <u>on</u> [concrete]

TSA (Transportation Security Administration) Rules: What Can I *Carry* **On** A Plane?
(Mathias, n.d.)

### Phrasal Verb: carry on [abstract]

The Pernod kids will all be lawyers. They want to **carry on** the family tradition
phrasal verb: <u>**carry on**</u> = to continue  [abstract]

*On* as a preposition signals the most basic meaning of *contact with a surface* (Figure 12.28).

From a temporal and aspectual perspective, *on* used as a phrasal verb particle typically signals *continuative aspect*, where the notion of "continuation" derives from the physical sense of "continuous contact with surface" (Figure 12.29).

Other examples of phrasal verbs with *on* signaling continuative aspect include:

| | |
|---|---|
| get on with | continue doing s.t. |
| keep on | continue doing s.t. |
| play on | continue playing |
| read on | continue reading |
| press on | continue doing s.t. |
| hang on | continue doing s.t., persevere |
| push on | continue doing s.t., persevere |
| drag on | continue for longer than one would like |
| urge on | encourage s.o. to continue doing s.t. |

These are considered *phrasal verbs* and not verb + preposition or verb + adverb, because both parts of this construction are necessary to evoke the meaning. Expressions like *urge on, push on, press on, play on* (i.e., keep playing), and *read on* (i.e., keep reading) are more emphatic expressions than their single-word lexical verb counterparts—*urge, push, press, play,* and *read*—and their meanings all evoke the notion of *continuation*.

Let's look at *press on* within multiple domains of meaning:

| | |
|---|---|
| If you *press* **on** *the gas pedal*, the car will move. | [concrete—V + prep] |
| Attorney Jones *pressed* Smith **on** his whereabouts on May 22. | [abstract—V + prep] |
| You are almost there! Don't give up. You must **press on**. | [abstract: **phrasal verb**] |

*Figure 12.29 on* as a phrasal verb particle: continuative aspect, continuous metaphorical contact
From Strauss, Chang, and Yoon (forthcoming)

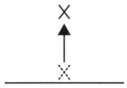

*Figure 12.30 off:* disconnect from surface

*Figure 12.31 off* as a phrasal verb particle: completive aspect—complete metaphorical disconnect

From Strauss, Chang, and Yoon (forthcoming)

We can illustrate similar patterns with the preposition *off*, used as a preposition in the concrete and abstract domains of meaning and as a particle in phrasal verb constructions. The examples illustrate the use of *took off* as a verb + preposition construction and then as a phrasal verb. In each case, note that the core conceptual meaning for *off* is still discernible even in the most abstract, figurative phrasal verb expressions (Figure 12.30).

*Off* used as a preposition and as a phrasal verb particle retains its core conceptual meaning of *disconnect from a surface*.

| | |
|---|---|
| Ezekiel *took* **off** <u>his jacket</u> and poured himself some lemonade. | [concrete—V + prep] |
| Pan was warned because he *took* **off** <u>too much time during the holidays</u>. | [abstract—V + prep] |
| United Airlines Flight 322 **took off** on schedule this morning. | [abstract: **phrasal verb**] |
| The carjacker **took off** before anyone could identify him.<br>[ran away—from the location and out of sight] | [abstract: **phrasal verb**] |
| Pokémon Go **took off** like a rocket in the summer of 2016.<br>[became very successful] | [abstract: **phrasal verb**] |

And the same conceptual meaning is evident in the following (and other) phrasal verbs with *off*. Note that in each case, there is either a focus on a change of state in the form of *disconnect from a current surface/state*, either emphasizing the end point of that change (e.g., *call off, pay off, write off, write off*) or the initial stage of that change (e.g., *doze off, set off, go off, kick off*). These expressions signal a type of *completive aspect*, designating that an action or event has taken place "thoroughly and to completion," or its incipient state has commenced "and is complete" (Bybee et al., 1994). These expressions evoke conceptual notions of totality, complete separation, complete removal, complete disappearance, and complete change from one state to another (*doze off, nod off, set off*, etc.) (Figure 12.31).

| | |
|---|---|
| call off | cancel |
| pay off | pay completely (to the end) |
| write off | cancel an account, subtract |
| sign off | agree to in full |
| drift off | to move away from, to fall asleep (to separate from state of being awake) |
| doze off | fall asleep (to separate from state of being awake) |
| nod off | fall asleep (to separate from state of being awake) |
| dry off | remove moisture completely from a surface |

wipe off        remove something from a surface completely
go off          explode (separate from a surface)
cut off         detach
kick off        begin
throw off       to stop s.t. from happening by leading astray, confounding
take off        leave the runway, succeed
set off         initiate

Other phrasal verb constructions that signal various characteristics of *completive aspect* include those formed with *out*, *away*, and *up*.

**Examples of phrasal verbs with *out* (Figure 12.32):**

call out        reprimand for a wrongdoing
pull out        leave, sever oneself from
write out       write something completely (i.e., not abbreviatedly)
dry out         dry completely
wipe out        take away completely, to erase, to annihilate
turn out        result in, produce
tire out        to get completely tired or to tire completely
sell out        to sell everything and have no items left
flicker out     to become extinguished, dark; focus on the end of the process
go out          (lights, candle) to become dark, to become extinguished

**Examples of phrasal verbs with *up* (Figure 12.33):**

burn up         to burn completely, to become very warm
eat up          to eat completely
tear up         to rip, tear completely
stir up         to mix completely, to incite
break up        to separate completely (into pieces)
give up         to become completely discouraged and stop
show up         to appear—with a focus on the end point of the appearance
blow up         to explode completely
come up with    to invent using mental processes, focus on the end point

*Figure 12.32 out:* beyond an enclosure; *out* as a phrasal verb particle: completive aspect, completely beyond metaphorical enclosure

*Figure 12.33 up:* toward a higher vertical position (as a preposition or adverb); *up* as a phrasal verb particle: completely, to the extreme metaphorical upper limit

*Figure 12.34 down:* toward a lower vertical position (as a preposition or adverb); *down* as a phrasal verb particle: completive aspect, to the extreme metaphorical lower limit as a gradual process

**Examples of phrasal verbs with *down* (Figure 12.34):**

| | |
|---|---|
| hold down | to apply pressure onto something completely |
| quiet down | to reduce noise completely, yet gradually |
| shut down | to stop an operation with force or authority, completely |
| take down | to remove from, to cause failure of, completely |
| cool down | to reduce in temperature, completely yet gradually |
| calm down | to reduce anger or anxiety, completely yet gradually |
| chase down | to run after, to follow and ultimately catch |
| melt down | to move to a liquid state, completely yet gradually |

## 12.5 Prepositions and Verbs That Often Combine Into Phrasal Verb Constructions

The meanings of phrasal verbs can be traced back to the meanings of the prepositions from which the phrasal verb particles evolved. And because those core meanings are still quite transparent within the phrasal verbs in general and the particles in particular, it should not be at all necessary to memorize endless lists of phrasal verb constructions.

In this section, we provide collections of prepositions that commonly transform into phrasal verb particles in addition to collections of verbs that commonly become full phrasal verb expressions.

First, read through the list of prepositions, and think about the core conceptual meanings for each. In the cases of prepositions for which we did not provide graphic representations, try to design your own, starting with the domain of concrete space, and then alter the graphic slightly to reflect a more abstract sense as the word is used as a phrasal verb particle.

**Prepositions that often become phrasal verb particles**

in, on, off, out, up, down, over, through, around, about, along, apart, after, away, by, into

**Verbs that often serve as phrasal verbs with a wide variety of particles**

go: go in, go on, go off, go out, go up, go down, go over, go through, go around, go about, go along, go after, go away, go by, go into

| | |
|---|---|
| get: | get in, get on, get off, get out, get up, get down, get over, get through, get around, get after, get away, get by, get into |
| turn: | turn in, turn on, turn off, turn out, turn up, turn down, turn over, turn around, turn about, turn away, turn into |
| take: | take in, take on, take off, take out, take up, take down, take over, take along, take apart, take after, take away |
| blow: | blow in, blow off, blow out, blow up, blow over, blow through, blow around, blow apart, blow away |
| stand: | stand in, stand on, stand off, stand out, stand up, stand down, stand around, stand about, stand by |
| break: | break in, break off, break out, break up, break down, breath through, break apart, break into |
| play: | play on, play off, play out, play up, play down, play over, play around, play along, play into |
| carry: | carry on, carry off, carry out, carry over, carry through, carry around, carry away |
| burn: | burn on, burn off, burn out, burn up, burn down, burn through, burn apart, burn away |
| run: | run on, run off, run up, run down, run over, run through, run around, run about, run along, run apart, run after, run away, run by, run into |
| pass: | pass off, pass out, pass up, pass over, pass through, pass around, pass away |
| cut: | cut in, cut off, cut out, cut up, cut down, cut through, cut away, cut into |
| show: | show off, show up, show down, show through, show around |
| give: | give in, give off, give up, give away, give into |
| hang: | hang on, hang up, hang around, hang about |
| hold: | hold on, hold off, hold out, hold up, hold down, hold over |
| grow: | grow out, grow up, |
| try: | try on, try out |
| make: | make off, make out, make up |
| fill: | fill out, fill up, fill into |

Let's examine a few examples of verb + preposition and phrasal verb constructions to see how the meanings change from the domain of the physical and concrete to the domain of the abstract and metaphorical.

### 12.5.1 Fall Through (Figure 12.35)

The dresser *fell* **through** the plywood floor because it was weakened by water damage.
        [concrete: verb *fell* + preposition **through**]

Hazel was hoping to buy a new car this year, but her loan **fell through** at the last minute.
        [phrasal verb: *fall through:* to fail after prolonged attempts]

### 12.5.2 Stand By (Figure 12.36)

To better engage with your audience, you should *stand* **by** the podium, not behind it.
        [concrete: verb *stand* + preposition **by**]

The candidate assured the public that he will ***stand*** **by** every word that he uttered in his speech.
        [phrasal verb: *stand by* = support, maintain]

The press was **standing by** as the crew prepared the secretary's mike for the conference.
        [phrasal verb: *stand by* = wait in readiness to act, be in *pause* mode]

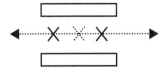

*Figure 12.35 through* as a preposition: movement traversing an entire trajectory within an enclosure or partial enclosure; *through* as a phrasal verb particle: movement traversing a metaphorical trajectory within an enclosure or partial enclosure

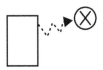

*Figure 12.36 by:* as a preposition: connection to a place, an action, an idea; *by* as a phrasal verb particle: metaphorical connection to a place, an action, an idea, a duration

### 12.5.3 Run After (Figure 12.37 on the next page)

George will run first. You can *run* **after** him.
[concrete: verb *run* + preposition **after**]

Mercedes tried to **run after** the thief who snatched her purse, but he got away.
[phrasal verb: *run after* = pursue, chase]

\*\*\*\*\*\*\*\*

### PRACTICE WITH DATA ANALYSIS: PUTTING IT ALL TOGETHER

1   Think about phrasal verb particles that evoke completive aspect, like *up*, *away*, *out*, and *off*. It might help to pinpoint the various meanings of these particles by analyzing their occurrences with the identical lexical verb. Let's try it with the verb *wipe*:

   wipe up, wipe off, wipe out, wipe away

In what situation or context would each be used? How could you articulate the differences in meaning for each phrasal verb?

2   Think about *up* as a phrasal verb particle. It occurs in many expressions:

   clean up, clear up, mess up, end up, show up, write up, play up, blow up, get up, call up.

We also find *up* as a phrasal verb particle in instances of conversion, whereby a noun takes on the meaning of a verb:

   lather up, soap up, queue up, gas up, mike (from *microphone*) up

These expressions are in addition to others such as *man up* and *lawyer up*. What is *up* doing here, especially as it is used with a noun, the whole of which is converted to a phrasal verb? What element of meaning does *up* contribute to these expressions?

*Figure 12.37 after* as a preposition: sequentially next, following; *after* as a phrasal verb particle: metaphorical sequence of next or following

How about these advertising taglines by Jell-O?

> Fun it Up
> Fun Things Up

In addition to the use of the particle *up*, what types of grammatical creativity come into play in these taglines? Think about the traditional notion of *parts of speech* as you formulate your responses.

3  What do you think is the difference between *write it up* and *write it down*?

As you work on answering this question, think about as many contexts as possible in which you might use each expression. (Hint: The notion of verticality will not gain you much mileage.)

This is not an easy question, so do try to find as many examples and potential contexts or scenarios as possible so that you can provide a design a solid and well-thought-out response.

4  The following plot overview of William Golding's classic allegorical 1954 novel *Lord of the Flies* contains a number of prepositions and a handful of phrasal verbs. The target forms appear in bold. Make a list of the prepositions, and indicate whether they evoke concrete space or more abstract domains of meaning. Identify the phrasal verbs. Discuss how the meanings of each phrasal verb particle can be traced back to the core conceptual meaning of its prepositional use.

> **In** the midst of a raging war, a plane evacuating a group of schoolboys **from** Britain is shot down **over** a deserted tropical island. Two **of** the boys, Ralph and Piggy, discover a conch shell **on** the beach, and Piggy realizes it could be used **as** a horn to summon the other boys. Once assembled, the boys **set about** electing a leader and devising a way to be rescued. They choose Ralph **as** their leader, and Ralph appoints another boy, Jack, to be **in** charge **of** the boys who will hunt food **for** the entire group.
>
> Ralph, Jack, and another boy, Simon, **set off on** an expedition to explore the island. When they return, Ralph declares that they must light a signal fire to attract the attention **of** passing ships. The boys succeed **in** igniting some dead wood **by** focusing sunlight **through** the lenses **of** Piggy's eyeglasses. However, the boys pay more attention **to** playing **than to** monitoring the fire, and the flames quickly engulf the forest. A large swath **of** dead wood burns **out of** control, and one **of** the youngest boys in the group disappears, presumably having burned **to** death.
>
> ("*Lord of the Flies*–plot summary," n.d.)

5  The following excerpt is from James McBride's best-selling (1996/2006) autobiography, *The Color of Water: A Black Man's Tribute to His White Mother*. The writing contains a number of grammatical constructions that we have addressed thus far: sentence types (simple, compound, complex); ellipsis; reference (multiple ways of naming entities in discourse—nouns, noun phrases, pronouns); nouns (Type 1 and Type 2); determiners; verbs (transitive,

intransitive, ditransitive); tense, aspect, and modality (especially simple past and modals *would* and *could*); negation (full form, contracted, *never*); and contrast/juxtaposition. Of course, it also contains prepositions and phrasal verbs.

Read through the text to see how various categories of grammar work together to create this past time narrative of McBride's memory. Here, we can envision the scene, recounted as an adult, but through the eyes or perspective of a child.

As you work through the text with this goal in mind, also attend to all prepositions and phrasal verbs. List the prepositions. List the phrasal verbs. Again, how do the phrasal verb particles reflect the meanings of the words as prepositions? How do these phrasal verbs contribute to the narrative as discussed in the introductory paragraph?

> Ma often lamented the fact that she could not afford to buy us fruit, sometimes for weeks at a time, but we didn't mind. We spent every penny we had on junk food. "If you eat that stuff your teeth will drop out," Mommy warned. We ignored her. "If you chew gum and swallow it, your behind will close up," she said. We listened and never swallowed gum. We learned to eat standing up, sitting down, lying down, and half asleep, because there were never enough places at the table for everyone to sit, and there was always a mad scramble for Ma's purse when she showed up at two A.M. from work. The cafeteria at the Chase Manhattan Bank where she worked served dinner to the employees for free, so she would load up with bologna sandwiches, cheese, cakes, whatever she could pillage, and bring it home for the hordes to devour. If you were the first to grab the purse when she got home, you ate. If you missed it, well, sleep tight.
> (McBride, 1996/2006)

6 Here is a headline from CNN.com about James Comey, the FBI director who was fired by Donald Trump in the midst of the 2017 investigation into the Trump administration's involvement in possible deals with Russia:

> COMEY MAY FIND HIMSELF BOXED IN . . . BY HIMSELF.
> (Callan, 2017)

What is the phrasal verb here?

How does Callan play with the reflexive (i.e., himself) and passive voice? That is, there is a double meaning of the phrase *by himself*. How is that meaning achieved through grammar?

## COMMON ERRORS, BUMPS, AND CONFUSIONS

Identify the errors or "bumps" in the following sentences or paragraphs. Use the concepts and terminology that you learned in this and other chapters to articulate what might be grammatically or pragmatically problematic. Suggest ways that each can be re-written more clearly and more accurately. (Note: While all bumps do involve some element of prepositions and phrasal verbs, they are not limited to only that.)

1 This car is not for sell.
2 Where are you at right now?
3 Xander need to repay to his boss for the money he borrowed him.
4 Let me know if this is something you want to be apart of.
5 Do you have an idea regarding where you are going to?
6 The CEO will talk on collaboration and ways to bringing more business with company.

396  *Prepositions and Phrasal Verbs*

7  My parents look forward meet you on next week when you coming by our house.

8  Kids nowadays do not acknowledge for the hard work their parents did to them.

9  From peer review, I learned to look in my essay with different point from view.

10  We walk and walk about the park one hour but never find out my lost bracelet.

## SUGGESTED ACTIVITIES

1  Have a look at the caption for Figure 12.38. The woman's words make a strong connection between the food items piled on the table and their health value.

Cover up the caption and view the cartoon without words. Now, invent your own caption so that it fits the drawing but expresses content that is completely different from what you see in the caption. That is, think of a humorous line that the woman can utter to the man that explains why she has that pile of food on the table. Invent a few captions, and have the class share their responses. You can also turn this activity into a "re-write the caption contest" and have the entire class (or teams) compete to write the best caption, voted on by a team of judges.

2  In an earlier section, we presented descriptions of pieces of art, written especially for persons with visual impairments (Matisse's *The Red Studio* and the Hans Christian Andersen sculpture in New York's Central Park).

Do the same activity, this time composing your own verbal description of Hokusai's world-famous woodblock print (*ukiyo-e*) *The Great Wave Off Kanagawa*. As you work through the

"I'm supposed to eat kale for smoother skin, turkey for stronger nails, fish for thinner thighs, oats for cardiovascular benefits, cabbage for leaner abdominals, salmon for softer hair, beets for a healthier colon, steak for muscle tone, blueberries for lower cholesterol, pasta for greater endurance, cheese for younger teeth and bones ...."

*Figure 12.38* "I'm supposed to eat kale for smother skin, turkey for stronger nails, fish for thinner thighs, oats for cardiovascular benefits...."

© Randy Glasbergen. Reproduced with permission of Glasbergen Cartoon Service.

task, pay attention to the categories of grammar that you need to use as you compose this description (in addition to prepositions and phrasal verbs).

3   This is a game idea to practice the meanings of phrasal verbs and also to get a sense of register, by comparing a phrasal verb construction to possible lexical verbs (i.e., one-word verbs) that may have similar conceptual meanings (e.g., *eat up* and *devour*).

Make a list of 50 (or more) phrasal verbs, making sure to use a variety of phrasal verb particles. Then, think of one or two lexical verbs that best correspond to the basic meaning of that phrasal verb. Using note cards (e.g., 3" × 5" cards), write the phrasal verb on one side and the lexical verb(s) on the other.

Divide the class into teams, and turn the activity into a competition. One team will read either the phrasal verb or the lexical verb aloud, and the other team needs to try to guess the target word.

For register, students can invent sentences using the phrasal verb and then using the lexical verb and consider such discursive features as genre and audience. In what types of contexts might the phrasal verb expression work better than the lexical verb? In what types of contexts might the lexical verb work better than the phrasal verb? Why?

4   Prepositions in slogans or taglines

We find taglines in many areas of public discourse: Corporations have taglines that we often hear in advertising. Universities have them, as do cities, towns, and charitable foundations.
In the following selection of taglines, the A group contains taglines from a number of charitable foundations. Think about how prepositions enhance the meanings of the taglines for each organization. First, find the organization that is represented by each slogan by searching the internet. Then, think about the meanings of the prepositions and how they relate to the foundation's goals. Are there multiple meanings at play in any of the prepositions?

   a   **Charitable foundations:**

       Don't Die of Ignorance
       The Power of Humanity
       Be Part of a Change in the World.
       Believe in Tomorrow.
       Don't Turn Your Back to Those in Need.
       Don't Turn Your Back on Those in Need.
       Empowering the youth for a better tomorrow
       Lifting up with hands of help.
       No one has ever become poor by giving.
       Turn up the pink
       Get your pink on
       Race for the cure
       We run for hope
       Join us in the fight

You can do the same with the B group that lists slogans of US cities. This time, first match the slogan in the left-hand column with the city and state in the right-hand column. Determine why each city has that slogan. How do the prepositions enhance the meaning of each city's slogan?

b **Slogans or taglines for US cities**—Matching Game (the column on the left is not the city that corresponds to the column on the right)

| | |
|---|---|
| Always Turned On. | Happy, TX |
| The Sweetest Place on Earth. | Peculiar, MO |
| City With Sol. | Bushnell, SD |
| Where Your Ship Comes In. | Spring Lake, MI |
| Lose Your Heart to the Hills. | Show Low, AZ |
| The Town Without a Frown. | Atlantic City, NJ |
| Where the Stars Come Out to Play. | Saratoga, WY |
| Named for the Turn of a Card. | Kerrville, TX |
| Where Nature Smiles for Seven Miles. | Gravity, IA |
| It's Not the End of the Earth, But You Can See It From Here. | San Diego, CA |
| Where the "Odds" Are With You | Moscow, ME |
| Where the Trout Leap in Main Street. | Fort Davis, TX |
| Best Town by a Dam Site. | Hershey, PA |
| We're down to earth. If gravity goes, we all go. | Gulfport, MS |

("15 Delightful. . .," n.d.; "U.S. city motto & moniker list," n.d.)

As you work with the slogans in a and b, also pay attention to such grammatical features as imperatives, noun types (proper, common, Type 1, Type 2), pronouns, and adjectives (see Chapter 13).

Some of the slogans or taglines might be more transparent than others. Research why/how each city's tagline came about.

5 Class game (or team/pair game) for practice with prepositions—information gap with line drawing activities (Figures 12.39–12.42)

For a class game, ask three volunteers go to the board to make a drawing based on the instructions they will be receiving from their classmates. The three volunteer "artists" will need to keep their backs to the class while the class views the image. Students can take turns providing instructions to the volunteers who are drawing on the board. The images in Figures 12.39 and 12.40 are static. That is, there is no action taking place. Grammatical features for these two descriptions might involve such constructions as *there is/there are*; *you see a* _____; passive voice, for example, *be located*, \_(noun or NP) *is/was placed* _____; and imperatives (*draw a horizontal line . . .*), as well as a wide variety of locational prepositions, such as *to the left of*, *above*, *to the right of*, *next to*, *below*, *about two inches away from*, and *on top of*.

In contrast, the images in Figures 12.41 and 12.42 depict some sort of motion, so in addition to prepositions and the other grammatical categories noted, the activity can also help review verbs as well as tense and aspect (including progressive and possibly perfect). You can use these line drawings or make your own. There are also many line drawings like these that you can find on the internet.

*Figure 12.39* Line drawing for preposition activity #5

*Figure 12.40* Line drawing for preposition activity #5

*Figure 12.41* Line drawing for preposition activity #5

*Figure 12.42* Line drawing for preposition activity #5

## Notes

1 Unlike any other preposition, *to* is also the word that is used for signaling the infinitive form of a verb or phrasal verb (We *plan* **to** *buy land in the countryside*, That *is enough food* **to** *feed the entire state of Maine*, You *have* **to** *stir the hot chocolate powder* into the water, I *used* **to** *be able* **to** *play "Für Elise"* on the piano). While this infinitival use of *to* is not considered a "preposition" *per se* by mainstream grammarians (it is not followed by a noun or NP), note that its meaning as an infinitive marker still evokes the same graphic representation as the core conceptual meaning of the preposition.
2 See Strauss, Yoon, and Chang (forthcoming) for a more detailed discussion of *on* and *off* based on the same basic concepts presented here.
3 See Buescher and Strauss (2015, 2016) for a detailed account of French prepositions *à*, *dans*, and *en* using a similar approach and similar sets of line diagrams.

## Academic References

Biber, D. Johansson, S. Leech, G., Conrad, S., & Finegan, E. (1999). *Longman grammar of spoken and written English*. Halow: Pearson Education.

Boers, F. (2004). Expanding learners' vocabulary through metaphor awareness: What expansion, what learners, what vocabulary? In S. Niemeier & M. Achard (Eds.), *Cognitive linguistics, second language acquisition, and foreign language teaching* (pp. 211–234). Berlin and New York: Mouton de Gruyter.

Buescher, K., & Strauss, S. (2015). A cognitive linguistic analysis of French prepositions *à*, *dans*, and *en* and a sociocultural theoretical approach to teaching them. In K. Masuda, C. Arnett, & A. Labarca (Eds.), *Cognitive linguistics and sociocultural theory: Applications for second and foreign language teaching* (pp. 155–181). Berlin, Germany: Walter de Gruyter.

Buescher, K., & Strauss, S. (2016). A cognitive linguistic analysis of French prepositions à, dans, and en and a sociocultural theoretical approach to teaching them. In L. Ortega, A. Tyler, H. Park, & M. Uno (Eds.), *Usage-inspired L2 instruction: Researched pedagogy*. Amsterdam: John Benjamins.

Bybee, J. L., Perkins, R., & Pagliuca, W. (1994). *The evolution of grammar: Tense, aspect and modality in the languages of the world*. Chicago: The University of Chicago Press.

Carter, R., & McCarthy, M. (2006). *Cambridge grammar of English: A comprehensive guide. Spoken and written English grammar and usage*. Cambridge: Cambridge University Press.

Davies, M. (2008–). *The corpus of contemporary American English (COCA): 520 million words, 1990–present*. Retrieved from http://corpus.byu.edu/coca/.

Gardner, D., & Davies, M. (2007). Pointing out frequent phrasal verbs: A corpus-based analysis. *TESOL Quarterly, 41*(2), 339–359.

Jackendoff, R. (1997). *The architecture of the language faculty*. Cambridge, MA: MIT Press.

Lakoff, G. (1987). *Women, fire and dangerous things: What categories reveal about the mind*. Chicago, IL: Chicago University Press.

Lakoff, G., & Johnson, M. (1980). *Metaphors we live by*. Chicago: University of Chicago.

Langacker, R. W. (1987). *Foundations of cognitive grammar: Vol. 1. Theoretical prerequisites*. Stanford, CA: Stanford University Press.

Langacker, R. W. (2002 [1991]). *Concept, image, and symbol: The cognitive basis of grammar*. Berlin and New York: Mouton de Gruyter.

Larsen-Freeman, D., & Celce-Murcia, M. (2016). *The grammar book: Form, meaning, and use for English language teachers*. Boston, MA: National Geographic and Heinle.

Lindstromberg, S. (2010). *English prepositions explained*. Amsterdam: John Benjamins.

Liu, D. (2011). The most frequently used English phrasal verbs in American and British English: A multicorpus examination. *TESOL Quarterly, 45*(4), 661–688.

Quirk, R., Greenbaum, S., Leech, G., & Svartvik, J. (1985). *A comprehensive grammar of the English language*. New York: Longman.

Radden, G., & Dirven, R. (2007). *Cognitive English grammar*. Philadelphia and Amsterdam: John Benjamins.

Strauss, S., Chang, H., & Yoon, J. (forthcoming). The speech went on (and on) as Kerry dozed off (*and off): A conceptual grammar approach to on and off. In V. Evans & L. Pickering (Eds.), *Language learning discourse and cognition: Studies in the tradition of Andrea Tyler*. Philadelphia: John Benjamins.

Talmy, L. (2000). *Toward a cognitive semantics: Vol. II. Typology and process in concept structuring*. Cambridge, MA: The MIT Press.

Tyler, A., & Evans, V. (2001). Reconsidering prepositional polysemy networks: The case of over. *Language, 77*(4), 724–765.

Tyler, A., & Evans, V. (2003). *The semantics of English prepositions: Spatial scenes, embodied meaning, and cognition*. Cambridge: Cambridge University Press.

Tyler, A., & Evans, V. (2004). Applying cognitive linguistics to pedagogical grammar: The case of over. In M. Achard & S. Niemeier (Eds.), *Cognitive linguistics, second language acquisition, and foreign language teaching* (pp. 257–280). Berlin: Mouton de Gruyter.

## Data References

Allrecipes.com. (n.d.). Retrieved March 1, 2017, from http://allrecipes.com/

Callan, P. (2017). Comey may find himself boxed in . . . by himself. CNN. Retrieved June 3, 2017, from www.cnn.com/2017/06/02/opinions/what-to-expect-from-comey-callan/index.html

Cisneros, S. (1984). *The house on Mango Street*. New York. Knopf Doubleday.

Exploring south bay. (2016, September). *WHERE Los Angeles Magazine*. SoCalPulse.com.

15 delightful, quirky town slogans. (n.d.). Retrieved March 1, 2017, from http://mentalfloss.com/article/58336/15-delightfully-quirky-town-slogans

Hans Christian Anderson sculpture. (n.d.). New York beyond sight. Retrieved May 20, 2017, from www.nybeyondsight.org/hans-christian.shtml

Lai, T. (2017, April 21). Raising children inside a war. *The New York Times*. Retrieved February 20, 2017, from www.nytimes.com/2017/04/21/opinion/raising-children-inside-a-war.html?_r=0

*Lord of the flies*—plot summary. (n.d.). Retrieved May 1, 2017, from www.sparknotes.com/lit/flies/summary.html

Maclean, N. (1976). *A river runs through it*. Chicago: University of Chicago Press.

Mathias, S. (n.d.). TSA rules: What can I carry on a plan? Retrieved March 1, 2017, from www.ebags.com/buyingguides/luggage-and-travel/tsa-rules

McBride, J. (1996/2006). *The color of water: A Black man's tribute to his White mother*. New York: New York. The Penguin Group.

OurOpenRoad. (n.d.). In the spirit of adventure//Peru into Chile. Retrieved January 22, 2017, from http://ouropenroad.com/category/field-notes/

Pistorius, M. (2013). *Ghost boy: The miraculous escape of a misdiagnosed boy trapped inside his own body*. Nashville, TN: Thomas Nelson.

Provine, R. R. (2012). *Curious behavior: Yawning, laughing, hiccupping, and beyond*. Cambridge, MA: Belknap Press.

Quintanilla, C. (Producer), & CNBC (Studio). (2007). *BIG MAC: Inside the McDonald's empire* [TV Original Documentary]. United States: CNBC.

The Red Studio. (n.d.). Art beyond sight. Retrieved May 20, 2017, from www.artbeyondsight.org/handbook/text-v-red-studio.shtml

Rojas-Sebesta, C. I., & Axel, E. (Writers). (n.d.). Arts beyond sight. Retrieved March 1, 2017, from www.artbeyondsight.org/

Sagan, C., Druyan, A., Soter, S. (Writer), & Malone, A. (Director). (1980). The persistence of memory [TV Series Episode]. In G. Andofer & R. McCain (Producer), *Cosmos*. Los Angeles, CA: PBS.

U.S. city motto & moniker list. (n.d.). Retrieved March 1, 2017, from http://taglineguru.com/mottolist.html

# 13 The Exquisite Grammar of Descriptions—Being Bellicose or Bubbly, Feckless, or Fearless

## Adjectives

*Figure 13.1* "I should go on a diet, but I'm afraid my brain will get thinner and I'll become narrow-minded!"

© Randy Glasbergen. Reproduced with permission of Glasbergen Cartoon Service.

Adjectives are words that describe nouns in terms of size, shape, weight, age, color, texture, and an almost infinite array of other qualities or characteristics. Adjectives help speakers and writers provide descriptive details about things, people, ideas, and concepts. They help portray individuals and depict events, upgrading them; downplaying them; capturing them with the finest, most minute aspects of realism; or painting them with broad impressionistic brushstrokes. Adjectives are different from determiners in that determiners only depict such concepts as identifiability, specifiability, possession, gender, and number (see Chapter 4). The descriptive power of adjectives vastly exceeds the very limited types of descriptions of nouns that determiners evoke.

## 13.1 Adjective Categories

The following examples are adjectives that fit into such categories of common description, from size to evaluation, and from physical traits to abstract ones. Note that some adjective pairs evoke various types of polar meanings (e.g., large vs. small; old vs. young; more positive vs. more negative).

**size:** large in size:
large, big, enormous, great, gigantic, huge, sizable, mammoth, massive, substantial, significant, vast, wide, expansive, tall, towering, high, major
small in size:
small, little, wee, tiny, miniature, modest, compact, brief, mini, baby, diminutive, inconsequential, unimportant, narrow, short, minor

**shape:** round, square, rectangular, oval, triangular, curved, angular, straight, linear

**weight:** heavy, hefty, massive, dense, burdensome, light, fluffy, buoyant, feathery

**age:** old, ancient, aged, mature, traditional, young, youthful, fledgling, green

**color:** green, red, blue, white, black, hazel, crimson, sapphire, ivory, ebony

**texture:** soft, hard, rough, smooth, shiny, matte, glossy, slick, mushy, fluffy, velvety

**evaluation:** more positive in meaning:
good, beautiful, lovely, upright, right, righteous, wise, lively, amazing, incredible, awesome, phenomenal, impressive, grand, healthy, fresh

more negative in meaning:
bad, spoiled, unusable, awful, ghastly, unappealing, wrong, morose, horrible, terrible, unseemly, unpleasant, deficient, sloppy, shoddy, heedless

## 13.2 Forming Adjectives From Other Parts of Speech

Adjectives can be formed by adding suffixes (both derivational and inflectional morphemes—see Chapter 2) to a root word.

### 13.2.1 Adjectives Formed From Nouns

| noun + -*ly* | → | adjective |
| --- | --- | --- |
| heaven | | heavenly |
| cost | | costly |
| man | | manly |
| day, month, year | | daily, monthly, yearly |
| coward | | cowardly |
| ghost | | ghostly |
| friend, brother, sister, mother | | friendly, brotherly, sisterly, motherly |

**Examples:**

The city name Philadelphia means "The City of <u>*Brotherly*</u> **Love**."
                                                         adj.     noun

Daniel Murphy made a <u>*costly*</u> **error** for the New York Mets in the 2015 World Series.
                          adj.   noun

**noun + -y** → **adjective**

| | |
|---|---|
| salt | salty |
| water | watery |
| ice | icy |
| rock | rocky |
| bump | bumpy |
| soap | soapy |
| oil | oily |
| rain, snow, wind, cloud | rainy, snowy, windy, cloudy |
| sun, fog | sunny, foggy [note double consonants] |

Examples:

Can someone explain why **yogurt** sometimes turns *watery* in the fridge?
                          noun                     adj.

When I wash the dishes, should I use warm or hot, *soapy* **water**?
                               adj.     adj.  adj.  noun


**noun + -al** → **adjective**

| | |
|---|---|
| nation, region | national, regional |
| accident | accidental |
| margin | marginal |
| environment | environmental |
| profession | professional |
| anecdote | anecdotal |

Example:

What is the difference between *regional* and *national* **universities**?
                                  adj.        adj.     noun


**noun + -ful** → **adjective**

| | |
|---|---|
| care | careful |
| delight | delightful |
| bounty | bountiful |
| beauty | beautiful |
| remorse | remorseful |

Examples:

**Halloween** can be both *frightful* and *delightful*. It is truly a *candy-ful* **holiday**.
 noun                       adj.       adj.                  adj.   noun

What do all *powerful* **leaders** have in common?
              adj.   noun

| noun + -*ish* → | adjective (with some adjectives, more negative connotations) |

| | | |
|---|---|---|
| child | childish | [more negative] |
| fool | foolish | [more negative] |
| baby | babyish | [more negative] |
| sheep | sheepish | [more negative] |
| Spain | Spanish | [neutral, objective] |
| Turk | Turkish | [neutral, objective] |

**Examples:**

"The <u>*foolish*</u> **man** seeks happiness in the distance. The *wise* [**man**] grows it under his feet."
    adj.  noun                                       adj.  noun

                                                                       (James Oppenheim, n.d.)

Don has always been a <u>*selfish*</u> **person**.
                           adj.  noun

## 13.2.2 Adjectives Formed From Other Adjectives

| adjective + -*ish* → | adjective ("sort of, but not exactly") |

| | |
|---|---|
| cold, warm | coldish, warmish |
| red, blue, white | reddish, bluish, whitish |
| new | newish |

**Examples:**

Cyan and teal are names for **colors** that are <u>*bluish-green*</u> or <u>*greenish-blue*</u>.
                                 noun               adj.        adj.

Paxton was upset because he discovered a lot of rust on his <u>*newish*</u> **car**.
                                                                adj.   noun

## 13.2.3 Adjectives Formed From Verbs

Some adjectives are derived from the past participle or present-participle forms of verbs. As discussed in Chapter 2, the present participle is a form of the verb that ends in -*ing*, and for many verbs, the past participle ends in -*en* or -*ed*.

| verb + -*en*/-*ed* [past participle] → | adjective |

| | |
|---|---|
| eat | eaten |
| wear | worn |
| worry | worried |
| write | written |

| | |
|---|---|
| tire | tired |
| excite | excited |
| surprise | surprised |
| horrify | horrified |
| interest | interested |
| advance | advanced |
| exhaust | exhausted |
| annoy | annoyed |

**Examples:**

The **man** was wearing a pair of *well-worn* boots and a *moth-eaten* sweater.
    noun                       past part. adj.   noun      past part. adj. noun

My **parents** were *worried* that we'd be late for dinner because of the *icy* roads.
    noun         past part. adj.                                    adj. noun

| verb + *-ing* [present participle] → | adjective |
|---|---|
| annoy | annoying |
| interest | interesting |
| burn | burning |
| tire | tiring |
| excite | exciting |
| surprise | surprising |
| promise | promising |
| bore | boring |
| miss | missing |
| develop | developing |
| horrify | horrifying |

**Examples:**

Dr. Kwon offered *promising* solutions to a *baffling behavioral* problem: speeding.
                          pres. part. adj.   noun   pres. part. adj.    adj.      noun

Children often find **preschool** to be both *exciting* and *overwhelming* at first.
                            noun                     pres. part. adj.   pres. part. adj.

    Many of the adjectives in both previously listed categories (e.g., *interesting, interested, boring, bored, annoying, annoyed*) are formed by adding *-ing* and *-ed* suffixes to verbs that express feelings toward and reactions to various situations and stimuli (Yule, 1998).
    In such cases, the ***present participle form*** occurs with the noun entity that ***causes*** that feeling, e.g., The teacher was **amusing.** [*the teacher* = cause of amusement], while ***the past participle*** describes that feeling *as experienced by the sentient being* (Yule, 1998, p. 6), e.g., The students were **amused.** [*the students* = experiencers of amusement].

## 13.3 Placements of Adjectives

Adjectives are categorized into two main groups, depending on their placement within a clause (Bolinger, 1967; Englebretson, 1997; Thompson, 1989; Truswell, 2004):

| category | placement |
|---|---|
| attributive | before the noun |
| predicative | after the copular verb, associated with the copular verb |

As evident in the following examples, sometimes the adjective is <u>placed directly before the noun</u>, in which case it is **attributive**. When an adjective is <u>placed after a copular verb</u>, it is **predicative.**

**adjective (+ adjective) + noun combinations (attributive)**

<u>brotherly</u> **love**
<u>costly</u> **error**
<u>hot, soapy</u> **water**
<u>regional</u> **competition**
<u>primary</u> **cause**
<u>promising</u> **solutions**
<u>baffling behavioral</u> **problem**

**Attributive** adjectives that directly precede nouns evoke a more permanent, stable, or defining quality or attribute of that noun. While attributive adjectives typically precede *common nouns*, they can also occur before proper nouns and pronouns (Biber et al., 2002), as in the following examples:

<u>Poor</u> **Chad**! He missed his flight to Sydney today.
This is a <u>new</u> **me**, a <u>healthier</u> **me**.

On the other hand, adjectives that follow a copular construction (e.g., *be*, *become*, *turn*, *get*, *sound*, *look*, *appear*, *taste*; see Chapter 6) are called **predicative adjectives**, because they follow the verb or predicate of the sentence or clause. In contrast with the attributive adjective, the predicative type evokes a less permanent quality or characteristic associated with that noun. As such, the descriptive characteristics surrounding the noun in question may evoke a more temporary, changing, and/or less definitive characteristic (Quirk et al., 1985).

| **noun (NP) +** | *copular verb +* | <u>*adjective*</u> | (predicative) |
|---|---|---|---|
| **My parents** | *are* | <u>*worried*</u>. | [now, but maybe not always] |
| **The weather** | *looks* | <u>*frightful*</u>. | |
| **The fire** | *feels* | <u>*delightful*</u>. | |

In the following sentence pairs, compare how the nouns or NPs are characterized by each adjective, and also determine how the meanings change by virtue of adjective placement, either in **predicative position** (after the copular verb) or in the **attributive position** (preceding the main noun). Note the possible shifts in assumptions about and stances toward each modified noun (sometimes strongly and sometimes subtly), depending on the placement of the adjective.

| | |
|---|---|
| **My parents** *were* worried, and they phoned me every hour. | predicative |
| **My** worried **parents** phoned me every hour. | attributive |
| **The weather** *looks* frightful, and it has caused many traffic accidents. | predicative |
| **The** frightful **weather** has caused many traffic accidents. | attributive |
| **Companies** *become* successful thanks to their employees' creativity. | predicative |
| Successful **companies** rely on their employees' creativity. | attributive |

### 13.3.1 Adjectives That Are Only Attributive

Some adjectives are only placed in the attributive position in English. Examples of these are as follows:

> main, mere, utter, sheer, eastern, western, favorite, ultimate, wayward, right-hand, left-hand, center, middle, outermost, innermost, exterior, interior

> **The** exterior **walls** are made of wood and stucco.
> Slower-moving vehicles must stay in **the** right-hand **lane** of the road.
> **The** main **idea** of an essay is typically expressed in the thesis statement.
> We met the lead guitarist in The Aces by sheer **coincidence**.

Note that the use of these adjectives in the predicative position yields an ungrammatical phrase, clause, or sentence:

> *the **walls** *are* exterior
> *the **idea** *is* main
> *the **lane** *is* right-hand
> *the **coincidence** *was* sheer

### 13.3.2 Adjectives That Are Only Predicative

Some adjectives are only placed in the predicative position. Examples of these are as follows:

> asleep, awake, aware, alive, alone, alike, afraid, aboard, ashamed, akin, agasp

Note that the core adjectives here all begin with the prefix *a-*. Etymologically, some of these adjectives derived from older versions of the words where the original prefix *a-* took on the meaning of the preposition *on*, affixed to verbs, nouns, and other adjectives.

> Is there a name for **the state when a person** *is* not awake but also not asleep?
> **Our school guidance counselor** *was* aghast at the number of bullying incidents.
> **Mr. Jackson** *felt* ashamed and sorry for what he had done.

## 13.4 Gradable and Absolute Upper/Lower Limit Adjectives

The term *gradable* refers to the types of adjectives that can naturally be intensified with adverbial intensifiers like *very*, *really*, and *extremely*. The gradability of adjectives simply means that the descriptor can naturally evoke varying degrees of that quality, as in the following examples:

### Gradable adjectives

| | | |
|---|---|---|
| tired | → | *very* <u>tired</u> |
| happy | → | *extremely* <u>happy</u> |
| bored | → | *really* <u>bored</u> |
| cold | → | *very* <u>cold</u> |
| large | → | *really quite* <u>large</u> |
| small | → | *very* <u>small</u> |
| red | → | *extremely* <u>red</u> |

In contrast, the meanings of some adjectives inherently evoke upper or lower limits of meaning. When upper/lower limit adjectives occur with an intensifying adverb, the expression can sound quite odd and marked in discourse, displaying a stance of exaggeration, hyperbole, and even sarcasm.

| *Gradable* | *Absolute, upper/lower limit* | *?Odd-sounding/exaggeration (marked)* |
|---|---|---|
| cool | freezing | ?very freezing |
| big | huge | ?very huge |
| small | miniscule | ?very miniscule |
| hungry | famished | ?very famished |
| glad | delighted | ?very delighted |
| famous | legendary, renowned | ?very legendary, very renowned |
| difficult | impossible | ?very impossible |
| surprising | astonishing | ?very astonishing |

---

### Mini Review and Practice

1  Have a look at the following excerpt from Maya Angelou's *I Know Why the Caged Bird Sings*.

>  . . . The free bird thinks of another breeze
>  and the trade winds soft through the sighing trees
>  and the fat worms waiting on a dawn-bright lawn
>  and he names the sky his own.
>  But a caged bird stands on the grave of dreams
>  his shadow shouts on a nightmare scream
>  his wings are clipped and his feet are tied
>  so he opens his throat to sing

> The caged bird sings
> with a fearful trill
> of things unknown
> but longed for still
> and his tune is heard
> on the distant hill
> for the caged bird
> sings of freedom.
>
> (Angelou, 1969)

Identify all of the adjectives. Then determine whether they are attributive or predicative. (Note: *Things unknown* can be considered *predicative*, because it is an elliptical form of "things [that are] unknown," cf. *unknown things*). Angelou constructs the entire poem based on the juxtaposition between the <u>caged</u> bird and the <u>free</u> bird.

What type of imagery is depicted for the *caged bird*? What type of imagery is depicted for the *free bird*? To answer this, in addition to your analysis of the adjectives, also consider nouns; pronouns; verbs; voice (active, passive, or middle); and the conjunctions *and*, *so*, and *for* (see Chapter 14). How does each set of linguistic elements combine to portray the *caged bird*? How does each set combine to portray the *free bird*?

2  The following quote by C. Joybell contains a number of adjectives. Some are attributive; that is, they directly precede the noun. Some are predicative; that is, they follow copular verbs. Some just stand alone without any overt noun or verb.

> When I was a little girl, everything in the world fell into either of these two categories: wrong or right. Black or white. Now that I am an adult, I have put childish things aside and now I know that some things fall into wrong and some things fall into right. Some things are categorized as black and some things are categorized as white. But most things in the world aren't either! Most things in the world aren't black, aren't white, aren't wrong, aren't right, but most of everything is just different. And now I know that there's nothing wrong with different, and that we can let things be different, we don't have to try and make them black or white, we can just let them be grey.
>
> (Joybell, n.d.)

First, identify all of the adjectives in the excerpt. Then, identify which are clearly used in attributive position, which are in predicative position, and which stand alone. How does the descriptive power of the attributive adjectives differ from that of the predicative adjectives? Would it be possible to re-write this passage and alter the adjective positions—that is, turn the attributive adjectives into predicative ones and vice versa? How does the meaning, stance, and purpose of the writing change with that type of alteration in adjective placement?

**Answers: head noun/NP (bold), <u>adjective</u> (underline), *verb* (italics)**

attributive:    *little* **girl**, *childish* **things**
predicative:   **some things** *are categorized as* <u>black</u>, **some things** *are categorized as* <u>white</u>, **most things** in the world *aren't* <u>black</u>, *aren't* <u>white</u>, *aren't*

wrong, *aren't* right, **most of everything** *is* just different, we can let **things** *be* different, we don't have to try and *make* **them** black or white, we can just *let* **them** *be* grey

stand alone:     wrong, right, black, white

3    Figure 13.1 shows a couple having a meal together. Their meal includes fries (or onion rings). The man's plate has more food on it than his companion's does, and he is holding bread (or a sandwich) in his hand. His dialogue line says this: "I should go on a diet, but I'm afraid my brain will get thinner and I'll become narrow-minded!" What is the source of humor? How would you analyze the adjective placements in this cartoon? Attributive? Predicative? What are the copular verbs in each of the two lines? What kinds of copular verbs are they? (See Chapter 6.)

4    The Great Courses is the name of a company that provides media-based (DVD, CD, digital video, and digital audio) college-level courses taught by actual university professors (www.thegreatcourses.com). The company name uses the attributive adjective *great*. How would the corporate image and marketing appeal change if the name were instead based on the predicative use of *great* in its name? Also, thinking back to the discussion of determiners in Chapter 4, how does the use of the definite article *the* also enhance the meaning and marketing appeal of this company's name?

5    The following sentence is a version of a recorded message from an auto repair shop. It goes like this:

"Thank you for calling John Dover Nissan. We are the only Nissan-certified shop in central Michigan, and we are very eco-friendly."

We have underlined the four adjectives. The fourth adjective, eco-friendly, appears in the predicative position and is preceded by the adverbial intensifier *very* (see Chapter 15). Does the adjective *eco-friendly* seem to belong to the gradable category or to the absolute or upper/lower limit category? In your opinion, how does the intensification with *very* add to or detract from this company's claim? Search the internet for other discursive contexts in which the adjectival phrase *very eco-friendly* occurs: What types of head nouns (for retail establishments, services, etc.) does it modify? What sort of stance does this adjective phrase evoke in discourse?

6    Here is a list of 10 recent email subject lines, all of which contain adjectives:

| **Sender** | **Subject line** |
|---|---|
| Lowe's Home Improvement | Sensational **savings** for **your** entire **home** |
| PayPal | Shop trendy small **businesses** this spring |
| American Girl | Save 50% off select **doll** outfits |
| The Great Courses | Gain valuable **insights** into unanswerable **questions** |
| Marriott Rewards | Win free **travel** for life |
| Chase | Say goodbye to misplaced **statements** |
| TheatreMania | Miss Saigon: On Broadway for a limited **time** |

> Alan English                    4 <u>smart</u> **ways** to kill <u>sugar</u> **cravings**
> AAA Southern Pennsylvania       **Our emails** are going <u>unnoticed</u>
> Bath & Body Works               **Your future** is looking <u>bright</u>
>
> We have indicated the head noun or NP (determiner + noun) in boldface type, and we have underlined the adjectives. Determine first whether each adjective appears in the attributive position or the predicative position. If in the predicative position, what is the copular verb? Is it possible to change the order of any of these adjectives such that the attributive adjectives become predicative? (One example: **Savings** are <u>sensational</u>, *<u>your</u> **home** is <u>entire</u>) Some adjectives can be rearranged and used in the opposite placement pattern. Others cannot. Which are which? Explain. Some nouns are used as adjectives in their original noun forms. Which ones? Explain how nouns can indeed function as adjectives, providing examples from discourse beyond the handful that you see listed previously.

## 13.5 Simple Comparative (*-er*) and Simple Superlative (*-est*)

English grammar provides a few options for comparing people, ideas, entities, groups, or concepts from the point of view of their qualities or characteristics.

### 13.5.1 Simple Comparative (*-er*)

If two entities, groups, states, or ideas are being compared, the simple comparative inflectional morpheme *-er* is added to the adjective. The preposition *than* typically follows the comparative adjective and precedes the noun or NP that is being compared. (See Chapter 12.)

**The sushi in Tokyo** seemed <u>fresher</u> **than the sushi in Los Angeles**.
[two entities being compared: sushi in Tokyo vs. sushi in Los Angeles]

The expression $x > y$ means that **the value of** $x$ is <u>greater</u> **than the value of** $y$.
[two entities being compared: the value of $x$ and the value of $y$]

**Penny's sister** is <u>younger</u> *than* **Fadi**.
[two entities being compared: Penny's sister's age vs. Fadi's age]

### 13.5.2 Simple Superlative (*-est*)

In the case of comparing three or more entities or ideas, where the goal is to pinpoint the one entity or group that exhibits the uppermost or lower most degree of that characteristic or quality, then the simple superlative form (adjective + *-est*) is used, and often with definite article *the* (see Chapter 4).

The sushi in Yokohama was **the** <u>freshest</u> **sushi** I had ever eaten.
Of $x$, $y$, and $z$, $x$ has **the** <u>greatest</u> **value**.
Penny's sister is **the** <u>youngest</u> **of all the children in her class**.

The simple comparative or simple superlative forms are commonly used with one-syllable adjectives and some two-syllable adjectives.

| adjective | two things compared | three or more superlative | |
|---|---|---|---|
| | | (often with determiner *the* or possessive determiner) | |
| good | better (irregular) | (the) best (irregular) | |
| bad | worse (irregular) | (the) worst (irregular) | |
| far | farther (irregular) | (the) farthest (irregular) | |
| cool | cooler | (the) coolest | |
| fresh | fresher | (the) freshest | |
| big | bigger | (the) biggest | [note double consonants] |
| red | redder | (the) reddest | [note double consonants] |
| hot | hotter | (the) hottest | [note double consonants] |
| nice | nicer | (the) nicest | [note dropping of -*e* from adj.] |
| late | later | (the) latest | [note dropping of -*e* from adj.] |
| simple | simpler | (the) simplest | [note dropping of -*e* from adj.] |
| pretty | prettier | (the) prettiest | [note *y* → *i* + -*er*/-*est*] |
| happy | happier | (the) happiest | [note *y* → *i* + -*er*/-*est*] |
| friendly | friendlier | (the) friendliest | [note *y* → *i* + -*er*/-*est*] |

For some two-syllable adjectives and for all adjectives with three or more syllables, comparative and superlative concepts are expressed in compound forms, with *more/less* + adjective for the comparative and *most/least* for the superlative.

| | more/less + adjective | (*the*) most/least + adjective |
|---|---|---|
| | | (often with determiner *the*, possessive determiner) |
| unique | more/less unique | (*the*) most/least unique |
| recent | more/less recent | (*the*) most/least recent |
| famous | more/less famous | (*the*) most/least famous |
| sincere | more/less sincere | (*the*) most/least sincere (or sincerest) |
| curious | more/less curious | (*the*) most/least curious |
| predictable | more/less predictable | (*the*) most/least predictable |
| unusual | more/less unusual | (*the*) most/least unusual |
| reprehensible | more/less reprehensible | (*the*) most/least reprehensible |
| democratic | more/less democratic | (*the*) most/least democratic |

**Andrea's apology** *sounded* <u>less sincere</u> **than Mark's**.
But, then again, **Andrea** *is* <u>the most sincere</u> **person** I have ever met.
<u>My</u> <u>most vivid</u> **memories of Europe** *are* from my trip to Heidelberg.

The creatively notable use of an exception to this is from *Alice in Wonderland* (Carroll, 1869), Chapter 2, "The Pool of Tears":

> "**Curiouser** and **Curiouser!**" cried Alice.
> (she was so much surprised, that for the moment she quite forgot how to speak good English).
>
> (Carroll, 1869)

## 13.6 Near "Synonyms": More on Meanings of Adjectives

The notion of synonymy in language and discourse relates to the fact that many words in a language have similar meanings to other words. It is important to remember that **no two words have the exact same meanings** in any language.

Near synonyms exist in every language. Sometimes, certain words appear to be more or less "interchangeable" with each other. Sometimes, they clearly are not.

Let's take a look at a few such word pairs that might be considered "synonyms"—words like *high* and *tall*, *big* and *large*, and *little* and *small*.

## 13.6.1 High *and* Tall

Both of these adjectives relate to a meaning connected with verticality and specifically the upper end of a vertical relationship. These words are often considered "pure synonyms," because in some cases, either can be used to express the meaning of an upper end of a vertical relationship.

| | | |
|---|---|---|
| tall mountains | high mountains | [*high* is more common, according to COCA (Davies, 2008–)] |
| tall peaks | high peaks | [*high* is more common, according to COCA (Davies, 2008–)] |
| 18 feet tall | 18 feet high | [both *tall* and *high* are common] |
| tall building | ?high building | |
| tall person | ?high person | |
| tall tree | *high tree | |
| ?tall branch | high branch | |
| *tall ceiling | high ceiling | |
| *tall blood pressure | high blood pressure | |

In examining the conceptual representations of verticality in the previous list, what strikes you about the meaning that *tall* evokes that *high* does not and vice versa? That is, if *tall* collocates naturally with *person*, *tree*, and *building* and if *high* collocates naturally with *ceiling*, *branch*, and *blood pressure*, what spatial meaning does *tall* evoke that *high* does not?

Here we propose a preliminary analysis of the semantic contrasts:

### Contrasts between core conceptual meanings between *tall* and *high*

**core conceptual meaning of *tall*:** vertical measurement that <u>*spans from*</u> the lowest point and extends <u>*to*</u> the uppermost point

**core conceptual meaning of *high*:** vertical measurement that focuses on the uppermost area or point

Such distinctions between core conceptual meanings help explain why one adjective might be preferred in collocation with certain nouns and why it might not be preferred with other nouns.

## 13.6.2 Big *and* Large

These two adjectives evoke a meaning of "considerable size." Here are some ways in which *big* and *large* collocate with nouns:

| | | |
|---|---|---|
| big package | large package | [both *big* and *large* are common] |
| big nose | large nose | |
| big family | large family | |

| | |
|---|---|
| big building | large building |
| big idea | *large idea |
| big day | *large day |
| big question | *large question |
| *big coffee | large coffee |
| *big sample | large sample |
| *big scale | large scale |
| *big cell carcinoma | large cell carcinoma |

In this case, what does *big* mean that *large* does not?
In what way does *big* evoke more than measurable, physical size? What else does it evoke?

### Contrasts between core conceptual meanings between *big* and *large*

| | |
|---|---|
| core conceptual meaning of *big*: | considerable size, *more subjective in meaning* in terms of both size and relative importance; major, important, relatively large size in comparison to other possible sizes (e.g., small coffee, medium coffee) |
| core conceptual meaning of *large*: | considerable size, *more objective in meaning*, more associated commonly with size only |

## 13.7 Order of Attributive Adjectives

Ideas, people, concepts, events, and things are often described in discourse with more than one adjective. When attributive adjectives appear in strings, there are a number of rules of thumb regarding the ordering of these adjectives according to basic semantic category. Celce-Murcia and Larsen-Freeman (1999, pp. 393–394) suggest the following order of semantic categories for adjective strings. This order is echoed in Cowan (2008, p. 260).

**determiner + subjective or evaluative adjective + size + color + material + head noun**

> The poor little pink plastic **doll**.
>
> (Celce-Murcia & Larsesn-Freeman, 1999, p. 393)

> An ugly old gray wooden **statue**.
> Three nice little oval antique Spanish **dressers**.
> A huge round modern plastic **table**.
>
> (Cowan, 2008, p. 260)

While the order may be a good rule of thumb, it should not be considered as a hard-and-fast rule to always follow or memorize. Adjectives serve to foreground certain characteristics of nouns.

Sometimes, the order is flexible, depending on which characteristic is being foregrounded, emphasized, or distinguished. Also, the categories of descriptors, from "subjective or evaluative adjective" through "material," cover only a limited range of the descriptor types that we find in actual discourse, and it is often difficult to categorize adjectives according to these rubrics. Other possible semantic categories of meaning for adjectives include process, temporal/frequency, purpose, and so forth. Often, multiple adjectives from the same category occur in succession within discourse.

A huge round modern plastic **table**. (Cowan's [2008, p. 260] original)
   size, shape,   ?   material **noun**

Possible variation (grammatical): A modern, round, huge plastic **table**
                     ?   shape, size material **noun**

**Other examples—variation is both possible and natural-sounding:**

A sterling silver handmade custom **flute**
   material     process     process **noun**

easy,    healthy, and quick    weeknight **dinners**
evaluation evaluation evaluation temporal

**Adjective strings from actual discourse:**

### From *The BFG* by Roald Dahl

> . . . The awful thing was that Sophie knew exactly what was going on although she couldn't see it happening. She knew that a Monster (or Giant) with an enormous long pale wrinkly **face** and dangerous eyes had plucked her from her bed in the middle of the witching hour and was now carrying her out through the window smothered in a blanket.
>
> (Dahl, 1982, p. 17)

**original:**
   an *enormous long pale wrinkly* **face**
**variations:**
   a pale wrinkly long *enormous* **face**
   a long pale enormous *wrinkly* **face**

(These are perfectly grammatical, but they foreground different characteristics of the Giant's face.)

With regard to adjective order, when multiple adjectives are used, often the *adjective that is closest to the noun* is foregrounded in terms of its descriptive quality and strength:

Head noun: **shoes**, preceded by five attributive adjectives
Discover our range of comfortable colorful custom handmade *leather* **shoes**.
                                                    ("Those shoes," n.d.)

Head noun: **flute**, preceded by four attributive adjectives ( . . . custom **flute**)
Powell sterling silver handmade *custom* **flute**, with soldered toneholes
                                                    ("Powell flutes," n.d.)

Head noun: **flute**, preceded by five attributive adjectives ( . . . sterling silver **flute**)
Powell 112000PL/91106 handmade custom *sterling silver* **flute**
                                                    (Chucklevins, n.d.)

## 13.8 Adjectives as Collective Nouns (Type 3b)

Sometimes adjectives can be used as collective nouns with the definite article *the* to refer to a group of people characterized and generalized by that quality evoked by the particular adjective.

418   *The Grammar of Descriptions—Adjectives*

Here are a few examples:

    We need more shelters for *the homeless.*     [= homeless people]

    "Blessed are *the meek*, for they shall inherit the earth."     [= meek people]
                                                                                            (Matthew 5:5)

How great is the employment gap between *the educated* and *the uneducated*?

    "What Becomes of *the Broken-Hearted*?"
                            (Song written by W. Weatherspoon, P. Riser, and James Dean)

Other examples: the poor, the able-bodied, the deaf, the blind, the disabled, the elite, the fair-minded, the disenfranchised, the powerful, the powerless, the righteous, the forgotten

   Essentially, this is a conversion process (see Chapter 2) in which an adjective that describes particular qualities and/or characteristics of humans becomes a Type 3b noun in discourse.

   Such Type 3b nouns (derived from adjectives) must always co-occur with the definite article determiner *the* because reference to this group of individuals suggests a generalized inclusion of every member that fits this category (see Chapters 3 and 4). It also requires the **verb form** to **be plural**, since the conceptual focus for this group or category of people is on the *individuals* and not on the *group as a unit.*

Plural verb form with *the* + adjective = Type 3b noun:

    <u>*The homeless*</u> ***represent*** the forgotten voices of society.
    <u>*The wealthy*</u> actually ***benefit*** somewhat less under this new tax plan.

## 13.9 Relative Clauses as Noun Modifiers

A relative clause is the dependent clause in a complex sentence type that serves to modify or describe nouns (see Chapter 2). Given this purpose of the relative clause, it can also be considered as fulfilling an adjectival function. In the following examples, the main nouns that are modified by a relative clause appear in boldface type. The relative clauses are underlined.

    This is **the project** <u>that I developed for my linguistics class</u>.
    Chuck Feeney was **the billionaire** <u>who anonymously gave away billions of dollars</u>.
    What is **the name of the person** <u>to whom I should send my letter of recommendation?</u>
    **The hospital** <u>where Barack Obama was born</u> is Kapiolani Medical Center.
    **The season** <u>in which wine grapes are best harvested</u> is late summer to early autumn.
    The Newberry Medal is given to **authors** <u>whose books contribute to children's literature</u>.
    That souvenir reminds me of **the time** <u>that/when we went to the Contra Costa County Fair</u>.

The **relative pronouns** that start a relative clause are *that, who, whom, where, which, whose,* and *when.*

    **the project** <u>*that* I developed</u>
    **the billionaire** <u>*who* gave away</u>
    **the person** <u>*to whom* I should send my letter</u>
    **the hospital** <u>*where Barack Obama was born*</u>
    **the season** <u>*in which* grapes are harvested</u>

authors *whose* books contribute to children's literature.
the time *that/when* we went to the Contra Costa County Fair

There are two basic types of relative clauses: restrictive and non-restrictive.

**Restrictive relative clauses** designate a **specific entity or sub-group from among other possible members**. These are called "restrictive" because of how the meaning becomes limited to a small set of possible entities. Note in the following examples that "restrictive" means "*not all* . . . but *only/just* the ones designated by the relative clause." That is, restrictive relative clauses identify the target noun from among other possible referents.

We have invited **Penn State professors** who published articles this year.
    Who is invited?
    **Not all** Penn State professors. . .
    . . . **only** those who published articles this year.

This weekend, we'll be fixing up **the scooters** that the church donated to the orphanage.
    What will we be fixing up?
    **Not all** the scooters. . .
    . . . **just** the ones that the church donated.

We bought some new equipment for **my brother** who is on the soccer team.
    Who is the new equipment for?
    **Not all** of my brothers . . .
    . . . **just** the one on the soccer team (not my other brother [who is] on the golf team).

**Non-restrictive relative clauses** do not restrict any meaning. In fact, they refer to **the very same entity or individual as the main noun in its entirety**. This type of clause serves simply to elaborate on the noun just referred to—whether that noun denotes and individual entity or a group of entities.

**Non-restrictive relative clauses** require a **comma** between the noun and the relative clause, [← note the comma here] which serves to offset the discourse and essentially **equate** the named entity or clause with the information in the relative clause.

Let's compare and contrast **restrictive** and **non-restrictive** relative clauses for both form and meaning:

We have invited **Penn State professors** who published articles this year.
[Restrictive—**only** those professors who published articles]

We have invited **Penn State professors,** [← note the comma here] who published articles this year.

[Non-restrictive—According to this, **all** Penn State professors published articles this year. The added information does not change the designation of who the main noun refers to.]

**The exams** that the TA graded were returned yesterday. Professor Smith still has the exams that she graded.

[Restrictive—There were exams. **Of the full set** of exams, the TA graded some, and Professor Smith graded some. **Only** the ones that the TA graded were returned.]

**The exams,** ← [comma] which the TA graded, ← [comma] were returned to the students yesterday.

[Non-restrictive—There were exams. The TA graded **all** of the exams and returned them to the students yesterday.]

**A note on relative pronoun choice for <u>non</u>-restrictive relative clauses:** When faced with the choice between *that* and *which*, choose *which*. Also be sure to place a comma before *which*. *That* <u>cannot</u> **be used** as a relative pronoun **in a <u>non</u>-restrictive relative clause**.

*Our Ford Mustang, **that** had a huge dent in the fender, was stolen.   [error: that]
Our Ford Mustang, **which** had a huge dent in the fender, was stolen.   [correct: which]

A sub-category of the **non-restrictive relative clause** is that of the **appositive**. The function of the appositive is to simply add another name to a just mentioned noun. Again, a comma is needed here. Look at the following examples:

Israel Kamakawiwoʻole, the Hawaiian vocalist, passed away in 1997.
noun [comma] another name (appositive) [comma]

Haile Selassie, emperor of Ethiopia from 1930 to 1974, was loved by many.
noun [comma] another name (appositive) [comma]

Sam Gribley, the protagonist of *My Side of the Mountain*, left home to live in the woods.
noun [comma] another name (appositive) [comma]

### 13.9.1 *Relative Clauses in Discourse*

Relative clause constructions as noun modifiers pervade all types of English discourse, from everyday conversation to news reports, and from personal narratives to religious sermons, children's books, lectures, TED Talks, and academic writing. Of the two types, corpus studies reveal that **restrictive relative clauses** are generally more frequent throughout all discourse types, while **non-restrictive relative** clauses are **common in news reporting discourse** (Biber et al., 2002, p. 280).

One unique genre of discourse that plays creatively with relative clauses is the *cumulative tale*. Using consecutive strings of **restrictive relative clause** constructions, the cumulative tale builds a potentially infinite narrative with bits of storyline and bits of grammar that combine to cumulatively construct a creative and largely repetitive story. From the point of view of grammar, the sentence becomes longer and longer, because of the serial building of the relative clause. Examples of cumulative tales include the classic nursery rhymes "This Is the House That Jack Built" and "There Was an Old Lady Who Swallowed a Fly." More recent variations include *The Bag I'm Taking to Grandma's* (Neitzel, 1998), *The Jacket I Wear in the Snow* (Neitzel, 1989), and *There Was an Old Lady Who Swallowed a Frog!* (Colandro, 2015).

Note how the cumulative tale works using strings of restrictive relative clauses:

**"This Is the House That Jack Built"**

This is **the house** that Jack built.
This is **the malt** that lay in **the house** that Jack built.
This is **the rat** that ate **the malt** that lay in **the house** that Jack built.
("This is the house that Jack built," n.d.)

Restrictive and non-restrictive relative clauses pervade discourse in less marked genres.

An example from everyday conversation adapted from the UC Santa Barbara Corpus will illustrate one typical use of a restrictive relative clause [relative pronoun = *who*]:

| | |
|---|---|
| Pamela: | Natalie asked me about Santa Claus today. |
| Darryl: | What did she say? |
| Pamela: | She said, Mom, . . . Is there a for real Santa Claus? |
| → | [and I said] You mean **a man** <u>who lives at the North Pole?</u> |

(UC Santa Barbara Corpus, n.d.)

Another example is adapted from COCA (Davies, 2008–), involving a 2015 interview by NBC's Hoda Kotb with celebrity guest Kathie Lee Gifford [relative pronouns = *that*]:

| | |
|---|---|
| Gifford: | That was **a selfie** *that* <u>we took in the house</u>, and look at **the cake** *that* <u>I bought from Publix</u> ((a grocery store name)). |
| Kotb: | By the way, Publix birthday cakes. . . |
| Gifford: | They're delicious. |
| Kotb: | . . . are unbelievable. |

(Davies, 2008–)

The following three examples illustrate the use of both restrictive and non-restrictive relative clauses in written registers. First, try to locate the relative pronoun (e.g., *that*, *which*, *who*, *when*). Next, determine whether there is a comma after the relative pronoun. If not, you can assume that it is **a restrictive relative clause**, as in the following VW example.

Associated Press: An attorney for **300 VW owners** <u>who have opted out of a larger court settlement objected to the penalty</u>.

("Volkswagen pleads guilty. . .," 2017)

You may find a noun that is followed by a comma and then discourse that provides additional details about that noun but without a discernible relative pronoun like *which* or *who*. The following ransomware example illustrates the discursive use of the **appositive**, one type of a **non-restrictive relative clause**. Note, too, that this appositive is further specified by a **restrictive relative clause** with *that*:

CNN: The hospital got hit with ransomware, a particularly nasty type of computer virus that encrypts computer files.

(Paglieri, 2016)

[full form variation: non-restrictive relative clause]
ransomware, *which is* a particularly nasty type of computer virus. . .

[restrictive relative clause—with *that*]
a particularly nasty type of computer virus *that* encrypts computer files

Even more complex examples of restrictive and non-restrictive relative clauses occur together quite naturally in discourse (italics, bold, and underline added). Have a look at the following excerpt from biosciences writer Janine M Benyus's thought-provoking and idea-inspiring non-fictional book (1997) *Biomimicry: Innovation Inspired by Nature*.

422    *The Grammar of Descriptions—Adjectives*

> One of the most promising ways to explore the natural world, and to further narrow our search, is called biorational drug prospecting, <u>a strategy advocated by Dan Janzen and Tom Eisner</u>. . . .
>
> Tom Eisner's father was **a chemist** *who* <u>used to make cosmetics in his basement</u>. . . . When prospecting for possible drugs . . . Eisner will look for **plants** *that* <u>are notably free of damage</u>. **Plants** *that* <u>insects avoid eating</u> must have potent defenses, he reasons, and should be screened for bioactive secondary compounds. . . .
>
> Other ways to find drugs from bugs is to watch how venomous animals handle both their enemies and their prey. **Any substance** *that* <u>can have such a profound effect on the victim</u> . . . is bound to have powerful biochemical or pharmaceutical properties. Natural Product Sciences in Salt Lake City . . . is looking into the toxins of spiders, snakes, and scorpions. **These compounds**, *which* <u>attack specific neurochemical targets</u>, are already helping researchers identify **tiny openings in the membranes of human neurons** *that* <u>admit charged molecules called ions</u>.
>
> (Benyus, 1997, pp. 178–179)

appositive (non-restrictive):
   . . . biorational drug prospecting, a strategy advocated by Dan Janzen and Tom Eisner.

restrictive relative clauses:
   . . . **a chemist** *who* <u>used to make cosmetics in his basement</u> . . .
   **plants** *that* <u>are notably free of damage</u>.
   **Plants** *that* <u>insects avoid eating</u> . . .
   **Any substance** *that* <u>can have such a profound effect on the victim</u> . . .
   . . . **tiny openings in the membranes of human neurons** *that* <u>admit charged molecules called ions</u>.

non-restrictive relative clauses:
   **These compounds**, *which* <u>attack specific neurochemical targets</u>.

(non-restrictive) reduced relative clauses:
   **charged molecules** <u>called ions</u>.

both non-restrictive and restrictive relative clauses in the same sentence:
   **These compounds**, [← note the comma here] *which* <u>attack specific neurochemical targets</u>, [← note the comma here] are already helping researchers identify **tiny openings in the membranes of human neurons** *that* <u>admit charged molecules called ions</u>.

## 13.10  Nouns Modified With Prepositional Phrases

As we have seen throughout this book, the traditional parts of speech in grammar can actually be quite fluid, such that their essential categories shift according to their functions in discourse: nouns function as adjectives, adjectives as nouns, verbs as nouns, nouns as verbs, relative clauses as adjectives, and so forth. Prepositional phrases can also function as adjectives, typically in the context of reduced relative clauses and in prepositional phrases that serve to describe nouns (e.g., all the **furniture** <u>in the house</u> // all the furniture [that was/is] in the house).

### 13.10.1  Prepositional Phrases From Reduced Relative Clauses as Adjectives

When we situate entities within space and time, we often use prepositions to designate their existence, their locations, and their states (see Chapter 12). Often, when the time/space designation modifies the head noun, it is achieved through a relative clause construction, with relative pronouns like *that* and *which*.

**The printer** <u>*that* is in the grad students' office</u> is <u>broken</u>.
[restrictive]

More commonly, however, the expression would be reduced by deleting the words *that is*.

**The printer** <u>in the grad students' office</u> is <u>broken</u>.

Here are some additional examples of reduced relative clauses:

**The wheels** <u>on the bus</u> go round and round
　　　**The wheels** <u>(that are) on the bus</u>

**A bird** <u>in the hand</u> is <u>worth</u> **two** <u>in the bush</u>.
　　　**A bird** (that is) <u>in the hand</u> is <u>worth</u> **two** (**birds** that are) <u>in the bush</u>.

### 13.10.2 Prepositional Phrases That Modify Nouns

Prepositional phrases that are not reduced relative clauses can also modify nouns. Here are some examples:

at:　**the public** <u>at large</u>, **a nation** <u>at risk</u>, **the world** <u>at peace</u>

of:　**the dangers** <u>of smoking</u>, **the purpose** <u>of the experiment</u>, **a matter** <u>of time</u>, **the city** <u>of love</u>

with:　**people** <u>with blue eyes</u>, **a room** <u>with a view</u>, **shirts** <u>with buttons</u>, *The Girl* <u>With the Dragon Tattoo</u>

to:　**a solution** <u>to the problem</u>, **the entrance** <u>to the building</u>, **the road** <u>to recovery</u>

According to Biber et al. (2002, p. 269), prepositional phrases as modifiers are particularly common in the more formal registers (i.e., academic discourse and news reports), followed by fiction.

## 13.11 Adjective Phrases

**Adjective phrases** can also modify nouns. Adjective phrases typically include a head adjective and other words (e.g., adverbs) that modify or complement the adjective (Biber et al., 2002; Quirk et al., 1985). The adjective phrases in the following examples are in italics (adjectives are also underlined), and the nouns modified by the adjective phrase are in bold:

| a | You're asking a | *totally* | *<u>different</u>* | **question**. |
|---|---|---|---|---|
|   |   | modifier (adverb) | head adjective |   |
| b | **Dave** must feel | *so* | *incredibly* | *<u>lucky</u>*. |
|   |   | modifier (adverb) | modifier (adverb) | head adjective |

As seen in the previous examples, adjective phrases can be attributive (a) or predicative (b).

## 13.12 Nouns Functioning as Adjectives

As we observed in Chapter 3, often nouns in English function in ways to modify or describe other nouns.

424 *The Grammar of Descriptions—Adjectives*

"The good news is, you'll be spending Thanksgiving with a large group of happy people."

*Figure 13.2* "The good news is, you'll be spending Thanksgiving with a large group of happy people."
© Randy Glasbergen. Reproduced with permission of Glasbergen Cartoon Service.

## Noun (functioning as adjective) + Noun

earth tones
music classes
steel frame
glass windows
agenda item
pencil lead
fish hook
dining experience
winding road

wall hanging
press conference
coffee cup
baby food
down pillow
savings account
vocabulary test
listening pleasure
meandering river

\*\*\*\*\*\*\*\*

### PRACTICE WITH DATA ANALYSIS: PUTTING IT ALL TOGETHER

1   Above is another cartoon. It depicts a fortune-teller reading her crystal ball and predicting the future for the turkey who is sitting across from her at the table.

Identify the adjectives here. Are they attributive? Are they predicative? What is the source of humor in this cartoon? What might the *bad news* be? Also think about the use of tense and aspect marking in the caption. What types of verbs are used? What are the categories of tense and aspect? (See Chapter 7.)

2   Corpus analysis shows that *good* and *nice* are two of the most commonly used adjectives in conversation (Conrad & Biber, 2009). Why do you think this is the case?

Think about the adjective *good*. What does *good* mean? Now, brainstorm, either alone or in groups, and try to find as many synonyms of *good* as possible. Try to generate as exhaustive a list as possible. As you do this, think about contexts that would be necessary to understand the various meanings of *good*.

For example: good = delicious, tasty
                    [referring to food, drink]

Contexts: dinner table, advertisements, etc.
> good = kind, saintly, obedient
> [referring to people in general, children, students]

Contexts: school, news reports, etc.
> good = healthy, working
> [referring to body parts, machine parts; in opposition to *bad*=not working]

Contexts: medical encounters, sports discourse, machine/technology repairs, etc.
> good = suitable, appropriate
> [referring to behavior, word choice, dress/fashion, responses]

Contexts: school, public vs. private, interviews etc.
> good = sufficient, enough
> [referring to quantity]

Contexts: cooking, mealtime, construction/craft projects, etc.

Keep the list going, and try to find as many different "near synonyms" for *good* as you can while at the same time specifying the types of contexts in which this adjective might occur. You can use the internet to help stimulate more ideas for a richer selection of near synonyms. Be sure to couple each use of *good* as an adjective with at least one appropriate noun, if not a full phrase or clause, to help solidify each meaning of *good* in a particular context.

Note that *good* can also be used as a noun (e.g., *the public good, for the good of, goods and services*). You can also incorporate an analysis of *good* used as a noun in English discourse into your work.

Then, do the same thing with a selection of other seemingly common adjectives that can take on a wide range of meanings, some of which can also be highly subjective, like *nice, big, little,* and *easy*. Again, think about the importance of context in word meaning. Also be sure to think about connotations. (See Chapter 2.)

3   Nouns can also become adjectives with slight changes to their forms (e.g., by adding *-y, -ly, -ish, -like,* or *-ful*). And this can be accomplished within multiple categories of nouns, like weather: *rain → rainy, snow → snowy, drizzle → drizzly, sleet → sleety, ice → icy*.

Animal- and insect-related nouns can also be transformed into adjectives:

| fox      | →  | foxy       |
| beast    | →  | beastly    |
| bee      | →  | beelike    |
| sheep    | →  | sheepish   |
| elephant | →  | elephantine |

In the animated film *Rio 2* (Smith, 2014), the blue macaw named Blu says this line: "I'm not **the birdliest** bird in the flock." Blu is not a particularly good flier. He wears a fanny pack, and he needs a GPS to navigate. Why do you think that Blu characterizes himself in this way? Why does he use the simple superlative form?

Other adjectives that are derived from animal and insect names are as follows:

| *Girls Acting Catty* (book title) | noun: cat → adj. = catty |
| *Something's Fishy at Ash Lake* (book title) | noun: fish → adj. = fishy |
| *The Magic School Bus: Going Batty* (book title) | noun: bat → adj. = batty |
| *A Stark and Wormy Knight* (book title) | noun: worm → adj. = wormy |

426  *The Grammar of Descriptions—Adjectives*

What other animal and/or insect adjectives can you think of—creature nouns that end with *-y*, *-ly*, *-ish*, *-like*, and *-ine*? What do those specific adjectives derived from nouns mean? Try and locate instances of these expressions in actual discourse (e.g., children's books, novels, essays, blogs, websites, general internet searches). In what way do the meanings of these words seem to expand when you see how they are used in discourse as opposed to their occurrences simply as words in a list? Explain.

4  Adjectives (including full and reduced relative clauses) are an important category of discourse in many genres such as product advertising (websites, print ads, commercials, billboards), reviews (books, movies, travel destinations, hotels, restaurants), retail catalogs (online, printed volumes), and so forth.

The following excerpt is a description of the Bellagio hotel in Las Vegas from the Event website for hotels and venues:

Bellagio Las Vegas: <u>Inspired</u> by **the** <u>beautiful</u> **villages** <u>of Europe</u>, **the** <u>AAA Five Diamond Award-winning</u> **Bellagio** overlooks **a** <u>Mediterranean-blue</u> <u>eight-acre</u> **lake** <u>in which fountains perform</u> **a** <u>magnificent</u> <u>aquatic</u> **ballet**. Within Bellagio, <u>award-winning</u> **dining**, <u>sophisticated</u> **nightlife**, a <u>world-class</u> <u>art</u> **gallery**, <u>exquisite</u> **gardens**, Cirque-du-Soleil's <u>stunning</u> **performance** <u>of O</u>™, a <u>luxurious</u> **spa and salon** and <u>upscale</u> **shopping** all add to **the** <u>extraordinary</u> **Bellagio** **experience**.

("Bellagio hotel and casino," n.d.)

Analyze how the adjectives are used in this passage. Do your best to use the types of grammatical categories we have introduced here: attributive, predicative, nouns used as adjectives, nouns derived from past or present participles, and relative clauses (full form or reduced).

What is the pattern in terms of the descriptions of the nouns? That is, is there an adjective preceding every noun? One adjective? Two? What kind of visual imagery is captured by this description (e.g., evaluation, color, size, and more)?

Based on this excerpt, do you sense that this is an expensive hotel or a lower budget one? Why? Who do you feel is the target audience? Explain your responses in detail, using excerpts from the description to support your answer.

5  Along these same lines, let's continue our exploration into how adjectives (and other parts of speech) are used by retailers to describe products for use by potential consumers or customers. For this comparison, we have selected two excerpts of promotional discourse for hand-cream products: Avon, a classic US skin care and beauty products brand, and Estée Lauder, a New York–based designer brand of high-end cosmetics.

  a  **Avon:** Price: Approximately $5.00

    **"Moisture Therapy Intensive Healing & Repair Hand Cream"**

    Do you have such dry skin you've lost hope? Even if you don't, you'll be sure to benefit from Moisture Therapy Intensive Healing & Repair Hand Cream. This restorative cream for dry hands moisturizes for days with Hydraboost Technology that lasts for 72 hours. Fragrance-Free formula is non-irritating and reduces redness! Comes in a 4.2 fl oz container.

BENEFITS

- Hand cream reduces redness
- Moisturizes skin for 72 hours with Hydraboost Technology
- Softens and soothes rough skin
- Hypoallergenic
- Dermatologist tested

(Avon, n.d.)

b   **Estée Lauder:** Price: Approximately $65.00

"Estée Lauder Re-Nutriv"
**Intense Smoothing Hand Crème (Crème main lissante confort intense)** [French wording also appears on the package] 3.4 oz.

**Product Details**

Slip on one of the most indulgent hand cremes ever created.
Sumptuous moisturizing ingredients deeply hydrate. Advanced anti-spot technology helps reduce the look of dark spots and even out skin tone.
Hands look younger and suppler. Crepiness is visibly smoothed. Skin remains soft and moisturized, ever after multiple washings.

HOW TO USE

Apply as needed

BENEFITS

Deeply hydrates. Reduces the look of spots.

LUXURY CARE FOR

- Dry, dehydrated hands
- Crepey texture
- Loss of firmness, tone
- Uneven skintone, spots

FORMULA FACTS

—Dermatologist tested.

(Avon, n.d.)

Compare and contrast the discourse from these two similar products. The discourse surrounding the Avon product addresses an audience of everyday users. The discourse surrounding the Estée Lauder product addresses a very different audience, but with the same basic needs. At first glance, you can discern the different target audiences just by looking at the respective prices. Beyond price, the discourse is clearly different. In what way?

As you work through your analysis, focus primarily on the nouns and adjectives in line with the topic of the current chapter. But do feel free to bring in other bits of grammar from the discourse to help you structure your analysis (e.g., questions, verbs [and verb types], and even punctuation) as you compare and contrast each product description. Also, in the Estée Lauder description, what does the term *crepey* and *crepiness* refer to? Hint: *crepe*: a thin, wrinkled fabric or paper.

428  *The Grammar of Descriptions—Adjectives*

6. The following excerpt is from the opening lines of the novel *The Giver* by Lois Lowry. The passage introduces the importance of accurate use of language and precisely appropriate word choice that is so highly valued by the community in which Jonas, the protagonist of the novel, lives. The passage is replete with a wide variety of adjective types: attributive, predicative, adjectives formed from past and present participles, restrictive relative clauses (both full forms and reduced [i.e., without *that* or *that is, was*]), and prepositional phrases functioning as adjectives.

> It was almost December, and Jonas was beginning to be frightened. No. Wrong word, Jonas thought. Frightened meant that deep, sickening feeling of something terrible about to happen. Frightened was the way he had felt a year ago when an unidentified aircraft had overflown the community twice. He had seen it both times. Squinting toward the sky, he had seen the sleek jet, almost a blur at its high speed, go past, and a second later heard the blast of sound that followed. Then one more time, a moment later, from the opposite direction, the same plane.
>
> At first, he had been only fascinated. . . .
>
> But the aircraft a year ago had been different. It was not a squat, fat-bellied cargo plane but a needle-nosed single-pilot jet. Jonas, looking around anxiously, had seen others—adults as well as children—stop what they were doing and wait, confused, for an explanation of the frightening event.
>
> (Lowry, 1993, p. 1)

First, identify as many of the adjectives as you can, including the prepositional phrases and relative clauses. Are the adjectives attributive? Are they predicative? Also, identify the determiners. How do determiners differ in terms of meaning and function from adjectives? Explain and provide examples.

Here are a few examples to start you off:

**Adjectives:**

| | |
|---|---|
| Jonas was beginning to be *frightened* | predicative adjective |
| *Wrong* word. | attributive adjective |
| *Frightened* meant. . .(i.e., "to be/feel frightened) | predicative adjective |
| . . . that <u>deep, sickening</u> feeling | attributive adjectives |
| something [that was] about to happen | reduced relative clause |

**Determiners:** (Be sure to include ∅ in your list and analysis.)
*that* deep, sickening feeling; *a* year ago; *an* unidentified aircraft; *both* times; *the* sky; *its* high speed

How does this passage portray descriptions of feelings—especially those related to mental states of understanding (or not understanding) and fear? How does the passage underscore the issues that we have discussed previously concerning *near synonymy*? How does Lowry construct comparisons and contrasts in the imagery in this passage?

7   Have a look at the following passage from Neil Gaiman's (2008) *The Graveyard Book*:

> We who make stories know that we tell lies for a living. But they are good lies that say true things, and we owe it to our readers to build them as best we can. Because somewhere out there is someone who needs that story. Someone who will grow up with a different landscape, who without that story will be a different person. And who with that story may have hope, or wisdom, or kindness, or comfort. And that is why we write.
>
> (Gaiman, 2008, p. 14)

What is Gaiman's point, and how does he structure it? Relative clauses play a big part in how he builds his idea. Identify the relative clauses. What are the subjects of the clauses? How are those noun or pronoun subjects modified with relative clauses? It's helpful to look for relative pronouns for the relative clauses to stand out more saliently. How do the relative clauses help Gaiman express his point?

8   Have a look at the following excerpts from various genres of public discourse: (a) an email in a public listserv by an owner seeking to rent a house, (b) a non-professional reader review of the novel *Little Bee*, and (c) an anonymized entry from RateMyProfessors.com—a website where students indicate their opinions about professors at any US university.

Compare and contrast each genre sample from the point of view of imagined audience/addressee, purpose, structure, register (including area-specific language), ellipsis, descriptors (adjectives/adjective types, including relative clauses), and word choice. As you work through these excerpts, focus on relevant instances of nouns, pronouns, determiners, verbs, tense and aspect, negation, and other bits of language that help construct these texts.

   a   **Email subject line: House For Rent**

   > Charming bright modernized period house for rent on farm. 3 bedrooms, study, living, kitchen, sitting room. Ample parking. Laundry. Plenty of basement and attic storage. Partially furnished or unfurnished. Beautiful views on private acreage from deck and front porch. 20 minutes drive from campus, State College School District. Available may/june on annual lease. $1350 per month + some utilities. For further details and pictures e-mail me at. . .
   >
   > ("House for Rent," n.d.)

   b   **Review of *Little Bee* by Chris Cleave**

   > Like Ian McEwan's propulsive novel "Enduring Love," in which a fatal hot-air balloon accident binds together two strangers who witness it, "Little Bee," by Guardian columnist Chris Cleave, hinges on a single horrific encounter. On a beach in Nigeria, the lives of Little Bee, a teenager from a small village, and Sara O'Rourke, editor of a posh British women's magazine, are brought into brutal conjunction.
   >
   > (Courteau, 2009)

c    RateMyProfessors.com—Robert Sandoval, Westward University (pseudonyms)

> Amazing class. I'd highly recommend this course to anyone contemplating the pursuit of any dramatic studies. Professor Sandoval is not only knowledgeable and experience, but he draws the best out of every student. p.s. Good luck with getting into this course as it's extremely competitive.
>
> (Rate My Professors, n.d.)

In what ways are these descriptive texts similar? In what ways are they different? What role do adjectives play in these three discourse excerpts? What is the purpose of each excerpt? Why are adjectives so crucial to these genres of discourse?

9   In Chapter 12, we looked at advertising slogans and taglines from the perspective of prepositions. You can also look at the same discourse genre and focus on adjectives.

Here is one example from the Toys"R"Us/Babies"R"Us retail line in response to issues surrounding the question "How prepared are you/were you to become a parent?"

BE PREPARED-ISH

What is the meaning of this tagline? How is it structured? You can search the internet to gain more insights about the history of this tagline and what it means today.

## COMMON ERRORS, BUMPS, AND CONFUSIONS

Identify the errors or "bumps" in the following sentences or paragraphs. Use the concepts and terminology that you learned in this and other chapters to articulate what might be grammatically or pragmatically problematic. Suggest ways that each can be re-written more clearly and more accurately. (Note: While all bumps do involve some element of adjectives and relative clauses, they are not limited to only that.)

1   Thanks for asking to me. I am very delighted to helping.

2   The tourists which we've met are interesting to sightsee the Gateway Arch at St. Louis.

3   I am so disappointing that people became bias and prejudice from young age.

4   The person, who have inspired me most, is John Wooden.

5   It's extremely freezing where I stay in the New York City.

6   The UN representatives, that are responsible for maintenance peace in the region, say they has troubles to communicating to the local residents.

7   Here are list of protestoring athlete's who join Colin Kaepernicks national anthem protest.

## SUGGESTED ACTIVITIES

1   Restrictive and non-restrictive relative clauses: Which is which, and why? How does the meaning change between the a versions and the b versions of the following sentences? Explain the concept of *restrictiveness* in terms of the referent subject of the relative clause.

a   The hospital, which has 335 beds, is going to close next month.
b   The hospital that has 335 beds is going to close next month.

a   Our Collie, which is still a puppy, needs shots.
b   Our Collie that/which/who is still a puppy needs shots.

2   Now, identify the relative clauses in the first five pages of this chapter. List them.

Are they restrictive relative clauses or non-restrictive relative clauses?
Do you find any instances of reduced relative clauses?

3   Relative clauses coupled with adjectives are often used in definitions and elaborations of concepts or things, much like what we observed earlier in the example with the appositive for ransomware:

> . . . ransomware, a particularly nasty type of computer virus **that** <u>encrypts computer files</u>.
> (appositive)                                                                    restrictive relative clause

Here is the *Merriam-Webster* definition of *virus* (related to computers):
> a computer program **that** <u>is usually hidden within another seemingly innocuous program</u> and **that** <u>produces copies of itself and inserts them into other programs and usually performs a malicious action</u> (such as destroying data).

Below you will find three definitions of simple words repeated from Chapter 4, initially introduced to illustrate the conceptual meanings of determiners.

For the definitions of *virus*, *hammer*, *monument*, and *noodle*, note how all descriptors work together to provide a clear and concise depiction of the thing or concept they are defining.

hammer:       A hand tool consisting of **a handle with a head of metal or other heavy rigid material** *that* <u>is attached at a right angle, used for striking or pounding</u>. ("Hammer," n.d.)
monument:     **A building or a statue** *that* <u>honors a person or an event, a building or a place</u> *that* <u>is important because of when it was built or because of something that happened there</u>. (adapted from "Monument," n.d.)
noodle:       **A narrow, ribbon-like strip of dough**, [*that is*] <u>usually made of flour, eggs, and water</u>. ("Noodle," n.d.)

Now, have a look that at the following five SAT words:

morass
alias
litigant
contusion
aberration

Write a definition for each (you may need to look up the words). What kinds of adjectives and adjective phrases do you need to define these words? Do you find yourself using relative clauses for any or all of the definitions?

4   Locate the relative clauses in the following John Wooden quotes:

"Things turn out best for the people who make the best of the way things turn out."
"Adversity is the state in which man most easily becomes acquainted with himself, being especially free of admirers then."
"You can't live a perfect day without doing something for someone who will never be able to repay you."
"A coach is someone who can give correction without causing resentment."
"It's the little details that are vital. Little things make big things happen."
"Success is never final; failure is never fatal. It's courage that counts."

What does each quote mean? Try to paraphrase each into your own words.

Find five quotes by someone who has inspired you to do your best. Be sure that all five quotes do contain relative clauses. Analyze how those relative clauses are used in the quotes. What do the quotes mean?

5   Analyze adjectives and relative clauses in news articles. Select a major news story that is covered by mainstream national news as well as local news and even some tabloid news outlets like *Globe*, *New York Post*, *Daily Star*, and *The Sun*. Conduct a three-way comparison-and-contrast study of the same story as reported in the three different venues (i.e., national, local, tabloid). How do these articles compare and contrast with each other from the point of view of register, information structure (what is assumed as *given*, and what is assumed as *new*? [see Chapter 4 for a discussion of *given* and *new* information]), adjectives (attributive/predicative), and relative clauses. Do you find any sort of skewing in terms of uses of attributive adjectives vs. predicative adjectives in the various news outlets? How are relative clauses structured in the news stories? You can build on this foundation and continue your inquiry using other news stories that are covered by all three types of news outlets.

6   The following is a list of titles of US TV series and movies. Each title contains at least one adjective. You may find attributive adjectives, predicative adjectives, adjectives that can only be used attributively, adjectives derived from past and present participles, adjectives used as nouns, adjectives that are reduced relative clauses, and nouns used as adjectives. You can design a game in which you switch the adjective type (i.e., from predicative to attributive or from attributive to predicative) and ask the class to identify the actual title from the mixed-up one. In some of the examples, you may need to turn the original titles into relative clauses (e.g., *Stranger Things* → *Things That Are Stranger* or *Things That Are Associated With A Stranger Or Strangers*). A variation of this game could be to design titles using near synonyms and have the class guess the titles.

**TV series:**

*Stranger Things*
*The Walking Dead*
*Arrested Development*
*The Young and the Restless*
*Orange Is the New Black*

**Movies:**

*Mean Girls*
*The Departed*
*The Dark Knight*
*The Good, the Bad, and the Ugly*
*The Boy in the Striped Pajamas*
*Raging Bull*
*The Man Who Would Be King*
*Eternal Sunshine of the Spotless Mind*
*Primal Fear*
*Little Women*
*Hidden Figures*

7   Think of the best teacher or professor you have had in recent years. What are his or her most positive qualities? Why was he or she such a good teacher? Brainstorm those ideas and then write a "review" of that person as if you were going to post it on RateMyProfessors.com for others to see and to convince them to take a class with that teacher.

8   Descriptors in any form (e.g., adjectives and adjective phrases, relative clauses, analogies) in all genres of discourse are socio-culturally influenced. Just like most features of "grammar," we tend to take them for granted. That is, descriptors reveal much about the preferences of particular socio-cultural groups (socio-economic status, gender, nationality, region, etc.).

Conduct a discourse-based research study of your own by isolating a certain genre of discourse and focusing on how key concepts and things are described in it, as you work to uncover socio-culturally influenced patterns of preference.

First, identify the topic you would like to pursue (e.g., cars, food, sporting goods, stationery items, tablets, telephones, photography equipment, video gaming). Then, isolate a genre of discourse for you to study.

Start with three to five exemplars of that genre, and identify the various ways that your target item or concept is described. Make an inventory of these descriptions and determine what is most salient: patterns of how nouns are used, patterns and varieties in adjective use, verbs that are associated with this item, determiners, tense and aspect, voice (active, passive, middle), and so forth.

Here are a few ideas to start you off—build on these or use this is a model to apply to other items, concepts, genres of discourse, and so forth.

Adjectives (in all forms) that describe various types of nouns—also consider determiners, nouns, verbs, tense and aspect, voice, and so forth where relevant:

## FOOD—taste terms (e.g., delicious, crunchy, ooey-gooey, melts in your mouth)

See Strauss (2005) and Jurafsky (2014) for actual language-based research conducted on this topic.

### Genres for discourse searches

- Television commercials
- Ads for fast-food restaurants
- Ads for health products
- Ads for pizza companies
- Menus for high-end restaurants
- Menus for coffee shops (e.g., Denny's)
- Reviews by diners on TripAdvisor, Yelp

### MOVIES (drama, sci-fi, documentary, movies based on books, etc.)

### Genres for discourse searches

- Reviews by professional reviewers
- Reviews by the general public (Rotten Tomatoes, Common Sense Media)

### HOTELS

### Genres for discourse searches

- High-end hotel websites
- Economy motel websites
- Reviews by guests on TripAdvisor, Yelp

### FURNITURE

### Genres for discourse searches

- Catalog entries in Gump's of San Francisco (high end) for sofas, coffee tables, dressers
- Catalog entries in Target (lower end) for sofas, coffee tables, dressers

## Academic References

Biber, D., Conrad, S., & Leech, G. (2002). *Longman student grammar of spoken and written English*. Essex: Pearson Education Limited.

Bolinger, D. (1967). Adjectives in English: Attribution and predication. *Lingua, 18*, 1–34.

Celce-Murcia, M., & Larsen-Freeman, D. (1999). *The grammar book: An ESL/EFL teacher's course*. Boston, MA: Heinle & Heinle.

Conrad, S., & Biber, D. (2009). *Real grammar: A corpus-based approach to grammar*. New York: Pearson Education.

Cowan, R. (2008). *The teacher's grammar of English: A course book and reference guide*. Cambridge: Cambridge University Press.

Davies, M. (2008–). *The corpus of contemporary American English: 520 million words, 1990-present*. Retrieved from http://corpus.byu.edu/coca/

Englebretson, R. (1997). Genre and grammar: Predicative and attributive adjectives in spoken English. *Annual Meeting of the Berkeley Linguistics Society, 23*(1), 411–421.

Jurafsky, D. (2014). *The language of food: A linguist reads the menu*. New York and London: W.W. Norton & Company.

Quirk, R., Greenbaum, S., & Leech, G., & Svartvik, J. (1985). *A comprehensive grammar of the English language*. London and New York: Longman.

Strauss, S. (2005). The linguistic aestheticization of food: A cross cultural look at food commercials in Japan, Korea, and the United States. *Journal of Pragmatics, 37*, 1427–1455.

Thompson, S. A. (1989). A discourse approach to the cross-linguistic category "adjective." *Linguistic Categorization, 61*, 245.

Truswell, R. (2004). *Attributive adjectives and the nominals they modify* (Doctoral dissertation). University of Oxford, Oxford, England, UK.

Yule, G. (1998). *Explaining English grammar: A guide to explaining grammar for teachers of English as a second or foreign language*. Oxford: Oxford University Press.

## Data References

Angelou, M. (1969). *I know why the caged bird sings*. New York: Random House.

Avon. (n.d.). Moisture therapy intensive healing & repair hand cream. Retrieved March 1, 2017, from www.avon.com/product/moisture-therapy-intensive-healing-repair-hand-cream-52855?c=repPWP&rep=mbertsch#!

Bellagio hotel and casino. (n.d.). Cvent network and supplier. Retrieved March 2, 2016, from www.cvent.com/rfp/las-vegas-hotels/bellagio-hotel-casino/venue-cfd60bd1954b4f63a5799c7ae-61c84cf.aspx

Benyus, J. (1997). *Biomimicry: Innovation inspired by nature*. New York: HarperCollins.

Carroll, L. (1869). *Alice in Wonderland*. Boston: Lee and Shepard.

Chucklevins. (n.d.). Powell Sterling silver flutes. Retrieved May 27, 2017, from www.chucklevins.com/products/powell-112000pl-91106-handmade-custom-sterling-silver-flute-with-inline-g-and-soloist-head-joint.html

Colandro, L. (2015). *There was an old lady who swallowed a frog!* New York: Cartwheel Books.

Courteau, S. (2009). Book review: "Little Bee" by Chris Cleave. *Washington Post*. Retrieved May 10, 2017, from www.washingtonpost.com/wp-dyn/content/article/2009/02/24/AR2009022403232.html

Dahl, R. (1982). *The BFG*. New York: Puffin Books.

Estée Lauder Re-Nutriv. (n.d.). Estée Lauder. Retrieved March 1, 2017, from www.esteelauder.com/product/661/3461/product-catalog/re-nutriv/re-nutriv/intensive-smoothing-hand-creme

Gaiman, N. (2008). *The graveyard book*. New York: HarperCollins.

Hammer. (n.d.). The free dictionary. Retrieved Feb. 23, 2017, from www.thefreedictionary.com/hammer.

Joybell, C. (n.d.). Quotes about right and wrong. Good reads. Retrieved February 3, 2017, from www.goodreads.com/quotes/tag/wrong-and-right.

Lowry, L. (1993). *The giver*. Boston, MA: Houghton Mifflin.

Monument. (n.d.). Wikipedia. Retrieved February 23, 2017, from https://en.wikipedia.org/wiki/Monument

Neitzl, Sh. (1989). *The jacket I wear in the snow*. New York: Greenwillow Books.

Neitzel, S. (1998). *The bag I'm taking to grandma's*. New York: William Morrow.

Noodle. (n.d.). The free dictionary. Retrieved Feb. 23, 2017, from www.thefreedictionary.com/noodle

Oppenheim, J. (n.d.). James Oppenheim quotes. Good reads. Retrieved January 29, 2017, from www.goodreads.com/quotes/194556-the-foolish-man-seeks-happiness-in-the-distance-the-wise.

Paglieri, J. (2016, March 28). U.S. hospitals are getting hit by hackers. CNN. Retrieved March 2, 2017, from http://money.cnn.com/2016/03/23/technology/hospital-ransomware/.

Powell flutes. (n.d.). Powell custom flutes. Retrieved May 27, 2017, from www.wwbw.com/Powell-Sterling-Silver-Handmade-Custom-Flute-with-Soldered-Toneholes-582523.wwbw

Rate My Professors. (n.d.). Retrieved Feb. 2, 2017, from ratemyprofessors.com.

Smith, K. (2014, April 9). Birds of a feather flock together in Rio 2. *New York Post*. Retrieved March 4, 2016, from http://nypost.com/2014/04/09/birds-of-a-feather-flock-together-in-lighthearted-rio-2.

This is the house that Jack built (n.d.). Retrieved May 10, 2017, from www.pitt.edu/~dash/type2035.html

Those shoes. (n.d.). Handmade leather shoes. Retrieved May 27, 2017, from www.thoseshoes.com

Volkswagen pleads guilty in U.S. diesel emissions scandal. (2017, March 10). *Los Angeles Times*.

# 14 The Grammar of Connecting, Adding, Conjoining, Contrasting, Indicating Alternatives, and Expressing Stance

## Conjunctions

*Figure 14.1* "I clawed my way to the top of the corporate ladder, but I couldn't get back down and they had to call the Fire Department."

© Randy Glasbergen. Reproduced with permission of Glasbergen Cartoon Service.

A conjunction is the part of speech that connects words, phrases, clauses, and sentences. Conjunctions can be categorized as coordinating conjunctions (i.e., *and, or, but, nor, yet, so, for*), correlative conjunctions (*either/or, neither/nor, both/and*), and subordinating conjunctions (e.g., *since, because, before, after, when, if, although, even though, while*). Subordinating conjunctions function as adverbials (see Chapters 2 and 15). Logical connectors like *however, moreover,* and *therefore* are also conjunctions that function as adverbials.

## 14.1 Coordinating Conjunctions

Coordinating conjunctions connect two or more words or bits of language that belong to the same category or part of speech (Larsen-Freeman & Celce-Murcia, 2016; Quirk et al,

1985). The well-known mnemonic for the seven coordinating conjunctions in English is FANBOYS:

F for
A and
N nor
B but
O or
Y yet
S so

And while the mnemonic can be generally helpful, it's not always accurate for a number of reasons. For example, *so*, *yet*, and *for* do not conjoin the full scope of constituent types, and other words in English in addition to these seven can also function to conjoin words, phrases, and clauses.

Of the seven, the most common coordinating conjunctions are *and*, *but*, and *or*.

**Examples:**

NP and/or/but NP
   **bacon** *and* **eggs**
   **friends, relatives,** *or* **acquaintances**
   **a hibiscus with blossoms** *but* **no leaves**

adjective *and* adjective
   red, white, *and* blue **snow cones**
   hot *or* cold **appetizers**
   His **management style** was tough *but* fair

verb phrase *and/or/but* verb phrase
   The crew just needed some time to relax *and* unwind.
   Taavi could not eat *or* drink anything after his surgery.
   How do I *save* an Instagram photo *but* *not* *post* it?

independent clause *and/or/but* independent clause (These form compound sentences; see Chapter 2)
   You can come watch our play *or* you can view it online.
   Politeness involves manners, *and* deference involves respect.
   I don't particularly agree with you, *but* you make good points.

The following sections will illustrate the basic meanings of each coordinating conjunction in addition to providing multiple examples of how they function in discourse.

As you read through the examples and others that you encounter in discourse, be sure to consider the various functions of **ellipsis**. Specifically, think about which words or word clusters have been ellipted and why (see Chapter 2).

### 14.1.1 And *(Additive, Sequence, Contrast)*

**Additive Meaning:**

   "Beauty *and* the Beast"
   Boys *and* Girls Clubs of America
   Follow us on Facebook *and* Twitter
   Slow *and* steady wins the race.

## Conjunctions

School meals accommodate most dietary restrictions *and* food allergies. Items are non-refundable, *and* all sales are final.

Priority seating is for seniors *and* customers with disabilities.

"(Zaha) Hadid studied at the Architectural Association in London, *and* is best known for her futuristic take on architecture." (Molinda, May 31, 2017)

"Although she contracted polio at the age of 6 *and* continued to have significant health issues throughout her life, Kahlo never stopped working *and* striving." ("Frida Kahlo's 103rd birthday," 2016)

**Sequential Meaning ("and then"):**

Kinsley did not want to leave the house *and* go to school.

I applied for *and* was granted a tuition waiver.

Amazon hinted it would buy Whole Foods, *and* on Friday, they announced the plan.

Soak the bread in the egg mixture, *and* place the soaked bread in the heated skillet.

"Did you ever stop to think *and* forget to start again?" (Milne, 1926)

**Contrastive Meaning ("but"):**

Card trick instructions: First, pick a card *and* don't let me see it.

Erica had her hair cut very short today, *and* she does not like it one bit.

Companies rarely test for nicotine use, *and* if yours does, you should be careful.

### 14.1.2 Or *(Choice, Alternative, Option, and Rephrasing of Reference Elements)*

The conjunction *or* signals a choice, an alternative, or an option (Schiffrin, 1987). For example, when ordering coffee in the summer at Dunkin' Donuts, the server may ask: "Iced *or* hot?"

These are some other choices that exist in service encounters in the US:

| | |
|---|---|
| grocery store: | paper *or* plastic? |
| ice cream shop: | cup *or* cone? |
| restaurant: | soup *or* salad? |
| | white, wheat, rye, *or* sourdough? (bread or toast choices) |
| | Italian, French, *or* blue cheese? (salad dressing choices) |
| retail express checkout: | 15 items *or* fewer [correct] |
| [special cash register that offers a shorter wait time for smaller purchases] | ?15 items *or* less [incorrect, but often used] |
| children's greeting on Halloween: | Trick *or* treat! |
| visa application: | Are you traveling with a partner, spouse, *or* dependent? |
| email instruction: | click here to reply *or* forward |

*or* **in affirmative or negative imperatives**

Call *or* text now for a free Geico Insurance quote.

Do NOT click on links in email *or* open attachments in suspicious emails.

*or* **in warnings or advice (meaning: "if you (don't), then . . ."; see Chapter 15**

Leave now *or* face the consequences. ["If you don't leave now, you will . . ."]

Take a coat *or* you'll get sick. ["If you don't take a coat, you'll get sick."]

440  *Conjunctions*

Put the leftovers in the fridge, <u>or</u> they'll spoil. ["If you don't put the leftovers . . ."]
Don't swim right after eating <u>or</u> you'll get a cramp. ["If you swim right after eating, you'll . . ."]
Don't put your hand in the subway door <u>or</u> it will get caught. ["If you put your hand . . ."]
Don't be home after 11:00 <u>or</u> there will be a curfew next weekend. ["If you are home . . ."]

**or in rephrasing reference elements ("in other words")**

Note that this use of *or* often functions like an appositive (see Chapter 13).

China has 1.4 billion people, <u>or</u> one fifth of the world's population.
The Frida Kahlo Museum, <u>or</u> La Casa Azul ('The Blue House'), is in Mexico City.
The aperture, <u>or</u> the lens diaphragm, allows light into the body of the camera.
Yuki Kuroda, <u>or</u> the father of modern Japanese linguistics, studied under Chomsky at MIT.

### 14.1.3 But *(Contrastive, Additive, "Only")*

*But* typically expresses contrasting, opposite, or juxtaposing ideas or concepts—for example, part/whole, number, quality, frequency, value, affirmative/negative (often occurring with *not*, *never*, and other expressions of negation), past/present (e.g., now vs. then) (Lakoff, 1971; Schiffrin, 1987; Van Dijk, 1979). *But* can also express an "additive" meaning, similar to *and*, but still evoking contrast. In the following examples, elements of contrast are underlined.

The city tour was offered to <u>the entire group</u>, *but* (*and*) <u>only a few</u> people participated.
Companies <u>rarely test for nicotine use</u>, *but* (*and*) <u>if yours does</u>, you should be careful.
Our house <u>sold for $500,000</u>, *but* (*and*) it had been <u>appraised for much less</u>.
Nova <u>wanted to say good-bye to Sean</u>, *but* (*and*) she <u>couldn't muster up the courage</u>.
Brielle's family <u>used to be poor</u>, *but* (*and*) <u>now they are comfortable</u>.
<u>The movie was excellent</u>, *but* (*and*) it's <u>not appropriate for children</u>.

Because of its essential meaning of contrast, *but* occurs often in conversation where speakers preface a disagreement or counter-stance in response to an interlocutor's statement or claim (Biber et al., 1999; Schiffrin, 1987).

a countering an interlocutor's statement or claim:

A: The golden rule is if the car is in reverse, you must look behind you (when you are backing up).
B: Yeah, <u>but</u> she said she did (look behind her).
[adapted from Biber et al. (1999, p. 238)]

b expression of positive stance + *but* + expression of negative stance:

Student: Have you had a chance to read my essay?
Tutor: Yes, and you have <u>some great points</u> ***but*** I think <u>they would be much clearer</u> if you explain in more detail and give the reader a concrete example or two.

Boy: Do you want to see a movie with me on Friday night?
Girl: <u>I'd really love to</u>, ***but*** <u>my cousins are visiting</u> from out of town (so <u>I can't</u> go with you).

c   but meaning "only":

> Even though it was snowing, Jacquie wore nothing *but* a thin sweater.
> Pip was *but* a toddler when his dad left for the war and never returned.
> Morris's financial support was *but* a drop in the bucket. His wife needed more.

## 14.1.4 For *(Reason)*

*For* used as a conjunction is rare in spontaneous spoken and informal or non-literary written discourse. Conjunciton *for* typically signals a formal or literary register. Its meaning can generally be paraphrased as "because" or "as."

**The following three examples are from COCA (Davies, 2008–).**

1 "His father bellowed his name again, demanding that he enter. Yet Jonathan hesitated *for* he was rarely invited into this room."

2 "He (Yonaguska) pulled out a pipe which he held out to Will. 'Now you have a pipe,' he said. 'Let's smoke.' . . . Will . . . lit the pipes. He was careful, *for* he had never smoked before, and he was afraid that he might cough or choke, but he did not."

3 "The reaction to the Boston Marathon bombings undoubtedly brought to light other examples of immediate courage . . . in the face of adversity. We must continue to highlight these stories *for* we need these moral exemplars and narratives of healing."

## 14.1.5 Nor *(Addition/Continuation of Commentary That Is Negative)*

*Nor* used as a coordinating conjunction serves to add commentary that is negative or to continue a logical thread by adding more negative commentary. *Nor* can connect phrasal units as well as clauses, as in the following example that connects two adverbs (see Chapter 15):

> Training takes time and it is not always offered regularly **nor** well. (adapted from Davies, 2008–)

When conjoining two independent clauses, the use of *nor* requires syntactic modifications to the second of the two clauses in which *nor* appears:

> Coaches *do not* diagnose severe injuries.   [independent clause 1]
> They *do* not *treat* them either.   [independent clause 2]

**To conjoin these two clauses:**

1   ADD *nor*.

2   Invert the subject and the verb.
    → Coaches *do not diagnose severe injuries*, **nor** *do they treat them.*

The meaning of *nor* here is ". . . *AND* + ADDITIONAL COMMENTARY + NOT *either.*"

1   The car didn't need service yesterday, **nor** did it need a smog inspection.
    [AND it did NOT need a smog inspection *either*]

2   There were never any miscommunications in the past, **nor** should there be any now.

3   Will shoppers ditch Costco and Amazon Prime for Jet? After all, Jet doesn't offer those in-store samples, same-day shipping, or video streaming, **nor** does it match those companies' incredible inventory. Let the shopping wars begin.

(Davies, 2008–)

## 14.1.6 Yet *(Concessive, Contrastive)*

*Yet* connects both phrasal units and clauses. It carries a meaning similar to the contrastive meaning of *but*. As we did with *but*, we have underlined the elements of contrast or juxtaposition. [Both examples are from COCA (Davies, 2008–).]

Caregivers need to remain <u>calm</u> **yet** <u>assertive</u>.

Students are in need of dealing with the following: homograph and homonym. <u>The former</u> are words that are <u>spelled the same</u>, for example, bow of the ship and bow and arrow. <u>The latter</u> are words with a <u>different spelling</u> **yet** <u>possess the same sound</u>, such as to, too, and two; plane and plain.

*Yet* also differs from *but* from the point of view of register, indicating a higher and more formal register than *but*. Thus, *yet* sometimes also expresses a meaning of contrast similar to *however* (see Section 14.4).

### 14.1.6.1 And Yet *("... and in Spite of This ...")*

As a variation of *yet*, *and yet* often expresses the notion of "and in spite of this" (i.e., the statement just made).

Clearly, it's winter, **and yet** young Pauline has a great business idea—a lemonade stand! (Davies, 2008–)

The question is still unanswerable, which is not to say futile. The greatest reward of this constant interrogation, of confrontation with the brutality of my country is that it has freed me from ghosts and myths. **AND YET** I AM STILL AFRAID. (emphasis original) (Davies, 2008–)

Internet meme—photo of dog(s) at the window, looking outside, longingly:

> "So far, my barking has saved Mom and Dad from murder by 40 mailmen, 16 UPS drivers, 3 girl scouts, 28 cats, and 1 sketchy looking plastic bag on the road...
> ... **and yet** they remain ungrateful."

## 14.1.7 So *(Sequential, Consequential, Inferential; Therefore, in Order That)*

*So* is a highly frequent conjunction (Biber et al., 1999, p. 887). Schiffrin (1987) categorizes *so* as a discourse marker of "result." Blakemore (1988, 2002) considers *so* as a marker of inferential conclusion. In this sense, *so* carries a meaning similar to that of *therefore*. *So* is used within all registers of discourse, whereas *therefore* is more formal and signals a higher register.

*So* **meaning "therefore":**

The conference room is not available, <u>so</u> we will meet in my office.
Shanshan is training for a marathon, <u>so</u> she's been very careful with her diet.

"As an immigrant child of eight, I had the illusion that I could already speak English. And *so* along with my classmates at P.S. No.8 in Brooklyn, I placed my hand over my heart, started at the stars and stripes, and proudly proclaimed 'I pledge a lesson to the frog of the United States of America and to the wee puppet for witches hands, on Asian, in the vestibule, with little tea and just rice for all.'" (Bette Bao Lord, 2000)

*So* **as an inferential conclusion marker:**

"In her early work, Hadid visualized her projects through paintings that resembled abstract modernist art. She famously said, 'There are 360 degrees, *so* why stick to one?'" ("Celebrating Zaha Hadid," 2017)

"I got interested in this other path to adulthood when I was myself a college student attending the University of Pennsylvania in the early 2000s. Penn sits within a historic African-American neighborhood. *So* you've got these two parallel journeys going on simultaneously: the kids attending this elite, private university, and the kids from the adjacent neighborhood, some of whom are making it to college, and many of whom are being shipped to prison." (Goffman, 2015)

*So* **meaning "in order that," "to assure," "to be sure that"**

Everyone please put your cell phone on the table or in your bag *so* there is no suspicion of cheating.

Read these tips *so* you will know how to create a professional-quality video.

"When planting roses, pruning is crucial to keep the center of the flower open, *so* sunshine can shine in." (Gelman, n.d.)

---

**Mini Review and Practice**

1   The following three quotes display interesting uses of conjunctions, each of which expresses some degree of wit or humor:

   All you need is love. *But* a little chocolate now *and* then doesn't hurt. (Charles M. Schulz)

   Beauty is in the eye of the beholder *and* it may be necessary from time to time to give a stupid *or* misinformed beholder a black eye. (Jim Henson)

   Instead of *either/or*, I discovered a whole world of *and*. (Steinem, 2015)

First, identify the conjunctions in each. Describe how the use of conjunctions is the essence of each message. What does each quote mean? Paraphrase each into your own words.
   Now, focus on the quote by Schulz. What is the contrast established between the two clauses? What is the humor in this quote?
   The second clause (sentence) contains *and* conjoining two adverbs whose meanings are somewhat opposite: now *and* then

Here are a few more examples:
   here *and* there
   inside *and* outside
   high *and* low

Think about the effect that this combination of words with seemingly opposite meanings creates in discourse.

2. The opening cartoon, Figure 14.1, depicts a cat as a corporate executive on the telephone telling a "success story" narrative. But it is not entirely a success story. There was one major complicating issue.

Part of the humor has to do with the expression "I clawed my way to the top." This can be interpreted literally, which would relate well to how a cat would climb a vertical structure, or it can be more figurative.

Paraphrase the caption in your own words, and think about the types of coordinating conjunctions you use as you do this. What is the difference between how you might use *and* and how you might use *but*?

3. Have a look at the following actual breakfast menu description from the Cozy Corner Restaurant and Pancake House (Cozy Corner Restaurant and Pancake House, n.d.):

   **EGGS**

   Two eggs (any style) served with hash browns **or** fresh fruit *and* toast **or** pancakes

   What are the possible serving options for this breakfast?
   The main element is the two eggs. Think about the various potential combinations for each menu order. What are they?

4. Have a look at Figure 14.2. What is the context? What does the caption mean? How does the use of *so* contribute to the humor and overall meaning of this cartoon? Again, paraphrase the meaning of the caption, and think about the possible coordinating conjunctions.

"Our ads promise you the biggest tax refund possible, so we're instructing your employer to withhold 300% of your paycheck this year."

*Figure 14.2* "Our ads promise you the biggest tax refund possible, so we're instructing your employer to withhold 300% of your paycheck this year."

© Randy Glasbergen. Reproduced with permission of Glasbergen Cartoon Service.

*Figure 14.3* "The college of my choice is very expensive, but when you graduate, they give you a home in the suburbs, a minivan, a lovely wife, two beautiful children and a golden retriever."

© Randy Glasbergen. Reproduced with permission of Glasbergen Cartoon Service.

5    Similar to number 4, here is another cartoon. What does the caption for Figure 14.3 mean? How is *but* used here to create both a sense of contrast and humor?

6    Think about the following two adjectives: *single, happy*.

Now, conjoin them with *and*, *but*, and *or*.
   SINGLE AND HAPPY
   SINGLE BUT HAPPY
   SINGLE OR HAPPY

What are the socio-cultural assumptions that underlie each phrase? Also, imagine a socio-cultural context in which each phrase might be used.

Now, do the same with the following adjectives pairs. That is, conjoin each with *and*, *but*, and then *or*. What types of socio-cultural assumptions might underlie each conjoined pair of adjectives with varying types of coordinating conjunctions?

   studious, fun-loving
   health-conscious, sedentary
   exciting, frightening

7    The following extract is adapted from an interview with Steve Jobs in 2007.

   Steve:          . . . There's a lot of things that are risky right now, which is always a good sign, you know, and you can see through them, you can see to the other side and go, "Yes, this could be huge," **but** there's a period of risk that, you know, nobody's ever done it before.
   Interviewer:   Do you have an example?
   Steve:          I do, **but** I can't say.

446  *Conjunctions*

> Interviewer: OK.
> Steve: **But** I *can* say, when you feel like that, that's a great thing.
> ("Bill Gates & Steve Jobs at D5," 2007)
>
> Explain how *but* is used in this excerpt. What does it mean? What is being contrasted?
>
> Listen for examples of *but* in everyday conversation, in TV dramas, and so on, and think about what *but* signals in these contexts of interaction. You can transcribe the longer stretches of discourse and listen for and analyze *and*, *but*, *yet*, *and yet*, *or*, *nor*, and *so*.

## 14.2 Correlative Conjunctions

From a structural perspective, correlative conjunctions occur in pairs, like *either . . . or*, *neither . . . nor*, and *both . . . and*. From a discourse perspective, correlative conjunctions highlight the speaker's or writer's stance by underscoring exclusion (*neither . . . nor*, *either . . . or*) or inclusion (*both/and*). The correlative component is often optional in terms of grammar, but it serves a strong discourse function.

### 14.2.1 Neither/Nor; Either/Or *(Highlighting Exclusion)*

The first three examples are adapted from COCA (Davies, 2008–).

1 These statements *neither* deny *nor* affirm what the patient is saying.
2 This is an act that I *neither* suggested *nor* prompted.
3 This kitchen is *neither* classic *nor* modern.
4 "N*either* rain *nor* snow could keep George from watching his favorite band perform in Endless Park." (adapted from "Curious George" the TV show, 2010)
5 "If you wonder where your plastic toothbrushes and cigarette lighters go after you trash them, here's your answer: Many end up in the ocean, which means that they *either* sink to the bottom *or* wash up on beaches—like this remote, uninhabited island in the middle of the Pacific Ocean." (Potenza, May 16, 2017)

### 14.2.2 Both/And *(Highlighting Inclusion)*

*Both* Babak *and* Ramin arrived late. [Babak and Ramin arrived late.]

She is *both* energetic *and* ambitious. [She is energetic and ambitious.]

"Teachers should impart knowledge, use grade assessment tools, and communicate student performance *both* objectively *and* subjectively." (Davies, 2008–)

### 14.2.3 Not Only/But Also

**Original:**

These recipes are *not only* delicious but *also* healthy.

**Variations:**

These recipes are *not only* delicious *but* healthy, *too*.

*Not only* are these recipes delicious, they are *also* healthy.

These recipes are *both* delicious *and* healthy.

"Those in possession (of drugs) *not only* pose a risk to themselves *but* everyone they come into contact with *as well*." (Mettler, May 16, 2017)

## 14.3 Subordinating Conjunctions

Unlike coordinating conjunctions that connect two or more categories or bits of language that are of equal grammatical status, subordinating conjunctions occur at the beginning of a dependent or subordinate clause, which is connected to a main or independent clause.

Examples of subordinating conjunctions include *if, when, unless, until, before, after, because, since, where, wherever, due to the fact that, although, even though, inasmuch as, as far as, provided that*, and so forth. These expressions are adverbial in function, and some are discussed in detail in Chapter 15. Subordinating conjunctions form complex sentences (see Chapters 2 and 15).

## 14.4 Logical Connectors

Logical connectors refer to the type of conjunction that is typically adverbial in nature and that serves to express such notions as *additive, temporal, causal, conditional,* and *adversative/concessive*. Note that the lists of exemplars here are not at all exhaustive.

### Examples of additive logical connectors:

and yet, and then, so that, moreover, further, furthermore, in addition, as well as, besides, in other words, likewise, similarly

### Examples of temporal logical connectors:

now, then, first, second, lastly, beforehand, afterward, finally, currently, until, when

### Examples of causal logical connectors:

therefore, so, thus, hence, as a result, consequently, to that end

### Examples of conditional logical connectors:

if, when, in the event that, provided that, unless

### Examples of adversative logical connectors:

however, nevertheless, actually, in effect, by contrast, on the one hand, at any rate, on the contrary, even though, although

### Logical connectors built with prepositions (see Chapter 12):

in: in addition (to), in other words, in sum, in conclusion, in so many words, in contrast, in effect

on: on the contrary, on the other hand, on account of
to: with respect to, due to, leading to
as: as a result, such as, as noted

(Quirk et al., 1985)

\*\*\*\*\*\*\*\*

## PRACTICE WITH DATA ANALYSIS: PUTTING IT ALL TOGETHER

1. Identify the various parts of speech and grammatical constructions in popular easy reading books like *The Rainbow Fish*, *Click, Clack, Moo*, and *The Giving Tree*. If you can't locate the actual book, you can find versions of the books online, often with animation or videos of someone reading the book. For this chapter, focus on how conjunctions are used in the texts. You'll also find that conjunctions might be possible between two constituents, but they were not used, and simply implied. As you work with the texts, also pay attention to other parts of speech and grammatical constructions as they relate to the story line (e.g., nouns, determiners, pronouns, verbs, tense and aspect, prepositions, adjectives [including relative clauses]).

2. Here are two excerpts taken from different discourse genres and representing different registers.

    a. "Shortsightedness <u>*or*</u> myopia, a condition where distant objects appear blurry while close objects appear normal, is an eye problem that is becoming increasingly serious among Chinese children. It is estimated that in China the myopia rate is 31%. *However*, among children and teenagers it can be as high as 90%."

    (Chelala, 2017)

    b. "There's no substitute for the hands-on, loving attention that an individual is going to give those pets. And that brings us to the Dog Lady of Geff, Illinois and the string of Catch-22s she inadvertently created. This was Pearl Foval's farm. The house is gone now, *but* 12 years ago, she lived here with 69 dogs she had rescued."

    (Davies, 2008–)

Review the grammatical differences that are associated with register and genre. (See Chapter 2).

3. How would you characterize the genre of excerpt a? How about the genre of excerpt b? What are the grammatical features that set the one apart from the other? Beyond genre and register, how is the use of *however* in excerpt a different from the use of *but* in excerpt b?

4. The following text is an actual oral narrative about a very frightening experience as told by Alan to a friend, in answer to the question "What was the scariest experience you have ever had?"

How did Alan establish the background of his narrative? How did he build the suspense of it? Were you able to envision the situation that he described? Which parts were especially vivid? Which parts, if any, were less clear? Why?

How did Alan use conjunctions to continue the story line through the end? How did he conclude his narrative?

Which conjunction was the most frequent? Why do you think this is so? What is the purpose of that conjunction? Does the meaning of the conjunction change at all throughout the story? If so, how? What other conjunctions does he use?

> When I was younger I was in Cub Scouts
> and on a field trip to the World Trade Center,
> and you know at the top of the building, they had an observatory platform that ended about two or three feet away from the actual glass,
> and then there were two steps down,
> and then a series of benches around
> so that people could sit and people behind them could still look out.
> And it was the first time I had been in anything higher than a three-story building.
> And I got up there and was easing my way to the top of the platform,
> and my mom, who of course had no understanding of my fear, pushed me a little, and
> I fell down those two steps and up against the window.
> But when you're falling you don't see the window.
> All you see is, y'know, all the way down to the street,
> and it was the longest couple of seconds that I've ever experienced,
> You know because honestly, you-
> I thought I was falling off the building.
> Y'know, so in those moments, I was really the scaredest I'd ever been in my whole life.
>
> (Alan, n.d.)

## COMMON ERRORS, BUMPS, AND CONFUSIONS

The following text is a version of an email from a student to a former ESL teacher sent during winter break. As you read through it, think about issues of genre, pragmatics, and grammar—including word choice, conjunctions, tense and aspect, overall sentence structure, and even punctuation. Also think about *authorial voice* and the degree of personal involvement that you hear in this message. Imagine that you are this student's current teacher and you want to use his or her actual discourse as a basis for teaching grammar and pragmatics, while at the same time helping students maintain their own voice, excitement, and passion.

From the point of view of grammar, which issues are more immediately noticeable? Which are more subtle and less noticeable?

Construct a lesson (or series of lessons) in which you have this student (and/or other students) revise and edit the email so that it sounds more grammatically correct and more pragmatically appropriate.

> Hello dearest professor,
>
> At first, I hoped you had a nice winter vacation, too and my vacation was fantastic! Actually, I took a trip from Key West in Florida to Augusta, Maine along east-coast line! Although it was a little bit freezing on north parts of our ride, the view or the mood of places were really different depending on cities! And I'm really happy with your mail because it means that you didn't forget us since the break. Your mail makes me remember the excitements in your classes but you give us many confidences as ESL students here in the US for first time.
> Thanks a lot,
> J.H.

## SUGGESTED ACTIVITIES

1  Work with narrative discourse to analyze the types of conjunctions that are used within a full narrative. Highlight all conjunctions, and determine which are the most frequent.

How does the narrative open? How does it develop? How are the key details made salient? Are there conjunctions within the sentences as well as between them?

Do you find cases where there is no *overt* conjunction in parts of the text, but readers can infer which conjunction might be used if there were one at that place? What effect is created by the *absence* of conjunctions?

One example to start with could be the following TED Talk by Tan Le:

### "My Immigration Story"

> My mother, my sister and I slept in the same bed. My mother was exhausted each night, but we told one another about our day and listened to the movements of my grandmother around the house. My mother suffered from nightmares, all about the boat. And my job was to stay awake until her nightmares came so I could wake her. She opened a computer store, then studied to be a beautician and opened another business. And the women came with their stories about men who could not make the transition (into Western culture), angry and inflexible, and troubled children caught between two worlds.
>
> Grants and sponsors were sought. Centers were established. I lived in parallel worlds. In one, I was the classic Asian student, relentless in the demands that I made on myself. In the other, I was enmeshed in lives that were precarious, tragically scarred by violence, drug abuse and isolation. But so many over the years were helped. And for that work, when I was a final-year law student, I was chosen as the Young Australian of the Year. And I was catapulted from one piece of the jigsaw to another, and their edges didn't fit.
> (Le, 2012)

Another example is Martin Pistorius's "How My Mind Came Back to Life—And No One Knew." This is an amazingly powerful story. We provide a short excerpt of Pistorius's autobiography in Chapter 12. www.ted.com/talks/martin_pistorius_how_my_mind_came_back_to_life_and_no_one_knew.

2  Examine and analyze the use of conjunctions in famous speeches and/or quotations.

How are the conjunctions used? What persuasive effects might those conjunctions have on the overall messages?

One salient example is George W. Bush's "Address to a Joint Session of Congress and the American People," from September 2001, just following the 9/11 attacks.

Here is a brief excerpt:

> "Every nation, in every region, now has a decision to make. Either you are with us, or you are with the terrorists." (Bush, 2001)

Analyze the full text of this speech by focusing first on conjunctions, and then on other parts of grammar (e.g., repetition, reference terms for peoples and nations, pronouns, demonstratives, tense and aspect, questions).

You can do this activity with other political/historical speeches to gain a deeper understanding of the speaker who delivered it and the context in which it was delivered, as well as the historical background behind its delivery.

## Academic References

Biber, D., Johansson, S., Leech, G., Conrad, S., & Finegan, E. (1999). *Grammar of spoken and written English*. Harlow: Longman.

Blakemore, D. (1988). "So" as a constraint on relevance. In R. M. Kempson (Ed.), *Mental representations: The interface between language and reality* (pp. 183–195). Cambridge: Cambridge University Press.

Blakemore, D. (2002). *Relevance and linguistic meaning: The semantics and pragmatics of discourse markers: Vol. 99*. Cambridge: Cambridge University Press.

Davies, M. (2008–). *The corpus of contemporary American English: 520 million words, 1990-present*. Retrieved form http://corpus.byu.edu/coca/.

Lakoff, R. (1971). If's, and's, and but's about conjunction. In C. J. Fillmore & D. T. Langendoen (Eds.), *Studies in linguistic semantics* (pp. 115–150). New York: Holt, Rinehart and Winston.

Larsen-Freeman, D., & Celce-Murcia, M. (2016). *The grammar book: Form, meaning, and use for English language teachers*. Boston, MA: National Geographic and Heinle.

Quirk, R., Greenbaum, S., Leech, G., & Svartvik, J. (1985). *A comprehensive grammar of the English language*. London: Longman.

Schiffrin, D. (1987). *Discourse markers*. Cambridge and New York: Cambridge University Press.

Van Dijk, T. (1979). Pragmatic connectives. *Journal of Pragmatics, 3*, 447–456.

## Data References

Bill Gates and Steve Jobs at D5 (Transcript). (2007, May). Retrieved May 1, 2017, from http://allthingsd.com/20070531/d5-gates-jobs-transcript/

Bush, G. (2001, September). Address to a joint session of congress and the American people. Retrieved June 1, 2017, from https://georgewbush-whitehouse.archives.gov/news/releases/2001/09/20010920-8.html

Celebrating Zaha Hadid. (2017, May 31). Google doodles archive. Retrieved June 1, 2017, from www.google.com/doodles/celebrating-zaha-hadid?hl=en

Chelala, C. (2017, June 7). Myopia is an increasingly serious problem among Chinese children. Retrieved June 10, 2017, from www.counterpunch.org/2017/06/07/myopia-is-an-increasingly-serious-problem-among-chinese-children/

Cozy Corner Restaurant and Pancake House. (n.d.). Retrieved May 1, 2017, from www.cozycornerrestaurant.com/

Curious George–George and Marco sound it out. (2010, September 7). PBS [TV Episode].

Frida Kahlo's 103rd birthday. (2010, July 6). Google doodles. Retrieved June 1, 2017, from www.google.com/doodles/frida-kahlos-103rd-birthday

Gelman, L. (n.d.). 10 expert gardening tips for beginners. Retrieved May 1, 2017, from www.rd.com/home/gardening/gardening-tips-for-beginners

Goffman, A. (2015). How we are priming some kids for college-and others for prison? Retrieved May 1, 2017, from www.ted.com/talks/alice_goffman_college_or_prison_two_destinies_one_blatant_injustice

Le, T. (2012, February). My immigration story. Retrieved June 1, 2017, from www.ted.com/talks/tan_le_my_immigration_story

Lord, B. B. (2000). As an immigrant child of eight . . . In PEN/Faulkner Foundation (Ed.), *Three minutes or less: Life lessons from America's greatest writers* (pp. 114–115). New York: Bloomsbury Publishing.

Markham, B. (1942). Good reads. Retrieved January 19, 2016, from www.goodreads.com/quotes/353737-if-a-man-has-any-greatness-in-him-it-comes

Mettler, K. (2017, May 16). "I was in shock": Ohio police officer accidentally overdoses after traffic stop. Retrieved June 1, 2017, from www.washingtonpost.com/news/morning-mix/wp/2017/05/16/i-was-in-total-shock-ohio-police-officer-accidentally-overdoses-after-traffic-stop

Milne, A. A. (1926). *Winnie-the-pooh*. London: Methuen Publishing Ltd.

Molina, B. (2017, May 31). Google doodle pays tribute to groundbreaking architect Zaha Hadid. Retrieved June 1, 2017, from www.usatoday.com/story/tech/talkingtech/2017/05/31/zaha-hadid-google-doodle-honors-architect/357679001/

Potenza, A. (2017, May 16). This Pacific island is covered in 38 million pieces of trash—mostly plastic. Retrieved May 1, 2017, fromwww.theverge.com/2017/5/16/15646800/henderson-island-pacific-ocean-plastic-trash-pollution

Steinem, G. (2015). *My life on the road*. London: Oneworld Publications.

# 15 The Grammar of Exquisitely Evoking Events, How Things Happen, When Things Happen, If Things Happen, and How We Portray Such Views in Discourse

Adverbs

"For richer or poorer, in sickness and health, until one little thing goes wrong and you give up on each other?"

*Figure 15.1* "For richer or poorer, in sickness and health, until one little thing goes wrong and you give up on each other?"

© Randy Glasbergen. Reproduced with permission of Glasbergen Cartoon Service.

Adverbs and adverbials are the lexical items and grammatical constructions that answer the four basic questions *How? When? Where?* and *Why?* and their variations like *What time? in what direction? for what? to what end? in what way? how often? to what degree?* and so forth.

Adverbs constitute the part of speech for single words that answer the same four basic questions—words like *calmly, absolutely, today, tomorrow, here,* and *there.* Adverbs also express aspects of speaker stance with regard to certainty or uncertainty, like *maybe, surely,* and *perhaps.* In addition to modifying the verbal or predicate elements within a clause or sentence, adverbs like *too, really, just,* and *exceptionally* also serve to modify adjectives, like <u>really</u> beautiful and <u>exceptionally</u> talented. And adverbs like *just, right,* and *straight* modify other adverbs, as in *He cooked the meat just <u>perfectly</u>* or *Go <u>straight ahead</u>.*

Adverbials function in essentially the same way as the adverb does as a basic part of speech, but adverbials consist of more than one word: a noun phrase (*next week, this semester, step-by-step*), a prepositional phrase (*in ten minutes, on your right*), an adverb phrase (*right away, straight ahead, hardly ever*), a present or past participial phrase (<u>*Trying to suppress her laughter,*</u> Pangiota took a

454  *Adverbs*

*deep breath*), or a subordinate adverbial clause (*when we travel to Japan, if you're still hungry, as I was saying*) (See Chapter 2).

Because of the wide variety of shapes that adverbials take, they have been referred to as the class of words "whose members are a good deal more heterogeneous than. . . [those of] . . . other primary classes" (Huddleston, 1984, p. 96), "the most diverse [grammatical structure] in their forms and syntactic positions" (Larsen-Freeman & Celce-Murcia, 2016, p. 509), and even as "the most nebulous and puzzling of the traditional word classes" with "great heterogeneity" (Quirk et al., 1985, p. 438).

## 15.1 Forms

**Single-word adverbs:**

a   Formed by adding the derivational morpheme *-ly* to adjectives (see Chapter 2):

| Adjective | → | Adverb | |
|---|---|---|---|
| frank | → | frankly | |
| absolute | → | absolutely | |
| pleasant | → | pleasantly | |
| plain | → | plainly | |
| easy | → | easily | (final *y* → *i*) |
| steady | → | steadily | (final *y* → *i*) |
| audible | → | audibly | (final *e* is dropped) |
| possible | → | possibly | (final *e* is dropped) |
| electric | → | electrically | (add *-al* + *ly*) |
| eccentric | → | eccentrically | (add *-al* + *ly*) |
| frantic | → | frantically | (add *-al* + *ly*) |

Exceptions to the simple rule of adding *-ly* to adjectives:

| **good** | → | **well** | (this is an irregular form [*goodly is not a word]) |

**adjectives that do not take *-ly* to form adverbs:**

| fast | → | fast | |
|---|---|---|---|
| early | → | early | |
| daily | → | daily | |
| weekly | → | weekly | |
| late | → | late | [*lately* has a different meaning] |
| hard | → | hard | [*hardly* has a different meaning] |

b   Other single-word adverbs:

here, there, ahead, outside, indoors, straight
now, then, often, again, still
therefore, thus, additionally, moreover
maybe, perhaps
just, only, too, really

**Examples:**

<u>Unfortunately</u>, we can't be at the meeting <u>today</u>.
Fahim was <u>definitely</u> going <u>somewhere</u>. We <u>just</u> didn't know <u>where</u>.

**Multiple-word adverbials:**

Multiple word adverbials are formed with noun phrases, prepositional phrases, adverb phrases, participial phrases, and adverbial clauses.

**Adverbials with:**

| | |
|---|---|
| Noun phrases: | step by step, one at a time, next summer |
| Prepositional phrases: | at noon, on the right, per person, with pleasure |
| Adverb phrases: | right away, quite frankly, just now |
| Participial phrases: | Matafu left, <u>gripping the candy he'd just purchased</u>. |
| | <u>*Mumbling to himself*</u>, Jean-Marc sat down at the table. |

With participial clauses, the subject of the main verb and the ellipted subject of the participial clause must be the same (i.e., *Matafu left/Matafu was gripping the candy // Jean-Marc sat down/Jean-Marc was mumbling to himself*).

This is an ungrammatical sentence:

*Colton wished he'd gone to Stanford instead of UCLA, having recently added an academic program in New York City to its curriculum.

Colton = subject of main clause
Stanford = ellipted or implied subject of participial phrase (i.e., the entity that added an academic program in NYC)

**Adverbial clauses:**

<u>*When it rains in California*</u>, everyone jumps for joy.
<u>*Because the book was late*</u>, the library charged a fine. (For an extended discussion of adverbial clauses, see Chafe, 1984; Ford, 1993.)

Adverbial clauses begin with adverbial subordinators like *when, if, because, due to the fact that, after,* and *before* and contain a subject and predicate, forming a subordinate or dependent clause (see Chapter 2).

## 15.2 Functions

The primary function of adverbs and adverbials is to modify the verbal part or the predicate of the clause or sentence, answering the four basic questions of *Where?, Why?, When?,* and *How?* In this sense, adverbs and adverbials can be classified into two basic categories: adverbials of *circumstance* and adverbials of *stance*, adapted from Biber et al. (2002).

### 15.2.1 Adverbs and Adverbials of Circumstance

Adverbs (single words) and adverbials (multiple words) of circumstance provide a detailed image of the state or event as evoked in the predicate or the verbal element of the clause or sentence. These words and constructions complement the meaning of the verb or predicate. They express the following details (adapted from Biber et al., 2002).

- **time, temporality, sequentiality, and frequency:**

  now, never, tomorrow, often, always, ever, first, next, then

  before noon, all the time, at 1:00 p.m., once in a while, ever since

  when Jorge arrives, until the bell rings, hardly ever, at the same time as, as she was baking cookies, as soon as it started to rain, since he was a boy.

**Examples:**

Gianna is <u>usually</u> not concerned about her grades, but <u>lately</u> she's been a little nervous.
       [adverb]                                        [adverb]

The names of the Pulitzer Prize winners will be announced <u>next week</u>.
                                                                            [noun phrase]

Dr. Masulto suggests postponing surgery <u>until</u>     <u>after the new year</u>.
                                                    [adverb]        [prepositional phrase]

We had to wait <u>*until* the manager approved my credit card</u> <u>*before* we could check in to the hotel</u>.
                [adverbial clause: *until* = ADV SUB]     [adverbial clause: *before* = ADV SUB]

Your children can play in IKEA's Småland play area <u>*while* you *shop*</u>.
                                                                     [adverbial clause: *while* = ADV SUB]

In-N-Out Burger has been in operation in the US <u>since 1948</u>.
                                                       [prepositional phrase]

Laurie and I have known each other <u>*since* we were 5 years old</u>.
                                    [adverbial clause: *since* = ADV SUB]

- **space, place, and direction:**

    far, home, halfway, inside, eastward, up, down, high, somewhere

    to the right, in the middle, halfway, toward the back

**Examples:**

Dominic waited <u>here</u>    <u>by this window</u> to better observe what was happening <u>outside</u>.
                      [adverb] [prepositional phrase]                                                    [adverb]

The puppy followed the children <u>*wherever* they went</u>.
                              [adverbial clause: *wherever* = ADV SUB]

I'll put your keys on the chair <u>*where* your jacket is.</u>
                            [adverbial clause: *where* = ADV SUB]

- **manner (how, in what way, using what, by whom/by what)**

    gently, slowly, fast, shyly, well, thoroughly, continually

    in ink, like a bunny, with caution, with a candlestick, without looking too fast, by the thief, on foot, by bike

    keeping his eye consistently on the ball, speaking English like an Australian, as we all know, as if he were the boss, like children do

**Examples:**

Aubrey was pouting and acting <u>like a spoiled child</u>.
                                        [prepositional phrase]

He speaks <u>much too fast</u>. He should enunciate <u>carefully</u>.
           [adverb phrase]                      [adverb]

Hudson ordered us around, <u>as if he were the person in charge</u>, but he is our equal.
[adverbial clause: *as* = ADV SUB]

Orion left the concert <u>in a very happy mood</u>, <u>whistling Mozart's *Eine kleine Nachtmusik.*</u>
[prepositional phrase] [participial phrase]

- **reason, purpose, target, goal, and cause:**

    to earn money, because of bad weather, for Mother's Day, to the charity, due to low enrollment

    since you won't be in town, because it was raining, so (that) you could study

**Examples:**

Some schools in the New York area are being closed <u>due to poor test performance by students.</u>
[adverbial prepositional phrase]

Wesley was fired <u>because of his continual absences</u>.
[adverbial prepositional phrase]

Babe Ruth played baseball <u>for the Boston Red Sox</u> and <u>(for) at least two other teams</u>.
[prepositional phrase] [prepositional phrase]

Camden was not allowed to use Eminem's lyrics in his paper *<u>since</u> some contain obscenities*.
[adverbial clause: *since* = ADV SUB]

I got a ticket yesterday *<u>because</u> I was going 50 miles per hour in a 35 mph zone*.
[adverbial clause: *because* = ADV SUB]

Mrs. Partridge has not passed the exam. <u>Therefore</u>, she will not be eligible for a driver's license.
[adverb]

- **condition or requirement:**

    if, provided that, unless, otherwise, as long as

**Examples:**

You cannot attend the lecture <u>unless you have a VIP ticket</u>.
[adverbial clause: *unless* = ADV SUB]

*<u>If you look at the sun too long</u>*, you will hurt your eyes.
[adverbial clause: *if* = ADV SUB]

I rated the Oasis Hotel a 2 because of the dirty pool. <u>Otherwise</u>, it would have been a 7.
[adverb]

Of course Betty can graduate after 3 years, *<u>provided that</u> she has enough credits*.
[adverbial clause: *provided that* = ADV SUB]

- **concession or contrast:**

    even though, although, in spite of, despite, in spite of the fact that, while, contrary to, on the contrary, in contrast, as opposed to

**Examples:**

*<u>Although</u> the results of the study are promising*, further research is still necessary.
[adverbial clause: *although* = ADV SUB]

The family would not accept his offer, despite his very good and honest intentions.
[prepositional phrase]

Notre Dame did not cancel the football game, in spite of the blizzard predictions.
[prepositional phrase]

*Even though* Maani had only slept for 2 hours last night, he performed wonderfully.
[adverbial clause: *even though* = ADV SUB]          [adverb]

- **degree (to what extent):**

    fully, entirely, very much, really, way, too, a little, somewhat, just, only, moreover, in addition

**Examples:**

Martita took an entirely different route than we did, and she got totally lost.
              [adverb]                                                [adverb]

The fry cook trainee ruined everyone's dishes somewhat, but the boss was not angry.
                                               [adverb]

We very much look forward to meeting you in person.
   [adverb phrase]                          [prepositional phrase]

### 15.2.2 Adverbs and Adverbials of (Epistemic and Affective) Stance

While all adverbs (and other parts of speech) have the potential of evoking a speaker's or writer's position, evaluation, or opinion vis-à-vis the statement made, topics, policies, films, books, hotels, restaurants, and so forth, there is a smaller sub-category of adverbs and adverbials that fulfill this function more explicitly.

Adverbs and adverbials of stance explicitly designate a speaker's or writer's position, evaluation, or opinion with regard to certainty or uncertainty (epistemic stance; Ochs, 1990, 1996; Strauss & Feiz, 2014) and emotions or feelings (affective stance; Ochs, 1990, 1996; Strauss & Feiz, 2014).

> By stance we mean the overt expression of an author's or speaker's attitudes, feelings, judgments, or commitment concerning the message. Adverbials are one of the primary lexical markers of stance in English.
>
> (Biber & Finegan, 1988, p. 1)

Adverbs that fall within this category typically indicate a speaker's or writer's stance with regard to an entire proposition or sentence. These include both epistemic and affective stance markers, listed as follows. Note that often these two categories of stance marking cross-cut each other. Some markers of epistemic stance also evoke affective stance and vice versa.

**Epistemic stance markers:**

surely, unquestionably, of course, by all means, certainly, maybe, perhaps, ironically, actually, frankly, strictly speaking, as a matter of fact, honestly, in all honesty, as it were

**Affective stance markers:**

personally, frankly, surprisingly, stunningly, amazingly, happily, sadly, unfortunately, fortunately, confidentially, if I may say so, if you want my opinion, for whatever it's worth

## Mini Review and Practice

1. The following sentences contain multiple adverbs and/or adverbials. We have underlined them here to make them more salient. First, identify the structural type of adverb or adverbial (e.g., adverb, noun phrase, adverb phrase, prepositional phrase, participial phrase, or adverbial clause). Adverbial subordinators that signal an adverbial clause appear in italics. Then, indicate the basic category of *circumstance* that each construction expresses (time, space, manner, degree, etc.).

As you work with the texts in this section, attend to all relevant grammatical categories and not just adverbs and adverbials (conjunctions, attributive and predicative adjectives, relative clauses, verbs, tense and aspect, etc.).

   a   From the perspective of the superintendent, the project proceeded fairly smoothly and at a rapid pace.

   b   In recent years, as we have all witnessed, the internet has revolutionized our daily lives, from the moment we wake up *until* the moment we to go sleep at night.

   c   From COCA (Davies, 2008–)

   Before the party, I had presented myself to him like a flamenco dancer, twirling *so* the skirt would take flight.

2. In Chapter 13 on adjectives, we observed in Section 13.10.2 that prepositional phrases can modify nouns, as in **a wish** for freedom, **Doctors** Without Borders (international humanitarian organization), **yogurt** with blueberries, and **the girl** with **stars** in her eyes.

Because of this structural similarity, it is sometimes challenging to identify the corresponding part of speech, and sometimes, the structural similarities create apparent ambiguities. That is, is the descriptor serving as an adjective or an adverb? However, the target of modification differs, as follows:

   adjectives   →   nouns
   adverbs      →   verbs, clauses, sentences, paragraphs, topics

Now have a look at the following quote by Martin Luther King Jr. Determine which of the word clusters are adjectives and which are adverbs. Think about the target of modification in each case (i.e., the *noun* element being modified [function = adjective] or the *verbal* element including full sentences, paragraphs, and even topics being modified [function = adverb). Explain why and how certain prepositional constructions serve as adjectives, and why and how certain prepositional constructions serve as adverbials. Note, too, that often adverbials consist of multiple adverbs or adverbials in the same construction.

Everyone has **the power** for greatness, not for fame but (for) greatness, *because greatness is determined* by service.

(Martin Luther King Jr., n.d.)

Now, do the same with the following quote by Beryl Markham (1942):

If a man has **any greatness** in him, it comes to light, not in one flamboyant hour, but in the **ledger** of his daily work.

(Markham, 1942)

3  Identify all adverbs and adverbials in the following text from COCA (Davies, 2008–). Determine the structural type of adverbial as well as the general category of meaning.

   a  "While there is so much science involved in our jobs, there are still many unknowns," she [meteorologist Jacqui Jeras] said. "So we get a chance **every day** to start fresh and give people a correct and accurate forecast."

Now, have a look at the following text (also from COCA). Identify the adverbs and adverbials from the points of view of structure and general category of meaning.

   b  "Craig remembered a focus on grammar and sentence mechanics in his high school writing courses, but he said that in his college course, the teacher used the topic of music to show students the relevance of writing to their **everyday** lives."

Also, how are the words *every day* in A different from the word *everyday* in B? Answer this question by focusing on function, meaning, and part of speech.

4  The following lines are from the children's song "Michael Finnegan." It is a repetitive song that can continue as you play with the lyrics. It also plays with rhymes and rhythm. The structure of the three stanzas shared here are built on adjectives and adverbs creatively repeated and rhyming, including the use of made-up words.

Try to find a version of this song online so that you can hear how it sounds.

> There was an old man
> named Michael Finnegan.
> He had whiskers on his chin-egan.
> The wind blew them off
> And then blew them on again.
> Poor old Michael Finnegan. Begin again. . .
> There was an old man
> named Michael Finnegan.
> He grew fat
> Wanted to be thin again.
> Went on a diet
> And got thin again.
> Poor old Michael Finnegan. Begin again. . .
> There was an old man
> named Michael Finnegan.
> He was so clumsy

> Banged his shin again.
> He shouted loud.
> Oh, what a din again!
> Poor old Michael Finnegan. Begin again. . .
>
> ("Michael Finnegan, n.d.)
>
> Locate the adjectives (predicative, attributive, preposition-based) and adverbs. Some expressions are also phrasal verbs. Identify those as well. What are the verb types? (See Chapter 6 for review.)

## 15.3 Conditionals

Conditional adverb clauses prototypically begin with *if*. The word *if* sets up a domain of irrealis, the unknown, or possible worlds (Dancygier & Sweetser, 2000).

There are three basic categories of conditional meaning:

**Factual:** indicating a natural or logical relationship between the two clauses

*If* there's no oxygen, there's no fire.
Water will boil *if* you heat it to 212°F at sea level.

**Future/predictive:** indicating that the main clause is contingent upon the occurrence of the event or state in the *if*-clause

*If* you eat that meat without cooking it, you'll get sick.
The steak will get chewy and tough *if* you overcook it.

**Imaginative conditionals:** indicating a possible world, either in **hypothetical** terms (not real now, but possible in the sense that the event or state *could* happen) or **counterfactual** terms (not real and impossible for the event or state to ever hold)

We would move to New York City *if* we could afford it. (hypothetical)
*If* you won the lottery, what is the first thing you would do? (hypothetical)
I would have said hello *if* I knew his name. (counterfactual)
*If* Susan were born a man, she might have chosen a different profession. (counterfactual)

### 15.3.1 Conditionals and Speech Acts: Threats, Warnings, Promises, Suggestions

It has been observed that across different languages, parents and caregivers commonly use predictive conditionals with their young children. Clancy et al. (1997) point out that in parents' discourse, these types of conditionals express the idea that an UNDESIRABLE act will lead to an UNDESIRABLE outcome, or that a DESIRABLE act will lead to a DESIRABLE outcome (Akatsuka, 1997):

"*If you touch that*, you'll get burned."　　　　　　　　　warning
undesirable　　→　　undesirable

"*If/when you finish your dinner*, you can have dessert."　　promise
desirable　　→　　desirable

Some expressions in English contain no actual adverbial subordinator of *condition*, yet the meaning is still clearly **conditional**.

As noted in Chapter 14, sometimes conjunctions *and* and *or* used with affirmative and negative imperatives can signal conditional meaning. These function much like imperatives and deontic modals (see Chapter 8):

Finish your homework *and* you can play outside, means:
"<u>If/when you finish your homework</u>, you can play outside."
OR: "You <u>have to/must</u> finish your homework before you can play outside."

Don't stay up too late *or* you'll be tired in the morning, means:
"<u>If/when you stay up too late</u> (at night), you will be tired in the morning."
OR: "You <u>shouldn't</u> stay up too late, because you will be tired in the morning."

Depending on the context, register, and the relationship between the speaker or writer and hearer or reader, such expressions can occur with very strong deontic meanings of threat or warning:

Do it, *or* else means:
"If you <u>*don't*</u> *do* it, there will be negative consequences."

Touch that antique once more *and* you will be asked to leave means:
"If you <u>*do*</u> <u>*touch*</u> that antique once more, you will not be permitted to stay here."

Note how the interactional/cognitive dynamic of (un)desirable leads to (un)desirable holds in these types of conditionals as well.

\*\*\*\*\*\*\*\*

## PRACTICE WITH DATA ANALYSIS: PUTTING IT ALL TOGETHER

1   As we have observed throughout this chapter, adverbs and adverbials are extremely pervasive in discourse. To illustrate this, have a look at the following quote by Anne Lamott (1994, p. 19):

> Thirty years ago my older brother, who was ten years old at the time, was trying to get a report written on birds that he'd had three months to write, which was due the next day. We were out at our family cabin in Bolinas, and he was at the kitchen table close to tears, surrounded by binder paper and pencils and unopened books about birds, immobilized by the hugeness of the task ahead. Then my father sat down beside him, put his arm around my brother's shoulder, and said, "Bird by bird, buddy. Just take it bird by bird."
>
> (Lamott, 1994, p. 19)

The descriptors here are adjectives (including relative clauses) and adverbs.

First, identify the adverbs or adverbials of time (e.g., *thirty years ago*, *at the time*), adverbs or adverbials of place (e.g., *out*, *at our family cabin*), manner (*bird by bird*), agent/cause (*by the hugeness of the task*), and purpose (*to write*). Are there other categories of adverbial meaning that you find? What are they? What are the adverbs or adverbials that express the meaning?

Then, think about the structure of the adverb or adverbial, especially single-word adverbs, noun phrases, and prepositional phrases. List each adverb or adverbial in each structural category.

Now think about adjectives. How do the adjectives here pattern differently from the adverbs in terms of meaning, function, and target of modification? Identify the attributive and predicative adjectives as well as the relative clauses.

And finally, think about conjunctions. How does the conjunction *and* function to depict the scene as well as tie the narrative together?

2   The opening cartoon, Figure 15.1, also contains a nice variety of adverbs and adverbials. The context is a wedding ceremony. Wedding ceremonies in the US typically include vows by both the bride and groom that include the phrase "for richer or (for) poorer" and end in the phrase "til death do us part." Identify all instances of adverbs and adverbials in the caption, and determine the basic category of meaning that each belongs to, as well as its structural type. What is the twist from the original set of marriage vows? What makes it humorous?

3   Analyze the next two cartoons from the point of view of adverbs or adverbials. Like Figure 15.1, the humor from Figures 15.2 and 15.3 (p. 465) is also tightly connected to both genre (lemonade stand sales, math word problems) and context. First, identify the adverbs and adverbials (meaning and structure). Think about how these constructions help develop the type of logic expressed in each cartoon and how that logic becomes humorous.

4   Similar to the imperatives used with conjunctions *and* and *or* that signal deontic meaning, the following expression, consisting solely of a series of three noun phrases, also evokes conditional/deontic meaning:

NO SHOES, NO SHIRTS, NO SERVICE

Signs that contain this message are still found in restaurants in the US. Paraphrase the meaning of this sign. How does it take on a clear deontic conditional meaning? Now, think about modals and deontic modality. What modals might be used in the various paraphrased meanings of this sign?

You might also want to search for the sign's origins to determine the history behind why dining establishments in the US used to post announcements like this.

5   Adverbials in discourse and literature—scene setting

What follows are the opening two paragraphs from the novel *Tuck Everlasting* (Babbitt, 1975). It is a beautifully written passage, thanks in large part to the use of adverbs and adverbials as a

"When your price is very high, people assume that your product must be very good!"

*Figure 15.2* "When your price is very high, people assume that your product must be very good!"
© Randy Glasbergen. Reproduced with permission of Glasbergen Cartoon Service.

464  *Adverbs*

means of setting the scene (both metaphorical and real) in terms of time and place. How does the simile ("like the highest seat of a Ferris wheel when it pauses in its turning") establish the author's perspective of the time?

How does her use of adverbs or adverbials contribute to this scene setting?

Use this passage as a way to review how the combination of adverbs or adverbials with other grammatical constructions in discourse (e.g., conjunctions, adjectives, relative clauses, nouns [Type 1 and Type 2], determines, pronouns, and verbs/verb types) work in concert with each other to so vividly depict the details in this opening scene.

> The first week of August hangs at the very top of summer, the top of the live-long year, like the highest seat of a Ferris wheel when it pauses in its turning. The weeks that come before are only a climb from balmy spring, and those that follow, a drop to the chill of autumn, but the first week of August is motionless, and hot. It is curiously silent, too, with blank white dawns and glaring noons, and sunsets smeared with too much color. Often at night there is lightning, but it quivers all alone. There is no thunder, no relieving rain. These are strange and breathless days, the dog days, when people are led to do things they are sure to be sorry for after.
> One day at that time, not so very long ago, three things happened and at first there appeared to be no connection between them.
>
> (Babbitt, 1975)

What is your favorite line from this excerpt? Why?

6   Adverbs and adverbials in promotional discourse

Analyze the adverbial constructions in the following promotions for Apple products:

- First, identify each adverb and adverbial and indicate its meaning type and structural category.
- Think about this genre of discourse as well as the register of each passage.

Other bits of grammar that you might want to attend to in these passages are negation, modals (simple modals and multi-word modals), adjectives, conjunctions, nouns and pronouns, demonstratives, and repetition of parallel constructions (e.g., if you ask. . . , to a doctor. . .).

The discourse is clearly persuasive. How would you describe the logic of the persuasive discourse in each segment? Who do you think is the target audience? Why? How does the concept of register help shed light on your observation regarding the target audience?

   a   *iPhone (2011)*

   If you don't have an iPhone, you don't have the App Store, so you don't have the world's largest selection of apps that are this easy to find and this easy to download right to your phone. So it can be almost anything, like a boarding pass. Or, do almost anything, like, pay for your coffee. Yup, if you don't have an iPhone, well, you don't have an iPhone.

   b   *iPad (2011)*

   If you ask a parent, they might call it intuitive. If you ask a musician, they might call it inspiring. To a doctor, it's groundbreaking. To a CEO, it's powerful. To a teacher, it's the future. If you ask a child, she might call it magic. And if you asked us—we'd say it's just getting started.

Adverbs 465

*Figure 15.3* "If a bus built in 1987 leaves Pittsburgh at 9:14 and Robert sets his crockpot to start cooking a 6-pound roast at 2:09, how long will it take your parents to stop helping with your homework?"

© Randy Glasbergen. Reproduced with permission of Glasbergen Cartoon Service.

7   The power of counterfactuals—adverbs and adverbials, conjunctions, modals, and counterfactual conditionals in discourse—flipping reality and expressing deep emotion (gratitude, regret, hope, relief) (See Chapter 8.)

As we observed in Chapter 8 on modals, it is not uncommon for speakers and writers to appeal to counterfactual thinking when expressing deep emotions, such as gratitude, regret, hope, and relief. Counterfactual constructions in language allow speakers to verbally portray versions of reality that are different from what actually happened. Have a look at the following two excerpts.

The excerpt in A expresses a multitude of emotions, including gratitude ( . . . this would not have been possible *without* . . .) and respect (as well as other deep emotions), all couched within a counterfactual framework. In B, the protagonist of the novel expresses deep regret and sadness over the loss of her husband.

In both cases, the speaker and writer flip their current realities through counterfactual conditionals.

In both excerpts (try to use the full text for Hanks's acceptance speech; see the link below, where you can access the full speech/video), first identify all adverbs and adverbials. Pay close attention to all conditional adverbials as well as modals. Then have a look at tense and aspect, conjunctions, and adjectives to see how these all work together to set the scene and express the feelings of the speaker or writer in each discourse excerpt.

a   **Tom Hanks's Academy Award acceptance speech** from the 66th Academy Awards ceremony in 1994 for his role in the groundbreaking 1993 film *Philadelphia*. You can view the full acceptance speech here: www.youtube.com/watch?v=bBuDMEpUc8k.

   Here's what I know: I could not be standing here without that undying love, that was just sung about by not Bruce [Springsteen], but Neil Young. . . .

> I should not be here, but I am, because of the union of such film makers as. . . .
>
> I would not be standing here, if it weren't for two very important men in my life. . . . I wish my babies could have the same sort of teacher, the same sort of friends.
>
> And there lies my dilemma here tonight. I know that my work in this case is magnified by the fact that the streets of are too crowded with angels.
>
> (Hanks, 1993)

b  *The Lost Concerto: A Novel*

> So many times, since her husband's death, she had forced herself to sit in front of the keyboard and begin the simple scales and chords that would stretch muscles grown stiff with disuse. But each time she tried to play, all she could see was the small shattered sailboat. And her fingers would freeze on the silent keys. If only I hadn't asked him to go. If only I'd gone with him. If only he hadn't gone sailing that day. If only, if only. Sometimes Maggie thought she would go mad with the compulsion to reshape the past.
>
> (Mario, 2015, p. 14)

What function do the counterfactual conditionals serve in each of these excerpts? You can find many instances of counterfactual conditionals in news reports and interviews—especially immediately after major catastrophic or major heroic events. These constructions capture such emotions of the speakers such as relief, sadness, guilt, joy. How does "flipping reality" through such grammatical features help speakers and writers put these and other emotions into words?

## COMMON ERRORS, BUMPS, AND CONFUSIONS

Identify the errors or "bumps" in the following sentences or paragraphs. Use the concepts and terminology that you learned in this and other chapters to articulate what might be grammatically or pragmatically problematic. Suggest ways that each can be re-written more clearly and more accurately. (Note: While all bumps do involve some element of adverbs and adverbials, they are not limited to only that.)

1   If I saw him, I am going to tell you.

2   Growing up in a chaotic family, teacher said I might to see a counselor when I become 21.

3   Venedictos would of completed his cross-country trip if there is not so many thunderstorms exploding in the Midwest.

4   Having stubbed the toe on the sofa, his wife re-arranged all the furnitures.

5   The Los Angeles Dodgers is winning bigly this season.

6   Email listserv announcement from a US art gallery that specializes in international artists:

>   Dear friends!
>
>   Good Day!
>
>   Today we like to update a few news.
>
>   Hu Weiyi's new exhibition is on in Morocco, a Grand Opening of Mo Abdi's International Art Center. Attention to all Hu Weiyi's collectors and lovers, here is a very good interview by an art magazine of Italy, please click on the link at the email's end.

It will help you understand more of his art and Chinese modern ink painting. We have update our exhibition site, please check it out

We will open daily from 12–5, close at Tuesday.
Please visit us during our hours. You can call us for any time you like to stop by.

7   Phishing scam emails: Perpetrators contact innocent recipients in the hopes that they will reply and provide their personal contact and financial information as a setup for identity theft. Often, these types of emails are filled with grammatical errors and bumps. Here is the actual text of one such email (though the return email address has been changed).

Greetings Sir,

I had written an earlier mail to you but without response. I have a client a citizen of your country who died on February 2011 on gas exploration he was an engineer. I am his lawyer, his bank wrote me that he made a deposit using his family as the beneficiary. I will give you more update as soon as I receive positive answer.

Contact me via my private email: notarealemailaddress@jmail.com

Sincerely,

Barr Thomas

## SUGGESTED ACTIVITIES

1   Analyze more recent versions of promotional discourse for Apple products. Compare and contrast your findings with those of the 2011 data presented here. Also, compare and contrast Apple product descriptions with those by its competitors, like Samsung and LG, for similar products. Focus on adverbs and adverbials, adjectives, modals, and conjunctions (and other grammatical patterns in discourse that become salient as you do your analysis). How would you describe the register of each—informal, formal, conversational, technical?

As a result of your analysis, try to determine what the stances of each company or corporation are (stances vis-à-vis the products, their customers, their competition, etc.).

2   Conditionals in general (not just counterfactual ones) function in such a way to express emotion. Think about how conditionals are used in English song titles and song lyrics.

Collect an inventory of song titles and also collect the lyrics. What genres of music tend to use the most conditionals?
What types of conditionals do you find—factual, predictive, imaginative (hypothetical or counterfactual)? Which type of conditional is the most frequent in your data?
Here are a few examples of song titles with counterfactuals to start you off: "If I Were a Boy" by Beyoncé, "If I Were a Rich Man" (from the musical *Fiddler on the Roof*), "If I Had My Way," and "If You Were the Only Girl (in the World)."
What are the types of situations that are portrayed in these songs that use counterfactual conditionals?

3   Think about how particular parts of speech function within various genres of discourse. For example, lease or rental agreements, traffic laws, policy documents, and game rules all are filled with adverbs and adverbials (including conditionals) and modals. Why do you think this is so?

Focus on one specific genre of discourse, and analyze its use of adverbs and adverbials and modals. How do these two categories relate to each other from a functional perspective?

For example, compare and contrast the return policies of various retail outlets—Saks Fifth Avenue, Macy's, and Target. These retail outlets represent a wide variety of merchandise and a broad spectrum of prospective shoppers, from high-end stores like Saks to lower-end stores like Target.

First, analyze through which grammatical constructions each store's conditions are established. Then, think about each company's stance vis-à-vis its products and its customers. Which discursive features (including register) lead you to these discoveries?

4  National Public Radio ran a special feature called "Ads for Nicer Living," in which they asked their listeners to be creative and write ads for things that make life better (but not products). Some examples are apple pie, clean sheets, cumulus clouds.

You can find more information about the project and sample "ads" here: www.npr.org/sections/thetwo-way/2016/12/15/505419422/ads-for-nicer-living-make-your-pitch-for-what-makes-life-better.

Write a 30-second ad or catchy jingle for something that makes life much better (e.g., your pet, sunflowers, sunsets, kindness). You can use any modality you like, though we suggest that you make a video to promote your ad.

5  Watch the video titled "Kindness Boomerang" by Life Vest Inside: www.youtube.com/watch?v=nwAYpLVyeFU.

Write up a short description or explain the film to a partner:

- What is the film about?
- What is its message?
- Why was it made? What is the relationship between the images and the music/lyrics? (Note: The song is called "One Day" by Matisyahu.)
- Do we need (more) films like this? Why?
- Can you think of another theme or set of events for a new film that would capture a similar message about helping us make the world a better place to live?

Now, think about adverbs and adverbials. What would happen to the meaning of your discussion if you deleted every adverbial?

You can do similar activities with other films with positive messages that have gone viral on the internet.

## Academic References

Akatsuka, N. (1997). Negative conditionality, subjectification, and conditional reasoning. In A. Athanasiadou & R. Dirven (Eds.), *On conditionals*. Amsterdam: John Benjamins.
Biber, D., Conrad, S., & Leech, G. (2002). *Student grammar of spoken and written English*. Essex: Pearson Education Limited.
Biber, D., & Finegan, E. (1988). Adverbial stance types in English. *Discourse Processes, 11*(1), 1–34.
Chafe, W. (1984, October). How people use adverbial clauses. *Annual Meeting of the Berkeley Linguistics Society, 10,* 437–449.
Clancy, P. M., Akatsuka, N., & Strauss, S. (1997). Deontic modality and conditionality in discourse: A cross-linguistic study of adult speech to young children. In A. Kamio (Ed.), *Directions in functional linguistics*. Amsterdam: John Benjamins.

Dancygier, B., & Sweetser, E. (2000). Constructions with if, since, and because: Causality, epistemic stance, and clause order. In B. Kortmann & E. Couper-Kuhlen (Eds.), *Cause, condition, concession, contrast*. Berlin: Mouton de Gruyter.

Ford, C. E. (1993). *Grammar in interaction: Adverbial clauses in American English conversations*. Cambridge: Cambridge University Press.

Huddleston, R. (1984). *Introduction to the grammar of English*. Cambridge: Cambridge University Press.

Larsen-Freeman, D., & Celce-Murcia, M. (2016). *The grammar book: Form, meaning, and use for English language teachers* (3rd ed.). Boston, MA: National Geographic.

Ochs, E. (1990). Cultural universals in the acquisition of language. *Papers and Reports on Child Language Development*, 29, 1–19.

Ochs, E. (1996). Linguistics resources for socializing humanity. In J. Gumperz & S. Levinson (Eds.), *Rethinking linguistic relativity* (pp. 407–438). Cambridge: Cambridge University Press.

Quirk, R., R., Greenbaum, S., Leech, G., & Svartvik, J. (1985). *A comprehensive grammar of the English language*. Harlow: Longman.

Strauss, S., & Feiz, P. (2014). *Discourse analysis: Putting our worlds into words*. New York: Routledge.

## Data References

Babbitt, N. (1975). *Tuck everlasting*. New York: Farar, Straus, Giroux.

Davies, M. (2008–). *The corpus of contemporary American English (COCA): 520 million words, 1990-present*. Retrieved from http://corpus.byu.edu/coca/

Hanks, T. (1993). Academy Award speech. Academy Award acceptance speech database. Retrieved July 5, 2017, from http://aaspeechesdb.oscars.org/link/066-1/

King, M. L. Jr. (n.d). Good reads. Retrieved June 12, 2017, from www.goodreads.com/quotes/432363-everyone-has-the-power-for-greatness-not-for-fame-but

Lamott, A. (1994). *Bird by bird: Some instructions on writing and life*. New York: Anchor.

Mario, H. (2015). *The lost concerto: A novel*. Longboat Key, FL: Oceanview Publishing.

# Index

Page numbers in italic indicate figures and in bold indicate tables on the corresponding pages.

*a-* (negation) 308–309
*a/an* (articles) 83–86
Aarts, B. 50
Abbott, G. 140n3
*about* (preposition) 372
absolute negation 301
absolute upper/lower limit adjectives 410
Achugar, M. 144
acronyms 19
active voice 265, 266; in discourse, conceptual focus of 268–269; to passive voice 269–270
activity/process verbs 144
adjective phrases 24–25, 423
adjectives 11, 20, 403; attributive 408–409; *a-* with 308–309; categories of 404; as collective nouns 417–418; determiners as not 107; for expressing modality 248; formed from nouns 404–406; formed from other adjectives 406; formed from other parts of speech 404–408; formed from verbs 406–408; gradable and absolute upper/lower limit 410; *in-, il-, im-, ir-* with 306–307; *non-* with 306; nouns functioning as 423–424; nouns modified with prepositional phrases as 422–423; order of 416–417; placement of 408–409; predicative 408–409; relative clauses as noun modifiers 418–422; simple comparative 413–414; simple superlative 413–414; suffixes to 14; synonymy 414–416; that are only attributive 409; that are only predicative 409; *un-* with 305
adverbial clauses 27–33; 455–459
adverbials 33; of circumstance 455–458; of (epistemic and affective) stance 458–459; multiple-word 455; in promotional discourse 464; for scene setting 463–464
adverb phrases 25
adverbs 11, 453–454; of circumstance 455–458; conditionals 461–462; of (epistemic and affective) stance 458–459; for expressing modality 248; forms 454–455; functions of 455–459; *in-, il-, im-, ir-* with 306–307; mitigating or intensifying stance 224–226; negative 304; in promotional discourse 464; single-word 454; suffixes to 14; *un-* with 305
affected entities 265–266; middle voice and 279
affixation 12–17
*after* (preposition) 374–375
agency 152, 265; tense, time, and 213–214
agency continuum 279
Aijmer, K. 225
Ainsworth-Vaughn, N. 325
Akatsuka, N. 461
Algeo, J. 68
Allen, C. L. 224
Allerton, D. J. 144
alternative questions 331–332
*and* (conjunction) 438–439
*and yet* (conjunction) 442
antecedent pronouns 118
appositives 420, 421
*around* (preposition) 371–372
articles: *a/an* 83–86; definite 86–90; indefinite 83–86
*as* (preposition) 372–373
aspect: perfect 197–201, 267–268; perfect progressive 201–207; progressive 193–197, 267; simple 178–193
*at* (preposition) 364–365, *366*
attributive adjectives 408–409; order of 416–417
Austin, J. L. 259n1
auxiliary verbs 29; *be* as, in questions 326; negation of 294–297; *never* with *be* as main verb 298; *not ever, n't ever* with 298–299

Bach, K. 259n1
Bardovi-Harlig, K. 259n1
Bauer, L. 68
*be:* as auxiliary verb 193, 201, 266; as copular verb 147–148; as main verb, in questions 326; with *never* as main verb and with all auxiliaries 298; *not, n't* negation 295; with *not ever, n't ever* as main verbs 298–299; passive voice 275–277, 283–284

*before* (preposition) 375–376
*be going to* 243–245; and *be about to* 245; and *will* 243–245
Beligon, S. 307
*be like* 164
Bell, A. 333
Berry, R. 53
Biber, D. 50, 69, 184, 243, 292, 303, 329, 333, 337, 387, 408, 420, 423–424, 440, 442, 455, 458
*big* (adjective) 415–416
Blakemore, D. 220, 442
blending 18, 22–23, 43; *see also* portmanteau
Blum-Kulka, S. 259n1
Blyth, C. 164
Bock, K. 68
Bodine, A. 140n3
Boers, F. 387
Bolinger, D. 408
*both/and* (conjunctions) 446
bound morphemes 12–17
Bowerman, M. 143
Brown, P. 143, 225, 260n3
Buescher, K. 400n3
*but* (conjunction) 440–441
Butterfield, S. 68
Bužarovska, E. 275
*by*+ overt agent 270–272; preposition 370–371
Bybee, J. 174, 177, 220, 260n3, 260n6, 389

Cameron, D. 140n3
*can*: deontic modality 234, 237–239; dynamic modality 236, 237–239; epistemic modality 235, 237–239
Carter, R. 92, 98, 248, 275, 314, 352, 354
Celce-Murcia, M. 92, 98, 103, 132, 164, 184, 224, 243, 303, 337, 352, 354, 416, 437, 454
Chafe, W. 53, 455
Chang, H. 362, 364, 387–388, 389, 400n2
change of state linking verbs 148, 184
Chappell, H. 275
Chesterman, A. 103
choice questions 331–332
Chung, S. 220
Clancy, P. M. 461
clauses 26–28, 30, 42; *see also* adverbial clauses; dependent clauses; independent clauses; nominal clauses; relative clauses; subordinate clauses
clipping 19
Cohen, A. 259n1
collective nouns, adjectives as 417–418
collectives (quantifiers) 99
collocation 38, 39, 99, 173
colloquialisms 37
colon (:) 41
comma (,) 40
common nouns 10, 20, 50–51; defined 50–51; type 1 53–55, 57–58; type 2 55–64; type 3 64–68; verbs derived from 161–162

communication, verbs related to 182–183
comparative adjectives, simple 413–414
comparatives 14
complex prepositions 379
complex sentences 28
complex transitive verbs 155–156
compounding 18
compound sentences 28
Comrie, B. 144, 177
conceptual imagery with type 1 and type 2 nouns 61–64
conditionals 461–462, 467
condition or requirement 457–458
conjunctions 11, 437–451; *and* 438–439; *but* 440–441; coordinating 437–443; correlative 446–447; *for* 441; logical connectors 447–448; negative 304; *nor* 441–442; *or* 439–440; *so* 442–443; subordinating 447; *yet* 442
connotational meanings 7–8
connotations 7–8
Conrad, S. 50, 69, 184, 243, 303, 329, 333, 337, 387, 408, 420, 423–424, 440, 442, 455
contradiction and negation 299
contrast and negation 299–300
conversion 17–18, 20, 43–44
coordinating conjunctions 437–443; *and* 438–439; *but* 440–441; *for* 441; *nor* 441–442; *or* 439–440; *so* 442–443; *yet* 442
copular verbs 147–148; negation of 295
correlative conjunctions 446–447
*could*: deontic modality 234, 237–239; dynamic modality 236, 237–239; epistemic modality 235, 237–239; in past time narrative 249–250
Coulthard, M. 324, 341
counterfactuals 201, 234, 242–243, 461
covert determiner Ø 79, 81, 82, 103–107; *see also* overt determiner
Cowan, R. 416, 417
Croft, W. 143
Crystal, D. 184, 275

Dancygier, B. 461
D'arcy, A. 164
Davidse, K. 279
Davies, M. 292–293, 316, 354, 356–361, 364–365, 371–379, 381, 387, 415, 421, 441–442, 446, 448
*de-* (negation) 307
declarative questions 336–337
declarative sentences 31
Declerck, R. 184, 186
definite articles 86–90
degree 458
demonstrative determiners 91–95
demonstrative pronouns 122–123
denotations 7–8
deontic modality 219–220, 231, 233–234, 237–239, 245–248

dependent clauses 26–27, 42
Depraetere, I. 68
derivational morphemes 15–17, 20–22, 41
determiner pronouns 121
determiners 10, 20, 29, 78–80; articles as 83–91; conceptual meanings 82–83; covert, Ø 103–107; demonstrative 91–95; interrogatives 31, 101–103; negative 303; in noun phrases 23; occurring in strings 107; possessive 95–98; quantifiers 98–101
Dik, S. C. 92
direct objects 24
Dirven, R. 50, 53, 177, 352–353
*dis-* (negation) 308
discourse: collocation in 38; genre in 33–35; grammar and 33–46; markedness in 39–40; pragmatics in 38–39; quantifiers in 100; register in 37–38; relative clauses in 420–422; stance and perspective in 36–37; used to (modal) in 249; would and could (modals) in 249–250
ditransitive verbs 24, 154–155; passive voice with 269–270
*don't, never, don't ever* (negative imperatives) 226–227
double negatives 318–319
dramatic present 186–187
dynamic modality 219–220, 231, 236, 237–239
dynamic verbs 143, 144–146, 149–152, 211

*each* 10, 99
Eberhard, K. M. 68
echo questions 336–337
*either/or* (conjunctions) 446
ellipsis 29–31; in echo questions 337; types of 30–31
Enfield, N. J. 325
Englebretson, R. 408
epistemic modality 219–220, 231, 234–236, 237–239, 245–248
ergative verbs 279
Evans, V. 353–354, 376
*every* 10, 99
exclamations using question words 337–338
exclamatory sentences 31

*fall through* (phrasal verb) 392, *393*
Feiz, P. 33, 36, 53, 93, 458
Fenn, P. 177
Ferris, D. C. 307
figurative interpretation of language 41
Fillmore, C. 92
Finegan, E. 50, 69, 184, 243, 303, 329, 333, 337, 387, 440, 442, 458
first-person pronouns 119–120
Fleisher, N. 275
Fludernik, M. 186
focus continuum 130–131
Foley, W. 260n3

*for:* conjunction 441; preposition 361
Ford, C. E. 455
formal register 38, 45–46
forming of words 12–23
*-free* (negation) 309–312
free morphemes 12
*from* (preposition) 355–356
full stop (.) 40
future events, simple present tense marking 186
future perfect 200–201
future time, simple 184–185

Garcia, E. 92–93
Gardner, D. 387
Gastil, J. 140n3
gender and stance 128–130
general quantifiers 98
genre 33–35
Gentner, D. 48
gerunds 31–32, 68; *not, never* phrases with 314
*get:* causative passive 277–278, 283–284; passive 275–277
Givón, T. 50, 184, 275, 327
Gledhill, C. J. 240
Goffman, E. 260n3
Goldberg, A. E. 144
*good* (adjective) 424–425
gradable adjectives 410
grammar rules 2
Greenbaum, S. 50, 92, 144, 164, 184, 220, 243, 275, 292, 303, 327, 332, 336, 338, 352, 354, 380, 408, 423, 437, 448, 458
Grice, H. P. 259n1

Halliday, M. A. K. 92, 144, 279
Hanks, W. F. 92
Hartford, B. 259n1
Hasan, R. 92
*have* as auxiliary in perfect aspect 197; in perfect progressive aspect 201; in causative passive 277–278; in questions 326
*have got to* 245–248
*have to* 245–248
Heinemann, T. 327
Heritage, J. C. 324–325, 327
*he/she* (pronouns) 128–129
Heyvaert, L. 279
*high* (adjective) 415
Hinkel, E. 325
Hirtle, W. H. 177
historical present 186–187; *see also* dramatic present
Holmes, J. 225
Hopper, P. J. 144, 150, 152, 157, 177
House, J. 224
Huddleston, R. 144, 454
Hudson, R. 164
Hundt, M. 68
Hyland, K. 164, 325, 338
hypothetical, modals expressing the 241

474  *Index*

*il-* (negation) 306–307
*im-* (negation) 306–307
immovable state linking verbs 147–148
imperatives 219–220; forms and conceptual meaning 221–222; + *just* 225–226; main features of 220–221; mitigating or intensifying 224–226; negative 226–227; objective 222–223; unmitigated 223–224
imperative sentences 31
*in-* (negation) 306–307
*in* (preposition) 356–357
indefinite articles 83–86
indefinite pronouns 121, 123
independent clauses 26, 41
indirect objects 24
infinitives 32–33; *not, never* phrases with 312–314; splitting 312–313
inflectional morphemes 12–15, 19–21, 41
informal register 37, 45–46
*inside* (preposition) 359
interrogative pronouns 121, 123
interrogatives 31, 101–103
*into* (preposition) 358–359
intonation 229, 232, 336–337
intransitive verbs 24, 156–157, 167–168, 265; distinguished from transitive verbs 157–161
*ir-* (negation) 306–307
irregular verbs: simple past tense 182; simple present tense 180
*it* (pronoun) 131–132

Jackendoff, R. 387
Jespersen, O. 292
Jiang, W. Y. 324
Johansson, S. 50, 69, 184, 243, 303, 329, 333, 337, 387, 440, 442
Johnson, M. 353
Johnstone, B. 128
Jordan, M. E. 324
Judd, E. L. 259n1
Jurafsky, D. 433
*just* (imperative) 225–226

Kasper, G. 259n1
Kemmer, S. 279
Kirsner, R. S. 93
Knight, C. 101

Lakoff, G. 144, 353
Lakoff, R. 275, 440
Lane, C. 325
Langacker, R. W. 53, 144, 150, 177, 353
*large* (adjective) 415–416
Larsen-Freeman, D. 92, 98, 103, 132, 164, 184, 224, 243, 303, 337, 352, 354, 416, 437, 454
Lauerbach, G. E. 325
Lee, D. 53

Lee, S. A. 324
Leech, G. N. 50, 69, 92, 144, 164, 184, 220, 243, 275, 292, 303, 327, 329, 332–333, 336–338, 352, 354, 380, 387, 408, 420, 423, 437, 440, 442, 448, 455, 458
Leech, J. 50, 177
*-less* (negation) 309–312
Levin, B. 144, 157
Levin, M. 68
Levinson, S. C. 126, 225, 260n3
lexical negation 302, 303–309
Li, C. N. 144
Licoppe, C. 324
*like* (preposition) 373, *374; see also be like*
limericks 34
Lindholm, C. 325
Lindstromberg, S. 354
Linell, P. 325
linking verbs 144, 146, 147–152
Liu, D. 387
logical connectors 447–448
Lucy, J. A. 144
Lyons, J. 279

Macauley, R. 164
MacCarthy, M. 92, 98, 248, 275, 314, 352, 354
MacCawley, J. D. 196
MacCawley, N. 337
MacKay, D. J. 140n3
Macnamara, J. 48
MacWhorter, J. 140n2
main verbs, negation of: *be* as, in questions 326; with *never* and *not ever/n't ever* 297–298; with *not* and *n't* 294–297; *not ever, n't ever* with 298–299
markedness 39–40
Martyna, W. 140n3
mass nouns 55; *see also* type 2 common nouns
Master, P. 103
Mathis, T. 144
*may*: deontic modality 234; epistemic modality 236
measurement units 99
Mehan, H. 324
Meyers, M. W. 140n3
Michaelis, L. A. 144
middle voice 278–280, 283
*might*: deontic modality 234; epistemic modality 235
*mis-* (negation) 308
Mitkovska, L. 275
modality 219, 259; deontic 219–220, 231, 233–234, 237–239, 245–248; dynamic 219–220, 231, 236, 237–239; epistemic 219–220, 231, 234–236, 237–239, 245–248; voice and 268
modals 24, 220, 231; in academic discourse 240; for counterfactual thinking 242–243; distancing from realis 241–242; expressing

the hypothetical 241; flipping reality 242–243; forms and conceptual meaning 231–236; gradient scale of meaning from strong obligation/certainty to weak suggestion/low likelihood 240–243; *have to, have got to, need to* 245–248; multi-word 243–248; simple 220, 232
mood 31, 219
Moore, E. 179, 333
morphemes: bound 12–17; derivational 15–17, 20–22, 41; free 12; inflectional 12–15, 19–21, 41
motion and manner of motion, verbs related to 144, 163, 168–169, 183
multiple-word adverbials 455
multi-word modal expressions 243–248
multi-word prepositions 379
Murphy, R. 50
*must*: deontic modality 234; epistemic modality 235

narratives: past time 248–250; of personal experience 187
*need to* 245–248
negation 289–319; absolute 301; contradiction and 299; contrast and 299–300; double 318–319; grammatical forms of 289–293; juxtaposition and 300–301; lexical 302, 303–309; negating the main verb or auxiliary with *not* or *n't* 294–297; *not, never* phrases with infinitives and gerunds 312–314; of other elements in discourse beyond the verb 302–312; rejection, and opposition 301–302; scope of 303; sentential 302; of utterances with *never* and *not ever/n't ever* 297–302
negative adverbs 304
negative conjunctions 304
negative connotations 8
negative declarative + affirmative tag 333
negative determiners 303
negative imperatives 226–227
negative prefixes 304, 315–318
negative prepositions 304
negative pronouns 304
negatives, double 318–319
negative suffixes 309–312, 315–318
*neither/nor* (conjunctions) 446
Nelson, K. 48
*never* (negation) 226–227, 293; with *be* as main verb and with all auxiliaries 298; negating utterances with 297–302; phrases with infinitives and gerunds 312–314
Nguyen, H. T. 324
nominal clauses 27
*non-* (negation) 306
non-restrictive relative clauses 419–422
*nor* (conjunction) 441–442
Norrick, N. R. 337

*not* (negation) 291–292; of main verb or auxiliary verb 294–297; phrases with infinitives and gerunds 312–314
*not ever* (negation) 291–292; negating utterances with 298–299
*not only/but also* (conjunctions) 446–447
noun phrases 23–24, 29–30; -based possessive determiners 95–96; demonstrative determiners in 92–93
nouns 10, 29–30, 48–75; adjectives as collective 417–418; categories of 48–49; common 10, 20, 50; concepts of English nouns 49–50, 68–69; conversion into verbs 17–18, 43; conversion of verbs into 18; functioning as adjectives 423–424; *in-, il-, im-, ir-* with 306–307; modified with prepositional phrases 422–423; for naming and conceptualizing things, people, ideas, values, objects, and concepts 49; *non-* with 306; proper 10, 20, 50–52, 69–70, 161–162; relative clauses modifying 418–422; suffixes to 12; type 1 53–55, 57–61; type 2 55–64; type 3 64–68; *un-* with 306; verbs derived from 161–162, 169–171
*n't ever* (negation) 297–302
Nuyts, J. 220, 231

objective imperatives 222–223
object pronouns 11, 29, 120, 121
obligation, verbs of 248
Ochs, E. 458
*of* (preposition) 356
*off* (preposition) 363
Ogiermann, E. 224
*on* (preposition) 362–363
onomatopoeia 9–10, 45
*onto* (preposition) 364
*or* (conjunction) 439–440
ordinal numbers and sequence 99
*ourselves* (pronoun) 120
*out* (preposition) 360
*outside* (preposition) 360
*over* (preposition) 376–377
overt determiner 104

Pagliuca, W. 174, 220, 260n6, 389
Palmer, F. R. 144, 220, 231
Park, Y. 324
parts of speech 10–11
passive voice 265, 266; active voice to 269–270; in discourse, conceptual focus of 268–269; with ditransitive verbs 269–270; *have* and *get* as causative passives 277–278; optional addition of *by* + overt agent in 270–272
past events, present tense marking 186
past participle 13–14; 406–407
past perfect 200
past tense, simple 180–184, 190–192; questions 326

past time narratives 248–250
perception, verbs related to 163–164, 166–167, 184
perception copula 148, 248
perfect aspect 197–201; voice and 267–268
perfect progressive aspect 201–207
period (.) 40
Perkins, R. 174, 220, 260n6, 389
personal possessive determiners 95
perspective and stance 36–37
phrasal verbs 387–391; prepositions and verbs that often combine into constructions of 391–395
phrases 23–25; noun 23–24, 29–30; other clauses and 30–31
*please* (imperative) 225
Podesva, R. 333
politeness 241–242
polysemy 353
portmanteau 18, 22–23, 43
Portner, P. 220
positive connotations 8
possessive determiners 95–98
possessive pronouns 120, 121
pragmatics 38–39
predicative adjectives 409
prefixes 15–16, 20–21; negative 304, 315–318
prepositional phrases 25; modifying nouns 422–423; and reduced relative clauses 422–423
prepositions 11, 29, 352–353; *about* 372; *after* 374–375; *around* 371–372; *as* 372–373; *at* 364–365, 366; *before* 375–376; *by* 370–371; complex 379; core meanings starting in concrete space 355–365; *for* 361; *from* 355–356; *in* 356–357; *inside* 359; *into* 358–359; *like* 373, 374; multi-word 379; negative 304; *of* 356; *off* 363; *on* 362–363; *onto* 364; *out* 360; *outside* 360; *over* 376–377; phrasal verbs and 387–391; *through* 373–374; *to* 357–358; *under* 377–378; and verbs that often combine into phrasal verb constructions 391–395; *with* 378–379, 381–382; *without* 379, 381–382
present perfect aspect 199–200
present progressive aspect 195–196
present tense, simple 178–180, 186–187, 190–191, 195–196; questions 326
progressive aspect 193–197; voice and 267
pronouns 11, 20, 29, 118–119; conceptual meanings and assumptions with 126–134; demonstrative 122–123; determiner 121; first-person 119–120; focus continuum with 130–131; forms of 119–125; gender 128–130; indefinite 121, 123; interrogative 121, 123; negative 304; object 11, 29, 120, 121; possessive 120, 121; quantifying 121, 123; reciprocal 121, 122; referential and non-referential *it* 131–132; reflexive 11, 120, 121; relative 29, 121, 124, 418, 420; second-person 119–120; subject 11, 29, 119–120, 121; third-person 119–120, 128–130; use assuming shared or given information regarding referents 126
proper nouns 10, 20, 50–51, 69–70; covert determiner Ø 104–105; verbs derived from 161–162
Proulx, S. 324
pseudo-agentive subject 278–280
Pullum, G. K. 144
punctuation 38, 43; basics of 40–41

quantifiers 98–101
quantifying pronouns 121, 123
question-like structures 336–340
questions 324–325; alternative or choice 331–332; echo 336–337; exclamations using questions words 337–338; question-like structures 336–340; rhetorical 338–340; statements with rising intonation as 336–337; tag 332–334; *wh-* 328–331, 340–341; *yes-no* 325–328
Quirk, R. 50, 69, 92, 144, 164, 184, 220, 243, 275, 292, 303, 327, 332, 336, 338, 352, 354, 379, 408, 423, 437, 448, 458

Radden, G. 50, 53, 177, 352–353
Ramsay, G. 324
Rappaport Hovav, M. 157
Raymond, G. 324, 327
reciprocal pronouns 11, 121, 122
Recktenwald, S. Jr. 164
reference 81–82; *see also* pronouns
reflexive pronouns 11, 120, 121
register 37–38, 45–46
regular verbs: simple past tense 182; simple present tense 179–180
relative clauses 27; in discourse 420–422; as noun modifiers 418–422; restrictive and non- restrictive 419–422
relative pronouns 29, 121, 124, 418, 420
reporting verbs 144, 164
restrictive relative clauses 419–422
rhetorical questions 338–340
Robinson, J. D. 324–325
Rose, K. R. 259n1
Roth, A. L. 325
*run after* (phrasal verb) 393
Rymes, B. 324, 341

Salager-Meyer, F. 240
scalar conceptual notions of degree 1
Schallert, D. 324
Schegloff, E. A. 327
Schiffrin, D. 439–440, 442
Schlenker, P. 186
Schleppegrell, M. J. 144
scope of negation 303

Searle, J. 259n1
second-person pronouns 119–120
Seedhouse, P. 324, 341
*self/selves* 121–122
semicolon (;) 41
sentences 28–31; complex 28; compound 28; functions of 31; punctuation and structure of 38, 40–41, 42–43; simple 28; types of 42
sentential negation 302
*shall*: deontic modality 233; epistemic modality 235
*she/he* (pronouns) 128–129
Shibatani, M. 269
shortening of words 19; *see also* clipping
*should*: deontic modality 234; epistemic modality 235
Silverstein, M. 144
simple aspect 178–193; simple future time 184–185; simple past tense 180–184; simple present tense 178–180; special uses of simple present tense 186–187; subject-verb agreement 187–188, 192–193
simple comparative adjectives 413–414
simple future time 184–185
simple modals 220, 232, 245–248
simple past tense 180–184, 190–192; questions 326
simple present tense 178–180, 186–187, 190–191, 195–196; questions 326
simple sentences 28
simple superlative adjectives 413–414
Sinclair, J. 279, 324, 341
single-word adverbs 454
slang 37
Sloat, C. 50
Slobin, D. I. 144
*so* (conjunction) 442–443
Song, K. 324
Sorjonen, M-L. 325
speech acts 39, 220, 227, 228, 252, 259, 336, 461–462; *see also* pragmatics
specificity of action 144
specific quantifiers 98
splitting infinitives 312–313
stable and unchanging physical states 146
stance: adverbs and adverbials of 458–459; perspective and 36–37
*stand by* (phrasal verb) 392–393
states of cognition, preference, and emotion 146
stative verbs 144, 146–147, 149–152, 211
Steensig, J. 327
Stivers, T. 325
Strauss, S. 33, 36, 53, 93, 131, 362, 364, 387–388, 389, 400nn2–3, 433, 458, 461
subject, pseudo-agentive 278–280
subject pronouns 11, 29, 119–120, 121
subject-verb agreement 187–188, 192–193, 208–210
subordinate clauses 26–27

subordinating conjunctions 447
subordinators 26
suffixes 12–15, 16–17, 21; negative 309–312, 315–318
Suh, K. 248
superlative adjectives, simple 413–414
superlatives 15
Sussex, R. 275
Svartvik, J. 50, 92, 144, 164, 184, 220, 243, 275, 292, 303, 327, 332, 336, 338, 352, 354, 379, 408, 423, 437, 448, 458
Swales, J. M. 240
Swan, M. 50, 248
Sweetser, E. E. 220, 461
synonyms 414–416

Tagliamonte, S. A. 164
tag questions 332–334
*tall* (adjective) 415
Talmy, L. 53, 144, 353
Taylor, J. R. 53
tense 177–178; simple future time 184–185; simple past 180–184, 190–192, 326; simple present 178–180, 186–187, 190–191, 195–196, 326; subject-verb agreement and 187–188, 192–193, 208–210; time, and agency 213–214; voice and 267
*that/those* (determiners) 92, 93–94
*the* (article) 86–90
*they* (pronoun) 129–130
third-person pronouns 119–120, 128–130
*this/that/it* (pronouns) 130–131
*this/these* (determiners) 92, 93–94
Thompson, S. A. 144, 150, 152, 154, 157, 408
*through* (preposition) 373–374
Timberlake, A. 220
time, temporality, sequentiality, and frequency 455–456
*to* (preposition) 357–358
transitive verbs 24, 152–157, 167–168, 265; complex 155–156; distinguished from intransitive verbs 157–161; voice and 282–283; *see also* ditransitive verbs
Truswell, R. 408
Tsunoda, T. 150
Tyler, A. 53, 353–354, 376
type 1 common nouns 55–64
type 2 common nouns 55–64
type 3 common nouns 64–68

*un-* (negative prefix): with adjectives and adverbs 305; with nouns 306; with verbs 304–305
*under* (preposition) 377–378
unmitigated imperatives 223–224
*used to* (in past time narratives) 248–249

van der Auwera, J. 220
Van Dijk, T. 440

Vantellini, L. 68
Vendler, Z. 144
verb phrases 24
verbs 11, 20, 143–144; adjectives formed from 406–408; auxiliary 29, 294–299, 326; change-of-state 148, 184, 199; of cognition and perception 163–164, 248; complex transitive 155–156; conversion into nouns 18; conversion of nouns into 17–18, 43; copular 147–149; derived from nouns 161–162, 169–171; *de-* with 307; *dis-* with 308; ditransitive 24, 154–155; dynamic 143, 144–146, 149–152, 211; ergative 279; for expressing modality 248; intransitive 156–157, 167–168, 265; linking 144, 146, 147–152; main 294–299, 326; *mis-* with 308; negating the main verb or auxiliary with *not* or *n't* 294–297; of obligation 248; of perception 148, 166–167; phrasal 387–391; progressive aspect 193–197; reporting 144, 164; similarities of action 164–165; simple aspect 178–193; simple present tense 179–180; stative 144, 146–147, 149–152, 211; suffixes to 13; transformed into nouns 31; transitive 24, 155–161, 167–168, 265, 282–283; transitivity and meaning of 24, 152–157; *un-* with 304–305
voice 264–265; active 265, 266; in discourse, conceptual focus of 268–269; *be*-passive *vs. get*-passive and 275–277, 283–284; in discourse, conceptual focus of 268–269; with ditransitive verbs 269–270; forms and meaning of active and passive 265–268; *have* and *get* as causative passives and 277–278; middle 278–280, 283; optional addition of *by* + overt agent in 270–272; passive 265, 266

Walsh, S. 324, 341
Walter, C. 248
Wang, J. 164
Waring, H. Z. 325
*we* (pronoun) 120
weather forecasts 35
White, P. R. R. 325, 338
*wh-* questions 328–331, 340–341; forms of 329–331
Wichmann, A. 224
Wierzbicka, A. 144
*will:* deontic modality 233; epistemic modality 235; simple future time 184–186
Williams, J. 347
*with* (preposition) 378–379, 381–382
*without* (preposition) 379, 381–382
Wolfson, N. 186
words 6–10; adding morphemes to 12–17; basic parts of speech 10–11; compounding of 18–20; connotations of 7–8; conversion of 18; defined 7; denotations 7–8; forming 12–23; onomatopoeia of 9–10, 45; portmanteau or blending 18, 22–23, 43; shortening or clipping and acronyms 19
*would:* deontic modality 234; epistemic modality 236; in past time narratives 249–250; in questions 332
writing prompts 348–349

Yang, L. 275
*yes-no* questions 325–328; functions of and answering 327–328
*yet* (conjunction) 442
Yoon, J. 362, 364, 387–388, 389, 400n2
*you, yours, yourself, yourselves* (pronouns) 126–128
Yule, G. 50, 53, 144, 184, 243, 260n3, 314, 407–408